LECTIONARY FOR MASSES WITH CHILDREN

LECTIONARY FOR MASSES WITH CHILDREN

**APPROVED FOR USE IN THE
DIOCESES OF THE UNITED STATES OF AMERICA
BY THE NATIONAL CONFERENCE OF CATHOLIC BISHOPS
AND CONFIRMED BY THE APOSTOLIC SEE**

**PREPARED BY THE COMMITTEE ON THE LITURGY
NATIONAL CONFERENCE OF CATHOLIC BISHOPS**

CATHOLIC BOOK PUBLISHING CO.
New York
1993

Concordat cum originali:
    Ronald F. Krisman, Executive Director
    Secretariat for the Liturgy
    National Conference of Catholic Bishops

Published by authority of the Committee on the Liturgy, National Conference of Catholic Bishops.

ACKNOWLEDGMENTS

Readings from the Old Testament, Book of Psalms, and a select number of the refrains for the responsorial psalms are taken from the *Contemporary English Version* © 1991 by the American Bible Society, New York, NY, and are used by license of the copyright owner. All rights reserved.

Readings from the New Testament are taken from the *Contemporary English Version, Bible for Today's Family: New Testament* © 1991 by the American Bible Society, New York, NY, and are used by license of the copyright owner. All rights reserved.

Introduction, order of readings, additional titles of the readings and psalm responses, sense-line format, and arrangement © 1991, United States Catholic Conference, 3211 Fourth Street, NE, Washington, DC 20017-1194 USA. All rights reserved.

The English translation of the titles of the readings, psalm responses, Alleluia verses, Lenten acclamations and verses before the gospel from the *Lectionary for Mass* © 1969, 1980, 1981, and 1992, International Committee on English in the Liturgy, Inc. (ICEL), 1275 K Street, NW, Washington, DC 20005-4097 USA. All rights reserved.

T-88

Illustrations and arrangement as well as Sunday Calendar, Index of Readings, Index of Responsorial Psalms, Index of Alleluia Verses and Verses before the Gospel, and Alphabetical Index of Celebrations
© 1993 by Catholic Book Publishing Co., N.Y.
International Copyright under International Copyright Union
Printed and bound in U.S.A.

NATIONAL CONFERENCE OF CATHOLIC BISHOPS
UNITED STATES OF AMERICA

DECREE

The *Lectionary for Masses with Children* for use in the dioceses of the United States of America was canonically approved by the members of the National Conference of Catholic Bishops on 13 November 1991 and was subsequently confirmed by the Apostolic See by decree of the Congregation for Divine Worship and the Discipline of the Sacraments on 27 May 1992 (Prot. N. 1259/91).

As of 1 September 1993 the *Lectionary for Masses with Children* may be published and used in the liturgy. The First Sunday of Advent, 28 November 1993, is hereby established as the effective date for use of the *Lectionary for Masses with Children* in the dioceses of the United States of America. From that day forward no other English lectionary for Masses with children may be used.

Given at the General Secretariat of the National Conference of Catholic Bishops, Washington, DC, on 28 December 1992, the feast of the Holy Innocents.

✢ William H. Keeler
Archbishop of Baltimore
President
National Conference of Catholic Bishops

Robert N. Lynch
General Secretary

CONGREGATION FOR DIVINE WORSHIP AND THE DISCIPLINE OF THE SACRAMENTS

Prot. N. 1259/91

This Congregation has examined the request of the National Conference of Catholic Bishops of the United States of America for the confirmation of the approval for the *Lectionary for Masses with Children*.

We grant permission for the experimental use of the cursus of the lectionary for children. After a three year period a full report of the experiment must be given and a renewal or definitive confirmation will be given.

The terms of the permission are as follows:

1 We ask that it be established as a first principle what is stated in paragraph 13 of the Introduction to the *Lectionary for Masses with Children:*

"Proper balance and consideration for the entire assembly should be observed. Therefore, priest celebrants should not use this *Lectionary for Masses with Children* exclusively or even preferentially at Sunday Masses, even though large numbers of children are present."

2a In granting permission for the cursus to be used, independently of any approved version of the Scripture, no approved version is *a priori* excluded from use. However, there is one small modification regarding the cursus.

b Before the readings for the following celebrations, Christmas Day, Epiphany, Sundays of Lent, Easter Sunday, Ascension, and Pentecost, it is asked that a rubric be added stating that, "these readings may be used only when the celebration of the liturgy of the word for the children is held in a place apart from the main assembly." This is to ensure that on these days in the assembly the universal lectionary will take precedence over the children's lectionary.

3 On the basis of the assurance given that the *Contemporary English Version* of the Bible does not present any doctrinal problems in the sphere of the issue of the inclusive language question at present under study we grant permission for its experimental use but without granting a formal confirmation.

From the Congregation for Divine Worship and the Discipline of the Sacraments, 27 May 1992.

✠ Antonio María Cardinal Javierre Ortas
Prefect

✠ Geraldo M. Agnelo
Archbishop Secretary

CONTENTS

Decree of the National Conference of Catholic Bishops 5
Decree of the Congregation for Divine Worship and the
   Discipline of the Sacraments 7
Foreword 11
Introduction 13
Sunday Calendars 24

PROPER OF SEASONS 31

SUNDAY READINGS 33
  Season of Advent 33
  Season of Christmas 65
  Season of Lent 81
  Season of Easter 145
  Ordinary Time 217

SOLEMNITIES OF THE LORD DURING ORDINARY TIME 505

COMMON TEXTS FOR SUNG RESPONSORIAL PSALMS 535

WEEKDAY READINGS 551
  Season of Advent 553
  Season of Lent 565
  Season of Easter 589
  Ordinary Time 611

**GOSPEL ACCLAMATIONS FOR WEEKDAYS
IN ORDINARY TIME** 695

PROPER OF SAINTS 699
  January 701
  February 708
  March 714
  April 720
  May 724
  June 733
  July 742
  August 748
  September 758
  October 766
  November 772
  December 781

COMMONS 789
Common for the Dedication of a Church 791
Common of the Blessed Virgin Mary 795
Common of Apostles 801
Common of Martyrs 804
Common of Pastors 808
Common of Doctors of the Church 812
Common of Saints 815

SACRAMENTS 823
Baptism 825
Confirmation (Holy Spirit) 830
Holy Eucharist 836
Reconciliation 841

MASSES FOR VARIOUS NEEDS AND OCCASIONS 847
Beginning of the School Year 849
End of the School Year 854
In Thanksgiving 857
For Vocations 860
For Unity of Christians 865
For Peace and Justice 869
For Productive Land and After the Harvest 873
For Refugees and Exiles 876
For the Sick 879
For the Dead 882

INDEXES 887
Index of Readings 888
Index of Responsorial Psalms 893
Index of Alleluia Verses and Verses Before the Gospel 894
Alphabetical Index of Celebrations 895

FOREWORD

Throughout his ministry, our Lord Jesus Christ had a special concern for children. When his disciples tried to prevent parents from bringing their children to Jesus to bless them, the Lord became angry and reminded the disciples: "Let the children come to me! Don't try to stop them. People who are like these little children belong to the kingdom of God" (Mk 10:14). The Gospels record other incidences when Jesus healed sick children and even raised them to life (e.g., Lk 8:40-56, Lk 9:37-43, Mt 17:14-18, Mk 9:14-27).

The Church too has manifested a special care and concern for children through the ages. From the time an infant is baptized the Church seeks to enfold it in its loving embrace so that the child may grow in the love of God. Parents are reminded: "It will be your duty to bring [your child] up to keep God's commandments as Christ taught us, by loving God and our neighbor." And in response to their affirmative answer, the minister addresses the child and says: "N., the Christian community welcomes you with great joy. In its name I claim you for Christ our Savior by the sign of his cross." The welcome of children by the Church must not be a one-time event; rather, the Church, in following the example of Christ, continues to welcome all children, but especially the young, into its midst and into its liturgical assemblies.

A concrete expression of the Church's concern for the pastoral care of children is found in the *Directory for Masses with Children*, published by the Congregation for Divine Worship in 1973 as a supplement to the *General Instruction of the Roman Missal*. This document provides for adaptations that can be made when the eucharist is celebrated with young children so that the words and actions of the Mass will be more suitable to the comprehension of the children. The Directory, in particular, provides for the adaptation of the liturgy of the word and recommends that individual conferences of bishops see to the composition of lectionaries for Masses with children.

At the recommendation of the Federation of Diocesan Liturgical Commissions and with its assistance, the Committee on the Liturgy of the National Conference of Catholic Bishops undertook the project of preparing a children's lectionary for Mass. The task group responsible for this work compared the existing lectionaries for children in other languages and, always keeping an eye on the Roman *Lectionary for Mass*, elaborated the *cursus* of readings that is found in this *Lectionary for Masses with Children* and prepared the introduction to the Lectionary. The work of the task group, which consisted of experts in liturgy, scripture, and catechetics, was ultimately approved by the NCCB Liturgy Committee and by the entire National Conference of

Catholic Bishops. The Congregation for Divine Worship and the Discipline of the Sacraments has approved the *Lectionary for Masses with Children* for experimental use for a period of three years at which time the approval will be renewed or a definitive decree of confirmation will be granted.

The *Lectionary for Masses with Children* is principally intended for use at Masses which are primarily for children and not the ordinary Sunday Mass. "Proper balance and consideration for the entire assembly should be observed. Therefore, priest celebrants should not use this *Lectionary for Masses with Children* exclusively or even preferentially at Sunday Masses, even though large numbers of children are present" (Introduction, no. 13).

It is the hope of the Liturgy Committee that the *Lectionary for Masses with Children* will enable children to hear the word of God in a manner more suited to their age and ability to understand. In providing this lectionary it is our sincere desire to enable young children to come to Christ, from whom they have received new life in baptism and who gives them the joy of salvation.

✢ Wilton D. Gregory
Auxiliary Bishop of Chicago
Chairman, Committee on the Liturgy
National Conference of Catholic Bishops

INTRODUCTION

I. THE LITURGICAL CELEBRATION OF THE WORD OF GOD

Living Word of God

1 God speaks to us the Word, who has become flesh in Jesus Christ our Lord. Through him all things came to be and were made.[1] The many words spoken throughout history for our salvation have their origin and end in Christ Jesus.[2] In the liturgy we are called together that in the Spirit we may listen to and respond to the word of God in Christ. "That word constantly proclaimed in the liturgy is always, then, a living, active word through the power of the Holy Spirit. It expresses the Father's love that never fails in its effectiveness toward us."[3]

Word of God in the Assembly

2 The liturgical assembly is a gathering of God's holy People. Christ is present in the very act of gathering.[4] Christ is also present in the proclamation of the word of God.[5] This proclamation, if it is to promote a deeper experience of Christ's presence, must be understood in its most complete sense. It must be prepared for and experienced as the specific kind of event it is, namely, a ritual celebration composed of reading, dialogue in song, silence, and reflection, with the use of appropriate gestures and symbols. The ability to give assent to God's Good News is deeply influenced by the manner in which the word is proclaimed and celebrated in the liturgical assembly.[6] The Church's deepest calling is to praise God. Members of the Church do this by conforming their lives to the message of the Scriptures that they have heard and by bringing to the celebration of the liturgy all that they have done.[7]

God's Word in Story

3 Christian communities discover, express, and deepen their identity by sharing the stories of our salvation that we read in the Scriptures. The way we pass these biblical stories on to children will also influence the way in which the message of the Scriptures is communicated to the children.

Liturgy of the Word

4 One of the clearest aims and achievements of the liturgical reform after the Second Vatican Council has been the renewal of the scriptural elements of liturgical prayer and the wider opening of the Scriptures within the full cycle of liturgical seasons and celebrations.[8] Every sacramental rite, blessing, and hour of prayer calls for the proclamation of the word of God in the form of a liturgy of the word. The most effective realization of this proclamation is the eucharist, the visible word or sacrament of the paschal mystery into which we have been baptized. Full nourishment comes from the tables of God's word and eucharist.[9]

---

[1] See John 1:1-3,14.
[2] See Hebrews 1:1-3.
[3] Lectionary for Mass [=OLM], Introduction, no. 4.
[4] See Matthew 18:19-20; see also Constitution on the Liturgy, *Sacrosanctum Concilium* [=SC], art. 7.
[5] See SC, art. 7.
[6] See Directory for Masses with Children [=DMC], no. 8.
[7] See OLM, no. 6 and DMC, no. 15.
[8] See SC, art. 24, 35, and 56.
[9] See SC, art. 2; see also OLM, no. 10.

Liturgical Ministries

5 In its liturgy the Christian community acts in its capacity as an "ordered diversity of members" and ministries.[10] The liturgy is a dialogue between God and the Church. This dialogue is effected by the Spirit's activity informing and inspiring the coordinated ministry of all who form the liturgical assembly (children as well as adults, including its bishops, presbyters, deacons, readers, musicians, and acolytes).[11]

II. THE CELEBRATION OF THE WORD OF GOD WITH CHILDREN

Scripture Never Omitted

6 The Directory for Masses with Children clearly sets forth the Church's desire that children, no less than other members of the community, be formed by the same word of God. Therefore, at Masses with adults in which children also participate and at Masses with children in which only a few adults participate "biblical reading should never be omitted."[12]

Separate Liturgy of the Word

7 In Masses with adults in which children also participate, "[s]ometimes, moreover, if the place itself and the nature of the community permit, it will be appropriate to celebrate the liturgy of the word, including a homily, with the children in a separate, but not too distant, room."[13]

8 When children are to participate in the liturgy of the word in a space separate from the main assembly, they first gather with the rest of the assembly to celebrate the introductory rites. At the conclusion of the opening prayer, but before the first reading is proclaimed, the presiding priest may formally send the children and their ministers to the place where they will celebrate their own liturgy of the word. This may be done by presenting the Lectionary to the one who will preside over the liturgy of the word with the children and/or by words of dismissal, such as the following:

A   Receive this book of readings
and proclaim God's word faithfully
to the children entrusted to your care.

B   My dear children,
you will now go to hear God's word,
to praise God in song,
and to reflect on the wonderful things God has done for us.
We will await your return
so that together we may celebrate the eucharist.

At the conclusion of their liturgy of the word, and before the liturgy of the eucharist begins, the children return to their families.

---

[10] OLM, no. 8.
[11] See DMC, nos. 22-24.
[12] DMC, no. 41.
[13] Ibid., no. 17.

Weekday Masses with Children

9 Although children are always to be led toward the parish's Sunday celebration of the eucharist, nevertheless, during the week Masses with children in which only a few adults participate are recommended.[14]

Homily or Explanation of the Readings

10 Because the explanation of the Scripture readings is so important at Masses with children, a homily should always be given. However, in order that they may not be deprived of the riches of God's word, especially if the priest finds it difficult to adapt himself to the mentality of children, and with the consent of the pastor or rector of the church, one of the adults participating in these celebrations may speak to the children after the gospel.[15]

III. THE LECTIONARY FOR MASSES WITH CHILDREN

A. ONE LECTIONARY

Purpose of Adaptation

11 This *Lectionary for Masses with Children* adheres as closely as possible to the selection and arrangement of readings for Sundays, solemnities, and feasts of the Lord in the *Lectionary for Mass*, while adapting them to the needs and capacities of children. In adapting the liturgy for use with children, the Church's goal is to nourish their faith and lead them to "active, conscious, and authentic" participation in the worship of the whole assembly,[16] but not to establish a different rite for children.[17]

Use of This Lectionary

12 In providing a lectionary for celebrations of the eucharist in which a considerable number of children are present, the Church intends to lead them into one community of faith, formed by the proclamation of the word of God. The scriptural readings contained in this Lectionary may be used at Sunday Masses when a large number of children are present along with adults, or when the children have a separate liturgy of the word, or for Masses at which most of the congregation consists of children (e.g., school Masses). The readings of this Lectionary are also a useful resource for those who wish to prepare other liturgical celebrations with children, and wish to do so within the context of the liturgical year.

13 Proper balance and consideration for the entire assembly should be observed. Therefore, priest celebrants should not use this *Lectionary for Masses with Children* exclusively or even preferentially at Sunday Masses, even though large numbers of children are present. In addition, this Lectionary may be used only when the liturgy of the word with the children is held in a place apart from the main assembly on Christmas Day, Epiphany, the Sundays of Lent, Easter Day, Ascension, and Pentecost. This is to ensure that on these days the Roman *Lectionary for Mass* will take precedence over the *Lectionary for Masses with Children* in the main assembly of the faithful.[18]

---

[14] See DMC, nos. 20-21.
[15] DMC, no. 24.
[16] Ibid., no. 12.
[17] See DMC, nos. 3 and 21.
[18] See letter of the Congregation for Divine Worship and the Discipline of the Sacraments granting permission for the experimental use of the *Lectionary for Masses with Children* (Prot. N. 1259/91).

Family Preparation

14 Although the Church permits the liturgy of the word to be celebrated in a place apart from the main Sunday assembly,[19] it seeks to protect and foster the domestic church which is the Christian family.[20] This might be weakened if all the Scripture readings heard by parents were substantially different from those heard by their children on the same Sunday. This Lectionary is intended to encourage families to prepare together those readings which will be used in common both by the adults and the children for the celebration of the Sunday Mass (at least the gospel) and to reflect after the celebration on the word proclaimed there.

B. Adapted for Particular Hearers of the Word

Age Level

15 The hearers of the word for whom this work is primarily intended are children of elementary grades [preadolescents].[21]

Number of Readings

16 "If three or even two readings appointed on Sundays or weekdays can be understood by children only with difficulty, it is permissible to read two or only one of them, but the reading of the gospel should never be omitted."[22]

Omission of Readings

17 In the preparation of this Lectionary, readings from the *Lectionary for Mass* which were judged to be too abstract were eliminated or shortened.[23] Also omitted were passages of Scripture containing images that could confuse or disturb children, or readings children could perceive as anti-Semitic or racist.[24]

Length of Readings

18 Length was not the sole criterion for elimination or abridgment.[25] In particular cases longer or shorter forms of readings have been provided. Liturgical planners, with the consent of the priest celebrant, may further adapt particularly long readings by choosing to use only that part of the selection which presents a particular biblical image or is directly related to the other reading(s).

Replacement of Readings

19 When one of the first two readings for Sundays or solemnities or feasts of the Lord was judged inappropriate for children, it was omitted and not replaced with another. In cases where both of the two first readings in the Lectionary have been dropped, a replacement has been provided. The gospel selections appointed in the Roman *Lectionary for Mass* have been retained although in particular cases they have been shortened or otherwise adapted.

---

[19] See DMC, no. 17.
[20] See DMC, no. 16.
[21] See DMC, no. 6.
[22] DMC, no. 42.
[23] See DMC, nos. 42-43.
[24] See DMC, no. 43.
[25] See DMC, no. 44.

Responsorial Psalms

20 The responsorial psalms of the Lectionary have been adapted in order to foster the singing of these texts.[26] Some refrains and psalms have been shortened or replaced. For the most part, the responsorial psalms are related to the first reading.[27] To make it easier for the assembly to join in singing the responsorial psalm, some common texts have been provided for the liturgical seasons and for the commons of saints. These may be used in place of the assigned responsorial psalms when they are sung.[28]

C. THAT THE WORD OF GOD MIGHT BE PROCLAIMED IN THE LITURGICAL CELEBRATION

Worthy Celebration

21 The liturgy has the power to form children and all believers in the paschal mystery. The worthy celebration of the liturgy itself is the best introduction to liturgy.[29]

Bodily Involvement

22 In order to engage children's authentic participation, liturgy must respect their need for physical involvement. They should be invited to participate in the actions of the liturgy whenever it is appropriate and possible.[30] Their internal life is still very much dependent upon what they experience through their senses. Therefore, ritual elements such as gestures and postures, processions, song, dialogue, silence, and the use of symbols are integral to their experience of the liturgy.

Ministers

23 Children imitate the behaviors and attitudes of adults. For this reason, adults who serve as ministers at liturgical celebrations where children are present should conduct the entire range of liturgical actions, gestures, and songs with dignity and care, yet without becoming distant or mechanical. All liturgical ministries are exercised for the sake of the prayer of the assembly. Therefore, ministers should be selected on the basis of liturgical competence. It should not be presumed that children should proclaim the word of God in the celebrations in which this Lectionary is used. Some younger children are able to read the Scriptures competently, but the witness of older children, teenagers, or adults, ministering graciously and reverently to young children engaged in liturgical prayer, is more conducive to the children's growing reverence for the word of God, than the peer ministry of embarrassed or ill-prepared children.[31]

Ritual Prayer

24 The Church's liturgy is first and foremost ritual prayer. The liturgy of the word is neither a catechetical session nor an introduction to biblical history. The liturgy celebrates the word of God in narrative and song, makes it visible in gesture and symbol and culminates in the celebration of the eucharist.

---

[26] See DMC, no. 30.
[27] See DMC, no. 46.
[28] See OLM, Introduction, no. 9.
[29] See DMC, no. 12.
[30] See DMC, nos. 33 and 34.
[31] See DMC, no. 24.

D. THROUGHOUT THE LITURGICAL YEAR

Introduction: Calendars Express and Shape Identity

25 A calendar marks the celebrations which shape, carry on and expand a particular community's common life. This Lectionary, like the Roman *Lectionary for Mass* of which it is an adaptation, is based on the Church's calendar called the liturgical year. Its faithful observance is vital to Catholic identity. This is true for children no less than for adults. Faithful observance of the calendar promotes formation and participation in the life of the Church.

Paschal Mystery

26 The Sundays, seasons and feasts of the liturgical year celebrate many facets of a single mystery. Each of them expresses from a different perspective the one great mystery of Christ's dying and rising yesterday, today and for ever. The mystery of redemption effected by Christ's incarnation, death, and resurrection is grounded in historical events of the past, yet leads to a future glory not yet fully revealed. The entire mystery, however, is present: God is now creating and redeeming in Christ. Each day Christ's Church is dying and coming to new life in him through the indwelling of the Spirit given at baptism. In ritual prayer, past and future are caught up into God's eternal present. Hence the liturgy is not an historical pageant trying to recreate a long-past event but rather is a true participation in Christ's death and resurrection, the paschal mystery. An understanding and appropriation of this mystery provides the essential starting point for preparing and celebrating the Church's liturgy.

Sunday

27 The shaping of time in the Church's tradition is related to the rhythms of nature, e.g., the relationship of morning and evening prayer to the daily rising and setting of the sun. The most fundamental shape of liturgical time, however, is the week. The first day of the week, Sunday, is the Lord's Day on which Christians assemble to celebrate the paschal mystery whose fullest expression is the celebration of the eucharist. Although it may be possible in appropriate ways to integrate a civil, diocesan, parochial, or domestic celebration within the Sunday liturgy, the full assembly's celebration of the Sunday eucharist must always take precedence over other special occasions. Fidelity to the Lectionary on Sundays, whether during the seasons or in Ordinary Time, is an indispensable element of Catholic formation. This Lectionary contains the readings for all the Sundays of the liturgical year in each year of the three year cycle of readings.

Weekdays

28 In addition to the readings for Sunday, this Lectionary provides thirty-six sets of readings for the weekdays in Ordinary Time. All four gospels are represented in these weekday selections. The readings provided for the weekdays of each season are generally taken from the respective Sundays and weekdays of the *Lectionary for Mass* so that the images fundamental to the understanding and celebration of that season are adequately represented. Each set of readings has a heading which points out the dominant theme of the readings.

The Seasons: Easter Triduum, Season of Easter, and Season of Lent

29 **The Triduum** The Easter Triduum or three days "begins with the evening Mass of the Lord's Supper on Holy Thursday, reaches its high point in the Easter Vigil, and closes with evening prayer on Easter Sunday."[32] The Sunday by Sunday celebration of our life in Christ finds its culmination in this annual celebration of Christ's passover from death to new life. These three days are best understood and celebrated as one liturgy which in its totality celebrates the paschal mystery. The liturgies of each day highlight the different facets of this mystery.

30 The duplication of the liturgies of Holy Thursday and Good Friday is permitted only with the permission of the Ordinary and, in the case of the Easter Vigil, is prohibited. These liturgies have a power and simplicity all of their own. No provision is made for a separate liturgy of the word for children on these occasions and this Lectionary has not provided adapted readings for these occasions. Nevertheless, care should be taken to insure that participation by children in these celebrations is both encouraged and fostered.

31 The united proclamation of Christ's death and resurrection first sounds in the entrance song of the Evening Mass of the Lord's Supper: "We should glory in the cross of our Lord Jesus Christ, for he is our salvation, our life and our resurrection; through him we are saved and made free."[33] It intensifies in the antiphon at the veneration of the cross on Good Friday: "We worship you, Lord, we venerate your cross, we praise your resurrection. Through the cross you brought joy to the world." It climaxes in the Easter Vigil Preface: "We praise you with greater joy than ever on this Easter night when Christ became our paschal sacrifice." It echoes in the reading for Evening Prayer of Easter Sunday, the closing liturgy of the Triduum: "Christ has offered one single sacrifice for sins.... By virtue of that one single offering he has achieved the eternal perfection of all whom he is sanctifying."[34]

32 The Easter Triduum should reflect our deepest belief that Christ has died once for all and that Holy Thursday evening, Good Friday and Holy Saturday are as much celebrations of the Lord's paschal mystery as is Easter Sunday, although each of these days may focus upon a particular aspect of that mystery which cannot be separated from the others.

33 **The Season of Easter** Following ancient tradition, the Church celebrates Easter for fifty days, from Easter Sunday to Pentecost. These fifty days are understood to be and are celebrated as one "great Sunday."[35] The Scripture readings, liturgical texts, and rites of these fifty days take precedence over civil, school, diocesan, parochial, or domestic celebrations. These events may be integrated with the celebration of the season of Easter, but this should be done with great care.

34. The primacy of the celebration of the Sundays of Easter is rooted in the traditional character of this period as a time for ongoing catechesis, especially in regard to the sacraments of initiation (baptism, confirmation, and eucharist)

---

[32] See General Norms for the Liturgical Year and the Calendar [=GNLYC], no. 19.
[33] Galatians 6:14.
[34] Hebrews 10:12-14.
[35] See GNLYC, no. 22.

and to the deeper spiritual meaning of the liturgical rites. This particular expression of the Church's formation process is called mystagogy.[36] Since most children have been baptized as infants and have received or soon will receive the eucharist, it is appropriate to draw out the meaning of these initiatory sacraments for the children during this season.

35 Throughout the season of Easter the first reading is from the Acts of the Apostles. In a three-year cycle of parallel and progressive selections, material is presented on the life of the primitive Church, its witness and growth.[37] For the second reading, passages are taken from I Peter in Year A, I John in Year B, the Revelation of John in Year C. "These are the texts that seem to fit in especially well with the spirit of joyous faith and sure hope proper to this season."[38] The gospel selections for the first three Sundays of Easter recount the appearances of the risen Christ. On the Fourth Sunday, the gospel is that of the Good Shepherd; on the Fifth, Sixth, and Seventh Sundays the Lord's discourse and prayer at the Last Supper are read. Eight sets of readings are provided for the weekdays of the Easter season.

36 **The Season of Lent** Lent extends from Ash Wednesday until just before the Holy Thursday Mass of the Lord's Supper. This season is a period of preparation for the celebration of the Easter Triduum.

37 The season of Lent takes its shape and meaning from the process and rites of conversion which lead to baptism. The process of initiation gave birth to the forty days of Lent. The privileged nature of the Triduum and the joyous celebration of Easter for fifty days can be adequately understood and maintained in worship only if Lent has led the community to the realization that this season celebrates the very nature of Christian life. As catechumens are enrolled on the First Sunday of Lent for baptism at the Easter Vigil, the word of God calls all Christians — children as well as adults — back to a deeper appreciation of their own baptism.

38 The readings, prayers, and Lenten seasonal practices are ultimately to be interpreted and celebrated in the light of our baptism into Christ's dying and rising. The gospels for the first two Sundays of Lent in all three cycles recount the Lord's temptation and transfiguration. The readings of Year A for the Third, Fourth, and Fifth Sundays of Lent are of major importance to Christian initiation and are always used when the Scrutinies are celebrated and may also be used in Years B and C even when there are no catechumens in the parish. "The Old Testament readings are about the history of salvation, which is one of the themes proper to the catechesis of Lent. The series of texts for each year presents the main elements of salvation history from its beginning until the promise of the New Covenant."[39] For the season of Lent only three selections from the letters of the apostles are included in this Lectionary. As in the *Lectionary for Mass*, these selections correspond to the gospel. Nine sets of readings are provided for the weekdays of Lent.

The Seasons: Advent – Christmas

39 **The Season of Advent** The first part of the Advent season extends from the First Sunday of Advent through December 16. The second part extends from December 17 through December 24.

---

[36] Rite of Christian Initiation of Adults, no. 247.
[37] See OLM, no. 100.
[38] OLM, no. 100.
[39] OLM, no. 97.

40 The reign of God is already among us but is not yet made manifest in its fullness. As Christians, we celebrate what already is while standing in expectation of what is yet to be revealed. Though we cannot bring about the fullness of God's reign through our efforts alone we can cooperate with God's grace to be ready and vigilant for its advent (coming). The Advent season is one of vigilant waiting but not of Lenten penitence. The first part of the season of Advent directs the eyes of our faith to the fullness yet to be revealed when the Spirit-inspired vision of the prophets, especially Isaiah and John the Baptist, will become full reality. The second part prepares us to celebrate Christ's coming in the flesh at Bethlehem. This sense of vigilance and expectation should not be anticipated by civil, diocesan, parochial, or school celebrations of Christmas during the season of Advent.

41 The Sunday gospels in Advent treat the Lord's coming at the end of time (First Sunday of Advent), John the Baptist (Second and Third Sundays), and the events that immediately prepare for the Lord's birth (Fourth Sunday). The Old Testament readings, especially those from Isaiah, are prophecies about the Messiah and the Messianic age. The readings from the apostles serve as exhortations and as proclamations, in keeping with the different themes of Advent.[40] For the weekdays of Advent this Lectionary provides four sets of readings which reflect some of the major themes of the season.

42 **The Season of Christmas** This season begins on the Vigil of Christmas and ends with the Feast of the Baptism of the Lord. The inauguration of the fullness we await was at long last disclosed in the incarnation and birth of Jesus (Christmas), born of Mary (Solemnity of Mary, Mother of God), who became a part of a human family (Feast of the Holy Family), was manifested to the nations (Epiphany), and revealed as God's own beloved child (Baptism of the Lord). The Christmas season celebrates the appearance of God among us in the birth, epiphany, and baptism of the Lord Jesus: the beginning of our salvation in Christ.

43 Christmas does not merely celebrate the birth of a child; rather this great feast celebrates the incarnation (birth) of the Lord of history in our world as God's own Word in our very flesh. It is the beginning of the paschal mystery and inevitably leads to his saving passion and resurrection from the dead. The full cycle of Christmas feasts, as surely as the celebration of the Easter Triduum, proclaims that God's "eternal Word has taken upon himself our human weakness."[41]

44. This is evident in the Gospel infancy narratives which, rather than being merely stories about the birth of a child, are anticipations of the acceptance and rejection which Jesus would meet throughout his ministry and unto his very death. Therefore Christmas is as integral to an adult understanding of faith as is Easter. Just as the Easter Triduum is one three-day celebration of Christ's paschal mystery, so the various feasts of the Christmas season are themselves celebrations of that same mystery made manifest in human history from the first moment of Jesus' birth. It is especially appropriate that the celebration of Christmas be prolonged throughout the Christmas season, rather than anticipating it as is so common in secular culture.

45 Only one set of readings for Christmas is provided in this Lectionary. These readings may be used for the Mass of the vigil, at midnight, at dawn, or during the day.

---

[40] See OLM, no. 93.
[41] *Roman Missal (Sacramentary)*, Preface of Christmas III.

Ordinary Time

46 Ordinary Time comprises the thirty-three or thirty-four weeks of the liturgical year which follow the major seasons of Christmas and Easter. There are two periods of Ordinary Time: one which extends from the end of the Christmas season to the beginning of Lent; a longer one which extends from the end of the Easter season to the beginning of Advent. Ordinary Time is devoted to the mystery of Christ in all its aspects.[42] During these weeks the Gospel accounts of Jesus' ministry and teaching are proclaimed and celebrated. This Lectionary provides thirty-six sets of readings for use on the weekdays in Ordinary Time. All four gospels are represented in these weekday selections.

The Proper of Saints

47 Throughout the centuries the Church has kept holy the memory of Mary, Mother of God, the apostles, the martyrs, and all the saints. The liturgy presents these men and women to us as intercessors and models. The entire Church joins in the celebrations of saints of universal significance, whereas other saints may be commemorated with optional celebrations by local churches or religious families.

48 Children's openness to the power of stories makes them ready listeners when they hear stories of the saints, the examples of whose lives give them a deeper appreciation of the gospel. This is especially true in the stories of saints of our time and nation. This Lectionary provides readings for all solemnities and for many feasts. Common readings are provided for use on other feasts and memorials.

IV. PARTICULAR ISSUES

Place of Celebration

49 The place where the liturgy of the word is celebrated may influence how the children receive God's word. It should be chosen carefully. Sometimes a space outside the usual place of worship may need to be chosen.[43] Even when classrooms or other non-liturgical spaces must be used for celebrations of the word with children every care must be taken that these spaces be well prepared, and that the environment is suitable for the worship of God.

The Lectionary and Other Objects Used in the Celebration

50 By their beauty and by the reverent way in which they are carried and handled the books used for the celebration of the word of God should be eloquent witnesses to the Church's reverence for the Scriptures.[44] The proclamation of the word transcends the mere communication of information and becomes a community-building celebration of God's saving mystery especially when candles, incense, banners, and processions magnify the word's impact on eyes and ears, in hearts and minds.

Music

51 The eucharistic liturgy requires the full use of music which is integral to the whole celebration, including the proclamation of the word of God. The responsorial psalm is normally sung by a cantor with the assembly singing the refrain. The gospel acclamation must always be sung. A sung response to the petitions of the general intercessions can enhance participation.

---

[42] GNLYC, no. 43.
[43] See DMC, no. 25.
[44] See OLM, no. 35.

Plays within the Liturgy of the Word

52 The Mass is not an historical reenactment of the events of salvation history and care should be taken not to give the impression that the liturgy of the word is a play. This is not to say that dramatic elements may not be used, e.g., the readings may at times be divided into parts distributed among the children;[45] however, the use of costumes, etc., is more appropriate in the context of other celebrations or services. Care should be taken especially at Christmas and during Holy Week and the Easter Triduum not to stage the various liturgies as plays. The Christmas Mass should not be presented as a birthday party for Jesus, nor should secular notions of Santa Claus be introduced into the Christmas liturgy.

Common Format

53 The preparation and celebration of liturgies for children begin with and flow from a clear desire to assist them to participate in the worship of the entire community. This is best accomplished when the basic shape of the ritual used with the children, its symbols, gestures, and language, is similar to that of the full assembly. The children are thus enabled to celebrate the paschal mystery of Christ on their own level of understanding and are led to the celebration of those same mysteries in the full assembly of the faithful.

Conclusion

54 Christ's particular care for children teaches us that they are capable of welcoming God's call and responding to it. Children's human and, therefore, religious experience is complete and whole in itself and is not determined simply by their potential for adulthood. The fullest reality of the liturgical assembly is children and adults together — not separate celebrations which run the risk of diminishing the place of children in the liturgical assembly. It should be noted that the same thing can happen if inadequate attention is given to their presence in the full assembly. Nevertheless, there will be occasions when a particular assembly is constituted almost entirely of children and other occasions where their numbers are so significant that the adaptations suggested by the Directory for Masses with Children should be applied for the sake of good pastoral care. This adaptation of the *Lectionary for Mass* is intended further to help those ministering to children. For them it provides the opportunity for deeper conversion as they attend to these young hearers of the word. The way in which the word of God is proclaimed and celebrated in the lives of children today will shape the future life of the Church.

---

[45] See DMC, no. 47.

SUNDAY CALENDAR
YEAR A

Page	Sunday or Feast	1995	1998	2001	2004	2007	2010
35	1st Sun. Advent	3 Dec.	29 Nov.	2 Dec.	28 Nov.	2 Dec.	28 Nov.
781	Immac. Concep.	8 Dec.	8 Dec.	8 Dec.	8 Dec.	8 Dec.	8 Dec.
42	2nd Sun. Advent	10 Dec.	6 Dec.	9 Dec.	5 Dec.	9 Dec.	5 Dec.
50	3rd Sun. Advent	17 Dec.	13 Dec.	16 Dec.	12 Dec.	16 Dec.	12 Dec.
59	4th Sun. Advent	24 Dec.	20 Dec.	23 Dec.	19 Dec.	23 Dec.	19 Dec.
67	Birth of the Lord	25 Dec.	25 Dec.	25 Dec.	25 Dec.	25 Dec.	25 Dec.
70	Holy Family	31 Dec.	27 Dec.	30 Dec.	26 Dec.	30 Dec.	26 Dec.
Page	**Sunday or Feast**	**1996**	**1999**	**2002**	**2005**	**2008**	**2011**
73	Mary, Mother of God	1 Jan.	1 Jan.	1 Jan.	1 Jan.	1 Jan.	1 Jan.
75	Epiphany of the Lord	7 Jan.	3 Jan.	6 Jan.	2 Jan.	6 Jan.	2 Jan.
78	Baptism of Lord	—	10 Jan.	13 Jan.	9 Jan.	13 Jan.	9 Jan.
219	2nd Ord. Sun.	14 Jan.	17 Jan.	20 Jan.	16 Jan.	20 Jan.	16 Jan.
227	3rd Ord. Sun.	21 Jan.	24 Jan.	27 Jan.	23 Jan.	27 Jan.	23 Jan.
235	4th Ord. Sun.	28 Jan.	31 Jan.	3 Feb.	30 Jan.	3 Feb.	30 Jan.
243	5th Ord. Sun.	4 Feb.	7 Feb.	10 Feb.	6 Feb.	—	6 Feb.
252	6th Ord. Sun.	11 Feb.	14 Feb.	—	—	—	13 Feb.
260	7th Ord. Sun.	18 Feb.	—	—	—	—	20 Feb.
269	8th Ord. Sun.	—	—	—	—	—	27 Feb.
276	9th Ord. Sun.	—	—	—	—	—	6 Mar.
83	1st Sun. of Lent	25 Feb.	21 Feb.	17 Feb.	13 Feb.	10 Feb.	13 Mar.
91	2nd Sun. of Lent	3 Mar.	28 Feb.	24 Feb.	20 Feb.	17 Feb.	20 Mar.
98	3rd Sun. of Lent	10 Mar.	7 Mar.	3 Mar.	27 Feb.	24 Feb.	27 Mar.
108	4th Sun. of Lent	17 Mar.	14 Mar.	10 Mar.	6 Mar.	2 Mar.	3 Apr.
118	5th Sun. of Lent	24 Mar.	21 Mar.	17 Mar.	13 Mar.	9 Mar.	10 Apr.
127	Passion (Palm) Sun.	31 Mar.	28 Mar.	24 Mar.	20 Mar.	16 Mar.	17 Apr.
147	Easter Sunday	7 Apr.	4 Apr.	31 Mar.	27 Mar	23 Mar.	24 Apr.
151	2nd Sun. Easter	14 Apr.	11 Apr.	7 Apr.	3 Apr.	30 Mar.	1 May
160	3rd Sun. Easter	21 Apr.	18 Apr.	14 Apr.	10 Apr.	6 Apr.	8 May
170	4th Sun. Easter	28 Apr.	25 Apr.	21 Apr.	17 Apr.	13 Apr.	15 May
178	5th Sun. Easter	5 May	2 May	28 Apr.	24 Apr.	20 Apr.	22 May

On the dates in bold, the Mass is as indicated on p. 30.

SUNDAY CALENDAR
YEAR A

Page	Sunday or Feast	1996	1999	2002	2005	2008	2011
188	6th Sun. Easter	12 May	9 May	5 May	1 May	27 Apr.	29 May
197	Ascension	16 May	13 May	9 May	5 May	1 May	2 June
206	7th Sun. Easter	19 May	16 May	12 May	8 May	4 May	5 June
214	Pentecost Sun.	26 May	23 May	19 May	15 May	11 May	12 June
507	Trinity Sun.	2 June	30 May	26 May	22 May	18 May	19 June
516	Body and Blood	9 June	6 June	2 June	29 May	25 May	26 June
525	Sacred Heart	14 June	11 June	7 June	3 June	30 May	1 July
276	9th Ord. Sun.	—	—	—	—	1 June	—
283	10th Ord. Sun.	—	—	9 June	5 June	8 June	—
293	11th Ord. Sun.	16 June	13 June	16 June	12 June	15 June	—
302	12th Ord. Sun.	23 June	20 June	23 June	19 June	22 June	—
310	13th Ord. Sun.	30 June	27 June	30 June	26 June	**29 June**	—
319	14th Ord. Sun.	7 July	4 July	7 July	3 July	6 July	3 July
328	15th Ord. Sun.	14 July	11 July	14 July	10 July	13 July	10 July
338	16th Ord. Sun.	21 July	18 July	21 July	17 July	20 July	17 July
346	17th Ord. Sun.	28 July	25 July	28 July	24 July	27 July	24 July
356	18th Ord. Sun.	4 Aug.	1 Aug.	4 Aug.	31 July	3 Aug.	31 July
364	19th Ord. Sun.	11 Aug.	8 Aug.	11 Aug.	7 Aug.	10 Aug.	7 Aug.
753	Assumption	15 Aug.	15 Aug.	15 Aug.	15 Aug.	15 Aug.	15 Aug.
373	20th Ord. Sun.	18 Aug.	—	18 Aug.	14 Aug.	17 Aug.	14 Aug.
381	21st Ord. Sun.	25 Aug.	22 Aug.	25 Aug.	21 Aug.	24 Aug.	21 Aug.
388	22nd Ord. Sun	1 Sept.	29 Aug.	1 Sept.	28 Aug.	31 Aug.	28 Aug.
397	23rd Ord. Sun.	8 Sept.	5 Sept.	8 Sept.	4 Sept.	7 Sept.	4 Sept.
405	24th Ord. Sun.	15 Sept.	12 Sept.	15 Sept.	11 Sept.	**14 Sept.**	11 Sept.
416	25th Ord. Sun.	22 Sept.	19 Sept.	22 Sept.	18 Sept.	21 Sept.	18 Sept.
423	26th Ord. Sun.	29 Sept.	26 Sept.	29 Sept.	25 Sept.	28 Sept.	25 Sept.
432	27th Ord. Sun.	6 Oct.	3 Oct.	6 Oct.	2 Oct.	5 Oct.	2 Oct.
441	28th Ord. Sun.	13 Oct.	10 Oct.	13 Oct.	9 Oct.	12 Oct.	9 Oct.
451	29th Ord. Sun.	20 Oct.	17 Oct.	20 Oct.	16 Oct.	19 Oct.	16 Oct.
458	30th Ord. Sun.	27 Oct.	24 Oct.	27 Oct.	23 Oct.	26 Oct.	23 Oct.
772	All Saints	1 Nov.	1 Nov.	1 Nov.	1 Nov.	1 Nov.	1 Nov.
466	31st Ord. Sun.	3 Nov.	31 Oct.	3 Nov.	30 Oct.	**2 Nov.**	30 Oct.
474	32nd Ord. Sun.	10 Nov.	7 Nov.	10 Nov.	6 Nov.	**9 Nov.**	6 Nov.
485	33rd Ord. Sun.	17 Nov.	14 Nov.	17 Nov.	13 Nov.	16 Nov.	13 Nov.
494	34th Ord. Sun.	24 Nov.	21 Nov.	24 Nov.	20 Nov.	23 Nov.	20 Nov.

SUNDAY CALENDAR
YEAR B

Page	Sunday or Feast	1993	1996	1999	2002	2005	2008
38	1st Sun. Advent	28 Nov.	1 Dec.	28 Nov.	1 Dec.	27 Nov.	30 Nov.
781	Immac. Concep.	8 Dec.	—	8 Dec.	—	8 Dec.	8 Dec.
45	2nd Sun. Advent	5 Dec.	8 Dec.	5 Dec.	8 Dec.	4 Dec.	7 Dec.
53	3rd Sun. Advent	12 Dec.	15 Dec.	12 Dec.	15 Dec.	11 Dec.	14 Dec.
61	4th Sun. Advent	19 Dec.	22 Dec.	19 Dec.	22 Dec.	18 Dec.	21 Dec.
67	Birth of the Lord	25 Dec.	25 Dec.	25 Dec.	25 Dec.	25 Dec.	25 Dec.
70	Holy Family	26 Dec.	29 Dec.	26 Dec.	29 Dec.	—	28 Dec.
Page	Sunday or Feast	1994	1997	2000	2003	2006	2009
73	Mary, Mother of God	1 Jan.	1 Jan.	1 Jan.	1 Jan.	1 Jan.	1 Jan.
75	Epiphany of the Lord	2 Jan.	5 Jan.	2 Jan.	5 Jan.	8 Jan.	4 Jan.
78	Baptism of Lord	9 Jan.	12 Jan.	9 Jan.	12 Jan.	—	11 Jan.
221	2nd Ord. Sun.	16 Jan.	19 Jan.	16 Jan.	19 Jan.	15 Jan.	18 Jan.
230	3rd Ord. Sun.	23 Jan.	26 Jan.	23 Jan.	26 Jan.	22 Jan.	25 Jan.
238	4th Ord. Sun.	30 Jan.	**2 Feb.**	30 Jan.	**2 Feb.**	29 Jan.	1 Feb.
246	5th Ord. Sun.	6 Feb.	9 Feb.	6 Feb.	9 Feb.	5 Feb.	8 Feb.
255	6th Ord. Sun.	13 Feb.	—	13 Feb.	16 Feb.	12 Feb.	15 Feb.
263	7th Ord. Sun.	—	—	20 Feb.	23 Feb.	19 Feb.	22 Feb.
272	8th Ord. Sun.	—	—	27 Feb.	2 Mar.	26 Feb.	—
278	9th Ord. Sun.	—	—	5 Mar.	—	—	—
86	1st Sun. of Lent	20 Feb.	16 Feb.	12 Mar.	9 Mar.	5 Mar.	1 Mar.
93	2nd Sun. of Lent	27 Feb.	23 Feb.	19 Mar.	16 Mar.	12 Mar.	8 Mar.
102	3rd Sun. of Lent	6 Mar.	2 Mar.	26 Mar.	23 Mar.	19 Mar.	15 Mar.
112	4th Sun. of Lent	13 Mar.	9 Mar.	2 Apr.	30 Mar.	26 Mar.	22 Mar.
122	5th Sun. of Lent	20 Mar.	16 Mar.	9 Apr.	6 Apr.	2 Apr.	29 Mar.
133	Passion (Palm) Sun.	27 Mar.	23 Mar.	16 Apr.	13 Apr.	9 Apr.	5 Apr.
147	Easter Sunday	3 Apr.	30 Mar.	23 Apr.	20 Apr.	16 Apr.	12 Apr.
154	2nd Sun. Easter	10 Apr.	6 Apr.	30 Apr.	27 Apr.	23 Apr.	19 Apr.
164	3rd Sun. Easter	17 Apr.	13 Apr.	7 May	4 May	30 Apr.	26 Apr.
173	4th Sun. Easter	24 Apr.	20 Apr.	14 May	11 May	7 May	3 May
182	5th Sun. Easter	1 May	27 Apr.	21 May	18 May	14 May	10 May

On the dates in bold, the Mass is as indicated on p. 30.

SUNDAY CALENDAR
YEAR B

Page	Sunday or Feast	1994	1997	2000	2003	2006	2009
191	6th Sun. Easter	8 May	4 May	28 May	25 May	21 May	17 May
200	Ascension	12 May	8 May	1 June	29 May	25 May	21 May
209	7th Sun. Easter	15 May	11 May	4 June	1 June	28 May	24 May
214	Pentecost Sun.	22 May	18 May	11 June	8 June	4 June	31 May
510	Trinity Sun.	29 May	25 May	18 June	15 June	11 June	7 June
519	Body and Blood	5 June	1 June	25 June	22 June	18 June	14 June
528	Sacred Heart	10 June	6 June	30 June	27 June	23 June	19 June
278	9th Ord. Sun.	—	—	—	—	—	—
286	10th Ord. Sun.	—	8 June	—	—	—	—
296	11th Ord. Sun.	12 June	15 June	—	—	—	—
304	12th Ord. Sun.	19 June	22 June	—	—	25 June	21 June
313	13th Ord. Sun.	26 June	**29 June**	2 July	**29 June**	2 July	28 June
322	14th Ord. Sun.	3 July	6 July	9 July	6 July	9 July	5 July
331	15th Ord. Sun.	10 July	13 July	16 July	13 July	16 July	12 July
341	16th Ord. Sun.	17 July	20 July	23 July	20 July	23 July	19 July
349	17th Ord. Sun.	24 July	27 July	30 July	27 July	30 July	26 July
359	18th Ord. Sun.	31 July	3 Aug.	**6 Aug.**	3 Aug.	**6 Aug.**	2 Aug.
367	19th Ord. Sun.	7 Aug.	10 Aug.	13 Aug.	10 Aug.	13 Aug.	9 Aug.
753	Assumption	15 Aug.	15 Aug.	15 Aug.	15 Aug.	15 Aug.	15 Aug.
375	20th Ord. Sun.	14 Aug.	17 Aug.	20 Aug.	17 Aug.	20 Aug.	16 Aug.
383	21st Ord. Sun.	21 Aug.	24 Aug.	27 Aug.	24 Aug.	27 Aug.	23 Aug.
391	22nd Ord. Sun.	28 Aug.	31 Aug.	3 Sept.	31 Aug.	3 Sept.	30 Aug.
400	23rd Ord. Sun.	4 Sept.	7 Sept.	10 Sept.	7 Sept.	10 Sept.	6 Sept.
409	24th Ord. Sun.	11 Sept.	**14 Sept.**	17 Sept.	**14 Sept.**	17 Sept.	13 Sept.
419	25th Ord. Sun.	18 Sept.	21 Sept.	24 Sept.	21 Sept.	24 Sept.	20 Sept.
426	26th Ord. Sun.	25 Sept.	28 Sept.	1 Oct.	28 Sept.	1 Oct.	27 Sept.
436	27th Ord. Sun.	2 Oct.	5 Oct.	8 Oct.	5 Oct.	8 Oct.	4 Oct.
444	28th Ord. Sun.	9 Oct.	12 Oct.	15 Oct.	12 Oct.	15 Oct.	11 Oct.
454	29th Ord. Sun.	16 Oct.	19 Oct.	22 Oct.	19 Oct.	22 Oct.	18 Oct.
460	30th Ord. Sun.	23 Oct.	26 Oct.	29 Oct.	26 Oct.	29 Oct.	25 Oct.
772	All Saints	1 Nov.	1 Nov.	1 Nov.	1 Nov.	1 Nov.	1 Nov.
469	31st Ord. Sun.	30 Oct.	**2 Nov.**	5 Nov.	**2 Nov.**	5 Nov.	—
478	32nd Ord. Sun.	6 Nov.	**9 Nov.**	12 Nov.	**9 Nov.**	12 Nov.	8 Nov.
487	33rd Ord. Sun.	13 Nov.	16 Nov.	19 Nov.	16 Nov.	19 Nov.	15 Nov.
498	34th Ord. Sun.	20 Nov.	23 Nov.	26 Nov.	23 Nov.	26 Nov.	22 Nov.

SUNDAY CALENDAR
YEAR C

Page	Sunday or Feast	1994	1997	2000	2003	2006	2009
40	1st Sun. Advent	27 Nov.	30 Nov.	3 Dec.	30 Nov.	3 Dec.	29 Nov.
781	Immac. Concep.	8 Dec.	8 Dec.	8 Dec.	8 Dec.	8 Dec.	8 Dec.
47	2nd Sun. Advent	4 Dec.	7 Dec.	10 Dec.	7 Dec.	10 Dec.	6 Dec.
56	3rd Sun. Advent	11 Dec.	14 Dec.	17 Dec.	14 Dec.	17 Dec.	13 Dec.
63	4th Sun. Advent	18 Dec.	21 Dec.	24 Dec.	21 Dec.	24 Dec.	20 Dec.
67	Birth of the Lord	25 Dec.	25 Dec.	25 Dec.	25 Dec.	25 Dec.	25 Dec.
70	Holy Family	—	28 Dec.	31 Dec.	28 Dec.	31 Dec.	27 Dec.

Page	Sunday or Feast	1995	1998	2001	2004	2007	2010
73	Mary, Mother of God	1 Jan.	1 Jan.	1 Jan.	1 Jan.	1 Jan.	1 Jan.
75	Epiphany of the Lord	8 Jan.	4 Jan.	7 Jan.	4 Jan.	7 Jan.	3 Jan.
78	Baptism of Lord	—	11 Jan.	—	11 Jan.	—	10 Jan.
224	2nd Ord. Sun.	15 Jan.	18 Jan.	14 Jan.	18 Jan.	14 Jan.	17 Jan.
232	3rd Ord. Sun.	22 Jan.	25 Jan.	21 Jan.	25 Jan.	21 Jan.	24 Jan.
240	4th Ord. Sun.	29 Jan.	1 Feb.	28 Jan.	1 Feb.	28 Jan.	31 Jan.
249	5th Ord. Sun.	5 Feb.	8 Feb.	4 Feb.	8 Feb.	4 Feb.	7 Feb.
257	6th Ord. Sun.	12 Feb.	15 Feb.	11 Feb.	15 Feb.	11 Feb.	14 Feb.
266	7th Ord. Sun.	19 Feb.	22 Feb.	18 Feb.	22 Feb.	18 Feb.	—
274	8th Ord. Sun.	26 Feb.	—	25 Feb.	—	—	—
281	9th Ord. Sun.	—	—	—	—	—	—
88	1st Sun. of Lent	5 Mar.	1 Mar.	4 Mar.	29 Feb.	25 Feb.	21 Feb.
95	2nd Sun. of Lent	12 Mar.	8 Mar.	11 Mar.	7 Mar.	4 Mar.	28 Feb.
105	3rd Sun. of Lent	19 Mar.	15 Mar.	18 Mar.	14 Mar.	11 Mar.	7 Mar.
114	4th Sun. of Lent	26 Mar.	22 Mar.	25 Mar.	21 Mar.	18 Mar.	14 Mar.
124	5th Sun. of Lent	2 Apr.	29 Mar.	1 Apr.	28 Mar.	25 Mar.	21 Mar.
138	Passion (Palm) Sun.	9 Apr.	5 Apr.	8 Apr.	4 Apr.	1 Apr.	28 Mar.
147	Easter Sunday	16 Apr.	12 Apr.	15 Apr.	11 Apr.	8 Apr.	4 Apr.
157	2nd Sun. Easter	23 Apr.	19 Apr.	22 Apr.	18 Apr.	15 Apr.	11 Apr.
167	3rd Sun. Easter	30 Apr.	26 Apr.	29 Apr.	25 Apr.	22 Apr.	18 Apr.
176	4th Sun. Easter	7 May	3 May	6 May	2 May	29 Apr.	25 Apr.
185	5th Sun. Easter	14 May	10 May	13 May	9 May	6 May	2 May

On the dates in bold, the Mass is as indicated on p. 30.

SUNDAY CALENDAR
YEAR C

Page	Sunday or Feast	1995	1998	2001	2004	2007	2010
194	6th Sun. Easter	21 May	17 May	20 May	16 May	13 May	9 May
203	Ascension	25 May	21 May	24 May	20 May	17 May	13 May
212	7th Sun. Easter	28 May	24 May	27 May	23 May	20 May	16 May
214	Pentecost Sun.	4 June	31 May	3 June	30 May	27 May	23 May
513	Trinity Sun.	11 June	7 June	10 June	6 June	3 June	30 May
522	Body and Blood	18 June	14 June	17 June	13 June	10 June	6 June
531	Sacred Heart	23 June	19 June	22 June	18 June	15 June	11 June
281	9th Ord. Sun.	—	—	—	—	—	—
290	10th Ord Sun.	—	—	—	—	—	—
299	11th Ord. Sun.	—	—	—	—	17 June	13 June
307	12th Ord Sun.	25 June	21 June	24 June	20 June	24 June	20 June
316	13th Ord. Sun.	2 July	28 June	1 July	27 June	1 July	27 June
325	14th Ord. Sun.	9 July	5 July	8 July	4 July	8 July	4 July
334	15th Ord. Sun.	16 July	12 July	15 July	11 July	15 July	11 July
343	16th Ord. Sun.	23 July	19 July	22 July	18 July	22 July	18 July
352	17th Ord. Sun.	30 July	26 July	29 July	25 July	29 July	25 July
362	18th Ord. Sun.	6 Aug.	2 Aug.	5 Aug.	1 Aug.	5 Aug.	1 Aug.
370	19th Ord. Sun.	13 Aug.	9 Aug.	12 Aug.	8 Aug.	12 Aug.	8 Aug.
753	Assumption	15 Aug.	15 Aug.	15 Aug.	15 Aug.	15 Aug.	15 Aug.
378	20th Ord. Sun.	20 Aug.	16 Aug.	19 Aug.	—	19 Aug.	—
386	21st Ord. Sun.	27 Aug.	23 Aug.	26 Aug.	22 Aug.	26 Aug.	22 Aug.
394	22nd Ord. Sun.	3 Sept.	30 Aug.	2 Sept.	29 Aug.	2 Sept.	29 Aug.
403	23rd Ord. Sun.	10 Sept.	6 Sept.	9 Sept.	5 Sept.	9 Sept.	5 Sept.
412	24th Ord. Sun.	17 Sept.	13 Sept.	16 Sept.	12 Sept.	16 Sept.	12 Sept.
421	25th Ord. Sun.	24 Sept.	20 Sept.	23 Sept.	19 Sept.	23 Sept.	19 Sept.
429	26th Ord. Sun.	1 Oct.	27 Sept.	30 Sept.	26 Sept.	30 Sept.	26 Sept.
438	27th Ord. Sun.	8 Oct.	4 Oct.	7 Oct.	3 Oct.	7 Oct.	3 Oct.
448	28th Ord. Sun.	15 Oct.	11 Oct.	14 Oct.	10 Oct.	14 Oct.	10 Oct.
456	29th Ord. Sun.	22 Oct.	18 Oct.	21 Oct.	17 Oct.	21 Oct.	17 Oct.
463	30th Ord. Sun.	29 Oct.	25 Oct.	28 Oct.	24 Oct.	28 Oct.	24 Oct.
772	All Saints	1 Nov.	1 Nov.	1 Nov.	1 Nov.	1 Nov.	1 Nov.
471	31st Ord. Sun.	5 Nov.	—	4 Nov.	31 Oct.	4 Nov.	31 Oct.
481	32nd Ord. Sun.	12 Nov.	8 Nov.	11 Nov.	7 Nov.	11 Nov.	7 Nov.
490	33rd Ord. Sun.	19 Nov.	15 Nov.	18 Nov.	14 Nov.	18 Nov.	14 Nov.
501	34th Ord. Sun.	26 Nov.	22 Nov.	25 Nov.	21 Nov.	25 Nov.	21 Nov.

LIST OF FEASTS THAT MAY REPLACE THE SUNDAY MASS

The following feasts from the Proper of the Saints may replace the Sunday Mass when they fall on Sunday. In such cases, their dates are printed in **bold** in the Calendar (pages 24-29), referring the reader to this section for the Mass to be celebrated and the page on which it is found. For convenience, the years in which these Masses are celebrated on Sundays are also given below. (Whenever March 19, March 25, or December 8 falls on a Sunday, the celebration will always be transferred to another day of the week.)

Page	Date	Feast	Date It Occurs on Sunday
708	February 2	The Presentation of the Lord	1997(B), 2003(B)
736	June 24	The Birth of John the Baptist	2001(C), 2007(C)
739	June 29	Peter and Paul	1997(B), 2003(B), 2008(A)
748	August 6	The Transfiguration of the Lord	1995(C), 2000(B), 2006(B)
753	August 15	The Assumption of the Virgin Mary into Heaven	1999(A), 2004(C), 2010(C)
758	September 14	The Holy Cross	1997(B), 2003(B), 2008(A)
772	November 1	All Saints	1998(C), 2009(B)
774	November 2	All Souls	1997(B), 2003(B), 2008(A)
774	November 9	The Dedication of the Lateran Basilica in Rome	1997(B), 2003(B), 2008(A)

PROPER OF SEASONS

SEASON OF ADVENT

[1] **FIRST SUNDAY OF ADVENT** **A**

FIRST READING

The Lord will gather all nations in eternal peace in the kingdom of God.

A reading from the book of the prophet Isaiah 2:1-5

This is the vision that Isaiah son of Amoz had
about Judah and Jerusalem:

In the future the mountain with the Lord's temple
will be the highest of all.
It will reach above the hills,
and every nation will rush to it.
Many people will come and say,
"Let's go to the mountain of the LORD God of Jacob
and worship in his temple."

The LORD will teach us his Law from Jerusalem.
He will settle the arguments of nations and of people.
They will pound their swords and their spears into garden tools.
And they will never make war or attack other nations.

People of Israel, let's live by the light of the LORD.

The word of the Lord.

RESPONSORIAL PSALM 122:1-2, 8-9

℟. (see 1) Let us go rejoicing to the house of the Lord.

It made me glad to hear them say,
"Let's go to the house of the LORD!"
Jerusalem, we are standing
inside your gates.

℟. Let us go rejoicing to the house of the Lord.

Because of my friends
and my relatives,
I will pray for peace.
And because of the house
of the LORD our God,
I will work for your good.

℟. Let us go rejoicing to the house of the Lord.

SECOND READING

The time has come, our salvation is near.

A reading from the letter of Paul to the Romans 13:11-13a

Brothers and sisters:
  You know what sort of times we live in,
  and so you should live properly.
It is time to wake up.
You know that the day when we will be saved
  is nearer now than when we first put our faith in the Lord.
Night is almost over, and day will soon appear.
We must stop behaving as people do in the dark
  and be ready to live in the light.
So behave properly, as people do in the day.

The word of the Lord.

ALLELUIA Psalm 85:8

℟. Alleluia, alleluia.

**Lord, show us your mercy and love,
and grant us your salvation.**

℟. Alleluia, alleluia.

GOSPEL

Stay awake, you must be ready.

✢ **A reading from the holy gospel according to Matthew** 24:37-44

Jesus said to his disciples:
  "When the Son of Man appears,
  things will be just as they were when Noah lived.
People were eating, drinking, and getting married
    right up to the day that the flood came
    and Noah went into the big boat.
They didn't know anything was happening
    until the flood came and swept them all away.
That is how it will be when the Son of Man appears.

"Two men will be in the same field,
    but only one will be taken.
The other will be left.
Two women will be together grinding grain,
    but only one will be taken.
The other will be left.

"So be on your guard!
You don't know when your Lord will come.
Homeowners never know when a thief is coming,
    and they are always on guard to keep one from breaking in.
Always be ready!
You don't know when the Son of Man will come."

The gospel of the Lord.

FIRST SUNDAY OF ADVENT   B

FIRST READING

The revelation we looked for, Christ Jesus our Lord.

A reading from the first letter of Paul to the Corinthians   1:3-9

Brothers and sisters:
My prayer is that God our Father and the Lord Jesus Christ
will be kind to you and will bless you with peace!

I never stop thanking my God
for being kind enough to give you Christ Jesus,
who helps you speak and understand so well.
Now you are certain that everything we told you
about our Lord Christ Jesus is true.

You are not missing out on any blessings,
as you wait for him to return.
And until the day Christ does return,
he will keep you completely innocent.

God can be trusted,
and he chose you to be partners with his Son,
our Lord Jesus Christ.

                                    The word of the Lord.

RESPONSORIAL PSALM   85:8, 9, 10

℟. (Sirach 36:16) Give peace, O Lord, to those who wait for you.

I will listen to you, Lord God,
because you promise peace
to those who are faithful
and no longer foolish.

℟. Give peace, O Lord, to those who wait for you.

You are ready to rescue
everyone who worships you,
so that you will live with us
in all of your glory.

℟. Give peace, O Lord, to those who wait for you.

Love and loyalty
will come together;
goodness and peace
will unite.

℟. Give peace, O Lord, to those who wait for you.

ALLELUIA   Psalm 85:8

℟. Alleluia, alleluia.

**Lord, show us your mercy and love,
and grant us your salvation.**

℟. Alleluia, alleluia.

GOSPEL

Stay awake! You never know when the Lord will come.

✣ A reading from the holy gospel according to Mark   13:33-37

Jesus said to his disciples:
  "Watch out and be ready!
You don't know when the time will come.
It is like what happens when a man goes away for a while
    and places his servants in charge of everything.
He tells each of them what to do,
    and he orders the watchmen to be on their guard.

"So be on your guard!
You don't know when the master of the house will come back.
It could be in the evening or at midnight
    or before dawn or in the morning.
But if he comes suddenly, don't let him find you asleep.
I tell everyone just what I have told you.
Be on your guard!"

                                    The gospel of the Lord.

FIRST SUNDAY OF ADVENT

FIRST READING

I will cause a good seed to spring forth from David.

A reading from the book of the prophet Jeremiah   33:14-16

I, the Lord, say this:
The time is coming when I will keep the promise I made
    to the people of Israel and Judah.
I will choose a ruler from the family of David,
    and he will be completely fair to everyone.
Judah will be safe.
Jerusalem will have peace, and it will be named,
"The Lord our Protector!"

The word of the Lord.

RESPONSORIAL PSALM   25:4-5, 8-9

℟. (1b) To you, O Lord, I lift my soul.

Show me your paths
and teach me to follow;
guide me by your truth
and instruct me.
You keep me safe,
and I always trust you.

℟. To you, O Lord, I lift my soul.

You are honest and merciful,
and you teach sinners
how to follow your path.
You lead humble people
to do what is right
and to stay on your path.

℟. To you, O Lord, I lift my soul.

ALLELUIA Psalm 85:8

℟. Alleluia, alleluia.

**Lord, show us your mercy and love,
and grant us your salvation.**

℟. Alleluia, alleluia.

GOSPEL

Your redemption is near at hand.

✢ **A reading from the holy gospel according to Luke** 21:25-28, 34-36

Jesus said to his disciples:
   "Strange things will happen to the sun, moon, and stars.
The nations on earth will be afraid of the roaring sea and tides,
   and they won't know what to do.
People will be so frightened that they will faint
   because of what is happening to the world.
Every power in the sky will be shaken.

"Then the Son of Man will be seen,
   coming in a cloud with great power and glory.
When all of this starts happening,
   stand up straight and be brave.
You will soon be set free.

"Don't spend all of your time thinking about eating or drinking
   or worrying about life.
If you do, the final day will suddenly catch you like a trap.
That day will surprise everyone on earth.

"Watch out and keep praying that you can escape
   all that is going to happen
   and that the Son of Man will be pleased with you."

                                    The gospel of the Lord.

SECOND SUNDAY OF ADVENT A

FIRST READING

He shall judge the poor with justice.

A reading from the book of the prophet Isaiah   11:1-4a, 5-6, 9b

The L̲ord says this:
Like a branch that sprouts from a stump,
   someone from David's family will someday be king.
The Spirit of the L̲ord will take control of him
   and give him understanding and wisdom and insight.
He will be powerful,
   and he will know and honor the L̲ord.
His greatest joy will be to worship the L̲ord.

He won't judge by appearances or listen to rumors.
The poor and the helpless will be treated
   with fairness and with justice.
Honesty and fairness will be his royal robes.

Leopards and young goats, and wolves and lambs
   will lie down and rest in the same field.
Calves and lions will eat together and be cared for by a child.

Just as water fills the sea,
   the land will be filled with people who know and honor the L̲ord.

                                  The word of the Lord.

RESPONSORIAL PSALM   72:1 and 8, 17

   ℟. (7) Justice shall flourish in his time,
      and fullness of peace for ever.

Please help the king
to be honest and fair
just like you, our God.
Let his kingdom reach
from sea to sea,
from the Euphrates River
across all the earth.

℟. Justice shall flourish in his time,
    and fullness of peace for ever.

**May the glory of the king
shine brightly forever
like the sun in the sky.
Let him make nations prosper
and learn to praise him.**

℟. Justice shall flourish in his time,
    and fullness of peace for ever.

SECOND READING

Christ, the hope of all people.

A reading from the letter of Paul to the Romans   15:4-6

Brothers and sisters:
The Scriptures were written to teach and encourage us by giving us hope.
God is the one who makes us patient and cheerful.
I pray that he will help you live at peace with each other,
    as you follow Christ.
Then all of you together will praise God,
    the Father of our Lord Jesus Christ.

The word of the Lord.

ALLELUIA   Luke 3:4, 6

℟. Alleluia, alleluia.

**Prepare the way of the Lord, make straight his paths:
all people shall see the salvation of God.**

℟. Alleluia, alleluia.

GOSPEL

Repent, for the kingdom of heaven is close at hand.

✣ A reading from the holy gospel according to Matthew 3:1-9, 11

John the Baptist started preaching in the desert of Judea.
He said, "Turn back to God!
The kingdom of heaven will soon be here."

John was the one the prophet Isaiah was talking about, when he said,

"In the desert someone is shouting,
'Get the road ready for the Lord!
Make a straight path for him.'"

John wore clothes made of camel's hair.
He had a leather strap around his waist
  and ate grasshoppers and wild honey.

From Jerusalem and all Judea and from the Jordan River Valley
  crowds of people went to John.
They told how sorry they were for their sins,
  and he baptized them in the river.

Many Pharisees and Sadducees also came to be baptized.
But John said to them: "You bunch of snakes!
Who warned you to run from the coming judgment?
Do something to show that you have really given up your sins.
And don't start telling yourselves
  that you belong to Abraham's family.
I tell you that God can turn these stones
  into children for Abraham.

"I baptize you with water so that you will give up your sins.
But someone more powerful is going to come,
  and I am not good enough even to carry his sandals.
He will baptize you with the Holy Spirit and with fire."

The gospel of the Lord.

SECOND SUNDAY OF ADVENT B

FIRST READING

Prepare the way for the Lord.

A reading from the book of the prophet Isaiah 40:3-5

A voice is shouting:
Clear a path in the desert for the Lord.
Build a straight road there for our God.

Fill in the valleys and flatten the mountains and hills.
Level the rough and rugged ground.

Then the glory of the Lord will appear for all to see.
The Lord has promised this!

The word of the Lord.

RESPONSORIAL PSALM 85:8-9, 10-11

℟. (8) Lord, show us your mercy and love,
and grant us your salvation.

I will listen to you, Lord God,
because you promise peace
to those who are faithful
and no longer foolish.
You are ready to rescue
everyone who worships you,
so that you will live with us
in all of your glory.

℟. Lord, show us your mercy and love,
and grant us your salvation.

Love and loyalty will come together;
goodness and peace will unite.
Loyalty will sprout
from the ground;
justice will look down
from the sky above.

℟. Lord, show us your mercy and love,
and grant us your salvation.

ALLELUIA
Luke 3:4, 6

℟. Alleluia, alleluia.

**Prepare the way of the Lord, make straight his paths:
all people shall see the salvation of God.**

℟. Alleluia, alleluia.

GOSPEL

Make straight the paths of the Lord.

✠ The beginning of the holy gospel according to Mark   1:1-8

**This is the good news about Jesus Christ, the Son of God.
It began just as God had said
   in the book written by Isaiah the prophet,**

    **"I am sending my messenger to get the way ready for you.
In the desert someone is shouting,
'Get the road ready for the Lord!
Make a straight path for him.' "**

**So John the Baptist showed up in the desert and told everyone,
"Turn back to God and be baptized!
Then your sins will be forgiven."**

**From all Judea and from Jerusalem crowds of people went to John.
They told how sorry they were for their sins,
   and he baptized them in the Jordan River.**

**John wore clothes made of camel's hair.
He had a leather strap around his waist
   and ate grasshoppers and wild honey.**

**John also told the people,
"Someone more powerful is going to come.
And I am not good enough even to stoop down and untie his sandals.
I baptize you with water,
   but he will baptize you with the Holy Spirit!"**

                                 The gospel of the Lord.

SECOND SUNDAY OF ADVENT   C

FIRST READING

Jerusalem, God will show your splendor.

A reading from the book of the prophet Baruch   5:1-5, 7

Jerusalem, exchange your robes of sorrow and suffering
    for those glorious garments God has given you forever.
Dress in the saving power of the eternal God,
    and wear his glory like a crown on your head.

God will show everyone on earth how wonderful you are.
And he has forever given you this name:
"Justice Leads to Peace, Obeying God Brings Honor."

Jerusalem, climb to the peaks of the highest mountains
    and see your people coming from the east and the west,
        at the command of God.
They are celebrating
    because they have been remembered by the Holy One.

God has commanded every tall and ancient mountain
        to be leveled to the ground and every valley filled in.
Then Israel will safely walk in the glory of God.

                                                The word of the Lord.

RESPONSORIAL PSALM   126:1-2ab, 2cde-3

    ℟. (3) The Lord has done great things for us;
        we are filled with joy.

It seemed like a dream
when the Lord brought us back
to the city of Zion.
We celebrated with laughter
and joyful songs.

    ℟. The Lord has done great things for us;
        we are filled with joy.

In foreign nations it was said,
"The LORD has worked miracles
for his people."
And so we celebrated
because the LORD had indeed
worked miracles for us.

℟. The Lord has done great things for us;
we are filled with joy.

SECOND READING

You share in spreading the good news.

A reading from the letter of Paul to the Philippians   1:4-6

Brothers and sisters:
Whenever I mention you in my prayers,
it makes me happy.
This is because you have taken part with me
    in spreading the good news
        from the first day you heard about it.
God is the one who began this good work in you,
    and I am certain that he won't stop before it is complete
        on the day that Christ Jesus returns.

                                                The word of the Lord.

ALLELUIA   Luke 3:4, 6

℟. Alleluia, alleluia.

Prepare the way of the Lord, make straight his paths:
all people shall see the salvation of God.

℟. Alleluia, alleluia.

GOSPEL

All people shall see the salvation of God.

✢ **A reading from the holy gospel according to Luke** 3:1a, 2-6

For fifteen years Emperor Tiberius had ruled that part of the world,
and Annas and Caiaphas were the Jewish high priests.
At that time God spoke to Zechariah's son John,
who was living in the desert.

So John went along the Jordan Valley, telling the people,
"Turn back to God and be baptized!
Then your sins will be forgiven."
Isaiah the prophet wrote about John when he said,

"In the desert someone is shouting,
'Get the road ready for the Lord!
Make a straight path for him!
Fill up every valley and level every mountain and hill.
Straighten the crooked paths and smooth out the rough roads.
Then everyone will see the saving power of God.'"

The gospel of the Lord.

THIRD SUNDAY OF ADVENT

FIRST READING

God will come and save you.

A reading from the book of the prophet Isaiah   35:1-2, 5-6ab, 10

Thirsty deserts will be glad,
   and barren lands will rejoice and blossom like flowers.
They will bloom everywhere and sing joyful songs.
They will be as majestic as Mount Lebanon
      and as glorious as Mount Carmel or the plain of Sharon.
Everyone will see the glory and the majesty of the Lord our God.

The blind will see, and the deaf will hear.
The disabled will leap about like deer,
   and tongues once silent will shout.

The people the Lord has rescued will come back singing,
   as they enter Zion.
Happiness will be a crown they will always wear.
They will rejoice and be glad,
   because all sorrows and worries will be gone.

The word of the Lord.

RESPONSORIAL PSALM   146:6d-7ab, 7c-8abc, 10

℞. (Isaiah 35:4) Lord, come and save us.

God always keeps his word.
He gives justice to the poor
and food to the hungry.

℞. Lord, come and save us.

The Lord sets prisoners free
and heals blind eyes.
He gives a helping hand
to everyone who falls.

℞. Lord, come and save us.

The LORD God of Zion
will rule forever!
Shout praises to the LORD!

℞. Lord, come and save us.

SECOND READING

You also must be patient; do not lose heart,
the Lord's coming will be soon.

A reading from the letter of James   5:7-10

My friends, be patient until the Lord returns.
Think of farmers who wait patiently for the spring and summer rains
  to make their valuable crops grow.
Be patient like those farmers and don't give up.
The Lord will soon be here!
Don't grumble about each other or you will be judged,
  and the judge is right outside the door.

My friends, follow the example of the prophets who spoke for the Lord.
They were patient,
  even when they had to suffer.

The word of the Lord.

ALLELUIA   Isaiah 61:1

℞. Alleluia, alleluia.

The Spirit of the Lord now upon me
has sent me to bring good news to the poor.

℞. Alleluia, alleluia.

GOSPEL

> Are you the one who is to come,
> or must we wait for someone else?

✢ A reading from the holy gospel according to Matthew 11:2-11

John was in prison when he heard what Christ was doing. So John sent some of his followers to ask Jesus, "Are you the one we should be looking for? Or must we wait for someone else?"

Jesus answered, "Go and tell John what you have heard and seen.
The blind are now able to see,
   and the lame can walk.
People with leprosy are being healed,
   and the deaf can hear.
The dead are raised to life,
   and the poor are hearing the good news.
God will bless everyone who does not reject me
      because of what I do."

As John's followers were going away,
   Jesus spoke to the crowds about John:

"What sort of person did you go out into the desert to see?
Was he like tall grass blown about by the wind?

"What kind of man did you go out to see?
Was he someone dressed in fine clothes?
People who dress like that live in the king's palace.

"What did you really go out to see?
Was he a prophet? He certainly was.
I tell you that he was more than a prophet.
In the Scriptures God says about him,

> 'I am sending my messenger ahead of you
>   to get things ready for you.'

"I tell you that no one ever born on this earth
   is greater than John the Baptist.
But whoever is least in the kingdom of heaven is greater than John."

The gospel of the Lord.

THIRD SUNDAY OF ADVENT

FIRST READING

The Spirit of the Lord has chosen me.

A reading from the book of the prophet Isaiah 61:1-2

The Spirit of the Lord God has come to me,
   because he has chosen me.
The Lord has sent me to tell the oppressed the good news,
   to heal the brokenhearted,
   and to announce freedom for prisoners and captives.

This is the year when the Lord God
   will show kindness to us and punish our enemies.
The Lord has sent me to comfort all who mourn.

The word of the Lord.

RESPONSORIAL PSALM Luke 1:47 and 49, 53-54

℟. (Isaiah 61:10b) My soul rejoices in my God.

With all my heart I praise the Lord,
and I am glad because of God my Savior.
God All-Powerful has done great things for me,
and his name is holy.

℟. My soul rejoices in my God.

God gives the hungry good things to eat,
and he sends the rich away with nothing in their hands.
He helps his servant Israel
and is always merciful to his people.

℟. My soul rejoices in my God.

SECOND READING

May you all be kept blameless, spirit, soul, and body,
for the coming of our Lord Jesus Christ.

A reading from the first letter of Paul to the Thessalonians 5:16-24

Brothers and sisters:
Always be joyful and never stop praying.
Whatever happens, keep thanking God because of Jesus Christ.
This is what God wants you to do.

Don't turn away God's Spirit or ignore prophecies.
Put everything to the test.
Accept what is good and don't have anything to do with evil.

I pray that God, who gives peace,
   will make you completely holy.
And may your spirit, soul, and body be kept healthy and faultless
   until our Lord Jesus Christ returns.
The one who chose you can be trusted,
   and he will do this.

The word of the Lord.

ALLELUIA   Isaiah 61:1

℟. Alleluia, alleluia.

The Spirit of the Lord now upon me
has sent me to bring good news to the poor.

℟. Alleluia, alleluia.

GOSPEL

>There stands among you, unknown to you,
>the one who is coming after me.

✠ A reading from the holy gospel according to John 1:19-28

The Jewish leaders in Jerusalem sent priests and temple helpers
>to ask John who he was.

He told them plainly, "I am not the Messiah."
Then when they asked him if he were Elijah,
>he said, "No, I am not!"

And when they asked if he were the Prophet,
>he also said "No!"

Finally, they said, "Who are you then?
We have to give an answer to the ones who sent us.
Tell us who you are!"

John answered in the words of the prophet Isaiah,

>>"I am only someone shouting in the desert,
>>'Get the road ready for the Lord!' "

Some Pharisees had also been sent to John.
They asked him, "Why are you baptizing people,
>if you are not the Messiah or Elijah or the Prophet?"

John told them, "I use water to baptize people.
But here with you is someone you don't know.
Even though I came first,
>I am not good enough to untie his sandals."

John said this as he was baptizing east of the Jordan River in Bethany.

>The gospel of the Lord.

[9] **THIRD SUNDAY OF ADVENT** C

FIRST READING

The Lord is at your side.

A reading from the book of the prophet Zephaniah 3:14-15

Everyone in Jerusalem and Judah,
 celebrate and shout with all your heart.
You won't be punished now.
The Lord has made your enemies retreat.
The Lord is the king of Israel,
 and he is at your side.
You don't have to worry about any more troubles.

The word of the Lord.

RESPONSORIAL PSALM Isaiah 12:2, 4bcd, 6

℟. (6) Cry out with joy and gladness:
 for among you is the great and Holy One of Israel.

**I trust the Lord to save me,
and I won't be afraid.
My power and my strength come from the Lord God,
and he has saved me.**

℟. Cry out with joy and gladness:
 for among you is the great and Holy One of Israel.

**Our Lord, we are thankful, and we worship only you.
We will tell the nations how glorious you are
and what you have done.**

℟. Cry out with joy and gladness:
 for among you is the great and Holy One of Israel.

People of Jerusalem, celebrate and sing.
The famous L<small>ORD</small> God of Israel is here with you.

℞. Cry out with joy and gladness:
for among you is the great and Holy One of Israel.

SECOND READING

The Lord is near.

A reading from the letter of Paul to the Philippians   4:4-7

Brothers and sisters:
Always be glad because of the Lord!
I will say it again: Be glad.

Always be gentle with others.
The Lord will soon be here.
Don't worry about anything,
but pray about everything.

With thankful hearts offer up your prayers and requests to God.
Then, because you belong to Christ Jesus,
God will bless you with peace
that no one can completely understand.
And this peace will control the way you think and feel.

The word of the Lord.

ALLELUIA   Isaiah 61:1

℞. Alleluia, alleluia.

The Spirit of the Lord now upon me
has sent me to bring good news to the poor.

℞. Alleluia, alleluia.

GOSPEL

What, then, must we do?

✠ A reading from the holy gospel according to Luke 3:10-16, 18

The crowds asked John the Baptist, "What should we do?"
John told them,
"If you have two coats,
    give one to someone who doesn't have any.
If you have food,
    share it with someone else."

When tax collectors came to be baptized, they asked John,
"Teacher, what should we do?"
John told them, "Don't make people pay more than they owe."

Some soldiers asked him, "And what about us?
What do we have to do?"

John told them,
"Don't force people to pay money to make you leave them alone.
Be satisfied with your pay."

Everyone became excited and wondered,
"Could John be the Messiah?"

John said, "I am just baptizing with water.
But someone more powerful is going to come,
    and I am not good enough even to untie his sandals.
He will baptize you with the Holy Spirit and with fire."

In many different ways John preached the good news to the people.

                                              The gospel of the Lord.

FOURTH SUNDAY OF ADVENT **A**

FIRST READING

Jesus Christ, a descendant of David, is the Son of God.

A reading from the letter of Paul to the Romans 1:2-4

Brothers and sisters:
Long ago God promised the good news
    by what his prophets said in the holy Scriptures.
This good news is about his Son, our Lord Jesus Christ!
As a human, he was from the family of David.
But the Holy Spirit proved that Jesus is the powerful Son of God,
    because he was raised from death.

The word of the Lord.

RESPONSORIAL PSALM 24:1-2, 3-4abc

℟. (7c and 10b) Let the Lord enter; he is king of glory.

**The earth and everything on it
belong to the L**ORD**.
The world and its people
belong to him.
The L**ORD **placed it all
on the oceans and rivers.**

℟. Let the Lord enter; he is king of glory.

Who may climb the LORD**'s hill
or stand in his holy temple?
Only those who do right
for the right reasons,
and don't worship idols.**

℟. Let the Lord enter; he is king of glory.

ALLELUIA Matthew 1:23

℟. Alleluia, alleluia.

**A virgin will give birth to a son;
his name will be Emmanuel: God is with us.**

℟. Alleluia, alleluia.

GOSPEL

Jesus was born of Mary, the betrothed of Joseph, a son of David.

✛ **A reading from the holy gospel according to Matthew** 1:18-24

This is how Jesus Christ was born.
A young woman named Mary was engaged
    to Joseph from King David's family.
But before they were married,
    she learned that she was going to have a baby by God's Holy Spirit.

Joseph was a good man and did not want to embarrass Mary
    in front of everyone.
So he decided to quietly call off the wedding.

While Joseph was thinking about this,
    an angel from the Lord came to him in a dream.
The angel said, "Joseph, the baby that Mary will have
    is from the Holy Spirit.
Go ahead and marry her.
Then after her baby is born, name him Jesus,
    because he will save his people from their sins."

So God's promise came true, just as the prophet had said,

    "A virgin will have a baby boy,
    and he will be called Immanuel,"
    which means "God is with us."

After Joseph woke up, he and Mary were soon married,
    just as the Lord's angel had told him to do.

                                The gospel of the Lord.

[11] **FOURTH SUNDAY OF ADVENT** **B**

FIRST READING

The mystery kept secret for endless ages is now revealed.

A reading from the letter of Paul to the Romans 16:25-27

Brothers and sisters:
Praise God!
He can make you strong by means of my good news,
   which is the message about Jesus Christ.
For ages and ages this message was kept secret,
   but now at last it has been told.

The eternal God commanded his prophets to write about the good news,
   so that all nations would obey and have faith.
And now, because of Jesus Christ,
   we can praise the only wise God forever! Amen.

The word of the Lord.

RESPONSORIAL PSALM 47:1-2, 7-8

℟. (8) God is king of all the earth!

All of you nations,
clap your hands and shout
joyful praises to God.
The Lord Most High is fearsome,
the ruler of all the earth.

℟. God is king of all the earth!

God is ruler of all the earth!
Praise God with songs.
God rules the nations
from his sacred throne.

℟. God is king of all the earth!

ALLELUIA Luke 1:38

℟. Alleluia, alleluia.

I am the servant of the Lord:
let it be done to me according to your word.

℟. Alleluia, alleluia.

GOSPEL

You will conceive and bear a son.

✢ A reading from the holy gospel according to Luke 1:26-38

God sent the angel Gabriel to the town of Nazareth in Galilee
with a message for a virgin named Mary.
She was engaged to Joseph from the family of King David.
The angel greeted Mary and said,
"You are truly blessed! The Lord is with you."

Mary was confused by the angel's words
and wondered what they meant.
Then the angel told Mary, "Don't be afraid!
God is pleased with you, and you will have a son.
His name will be Jesus.
He will be great and will be called the Son of God Most High.
The Lord God will make him king,
as his ancestor David was.
He will rule the people of Israel forever,
and his kingdom will never end."

Mary asked the angel, "How can this happen?
I am not married!"

The angel answered, "The Holy Spirit will come down to you,
and God's power will come over you.
So your child will be called the holy Son of God.

"Your relative Elizabeth is also going to have a son,
even though she is old.
No one thought she could ever have a baby,
but in three months she will have a son.
Nothing is impossible for God!"

Mary said, "I am the Lord's servant!
Let it happen as you have said."

And the angel left her.

The gospel of the Lord.

FOURTH SUNDAY OF ADVENT

FIRST READING

Out of you will be born the one who is to rule over Israel.

A reading from the book of the prophet Micah 5:1-3

Town of Bethlehem Ephrathah,
    you are one of the smallest in the nation of Judah.
But I will choose one of your people to rule the nation.
And his family goes back to ancient times.

The Lord will abandon Israel only until this ruler is born
    and the rest of his family come back to join Israel.

He will stand like a shepherd feeding his sheep
    by the power and glorious name of the Lord his God.
His people will live in peace,
    and everyone on earth will know how great the Lord is.

The word of the Lord.

RESPONSORIAL PSALM 80:1acdef and 2c, 14-15ab

℟. (3) Rouse your power, O Lord, and come to save us.

Shepherd of Israel,
you sit on your throne
above the winged creatures.
Listen to our prayer
and let your light shine.
Save us by your power.

℟. Rouse your power, O Lord, and come to save us.

God All-Powerful,
please do something!
Look down from heaven
and see what's happening to this vine.
With your own hands
you planted its roots.

℟. Rouse your power, O Lord, and come to save us.

ALLELUIA
Luke 1:38

℟. Alleluia, alleluia.

**I am the servant of the Lord:
let it be done to me according to your word.**

℟. Alleluia, alleluia.

GOSPEL

Why should I be honored with a visit from the mother of my Lord?

✢ **A reading from the holy gospel according to Luke** 1:39-45

**Mary hurried to a town in the hill country of Judea.
She went into Zechariah's home,
  where she greeted Elizabeth.
When Elizabeth heard Mary's greeting,
  her baby moved within her.**

**The Holy Spirit came upon Elizabeth.
Then in a loud voice she said to Mary:
"God has blessed you more than any other woman!
He has also blessed the child you will have.
Why should the mother of my Lord come to me?
As soon as I heard your greeting,
  my baby became happy and moved within me.
The Lord has blessed you because you believed
  that he will keep his promise."**

The gospel of the Lord.

SEASON OF CHRISTMAS

[13]   December 25   

THE BIRTH OF THE LORD

The following readings may be used only when the celebration of the liturgy of the word for the children is held in a place apart from the main assembly.

FIRST READING

A son is given to us.

A reading from the book of the prophet Isaiah   9:2-4, 6-7

Those who walked in the dark have seen a bright light.
And it shines upon everyone who lives in the land of darkest shadows.

Our LORD, you have made your nation stronger.
Because of you, its people are glad and celebrate
    like workers at harvest time
    or soldiers dividing what they have taken.

You have broken the power
    of those who oppressed and enslaved your people.
You have rescued them as you did from Midian.

For us a child has been born.
A son has been given to us,
    and he will be our ruler.
His names will be:
    Wonderful Adviser and Mighty God,
    Eternal Father and Prince of Peace.

His power will never end,
    and peace will last forever.
He will rule David's kingdom and make it grow strong.
He will always rule with honesty and justice.
The LORD All-Powerful will make certain that all of this is done.

The word of the Lord.

RESPONSORIAL PSALM   96:1-2a, 2b-3, 11-12a

℟. (Luke 2:11) Today is born our Savior, Christ the Lord.

Sing a new song to the LORD!
Everyone on this earth,
sing praises to the LORD,
sing and praise his name.

℟. Today is born our Savior, Christ the Lord.

**Day after day announce,
"The LORD has saved us!"
Tell every nation on earth,
"The LORD is wonderful
and does marvelous things!"**

℟. Today is born our Savior, Christ the Lord.

**Tell the heavens and the earth
to be glad and celebrate!
Command the ocean to roar
with all of its creatures
and the fields to rejoice
with all of their crops.**

℟. Today is born our Savior, Christ the Lord.

SECOND READING

God's grace has been revealed to all people.

A reading from the letter of Paul to Titus   3:4-6

**Brothers and sisters:
God our Savior showed us how good and kind he is.
He saved us because of his mercy,
   and not because of any good things that we have done.**

**God washed us by the power of the Holy Spirit.
He gave us new birth and a fresh beginning.
God sent Jesus Christ our Savior to give us his Spirit.**

The word of the Lord.

ALLELUIA   Luke 2:10-11

℟. Alleluia, alleluia.

**Good news and great joy to all the world:
today is born our Savior, Christ the Lord.**

℟. Alleluia, alleluia.

GOSPEL

Today a Savior has been born for you.

✢ A reading from the holy gospel according to Luke   2:1-14

Emperor Augustus gave orders for the names of all the people
    to be listed in record books.
These first records were made when Quirinius was governor of Syria.

Everyone had to go to their own hometown to be listed.
So Joseph had to leave Nazareth in Galilee and go to Bethlehem in Judea.
Long ago Bethlehem had been King David's hometown,
    and Joseph went there because he was from David's family.

Mary was engaged to Joseph and traveled with him to Bethlehem.
She was soon going to have a baby,
    and while they were there,
    she gave birth to her first-born son.
She dressed him in baby clothes and laid him in a manger,
    because there was no room for them in the inn.

That night in the fields near Bethlehem
    some shepherds were guarding their sheep.
All at once an angel came down to them from the Lord,
    and the brightness of the Lord's glory flashed around them.
The shepherds were frightened.
But the angel said, "Don't be afraid!
I have good news for you, which will make everyone happy.
This very day in King David's hometown a Savior was born for you.
He is Christ the Lord.
You will know who he is,
    because you will find him dressed in baby clothes
        and lying in a manger."

Suddenly many other angels came down from heaven
    and joined in praising God.
They said: "Praise God in heaven!
Peace on earth to everyone who pleases God."

                                    The gospel of the Lord.

[14] Sunday in the Octave of Christmas

THE HOLY FAMILY

FIRST READING

Those who fear the Lord honor their parents.

A reading from the book of Sirach 3:2-6

Children, the LORD expects you to honor your father,
 and has given your mother authority over you.
If you honor your father,
 your sins will be forgiven.
If you praise your mother,
 treasure will be stored up in heaven for you.

If you honor your father,
 your own children will make you happy,
 and all of your prayers will be answered.
If you respect your father,
 you will live a long life,
 and if you listen to the LORD,
 your mother can relax.

The word of the Lord.

RESPONSORIAL PSALM 128:1-2, 3, 4-5

℟. (see 1) Happy are those who fear the Lord and walk in his ways.

**The LORD will bless you
if you respect him
and obey his laws.
Your fields will produce,
and you will be happy
and all will go well.**

℟. Happy are those who fear the Lord and walk in his ways.

**Your wife will be as fruitful
as a grapevine,**

and just as an olive tree
is rich with olives,
your home will be rich
with healthy children.

℟. Happy are those who fear the Lord and walk in his ways.

That is how the LORD will bless
everyone who respects him.
I pray that the LORD
will bless you from Zion
and let Jerusalem prosper
as long as you live.

℟. Happy are those who fear the Lord and walk in his ways.

SECOND READING

Concerning the Christian life in the world.

A reading from the letter of Paul to the Colossians 3:12-17

Brothers and sisters:
God loves you and has chosen you as his own special people.
So be gentle, kind, humble, meek, and patient.
Put up with each other,
    and forgive anyone who does you wrong,
    just as Christ has forgiven you.
Love is more important than anything else.
It is what ties everything completely together.

Each one of you is part of the body of Christ,
    and you were chosen to live together in peace.
So let the peace that comes from Christ control your thoughts.
And be grateful.

Let the message about Christ completely fill your lives,
    while you use all your wisdom to teach and instruct each other.
With thankful hearts,
    sing psalms, hymns, and spiritual songs to God.
Whatever you say or do should be done in the name of the Lord Jesus,
    as you give thanks to God the Father because of him.

The word of the Lord.

ALLELUIA
Colossians 3:15a, 16

℟. Alleluia, alleluia.

May the peace of Christ rule in your hearts,
and the fullness of his message live within you.

℟. Alleluia, alleluia.

GOSPEL

Take the child and his mother, and flee to Egypt.

✜ A reading from the holy gospel according to Matthew   2:13-15, 19-23

An angel from the Lord appeared to Joseph in a dream.
The angel said, "Get up!
Hurry and take the child and his mother to Egypt!
Stay there until I tell you to return,
   because Herod is looking for the child and wants to kill him."

That night Joseph got up and took his wife and the child to Egypt,
   where they stayed until Herod died.
So the Lord's promise came true, just as the prophet had said,
"I called my son out of Egypt."

After King Herod died,
   an angel from the Lord appeared in a dream to Joseph
   while he was still in Egypt.
The angel said, "Get up and take the child and his mother
   back to Israel.
The people who wanted to kill him are now dead."

Joseph got up and left with them for Israel.
But when he heard that Herod's son Archelaus was now ruler of Judea,
   he was afraid to go there.
Then in a dream he was told to go to Galilee,
   and they went to live there in the town of Nazareth.

So the Lord's promise came true,
   just as the prophet had said,
"He will be called a Nazarene."

                        The gospel of the Lord.

[15]   **January 1**   **A B C**
Octave of Christmas

MARY, MOTHER OF GOD

FIRST READING

*They will call down my name on the children of Israel,
and I will bless them.*

A reading from the book of Numbers   6:22-27

The LORD told Moses to tell Aaron and his sons what they must say to bless the people of Israel. It was:

"I pray that the LORD will bless and protect you.
May the LORD show kindness and mercy to you.
May he be good to you and give you peace."

Then the LORD said,
"If they speak in my name to the people of Israel,
I will bless them."

The word of the Lord.

RESPONSORIAL PSALM   67:1-2, 5 and 7

℟. (2a) May God bless us in his mercy.

**Our God, be kind and bless us!
Be pleased and smile.
Then everyone on earth
will learn to follow you,
and all nations will see
your power to save us.**

℟. May God bless us in his mercy.

**Make everyone praise you
and shout your praises.
Pray for his blessings to continue
and for everyone on earth
to worship our God.**

℟. May God bless us in his mercy.

ALLELUIA

Hebrews 1:1-2

℟. Alleluia, alleluia.

In the past God spoke to our ancestors through the prophets; now God speaks to us through the Son.

℟. Alleluia, alleluia.

GOSPEL

The shepherds found Mary and Joseph, and the baby lying in the manger.... When the eighth day came they gave him the name Jesus.

✢ A reading from the holy gospel according to Luke

2:16-21

The shepherds hurried off and found Mary and Joseph, and they saw the baby lying in the manger.

When the shepherds saw Jesus,
 they told his parents what the angel had said about him.
Everyone listened and was surprised.
But Mary kept thinking about all this and wondering what it meant.

As the shepherds returned to their sheep,
 they were praising God and saying wonderful things about him.
Everything they had seen and heard was just as the angel had said.

Eight days later Jesus' parents did for him
  what the Law of Moses commands.
And they named him Jesus,
  just as the angel had told Mary
   when he promised she would have a baby.

The gospel of the Lord.

[16] # THE EPIPHANY OF THE LORD   **A B C**

The following readings may be used only when the celebration of the liturgy of the word for the children is held in a place apart from the main assembly.

FIRST READING

The glory of the Lord shines upon you.

A reading from the book of the prophet Isaiah 60:1-6

Jerusalem, stand up and shine!
  Your new day is dawning.
And the glory of the Lord shines brightly on you.
The earth and its people are covered with darkness,
  but the glory of the Lord is shining over you.
Nations and kings will come to the light of your dawning day.

Open your eyes and look around!
Crowds are on their way.
Your sons are coming from distant lands,
  and your daughters are being carried like young children.
When you see this, your faces will glow.
Your hearts will beat fast and swell with pride.

Treasures from over the sea
  and the wealth of nations will be brought to you.
Your country will be covered with caravans of young camels
    from Midian and Ephah.
And the people of Sheba will bring gold and spices
    in praise of the Lord.

The word of the Lord.

RESPONSIONAL PSALM
72:1, 2, 10abc, 10de-11

℟. (see 11) Lord, every nation on earth will adore you.

**Please help the king
to be honest and fair
just like you, our God.**

℟. Lord, every nation on earth will adore you.

**Let him be honest and fair
with all your people,
especially the poor.**

℟. Lord, every nation on earth will adore you.

**Force the rulers of Tarshish
and of the islands
to pay taxes to him.**

℟. Lord, every nation on earth will adore you.

**Make the kings of Sheba
and of Seba bring gifts.
Make other rulers bow down
and all nations serve him.**

℟. Lord, every nation on earth will adore you.

ALLELUIA
Matthew 2:2

℟. Alleluia, alleluia.

**We have seen his star in the east
and have come to adore the Lord.**

℟. Alleluia, alleluia.

GOSPEL

We have come from the east to worship the king.

✛ A reading from the holy gospel according to Matthew   2:1-12

When Jesus was born in the village of Bethlehem in Judea,
Herod was king.
During this time some wise men from the east came to Jerusalem and said,
"Where is the child born to be king of the Jews?
We saw his star in the east and have come to worship him."

When King Herod heard about this, he was worried,
    and so was everyone else in Jerusalem.
Herod brought together all the chief priests and the teachers
    of the Law of Moses and asked them,
"Where will the Messiah be born?"

They told him,
"He will be born in Bethlehem, just as the prophet wrote,

    'Bethlehem in the land of Judea,
    you are very important among the towns of Judea.
    From your town will come a leader,
    who will be like a shepherd for my people Israel.' "

Herod secretly called in the wise men
    and asked them when they had first seen the star.
He told them, "Go to Bethlehem and search carefully for the child.
As soon as you find him, let me know.
I want to go and worship him too."

The wise men listened to what the king said and then left.
And the star they had seen in the east went on ahead of them
    until it stopped over the place where the child was.
They were thrilled and excited to see the star.

When the men went into the house
    and saw the child with Mary, his mother,
    they kneeled down and worshiped him.
They took out their gifts of gold, frankincense, and myrrh
    and gave them to him.
Later they were warned in a dream not to return to Herod,
    and they went back home by another road.

                                The gospel of the Lord.

[17]   Sunday after January 6   

THE BAPTISM OF THE LORD
(First Sunday in Ordinary Time)

FIRST READING

Here is my servant, my chosen one in whom I am well pleased.

A reading from the book of the prophet Isaiah   42:1-2, 4, 6-7

Here is my servant!
I have made him strong.
He is my chosen one, and I am pleased with him.
I will give him my Spirit,
    and he will bring justice to the nations.
He won't shout or yell or call out in the streets.
He won't quit or give up until he brings justice to all the earth,
    and people in foreign lands long for his teaching.
I, the LORD, chose you because of my kindness,
    and I am here at your side.
I created and appointed you
      to bring light and my promise of hope to the nations.
You will give sight to the blind
    and set prisoners free from dark dungeons.

                                 The word of the Lord.

RESPONSORIAL PSALM   29:3abde-4, 3cde and 9ef-10

℟. (11b) The Lord will bless his people with peace.

**The voice of the LORD
echoes over the oceans.
He thunders above the roar
of the raging seas,
and his voice is mighty
and marvelous.**

℟. The Lord will bless his people with peace.

The glorious LORD God
thunders above the roar
of the raging seas,
and the temple is filled
with shouts of praise.
The LORD rules on his throne,
king of the flood forever.

℟. The Lord will bless his people with peace.

SECOND READING

God anointed Jesus of Nazareth with the Holy Spirit and with power.

A reading from the Acts of the Apostles   10:34-38

Peter said to Cornelius and his household:
"Now I am certain that God treats all people alike.
God is pleased with everyone who worships him and does right,
   no matter what nation they come from.
This is the same message that God gave to the people of Israel,
   when he sent Jesus Christ, the Lord of all, to offer peace to them.

"You surely know what happened everywhere in Judea.
It all began in Galilee after John had told everyone to be baptized.
God gave the Holy Spirit and power to Jesus from Nazareth.
He was with Jesus,
   as he went around doing good
      and healing everyone who was under the power of the devil."

The word of the Lord.

ALLELUIA   See Mark 9:7

℟. Alleluia, alleluia.

**The heavens were opened and the Father's voice was heard:
This is my beloved Son, hear him.**

℟. Alleluia, alleluia.

GOSPEL

When Jesus had been baptized and had been praying,
the heavens were opened and the Holy Spirit came upon him.

✛ **A reading from the holy gospel according to Luke**　　3:15-16, 21-22

Everyone became excited and wondered,
"Could John be the Messiah?"

John said, "I am just baptizing with water.
But someone more powerful is going to come,
　　and I am not good enough even to untie his sandals.
He will baptize you with the Holy Spirit and with fire."

After everyone else had been baptized,
　　Jesus himself was baptized.
Then as he prayed, the sky opened up,
　　and the Holy Spirit came down upon him in the form of a dove.
A voice from heaven said,
"You are my own dear Son, and I am pleased with you."

　　　　　　　　　　　　　　　　　　　The gospel of the Lord.

SEASON OF LENT

FIRST SUNDAY OF LENT A

[18]

The following readings may be used only when the celebration of the liturgy of the word for the children is held in a place apart from the main assembly.

FIRST READING

Creation of our first parents, and sin.

A reading from the book of Genesis 2:7-9; 3:1-7

The Lord God took some earth and used it to make a man.
God breathed into the man's nose,
    and the man started breathing.
The Lord God had made a garden in a place called Eden,
    which was in the east,
    and he put the man there.

The Lord made all kinds of beautiful trees
    and all kinds of fruit trees grow in the garden.
Two other trees were in the middle of the garden.
One of the trees gave life,
    and the other showed the difference between right and wrong.

The snake was sneakier than any of the other wild animals
    that the Lord God had made.
One day it came to the woman and asked,
"Did God tell you not to eat fruit from any tree in the garden?"

The woman answered,
"God said we could eat fruit from any tree in the garden
    except the one in the middle.
He told us not to eat fruit from that tree or even touch it.
If we do, we will die."

"No, you won't die!" the snake replied.
"God understands what will happen
    on the day you eat fruit from that tree.
You will see what you have done,
    and you will know the difference between right and wrong,
    just as God does."

The woman stared at the fruit.
It looked beautiful and tasty.
She wanted the wisdom that it would give her,
    and she ate some of the fruit.
She gave some to her husband Adam, and he ate it too.
At once they saw what they had done,
    and they realized that they were naked.
So they sewed fig leaves together to make clothes for themselves.

The word of the Lord.

RESPONSORIAL PSALM   51:1, 10, 12, 15

℟. (3a) Be merciful, O Lord, for we have sinned.

You are kind, God!
Please have pity on me.
You are always merciful!
Please wipe away my sins.

℟. Be merciful, O Lord, for we have sinned.

Create pure thoughts in me
and make me faithful again.

℟. Be merciful, O Lord, for we have sinned.

Make me as happy as you did
when you saved me; make me want to obey!

℟. Be merciful, O Lord, for we have sinned.

Help me to speak,
and I will praise you, Lord.

℟. Be merciful, O Lord, for we have sinned.

VERSE BEFORE THE GOSPEL   Matthew 4:4b

℟. Glory and praise to you, Lord Jesus Christ.

No one lives on bread alone,
but on every word that comes from the mouth of God.

℟. Glory and praise to you, Lord Jesus Christ.

GOSPEL

Jesus fasted for forty days and nights and was tempted.

✢ **A reading from the holy gospel according to Matthew**   4:1-11

The Holy Spirit led Jesus into the desert,
    so that the devil could test him.
After Jesus went without eating for forty days and nights,
    he was very hungry.
Then the devil came to him and said,
"If you are God's Son,
    tell these stones to turn into bread."

Jesus answered,
"The Scriptures say: 'No one can live only on food.
People need every word that God has spoken.' "

Next, the devil took Jesus to the holy city
    and had him stand on the highest part of the temple.

The devil said, "If you are God's Son, jump off.
The Scriptures say: 'God will give his angels orders about you.
They will catch you in their arms,
    and you will not hurt your feet on the stones.' "

Jesus answered, "The Scriptures also say,
'Don't try to test the Lord your God!' "

Finally, the devil took Jesus up on a very high mountain
    and showed him all the kingdoms on earth and their power.
The devil said to him, "I will give all this to you,
    if you will bow down and worship me."

Jesus answered, "Go away, Satan!
The Scriptures say: 'Worship the Lord your God and serve only him.' "

Then the devil left Jesus,
    and angels came to help him.

The gospel of the Lord.

[19] # FIRST SUNDAY OF LENT   **B**

The following readings may be used only when the celebration of the liturgy of the word for the children is held in a place apart from the main assembly.

FIRST READING

The covenant of God when Noah was delivered from the flood.

A reading from the book of Genesis   9:8-15

God told Noah and his sons:
"I am going to make a solemn promise to you
   and to all who will live after you.
This includes the birds and animals that came out of the boat.
I promise every living creature on earth
   that the earth and those living on it
      will never again be destroyed by a flood.

"The rainbow that I have put in the sky will be my sign
   to you and to every living creature on earth.
It will tell you that I will keep this solemn promise forever.
When I send clouds to cover the earth,
   and the rainbow appears in the sky,
   I will remember my promise
      to you and to all other living creatures.
Never again will I let flood waters destroy all life."

The word of the Lord.

RESPONSORIAL PSALM   25:4-5abc, 6 and 7cd

℟. (see 10) Your ways, O Lord, are love and truth
   to those who keep your covenant.

Show me your paths
and teach me to follow;
guide me by your truth
and instruct me.
You keep me safe.

℟. Your ways, O Lord, are love and truth
   to those who keep your covenant.

Please, LORD, remember,
you have always
been patient and kind.
Show how truly kind you are
and remember me.

℟. Your ways, O Lord, are love and truth
to those who keep your covenant.

VERSE BEFORE THE GOSPEL   Matthew 4:4b

℟. Glory and praise to you, Lord Jesus Christ.

No one lives on bread alone,
but on every word that comes from the mouth of God.

℟. Glory and praise to you, Lord Jesus Christ.

GOSPEL

Jesus was tempted by Satan, and the angels looked after him.

✠ **A reading from the holy gospel according to Mark**   1:12-15

Right away God's Spirit made Jesus go into the desert.
He stayed there for forty days while Satan tested him.
Jesus was with the wild animals,
    but angels took care of him.

After John was arrested,
    Jesus went to Galilee and told the good news that comes from God.
He said, "The time has come!
God's kingdom will soon be here.
Turn back to God and believe the good news!"

                              The gospel of the Lord.

FIRST SUNDAY OF LENT

The following readings may be used only when the celebration of the liturgy of the word for the children is held in a place apart from the main assembly.

FIRST READING

The confession of faith of the chosen people.

A reading from the book of Deuteronomy 26:4-10

Moses said to the people:
"The priest will take the baskets of grain from your hands
 and put them in front of the altar of the Lord your God.
And there, in the presence of the Lord your God, you must say,

> 'My ancestor was merely a homeless Aramean,
> who went to live in Egypt.
> Although his family was small,
> they became great and powerful,
> a nation of many people.
>
> 'The Egyptians showed no pity!
> They oppressed our people and were very cruel to us.
> Then we called out for help to you,
> the Lord God of our ancestors.
> You heard our cries and knew that we were in trouble,
>   distressed and oppressed.
>
> 'You reached out your mighty arm and rescued us from Egypt.
> You did fearsome things,
> and you worked miracles and all kinds of wonders.

> 'You brought us here
> and gave us this land rich in milk and honey.
> Now, LORD, I bring to you the best part of the crops
> that you have given to me.'

"Leave your baskets there in the presence of the LORD your God
and bow down to worship him."

The word of the Lord.

RESPONSORIAL PSALM 91:1-2, 10-11

℟. (see 15b) Be with me, Lord, when I am in trouble.

**Live under the protection
of God Most High
and stay in the shadow
of God All-Powerful.
Then you will say to the LORD,
"You are my fortress,
my place of safety;
you are my God, and I trust you."**

℟. Be with me, Lord, when I am in trouble.

**No terrible disasters
will strike you or your home.
God will command his angels
to protect you wherever you go.**

℟. Be with me, Lord, when I am in trouble.

VERSE BEFORE THE GOSPEL Matthew 4:4b

℟. Glory and praise to you, Lord Jesus Christ.

**No one lives on bread alone,
but on every word that comes from the mouth of God.**

℟. Glory and praise to you, Lord Jesus Christ.

GOSPEL

> Filled with the Holy Spirit, Jesus was led by the Spirit
> through the wilderness where he was tempted.

✢ A reading from the holy gospel according to Luke 4:1-13

When Jesus returned from the Jordan River,
the power of the Holy Spirit was with him,
and the Spirit led him into the desert.
For forty days Jesus was tested by the devil,
and during that time he went without eating.
When it was all over, he was hungry.

The devil said to Jesus,
"If you are God's Son, tell this stone to turn into bread."

Jesus answered, "The Scriptures say,
'No one can live only on food.' "

Then the devil led Jesus up to a high place
and quickly showed him all the nations on earth.
The devil said, "I will give all this power and glory to you.
It has been given to me,
and I can give it to anyone I want to.
Just worship me, and you can have it all."

Jesus answered, "The Scriptures say:
'Worship the Lord your God and serve only him!' "

Finally, the devil took Jesus to Jerusalem
and had him stand on top of the temple.
The devil said, "If you are God's Son, jump off.
The Scriptures say: 'God will tell his angels to take care of you.
They will catch you in their arms,
and you will not hurt your feet on the stones.' "

Jesus answered, "The Scriptures also say,
'Don't try to test the Lord your God!' "

After the devil had finished testing Jesus in every way possible,
he left him for a while.

The gospel of the Lord.

SECOND SUNDAY OF LENT **A**

[21]

The following readings may be used only when the celebration of the liturgy of the word for the children is held in a place apart from the main assembly.

FIRST READING

The call of Abraham, the father of God's people.

A reading from the book of Genesis   12:1-4a

The Lord said to Abraham,
"Leave your country, your family, and your relatives
and go to the land that I will show you.

"I will bless you and make you into a great nation.
You will become famous and be a blessing to others.
I will bless the people who say good things about you,
    but I will put a curse on anyone who says evil things about you.
Everyone on earth will be blessed because of you."

So Abraham left, just as the Lord had told him to do.

The word of the Lord.

RESPONSORIAL PSALM   33:4-5, 20 and 22

℟. (22) Lord, let your mercy be on us,
    as we place our trust in you.

**The Lord is truthful;
he can be trusted.
He loves justice and fairness,
and he is kind to everyone
everywhere on earth.**

℟. Lord, let your mercy be on us,
    as we place our trust in you.

**We depend on you, Lord,
to help and protect us.
Be kind and bless us!
We depend on you.**

℟. Lord, let your mercy be on us,
    as we place our trust in you.

VERSE BEFORE THE GOSPEL See Matthew 17:5

℟. Glory and praise to you, Lord Jesus Christ.

From the shining cloud the Father's voice is heard:
This is my beloved Son, hear him.

℟. Glory and praise to you, Lord Jesus Christ.

GOSPEL

Jesus' face shone like the sun.

✛ A reading from the holy gospel according to Matthew 17:1-9

Jesus took Peter and the brothers James and John with him.
They went up on a very high mountain where they could be alone.
There in front of the disciples Jesus was completely changed.
His face was shining like the sun,
    and his clothes became white as light.

All at once Moses and Elijah were there talking with Jesus.
So Peter said to him, "Lord, it is good for us to be here!
Let us make three shelters,
    one for you, one for Moses, and one for Elijah."

While Peter was still speaking,
    the shadow of a bright cloud passed over them.
From the cloud a voice said,
"This is my own dear Son, and I am pleased with him.
Listen to what he says!"

When the disciples heard the voice,
    they were so afraid that they fell flat on the ground.
But Jesus came over and touched them.
He said, "Get up and don't be afraid!"
When they opened their eyes, they saw only Jesus.

On their way down from the mountain,
    Jesus warned his disciples not to tell anyone what they had seen
    until after the Son of Man had been raised from death.

                                                The gospel of the Lord.

[22] **SECOND SUNDAY OF LENT** B

The following readings may be used only when the celebration of the liturgy of the word for the children is held in a place apart from the main assembly.

FIRST READING

Nothing can separate us from God's love in Christ.

A reading from the letter of Paul to the Romans 8:31, 38-39

Brothers and sisters:
What can we say about all this?
If God is on our side, can anyone be against us?

I am sure that nothing can separate us from God's love —
 not life or death, not angels or spirits,
 not the present or the future,
 and not powers above or powers below.
Nothing in all creation can separate us from God's love for us
 in Christ Jesus our Lord!

The word of the Lord.

RESPONSORIAL PSALM 103:1-2, 8 and 11

℟. (8a) The Lord is kind and merciful.

**With all my heart
I praise the L**ORD**,
and with all that I am
I praise his holy name!
With all my heart
I praise the L**ORD**!
I will never forget
how kind he has been.**

℟. The Lord is kind and merciful.

The LORD **is merciful!
He is kind and patient,
and his love never fails.
How great is God's love for all
who worship him?
Greater than the distance
between heaven and earth!**

℟. The Lord is kind and merciful.

VERSE BEFORE THE GOSPEL
See Matthew 17:5

℟. Glory and praise to you, Lord Jesus Christ.

**From the shining cloud the Father's voice is heard:
This is my beloved Son, hear him.**

℟. Glory and praise to you, Lord Jesus Christ.

GOSPEL

This is my beloved Son.

✢ A reading from the holy gospel according to Mark
9:2-10

Jesus took Peter, James, and John with him
   and went up on a high mountain,
   where they could be alone.
There in front of the disciples,
   Jesus was completely changed.
And his clothes became much whiter
   than any bleach on earth could make them.
Then Moses and Elijah were there talking with Jesus.

Peter said to Jesus, "Teacher, it is good for us to be here!
Let us make three shelters,
   one for you, one for Moses, and one for Elijah."
But Peter and the others were terribly frightened,
   and he did not know what he was talking about.

The shadow of a cloud passed over and covered them.
From the cloud a voice said, "This is my Son, and I love him.
Listen to what he says!"
At once the disciples looked around,
   but they saw only Jesus.

As Jesus and his disciples were coming down the mountain,
   he told them not to say a word about what they had seen,
   until the Son of Man had been raised from death.
So they kept it to themselves.
But they wondered what he meant by the words "raised from death."

The gospel of the Lord.

[23] **SECOND SUNDAY OF LENT**

The following readings may be used only when the celebration of the liturgy of the word for the children is held in a place apart from the main assembly.

FIRST READING

*Christ will transfigure these bodies of ours
into copies of his glorious body.*

A reading from the letter of Paul to the Philippians 3:20—4:1

B rothers and sisters:
 We are citizens of heaven
  and are eagerly waiting for our Savior to come from there.
Our Lord Jesus Christ has power over everything,
 and he will make these poor bodies of ours
  like his own glorious body.

Dear friends, I love you and long to see you.
Please keep on being faithful to the Lord.
You are my pride and joy.

The word of the Lord.

RESPONSORIAL PSALM 147:1, 3-4, 5 and 7

℟. (Is 30:18) Happy are all who long for the coming of the Lord.

**Shout praises to the LORD!
Our God is kind,
and it is right and good
to sing praises to him.**

℟. Happy are all who long for the coming of the Lord.

**He renews our hopes
and heals our bodies.
He decided how many stars
there would be in the sky
and gave each one a name.**

℟. Happy are all who long for the coming of the Lord.

Our LORD is great and powerful!
He understands everything.
Celebrate and sing!
Play your harps
for the LORD our God.

℟. Happy are all who long for the coming of the Lord.

VERSE BEFORE THE GOSPEL See Matthew 17:5

℟. Glory and praise to you, Lord Jesus Christ.

**From the shining cloud the Father's voice is heard:
This is my beloved Son, hear him.**

℟. Glory and praise to you, Lord Jesus Christ.

GOSPEL

As Jesus prayed, the aspect of his face was changed,
and his clothing became brilliant as lightning.

✣ **A reading from the holy gospel according to Luke** 9:28-36

Jesus took Peter, John, and James with him
and went up on a mountain to pray.
While he was praying,
his face changed, and his clothes became shining white.
Suddenly Moses and Elijah were there speaking with him.
They appeared in heavenly glory
and talked about all that Jesus' death
in Jerusalem would mean.

Peter and the other two disciples had been sound asleep.
All at once they woke up and saw how glorious Jesus was.
They also saw the two men who were with him.

Moses and Elijah were about to leave, when Peter said to Jesus,
"Master, it is good for us to be here!
Let us make three shelters,
one for you, one for Moses, and one for Elijah."
But Peter did not know what he was talking about.

While Peter was still speaking,
>   a shadow from a cloud passed over them,
>   and they were frightened as the cloud covered them.
> From the cloud a voice spoke, "This is my chosen Son.
> Listen to what he says!"

After the voice had spoken,
>   Peter, John, and James saw only Jesus.
> For some time they kept quiet
>   and did not say anything about what they had seen.

The gospel of the Lord.

THIRD SUNDAY OF LENT **A**

[24]

The following readings may be used only when the celebration of the liturgy of the word for the children is held in a place apart from the main assembly.

FIRST READING

Give us water to drink (Exodus 17:2).

A reading from the book of Exodus 17:3-7

The people of Israel were thirsty and kept on complaining.
They said, "Moses, did you bring us out of Egypt
   just to let us and our families and our animals die of thirst?"

Then Moses prayed, "LORD, what am I going to do with these people?
They are about to stone me to death."

The LORD answered, "Take some of the leaders with you
   and go on ahead of the rest of the people.
Take along the walking stick that you used to strike the Nile River,
   and when you get to the rock at Sinai,
   I will be there with you.
Strike the rock with the stick,
   and water will pour out for the people to drink."

Moses did this while the leaders of the people watched.
He named that place Massah and Meribah.
This was because the people complained and tested the LORD by asking,
"Is the LORD really with us?"

The word of the Lord.

RESPONSORIAL PSALM   95:1-2, 7e-9c

℟. (8) If today you hear God's voice, harden not your hearts.

**Sing joyful songs to the LORD!
Praise the mighty rock
where we are safe.
Come to worship him
with thankful hearts
and songs of praise.**

℟. If today you hear God's voice, harden not your hearts.

**Listen to God's voice today!
Don't be stubborn and rebel
as your ancestors did
at Meribah and at Massah
out in the desert.
They tested God and saw
the things he did.**

℟. If today you hear God's voice, harden not your hearts.

VERSE BEFORE THE GOSPEL   See John 2:42, 15

℟. Glory and praise to you, Lord Jesus Christ.

**Lord, you are truly the Savior of the world;
give me living water, that I may never thirst again.**

℟. Glory and praise to you, Lord Jesus Christ.

GOSPEL

The water that I shall give will become a spring of eternal life.

✣ A reading from the holy gospel according to John

4:5-15, 19b-26, 39a, 40-42

On his way to Galilee,
Jesus came to the town of Sychar.
It was near the field that Jacob had long ago given to his son Joseph.
The well that Jacob had dug was still there,
    and Jesus sat down beside it
    because he was tired from traveling.
It was noon,
    and after Jesus' disciples had gone into town to buy some food,
    a Samaritan woman came to draw water from the well.

Jesus asked her, "Would you please give me a drink of water?"

"You are a Jew," she replied,
    "and I am a Samaritan woman.
How can you ask me for a drink of water
    when Jews and Samaritans won't have anything to do
        with each other?"

Jesus answered, "You don't know what God wants to give you,
    and you don't know who is asking you for a drink.
If you did, you would ask him for the water that gives life."

"Sir," the woman said,
    "you don't even have a bucket, and the well is deep.
Where are you going to get this life-giving water?
Our ancestor Jacob dug this well for us,
    and his family and animals got water from it.
Are you greater than Jacob?"

Jesus answered,
"Everyone who drinks this water will get thirsty again.
But no one who drinks the water I give will ever be thirsty again.
The water I give is like a flowing fountain that gives eternal life."

The woman replied, "Sir, please give me a drink of that water!
Then I won't get thirsty and have to come to this well again."

She also told him,
"Sir, I can see that you are a prophet.
My ancestors worshiped on this mountain,
    but you Jews say Jerusalem is the only place to worship."

Jesus said to her: "Believe me,
    the time is coming when you won't worship God
        either on this mountain or in Jerusalem.
You Samaritans don't really know the one you worship.
But we Jews do know the God we worship,
    and by using us God will save the world.
But a time is coming, and it is already here!
Even now the true worshipers are being led by the Spirit
    to worship the Father according to the truth.
These are the ones the Father is seeking to worship him.
God is Spirit,
    and those who worship God must be led by the Spirit
        to worship him according to the truth."

The woman said, "I know that the Messiah will come.
He is the one we call Christ.
When he comes, he will explain everything to us."

"I am that one," Jesus told her,
    "and I am speaking to you now."

A lot of Samaritans in that town put their faith in Jesus.
They came and asked him to stay in their town,
    and he stayed on for two days.

Many more Samaritans put their faith in Jesus
    because of what they heard him say.
They told the woman, "We no longer have faith in Jesus
    just because of what you told us.
We have heard him ourselves,
    and we are certain that he is the Savior of the world!"

                                    The gospel of the Lord.

[25] **THIRD SUNDAY OF LENT** B

The following readings may be used only when the celebration of the liturgy of the word for the children is held in a place apart from the main assembly.

FIRST READING

The law was given through Moses.

A reading from the book of Exodus   20:1-3, 7-8, 12-17

The Lord gave Moses these commandments:
I am the Lord your God.
I brought you out of Egypt, where you were slaves.
Do not worship any god except me.

Do not misuse my name.
I am the Lord your God,
　　and I will punish anyone who misuses my name.

Remember that the Sabbath Day belongs to me.

Respect your father and your mother,
　　and you will live a long time in the land that I am giving you.

Do not murder.
Be faithful in marriage.
Do not steal.
Do not tell lies about others.

Do not want what belongs to someone else.
Do not want anyone's house or wife or slaves
　　or cattle or donkeys or anything else.

　　　　　　　　　　　　　　　　　　The word of the Lord.

RESPONSORIAL PSALM

19:7, 8, 9cd-10ab

℟. (John 6:68c) Lord, you have the words of everlasting life.

The Law of the Lord is perfect;
it gives us new life.
His teachings last forever,
and they give wisdom
to ordinary people.

℟. Lord, you have the words of everlasting life.

The Lord's instruction is right;
it makes our hearts glad.
His commands shine brightly,
and they give us light.

℟. Lord, you have the words of everlasting life.

All of his decisions
are correct and fair.
They are worth more
than the finest gold.

℟. Lord, you have the words of everlasting life.

VERSE BEFORE THE GOSPEL

Ezekiel 18:31

℟. Glory and praise to you, Lord Jesus Christ.

Rid yourselves of all your sins
and make a new heart and a new spirit.

℟. Glory and praise to you, Lord Jesus Christ.

GOSPEL

Destroy this temple, and in three days I will raise it up.

✤ A reading from the holy gospel according to John   2:13-22

Not long before the Jewish festival of Passover,
    Jesus went to Jerusalem.
There he found people selling cattle, sheep, and doves in the temple.
He also saw moneychangers sitting at their tables.
So he took some rope and made a whip.
Then he chased everyone out of the temple,
    together with their sheep and cattle.
He turned over the tables of the moneychangers
    and scattered their coins.

Jesus said to the people who had been selling doves,
"Get those doves out of here!
Don't make my Father's house a marketplace."

The disciples then remembered that the Scriptures say,
"My love for your house burns in me like a fire."

The Jewish leaders asked Jesus,
"What miracle will you work to show us why you have done this?"

"Destroy this temple," Jesus answered,
    "and in three days I will build it again!"

The leaders replied, "It took forty-six years to build this temple.
What makes you think you can rebuild it in three days?"

But Jesus was talking about his body as a temple.
And when he was raised from death,
    his disciples remembered what he had told them.
Then they believed the Scriptures and the words of Jesus.

                                        The gospel of the Lord.

[26] **THIRD SUNDAY OF LENT** **C**

The following readings may be used only when the celebration of the liturgy of the word for the children is held in a place apart from the main assembly.

FIRST READING

> This is what you must say to the children of Israel:
> I AM has sent me to you.

A reading from the book of Exodus   3:1-8a, 13-15

One day Moses was taking care of the sheep of Jethro his father-in-law,
 who was the priest of Midian.
Moses led the sheep along the edge of the desert to Sinai,
  the mountain of God.
Suddenly the Lord's angel appeared to him from a burning bush.
Moses saw that the bush was on fire,
 but it was not burning up.
He said to himself, "This is strange!
I'll go over and see why the bush is not burning up."

When the Lord saw Moses coming near the bush,
 he called out to him.

Moses answered, "Lord, here I am."

God replied, "Don't come any closer.
Take off your sandals,
 because the ground where you are standing is holy.
I am the God who was worshiped by your ancestors,
  Abraham, Isaac, and Jacob."

Moses was too afraid to look at God, and he hid his face.

The Lord said, "I have seen how my people are suffering in Egypt,
 and I have heard them cry out to me because of those slave bosses.
I am sorry for them,
 and so I have come down to rescue them
  from the power of the Egyptians.
I will bring my people out of Egypt
  into a country where there is good land
  and plenty of milk and honey."

Moses answered, "I will tell the people of Israel
> that the God of their ancestors has sent me to them.
But what should I say, if they ask me who you are?"

God said to Moses, "I am who I am.
So tell them that the one whose name is 'I Am' has sent you.
Say that the God of their ancestors,
> the God of Abraham, Isaac, and Jacob,
>> has sent you to them.
This is my name forever,
> and it is the name that people must use from now on."

The word of the Lord.

RESPONSORIAL PSALM 103:1-2, 6-7, 8 and 11

℟. (8a) The Lord is kind and merciful.

With all my heart
I praise the LORD,
and with all that I am
I praise his holy name!
With all my heart
I praise the LORD!
I will never forget
how kind he has been.

℟. The Lord is kind and merciful.

For all who are mistreated,
the LORD brings justice.
He taught his Law to Moses
and showed all Israel
what he could do.

℟. The Lord is kind and merciful.

The LORD is merciful!
He is kind and patient,
and his love never fails.
How great is God's love for all
who worship him?
Greater than the distance
between heaven and earth!

℟. The Lord is kind and merciful.

VERSE BEFORE THE GOSPEL
Matthew 4:17

℟. Glory and praise to you, Lord Jesus Christ.

**Repent, says the Lord;
the kingdom of heaven is at hand.**

℟. Glory and praise to you, Lord Jesus Christ.

GOSPEL

Leave the tree for another year and I will try to help it grow.

✧ **A reading from the holy gospel according to Luke** 13:6-9

Jesus told the people this story:
"A man had a fig tree growing in his vineyard.
One day he went out to pick some figs,
 but he didn't find any.
So he said to the gardener,
'For three years I have come looking for figs on this tree,
 and I haven't found any yet.
Chop it down!
Why should it take up space?'

"The gardener answered,
'Master, leave it for another year.
I'll dig around it and put some manure on it to make it grow.
Maybe it will have figs on it next year.
If it doesn't, you can have it cut down.' "

The gospel of the Lord.

[27] **FOURTH SUNDAY OF LENT** **A**

The following readings may be used only when the celebration of the liturgy of the word for the children is held in a place apart from the main assembly.

FIRST READING

David is anointed king of Israel.

A reading from the first book of Samuel   16:1b, 6-7, 10-13a

The Lord said to Samuel:
"Take some olive oil with you
   and go to a man named Jesse who lives in Bethlehem.
I have chosen one of his sons to be king."

When Jesse and his sons got there,
   Samuel saw Jesse's oldest son, Eliab, and thought,
"He must be the one the Lord has chosen."

But the Lord told Samuel,
"Don't choose him just because he is tall and handsome.
He isn't the one I have chosen.
People judge others by what they look like, but I don't.
I judge by what is in a person's heart."

Jesse sent seven of his sons to Samuel,
   but each time Samuel would say,
"The Lord has not chosen him."

Finally, Samuel asked Jesse,
"Do you have any more sons?"

Jesse answered,
"Yes, my youngest son David is out taking care of the sheep."

Samuel said, "Send for him.
We won't start until he gets here."

Jesse sent for David, and he came.
He was a healthy, good-looking boy with a sparkle in his eye.
The Lord told Samuel, "This is the one.
Pour the olive oil on his head."

Samuel poured the oil on David's head while his brothers watched.
At that moment the LORD's Spirit took control of David
   and stayed with him from then on.

> The word of the Lord.

RESPONSIONAL PSALM 23:1-3a, 3b-4, 5b-6c

℟. (1) The Lord is my shepherd; there is nothing I shall want.

You, LORD, are my shepherd.
I will never be in need.
You let me rest in fields
of green grass.
You lead me to streams
of peaceful water,
and you refresh my life.

℟. The Lord is my shepherd; there is nothing I shall want.

You are true to your name,
and you lead me
along the right paths.
I may walk through valleys
as dark as death,
but I won't be afraid.
You are with me,
and your shepherd's rod
makes me feel safe.

℟. The Lord is my shepherd; there is nothing I shall want.

While my enemies watch,
you honor me as your guest,
and you fill my cup
until it overflows.
Your kindness and love
will always be with me
each day of my life.

℟. The Lord is my shepherd; there is nothing I shall want.

SECOND READING

You are people of the light.

A reading from the letter of Paul to the Ephesians   5:1-2, 8-10

Brothers and sisters:
Do as God does.
After all, you are his dear children.
Let love be your guide.
Christ loved us and offered his life for us
    as a sacrifice that pleases God.

You used to be like people living in the dark,
    but now you are people of the light
    because you belong to the Lord.
So act like people of the light
    and make your light shine.
Be good and honest and truthful,
    as you try to please the Lord.

The word of the Lord.

VERSE BEFORE THE GOSPEL   John 8:12

℟. Glory and praise to you, Lord Jesus Christ.

**I am the light of the world, says the Lord;
whoever follows me will have the light of life.**

℟. Glory and praise to you, Lord Jesus Christ.

GOSPEL

*The man who was blind went off and washed himself
and came away with his sight restored.*

✢ **A reading from the holy gospel according to John**   9:1, 6-12, 35-38

One day as Jesus walked along,
he saw a man who had been blind since birth.
Jesus spit on the ground.
He made some mud and smeared it on the man's eyes.

Then he said, "Go and wash off the mud in Siloam Pool."
The man went and washed in Siloam,
> which means "One Who Is Sent."

When he had washed off the mud, he could see.

The man's neighbors and the people who had seen him begging
> wondered if he really could be the same man.

Some of them said he was the same beggar,
> while others said he only looked like him.

But he told them, "I am that man."

"Then how can you see?" they asked.

He answered,
"Someone named Jesus made some mud and smeared it on my eyes.
He told me to go and wash it off in Siloam Pool.
When I did, I could see."

"Where is he now?" they asked.
"I don't know," he answered.

When Jesus heard what had happened,
> he went and found the man.

Then Jesus asked, "Do you have faith in the Son of Man?"
He replied, "Sir, if you will tell me who he is,
> I will put my faith in him."

"You have already seen him," Jesus answered,
> "and right now he is talking with you."

The man said, "Lord, I put my faith in you!"
Then he worshiped Jesus.

The gospel of the Lord.

FOURTH SUNDAY OF LENT — B

[28]

The following readings may be used only when the celebration of the liturgy of the word for the children is held in a place apart from the main assembly.

FIRST READING

When we were dead through sin, Christ brought us to life.

A reading from the letter of Paul to the Ephesians   2:4-10

Brothers and sisters:
God was merciful!
We were dead because of our sins,
    but God loved us so much that he made us alive with Christ,
    and God's kindness is what saves you.

God raised us from death to life with Christ Jesus,
    and he has given us a place beside Christ in heaven above.
God did this so that in the future world he could show
      how truly good and kind he is to us
      because of what Christ Jesus has done.

You were saved by faith in God
    who treats us better than we deserve.
This is God's gift to you,
    and not anything you have done on your own.
It isn't something you have earned,
    so there is nothing you can brag about.

God planned for us to do good things
    and to live as he has always wanted us to live.
That's why he sent Christ to make us what we are.

                                       The word of the Lord.

RESPONSORIAL PSALM   25:4-5abc, 6 and 7cd

    ℟. (6a) Remember your mercies, O Lord.

Show me your paths
and teach me to follow;
guide me by your truth
and instruct me.
You keep me safe.

    ℟. Remember your mercies, O Lord.

Please, LORD, remember,
you have always
been patient and kind.
Show how truly kind you are
and remember me.

℟. Remember your mercies, O Lord.

VERSE BEFORE THE GOSPEL   John 3:16

℟. Glory and praise to you, Lord Jesus Christ.

**God loved the world so much, he gave his only Son,
that all who believe in him might have eternal life.**

℟. Glory and praise to you, Lord Jesus Christ.

GOSPEL

God sent his Son into the world, that we might be saved through him.

✚ **A reading from the holy gospel according to John**   3:16-17

Jesus told Nicodemus:
"God loved the people of this world so much
    that he gave his only Son,
so that everyone who has faith in him
    will have eternal life and never die.
God did not send his Son into the world to condemn its people.
He sent him to save them!"

The gospel of the Lord.

[29] **FOURTH SUNDAY OF LENT**

The following readings may be used only when the celebration of the liturgy of the word for the children is held in a place apart from the main assembly.

FIRST READING

God reconciled us to himself through Christ.

A reading from the second letter of Paul to the Corinthians 5:17-19

Brothers and sisters:
Anyone who belongs to Christ is a new person.
The past is forgotten,
  and everything is new.

God has done it all!
He sent Christ to make peace between himself and us,
  and he has given us the work of making peace
    between himself and others.

What we mean is that God was in Christ,
  offering peace and forgiveness to the people of this world.
And he has given us the work of sharing his message about peace.

The word of the Lord.

RESPONSORIAL PSALM   85:8, 9, 10

℟. (9b) The Lord speaks of peace to his people.

I will listen to you, LORD God,
because you promise peace
to those who are faithful
and no longer foolish.

℟. The Lord speaks of peace to his people.

You are ready to rescue
everyone who worships you,
so that you will live with us
in all of your glory.

℟. The Lord speaks of peace to his people.

Love and loyalty
will come together;
goodness and peace
will unite.

℟. The Lord speaks of peace to his people.

VERSE BEFORE THE GOSPEL Luke 15:18

℟. Glory and praise to you, Lord Jesus Christ.

**I will rise and go to my father and tell him:
Father, I have sinned against heaven and against you.**

℟. Glory and praise to you, Lord Jesus Christ.

GOSPEL

Your brother here was dead and has come to life.

✛ A reading from the holy gospel according to Luke   15:1-3, 11b-32

Tax collectors and sinners were all crowding around to listen to Jesus. So the Pharisees and the teachers of the Law of Moses started grumbling, "This man is friendly with sinners.
He even eats with them."

Then Jesus told them this story:

"Once a man had two sons.
The younger son said to his father,
'Give me my share of the property.'
So the father divided his property between his two sons.

"Not long after that,
    the younger son packed up everything he owned
        and left for a foreign country,
    where he wasted all his money in wild living.
He had spent everything,
    when a bad famine spread through that whole land.
Soon he had nothing to eat.

"He went to work for a man in that country,
    and the man sent him out to take care of his pigs.
He would have been glad to eat what the pigs were eating,
    but no one gave him a thing.

"Finally, he came to his senses and said,
'My father's workers have plenty to eat,
    and here I am, starving to death!
I will leave and go to my father and say to him,
"Father, I have sinned against God in heaven and against you.
I am no longer good enough to be called your son.
Treat me like one of your workers." '

"The younger son got up and started back to his father.
But when he was still a long way off,
    his father saw him and felt sorry for him.
He ran to his son and hugged and kissed him.

"The son said,
'Father, I have sinned against God in heaven and against you.
I am no longer good enough to be called your son.'

"But his father said to the servants,
'Hurry and bring the best clothes and put them on him.
Give him a ring for his finger and sandals for his feet.
Get the best calf and prepare it,
    so we can eat and celebrate.
This son of mine was dead,
    but has now come back to life.
He was lost and has now been found.'
And they began to celebrate.

"The older son had been out in the field.
But when he came near the house,
    he heard the music and dancing.
So he called one of the servants over and asked,
'What's going on here?'

"The servant answered,
'Your brother has come home safe and sound,
    and your father ordered us to kill the best calf.'
The older brother got so mad
    that he would not even go into the house.

"His father came out and begged him to go in.
But he said to his father,
'For years I have worked for you like a slave
    and have always obeyed you.
But you have never even given me a little goat,
    so that I could give a dinner for my friends.
This other son of yours wasted your money on bad women.
And now that he has come home,
    you ordered the best calf to be killed for a feast.'

"His father replied,
'My son, you are always with me,
    and everything I have is yours.
But we should be glad and celebrate!
Your brother was dead,
    but he is now alive.
He was lost and has now been found.' "

                                       The gospel of the Lord.

[30] # FIFTH SUNDAY OF LENT

The following readings may be used only when the celebration of the liturgy of the word for the children is held in a place apart from the main assembly.

FIRST READING

I shall put my spirit in you, and you will live.

A reading from the book of the prophet Ezekiel   37:12-14

The Lord said to Ezekiel:
Tell the people that I, the Lord God,
   promise to open their graves and set them free,
so they can go home to their land.
When I let them out of their graves,
   they will know that I am the Lord.
My Spirit will give them breath.
They will live again,
   and I will bring them back home.
Then they will know that I, the Lord God,
   have kept my promise.

The word of the Lord.

RESPONSORIAL PSALM   130:1-2, 5 and 7bcd

℟. (7bc) With the Lord there is mercy and fullness of redemption.

From a sea of troubles
I call out to you, Lord.
Won't you please listen
as I beg for mercy?

℟. With the Lord there is mercy and fullness of redemption.

With all my heart,
I am waiting, Lord, for you!
I trust your promises.
God is always merciful,
and he has the power to save you.

℟. With the Lord there is mercy and fullness of redemption.

VERSE BEFORE THE GOSPEL
John 11:25, 26

℟. Glory and praise to you, Lord Jesus Christ.

**I am the resurrection and the life, says the Lord;
whoever believes in me will not die for ever.**

℟. Glory and praise to you, Lord Jesus Christ.

GOSPEL

I am the resurrection and the life.

✤ **A reading from the holy gospel according to John** 11:3-7, 17, 20-27, 31-45

Martha and her sister Mary sent a message to the Lord
and told him that his good friend Lazarus was sick.

When Jesus heard this, he said,
"His sickness won't end in death.
It will bring glory to God and his Son."

Jesus loved Martha and her sister and brother.
But he stayed where he was for two more days.
Then he said to his disciples,
"Now we'll go back to Judea."

When Jesus got to Bethany,
he found that Lazarus had already been in the tomb four days.

When Martha heard that Jesus had arrived,
she went out to meet him,
but Mary stayed in the house.
Martha said to Jesus, "Lord, if you had been here,
my brother would not have died.
Yet even now I know that God will do anything you ask."

Jesus told her, "Your brother will live again!"

Martha answered,
"I know that he will be raised to life on the last day,
when all the dead are raised."

Jesus then said,
"I am the one who raises the dead to life!

Everyone who has faith in me will live,
    even if they die.
And everyone who lives because of faith in me will never die.
Do you believe this?"

"Yes, Lord!" she replied.
"I believe that you are Christ, the Son of God.
You are the one we hoped would come into the world."

Many people had come to comfort Mary,
    and when they saw her quickly leave the house,
        they thought she was going out to the tomb to cry.
So they followed her.

Mary went to where Jesus was.
Then as soon as she saw him,
    she kneeled at his feet and said,
"Lord, if you had been here,
    my brother would not have died."

When Jesus saw that Mary and the people with her were crying,
    he was terribly upset and asked,
"Where have you put his body?"

They replied, "Lord, come and you will see."

Jesus started crying, and the people said,
"See how much he loved Lazarus."

Some of them said, "He gives sight to the blind.
Why couldn't he have kept Lazarus from dying?"

Jesus was still terribly upset.
So he went to the tomb,
    which was a cave with a stone rolled against the entrance.
Then he told the people to roll the stone away.
But Martha said, "Lord, you know that Lazarus has been dead four days,
    and there will be a bad smell."

Jesus replied, "Didn't I tell you that if you had faith,
    you would see the glory of God?"

After the stone had been rolled aside,
    Jesus looked up toward heaven and prayed,
"Father, I thank you for answering my prayer.
I know that you always answer my prayers.
But I said this,
    so that the people here would believe that you sent me."

When Jesus had finished praying, he shouted,
"Lazarus, come out!"
The man who had been dead came out.
His hands and feet were wrapped with strips of burial cloth,
    and a cloth covered his face.

Jesus then told the people, "Untie him and let him go."

Many of the people who had come to visit Mary
    saw the things that Jesus did,
  and they put their faith in him.

The gospel of the Lord.

[31] **FIFTH SUNDAY OF LENT** B

The following readings may be used only when the celebration of the liturgy of the word for the children is held in a place apart from the main assembly.

FIRST READING

The days are coming when I will make a new covenant with Israel and I will forgive their iniquity.

A reading from the book of the prophet Jeremiah 31:31-34

The Lord says,
"The time is coming when I will make a new agreement
　　with the people of Israel and Judah.
It will be different from the agreement
　　that I made with their ancestors,
　when I led them out of Egypt.
Although I was their God, they broke their agreement with me.

"This is the agreement that I, the Lord,
　　will make with the people of Israel:
I will write my laws on their hearts and minds.
I will be their God, and they will be my people.

"No longer will they have to teach each other to obey me.
I, the Lord, promise that all of them will obey me,
　　no matter who they are.
I will forgive their sins and forget the evil things they have done."

　　　　　　　　　　　　　　　　　　　　　The word of the Lord.

RESPONSORIAL PSALM 51:1, 10, 12

　℟. (12a) Create a clean heart in me, O God.

You are kind, God!
Please have pity on me.
You are always merciful!
Please wipe away my sins.

　℟. Create a clean heart in me, O God.

Create pure thoughts in me
and make me faithful again.

℟. Create a clean heart in me, O God.

**Make me as happy as you did
when you saved me;
make me want to obey!**

℟. Create a clean heart in me, O God.

VERSE BEFORE THE GOSPEL
John 12:26

℟. Glory and praise to you, Lord Jesus Christ.

**If you serve me, follow me, says the Lord;
and where I am, my servant will also be.**

℟. Glory and praise to you, Lord Jesus Christ.

GOSPEL

If a grain of wheat falls on the ground and dies,
it yields a rich harvest.

✣ A reading from the holy gospel according to John   12:24-26

**Jesus said to his disciples:
"I tell you for certain that a grain of wheat that falls on the ground
will never be more than one grain unless it dies.
But if it dies, it will produce lots of wheat.**

**"If you love your life, you will lose it.
If you give it up in this world,
you will be given eternal life.**

**"If you serve me, you must go with me.
My servants will be with me wherever I am.
If you serve me, my Father will honor you."**

The gospel of the Lord.

FIFTH SUNDAY OF LENT

The following readings may be used only when the celebration of the liturgy of the word for the children is held in a place apart from the main assembly.

FIRST READING

I am doing a new thing and I will give drink to my people.

A reading from the book of the prophet Isaiah   43:18-21

The Lord says this:
Forget what happened long ago!
Don't think about the past.
I am creating something new.
There it is! Do you see it?
I have put a road in the desert and streams in thirsty land.
Every wild animal honors me,
    even the jackals and owls.
I provide water in the desert
    and streams in a thirsty land for my chosen people.
I made them my own nation,
    so they would praise me.

The word of the Lord.

RESPONSORIAL PSALM   126:1-2ab, 2cd-3

    ℟. (3a) The Lord has done great things for us.
or:
    ℟. (3) The Lord has done great things for us;
        we are filled with joy.

**It seemed like a dream
when the Lord brought us back
to the city of Zion.
We celebrated with laughter and joyful songs.**

    ℟. The Lord has done great things for us.
or:
    ℟. The Lord has done great things for us;
        we are filled with joy.

In foreign nations it was said,
"The LORD has worked miracles
for his people."
And so we celebrated
because the LORD had indeed
worked miracles for us.

> ℟. The Lord has done great things for us.
>
> **or:**
>
> ℟. The Lord has done great things for us;
> we are filled with joy.

SECOND READING

I struggle for what is ahead; I run for the goal.

A reading from the letter of Paul to the Philippians   3:12-14

Brothers and sisters:
> I have not yet reached my goal,
> and I am not perfect.

But Christ has taken hold of me.
So I keep on running and struggling to take hold of the prize.
My friends, I don't feel that I have already arrived.
But I forget what is behind,
> and I struggle for what is ahead.

I run toward the goal,
> so that I can win the prize of being called to heaven.

This is the prize that God offers
> because of what Christ Jesus has done.

The word of the Lord.

VERSE BEFORE THE GOSPEL   Joel 2:12-13

> ℟. Glory and praise to you, Lord Jesus Christ.
>
> **With all your heart turn to me, says the Lord;
> for I am tender and compassionate.**
>
> ℟. Glory and praise to you, Lord Jesus Christ.

GOSPEL

Let the person among you without sin be the first to throw a stone.

✢ A reading from the holy gospel according to John   8:2-11

Jesus spent the night on the Mount of Olives.
Then early the next morning he went to the temple.
The people came to him,
> and he sat down and started teaching them.

The Pharisees and the teachers of the Law of Moses
> > brought in a woman who had been caught in bed
> > with a man who was not her husband.

They made her stand in the middle of the crowd.
Then they said, "Teacher, this woman was caught
> sleeping with a man who is not her husband.

The Law of Moses teaches
> that a woman like this should be stoned to death!

What do you say?"

They asked Jesus this question,
> because they wanted to test him and bring some charge against him.

But Jesus simply bent over
> and started writing on the ground with his finger.

The crowd kept on asking Jesus about the woman.
Finally, he stood up and said,
"If any of you have never sinned,
> then go ahead and throw the first stone at her!"

Once again he bent over and began writing on the ground.
The people left one by one,
> beginning with the oldest one in the crowd.

Finally, Jesus and the woman were there alone.

Jesus stood up and asked her, "Where is everyone?
Isn't there anyone left to accuse you?"

"No, sir," the woman answered.

Then Jesus told her,
"I am not going to accuse you either.
You may go now, but don't sin anymore."

The gospel of the Lord.

[33]

PASSION SUNDAY
(Palm Sunday)
The Procession with Palms

GOSPEL

Blessed is the one who comes in the name of the Lord.

✠ A reading from the holy gospel according to Matthew   21:1-11

When Jesus and his disciples came near to Jerusalem,
   he went to Bethphage on the Mount of Olives
      and sent two of his disciples on ahead.
He told them, "Go into the next village,
   where you will at once find a donkey and her colt.
Untie the two donkeys and bring them to me.
If anyone asks why you are doing that, just say,
'The Lord needs them.'
Right away he will let you have the donkeys."

So God's promise came true,
   just as the prophet had said,

      "Announce to the people of Jerusalem:
      'Your king is coming to you!
      He is humble and rides on a donkey.
      He comes on the colt of a donkey.'"

The disciples left and did what Jesus had told them to do.
They brought the donkey and its colt
   and laid some clothes on their backs.
Then Jesus got on.

Many people spread clothes in the road,
   while others put down branches which they had cut from trees.
Some people walked ahead of Jesus and others followed behind.
They were all shouting, "Hosanna for the Son of David!
God bless the one who comes in the name of the Lord.
Hooray for God in heaven above!"

When Jesus came to Jerusalem,
   everyone in the city was excited and asked,
"Who can this be?"

The crowd answered,
"This is Jesus, the prophet from Nazareth in Galilee."

The gospel of the Lord.

MASS

The following readings may be used only when the celebration of the liturgy of the word for the children is held in a place apart from the main assembly.

FIRST READING

> I did not cover my face against insult
> and I know I will not be ashamed
> (third oracle of the Servant of the Lord).

A reading from the book of the prophet Isaiah 50:6-7

I let them beat my back and pull out my beard.
I didn't turn aside when they made fun of me and spit in my face.

But the Lord God keeps me from being embarrassed.
And I refuse to give up,
> because I know I will never be ashamed.

The word of the Lord.

RESPONSORIAL PSALM 22:7-8, 16c-17a and 18, 19 and 22

℟. (2a) My God, my God, why have you abandoned me?

Everyone who sees me
makes fun and sneers.
They shake their heads,
and say, "Trust the Lord!
If you are his favorite,
let him protect you and keep you safe."

℟. My God, my God, why have you abandoned me?

My enemies have tied up
my hands and my feet.
I can count all my bones!
They took my clothes
and gambled for them.

℟. My God, my God, why have you abandoned me?

Don't stay far away, LORD!
My strength comes from you,
so hurry and help.
And when your people meet,
I will praise you, LORD.

℟. My God, my God, why have you abandoned me?

VERSE BEFORE THE GOSPEL   Philippians 2:8-9

℟. Glory and praise to you, Lord Jesus Christ.

**Christ became obedient for us even to death,
dying on the cross.
Therefore God raised him on high
and gave him a name above all other names.**

℟. Glory and praise to you, Lord Jesus Christ.

GOSPEL

The passion of our Lord Jesus Christ.

The passion of our Lord Jesus Christ according to Matthew   27:11-54

Jesus was brought before Pilate the governor, who asked him, "Are you the King of the Jews?"

"Those are your words!" Jesus answered.
And when the chief priests and leaders
    brought their charges against him,
  he did not say a thing.

Pilate asked him, "Don't you hear what crimes they say you have done?"
But Jesus did not say anything,
  and the governor was greatly amazed.

During Passover the governor always freed
    a prisoner chosen by the people.
At that time a well-known terrorist named Jesus Barabbas
    was in jail.
So when the crowd came together, Pilate asked them,
"Which prisoner do you want me to set free?
Do you want Jesus Barabbas or Jesus who is called the Messiah?"

Pilate knew that the leaders had brought Jesus to him
    because they were jealous.

While Pilate was judging the case,
    his wife sent him a message.
It said, "Don't have anything to do with that innocent man.
I have had nightmares because of him."

But the chief priests and the leaders convinced the crowds
        to ask for Barabbas to be set free and for Jesus to be killed.
Pilate asked the crowd again,
"Which of these two men do you want me to set free?"

"Barabbas!" they replied.
Pilate asked them, "What am I to do with Jesus,
    who is called the Messiah?"
They all yelled, "Nail him to a cross!"

Pilate answered, "But what crime has he done?"
"Nail him to a cross!" they yelled even louder.

Pilate saw that there was nothing he could do
      and that the people were starting to riot.
So he took some water and washed his hands in front of them
    and said,
"I won't have anything to do with killing this man.
You are the ones doing it!"

Everybody answered,
"We and our descendants will take the blame for his death!"

Pilate set Barabbas free.
Then he ordered his soldiers to beat Jesus with a whip
    and nail him to a cross.

The governor's soldiers led Jesus into the fortress
    and brought together the rest of the troops.
They stripped off Jesus' clothes and put a scarlet robe on him.
They made a crown out of thorn branches and placed it on his head,
    and they put a stick in his right hand.
The soldiers kneeled down and pretended to worship him.
They made fun of him and shouted,
"Hey, you king of the Jews!"

Then they spit on him.
They took the stick from him and beat him on the head with it.

When the soldiers had finished making fun of Jesus,
    they took off the robe.
They put his own clothes back on him
        and led him off to be nailed to a cross.
On the way they met a man from Cyrene named Simon,
    and they forced him to carry Jesus' cross.

They came to a place named Golgotha,
    which means "Place of the Skull."
There they gave Jesus some wine mixed with a drug to ease the pain.
But when Jesus tasted what it was,
    he refused to drink it.

The soldiers nailed Jesus to a cross
        and gambled to see who would get his clothes.
Then they sat down to guard him.
Above his head they put a sign that told why he was nailed there.
It said, "This is Jesus, the King of the Jews."
The soldiers also nailed two criminals on crosses,
        one to the right of Jesus and the other to his left.

People who passed by said terrible things about Jesus.
They shook their heads and shouted,
"So you're the one who claimed you could tear down the temple
    and build it again in three days!
If you are God's Son,
    save yourself and come down from the cross!"

The chief priests, the leaders, and the teachers of the Law of Moses
    also made fun of Jesus.
They said, "He saved others, but he can't save himself.
If he is the king of Israel,
    he should come down from the cross!
Then we will believe him.
He trusted God,
    so let God save him, if he wants to.
He even said he was God's Son."

The two criminals also said cruel things to Jesus.

At noon the sky turned dark and stayed that way until three o'clock.
Then about that time Jesus shouted,

> "Eli, Eli, lema sabachthani?"
> which means, "My God, my God, why have you deserted me?"

Some of the people standing there heard Jesus and said,
"He's calling for Elijah."
One of them at once ran and grabbed a sponge.
He soaked it in wine,
> then put it on a stick and held it up to Jesus.

Others said, "Wait!
Let's see if Elijah will come and save him."
Once again Jesus shouted,
> and then he died.

At once the curtain in the temple was torn in two from top to bottom.
The earth shook, and rocks split apart.
Graves opened,
> and many of God's people were raised to life.
Then after Jesus had risen to life,
> they came out of their graves and went into the holy city,
> where many people saw them.

The officer and the soldiers guarding Jesus felt the earthquake
> and saw everything else that happened.
They were frightened and said,
"This man really was God's Son!"

The gospel of the Lord.

[34] **PASSION SUNDAY**
(Palm Sunday)

The Procession with Palms

GOSPEL

Blessed is the one who comes in the name of the Lord.

✠ A reading from the holy gospel according to Mark   11:1-10

Jesus and his disciples reached Bethphage and Bethany
    near the Mount of Olives.
When they were getting close to Jerusalem,
    Jesus sent two of them on ahead.
He told them, "Go into the next village.
As soon as you enter it,
    you will find a young donkey that has never been ridden.
Untie the donkey and bring it here.
If anyone asks why you are doing that,
    say, 'The Lord needs it and will soon bring it back.' "

The disciples left and found the donkey
        tied near a door that faced the street.
While they were untying it,
    some of the people standing there asked,
"Why are you untying the donkey?"
They told them what Jesus had said,
    and the people let them take it.

The disciples led the donkey to Jesus.
They put some of their clothes on its back,
    and Jesus got on.
Many people spread clothes on the road,
    while others went to cut branches from the fields.

In front of Jesus and behind him,
    people went along shouting, "Hosanna!
God bless the one who comes in the name of the Lord!
God bless the coming kingdom of our ancestor David.
Hosanna to God in heaven above!"

                              The gospel of the Lord.

PASSION SUNDAY (PALM SUNDAY) — B

MASS

The following readings may be used only when the celebration of the liturgy of the word for the children is held in a place apart from the main assembly.

FIRST READING

> I did not cover my face against insult
> and I know I will not be ashamed
> (third oracle of the Servant of the Lord).

A reading from the book of the prophet Isaiah 50:6-7

**I let them beat my back and pull out my beard.
I didn't turn aside when they made fun of me and spit in my face.**

**But the LORD God keeps me from being embarrassed.
And I refuse to give up,
because I know I will never be ashamed.**

The word of the Lord.

RESPONSORIAL PSALM 22:7-8, 16c-17a and 18, 19 and 22

℟. (2a) My God, my God, why have you abandoned me?

**Everyone who sees me
makes fun and sneers.
They shake their heads,
and say, "Trust the LORD!
If you are his favorite,
let him protect you and keep you safe."**

℟. My God, my God, why have you abandoned me?

**My enemies have tied up
my hands and my feet.
I can count all my bones!
They took my clothes
and gambled for them.**

℟. My God, my God, why have you abandoned me?

**Don't stay far away, LORD!
My strength comes from you,
so hurry and help.**

And when your people meet,
I will praise you, LORD.

℟. My God, my God, why have you abandoned me?

VERSE BEFORE THE GOSPEL Philippians 2:8-9

℟. Glory and praise to you, Lord Jesus Christ.

Christ became obedient for us even to death,
dying on the cross.
Therefore God raised him on high
and gave him a name above all other names.

℟. Glory and praise to you, Lord Jesus Christ.

GOSPEL

The passion of our Lord Jesus Christ.

The passion of our Lord Jesus Christ according to Mark 15:1-39

Early in the morning the chief priests, the nation's leaders,
and the teachers of the Law of Moses
met together with the whole Jewish council.
They tied up Jesus and led him off to Pilate.

He asked Jesus, "Are you the king of the Jews?"

"Those are your words," Jesus answered.

The chief priests brought many charges against Jesus.
Then Pilate questioned him again,
"Don't you have anything to say?
Don't you hear what crimes they say you have done?"
But Jesus did not answer, and Pilate was amazed.

During Passover, Pilate always freed one prisoner chosen by the people.
And at that time there was a prisoner named Barabbas.
He and some others had been arrested for murder during a riot.
The Jewish people now came and asked Pilate to set a prisoner free,
    just as he usually did.

Pilate asked them, "Do you want me to free the king of the Jews?"
Pilate knew that the chief priests had brought Jesus to him
    because they were jealous.

But the chief priests told the crowd to ask Pilate to free Barabbas.
Then Pilate asked the crowd,
"What do you want me to do with this man
        you say is the king of the Jews?"

They yelled, "Nail him to a cross!"

Pilate asked, "But what crime has he done?"

"Nail him to a cross!" they yelled even louder.

Pilate wanted to please the crowd.
So he set Barabbas free.
Then he ordered his soldiers to beat Jesus with a whip
        and nail him to a cross.

The soldiers led Jesus inside the courtyard of the fortress
        and called together the rest of the troops.
They put a purple robe on him,
    and on his head they placed a crown
        that they had made out of thorn branches.
They made fun of Jesus and shouted,
"Hey, you king of the Jews!"
Then they beat him on the head with a stick.
They spit on him and kneeled down and pretended to worship him.

When the soldiers had finished making fun of Jesus,
    they took off the purple robe.
They put his own clothes back on him
        and led him off to be nailed to a cross.
Simon from Cyrene happened to be coming in from a farm,
    and they forced him to carry Jesus' cross.
Simon was the father of Alexander and Rufus.

The soldiers took Jesus to Golgotha,
    which means "Place of a Skull."
There they gave him some wine mixed with a drug to ease the pain,
    but he refused to drink it.

They nailed Jesus to a cross
        and gambled to see who would get his clothes.
It was about nine o'clock in the morning
        when they nailed him to the cross.

On it was a sign that told why he was nailed there.
It read, "This is the King of the Jews."
The soldiers also nailed two criminals on crosses,
      one to the right of Jesus and the other to his left.
So the Scriptures came true which say,
"He was accused of being a criminal."

People who passed by said terrible things about Jesus.
They shook their heads and shouted,
"Ha! So you're the one who claimed you could tear down the temple
      and build it again in three days.
Save yourself and come down from the cross!"

The chief priests and the teachers of the Law of Moses
      also made fun of Jesus.
They said to each other,
"He saved others, but he can't save himself.
If he is the Messiah, the king of Israel,
   let him come down from the cross!
Then we will see and believe."
The two criminals also said cruel things to Jesus.

About noon the sky turned dark
      and stayed that way until around three o'clock.
Then about that time Jesus shouted,

      "Eloi, Eloi, lema sabachthani?"
      which means, "My God, my God, why have you deserted me?"

Some of the people standing there heard Jesus and said,
"He is calling for Elijah."
One of them ran and grabbed a sponge.
After he had soaked it in wine,
   he put it on a stick and held it up to Jesus.
He said, "Let's wait and see if Elijah will come and take him down!"
Jesus shouted and then died.

At once the curtain in the temple tore in two from top to bottom.

A Roman army officer was standing in front of Jesus.
When the officer saw how Jesus died,
   he said, "This man really was the Son of God!"

                                   The gospel of the Lord.

PASSION SUNDAY
(Palm Sunday)
The Procession with Palms

GOSPEL

Blessed is the one who comes in the name of the Lord.

✛ A reading from the holy gospel according to Luke 19:28-40

Jesus went toward Jerusalem.
As he was getting near to Bethphage and Bethany
   on the Mount of Olives,
   he sent two of his disciples on ahead.
He told them, "Go into the next village,
   where you will find a young donkey that has never been ridden.
Untie the donkey and bring it here.
If anyone asks why you are doing that, just say,
'The Lord needs it.' "

They went off and found everything just as Jesus had said.
While they were untying the donkey,
   its owners asked, "Why are you doing that?"

They answered, "The Lord needs it."

Then they led the donkey to Jesus.
They put some of their clothes on its back and helped Jesus get on.
And as he rode along,
   the people spread clothes on the road in front of him.
When Jesus was starting down the Mount of Olives,
   his large crowd of disciples were happy and praised God
      because of all the miracles they had seen.
They shouted, "Blessed is the king who comes in the name of the Lord!
Peace in heaven and glory to God."

Some Pharisees in the crowd said to Jesus,
"Teacher, make your disciples stop shouting!"

But Jesus answered,
"If they keep quiet, these stones will start shouting."

The gospel of the Lord.

MASS

The following readings may be used only when the celebration of the liturgy of the word for the children is held in a place apart from the main assembly.

FIRST READING

I did not cover my face against insult
and I know I will not be ashamed
(third oracle of the Servant of the Lord).

A reading from the book of the prophet Isaiah 50:6-7

I let them beat my back and pull out my beard.
I didn't turn aside when they made fun of me and spit in my face.

But the LORD God keeps me from being embarrassed.
And I refuse to give up,
 because I know I will never be ashamed.

The word of the Lord.

RESPONSORIAL PSALM 22:7-8, 16c-17a and 18, 19 and 22

℟. (2a) My God, my God, why have you abandoned me?

Everyone who sees me
makes fun and sneers.
They shake their heads,
and say, "Trust the LORD!
If you are his favorite,
let him protect you and keep you safe."

℟. My God, my God, why have you abandoned me?

My enemies have tied up
my hands and my feet.
I can count all my bones!
They took my clothes
and gambled for them.

℟. My God, my God, why have you abandoned me?

Don't stay far away, LORD!
My strength comes from you,
so hurry and help.
And when your people meet,
I will praise you, LORD.

℟. My God, my God, why have you abandoned me?

VERSE BEFORE THE GOSPEL   Philippians 2:8-9

℟. Glory and praise to you, Lord Jesus Christ.

Christ became obedient for us even to death,
dying on the cross.
Therefore God raised him on high
and gave him a name above all other names.

℟. Glory and praise to you, Lord Jesus Christ.

GOSPEL

The passion of our Lord Jesus Christ.

The passion of our Lord Jesus Christ according to Luke   23:1-49

Everyone in the council led Jesus off to Pilate.
They started accusing him and said,
"We caught this man trying to get our people to riot
    and stop paying taxes to the Emperor.
He also claims that he is the Messiah, our king."

Pilate asked Jesus, "Are you the king of the Jews?"

"Those are your words," Jesus answered.

Pilate told the chief priests and the crowd,
"I don't find him guilty of anything."

But they all kept on saying,
"He has been teaching and causing trouble all over Judea.
He started in Galilee and has now come all the way here."

When Pilate heard this, he asked,
"Is this man from Galilee?"
After Pilate learned that Jesus came from the region ruled by Herod,
    he sent him to Herod, who was in Jerusalem at that time.

For a long time Herod had wanted to see Jesus
    and was very happy because he finally had this chance.
He had heard many things about Jesus
    and hoped to see him work a miracle.

Herod asked him a lot of questions,
    but Jesus did not answer.
Then the chief priests and the teachers of the Law of Moses
    stood up and accused him of all kinds of bad things.

Herod and his soldiers made fun of Jesus and insulted him.
They put a fine robe on him and sent him back to Pilate.
That same day Herod and Pilate became friends,
    even though they had been enemies before this.

Pilate called together the chief priests, the leaders, and the people.
He told them, "You brought Jesus to me and said he was a troublemaker.
But I have questioned him here in front of you,
    and I have not found him guilty
        of anything that you say he has done.
Herod didn't find him guilty either and sent him back.
This man doesn't deserve to be put to death!
I will just have him beaten with a whip and set free."

Pilate said this,
    because at every Passover
        he was supposed to set one prisoner free
            for the Jewish people.

But the whole crowd shouted, "Kill Jesus!
Give us Barabbas!"
Now Barabbas was in jail because he had started a riot in the city
    and had murdered someone.

Pilate wanted to set Jesus free,
    so he spoke again to the crowds.
But they kept shouting, "Nail him to a cross!
Nail him to a cross!"

Pilate spoke to them a third time,
"But what crime has he done?
I have not found him guilty of anything
> for which he should be put to death.
I will have him beaten with a whip and set free."

The people kept on shouting as loud as they could
> for Jesus to be put to death.
Finally, Pilate gave in.
He freed the man who was in jail for rioting and murder,
> because he was the one the crowd wanted to be set free.
Then Pilate handed Jesus over
> for them to do what they wanted with him.

As Jesus was being led away,
> some soldiers grabbed hold of a man from Cyrene named Simon.
He was coming in from the fields,
> but they put the cross on him and made him carry it behind Jesus.

A large crowd was following Jesus,
> and in the crowd a lot of women were crying and weeping for him.
Jesus turned to the women and said:
"Women of Jerusalem, don't cry for me!
Cry for yourselves and for your children.
Someday people will say,
'Women who never had children are really fortunate!'
At that time everyone will say to the mountains, 'Fall on us!'
They will say to the hills, 'Hide us!'
If this can happen when the wood is green,
> what do you think will happen when it is dry?"

Two criminals were led out to be put to death with Jesus.
When the soldiers came to a place called "The Skull,"
> they nailed Jesus to a cross.
They also nailed the two criminals to crosses,
> one on each side of Jesus.

Jesus said, "Father, forgive these people!
They don't know what they're doing."

While the people stood there watching Jesus,
> the soldiers gambled for his clothes.

The leaders insulted him by saying, "He saved others.
Now he should save himself,
    if he really is God's chosen Messiah!"

The soldiers made fun of Jesus and brought him some wine.
They said, "If you are the king of the Jews, save yourself!"

Above him was a sign that said,
"This is the King of the Jews."

One of the criminals hanging there also insulted Jesus by saying,
"Aren't you the Messiah?
Save yourself and save us!"

But the other criminal told the first one off,
"Don't you fear God?
Aren't you getting the same punishment as this man?
We got what was coming to us,
    but he didn't do anything wrong."
Then he said to Jesus,
"Remember me when you come into power!"

Jesus replied,
"I promise that today you will be with me in paradise."

Around noon the sky turned dark and stayed that way
    until the middle of the afternoon.
The sun stopped shining,
    and the curtain in the temple split down the middle.
Jesus shouted, "Father, I put myself in your hands!"
Then he died.

When the Roman officer saw what had happened,
    he praised God and said,
"Jesus must really have been a good man!"

A crowd had gathered to see the terrible sight.
After they saw it,
    they felt brokenhearted and went home.
All of Jesus' close friends
    and the women who had come with him from Galilee
    stood at a distance and watched.

                            The gospel of the Lord.

SEASON OF EASTER

EASTER SUNDAY

The following readings may be used only when the celebration of the liturgy of the word for the children is held in a place apart from the main assembly.

FIRST READING

*After Jesus was raised from the dead,
we ate and drank with him.*

A reading from the Acts of the Apostles   10:34a, 37-43

Peter said to Cornelius and his household:
"You surely know what happened everywhere in Judea.
It all began in Galilee after John had told everyone to be baptized.
God gave the Holy Spirit and power to Jesus from Nazareth.
He was with Jesus,
   as he went around doing good
      and healing everyone who was under the power of the devil.
We all saw what Jesus did both in Israel and in the city of Jerusalem.

"Jesus was put to death on a cross.
But three days later,
   God raised him to life and let him be seen.
Not everyone saw him.
He was seen only by us,
   who ate and drank with him after he was raised from death.
We were the ones God chose to tell others about him.

"God told us to announce clearly to the people
   that Jesus is the one he has chosen
      to judge the living and the dead.

"Every one of the prophets has said
   that all who have faith in Jesus
      will have their sins forgiven in his name."

                              The word of the Lord.

RESPONSIONAL PSALM 118:1-2, 15c-16ab and 17, 22-23

> ℟. (24) This is the day the Lord has made;
>   let us rejoice and be glad.

or:

> ℟. Alleluia.

Tell the Lord
how thankful you are,
because he is kind
and always merciful.
Let Israel shout,
"God is always merciful!"

> ℟. This is the day the Lord has made;
>   let us rejoice and be glad.

or:

> ℟. Alleluia.

The Lord is powerful!
With his mighty arm
the Lord wins victories!
And so my life is safe,
and I will live to tell
what the Lord has done.

> ℟. This is the day the Lord has made;
>   let us rejoice and be glad.

or:

> ℟. Alleluia.

The stone that the builders
tossed aside
has now become
the most important stone.
The Lord has done this,
and it is amazing to us.

> ℟. This is the day the Lord has made;
>   let us rejoice and be glad.

or:

> ℟. Alleluia.

EASTER SUNDAY — A, B, C

SECOND READING

A Look for the things that are in heaven, where Christ is.

A reading from the letter of Paul to the Colossians 3:1-4

Brothers and sisters:
You have been raised to life with Christ.
Now set your heart on what is in heaven,
    where Christ rules at God's right side.
Think about what is up there,
    not about what is here on earth.

You died, which means that your life is hidden with Christ,
    who sits beside God.
Christ gives meaning to your life,
    and when he appears,
        you will also appear with him in glory.

                The word of the Lord.

OR

B Throw away the old yeast, that you may be new dough.

A reading from the first letter of Paul to the Corinthians 5:6b-8

Brothers and sisters:
Don't you know how a little yeast can spread
    through the whole batch of dough?
Get rid of the old yeast!
Then you will be like fresh bread made without yeast,
    and that is what you are.

Our Passover lamb is Christ,
    who has already been sacrificed.
So don't celebrate the festival by being evil and sinful,
    which is like serving bread made with yeast.
Be pure and truthful and celebrate by using bread made without yeast.

                The word of the Lord.

ALLELUIA   1 Corinthians 5:7b-8a

℟. Alleluia, alleluia.

**Christ has become our paschal sacrifice;
let us feast with joy in the Lord.**

℟. Alleluia, alleluia.

GOSPEL

The teaching of Scripture is that Jesus must rise from the dead.

✠ **A reading from the holy gospel according to John**   20:1-9

**On Sunday morning while it was still dark,
Mary Magdalene went to the tomb
     and saw that the stone had been rolled away from the entrance.
She ran to Simon Peter and to Jesus' favorite disciple and said,
"They have taken the Lord from the tomb!
We don't know where they have put him."**

**Peter and the other disciple started for the tomb.
They ran side by side,
     until the other disciple ran faster than Peter and got there first.
He bent over and saw the strips of linen cloth lying inside the tomb,
     but he did not go in.**

**When Simon Peter got there,
     he went into the tomb and saw the strips of cloth.
He also saw the piece of cloth that had been used to cover Jesus' face.
It was rolled up and in a place by itself.
The disciple who got there first then went into the tomb,
     and when he saw it, he believed.
At that time Peter and the other disciple did not know
          that the Scriptures said Jesus would rise to life.**

                                             The gospel of the Lord.

[37] SECOND SUNDAY OF EASTER   **A**

FIRST READING

All those who believed were equal and held everything in common.

A reading from the Acts of the Apostles   2:42-47

The followers of Jesus spent their time learning from the apostles,
and they were like family to each other.
They also broke bread and prayed together.

Everyone was amazed at the many miracles and wonders
   that the apostles worked.

All the Lord's followers often met together,
   and they shared everything they had.
They would sell their property and possessions
     and give the money to whoever needed it.
Day after day they met together in the temple.
They broke bread together in different homes
     and shared their food happily and freely,
         while praising God.
Everyone liked them,
     and each day the Lord added to their group
         others who were being saved.

                                  The word of the Lord.

RESPONSORIAL PSALM   118:2-4, 22-24

   ℟. (1) Give thanks, for the Lord is good,
       God's love is everlasting.
  or:
   ℟. Alleluia.

**Let Israel shout,
"God is always merciful!"
Let the family of Aaron
the priest shout,
"God is always merciful!"
Let every true worshiper
of the L**ORD** shout,
"God is always merciful!"**

> ℟. Give thanks, for the Lord is good,
>   God's love is everlasting.
> **or:**
> ℟. Alleluia.

**The stone that the builders
tossed aside
has now become
the most important stone.
The Lord has done this,
and it is amazing to us.
This day belongs to the Lord!
Let's celebrate and be glad today.**

> ℟. Give thanks, for the Lord is good,
>   God's love is everlasting.
> **or:**
> ℟. Alleluia.

SECOND READING

God has given us a new birth as his children,
by raising Jesus Christ from the dead.

A reading from the first letter of Peter   1:3-4

Brothers and sisters:
**Praise God, the Father of our Lord Jesus Christ.
God is so good,**
   and by raising Jesus from death,
      he has given us new life and a hope that lives on.

God has something stored up for you in heaven,
   where it will never decay or be ruined or disappear.

The word of the Lord.

ALLELUIA   John 20:29

> ℟. Alleluia, alleluia.

**You believe in me, Thomas, because you have seen me;
happy those who have not seen me, but still believe!**

> ℟. Alleluia, alleluia.

GOSPEL

After eight days Jesus came in and stood among them.

✢ A reading from the holy gospel according to John   20:19-29

The disciples were afraid of the Jewish leaders,
and on the evening of that same Sunday
    they locked themselves in a room.
Suddenly, Jesus appeared in the middle of the group.
He greeted them and showed them his hands and his side.
When the disciples saw the Lord,
    they became very happy.

After Jesus had greeted them again, he said,
"I am sending you, just as the Father has sent me."
Then he breathed on them and said,
"Receive the Holy Spirit.
If you forgive anyone's sins,
    they will be forgiven.
But if you don't forgive their sins,
    they will not be forgiven."

Although Thomas the Twin was one of the twelve disciples,
    he was not with the others when Jesus appeared to them.
So they told him, "We have seen the Lord!"

But Thomas said, "First, I must see the nail scars in his hands
    and touch them with my finger.
I must put my hand where the spear went into his side.
I won't believe unless I do this!"

A week later the disciples were together again.
This time Thomas was with them.
Jesus came in while the doors were still locked
    and stood in the middle of the group.
He greeted his disciples and said to Thomas,
"Put your finger here and look at my hands!
Put your hand into my side.
Stop doubting and have faith!"

Thomas replied, "You are my Lord and my God!"

Jesus said, "Thomas, do you have faith because you have seen me?
The people who have faith in me without seeing me
    are the ones who are really blessed!"

                                                  The gospel of the Lord.

SECOND SUNDAY OF EASTER — B

FIRST READING

The whole group of believers was united, heart and soul.

A reading from the Acts of the Apostles 4:32-35

The followers of Jesus all felt the same way about everything. None of them claimed that their belongings were their own, and they shared everything they had with each other.

In a powerful way the apostles told everyone
   that the Lord Jesus was now alive.

God greatly blessed his followers,
   and no one went in need of anything.
Everyone who owned land or houses would sell them
   and bring the money to the apostles.
Then they would give the money to anyone who needed it.

The word of the Lord.

RESPONSORIAL PSALM 118:2-4, 22-24

℟. (1) Give thanks, for the Lord is good,
   God's love is everlasting.

or:

℟. Alleluia.

Let Israel shout,
"God is always merciful!"
Let the family of Aaron
the priest shout,
"God is always merciful!"
Let every true worshiper
of the LORD shout,
"God is always merciful!"

℟. Give thanks, for the Lord is good,
   God's love is everlasting.

or:

℟. Alleluia.

The stone that the builders
tossed aside
has now become
the most important stone.
The LORD has done this,
and it is amazing to us.
This day belongs to the LORD!
Let's celebrate and be glad today.

> ℟. Give thanks, for the Lord is good,
> God's love is everlasting.

or:

> ℟. Alleluia.

SECOND READING

We are God's children.

A reading from the first letter of John 5:1-3

Beloved:
If we believe that Jesus is truly Christ,
we are God's children.
Everyone who loves the Father will also love his children.
If we love and obey God,
> we know that we will love his children.
We show our love for God by obeying his commandments,
> and they are not hard to follow.

The word of the Lord.

ALLELUIA

John 20:29

> ℟. Alleluia, alleluia.

You believe in me, Thomas, because you have seen me;
happy those who have not seen me, but still believe!

> ℟. Alleluia, alleluia.

GOSPEL

After eight days Jesus came in and stood among them.

✣ A reading from the holy gospel according to John   20:19-29

The disciples were afraid of the Jewish leaders,
   and on the evening of that same Sunday
      they locked themselves in a room.
Suddenly, Jesus appeared in the middle of the group.
He greeted them and showed them his hands and his side.
When the disciples saw the Lord,
   they became very happy.

After Jesus had greeted them again, he said,
"I am sending you, just as the Father has sent me."
Then he breathed on them and said,
"Receive the Holy Spirit.
If you forgive anyone's sins,
   they will be forgiven.
But if you don't forgive their sins,
   they will not be forgiven."

Although Thomas the Twin was one of the twelve disciples,
   he was not with the others when Jesus appeared to them.
So they told him, "We have seen the Lord!"

But Thomas said, "First, I must see the nail scars in his hands
   and touch them with my finger.
I must put my hand where the spear went into his side.
I won't believe unless I do this!"

A week later the disciples were together again.
This time Thomas was with them.
Jesus came in while the doors were still locked
   and stood in the middle of the group.
He greeted his disciples and said to Thomas,
"Put your finger here and look at my hands!
Put your hand into my side.
Stop doubting and have faith!"

Thomas replied, "You are my Lord and my God!"

Jesus said, "Thomas, do you have faith because you have seen me?
The people who have faith in me without seeing me
   are the ones who are really blessed!"

                                        The gospel of the Lord.

[39] **SECOND SUNDAY OF EASTER** C

FIRST READING

The numbers of men and women who came to believe in the Lord increased steadily.

A reading from the Acts of the Apostles 5:12-16

The apostles worked many miracles and wonders among the people.
All of the Lord's followers
    often met in the part of the temple known as Solomon's Porch.
No one outside their group dared join them,
    even though everyone liked them very much.

Many men and women started having faith in the Lord.
Then sick people were brought out to the road
    and placed on cots and mats.
It was hoped that Peter would walk by,
    and his shadow would fall on them and heal them.
A lot of people living in the towns near Jerusalem
    brought those who were sick or troubled by evil spirits,
and they were all healed.

The word of the Lord.

RESPONSORIAL PSALM 118:2 and 4, 13-14

℟. (1) Give thanks, for the Lord is good,
    God's love is everlasting.

or:

℟. Alleluia.

Let Israel shout,
"God is always merciful!"
Let every true worshiper
of the LORD **shout,**
"God is always merciful!"

℟. Give thanks, for the Lord is good,
    God's love is everlasting.

or:

℟. Alleluia.

The nations attacks were so fierce
that I nearly fell,
but the LORD helped me.
My power and my strength
come from the LORD,
and he has saved me.

> ℟. Give thanks, for the Lord is good,
> God's love is everlasting.
>
> **or:**
>
> ℟. Alleluia.

ALLELUIA
John 20:29

> ℟. Alleluia, alleluia.

**You believe in me, Thomas, because you have seen me;
happy those who have not seen me, but still believe!**

> ℟. Alleluia, alleluia.

GOSPEL

After eight days Jesus came in and stood among them.

✛ **A reading from the holy gospel according to John**   20:19-29

The disciples were afraid of the Jewish leaders,
and on the evening of that same Sunday
    they locked themselves in a room.
Suddenly, Jesus appeared in the middle of the group.
He greeted them and showed them his hands and his side.
When the disciples saw the Lord,
    they became very happy.

After Jesus had greeted them again, he said,
"I am sending you, just as the Father has sent me."
Then he breathed on them and said,
"Receive the Holy Spirit.
If you forgive anyone's sins,
    they will be forgiven.
But if you don't forgive their sins,
    they will not be forgiven."

Although Thomas the Twin was one of the twelve disciples,
    he was not with the others when Jesus appeared to them.
So they told him, "We have seen the Lord!"

But Thomas said, "First, I must see the nail scars in his hands
        and touch them with my finger.
I must put my hand where the spear went into his side.
I won't believe unless I do this!"

A week later the disciples were together again.
This time Thomas was with them.
Jesus came in while the doors were still locked
    and stood in the middle of the group.
He greeted his disciples and said to Thomas,
"Put your finger here and look at my hands!
Put your hand into my side.
Stop doubting and have faith!"

Thomas replied, "You are my Lord and my God!"

Jesus said, "Thomas, do you have faith because you have seen me?
The people who have faith in me without seeing me
    are the ones who are really blessed!"

                                      The gospel of the Lord.

THIRD SUNDAY OF EASTER

A

FIRST READING

It was impossible for Jesus to be held by the power of Hades.

A reading from the Acts of the Apostles   2:14, 22-24

On the day of Pentecost,
>Peter stood with the eleven apostles
>>and spoke in a loud and clear voice to the crowd:

"Friends and everyone else living in Jerusalem,
>listen carefully to what I have to say!

"Now, listen to what I have to say about Jesus from Nazareth.
God proved that he sent Jesus to you
>by having him work miracles, wonders, and signs.
All of you know this.

"God had already planned and decided
>that Jesus would be handed over to you.
So you took him and had evil men put him to death on a cross.

"But God set him free from death and raised him to life.
Death could not hold him in its power."

The word of the Lord.

RESPONSORIAL PSALM   18:1-2, 46 and 50ab

> ℟. (2) I love you, Lord, my strength.
> **or:**
> ℟. Alleluia.

I love you, LORD God,
and you make me strong.
You are my mighty rock,
my fortress, my protector,
the rock where I am safe,
my shield, my powerful weapon,
and my place of shelter.

> ℟. I love you, Lord, my strength.
> **or:**
> ℟. Alleluia.

You are the living LORD!
I will praise you.
You are a mighty rock.
I will honor you
for keeping me safe.
You give glorious victories to your chosen king.

> ℟. I love you, Lord, my strength.
>
> or:
>
> ℟. Alleluia.

ALLELUIA
See Luke 24:32

> ℟. Alleluia, alleluia.

**Lord Jesus, make your word plain to us;
make our hearts burn with love when you speak.**

> ℟. Alleluia, alleluia.

GOSPEL

They recognized Jesus in the breaking of the bread.

✢ A reading from the holy gospel according to Luke   24:13-35

Two of Jesus' disciples were going to the village of Emmaus,
which was about seven miles from Jerusalem.
As they were talking and thinking about what had happened,
    Jesus came near and started walking along beside them.
But they did not know who he was.

Jesus asked them, "What were you talking about as you walked along?"

The two of them stood there looking sad and gloomy.
Then the one named Cleopas asked Jesus,
"Are you the only person from Jerusalem
    who didn't know what was happening there these last few days?"

"What do you mean?" Jesus asked.

They answered:
"Those things that happened to Jesus from Nazareth.
By what he did and said
    he showed that he was a powerful prophet,
        who pleased God and all the people.
Then the chief priests and our leaders
        had him arrested and sentenced to die on a cross.
We had hoped that he would be the one to set Israel free!

"But it has already been three days since all this happened.
Some women in our group surprised us.
They had gone to the tomb early in the morning,
    but did not find the body of Jesus.
They came back,
    saying that they had seen a vision of angels
    who told them that he is alive.
Some men from our group went to the tomb
        and found it just as the women had said.
But they didn't see Jesus either."

Then Jesus asked the two disciples,
"Why can't you understand?
How can you be so slow to believe all that the prophets said?
Didn't you know that the Messiah would have to suffer
    before he was given his glory?"

Jesus then explained everything written about himself
      in the Scriptures,
    beginning with the Law of Moses and the Books of the Prophets.

When the two of them came near the village where they were going,
    Jesus seemed to be going farther.
They begged him, "Stay with us!
It's already late, and the sun is going down."
So Jesus went into the house to stay with them.

After Jesus sat down to eat,
> he took some bread.
He blessed it and broke it.
Then he gave it to them.
At once they knew who he was,
> but he disappeared.

They said to each other,
"When he talked with us along the road
>> and explained the Scriptures to us,
> didn't it warm our hearts?"
So they got right up and returned to Jerusalem.

The two disciples
> found the eleven apostles and the others gathered together.
And they learned from the group
> that the Lord was really alive and had appeared to Peter.

Then the disciples from Emmaus told what happened on the road
> and how they knew he was the Lord
> when he broke the bread.

The gospel of the Lord.

[41] **THIRD SUNDAY OF EASTER** B

FIRST READING

>You have killed the Author of life;
>God, however, raised Jesus from the dead.

A reading from the Acts of the Apostles 3:13-15, 17-19

Peter told the people:
"The God that Abraham, Isaac, Jacob, and our other ancestors worshiped
   has brought honor to his Servant Jesus.
He is the one you betrayed.
You turned against him when he was being tried by Pilate,
   even though Pilate wanted to set him free.

"You rejected Jesus,
   who was holy and good.
You asked for a murderer to be set free,
   and you killed the one who leads people to life.
But God raised him from death,
   and all of us can tell you what he has done.

"My friends,
   I am sure that you and your leaders
      didn't know what you were doing.
But God had his prophets tell that his Messiah would suffer,
   and now he has kept that promise.
So turn to God!
Give up your sins, and you will be forgiven."

                              The word of the Lord.

RESPONSORIAL PSALM   4:1ab and 1ef, 3, 6cd-7a

℟. (7b) Lord, let your face shine on us.
or:
℟. Alleluia.

You are my God and protector.
Please answer my prayer.
Now have pity and listen as I pray.

℟. Lord, let your face shine on us.
or:
℟. Alleluia.

The LORD has chosen
everyone who is faithful
to be his very own,
and he answers my prayers.

℟. Lord, let your face shine on us.
or:
℟. Alleluia.

Let your kindness, LORD,
shine brightly on us.
You brought me happiness.

℟. Lord, let your face shine on us.
or:
℟. Alleluia.

ALLELUIA   See Luke 24:32

℟. Alleluia, alleluia.

Lord Jesus, make your word plain to us;
make our hearts burn with love when you speak.

℟. Alleluia, alleluia.

GOSPEL

*It was written that the Christ would suffer
and on the third day rise from the dead.*

✣ A reading from the holy gospel according to Luke 24:35-48

The disciples from Emmaus told what happened on the road
and how they knew he was the Lord when he broke the bread.

While Jesus' disciples were talking about what had happened,
   Jesus appeared to them and said,
"May God give you peace!"
They were frightened and terrified
   because they thought they were seeing a ghost.

But Jesus said, "Why are you so frightened?
Why do you doubt?
Look at my hands and my feet and see who I am!
Touch me and find out for yourselves.
Ghosts don't have flesh and bones as you see I have."

After Jesus said this,
   he showed them his hands and his feet.
The disciples were so glad and amazed that they could not believe it.

Jesus then asked them, "Do you have something to eat?"
They gave him a piece of baked fish.
He took it and ate it as they watched.

Jesus said to them,
"While I was still with you,
   I told you that everything written about me
      in the Law of Moses, the Books of the Prophets,
      and in the Psalms had to happen."

Then he helped them understand the Scriptures.
He told them:
"The Scriptures say that the Messiah must suffer,
   then three days later he will rise from death.
They also say that all people of every nation
      must be told in my name to turn to God,
      in order to be forgiven.
So beginning in Jerusalem,
   you must tell everything that has happened."

The gospel of the Lord.

THIRD SUNDAY OF EASTER C

FIRST READING

We are witnesses of these words and so is the Holy Spirit.

A reading from the Acts of the Apostles   5:27b-32, 40b-41

The high priest said to the apostles,
"We told you plainly not to teach in the name of Jesus.
But look what you have done!
You have been teaching all over Jerusalem,
    and you are trying to blame us for his death."

Peter and the apostles replied:
"We don't obey people. We obey God.
You killed Jesus by nailing him to a cross.
But the God our ancestors worshiped raised him to life
        and made him our Leader and Savior.
Then God gave him a place at his right side,
        so that the people of Israel would turn back to him
            and be forgiven.
We are here to tell you about all this,
    and so is the Holy Spirit,
    who is God's gift to everyone who obeys God."

They had the apostles beaten with a whip
    and warned them not to speak in the name of Jesus.
Then they let them go.
The apostles left the council and were happy,
    because God had considered them worthy
        to suffer for the sake of Jesus.

The word of the Lord.

RESPONSORIAL PSALM   30:1ab and 2 and 4, 10-11ab and 12bcd

℟. (2a) I will praise you, Lord,
        for you have rescued me.
or:
℟. Alleluia.

I will praise you, L ORD!
You saved me from the grave.
I prayed to you, L ORD God,
and you healed me.
Your faithful people, L ORD,
will praise you with songs
and honor your holy name.

> ℟. I will praise you, Lord,
>   for you have rescued me.

or:

> ℟. Alleluia.

Have pity, L ORD! Help!
You have turned my sorrow
into joyful dancing.
I will never stop
singing your praises,
my L ORD and my God.

> ℟. I will praise you, Lord,
>   for you have rescued me.

or:

> ℟. Alleluia.

ALLELUIA
See Luke 24:32

> ℟. Alleluia, alleluia.

Lord Jesus, make your word plain to us;
make our hearts burn with love when you speak.

> ℟. Alleluia, alleluia.

GOSPEL

*Jesus came and took the bread and gave it to them,
and did the same with the fish.*

✤ A reading from the holy gospel according to John   21:1-14

Jesus later appeared to his disciples along the shore of Lake Tiberias. Simon Peter, Thomas the Twin, Nathanael from Cana in Galilee,
  and the two sons of Zebedee, were there,
    together with two other disciples.
Simon Peter said, "I'm going fishing!"

The others said, "We'll go with you."
They went out in their boat.
But they didn't catch a thing that night.

Early the next morning Jesus stood on the shore,
    but the disciples did not realize who he was.
Jesus shouted, "Friends, have you caught anything?"

"No!" they answered.

So he told them,
"Let your net down on the right side of your boat,
    and you will catch some fish."
They did,
    and the net was so full of fish
        that they could not drag it up into the boat.

Jesus' favorite disciple told Peter, "It's the Lord!"
When Simon heard that it was the Lord,
    he put on the clothes that he had taken off while he was working.
Then he jumped into the water.
The boat was only about a hundred yards from shore.
So the other disciples stayed in the boat
    and dragged in the net full of fish.

When the disciples got out of the boat,
    they saw some bread and a charcoal fire with fish on it.
Jesus told his disciples,
"Bring some of the fish you just caught."
Simon Peter got back into the boat
    and dragged the net to shore.
In it were one hundred fifty-three large fish,
    but still the net did not rip.

Jesus said, "Come and eat!"
But none of the disciples dared ask who he was.
They knew he was the Lord.
Jesus took the bread in his hands
    and gave some of it to his disciples.
He did the same with the fish.

This was the third time that Jesus appeared to his disciples
    after he was raised from death.

                      The gospel of the Lord.

[43]   **FOURTH SUNDAY OF EASTER**   **A**

FIRST READING

God has made Jesus both Lord and Christ.

A reading from the Acts of the Apostles   2:14a, 36-41

On the day of Pentecost,
    Peter stood with the eleven apostles
        and spoke in a loud and clear voice to the crowd:

"Everyone in Israel should know for certain
        that God has made Jesus both Lord and Christ,
    even though you put him to death on a cross."

When the people heard this, they were very upset.
They asked Peter and the other apostles,
"Friends, what shall we do?"

Peter said, "Turn back to God!
Be baptized in the name of Jesus Christ,
    so that your sins will be forgiven.
Then you will be given the Holy Spirit.
This promise is for you and your children.
It is for everyone our Lord God will choose,
    no matter where they live."

Peter told the people many other things as well.
Then he said, "I beg you to save yourselves
        from what will happen to all these evil people."

On that day about three thousand believed his message
    and were baptized.

                                    The word of the Lord.

RESPONSORIAL PSALM   23:1-3a, 3b-4, 6

    ℞. (1) The Lord is my shepherd; there is nothing I shall want.
    or:
    ℞. Alleluia.

You, LORD, are my shepherd.
I will never be in need.
You let me rest in fields of green grass.

You lead me to streams of peaceful water,
and you refresh my life.

> ℟. The Lord is my shepherd; there is nothing I shall want.
> or:
> ℟. Alleluia.

You are true to your name,
and you lead me
along the right paths.
I may walk through valleys
as dark as death,
but I won't be afraid.
You are with me,
and your shepherd's rod
makes me feel safe.

> ℟. The Lord is my shepherd; there is nothing I shall want.
> or:
> ℟. Alleluia.

Your kindness and love
will always be with me
each day of my life,
and I will live forever
in your house, LORD.

> ℟. The Lord is my shepherd; there is nothing I shall want.
> or:
> ℟. Alleluia.

ALLELUIA
John 10:14

> ℟. Alleluia, alleluia.

**I am the good shepherd, says the Lord;
I know my sheep, and mine know me.**

> ℟. Alleluia, alleluia.

GOSPEL

I am the gate of the sheepfold.

✢ A reading from the holy gospel according to John   10:1-10

Jesus said to his disciples:
"I tell you for certain
    that only thieves and robbers climb over the fence
    instead of going in through the gate to the sheep pen.
But the gatekeeper opens the gate for the shepherd,
    and he goes in through it.
The sheep know their shepherd's voice.
He calls each of them by name and leads them out.

"When he has led out all of his sheep,
    he walks in front of them,
    and they follow, because they know his voice.
The sheep will not follow strangers.
They don't recognize a stranger's voice,
    and they run away."

Jesus told the people this story.
But they did not understand what he was talking about.

Then Jesus said:
"I tell you for certain that I am the gate for the sheep.
Everyone who came before me was a thief or a robber,
    and the sheep did not listen to any of them.
I am the gate.
All who come in through me will be saved.
Through me they will come and go and find pasture.

"A thief comes only to rob, kill, and destroy.
I came so that everyone would have life,
    and have it in its fullest."

The gospel of the Lord.

[44] **FOURTH SUNDAY OF EASTER** B

FIRST READING

This is the only name by which we can be saved.

A reading from the Acts of the Apostles   4:8-12

Peter was filled with the Holy Spirit
and told the nation's leaders and the elders:

"You are questioning us today about a kind deed
in which a crippled man was healed.
But there is something we must tell you and everyone else in Israel.
This man is standing here completely well
because of the power of Jesus Christ from Nazareth.

"You put Jesus to death on a cross,
but God raised him to life.
He is the stone that you builders thought was worthless,
and now he is the most important stone of all.
Only Jesus has the power to save!
His name is the only one in all the world that can save anyone."

The word of the Lord.

RESPONSORIAL PSALM   118:1 and 21, 22-23

℟. (22) The stone rejected by the builders
has become the cornerstone.
or:
℟. Alleluia.

Tell the Lord
how thankful you are,
because he is kind
and always merciful.
I praise the Lord
for answering my prayers
and saving me.

℟. The stone rejected by the builders
has become the cornerstone.
or:
℟. Alleluia.

The stone that the builders
tossed aside
has now become
the most important stone.
The Lord has done this,
and it is amazing to us.

> ℟. The stone rejected by the builders
> has become the cornerstone.
> **or:**
> ℟. Alleluia.

SECOND READING

We shall see God as he really is.

A reading from the first letter of John 3:1-2

Beloved:
Think how much the Father loves us.
He loves us so much that he lets us be called his children,
as we truly are.
But since the people of this world did not know who Christ is,
they don't know who we are.

My dear friends, we are already God's children,
though what we will be has not yet been seen.
But we do know that when Christ returns,
we will be like him,
because we will see him as he truly is.

The word of the Lord.

ALLELUIA John 10:14

℟. Alleluia, alleluia.

**I am the good shepherd, says the Lord;
I know my sheep, and mine know me.**

℟. Alleluia, alleluia.

GOSPEL

The good shepherd lays down his life for his sheep.

✣ A reading from the holy gospel according to John   10:11-16

Jesus said to his disciples:
"I am the good shepherd,
    and the good shepherd gives up his life for his sheep.

"Hired workers are not like the shepherd.
They don't own the sheep,
    and when they see a wolf coming,
    they run off and leave the sheep.
Then the wolf attacks and scatters the flock.

"Hired workers run away because they don't care about the sheep.

"I am the good shepherd.
I know my sheep, and they know me.
Just as the Father knows me,
    I know the Father,
    and I give up my life for my sheep.

"I have other sheep that are not in this sheep pen.
I must bring them together too,
    when they hear my voice.
Then there will be one flock of sheep and one shepherd."

                                              The gospel of the Lord.

[45]   **FOURTH SUNDAY OF EASTER**   **C**

FIRST READING

We are now turning to the Gentiles.

A reading from the Acts of the Apostles   13:43-44, 47-48

After the Sabbath service,
   many Jews and a lot of Gentiles who worshiped God
      went with Paul and Barnabas.
They begged the people to remain faithful to God,
   who had been so kind to them.

The next Sabbath almost everyone in town
   came to hear the message about the Lord.

Paul and Barnabas told them,
"The Lord has given this command,

      'I have placed you here as a light for the Gentiles.
      You are to take the saving power of God
         to people everywhere on earth.' "

This message made the Gentiles glad,
   and they praised what they had heard about the Lord.
Everyone who had been chosen for eternal life
   then put their faith in the Lord.

                The word of the Lord.

RESPONSORIAL PSALM   100:1-2, 3, 5

   ℟. (3c) We are God's people, the sheep of his flock.
   or:
   ℟. Alleluia.

Shout praises to the Lord,
everyone on this earth.
Be joyful and sing
as you come in to worship the Lord!

   ℟. We are God's people, the sheep of his flock.
   or:
   ℟. Alleluia.

You know the Lord is God!
He created us,
and we belong to him;
we are his people,
the sheep in his pasture.

> ℟. We are God's people, the sheep of his flock.
> or:
> ℟. Alleluia.

The Lord is good!
His love and faithfulness
will last forever.

> ℟. We are God's people, the sheep of his flock.
> or:
> ℟. Alleluia.

ALLELUIA
John 10:14

> ℟. Alleluia, alleluia.
>
> **I am the good shepherd, says the Lord;
> I know my sheep, and mine know me.**
>
> ℟. Alleluia, alleluia.

GOSPEL

I give my sheep eternal life.

✠ **A reading from the holy gospel according to John**   10:27-30

Jesus said to his disciples:
"My sheep know my voice, and I know them.
They follow me,
    and I give them eternal life,
    so that they will never be lost.
No one can snatch them out of my hand.
My Father gave them to me,
    and he is greater than all others.
No one can snatch them from his hands,
    and I am one with the Father."

The gospel of the Lord.

FIFTH SUNDAY OF EASTER

FIRST READING

They chose seven men filled with the Spirit.

A reading from the Acts of the Apostles   6:1-7a

A lot of people were becoming followers of the Lord.
But some of the ones who spoke Greek started complaining
    about the ones who spoke Aramaic.
They complained that the Greek-speaking widows
    were not given their share
    when the food supplies were handed out each day.

The twelve apostles called the whole group of followers together
    and said,
"We should not give up preaching God's message
    in order to serve at tables.
My friends, choose seven men who are respected and wise
    and filled with God's Spirit.
We will put them in charge of these things.
We can spend our time praying and serving God by preaching."

This suggestion pleased everyone,
    and they began by choosing Stephen.
He had great faith and was filled with the Holy Spirit.

Then they chose Philip, Prochorus, Nicanor, Timon, Parmenas,
    and also Nicolaus,
    who worshiped with the Jewish people in Antioch.
These men were brought to the apostles.
Then the apostles prayed and placed their hands on the men
    to show that they had been chosen to do this work.

God's message spread,
    and many more people in Jerusalem became followers.

                                        The word of the Lord.

RESPONSIONAL PSALM

145:10-11, 15-16, 17-18

℟. (16) You open your hand to feed us, Lord;
　　 you answer all our needs.
or:
℟. Alleluia.

**All creation will thank you,
and your loyal people will praise you.
They will tell about
your marvelous kingdom and your power.**

℟. You open your hand to feed us, Lord;
　　 you answer all our needs.
or:
℟. Alleluia.

**Everyone depends on you,
and when the time is right,
you provide them with food.
By your own hand you satisfy
the desires of all who live.**

℟. You open your hand to feed us, Lord;
　　 you answer all our needs.
or:
℟. Alleluia.

**Our Lord, everything you do
is kind and thoughtful,
and you are near to everyone
whose prayers are sincere.**

℟. You open your hand to feed us, Lord;
　　 you answer all our needs.
or:
℟. Alleluia.

ALLELUIA

John 14:6

℟. Alleluia, alleluia.

**I am the way, the truth, and the life, says the Lord;
no one comes to the Father, except through me.**

℟. Alleluia, alleluia.

GOSPEL

I am the way, the truth, and the life.

✣ **A reading from the holy gospel according to John**

14:1-12

**Jesus said to his disciples,
"Don't be worried!
Have faith in God and have faith in me.
There are many rooms in my Father's house.
I wouldn't tell you this, unless it was true.
I am going there to prepare a place for each of you.
After I have done this,
   I will come back and take you with me.
Then we will be together.
You know the way to where I am going."**

**Thomas said, "Lord, we don't even know where you are going!
How can we know the way?"**

**"I am the way, the truth, and the life!" Jesus answered.
"Without me, no one can go to the Father.
If you had known me,
   you would have known the Father.
But from now on, you do know him,
   and you have seen him."**

**Philip said, "Lord, show us the Father.
That is all we need."**

**Jesus replied:
"Philip, I have been with you for a long time.
Don't you know who I am?
If you have seen me, you have seen the Father.**

How can you ask me to show you the Father?
Don't you believe that I am one with the Father
    and that the Father is one with me?
What I say is not said on my own.
The Father who lives in me does these things.

"Have faith in me when I say that the Father is one with me
    and that I am one with the Father.
Or else have faith in me simply because of the things I do.

"I tell you for certain that if you have faith in me,
    you will do the same things that I am doing.
You will do even greater things,
    now that I am going back to the Father."

                                        The gospel of the Lord.

FIFTH SUNDAY OF EASTER B

FIRST READING

Barnabas explained to the apostles how the Lord appeared to Saul and spoke to him on his journey.

A reading from the Acts of the Apostles 9:26-28

When Saul arrived in Jerusalem,
he tried to join the followers.
But they were all afraid of him,
    because they did not believe he was a true follower.

Then Barnabas helped him by taking him to the apostles.
He explained how on the road to Damascus,
    Saul had seen the Lord and how the Lord had spoken to Saul.
Barnabas also said that when Saul was in Damascus,
    he had spoken bravely in the name of Jesus.

Saul moved about freely with the followers in Jerusalem
    and told everyone about the Lord.

The word of the Lord.

RESPONSORIAL PSALM 22:27, 30-31

℟. (26a) I will praise you, Lord, in the assembly of your people.
or:
℟. Alleluia.

Everyone on this earth
will remember you, Lord.
People all over the world
will turn and worship you.

℟. I will praise you, Lord, in the assembly of your people.
or:
℟. Alleluia.

**In the future, everyone will worship and learn
about you, our Lord.
People not yet born
will be told,
"The Lord has saved us!"**

℟. I will praise you, Lord, in the assembly of your people.
or:
℟. Alleluia.

SECOND READING

God's commandment is this: love others by helping them.

A reading from the first letter of John 3:18

Children, you show love for others by truly helping them, and not merely by talking about it.

The word of the Lord.

ALLELUIA John 15:4a, 5b

℟. Alleluia, alleluia.

**Live in me and let me live in you, says the Lord;
my branches bear much fruit.**

℟. Alleluia, alleluia.

GOSPEL

All who live in me, and I in them, bear much fruit.

✤ **A reading from the holy gospel according to John** 15:1-5, 7-8

Jesus said to his disciples:
"I am the true vine,
   and my Father is the gardener.
He cuts away every branch of mine that does not produce fruit.
But he trims clean every branch that does produce fruit,
   so that it will produce even more fruit.

"You are already clean because of what I have said to you.

"Stay joined to me,
   and I will stay joined to you.
Just as a branch cannot produce fruit
     unless it stays joined to the vine,
   you cannot produce fruit unless you stay joined to me.

"I am the vine, and you are the branches.
If you stay joined to me, and I stay joined to you,
   then you will produce lots of fruit.
But you cannot do anything without me.

"Stay joined to me and let my teachings become part of you.
Then you can pray for whatever you want,
   and your prayer will be answered.

"When you become fruitful disciples of mine,
   my Father will be honored."

The gospel of the Lord.

[48] # FIFTH SUNDAY OF EASTER   **C**

FIRST READING

*They assembled the Church
and gave an account of all that God had done with them.*

A reading from the Acts of the Apostles   14:21-27

Paul and Barnabas preached the good news in Derbe
    and won some people to the Lord.
Then they went back to Lystra, Iconium, and Antioch in Pisidia.
They encouraged the followers and begged them to remain faithful.
They told them,
"We have to suffer a lot before we can get into God's kingdom."

Paul and Barnabas chose some of those who had faith in the Lord
    to be leaders for each of the churches.
Then they went without eating
    and prayed that the Lord would take good care
    of these leaders.

Paul and Barnabas went on through Pisidia to Pamphylia,
    where they preached in the town of Perga.
Then they went down to Attalia and sailed to Antioch in Syria.
It was there that they had been placed in God's care
    for the work they had now completed.

After arriving in Antioch,
    they called the church together.
They told the people what God had helped them do
    and how he had made it possible for the Gentiles to believe.

The word of the Lord.

RESPONSORIAL PSALM   145:8-9, 10 and 12

℟. (see 1) I will praise your name for ever, my king and my God.
or:
℟. Alleluia.

You are merciful, LORD!
You are kind and patient
and always loving.

You are good to everyone,
and you take care
of all your creation.

> ℟. I will praise your name for ever, my king and my God.
> or:
> ℟. Alleluia.

All creation will thank you,
and your loyal people
will praise you.
Then everyone will know about
the mighty things you do
and your glorious kingdom.

> ℟. I will praise your name for ever, my king and my God.
> or:
> ℟. Alleluia.

SECOND READING

God will wipe away all tears from their eyes.

A reading from the book of Revelation   21:1-4

I, John, saw a new heaven and a new earth.
The first heaven and the first earth had disappeared,
  and so had the sea.
Then I saw New Jerusalem, that holy city,
  coming down from God in heaven.
It was like a bride dressed in her wedding gown
  and ready to meet her husband.

I heard a loud voice shout from the throne:
"God's home is now with his people.
He will live with them,
  and they will be his own.
Yes, God will make his home among his people.
He will wipe all tears from their eyes,
  and there will be no more death, suffering, crying, or pain.
These things of the past are gone forever."

The word of the Lord.

ALLELUIA
John 13:34

℟. Alleluia, alleluia.

**I give you a new commandment:
love one another as I have loved you.**

℟. Alleluia, alleluia.

GOSPEL

I give you a new commandment: love one another.

✤ **A reading from the holy gospel according to John**   13:31a, 33-35

After Judas had gone, Jesus said:
"My children, I will be with you for a little while longer.
Then you will look for me,
   but you won't find me.
I tell you just as I told the people,
'You cannot go where I am going.'

"But I am giving you a new command.
You must love each other,
   just as I have loved you.
If you love each other,
   everyone will know that you are my disciples."

The gospel of the Lord.

SIXTH SUNDAY OF EASTER

FIRST READING

Peter and John laid hands on them, and they received the Holy Spirit.

A reading from the Acts of the Apostles   8:5-8, 14-17

Philip went to the town of Samaria and told the people about Christ.
They crowded around Philip
   because they were eager to hear what he was saying
      and to see him work miracles.
Many people with evil spirits were healed,
   and the spirits went out of them with a shout.
A lot of crippled and lame people were also healed.
Everyone in that city was very glad because of what was happening.

When the apostles in Jerusalem
      heard that some people in Samaria had accepted God's message,
   they sent Peter and John.
When the two apostles arrived,
   they prayed that the people would be given the Holy Spirit.

Before this, the Holy Spirit had not been given to anyone in Samaria
      though some of them had been baptized
      in the name of the Lord Jesus.

Peter and John then placed their hands
      on everyone who had faith in the Lord,
   and they were given the Holy Spirit.

The word of the Lord.

RESPONSORIAL PSALM   66:1-3ab, 4-5, 16 and 20

℟. (1) Let all the earth cry out to God with joy.
or:
℟. Alleluia.

Tell everyone on this earth
to shout praises to God!
Sing about his glorious name.
Honor him with praises.
Say to God, "Everything you do is fearsome!"

℟. Let all the earth cry out to God with joy.
or:
℟. Alleluia.

"You are worshiped by everyone!
We all sing praises to you."
Come and see the fearsome things
our God has done!

℟. Let all the earth cry out to God with joy.
or:
℟. Alleluia.

All who worship God,
come here and listen;
I will tell you everything
God has done for me.
Let's praise God!
He listened when I prayed,
and he is always kind.

℟. Let all the earth cry out to God with joy.
or:
℟. Alleluia.

ALLELUIA John 14:23

℟. Alleluia, alleluia.

All who love me will keep my words,
and my Father will love them,
and we will come to them.

℟. Alleluia, alleluia.

GOSPEL

I shall ask the Father and he will give you another Advocate.

✠ A reading from the holy gospel according to John   14:15-21

Jesus said to his disciples:
"If you love me, you will do as I command.
Then I will ask the Father to send you the Holy Spirit
    who will help you and always be with you.
The Spirit will show you what is true.

"The people of this world cannot accept the Spirit,
    because they don't see or know him.
But you know the Spirit, who is with you
    and will keep on living in you.

"I won't leave you like orphans.
I will come back to you.
In a little while the people of this world won't be able to see me,
    but you will see me.
And because I live, you will live.
Then you will know that I am one with the Father.
You will know that you are one with me,
    and I am one with you.

"If you love me, you will do what I have said,
    and my Father will love you.
I will also love you and show you what I am like."

The gospel of the Lord.

SIXTH SUNDAY OF EASTER   B

FIRST READING

The gift of the Holy Spirit was poured out upon the Gentiles also.

A reading from the Acts of the Apostles   10:25-26, 34-35, 44-48

When Peter arrived, Cornelius greeted him.
Then he kneeled at Peter's feet and started worshiping him.
But Peter took hold of him and said, "Stand up!
I am nothing more than a human."

Peter then said,
"Now I am certain that God treats all people alike.
God is pleased with everyone who worships him and does right,
    no matter what nation they come from."

While Peter was still speaking,
    the Holy Spirit took control of everyone who was listening.
Some Jewish followers of the Lord had come with Peter,
    and they were surprised
       that the Holy Spirit had been given to Gentiles.
Now they were hearing Gentiles speaking unknown languages
    and praising God.

Peter said, "These Gentiles have been given the Holy Spirit,
    just as we have!
I am certain that no one would dare stop us from baptizing them."

Peter ordered them to be baptized in the name of Jesus Christ,
    and they asked him to stay on for a few days.

                                            The word of the Lord.

RESPONSORIAL PSALM   98:1-2, 3cd-4

℟. (see 2b) **The Lord has revealed to the nations his saving power.**
or:
℟. **Alleluia.**

Sing a new song to the LORD!
He has worked miracles,
and with his own powerful arm,
he has won the victory.

**The LORD has shown the nations
that he has the power to save
and to bring justice.**

> ℟. The Lord has revealed to the nations his saving power.
> **or:**
> ℟. Alleluia.

**God's saving power is seen
everywhere on earth.
Tell everyone on this earth
to sing happy songs
in praise of the LORD.**

> ℟. The Lord has revealed to the nations his saving power.
> **or:**
> ℟. Alleluia.

SECOND READING

God is love.

A reading from the first letter of John   4:7-10

My dear friends, we must love each other.
Love comes from God,
   and when we love each other,
     it shows that we have been given new life.

We are now God's children, and we know him.

God is love,
   and anyone who doesn't love others has never known him.

God showed his love for us
   when he sent his only Son into the world to give us life.

Real love is not our love for God, but his love for us.
God sent his Son to be the sacrifice by which our sins are forgiven.

The word of the Lord.

ALLELUIA
John 14:23

℟. Alleluia, alleluia.

**All who love me will keep my words,
and my Father will love them,
and we will come to them.**

℟. Alleluia, alleluia.

GOSPEL

No one can have greater love
than to lay down one's life for one's friends.

✢ **A reading from the holy gospel according to John** 15:9-14

Jesus said to his disciples:
  "I have loved you,
    just as my Father has loved me.
So make sure that I keep on loving you.
If you obey me,
  I will keep loving you,
    just as my Father keeps loving me,
    because I have obeyed him.

"I have told you this to make you as completely happy as I am.
Now I tell you to love each other,
  as I have loved you.
The greatest way to show love for friends is to die for them.
And you are my friends,
  if you obey me."

The gospel of the Lord.

[51]   **SIXTH SUNDAY OF EASTER**

FIRST READING

The angel showed me the holy city coming down out of heaven.

A reading from the book of Revelation   21:10-14, 22-23

With the help of the Spirit,
   the angel took me to the top of a very high mountain.
There he showed me the holy city of Jerusalem
     coming down from God in heaven.

The glory of God made the city bright.
It was dazzling and crystal clear like a precious jasper stone.
The city had a high and thick wall with twelve gates,
   and each one of them was guarded by an angel.
On each of the gates was written
     the name of one of the twelve tribes of Israel.
Three of these gates were on the east,
     three were on the north,
     three more were on the south,
     and the other three were on the west.
The city was built on twelve foundation stones.
On each of the stones was written
     the name of one of the Lamb's twelve apostles.

I did not see a temple there.
The Lord God All-Powerful and the Lamb were its temple.
And the city did not need the sun or the moon.
The glory of God was shining on it,
   and the Lamb was its light.

                                                 The word of the Lord.

RESPONSIVE PSALM

RESPONSORIAL PSALM 67:1-2, 4, 5 and 7

℟. (6a) O God, let all the nations praise you!
or:
℟. Alleluia.

Our God, be kind and bless us!
Be pleased and smile.
Then everyone on earth
will learn to follow you,
and all nations will see
your power to save us.

℟. O God, let all the nations praise you!
or:
℟. Alleluia.

Let the nations celebrate
with joyful songs,
because you judge fairly
and guide all nations.

℟. O God, let all the nations praise you!
or:
℟. Alleluia.

Make everyone praise you
and shout your praises.
Pray for his blessings to continue
and for everyone on earth
to worship our God.

℟. O God, let all the nations praise you!
or:
℟. Alleluia.

ALLELUIA
John 14:23

℟. Alleluia, alleluia.

**All who love me will keep my words,
and my Father will love them,
and we will come to them.**

℟. Alleluia, alleluia.

GOSPEL

The Holy Spirit will teach you everything
and remind you of all I have said to you.

✤ **A reading from the holy gospel according to John**   14:23-26

**Jesus said:
"If anyone loves me, they will obey me.
Then my Father will love them,
   and we will come to them and live in them.
But anyone who doesn't love me,
   won't obey me.
What they have heard me say doesn't really come from me,
   but from the Father who sent me.**

**"I have told you these things while I am still with you.
But the Holy Spirit will come and help you,
   because the Father will send the Spirit to take my place.
The Spirit will teach you everything
      and will remind you of what I said while I was with you."**

The gospel of the Lord.

[52] THE ASCENSION OF THE LORD **A**

The following readings may be used only when the celebration of the liturgy of the word for the children is held in a place apart from the main assembly.

FIRST READING

Why are you standing here looking at the sky?
Jesus has been taken into heaven.

A reading from the Acts of the Apostles 1:8-11

Jesus told his disciples:
"The Holy Spirit will come upon you and give you power.
Then you will tell everyone about me in Jerusalem,
 in all Judea, in Samaria, and everywhere in the world."

After Jesus had said this and while they were watching,
 he was taken up into a cloud.
They could not see him, but as he went up,
 they kept looking up into the sky.

Suddenly two men dressed in white clothes
 were standing there beside them.
They said, "Why are you men from Galilee
 standing here and looking up into the sky?
Jesus has been taken to heaven.
But he will come back in the same way that you have seen him go."

The word of the Lord.

RESPONSORIAL PSALM 47:1-2, 5-6, 7-8

℟. (6a) God mounts the throne to shouts of joy.
or:
℟. Alleluia.

All of you nations,
clap your hands and shout
joyful praises to God.
The LORD Most High is fearsome,
the ruler of all the earth.

℟. God mounts the throne to shouts of joy.
or:
℟. Alleluia.

God goes up to his throne,
as people shout
and trumpets blast.
Sing praises to God our King.

> ℟. God mounts the throne to shouts of joy.
> or:
> ℟. Alleluia.

God is ruler of all the earth!
Praise God with songs.
God rules the nations
from his sacred throne.

> ℟. God mounts the throne to shouts of joy.
> or:
> ℟. Alleluia.

SECOND READING

God seated Jesus at his right hand in heaven.

A reading from the letter of Paul to the Ephesians　　　1:17-21

Brothers and sisters:
I ask the glorious Father and God of our Lord Jesus Christ
    to give you his Spirit.
The Spirit will make you wise and let you understand
    what it means to know God.

My prayer is that light will flood your hearts
    and that you will understand the hope that was given to you
    when God chose you.
Then you will discover the glorious blessings that will be yours
    together with all of God's people.

I want you to know about the great and mighty power
    that God has for us followers.
It is the same wonderful power he used when he raised Christ from death
    and let him sit at his right side in heaven.
There Christ rules over all forces, authorities, powers, and rulers.
He rules over all beings in this world
    and will rule in the future world as well.

                              The word of the Lord.

ALLELUIA
Matthew 28:19a, 20b

℟. Alleluia, alleluia.

Go and teach all people my gospel;
I am with you always, until the end of the world.

℟. Alleluia, alleluia.

GOSPEL

All authority in heaven and on earth has been given to me.

✝ **A reading from the holy gospel according to Matthew**   28:16-20

Jesus' eleven disciples went to a mountain in Galilee,
> where Jesus had told them to meet him.

They saw him and worshiped him,
> but some of them doubted.

Jesus came to them and said:
"I have been given all authority in heaven and on earth!
Go to the people of all nations and make them my disciples.
Baptize them in the name of the Father,
> the Son, and the Holy Spirit,
> and teach them to do everything I have told you.

"I will be with you always,
> even until the end of the world."

The gospel of the Lord.

[53] **THE ASCENSION OF THE LORD** **B**

The following readings may be used only when the celebration of the liturgy of the word for the children is held in a place apart from the main assembly.

FIRST READING

Why are you standing here looking at the sky?
Jesus has been taken into heaven.

A reading from the Acts of the Apostles 1:8-11

Jesus told his disciples:
"The Holy Spirit will come upon you and give you power.
Then you will tell everyone about me in Jerusalem,
    in all Judea, in Samaria, and everywhere in the world."

After Jesus had said this and while they were watching,
    he was taken up into a cloud.
They could not see him, but as he went up,
    they kept looking up into the sky.

Suddenly two men dressed in white clothes
    were standing there beside them.
They said, "Why are you men from Galilee
    standing here and looking up into the sky?
Jesus has been taken to heaven.
But he will come back in the same way that you have seen him go."

The word of the Lord.

RESPONSORIAL PSALM 47:1-2, 5-6, 7-8

℟. (6a) God mounts the throne to shouts of joy.
or:
℟. Alleluia.

All of you nations,
clap your hands and shout
joyful praises to God.
The Lord Most High is fearsome,
the ruler of all the earth.

℟. God mounts the throne to shouts of joy.
or:
℟. Alleluia.

God goes up to his throne,
as people shout
and trumpets blast.
Sing praises to God our King.

> ℟. God mounts the throne to shouts of joy.
> **or:**
> ℟. Alleluia.

God is ruler of all the earth!
Praise God with songs.
God rules the nations
from his sacred throne.

> ℟. God mounts the throne to shouts of joy.
> **or:**
> ℟. Alleluia.

SECOND READING

God seated Jesus at his right hand in heaven.

A reading from the letter of Paul to the Ephesians 1:17-21

Brothers and sisters:
 I ask the glorious Father and God of our Lord Jesus Christ
> to give you his Spirit.
The Spirit will make you wise and let you understand
> what it means to know God.

My prayer is that light will flood your hearts
> and that you will understand the hope that was given to you
> when God chose you.
Then you will discover the glorious blessings that will be yours
> together with all of God's people.

I want you to know about the great and mighty power
> that God has for us followers.
It is the same wonderful power he used when he raised Christ from death
> and let him sit at his right side in heaven.
There Christ rules over all forces, authorities, powers, and rulers.
He rules over all beings in this world
> and will rule in the future world as well.

The word of the Lord.

THE ASCENSION OF THE LORD — B

ALLELUIA Matthew 28:19a, 20b

℟. Alleluia, alleluia.

Go and teach all people my gospel;
I am with you always, until the end of the world.

℟. Alleluia, alleluia.

GOSPEL

*The Lord Jesus was taken into heaven
and is seated at the right hand of God.*

✢ A reading from the holy gospel according to Mark   16:15-20

Jesus told his disciples:
"Go and preach the good news to everyone in the world.
Anyone who believes me and is baptized will be saved.
But anyone who refuses to believe me will be condemned.

"Everyone who believes me will be able to do wonderful things.
By using my name they will force out demons,
    and they will speak new languages.
They will handle snakes and will drink poison and not be hurt.
They will also heal sick people by placing their hands on them."

After the Lord Jesus had said these things to the disciples,
    he was taken back up to heaven
    where he sat down at the right side of God.
Then the disciples left and preached everywhere.
The Lord was with them,
    and the miracles they worked proved that their message was true.

The gospel of the Lord.

[54] **THE ASCENSION OF THE LORD** **C**

The following readings may be used only when the celebration of the liturgy of the word for the chidren is held in a place apart from the main assembly.

FIRST READING

Why are you standing here looking at the sky?
Jesus has been taken into heaven.

A reading from the Acts of the Apostles 1:8-11

Jesus told his disciples:
"The Holy Spirit will come upon you and give you power.
Then you will tell everyone about me in Jerusalem,
   in all Judea, in Samaria, and everywhere in the world."

After Jesus had said this and while they were watching,
   he was taken up into a cloud.
They could not see him, but as he went up,
   they kept looking up into the sky.

Suddenly two men dressed in white clothes
   were standing there beside them.
They said, "Why are you men from Galilee
   standing here and looking up into the sky?
Jesus has been taken to heaven.
But he will come back in the same way that you have seen him go."

The word of the Lord.

RESPONSORIAL PSALM 47:1-2, 5-6, 7-8

℟. (6a) God mounts the throne to shouts of joy.
or:
℟. Alleluia.

All of you nations,
clap your hands and shout
joyful praises to God.
The LORD Most High is fearsome,
the ruler of all the earth.

℟. God mounts the throne to shouts of joy.
or:
℟. Alleluia.

God goes up to his throne,
as people shout
and trumpets blast.
Sing praises to God our King.

> ℟. God mounts the throne to shouts of joy.
> or:
> ℟. Alleluia.

God is ruler of all the earth!
Praise God with songs.
God rules the nations
from his sacred throne.

> ℟. God mounts the throne to shouts of joy.
> or:
> ℟. Alleluia.

SECOND READING

God seated Jesus at his right hand in heaven.

A reading from the letter of Paul to the Ephesians   1:17-21

Brothers and sisters:
I ask the glorious Father and God of our Lord Jesus Christ
    to give you his Spirit.
The Spirit will make you wise and let you understand
    what it means to know God.

My prayer is that light will flood your hearts
    and that you will understand the hope that was given to you
    when God chose you.
Then you will discover the glorious blessings that will be yours
    together with all of God's people.

I want you to know about the great and mighty power
    that God has for us followers.
It is the same wonderful power he used when he raised Christ from death
    and let him sit at his right side in heaven.
There Christ rules over all forces, authorities, powers, and rulers.
He rules over all beings in this world
    and will rule in the future world as well.

The word of the Lord.

ALLELUIA

Matthew 28:19a, 20b

℟. Alleluia, alleluia.

Go and teach all people my gospel;
I am with you always, until the end of the world.

℟. Alleluia, alleluia.

GOSPEL

Jesus blessed them, withdrew from them, and was carried to heaven.

✞ A reading from the holy gospel according to Luke   24:50-53

Jesus led his disciples out to Bethany,
   where he raised his hands and blessed them.
As he was doing this,
   he left and was taken up to heaven.

After his disciples had worshiped him,
   they returned to Jerusalem and were very happy.
They spent their time in the temple, praising God.

The gospel of the Lord.

[55] **SEVENTH SUNDAY OF EASTER** A

FIRST READING

They all joined together in continuous prayer in the upper room.

A reading from the Acts of the Apostles 1:12-14

The Mount of Olives was about half a mile from Jerusalem.
The apostles who had gone there were Peter, John, James, Andrew,
    Philip, Thomas, Bartholomew, Matthew,
    James the son of Alphaeus,
    Simon, known as the Eager One,
    and Judas the son of James.
After the apostles returned to the city,
    they went upstairs to the room where they had been staying.
The apostles often met together
    and prayed with a single purpose in mind.
The women and Mary the mother of Jesus would meet with them,
    and so would his brothers.

The word of the Lord.

RESPONSORIAL PSALM 27:1, 4abc, 7-8

℟. (13a) I believe that I shall see the good things of the Lord.
or:
℟. Alleluia.

You, Lord, are the light
that keeps me safe.
I am not afraid of anyone.
You protect me,
and I have no fears.

℟. I believe that I shall see the good things of the Lord.
or:
℟. Alleluia.

I ask only one thing, Lord:
Let me live in your house
every day of my life.

℞. I believe that I shall see the good things of the Lord.
or:
℞. Alleluia.

**Please listen when I pray!
Have pity. Answer my prayer.
My heart tells me to pray.
I am eager to see your face.**

℞. I believe that I shall see the good things of the Lord.
or:
℞. Alleluia.

SECOND READING

It is a blessing for you when they insult you
for bearing the name of Christ.

A reading from the first letter of Peter　　　　　　　　4:13-16

Brothers and sisters:
　Be glad for the chance to suffer as Christ suffered.
**It will prepare you for even greater happiness
　　when he makes his glorious return.**

Count it a blessing when you suffer for being a Christian.
This shows that God's glorious Spirit is with you.
But you deserve to suffer if you are a murderer, a thief,
　　a crook, or a busybody.
Don't be ashamed to suffer for being a Christian.
Praise God that you belong to him.

　　　　　　　　　　　　　　　　　　The word of the Lord.

ALLELUIA　　　　　　　　　　　　　　　　　　See John 14:18

℞. Alleluia, alleluia.

**The Lord says: I will not leave you orphans.
I will come back to you, and your hearts will rejoice.**

℞. Alleluia, alleluia.

GOSPEL

My followers belong to you, and I am praying for them.

✜ **A reading from the holy gospel according to John** 17:6-9

Jesus prayed to God:
"You have given me some followers from this world,
   and I have shown them what you are like.

"They were yours,
   but you gave them to me,
   and they have obeyed you.
They know that you gave me everything I have.

"I told my followers what you told me,
   and they accepted it.
They know that I came from you,
   and they believe that you are the one who sent me.

"I am praying for them,
   but not for those who belong to this world.
My followers belong to you,
   and I am praying for them."

                             The gospel of the Lord.

[56] **SEVENTH SUNDAY OF EASTER** B

FIRST READING

> We must therefore choose someone who has been with us the whole time,
> and he can act with us as a witness to Christ's resurrection.

A reading from the Acts of the Apostles 1:15-17, 20a, 20c-26

One day there were about a hundred and twenty of the Lord's followers meeting together,
and Peter stood up to speak to them.

He said:
"My friends, long ago by the power of the Holy Spirit,
David said something about Judas,
and what he said has now happened.
Judas was one of us and had worked with us,
but he brought the mob to arrest Jesus.
In the book of Psalms David said,
'Leave his house empty.'

"It also says, 'Let someone else have his job.'

"So we need someone else to help us tell others
that Jesus has been raised from death.
He must also be one of the men who was with us from the very beginning.
He must have been with us
from the time the Lord Jesus was baptized by John
until the day he was taken to heaven."

Two men were suggested:
One of them was Joseph Barsabbas, known as Justus,
and the other was Matthias.
Then they all prayed,
"Lord, you know what everyone is like!
Show us the one you have chosen to be an apostle
and to serve in place of Judas,
who got what he deserved."
They drew names,
and Matthias was chosen to join the group of the eleven apostles.

The word of the Lord.

RESPONSIONAL PSALM

103:1-2, 19-20ac

℟. (19a) The Lord has set his throne in heaven.
or:
℟. Alleluia.

With all my heart
I praise the LORD,
and with all that I am
I praise his holy name!
With all my heart
I praise the LORD!
I will never forget
how kind he has been.

℟. The Lord has set his throne in heaven.
or:
℟. Alleluia.

God has set up his kingdom in heaven,
and he rules the whole creation.
All of you mighty angels,
come and praise your LORD!

℟. The Lord has set his throne in heaven.
or:
℟. Alleluia.

SECOND READING

God lives in us.

A reading from the first letter of John

4:11-13

Dear friends,
since God loved us this much,
we must love each other.

No one has ever seen God.
But if we love each other,
God lives in us,
and his love is truly in our hearts.

God has given us his Spirit.
That is how we know that we are one with him,
> just as he is one with us.

The word of the Lord.

ALLELUIA See John 14:18

℟. Alleluia, alleluia.

**The Lord says: I will not leave you orphans.
I will come back to you, and your hearts will rejoice.**

℟. Alleluia, alleluia.

GOSPEL

Then they will be one.

✢ A reading from the holy gospel according to John 17:11

Jesus prayed to God:
"Holy Father, I am no longer in the world.
I am coming to you,
> but my followers are still in the world.
So keep them safe by the power of the name that you have given me.
Then they will be one with each other,
> just as you and I are one."

The gospel of the Lord.

[57] **SEVENTH SUNDAY OF EASTER** C

FIRST READING

I can see the heavens thrown open
and the Son of Man standing at the right hand of God.

A reading from the Acts of the Apostles 7:55-60

Stephen was filled with the Holy Spirit.
He looked toward heaven,
  where he saw our glorious God and Jesus standing at his right side.
Then Stephen said, "I see heaven open
  and the Son of Man standing at the right side of God!"

The council members shouted and covered their ears.
At once they all attacked Stephen and dragged him out of the city.
Then they started throwing stones at him.
The men who had brought charges against him
  put their coats at the feet of a young man named Saul.

As Stephen was being stoned to death, he called out,
"Lord Jesus, please welcome me!"
He kneeled down and shouted,
"Lord, don't blame them for what they have done."
Then he died.

The word of the Lord.

RESPONSORIAL PSALM 97:1, 6, 9

℟. (1a and 9a) The Lord is king, the most high over all the earth.
or:
℟. Alleluia.

The LORD is King!
Tell the earth to celebrate
and all islands to shout.

℟. The Lord is king, the most high over all the earth.
or:
℟. Alleluia.

The heavens announce,
"The LORD brings justice!"
Everyone sees God's glory.

℟. The Lord is king, the most high over all the earth.
or:
℟. Alleluia.

The LORD rules the whole earth,
and he is more glorious
than all the false gods.

℟. The Lord is king, the most high over all the earth.
or:
℟. Alleluia.

ALLELUIA
See John 14:18

℟. Alleluia, alleluia.

The Lord says: I will not leave you orphans.
I will come back to you, and your hearts will rejoice.

℟. Alleluia, alleluia.

GOSPEL

May they be completely one.

✢ A reading from the holy gospel according to John   17:20-21

Jesus prayed to God:
"Father, I am not praying just for these followers.
I am also praying for everyone else who will have faith
    because of what my followers will say about me.
I want all of them to be one with each other,
    just as I am one with you
    and you are one with me.
I also want them to be one with us.
Then the people of this world will believe that you sent me."

The gospel of the Lord.

PENTECOST SUNDAY

[58]

The following readings may be used only when the celebration of the liturgy of the word for the children is held in a place apart from the main assembly.

FIRST READING

*They were all filled with the Holy Spirit,
and began to speak different languages.*

A reading from the Acts of the Apostles   2:1-11

On the day of Pentecost
    all the Lord's followers were together in one place.
Suddenly there was a noise from heaven like the sound of a mighty wind!
It filled the house where they were meeting.
Then they saw what looked like fiery tongues moving in all directions,
    and a tongue came and settled on each person there.
The Holy Spirit took control of everyone,
    and they began speaking
        whatever languages the Spirit let them speak.

Many religious Jews from every country in the world
    were living in Jerusalem.
And when they heard this noise, a crowd gathered.
But they were surprised,
    because they were hearing everything in their own languages.

They were excited and amazed, and said:
"Don't all these who are speaking come from Galilee?
Then why do we each hear them speaking our very own languages?
Some of us are from Parthia, Media, and Elam.
Others are from Mesopotamia, Judea,
    Cappadocia, Pontus, Asia,
    Phrygia, Pamphylia, Egypt,
    parts of Libya near Cyrene,
    Rome, Crete, and Arabia.
Some of us were born Jews,
    and others of us have chosen to be Jews.
Yet we all hear them using our own languages
    to tell the wonderful things God has done."

                                        The word of the Lord.

RESPONSIAL PSALM 104:1abc and 24, 30-31

℟. (see 30) Lord, send out your Spirit, and renew the face of the earth.
or:
℟. Alleluia.

**I praise you, Lord God,
with all my heart.
You are glorious and majestic.
Our Lord, by your wisdom
you made so many things;
the whole earth is covered
with your living creatures.**

℟. Lord, send out your Spirit, and renew the face of the earth.
or:
℟. Alleluia.

**You created all of them
by your Spirit,
and you give new life
to the earth.
Our Lord, we pray
that your glory will last for ever
and that you will be pleased
with what you have done.**

℟. Lord, send out your Spirit, and renew the face of the earth.
or:
℟. Alleluia.

SECOND READING

In the one Spirit we were all baptized into one body.

A reading from the first letter of Paul to the Corinthians 12:4-7, 12-13

Brothers and sisters:
There are different kinds of spiritual gifts,
  but they all come from the same Spirit.
There are different ways to serve the same Lord,
  and we can each do different things.
Yet the same God works in all of us and helps us in everything we do.

The Spirit has given each of us a special way of serving others.

The body of Christ has many different parts,
> just as any other body does.
Some of us are Jews,
> and others are Gentiles.
Some of us are slaves,
> and others are free.
But God's Spirit baptized each of us
> and made us part of the body of Christ.
Now we each drink from that same Spirit.

The word of the Lord.

ALLELUIA

℟. Alleluia, alleluia.

**Come, Holy Spirit, fill the hearts of your faithful
and kindle in them the fire of your love.**

℟. Alleluia, alleluia.

GOSPEL

As the Father sent me, so I send you. Receive the Holy Spirit.

✣ A reading from the holy gospel according to John   20:19-23

The disciples were afraid of the Jewish leaders,
> and on the evening of that same Sunday
>> they locked themselves in a room.

Suddenly, Jesus appeared in the middle of the group.
He greeted them and showed them his hands and his side.
When the disciples saw the Lord,
> they became very happy.

After Jesus had greeted them again, he said,
"I am sending you, just as the Father has sent me."
Then he breathed on them and said,
"Receive the Holy Spirit.
If you forgive anyone's sins,
> they will be forgiven.
But if you don't forgive their sins,
> they will not be forgiven."

The gospel of the Lord.

ORDINARY TIME

[59] SECOND SUNDAY IN ORDINARY TIME — A

FIRST READING

*I will make you the light of the nations,
so that my salvation may reach to the ends of the earth.*

A reading from the book of the prophet Isaiah 49:3, 5-6

The LORD said to me,
"Israel, you are my servant,
 and because of you I will be highly honored."

Even before I was born,
 the LORD chose me to serve him
  and to bring back the people of Israel.
The LORD God has honored me and made me strong.

Now the LORD says to me,
"It isn't enough for you to be merely my servant.
You must do more than lead back
  those from the tribes of Israel who have survived.
I have placed you here as a light for the Gentiles.
You are to take my saving power everywhere on earth."

The word of the Lord.

RESPONSORIAL PSALM 40:1 and 3ab, 8 and 11

℟. (8a and 9a) Here am I, Lord;
 I come to do your will.

**I patiently waited, LORD,
for you to hear my prayer.
You listened
and you gave me a new song,
a song of praise to you.**

℟. Here am I, Lord;
 I come to do your will.

**" 'I enjoy pleasing you.
Your Law is in my heart.' "
You, LORD, never fail
to have pity on me;**

your love and faithfulness
always keep me secure.

> ℟. Here am I, Lord;
> I come to do your will.

ALLELUIA
John 1:14a, 12a

> ℟. Alleluia, alleluia.

The Word of God became flesh and dwelt among us.
He enabled those who accepted him
to become the children of God.

> ℟. Alleluia, alleluia.

GOSPEL

> This is the Lamb of God who takes away the sins of the world.

✠ A reading from the holy gospel according to John 1:29-34

John saw Jesus coming toward him and said:
"Here is the Lamb of God who takes away the sin of the world!
He is the one I told you about when I said,

> 'Someone else will come.
> He is greater than I am,
> because he was alive before I was born.'

"I didn't know who he was.
But I came to baptize you with water,
> so that everyone in Israel would see him.

"I was there and saw the Spirit come down on him
> like a dove from heaven.
And the Spirit stayed on him.
Before this I didn't know who he was.
But the one who sent me to baptize with water had told me,
'You will see the Spirit come down and stay on someone.
Then you will know that he is the one
> who will baptize with the Holy Spirit.'

"I saw this happen,
> and I tell you that he is the Son of God."

The gospel of the Lord.

[60] SECOND SUNDAY IN ORDINARY TIME — B

FIRST READING

       Speak, O Lord, your servant is listening.

A reading from the first book of Samuel   3:4-10, 19

Samuel was sleeping in the temple
when the LORD called out to him.
"Here I am," Samuel answered.
He ran to Eli and said,
"Here I am, sir. What can I do for you?"

Eli replied, "I didn't call you. Go back to bed."
So Samuel went back.

Once more the LORD called Samuel's name.
Samuel got up.
He went to Eli and said,
"Here I am. What can I do for you?"

But Eli told him, "Son, I didn't call you.
Now go back to sleep."

Samuel did not realize that the LORD was speaking,
    because this was the first time the LORD had spoken to him.
When the LORD spoke a third time that night,
    Samuel again went to Eli and said,
"Here I am. What can I do for you?"

Eli now knew that it was the LORD who was speaking to Samuel.
So Eli told him, "Go back to bed.
If someone speaks to you again,
    answer, 'LORD, I am your servant.
Speak, and I will listen.' "
Once again Samuel went back and lay down.

The LORD came and stood beside Samuel.
Then he called out as he had done before, "Samuel! Samuel!"

The boy replied, "LORD, I am your servant.
Speak, and I will listen."

As Samuel grew up,
 the LORD was with him and made everything he said come true.

              The word of the Lord.

RESPONSORIAL PSALM   40:1 and 3ab, 8 and 11

  ℟. (8a and 9a) Here am I, Lord;
    I come to do your will.

**I patiently waited, LORD,
for you to hear my prayer.
You listened
and you gave me a new song,
a song of praise to you.**

  ℟. Here am I, Lord;
    I come to do your will.

**" 'I enjoy pleasing you.
Your Law is in my heart.' "
You, LORD, never fail
to have pity on me;
your love and faithfulness
always keep me secure.**

  ℟. Here am I, Lord;
    I come to do your will.

ALLELUIA   John 1:41, 17b

  ℟. Alleluia, alleluia.

**We have found the Messiah:
Jesus Christ, who brings us truth and grace.**

  ℟. Alleluia, alleluia.

GOSPEL

They saw where Jesus lived, and they stayed with him.

✢ A reading from the holy gospel according to John 1:35-42

On one occasion John was with two of his followers.
When he saw Jesus walking by,
he said, "Here is the Lamb of God!"
John's two followers heard him,
and they went with Jesus.

When Jesus turned and saw them,
he asked, "What do you want?"

They answered, "Rabbi, where do you live?"
The Hebrew word "Rabbi" means "Teacher."

Jesus replied, "Come and see!"
It was already about four o'clock in the afternoon
when they went with him and saw where he lived.
So they stayed on for the rest of the day.

One of the two men who had heard John and had gone with Jesus
was Andrew, the brother of Simon Peter.
The first thing Andrew did was to find his brother and tell him,
"We have found the Messiah!"
The Hebrew word "Messiah" means the same as the Greek word "Christ."

Andrew brought his brother to Jesus.
And when Jesus saw him, he said,
"Simon son of John, you will be called Cephas."
This name can be translated as "Peter."

The gospel of the Lord.

[61] **SECOND SUNDAY IN ORDINARY TIME** C

FIRST READING

You will be a glorious crown in the hands of your God.

A reading from the book of the prophet Isaiah   62:1-3

Jerusalem, I will speak up for your good.
I will never be silent till you are safe and secure,
   sparkling like a flame.
Your great victory will be seen by every nation and king,
   and the LORD will give you a new name.
You will be a glorious crown and a royal headband
   in the hands of the LORD your God.

                                        The word of the Lord.

RESPONSORIAL PSALM   96:1-2a, 2b-3, 7-8a

℟. (3) Proclaim God's marvelous deeds to all the nations.

Sing a new song to the LORD!
Everyone on this earth,
sing praises to the LORD,
sing and praise his name.

℟. Proclaim God's marvelous deeds to all the nations.

Day after day announce,
"The LORD has saved us!"
Tell every nation on earth,
"The LORD is wonderful
and does marvelous things!"

℟. Proclaim God's marvelous deeds to all the nations.

Tell everyone of every nation,
"Praise the glorious power
of the LORD."
He is wonderful! Praise him!

℟. Proclaim God's marvelous deeds to all the nations.

SECOND READING

There is one and the same Spirit giving to each as the Spirit wills.

A reading from the first letter of Paul to the Corinthians   12:4-11

Brothers and sisters:
There are different kinds of spiritual gifts,
   but they all come from the same Spirit.
There are different ways to serve the same Lord,
   and we can each do different things.
Yet the same God works in all of us and helps us in everything we do.

The Spirit has given each of us a special way of serving others.
Some of us can speak with wisdom,
   while others can speak with knowledge,
   but these gifts come from the same Spirit.

To others the Spirit has given great faith
   or the power to heal the sick
   or the power to work mighty miracles.

Some of us are prophets,
   and some of us recognize when God's Spirit is present.
Others can speak different kinds of languages,
   and still others can tell what these languages mean.

But it is the Spirit who does all this
   and decides which gifts to give to each of us.

The word of the Lord.

ALLELUIA   See 2 Thessalonians 2:14

℟. Alleluia, alleluia.

**God has called us with the gospel,
to share in the glory of our Lord Jesus Christ.**

℟. Alleluia, alleluia.

GOSPEL

The first of the signs given by Jesus was at Cana in Galilee.

✤ A reading from the holy gospel according to John   2:1-12

Mary, the mother of Jesus,
    was at a wedding feast in the village of Cana in Galilee.
Jesus and his disciples had also been invited and were there.

When the wine was all gone, Mary said to Jesus,
"They don't have any more wine."

Jesus replied, "Mother, my time has not yet come!
You must not tell me what to do."

Mary then said to the servants,
"Do whatever Jesus tells you to do."

At the feast there were six stone water jars
    that were used by the people for washing themselves
    in the way that their religion said they must.
Each jar held about twenty or thirty gallons.
Jesus told the servants to fill them to the top with water.
Then after the jars had been filled, he said,
"Now take some water
    and give it to the man in charge of the feast."

The servants did as Jesus told them,
    and the man in charge drank some of the water
    that had now turned into wine.
He did not know where the wine had come from,
    but the servants did.
He called the bridegroom over and said,
"The best wine is always served first.
Then after the guests have had plenty,
    the other wine is served.
But you have kept the best until last!"

This was Jesus' first miracle,
    and he did it in the village of Cana in Galilee.
There Jesus showed his glory,
    and his disciples put their faith in him.
After this, he went with his mother, his brothers,
    and his disciples to the town of Capernaum,
    where they stayed for a few days.

                                The gospel of the Lord.

THIRD SUNDAY IN ORDINARY TIME

FIRST READING

The people have seen a great light.

A reading from the book of the prophet Isaiah 9:2-4

Those who walked in the dark have seen a bright light.
And it shines upon everyone who lives in the land of darkest shadows.

Our Lord, you have made your nation stronger.
Because of you, its people are glad and celebrate
    like workers at harvest time
    or soldiers dividing what they have taken.

You have broken the power
    of those who oppressed and enslaved your people.
You have rescued them as you did from Midian.

The word of the Lord.

RESPONSORIAL PSALM 27:1, 4abc

℟. (1a) The Lord is my light and my salvation.

**You, Lord, are the light
that keeps me safe.
I am not afraid of anyone.
You protect me,
and I have no fears.**

℟. The Lord is my light and my salvation.

**I ask only one thing, Lord:
Let me live in your house
every day of my life.**

℟. The Lord is my light and my salvation.

SECOND READING

> I appeal to you, my brothers and sisters,
> there should not be serious differences between you.

A reading from the first letter of Paul to the Corinthians 1:10-13, 17

My dear friends,
as a follower of our Lord Jesus Christ,
I beg you to get along with each other.
Don't take sides.
Always try to agree in what you think.

Several people from Chloe's family have already reported to me
that you keep arguing with each other.

They have said that some of you claim to follow me,
while others claim to follow Apollos or Peter or Christ.

Has Christ been divided up?
Was I nailed to a cross for you?
Were you baptized in my name?

Christ did not send me to baptize.
He sent me to tell the good news without using big words
that would make the cross of Christ lose its power.

The word of the Lord.

ALLELUIA   See Matthew 4:23

℟. Alleluia, alleluia.

**Jesus preached the good news of the kingdom
and healed all who were sick.**

℟. Alleluia, alleluia.

GOSPEL

Come with me.

✢ A reading from the holy gospel according to Matthew 4:17-23

Jesus started preaching, "Turn back to God!
The kingdom of heaven will soon be here."

While Jesus was walking along the shore of Lake Galilee,
>   he saw two brothers.
One was Simon, also known as Peter,
>   and the other was Andrew.
They were fishermen, and they were casting their net into the lake.

Jesus said to them, "Come with me!
I will teach you how to bring in people instead of fish."
Right then the two brothers dropped their nets and went with him.

Jesus walked on until he saw James and John, the sons of Zebedee.
They were in a boat with their father, mending their nets.
Jesus asked them to come with him too.
Right away they left the boat and their father and went with Jesus.

Jesus went all over Galilee,
>   teaching in the Jewish meeting places
>   and preaching the good news about God's kingdom.

He also healed every kind of disease and sickness.

>   The gospel of the Lord.

[63] THIRD SUNDAY IN ORDINARY TIME B

FIRST READING

The Ninevites renounced their evil ways.

A reading from the book of the prophet Jonah 3:1-5, 10

The Lord spoke to Jonah and said,
"Jonah, go to that great city of Nineveh and speak to them for me."

Jonah obeyed the Lord and went to Nineveh.
The city was so large that it took three days just to walk through it.
After walking for a day, Jonah told the people,
"Forty days from now Nineveh will be destroyed."

They believed God's message
    and they set a time when they would all go without eating.
Then everyone in the city, no matter who they were,
    also dressed in sackcloth.

When God saw that the people had stopped doing evil things,
    he had pity on them and did not destroy them, as he had said.

The word of the Lord.

RESPONSORIAL PSALM 25:4-5abc, 6 and 7cd, 8-9

℟. (4a) Teach me your ways, O Lord.

**Show me your paths
and teach me to follow;
guide me by your truth
and instruct me.
You keep me safe.**

℟. Teach me your ways, O Lord.

**Please, Lord, remember,
you have always
been patient and kind.
Show how truly kind you are
and remember me.**

℟. Teach me your ways, O Lord.

You are honest and merciful,
and you teach sinners
how to follow your path.
You lead humble people
to do what is right
and to stay on your path.

℞. Teach me your ways, O Lord.

ALLELUIA
Mark 1:15

℞. Alleluia, alleluia.

**The kingdom of God is near:
repent and believe the good news!**

℞. Alleluia, alleluia.

GOSPEL

Repent and believe the good news.

✝ **A reading from the holy gospel according to Mark** 1:14-20

After John was arrested,
Jesus went to Galilee and told the good news that comes from God.
He said, "The time has come!
God's kingdom will soon be here.
Turn back to God and believe the good news!"

As Jesus was walking along the shore of Lake Galilee,
he saw Simon and his brother Andrew.
They were fishermen and were casting their nets into the lake.
Jesus said to them, "Come with me!
I will teach you how to bring in people instead of fish."
Right then the two brothers dropped their nets and went with him.

Jesus walked on and soon saw James and John, the sons of Zebedee.
They were in a boat, mending their nets.
At once Jesus asked them to come with him.
They left their father in the boat with the hired workers
and went with him.

The gospel of the Lord.

THIRD SUNDAY IN ORDINARY TIME   C

FIRST READING

They read from the book of the law and they understood what was read.

A reading from the book of Nehemiah   8:1-4a, 5-6, 8-10

All the people came together
    and stood in the open area in front of the Water Gate.
They asked Ezra the teacher to read to them from the Law of Moses
    that the Lord had given for his people.

So on the first day of the seventh month
    Ezra the priest came with the Law
    and stood before the crowd of men and women.
Everyone who was able to understand was there.
From early morning till noon
    Ezra read the Law of Moses aloud in front of the Water Gate.
They all listened carefully,
    as Ezra stood and read from the wooden platform
    that had been built for him.

The platform was very high,
    and everyone could see Ezra as he opened the Book of the Law.
And when he opened it, they all stood up.
Ezra praised the wonderful Lord God,
    and the people shouted, "Amen! Amen!"
They bowed low to the ground and worshiped the Lord.

The men who were on the platform with him translated what he read
    and explained to the people what it meant.

Then Nehemiah the governor, Ezra the priest and teacher,
    and the Levites who had been teaching the people
    all said, "Don't be sad or cry!
This is a special day for the Lord your God."
They said this because the people cried when God's Law was read to them.

Nehemiah told the people,
"Enjoy your good food and wine
    and share what you have
        with everyone who didn't have any to bring.

Don't be sad!
This is a special day for the LORD,
   and he will make you happy and strong."

The word of the Lord.

RESPONSIBLE PSALM 19:7, 8, 14

℟. (see John 6:63c) Your words, Lord, are spirit and life.

The Law of the LORD is perfect;
it gives us new life.
His teachings last forever,
and they give wisdom
to ordinary people.

℟. Your words, Lord, are spirit and life.

The LORD's instruction is right;
it makes our hearts glad.
His commands shine brightly,
and they give us light.

℟. Your words, Lord, are spirit and life.

Let my words and my thoughts
be pleasing to you, LORD,
because you are my mighty rock
and my protector.

℟. Your words, Lord, are spirit and life.

SECOND READING

Together you are Christ's body,
but each of you is a different part of it.

A reading from the first letter of Paul to the Corinthians 12:12-14, 27

Brothers and sisters:
The body of Christ has many different parts,
   just as any other body does.
Some of us are Jews, and others are Gentiles.
Some of us are slaves, and others are free.
But God's Spirit baptized each of us
      and made us part of the body of Christ.
Now we each drink from that same Spirit.

Our bodies don't have just one part.
They have many parts.

Together you are the body of Christ.
Each one of you is part of his body.

The word of the Lord.

ALLELUIA Luke 4:18

℟. Alleluia, alleluia.

The Lord sent me to bring good news to the poor
and freedom to prisoners.

℟. Alleluia, alleluia.

GOSPEL

Today this scripture is being fulfilled.

✢ A reading from the holy gospel according to Luke 4:14-21

Jesus returned to Galilee with the power of the Spirit.
News about him spread everywhere.
He taught in the Jewish meeting places,
  and everyone praised him.

Jesus went back to Nazareth, where he had been brought up,
  and as usual he went to the meeting place on the Sabbath.
When he stood up to read from the Scriptures,
  he was given the book of Isaiah the prophet.
He opened it and read,

> "The Lord's Spirit has come to me,
> because he has chosen me
> to tell the good news to the poor.
> The Lord has sent me to announce freedom for prisoners,
> to give sight to the blind,
> to free everyone who suffers,
> and to say, 'This is the year the Lord has chosen.' "

Jesus closed the book,
  then handed it back to the man in charge and sat down.

Everyone in the meeting place looked straight at Jesus.
Then Jesus said to them,
"What you have just heard me read has come true today."

The gospel of the Lord.

[65] FOURTH SUNDAY IN ORDINARY TIME   **A**

FIRST READING

In your midst I will leave a humble and a lowly people.

A reading from the book of the prophet Zephaniah   2:3; 3:12-13

If you humbly obey the Lord,
    then come and worship him.
If you do right and are humble,
    you might be safe on that day when the Lord shows his anger.
I won't destroy any of you that are truly humble
    and come to me for safety.
The people of Israel who survive will live right
    and refuse to tell lies.
They will eat in peace,
    and no one will bother them.

The word of the Lord.

RESPONSORIAL PSALM   146:6d-7ab, 7c-9a

℟. (Matthew 5:3) Blessed are the poor in spirit;
    the kingdom of heaven is theirs!

God always keeps his word.
He gives justice to the poor
and food to the hungry.

℟. Blessed are the poor in spirit;
    the kingdom of heaven is theirs!

The Lord sets prisoners free
and heals blind eyes.
He gives a helping hand
to everyone who falls.
The Lord loves good people
and looks after strangers.

℟. Blessed are the poor in spirit;
    the kingdom of heaven is theirs!

SECOND READING

God has chosen what is weak by human reckoning.

A reading from the first letter of Paul to the Corinthians 1:26-31

My dear friends,
remember what you were when God chose you.
The people of this world didn't think that many of you were wise.
Only a few of you were in places of power,
    and not many of you came from important families.

But God chose the foolish things of this world to put the wise to shame.
He chose the weak things of this world to put the powerful to shame.

What the world thinks is worthless, useless, and nothing at all
    is what God has used
        to destroy what the world considers important.
God did all this to keep anyone from bragging to him.
You are God's children.
He sent Christ Jesus to save us
    and to make us wise, acceptable, and holy.
So if you want to brag,
    do what the Scriptures say and brag about the Lord.

The word of the Lord.

ALLELUIA
Matthew 5:12a

℟. Alleluia, alleluia.

**Rejoice and be glad;
your reward will be great in heaven.**

℟. Alleluia, alleluia.

GOSPEL

Blessed are the poor in spirit.

✣ **A reading from the holy gospel according to Matthew**   5:1-12ab

When Jesus saw the crowds,
   he went up on the side of a mountain and sat down.

Jesus' disciples gathered around him, and he taught them:

"God blesses those people who depend only on him.
They belong to the kingdom of heaven!

"God blesses those people who grieve.
They will find comfort!

"God blesses those people who are humble.
The earth will belong to them!

"God blesses those people who want to obey him
     more than to eat or drink.
They will be given what they want!

"God blesses those people who are merciful.
They will be treated with mercy!

"God blesses those people whose hearts are pure.
They will see him!

"God blesses those people who make peace.
They will be called his children!

"God blesses those people who are treated badly for doing right.
They belong to the kingdom of heaven.

"God will bless you when people insult you, mistreat you,
     and tell all kinds of evil lies about you because of me.
Be happy and excited!
You will have a great reward in heaven."

                                      The gospel of the Lord.

[66] **FOURTH SUNDAY IN ORDINARY TIME** **B**

FIRST READING

*I will put my words into the prophet's mouth,
and he will tell them all I command.*

A reading from the book of Deuteronomy 18:18-19

The Lord said to Moses:
I will choose one of their own people to be a prophet like you.
I will give my message to that prophet,
 who will tell the people exactly what I have said.
That prophet will speak in my name,
 and anyone who doesn't obey the message will have to answer to me.

The word of the Lord.

RESPONSORIAL PSALM 95:1-2, 6-7abcd

℟. (8) If today you hear God's voice,
 harden not your hearts.

Sing joyful songs to the LORD!
Praise the mighty rock
where we are safe.
Come to worship him
with thankful hearts
and songs of praise.

℟. If today you hear God's voice,
 harden not your hearts.

Bow down and worship
the LORD our Creator!
The LORD is our God,
and we are his people,
the sheep he takes care of
in his own pasture.

℟. If today you hear God's voice,
 harden not your hearts.

ALLELUIA
Matthew 4:16

℟. Alleluia, alleluia.

A people in darkness have seen a great light;
a radiant dawn shines on those lost in death.

℟. Alleluia, alleluia.

GOSPEL

Here was a teaching with authority behind it.

✠ A reading from the holy gospel according to Mark 1:21-28

Jesus and his disciples went to the town of Capernaum.
Then on the next Sabbath he went into the Jewish meeting place
    and started teaching.
Everyone was amazed at his teaching.
He taught with authority,
    and not like the teachers of the Law of Moses.

Suddenly a man with an evil spirit in him
    entered the meeting place and yelled,
"Jesus from Nazareth, what do you want with us?
Have you come to destroy us?
I know who you are!
You are God's Holy One."

Jesus told the evil spirit,
"Be quiet and come out of the man!"
The spirit shook him.
Then it gave a loud shout and left.

Everyone was completely surprised and kept saying to each other,
"What is this?
It must be some new kind of powerful teaching!
Even the evil spirits obey him."
News about Jesus quickly spread all over that part of Galilee.

                                            The gospel of the Lord.

[67] FOURTH SUNDAY IN ORDINARY TIME   C

FIRST READING

I have appointed you as prophet to the nations.

A reading from the book of the prophet Jeremiah   1:4-5, 17ab, 18-19

The LORD said to Jeremiah,
"Before I gave you life,
and before you were born,
I chose you to be a prophet to the nations.

"Jeremiah, get ready!
Go and tell those people everything I command you.
Don't be afraid of them.

"Today my power will make you as strong as a fortress
    or a tall column of iron or a wall of bronze.
You will be against everyone in Judah,
    its kings, leaders, priests, and all the common people.
They will fight against you,
    but they won't win,
    because I will be with you to protect you.
I, the LORD, have spoken."

                                          The word of the Lord.

RESPONSORIAL PSALM   71:1-2, 3abcd, 3ef and 5a

    ℟. (see 15ab) I will sing of your salvation.

I run to you, LORD,
for protection.
Don't disappoint me.
You do what is right,
so come to my rescue.
Listen to my prayer
and keep me safe.

    ℟. I will sing of your salvation.

Be my mighty rock, the place
where I can always run
for protection.
Save me by your command!

℟. I will sing of your salvation.

**You are my mighty rock
and my fortress.
I depend on you.**

℟. I will sing of your salvation.

SECOND READING

*There are three things that last: faith, hope, and love;
and the greatest of these is love.*

A reading from the first letter of Paul to the Corinthians 13:4-8a, 11-13

**Brothers and sisters:
Love is kind and patient,
   never jealous, boastful, proud, or rude.
Love isn't selfish or quick tempered.
It doesn't keep a record of wrongs that others do.
Love rejoices in the truth, but not in evil.
Love is always supportive, loyal, hopeful, and trusting.
Love never fails!**

**When we were children,
   we thought and reasoned as children do.
But when we grew up,
   we quit our childish ways.**

**Now all we can see of God is like a cloudy picture in a mirror.
Later we will see him face to face.
We don't know everything,
   but then we will,
      just as God completely understands us.**

**For now there are faith, hope, and love.
But of these three, the greatest is love.**

The word of the Lord.

ALLELUIA
Luke 4:18

℟. Alleluia, alleluia.

The Lord sent me to bring good news to the poor and freedom to prisoners.

℟. Alleluia, alleluia.

GOSPEL

No prophets are liked by the people of their own town.

✣ **A reading from the holy gospel according to Luke** 4:20b-24, 28-30

Everyone in the Jewish meeting place looked straight at Jesus.
Then Jesus said to them,
"What you have just heard me read has come true today."

All the people started talking about Jesus
    and were amazed at the wonderful things he said.
They kept on asking, "Isn't he Joseph's son?"

Jesus answered:
"You will certainly want to tell me this saying,
'Doctor, first make yourself well.'
You will tell me to do the same things here in my own hometown
    that you heard I did in Capernaum.
But you can be sure that no prophets are liked by the people
    of their own hometown."

When the people in the meeting place heard Jesus say this,
    they became so angry that they got up and threw him out of town.
They dragged him to the edge of the cliff on which the town was built,
    because they wanted to throw him down from there.
But Jesus slipped through the crowd and got away.

The gospel of the Lord.

FIFTH SUNDAY IN ORDINARY TIME

A

FIRST READING

Your light will shine like the dawn.

A reading from the book of the prophet Isaiah 58:7-10

The Lord says this:
Share your food with everyone who is hungry,
   and share your home with the poor and homeless.
Give clothes to all in need
   and don't turn away your own relatives.

Then your light will shine like the dawning sun,
   and you will quickly heal.
Your honesty will protect you as you advance,
   and the glory of the Lord will defend you from behind.
Then you will call for help,
   and the Lord will answer, "Here I am!"

Don't oppress others or falsely accuse them or say cruel things.
Give your food to the hungry,
   and care for the helpless.
Then your light will shine in the darkness,
   and your darkest hour will be like the noonday sun.

The word of the Lord.

RESPONSORIAL PSALM 112:4-5, 8ab and 9

℟. (4a) A light rises in the darkness for the upright.
or:
℟. Alleluia.

Those who worship the Lord
will be so kind and merciful and good,
that they will be a light
in the dark for others
who do the right thing.
Life will go well for those
who freely lend
and are honest in business.

℟. A light rises in the darkness for the upright.
or:
℟. Alleluia.

**They are dependable
and not afraid.
They will always be remembered
and greatly praised,
because they were kind
and freely gave to the poor.**

℟. A light rises in the darkness for the upright.
or:
℟. Alleluia.

SECOND READING

I have announced to you knowledge of Christ crucified.

A reading from the first letter of Paul to the Corinthians   2:1-5

Brothers and sisters:
**When I came and told you the mystery that God had shared with us,
I didn't use big words or try to sound wise.
In fact, while I was with you,
  I made up my mind to speak only about Jesus Christ,
  who had been nailed to a cross.**

At first, I was weak and trembling with fear.
When I talked with you or preached,
  I didn't try to prove anything by sounding wise.
I simply let God's Spirit show his power.
That way you would have faith because of God's power
  and not because of human wisdom.

The word of the Lord.

ALLELUIA   John 8:12

℟. Alleluia, alleluia.

**I am the light of the world, says the Lord;
whoever follows me will have the light of life.**

℟. Alleluia, alleluia.

GOSPEL

You are the light of the world.

✢ **A reading from the holy gospel according to Matthew** 5:13-16

Jesus said to his disciples:
"You are like salt for everyone on earth.
But if salt no longer tastes like salt,
    how can it make food salty?
All it is good for is to be thrown out and walked on.

"You are like light for the whole world.
A city built on top of a hill cannot be hidden,
    and no one would light a lamp and put it under a clay pot.
A lamp is placed on a lamp stand,
    where it can give light to everyone in the house.
Make your light shine,
    so that others will see the good that you do
        and will praise your Father in heaven."

The gospel of the Lord.

[69] FIFTH SUNDAY IN ORDINARY TIME B

FIRST READING

I am filled with sorrow all day long.

A reading from the book of Job   7:1-4, 6-7

Job responded to his friend and said:
Life on earth is slavery!
We spend our days like laborers.
I am only a slave in search of shade,
    a laborer waiting for his wages.

Each month of my life is meaningless,
    and all of my nights are miserable.
While lying in bed I ask,
"How long before time to get up?"
The night drags slowly on,
    as I toss and turn until the sun rises.

My days fly by more swiftly than the needle of a weaver,
    and they end without hope.
Remember that my life is merely a breath,
    and I will never be happy again.

The word of the Lord.

RESPONSORIAL PSALM   147:1, 4, 5 and 7

℟. (see 3a) Praise the Lord, who heals the brokenhearted.

Shout praises to the Lord!
Our God is kind,
and it is right and good
to sing praises to him.

℟. Praise the Lord, who heals the brokenhearted.

He decided how many stars
there would be in the sky
and gave each one a name.

℟. Praise the Lord, who heals the brokenhearted.

**Our LORD is great and powerful!
He understands everything.
Celebrate and sing!
Play your harps
for the LORD our God.**

℟. Praise the Lord, who heals the brokenhearted.

SECOND READING

Punishment will come to me if I do not preach the gospel.

A reading from the first letter of Paul to the Corinthians   9:16-18

Brothers and sisters:
**I don't have any reason to brag about preaching the good news.
Preaching is something God told me to do,
    and if I don't do it, I am doomed.
If I preach because I want to, I will be paid.
But even if I don't want to,
    it is still something that God has sent me to do.
What pay am I given?
It is the chance to preach the good news free of charge
    and not to use the privileges that are mine
        because I am a preacher.**

The word of the Lord.

ALLELUIA   Matthew 8:17

℟. Alleluia, alleluia.

**Christ bore our sickness,
and endured our suffering.**

℟. Alleluia, alleluia.

GOSPEL

Jesus healed many who were suffering from diseases.

✚ A reading from the holy gospel according to Mark   1:29-39

As soon as Jesus left the meeting place with James and John,
they went home with Simon and Andrew.
When they got there,
    Jesus was told that Simon's mother-in-law
        was sick in bed with fever.
Jesus went to her.
He took hold of her hand and helped her up.
The fever left her, and she served them a meal.

That evening after sunset,
    all who were sick or had demons in them were brought to Jesus.
In fact, the whole town gathered around the door of the house.
Jesus healed all kinds of terrible diseases
        and forced out a lot of demons.
But the demons knew who he was,
    and he did not let them speak.

Very early the next morning Jesus got up and went to a place
        where he could be alone and pray.
Simon and the others started looking for him.

And when they found him, they said,
"Everyone is looking for you!"

Jesus replied, "We must go to the nearby towns,
    so that I can tell the good news to those people.
This is why I have come."

Then Jesus went to Jewish meeting places everywhere in Galilee,
    where he preached and forced out demons.

The gospel of the Lord.

FIFTH SUNDAY IN ORDINARY TIME   C

FIRST READING

Here am I! Send me.

A reading from the book of the prophet Isaiah   6:1-2a, 3-8

In the year that King Uzziah died,
   I had a vision of the Lord.
He was on his throne high above,
   and his robe filled the temple.
Flaming creatures with six wings each were flying over him
   and shouted to each other,

   "Holy, holy, holy, Lord All-Powerful!
   The earth is filled with your glory."

As they shouted, the door of the temple shook,
   and the temple was filled with smoke.
Then I cried out, "I'm doomed!
Everything I say is sinful,
   and everyone around me is sinful too.
Yet I have seen the King, the Lord All-Powerful."

One of the flaming creatures flew over to me
     with a burning coal that it had taken from the altar
     with a pair of metal tongs.
It touched my lips with the hot coal and said,
"This has touched your lips.
Your sins are forgiven,
   and you are no longer guilty."

After this, I heard the Lord ask,
"Is there anyone I can send?
Will someone go for us?"

I replied, "Here I am! Send me."

                             The word of the Lord.

RESPONSORIAL PSALM   138:1acd-2a, 4-5

   ℟. (1c) In the sight of the angels I will sing your praises, Lord.

With all my heart
and in the presence of angels

I sing your praises.
I worship at your holy temple.

℟. In the sight of the angels I will sing your praises, Lord.

All kings on this earth
have heard your promises, LORD,
and they will praise you.
You are so famous
that they will sing about
the things you have done.

℟. In the sight of the angels I will sing your praises, Lord.

SECOND READING

We preached and this is what you believed.

A reading from the first letter of Paul to the Corinthians 15:3-8, 11

Brothers and sisters:
I told you the most important part of the message,
and you believed it.

That part is:
Christ died for our sins, as the Scriptures say.
He was buried,
and three days later he was raised to life, as the Scriptures say.
Christ appeared to Peter, then to the twelve.
After this, he appeared to more than five hundred other followers.
Most of them are still alive,
but some have died.
He also appeared to James, and then to all of the apostles.

Finally, he appeared to me,
even though I am like someone who was born at the wrong time.

But it doesn't matter if I preached or if they preached.
All of you believed the message just the same.

The word of the Lord.

ALLELUIA Matthew 4:19

℟. Alleluia, alleluia.

Come follow me, says the Lord,
and I will make you fishers of people.

℟. Alleluia, alleluia.

GOSPEL

They left everything and followed Jesus.

✢ A reading from the holy gospel according to Luke   5:1-11

Jesus was standing on the shore of Lake Gennesaret,
    teaching the people as they crowded around him
    to hear God's message.
Near the shore he saw two boats
    left there by some fishermen who had gone to wash their nets.
Jesus got into the boat that belonged to Simon
    and asked him to row it out a little way from the shore.
Then Jesus sat down in the boat to teach the crowd.

When Jesus had finished speaking, he told Simon,
"Row the boat out into the deep water
    and let your nets down to catch some fish."

"Master," Simon answered,
    "we have worked hard all night long and have not caught a thing.
But if you tell me to, I will let the nets down."

They did it and caught so many fish that their nets began ripping apart.
Then they signaled for their partners in the other boat
    to come and help them.
The men came,
    and together they filled the two boats so full
    that they both began to sink.

When Simon Peter saw this happen,
    he kneeled down in front of Jesus and said,
"Lord, don't come near me!
I am a sinner."

Peter and everyone with him
    were completely surprised at all the fish they had caught.
His partners James and John, the sons of Zebedee, were surprised too.

Jesus told Simon, "Don't be afraid!
From now on you will bring in people instead of fish."
The men pulled their boats up on the shore.
Then they left everything and went with Jesus.

                                           The gospel of the Lord.

[71] **SIXTH SUNDAY IN ORDINARY TIME** **A**

FIRST READING

The Lord never commanded anyone to be godless.

A reading from the book of Sirach 15:15-20

If you really want to,
   you can faithfully obey the Lord's commands.
The Lord gives you the choice between fire and water.
Take the one you want.
You can also choose between life and death.
The one you want is yours.
The Lord is very wise.
He can do anything,
   and he sees everything.
The Lord watches over everyone who respects him,
   and he knows everything that anyone does.
The Lord did not command us to sin and do wrong.

The word of the Lord.

RESPONSORIAL PSALM 119:1-2, 4-5, 33-34

℟. (1b) Happy are they who follow the law of the Lord!

Our LORD, you bless everyone
who lives right and obeys your Law.
You bless all of those
who follow your commands
from deep in their hearts.

℟. Happy are they who follow the law of the Lord!

You have ordered us always
to obey your teachings;
I don't ever want to stray
from your laws.

℟. Happy are they who follow the law of the Lord!

Point out your rules to me,
and I won't disobey
even one of them.
Help me to understand your Law;
I promise to obey it
with all my heart.

℟. Happy are they who follow the law of the Lord!

SECOND READING

God's wisdom predestined our glory before the ages began.

A reading from the first letter of Paul to the Corinthians 2:6-10

Brothers and sisters:
We use wisdom when speaking to people who are mature in their faith.
But it is not the wisdom of this world or of its rulers,
    who will soon disappear.
We speak of God's hidden and mysterious wisdom
    that God decided to use for our glory
        long before the world began.

The rulers of this world didn't know anything about this wisdom.
If they had known about it,
    they would not have nailed the glorious Lord to a cross.
But it is just as the Scriptures say,
"What God has planned for people who love him
    is more than eyes have seen or ears have heard.
It has never even entered our minds!"

God's Spirit has shown you everything.
His Spirit finds out everything,
    even what is deep in the mind of God.

                        The word of the Lord.

ALLELUIA   See Matthew 11:25

℟. Alleluia, alleluia.

Blessed are you, Father, Lord of heaven and earth;
you have revealed to little ones the mysteries of the kingdom.

℟. Alleluia, alleluia.

GOSPEL

Be reconciled before you offer your gift.

✜ **A reading from the holy gospel according to Matthew**   5:23-24

Jesus said to his disciples:
  "If you are about to place your gift on the altar
      and remember that someone is angry with you,
  leave your gift there in front of the altar.
Make peace with that person,
  then come back and offer your gift to God."

The gospel of the Lord.

[72] **SIXTH SUNDAY IN ORDINARY TIME** B

FIRST READING

Be imitators of me, as I am of Christ.

A reading from the first letter of Paul to the Corinthians 10:31—11:1

Brothers and sisters:
When you eat or drink or do anything else,
   always do it to honor God.
Don't cause problems for Jews or Greeks
   or anyone else who belongs to God's church.

I always try to please others instead of myself,
   in the hope that many of them will be saved.
You must follow my example,
   as I follow the example of Christ.

The word of the Lord.

RESPONSORIAL PSALM 32:1, 5ab, 11

℟. (7a) I turn to you, Lord, in time of trouble.

Our God, you bless everyone
whose sins you forgive and wipe away.

℟. I turn to you, Lord, in time of trouble.

So I confessed my sins
and told them all to you.

℟. I turn to you, Lord, in time of trouble.

And so your good people
should celebrate and shout.

℟. I turn to you, Lord, in time of trouble.

ALLELUIA Luke 7:16

℟. Alleluia, alleluia.

A great prophet has appeared among us;
God has visited his people.

℟. Alleluia, alleluia.

GOSPEL

The leprosy left him, and he was cured.

✢ A reading from the holy gospel according to Mark   1:40-45

A man with leprosy came to Jesus and kneeled down.
He begged, "You have the power to make me well,
if only you wanted to."

Jesus felt sorry for the man.
So he put his hand on him and said, "I want to!
Now you are well."
At once the man's leprosy disappeared,
   and he was well.

After Jesus strictly warned the man,
   he sent him on his way.
He said, "Don't tell anyone about this.
Just go and show the priest that you are well.
Then take a gift to the temple as Moses commanded,
   and everyone will know that you have been healed."

The man talked about it so much and told so many people,
   that Jesus could no longer go openly into a town.
He had to stay away from the towns,
   but people still came to him from everywhere.

                                       The gospel of the Lord.

[73] **SIXTH SUNDAY IN ORDINARY TIME** C

FIRST READING

A blessing on those who trust in the Lord.

A reading from the book of the prophet Jeremiah 17:7-8

The LORD blesses everyone who honestly trusts him.
They are like trees growing beside a stream,
> trees with roots that reach down to the water
>> and have leaves that are always green.
They always bear fruit
> and they don't worry about the lack of rain
>> during the dry season.

The word of the Lord.

RESPONSORIAL PSALM 40:1 and 2de, 3, 17

℟. (5a) Happy are they who hope in the Lord.

I patiently waited, Lord,
for you to hear my prayer.
You listened,
and you let me stand on a rock
with my feet firm.

℟. Happy are they who hope in the Lord.

You gave me a new song,
a song of praise to you.
Many will see this,
and they will honor and trust
you, the LORD God.

℟. Happy are they who hope in the Lord.

I am poor and needy,
but, LORD God, you care about me,
and you come to my rescue.
Please hurry and help.

℟. Happy are they who hope in the Lord.

SECOND READING

If Christ has not risen, your faith is in vain.

A reading from the first letter of Paul to the Corinthians 15:12, 16-20

Brothers and sisters:
If we preach that Christ was raised from death,
>how can some of you say
>>that the dead will not be raised to life?

If the dead won't be raised to life,
>Christ was not raised to life.

Unless Christ was raised to life,
>your faith is useless,
>and you are still living in your sins.

And those people who died after putting their faith in him
>are completely lost.

If our hope in Christ is good only for this life,
>we are worse off than anyone else.

But Christ has been raised to life!
And he makes us certain
>that others will also be raised to life.

The word of the Lord.

ALLELUIA Luke 6:23ab

℟. Alleluia, alleluia.

**Rejoice and be glad;
your reward will be great in heaven.**

℟. Alleluia, alleluia.

GOSPEL

Happy are the poor.

✣ A reading from the holy gospel according to Luke   6:17, 20-23

Jesus and his apostles went down from the mountain
    and came to some flat, level ground.
Many other disciples were there to meet him.
Large crowds of people from all over Judea, Jerusalem,
    and the coastal cities of Tyre and Sidon were there too.

Jesus looked at his disciples and said:
"God will bless you people who are poor.
His kingdom belongs to you!
God will bless you hungry people.
You will have plenty to eat!
God will bless you people who are crying.
You will laugh!

"God will bless you when others hate you
    and won't have anything to do with you.
God will bless you when people insult you
    and say cruel things about you,
        all because you are a follower of the Son of Man!
Long ago your own people did these same things to the prophets.

"So when this happens to you,
    be happy and jump for joy!
You will have a great reward in heaven."

            The gospel of the Lord.

SEVENTH SUNDAY IN ORDINARY TIME

FIRST READING

You must love your neighbor as yourself.

A reading from the book of Leviticus 19:1-2, 17-18

The LORD told Moses to say to all of the people of Israel:
Keep yourselves holy.
I am the LORD your God, and I am holy.

Don't secretly hate someone.

Correct anyone who does wrong,
    and you won't be guilty of that person's sin.

Don't try to get even.
And don't hold grudges.
You must love others as much as you love yourself.
I am the LORD your God.

                              The word of the Lord.

RESPONSORIAL PSALM 103:1-2, 3 and 13

    ℟. (8a) The Lord is kind and merciful.

With all my heart
I praise the LORD,
and with all that I am
I praise his holy name!
With all my heart
I praise the LORD!
I will never forget
how kind he has been.

    ℟. The Lord is kind and merciful.

The LORD forgives our sins,
heals us when we are sick.
Just as parents are kind
to their children,
the LORD is kind
to all who worship him.

℟. The Lord is kind and merciful.

SECOND READING

Do not fool yourselves.

A reading from the first letter of Paul to the Corinthians   3:18-20

Brothers and sisters:
Don't fool yourselves!
If any of you think you are wise in the things of this world,
   you will have to become foolish before you can be truly wise.
This is because God considers the wisdom of this world to be foolish.

It is just as the Scriptures say,
"God catches the wise when they try to outsmart him."
The Scriptures also say,
"The Lord knows that the plans made by wise people are useless."

The word of the Lord.

ALLELUIA   1 John 2:5

℟. Alleluia, alleluia.

**Whoever keeps the word of Christ,
grows perfect in the love of God.**

℟. Alleluia, alleluia.

GOSPEL

Love your enemies.

✣ A reading from the holy gospel according to Matthew   5:38-48

Jesus said to his disciples:
"You know that you have been taught,
'An eye for an eye and a tooth for a tooth.'
But I tell you not to try to get even
    with a person who has done something to you.

"When someone slaps your right cheek,
    turn and let that person slap your other cheek.
If someone sues you for your shirt,
    give up your coat as well.
If a soldier forces you to carry his pack one mile,
    carry it two miles.
When people ask you for something,
    give it to them.
When they want to borrow money,
    loan it to them.

"You have heard people say,
'Love your neighbors and hate your enemies.'
But I tell you to love your enemies
    and pray for anyone who mistreats you.
Then you will be acting like your Father in heaven.

"He makes the sun rise on both good and bad people.
And he sends rain for the ones who do right
    and for the ones who do wrong.

"If you love only those people who love you,
    will God reward you for that?
Even tax collectors love their friends.
If you greet only your friends,
    what's so great about that?
Don't even unbelievers do that?
But you must always act like your Father in heaven."

                                          The gospel of the Lord.

[75] **SEVENTH SUNDAY IN ORDINARY TIME** B

FIRST READING

On account of me your iniquities are blotted out.

A reading from the book of the prophet Isaiah 43:22-25

I, the Lord, said to Israel:
"You have not become tired from worshiping me.
You have not honored me by sacrificing sheep or other animals.
And I have not burdened you
　　with demands for sacrifices and sweet-smelling incense.
You have not bought delicious spices for me
　　or given me the best part of your sacrificed animals.
But you have burdened me down with your terrible sins.
Yet I wipe away your sins because of who I am.
And so, I will forget about your sins."

　　　　　　　　　　　　　　　　The word of the Lord.

RESPONSORIAL PSALM 41:1-2abcd, 3 and 13

℟. (5) Lord, heal my soul,
　　for I have sinned against you.

You, Lord God, bless everyone
who cares for the poor,
and you rescue those people
in times of trouble.
You protect them
and keep them alive.
You make them happy here
in this land.

℟. Lord, heal my soul,
　　for I have sinned against you.

You always heal them
and restore their strength
when they are sick.
You, the LORD God of Israel,
will be praised forever!
Amen and amen.

℟. Lord, heal my soul,
for I have sinned against you.

ALLELUIA
Luke 4:18

℟. Alleluia, alleluia.

**The Lord sent me to bring good news to the poor
and freedom to prisoners.**

℟. Alleluia, alleluia.

GOSPEL

The Son of Man has authority on earth to forgive sins.

✠ A reading from the holy gospel according to Mark 2:1-12

Jesus went to Capernaum,
and a few days later people heard that he was at home.
Then so many of them came to the house
that there was not even standing room
left in front of the door.

Jesus was still teaching when four people came up,
carrying a crippled man on a mat.
But because of the crowd,
they could not get him to Jesus.
So they made a hole in the roof above him
and let the man down in front of everyone.

When Jesus saw how much faith they had,
    he said to the crippled man,
"My friend, your sins are forgiven."

Some of the teachers of the Law of Moses were sitting there.
They started wondering, "Why would he say such a thing?
He must think he is God!
Only God can forgive sins."

Right away Jesus knew what they were thinking,
    and he said to them, "Why are you thinking such things?
Is it easier for me to tell this crippled man that his sins are forgiven
    or to tell him to get up and pick up his mat and go on home?
I will show you that the Son of Man
        has the right to forgive sins here on earth."
So Jesus said to the man, "Get up!
Pick up your mat and go on home."

The man got right up.
He picked up his mat and went out while everyone watched in amazement.
They praised God and said,
"We have never seen anything like this!"

                                          The gospel of the Lord.

[76] **SEVENTH SUNDAY IN ORDINARY TIME** **C**

FIRST READING

The Lord has put you in my power,
but I will not raise my hand against you.

A reading from the first book of Samuel   26:2, 7-9, 12-13, 22-23

One day Saul took three thousand of his best soldiers
    and went to look for David in the desert near Ziph.

That night David and Abishai went into the camp.
Saul was sleeping with his spear stuck in the ground near his head,
    while Abner and the soldiers were sleeping all around him.

Abishai whispered to David,
"This time God has given you the chance to kill your enemy.
I'll pin him to the ground with his own sword,
    and I won't have to try but once."

David whispered back, "Don't kill him!
The LORD will punish anyone who kills his chosen king."

David took the spear and the water jar,
    and then the two men left.
None of Saul's soldiers knew what had happened or even woke up,
    because the LORD had made them all fall sound asleep.

David and Abishai crossed the valley and went to the top of the hill,
    where they were at a safe distance.

David said, "Your Majesty, here is your spear.
Have one of your young men come and get it.
The LORD put you in my power today.
But you are his chosen king,
    and I refused to harm you,
        because the LORD rewards people who are honest and faithful."

                                      The word of the Lord.

RESPONSORIAL PSALM

103:1-2, 3 and 13

℟. (8a) The Lord is kind and merciful.

With all my heart
I praise the LORD,
and with all that I am
I praise his holy name!
With all my heart
I praise the LORD!
I will never forget
how kind he has been.

℟. The Lord is kind and merciful.

The LORD forgives our sins,
heals us when we are sick.
Just as parents are kind
to their children,
the LORD is kind
to all who worship him.

℟. The Lord is kind and merciful.

ALLELUIA

John 13:34

℟. Alleluia, alleluia.

I give you a new commandment:
love one another as I have loved you.

℟. Alleluia, alleluia.

GOSPEL

Be merciful as your Father is merciful.

✢ A reading from the holy gospel according to Luke

6:27-37

Jesus said to his disciples:
"This is what I say to all who will listen to me:
Love your enemies,
    and be good to everyone who hates you.
Ask God to bless anyone who curses you,
    and pray for everyone who is cruel to you.

If someone slaps you on one cheek,
>   don't stop that person from slapping you on the other cheek.
If someone wants to take your coat,
>   don't try to keep back your shirt.
Give to everyone who asks
>   and don't ask people to return what they have taken from you.
Treat others just as you want to be treated.

"If you love only someone who loves you,
>   will God praise you for that?
Even sinners love people who love them.
If you are kind only to someone who is kind to you,
>   will God be pleased with you for that?
Even sinners are kind to people who are kind to them.
If you lend money only to someone you think will pay you back,
>   will God be pleased with you for that?
Even sinners lend to sinners
>   because they think they will get it all back.

"But love your enemies and be good to them.

"Lend without expecting to be paid back.
Then you will get a great reward,
>   and you will be the true children of God in heaven.
He is good even to people who are unthankful and cruel.
Have pity on others,
>   just as your Father has pity on you.

"Don't judge others,
>   and God will not judge you.
Don't be hard on others,
>   and God will not be hard on you.
Forgive others,
>   and God will forgive you."

The gospel of the Lord.

EIGHTH SUNDAY IN ORDINARY TIME — A

FIRST READING

Even these may forget, says the Lord God; yet I will never forget you.

A reading from the book of the prophet Isaiah   49:14-15

The people of Jerusalem said,
"The L ORD has deserted us and forgotten all about us."

The L ORD replied:
"Could a mother forget a child that nurses at her breast
    or fail to love the one who came from her own body?
Even if a mother could forget,
    I will never forget you."

The word of the Lord.

RESPONSORIAL PSALM   62:1-2, 7-8abc

℟. (6a) Rest in God alone, my soul.

Only God can save me,
and I calmly wait for him.
God alone is the mighty rock
that keeps me safe
and the fortress
where I feel secure.

℟. Rest in God alone, my soul.

God saves me and honors me.
He is that mighty rock
where I find safety.
Trust God, my friends,
and always tell him
each one of your concerns.

℟. Rest in God alone, my soul.

ALLELUIA
Hebrews 4:12

℟. Alleluia, alleluia.

**The word of God is living and active;
it probes the thoughts and motives of our heart.**

℟. Alleluia, alleluia.

GOSPEL

Do not worry about tomorrow.

✣ **A reading from the holy gospel according to Matthew** 6:24-34

Jesus said to his disciples:
"You cannot be the slave of two masters!
You will like one more than the other
    or be more loyal to one than the other.
You cannot serve both God and money.

"I tell you not to worry about your life.
Don't worry about having something to eat, drink, or wear.
Isn't life more than food or clothing?
Look at the birds in the sky!
They don't plant or harvest.
They don't even store grain in barns.
Yet your Father in heaven takes care of them.
Aren't you worth more than birds?

"Can worry make you live longer?
Why worry about clothes?
Look how the wild flowers grow.
They don't work hard to make their clothes.
But I tell you that Solomon with all his wealth
    was not as well clothed as one of them.
God gives such beauty to everything that grows in the fields,
   even though it is here today and thrown into a fire tomorrow.
He will surely do even more for you!
Why do you have such little faith?

"Don't worry and ask yourselves,
'Will we have anything to eat?
Will we have anything to drink?
Will we have clothes to wear?'
Only people who don't know God are always worrying about such things.
Your Father in heaven knows that you need all of these.
But more than anything else,
    put God's work first and do what he wants.
Then all the other things will be yours as well.

"Don't worry about tomorrow.
It will take care of itself.
You have enough to worry about today."

The gospel of the Lord.

EIGHTH SUNDAY IN ORDINARY TIME **B**

FIRST READING

I will betroth you to myself for ever.

A reading from the book of the prophet Hosea   2:16b, 17b, 21-22

The LORD says this:
I will lead my people into the desert and speak gently to them.
They will turn back to me,
    as they did when they came out of Egypt.

I make you my people forever,
    and we will be joined together by fairness and justice,
       and by love and mercy.
I will make you faithful,
    and you will accept me as your LORD.

The word of the Lord.

RESPONSORIAL PSALM   103:1-2, 3 and 13

℟. (8a) The Lord is kind and merciful.

With all my heart
I praise the LORD,
and with all that I am
I praise his holy name!
With all my heart
I praise the LORD!
I will never forget
how kind he has been.

℟. The Lord is kind and merciful.

The LORD forgives our sins,
heals us when we are sick.
Just as parents are kind
to their children,
the LORD is kind
to all who worship him.

℟. The Lord is kind and merciful.

ALLELUIA
James 1:18

℟. Alleluia, alleluia.

**The Father gave us birth by his message of truth,
that we might be as the first fruits of his creation.**

℟. Alleluia, alleluia.

GOSPEL

The bridegroom is still with them.

✙ A reading from the holy gospel according to Mark   2:18-22

**The followers of John the Baptist and the Pharisees
    often went without eating.
Some people came and asked Jesus,
"Why do the followers of John and those of the Pharisees
    often go without eating,
  while your disciples never do?"**

**Jesus answered:
"The friends of a bridegroom don't go without eating
  while he is still with them.
But the time will come when he will be taken from them.
Then they will go without eating.**

**"No one patches old clothes by sewing on a piece of new cloth.
The new piece would shrink and tear a bigger hole.**

**"No one pours new wine into old wineskins.
The wine would swell and burst the old skins.
Then the wine would be lost,
  and the skins would be ruined.
New wine must be put into new wineskins."**

The gospel of the Lord.

[79] **EIGHTH SUNDAY IN ORDINARY TIME** C

FIRST READING

Do not praise people before they have spoken.

A reading from the book of Sirach 27:6-7

You know what a tree is like by its fruit.
You know what people are like by their words.
Words are a true test of character.
So never praise anyone before they speak.

The word of the Lord.

RESPONSORIAL PSALM 92:1-2, 12-13

℟. (see 2a) Lord, it is good to give thanks to you.

It is wonderful to be grateful
and to sing your praises,
LORD Most High!
It is wonderful each morning
to tell about your love
and at night to announce
how faithful you are.

℟. Lord, it is good to give thanks to you.

Good people will prosper
like palm trees,
and they will grow strong
like the cedars of Lebanon.
They will take root
in your house, LORD God,
and they will do well.

℟. Lord, it is good to give thanks to you.

ALLELUIA Philippians 2:15d,16a

℟. Alleluia, alleluia.

Shine on the world like bright stars;
you are offering it the word of life.

℟. Alleluia, alleluia.

GOSPEL

What a person says comes from what is in the heart.

✣ A reading from the holy gospel according to Luke 6:39-45

Jesus used some sayings as he spoke to the people.
He said: "Can one blind person lead another blind person?
Won't they both fall into a ditch?

"Are students better than their teacher?
But when they are fully trained,
    they will be like their teacher.

"You can see the speck in your friend's eye.
But you don't notice the log in your own eye.
How can you say,
'My friend, let me take the speck out of your eye,'
    when you don't see the log in your own eye?
You showoffs!
First, get the log out of your own eye.
Then you can see how to take the speck out of your friend's eye.

"A good tree cannot produce bad fruit,
    and a bad tree cannot produce good fruit.
You can tell what a tree is like by the fruit it produces.
You cannot pick figs or grapes from thorn bushes.
Good people do good things because of the good in their hearts.
Bad people do bad things because of the evil in their hearts.
Your words show what is in your hearts."

                                      The gospel of the Lord.

NINTH SUNDAY IN ORDINARY TIME   **A**

FIRST READING

I set before you today a blessing and a curse.

A reading from the book of Deuteronomy   11:18, 26-28

Moses said to the people:
"Remember these laws and think about them.
Wear them like a sign around your arm and on your forehead.

"Today I am giving you the choice of a blessing or a curse.
The Lord your God will bless you,
> if you obey the commands that I am giving you today.
But you will be under the Lord's curse,
> if you disobey these commands
>> and worship gods that are strange to you."

The word of the Lord.

RESPONSORIAL PSALM   31:1 and 2b, 3 and 16

℟. (3b) Lord, be my rock of safety.

I come to you, Lord,
for protection.
Don't let me be ashamed.
Do as you have promised
and rescue me,
and hurry to save me.

℟. Lord, be my rock of safety.

You, Lord God,
are my mighty rock
and my fortress.
Lead me and guide me,
so that your name
will be honored.
Smile on me, your servant.
Have pity and rescue me.

℟. Lord, be my rock of safety.

ALLELUIA John 15:5

℟. Alleluia, alleluia.

I am the vine and you are the branches, says the Lord;
those who live in me, and I in them, will bear much fruit.

℟. Alleluia, alleluia.

GOSPEL

The house built on rock is compared to the house built on sand.

✠ A reading from the holy gospel according to Matthew 7:21-27

Jesus said to his disciples:
"Not everyone who calls me their Lord
    will get into the kingdom of heaven.
Only the ones who obey my Father in heaven will get in.
On the day of judgment many will call me their Lord.
They will say, 'We preached in your name,
    and in your name we forced out demons and worked many miracles.'
But I will tell them,
'I will have nothing to do with you!
Get out of my sight, you evil people!'

"Anyone who hears and obeys these teachings of mine
    is like a wise person who built a house on solid rock.
Rain poured down, rivers flooded,
    and winds beat against that house.
But it did not fall,
    because it was built on solid rock.

"Anyone who hears my teachings and does not obey them
    is like a foolish person who built a house on sand.
The rain poured down, the rivers flooded,
    and the winds blew and beat against that house.
Finally, it fell with a crash."

                                      The gospel of the Lord.

[81] **NINTH SUNDAY IN ORDINARY TIME** B

FIRST READING

> Remember that you were a servant in the land of Egypt
> and that the Lord God brought you out.

A reading from the book of Deuteronomy   5:12-15

Moses said to the people:
"Keep the Sabbath Day holy,
  as the LORD your God commanded.
You have six days in which to do all your work.
But the seventh day of the week belongs to the LORD your God.
It is the Sabbath,
  and no one may work on that day.

"This includes you, your children,
    your servants, and your oxen and donkeys,
      as well as any other animals of yours.
Not even the foreigners who live in your cities are allowed to work
    on that day.
This will let your servants rest when you do.

"Don't forget that you were once slaves in Egypt.
But the LORD your God reached out his mighty arm
    and rescued you from there.
That's why he commands you to make the Sabbath a special day."

The word of the Lord.

RESPONSORIAL PSALM   81:2-3, 4-5abcd

℟. (2a) Sing with joy to God our help.

Sing as you play tambourines
and the lovely sounding
stringed instruments.
Sound the trumpets and start
the New Moon Festival.
We must celebrate
when the moon is full.

℟. Sing with joy to God our help.

This is the law in Israel,
and it was given to us
by the God of Jacob.
The descendants of Joseph
were told to obey it,
when God led them out
from the land of Egypt.

℟. Sing with joy to God our help.

SECOND READING

The life of Jesus is revealed in our body.

A reading from the second letter of Paul to the Corinthians   4:6-11

Brothers and sisters:
The Scriptures say, "God commanded light to shine in the dark."
Now God is shining in our hearts
  to let you know that his glory is seen in Jesus Christ.

We are like clay jars in which this treasure is stored.
The real power comes from God and not from us.

We often suffer,
  but we are never crushed.
Even when we don't know what to do,
  we never give up.
In times of trouble, God is with us,
  and when we are knocked down,
  we get up again.

We face death every day because of Jesus.
Our bodies show what his death was like,
  so that his life can also be seen in us.

The word of the Lord.

ALLELUIA
See John 17:17b, 17a

℟. Alleluia, alleluia.

**Your word, O Lord, is truth;
make us holy in the truth.**

℟. Alleluia, alleluia.

GOSPEL

The Son of Man is master even of the sabbath.

✢ **A reading from the holy gospel according to Mark** 2:23-28

One Sabbath Jesus and his disciples
were walking through some wheat fields.
His disciples were picking grains of wheat as they went along.
Some Pharisees asked Jesus,
"Why are your disciples picking grain on the Sabbath?
They are not supposed to do that!"

Jesus answered, "Haven't you read what David did
when he and his followers were hungry and in need?
It was during the time of Abiathar the high priest.
David went into the house of God and ate the sacred loaves of bread
that only priests are allowed to eat.
He also gave some to his followers."

Jesus finished by saying,
"People were not made for the good of the Sabbath.
The Sabbath was made for the good of people.
So the Son of Man is Lord over the Sabbath."

The gospel of the Lord.

NINTH SUNDAY IN ORDINARY TIME C

FIRST READING
When strangers come, hear them.

A reading from the first book of Kings 8:41-43

Solomon prayed to God and said:
"People who live in foreign lands
　　will hear about you and your mighty power,
　and they will come here to pray toward your temple.
When they do,
　　please answer their prayers from your home in heaven,
　　so that everyone on earth will know about you and worship you,
　　just as your people Israel do.
Then they will know that this temple I have built belongs to you."

　　　　　　　　　　　　　　　　　　　　　The word of the Lord.

RESPONSORIAL PSALM 117:1, 2

　℟. (Mark 16:15) Go out to all the world and tell the good news.
or:
　℟. Alleluia.

All of you nations,
come praise the LORD!
Let everyone praise him.

　℟. Go out to all the world and tell the good news.
or:
　℟. Alleluia.

His love for us is wonderful,
his faithfulness never ends.
Shout praises to the LORD!

　℟. Go out to all the world and tell the good news.
or:
　℟. Alleluia.

ALLELUIA John 3:16

　℟. Alleluia, alleluia.

God loved the world so much, he gave us his only Son,
that all who believe in him might have eternal life.

　℟. Alleluia, alleluia.

GOSPEL

Nowhere in Israel have I found as much faith.

✠ A reading from the holy gospel according to Luke 7:1-10

After Jesus had finished teaching the people,
he went to Capernaum.
In that town an army officer's servant was sick and about to die.
The officer liked this servant very much.
And when he heard about Jesus,
    he sent some Jewish leaders
        to ask him to come and heal the servant.

The leaders went to Jesus and begged him to do something.
They said, "This man deserves your help!
He loves our nation and even built us a meeting place."
So Jesus went with them.

When Jesus was not far from the house,
    the officer sent some friends to tell him,
"Lord, don't go to any trouble for me!
I am not good enough for you to come into my house.
And I am certainly not worthy to come to you.
Just say the word, and my servant will get well.
I have officers who give orders to me,
    and I have soldiers who take orders from me.
I can say to one of them, 'Go!' and he goes.
I can say to another, 'Come!' and he comes.
I can say to my servant, 'Do this!'
    and he will do it."

When Jesus heard this,
    he was so surprised
        that he turned and said to the crowd following him,
"In all of Israel I've never found anyone with this much faith!"

The officer's friends returned and found the servant well.

                              The gospel of the Lord.

[83] **TENTH SUNDAY IN ORDINARY TIME** A

FIRST READING

What I want is love, not sacrifice, says the Lord.

A reading from the book of the prophet Hosea   6:3-6

Let's try our best to know the LORD.
The coming of the LORD is as certain as the dawn.
He will bless us like showers in winter and spring.

People of Judah and Israel,
    what must I do with you?
Your love for me is merely a morning cloud or dew
    that quickly disappears.
I sent prophets to you with my message of doom,
    and my judgment against you struck like lightning.

When you show mercy and obey me,
    it pleases me more than sacrifices and gifts.

The word of the Lord.

RESPONSORIAL PSALM   50:8-9, 14-15

℟. (23b) To the upright I will show the saving power of God.

Although you offer sacrifices
and always bring gifts,
I won't accept your offerings
of bulls and goats.

℟. To the upright I will show the saving power of God.

I am God Most High!
The only sacrifice I want
is for you to be thankful
and to keep your word.
Pray to me in time of trouble.
I will rescue you,
and you will honor me.

℟. To the upright I will show the saving power of God.

SECOND READING

Abraham drew strength from his faith while giving glory to God.

A reading from the letter of Paul to the Romans 4:18-21

Brothers and sisters:
**God promised Abraham a lot of descendants.
And when it all seemed hopeless,
    Abraham still had faith in God
        and became the ancestor of many nations.**

**Abraham's faith never became weak,
    not even when he was nearly a hundred years old.
He knew that he was almost dead
    and that his wife Sarah could not have children.
But Abraham never doubted or questioned God's promise.
His faith made him strong,
    and he gave all the credit to God.**

Abraham was certain that God could do what he had promised.

The word of the Lord.

ALLELUIA Luke 4:18

℟. Alleluia, alleluia.

**The Lord sent me to bring good news to the poor
and freedom to prisoners.**

℟. Alleluia, alleluia.

GOSPEL

<small>I did not come to call the just, but sinners.</small>

✤ A reading from the holy gospel according to Matthew   9:9-13

As Jesus was leaving Capernaum,
he saw a tax collector named Matthew
   sitting at the place for paying taxes.
Jesus said to him, "Come with me."
Matthew got up and went with him.

Later, Jesus and his disciples were having dinner at Matthew's house.
Many tax collectors and other sinners were also there.
Some Pharisees asked Jesus' disciples,
"Why does your teacher eat with tax collectors and other sinners?"

Jesus heard them and answered,
"Healthy people don't need a doctor,
   but sick people do.
Go and learn what the Scriptures mean when they say,
'Instead of offering sacrifices to me,
I want you to be merciful to others.'
I didn't come to invite good people to be my followers.
I came to invite sinners."

The gospel of the Lord.

[84] TENTH SUNDAY IN ORDINARY TIME B

FIRST READING

I will put enmity between your offspring and her offspring.

A reading from the book of Genesis 3:9-15

The Lord called out to Adam and asked, "Where are you?"

Adam answered, "I was naked,
  and when I heard you walking through the garden,
  I was afraid and hid!"

"How did you know you were naked?" God asked.
"Did you eat from the tree I told you not to?"

Adam said, "It was that woman you put here with me!
She gave me some of the fruit, and I ate it."

The Lord God then asked her, "What have you done?"

The woman answered,
"The snake tricked me into eating some of that fruit."

The Lord God said to the snake:
"Because of what you have done,
  you will suffer a greater curse than the cattle
    and the wild animals.
For as long as you live,
  you will crawl on your stomach and eat dirt from the ground.
You and this woman will hate each other.
Your descendants and hers will always be enemies.
One of them will crush your head,
  and you will bite him on the heel."

The word of the Lord.

RESPONSORIAL PSALM 130:1-2, 3-4, 5 and 6d-7a

℟. (7b) With the Lord there is mercy.

From a sea of troubles
I call out to you, Lord.
Won't you please listen
as I beg for mercy?

℟. With the Lord there is mercy.

If you kept record of our sins,
no one could last long.
But you forgive us,
and so we will worship you.

℟. With the Lord there is mercy.

With all my heart,
I am waiting, LORD, for you!
I trust your promises.
Yes, I wait more eagerly
than a soldier on guard duty
waits for the dawn.
Israel, trust the LORD!

℟. With the Lord there is mercy.

SECOND READING

Our bodies are dying but we are being made stronger.

A reading from the second letter of Paul to the Corinthians 4:16—5:1

Brothers and sisters:
We never give up.
Our bodies are gradually dying,
   but we ourselves are being made stronger every day.
These little troubles are getting us ready for an eternal glory
   that will make all our troubles seem like nothing.

Things that are seen don't last forever,
   but things that are not seen are eternal.
That's why we keep our minds on the things that cannot be seen.

Our bodies are like tents that we live in here on earth.
But when these tents are destroyed,
   we know that God will give each of us a place to live.
These homes will not be buildings that someone has made,
   but they are in heaven and will last forever.

The word of the Lord.

ALLELUIA
John 12:31b-32

℟. Alleluia, alleluia.

The prince of this world will now be cast out,
and when I am lifted up from the earth
I will draw all to myself, says the Lord.

℟. Alleluia, alleluia.

GOSPEL

A   Long Form

It is the end of Satan

✠ A reading from the holy gospel according to Mark   3:20-26, 31-35

Jesus went back home,
   and once again such a large crowd gathered
      that there was no chance even to eat.
When Jesus' family heard what he was doing,
   they thought he was crazy and went to get him under control.

Some teachers of the Law of Moses came from Jerusalem and said,
"This man is under the power of Beelzebul, the ruler of demons!
He is even forcing out demons with the help of Beelzebul."

Jesus told the people to gather around him.
Then he spoke to them in riddles and said:
"How can Satan force himself out?
A nation whose people fight each other won't last very long.
And a family that fights won't last long either.
So if Satan fights against himself,
   that will be the end of him."

Jesus' mother and brothers came and stood outside.
Then they sent someone with a message for him to come out to them.
The crowd that was sitting around Jesus told him,
"Your mother and your brothers and sisters are outside
      and want to see you."

Jesus asked, "Who is my mother and who are my brothers?"
Then he looked at the people sitting around him and said,
"Here are my mother and my brothers.
Anyone who obeys God is my brother or sister or mother."

The gospel of the Lord.

OR

B Short Form

Who are my mother and my brothers?

✣ A reading from the holy gospel according to Mark   3:20-21, 31-35

Jesus went back home,
   and once again such a large crowd gathered
      that there was no chance even to eat.
When Jesus' family heard what he was doing,
      they thought he was crazy and went to get him under control.

Jesus' mother and brothers came and stood outside.
Then they sent someone with a message for him to come out to them.
The crowd that was sitting around Jesus told him,
"Your mother and your brothers and sisters are outside
      and want to see you."

Jesus asked, "Who is my mother and who are my brothers?"
Then he looked at the people sitting around him and said,
"Here are my mother and my brothers.
Anyone who obeys God is my brother or sister or mother."

The gospel of the Lord.

[85] **TENTH SUNDAY IN ORDINARY TIME** C

FIRST READING
> Look, said Elijah, your son is living.

A reading from the first book of Kings   17:17-24

After Elijah had stayed in the woman's house for a while,
her son got sick.
The boy kept getting worse and finally died.
The woman said to Elijah,
"You prophet of God, what have I done to you?
Why did you come here to remind me of my sins
    by taking the life of my son?"

"Bring the boy to me," he replied.

Elijah took the boy from her arms.
Then he carried him upstairs to the room where he was staying
    and laid him on the bed.
Elijah prayed, "My Lord and God,
  why have you done such a terrible thing to this widow
    in whose home I am staying?
Why did you take the life of her son?"
Elijah stretched out over the little boy three times and prayed,
"My Lord and God, bring the boy back to life!"

The Lord answered Elijah's prayer,
  and the boy began breathing again.
Elijah picked him up and took him downstairs.
He gave him to his mother and said,
"Look, your son is alive!"

The woman told Elijah,
"Now I am sure that you are God's prophet
    and that you really do speak for him."

The word of the Lord.

RESPONSORIAL PSALM   30:4 and 5def, 10-11ab and 12bcd

℟. (2a) I will praise you, Lord, for you have rescued me.

Your faithful people, Lord,
will praise you with songs
and honor your holy name.

At night we may cry,
but when morning comes
we will celebrate.

℟. I will praise you, Lord, for you have rescued me.

**Have pity, LORD! Help!
You have turned my sorrow
into joyful dancing.
I will never stop
singing your praises,
my LORD and my God.**

℟. I will praise you, Lord, for you have rescued me.

SECOND READING

*God has revealed his Son in me,
that I might preach the good news about Christ to the Gentiles.*

A reading from the letter of Paul to the Galatians   1:11-12, 15-19

My friends,
I want you to know that no one made up the message I preach.
It was not given or taught to me by some mere human.
My message came directly from Jesus Christ
   when he appeared to me.

But even before I was born,
   God had chosen me.
He was kind and had decided to show me his Son,
   so that I would announce his message to the Gentiles.

I didn't talk this over with anyone.
I didn't say a word,
   not even to the men in Jerusalem who were apostles before I was.
Instead, I went at once to Arabia,
   and afterwards I returned to Damascus.

Three years later I went to visit Peter in Jerusalem
   and stayed with him for fifteen days.
The only other apostle I saw was James, the Lord's brother.

The word of the Lord.

ALLELUIA   Luke 7:16

℟. Alleluia, alleluia.

A great prophet has appeared among us;
God has visited his people.

℟. Alleluia, alleluia.

GOSPEL

Young man, I say to you, arise.

✤ A reading from the holy gospel according to Luke   7:11-17

Jesus and his disciples were on their way to the town of Nain,
   and a big crowd was going along with them.
As they came near the gate of the town,
   they saw people carrying out the body of a widow's only son.
Many people from the town were walking along with her.

When the Lord saw the woman,
   he felt sorry for her and said, "Don't cry!"

Jesus went over and touched the stretcher
     on which the people were carrying the dead boy.
They stopped, and Jesus said,
"Young man, get up!"
The man sat up and began to speak.
Jesus then gave him back to his mother.

Everyone was frightened and praised God.
They said, "A great prophet is here with us!
God has come to his people."

News about Jesus spread all over Judea
     and everywhere else in that part of the country.

                                      The gospel of the Lord.

[86] ELEVENTH SUNDAY IN ORDINARY TIME   **A**

FIRST READING

You will be a kingdom of priests, a consecrated nation.

A reading from the book of Exodus   19:1-6a

The people of Israel left Rephidim.
And two months after leaving Egypt,
>they reached the desert near Mount Sinai.
They set up camp there at the foot of the mountain.

Moses went up the mountain to meet with the LORD God,
>who told him to say to the people:

"You saw what I, the LORD, did in Egypt.
You know how like a mighty eagle
>I brought you here to me.
Now if you will obey me and are faithful to me,
>you will be my people.
The whole world is mine.
But you will be mine in a special way
>>and serve me as priests."

The word of the Lord.

RESPONSORIAL PSALM   100:1-2, 3, 5

℟. (3c) We are his people: the sheep of his flock.

Shout praises to the LORD,
everyone on this earth.
Be joyful and sing
as you come in
to worship the LORD!

℟. We are his people: the sheep of his flock.

You know the LORD is God!
He created us,
and we belong to him;
we are his people,
the sheep in his pasture.

℟. We are his people: the sheep of his flock.

The LORD is good!
His love and faithfulness
will last forever.

℟. We are his people: the sheep of his flock.

SECOND READING

*We have been reconciled to God through the death of his Son;
we are saved by his life.*

A reading from the letter of Paul to the Romans 5:6-11

Brothers and sisters:
Christ died for us at a time when we were helpless and sinful.
No one is really willing to die for an honest person,
    though someone might be willing to die for a truly good person.
But God showed how much he loved us
    by having Christ die for us,
    even though we were sinful.

But there is more!
Now that God has accepted us because Christ sacrificed his life's blood,
    we will also be kept safe from God's anger.
Even when we were still God's enemies,
    he made peace with us,
    because his Son died for us.
Yet something even greater than friendship is ours.
Now that we are at peace with God,
    we will be saved by his Son's life.

And in addition to everything else,
    we are happy because God sent our Lord Jesus Christ
        to make peace with us.

The word of the Lord.

ALLELUIA Mark 1:15

℟. Alleluia, alleluia.

**The kingdom of God is near;
repent and believe the good news!**

℟. Alleluia, alleluia.

GOSPEL

Jesus summoned his twelve disciples, and sent them out.

✢ A reading from the holy gospel according to Matthew 9:36—10:8

When Jesus saw the crowds,
   he felt sorry for them.
They were confused and helpless,
   like sheep without a shepherd.

He said to his disciples,
"A large crop is in the fields,
   but there are only a few workers.
Ask the Lord in charge of the harvest
   to send out workers to bring it in."

Jesus called together his twelve disciples.
He gave them the power to force out evil spirits
   and to heal every kind of disease and sickness.

The first of the twelve apostles was Simon,
   better known as Peter.
His brother Andrew was an apostle,
   and so were James and John, the two sons of Zebedee.
Philip, Bartholomew, Thomas,
   Matthew the tax collector, James the son of Alphaeus,
   and Thaddaeus were also apostles.
The others were Simon, known as the Eager One,
   and Judas Iscariot, who later betrayed Jesus.

Jesus sent out the twelve apostles with these instructions:
"Stay away from the Gentiles
   and don't go to any Samaritan town.
Go only to the people of Israel,
   because they are like a flock of lost sheep.

"As you go,
   announce that the kingdom of heaven will soon be here.
Heal the sick, raise the dead to life,
   heal people who have leprosy,
   and force out demons.
You received without paying,
   now give without being paid."

                                   The gospel of the Lord.

[87] ELEVENTH SUNDAY IN ORDINARY TIME   B

FIRST READING

I have made the small tree great.

A reading from the book of the prophet Ezekiel   17:22-24

The Lord God said:
I will cut a tender twig from the very top of a cedar tree
    and plant it on the peak of a tall mountain.
I will plant it on the highest mountain in Israel.
It will put out branches
    and grow into a beautiful and useful cedar tree.
All kinds of birds will find shelter under it and shade in its branches.

Every tree in the forest will then know that I, the Lord,
    bring down tall trees and make short trees grow tall.
I dry up green trees and make dried up trees turn green again.
I, the Lord, have spoken!
And I will keep my word.

                              The word of the Lord.

RESPONSORIAL PSALM   92:1-2, 12-13

℟. (see 2a) Lord, it is good to give thanks to you.

**It is wonderful to be grateful
and to sing your praises,
Lord Most High!
It is wonderful each morning
to tell about your love
and at night to announce
how faithful you are.**

℟. Lord, it is good to give thanks to you.

**Good people will prosper
like palm trees,
and they will grow strong
like the cedars of Lebanon.**

They will take root
in your house, Lord God,
and they will do well.

℟. Lord, it is good to give thanks to you.

SECOND READING

*Whether we are living in the body or exiled from it,
we are intent on pleasing the Lord.*

A reading from the second letter of Paul to the Corinthians   5:6-10

Brothers and sisters:
Always be cheerful!
As long as we are in these bodies,
   we are away from the Lord.
But we live by faith, not by what we see.

We should be cheerful,
   because we would rather leave these bodies
     and be at home with the Lord.
But whether we are at home with the Lord or away from him,
   we still try our best to please him.
After all, Christ will judge each of us
     for the good or the bad that we do
     while living in these bodies.

The word of the Lord.

ALLELUIA

℟. Alleluia, alleluia.

**The seed is the word of God, Christ is the sower;
all who come to him will live for ever.**

℟. Alleluia, alleluia.

GOSPEL

*The mustard seed, the smallest of all the seeds,
grows into the biggest shrub of all.*

✢ **A reading from the holy gospel according to Mark** 4:30-34

Jesus said: "What is God's kingdom like?
What story can I use to explain it?
It is like what happens when a mustard seed is planted in the ground.
It is the smallest seed in all the world.
But once it is planted,
   it grows larger than any garden plant.
It even puts out branches
   that are big enough for birds to rest in its shade."

Jesus used many other stories when he spoke to the people,
   and he taught them as much as they could understand.
He did not tell them anything without using stories.
But when he was alone with his disciples,
   he explained everything to them.

The gospel of the Lord.

[88] **ELEVENTH SUNDAY IN ORDINARY TIME** C

FIRST READING

The Lord God forgave your sin; you will not die.

A reading from the second book of Samuel 12:7-10, 13-14

Nathan the prophet told David:
"You are that rich man!
Now listen to what the LORD God of Israel says to you:

" 'I chose you to be the king of Israel.
I kept you safe from Saul
    and even gave you his house and his wives.
I let you rule Israel and Judah,
    and if that had not been enough,
    I would have given you much more.
Why did you disobey me and do such a horrible thing?
You murdered Uriah the Hittite
    by having the Ammonites kill him,
    so you could take his wife.

" 'Because you wouldn't obey me and took Uriah's wife for yourself,
    your family will never live in peace.' "

David said to Nathan, "I have disobeyed the LORD!"

Nathan answered, "Yes, you have!
You showed you didn't care what the LORD wanted.
He has forgiven you,
    and you won't die.
But your son will."

The word of the Lord.

RESPONSORIAL PSALM 32:1 and 5ab, 7 and 11

℟. (see 5c) Lord, forgive the wrong I have done.

Our God, you bless everyone
whose sins you forgive
and wipe away.
So I confessed my sins
and told them all to you.

ELEVENTH SUNDAY IN ORDINARY TIME — C

℟. Lord, forgive the wrong I have done.

**You are my hiding place!
You protect me from trouble,
and you put songs in my heart
because you have saved me.
And so your good people
should celebrate and shout.**

℟. Lord, forgive the wrong I have done.

ALLELUIA   1 John 4:10b

℟. Alleluia, alleluia.

**God first loved us
and sent his Son to take away our sins.**

℟. Alleluia, alleluia.

GOSPEL

*Her many sins were forgiven her,
because she has shown great love.*

✚ **A reading from the holy gospel according to Luke**   7:36-50

A Pharisee invited Jesus to have dinner with him.
So Jesus went to the Pharisee's home and got ready to eat.

When a sinful woman in that town found out that Jesus was there,
    she bought an expensive bottle of perfume.
Then she came and stood behind Jesus.
She cried and started washing his feet with her tears
    and drying them with her hair.
The woman kissed his feet and poured the perfume on them.

The Pharisee who had invited Jesus saw this and said to himself,
"If this man really were a prophet,
    he would know what kind of woman is touching him!
He would know that she is a sinner."

Jesus said to the Pharisee,
"Simon, I have something to say to you."

"Teacher, what is it?" Simon replied.

Jesus told him, "Two people were in debt to a moneylender.
One of them owed him five hundred silver coins,
    and the other owed him fifty.
Since neither of them could pay him back,
    the moneylender said that they didn't have to pay him anything.
Which one of them will like him most?"

Simon answered,
"I suppose it would be the one who had owed more
    and didn't have to pay it back."

"You are right," Jesus said.

He turned toward the woman and said to Simon,
"Have you noticed this woman?
When I came into your home,
    you didn't give me any water so I could wash my feet.
But she has washed my feet with her tears
    and dried them with her hair.

"You didn't greet me with a kiss,
    but from the time I came in,
    she has not stopped kissing my feet.

"You didn't even pour olive oil on my head,
    but she has poured expensive perfume on my feet.

"So I tell you that all her sins are forgiven,
    and that is why she has shown great love.
But anyone who has been forgiven only a little
    will show only a little love."

Then Jesus said to the woman,
"Your sins are forgiven."

Some other guests started saying to one another,
"Who is this who dares to forgive sins?"

But Jesus told the woman,
"Because of your faith, you are now saved.
May God give you peace!"

                                          The gospel of the Lord.

[89] TWELFTH SUNDAY IN ORDINARY TIME **A**

FIRST READING

*The Lord has delivered the soul of the needy
from the hands of those who are evil.*

A reading from the book of the prophet Jeremiah 20:10-12a, 13

I heard the crowds whisper, "Everyone's afraid!
Tell on him! Tell on him!"
All of my friends are waiting for me to make a mistake.
They say, "He will slip up.
Then we can trap him and get even at last."

But the LORD is with me like a mighty soldier.
And those troublemakers will stumble,
    then fall down and fail.
They will be forever disgraced and terribly ashamed.

LORD All-Powerful, you test everyone who does right,
    and you know everything anyone thinks or feels.

Sing and praise the LORD!
He rescues the helpless from cruel oppressors.

The word of the Lord.

RESPONSORIAL PSALM 69:13, 16, 29b-30a

℟. (14c) Lord, in your great love, answer me.

I pray to you, LORD.
So when the time is right,
answer me and help me
with your wonderful love.

℟. Lord, in your great love, answer me.

Answer me, LORD!
You are kind and good.
Pay attention to me!
You are truly merciful.

℟. Lord, in your great love, answer me.

Protect me, God,
and keep me safe!
I will praise the LORD God
with a song.

℟. Lord, in your great love, answer me.

ALLELUIA
John 15:26b, 27a

℟. Alleluia, alleluia.

**The Spirit of truth will bear witness to me, says the Lord,
and you also will be my witnesses.**

℟. Alleluia, alleluia.

GOSPEL

Do not fear those who can kill the body.

✠ A reading from the holy gospel according to Matthew   10:26-31

Jesus said to his disciples:
"Don't be afraid of anyone!
Everything that is hidden will be found out,
   and every secret will be known.

"Whatever I say to you in the dark,
   you must tell in the light.
And you must announce from the housetops
      whatever I have whispered to you.

"Don't be afraid of people.
They can kill you,
   but they cannot harm your soul.
Instead, you should fear God
   who can destroy both your body and your soul in hell.

"Aren't two sparrows sold for only a penny?
But your Father knows when any one of them falls to the ground.
Even the hairs on your head are counted.
So don't be afraid!
You are worth much more than many sparrows."

The gospel of the Lord.

[90] TWELFTH SUNDAY IN ORDINARY TIME B

FIRST READING

Here I have set the boundaries of the sea.

A reading from the book of Job 38:1, 8-11

From the storm the Lord said to Job:
"After the ocean was born,
 I enclosed it with a wall.
I used the mist for its baby clothes and covered it with clouds.
I marked out its boundaries and locked it behind doors."

Then I said to the ocean,
"Your raging waves stop here!
This is as far as you go!"

The word of the Lord.

RESPONSORIAL PSALM 107:23-24, 25 and 28, 29-30

℟. (1b) Give thanks to the Lord, God's love is everlasting.
or:
℟. Alleluia.

Some of you made a living
by sailing the mighty sea,
and you saw the miracles
the Lord performed there.

℟. Give thanks to the Lord, God's love is everlasting.
or:
℟. Alleluia.

At his command a storm arose,
and waves covered the sea.
You were in serious trouble,
but you prayed to the Lord,
and he rescued you.

℟. Give thanks to the Lord, God's love is everlasting.
or:
℟. Alleluia.

He made the storm stop
and the sea be quiet.
You were happy because of this,
and he brought you to the port
where you wanted to go.

> ℟. Give thanks to the Lord, God's love is everlasting.

or:

> ℟. Alleluia.

SECOND READING

All things are made new.

A reading from the second letter of Paul to the Corinthians   5:14-17

Brothers and sisters:
We are ruled by Christ's love for us.
We are certain that if one person died for everyone else,
> then all of us have died.

And Christ did die for all of us.
He died so we would no longer live for ourselves,
> but for the one who died and was raised to life for us.

We are careful not to judge people by what they seem to be,
> though we once judged Christ in that way.

Anyone who belongs to Christ is a new person.
The past is forgotten,
> and everything is new.

The word of the Lord.

ALLELUIA   Luke 7:16

> ℟. Alleluia, alleluia.

**A great prophet has appeared among us;
God has visited his people.**

> ℟. Alleluia, alleluia.

GOSPEL

Who can this be? Even the wind and the sea obey him.

✢ **A reading from the holy gospel according to Mark** 4:35-41

Jesus said to his disciples, "Let's cross to the east side."
So they left the crowd,
   and his disciples started across the lake with him in the boat.

Some other boats followed along.
Suddenly a windstorm struck the lake.
Waves started splashing into the boat,
   and it was about to sink.

Jesus was in the back of the boat with his head on a pillow,
   and he was asleep.
His disciples woke him and said,
"Teacher, don't you care that we're about to drown?"

Jesus got up and ordered the wind and the waves to be quiet.
The wind stopped,
   and everything was calm.

Jesus asked his disciples, "Why were you afraid?
Don't you have any faith?"

Now they were more afraid than ever and said to each other,
"Who is this?
Even the wind and the waves obey him!"

                                          The gospel of the Lord.

[91] **TWELFTH SUNDAY IN ORDINARY TIME** C

FIRST READING

All, baptized in Christ, have put on Christ.

A reading from the letter of Paul to the Galatians 3:26-29

Brothers and sisters:
All of you are God's children because of your faith in Christ Jesus.
And when you were baptized,
> **it was as though you had put on Christ**
>> **in the same way you put on new clothes.**

Faith in Christ Jesus is what makes each of you equal with each other,
> **whether you are a Jew or a Greek,**
> **a slave or a free person,**
> **a man or a woman.**

So if you belong to Christ,
> **you are now part of Abraham's family,**
> **and you will be given what God has promised.**

The word of the Lord.

RESPONSORIAL PSALM 100:1-2, 3, 5

℟. (3c) We are his people, the sheep of his flock.

Shout praises to the Lord,
everyone on this earth.
Be joyful and sing
as you come in to worship the Lord!

℟. We are his people, the sheep of his flock.

You know the Lord is God!
He created us,
and we belong to him;
we are his people,
the sheep in his pasture.

℟. We are his people, the sheep of his flock.

The LORD is good!
His love and faithfulness
will last forever.

℟. We are his people, the sheep of his flock.

ALLELUIA
John 10:27

℟. Alleluia, alleluia.

My sheep listen to my voice, says the Lord;
I know them, and they follow me.

℟. Alleluia, alleluia.

GOSPEL

You are the Christ sent by God.
The Son of Man was destined to suffer much.

✠ A reading from the holy gospel according to Luke   9:18-24

When Jesus was alone praying,
his disciples came to him,
and he asked them, "What do people say about me?"

They answered,
"Some say that you are John the Baptist or Elijah
or a prophet from long ago who has come back to life."

Jesus then asked them, "But who do you say I am?"

Peter answered, "You are the Messiah sent from God."

Jesus strictly warned his disciples
not to tell anyone what had happened.

Jesus told his disciples,
"The nation's leaders, the chief priests,
and the teachers of the Law of Moses
will make the Son of Man suffer terribly.
They will reject him and kill him,
but three days later he will rise to life."

Then Jesus said to all the people:
"If any of you want to be my followers,
    you must forget about yourself.
You must take up your cross each day and follow me.
If you want to save your life,
    you will destroy it.
But if you give up your life for me,
    you will save it."

                        The gospel of the Lord.

[92] THIRTEENTH SUNDAY IN ORDINARY TIME A

FIRST READING

That is the holy man of God; let him remain there.

A reading from the second book of Kings   4:8-11, 14-16a

One day Elisha went to the town of Shunem.
A rich woman lived there,
   and she invited him for a meal.
Each time Elisha was in town after that,
   he would eat at her home.

The woman said to her husband,
"I'm sure that this man who comes by here so often
   is a holy man of God.
Let's build him a small room on our flat roof.
We can put a bed, a table, a chair, and an oil lamp in the room.
He can stay there whenever he comes to visit us."
The next time Elisha came to Shunem,
   he spent the night in his room.

Elisha asked his servant Gehazi,
"What can we do to repay this woman for being so kind?"

Gehazi answered,
"She doesn't have a son, and her husband is old."

Elisha said to Gehazi,
"Tell the woman to come here."
He told her,
   and she came and stood in the doorway of the room.

Elisha promised the woman,
"Next year about this time you will have a son of your own."

                                                   The word of the Lord.

RESPONSORIAL PSALM   89:1-2, 15-16

℟. (2a) For ever I will sing the goodness of the Lord.

Our LORD, I will sing
of your love forever.

Everyone yet to be born
will hear me praise
your faithfulness.
I will tell them, "God's love
can always be trusted,
and his faithfulness lasts
as long as the heavens."

℟. For ever I will sing the goodness of the Lord.

Our LORD, you bless those
who join in the festival
and walk in the brightness
of your presence.
We are happy all day
because of you,
and your saving power
brings honor to us.

℟. For ever I will sing the goodness of the Lord.

SECOND READING

*Buried with Christ in baptism,
we shall walk in the newness of life.*

A reading from the letter of Paul to the Romans 6:3-4, 8-9

Brothers and sisters:
Don't you know that all who share in Christ Jesus by being baptized
    also share in his death?
When we were baptized,
    we died and were buried with Christ.
We were baptized, so that we would live a new life,
    as Christ was raised to life by the glory of God the Father.

As surely as we died with Christ,
    we believe we will also live with him.
We know that death no longer has any power over Christ.
He died and was raised to life,
    never again to die.

The word of the Lord.

ALLELUIA
1 Peter 2:9

℟. Alleluia, alleluia.

You are a chosen race, a royal priesthood, a holy people.
Praise God who called you out of darkness
and into his marvelous light.

℟. Alleluia, alleluia.

GOSPEL

Anyone who welcomes you, welcomes me.

✢ A reading from the holy gospel according to Matthew   10:40-42

Jesus said to his disciples:
"Anyone who welcomes you welcomes me.
And anyone who welcomes me also welcomes the one who sent me.

"Anyone who welcomes a prophet, just because that person is a prophet,
   will be given the same reward as a prophet.
Anyone who welcomes a good person, just because that person is good,
   will be given the same reward as a good person.

"And anyone who gives one of my most humble followers
   a cup of cool water,
   just because that person is my follower,
   will surely be rewarded."

The gospel of the Lord.

[93] THIRTEENTH SUNDAY IN ORDINARY TIME B

FIRST READING

It was the devil's envy that brought death into the world.

A reading from the book of Wisdom 1:13-15; 2:23-24a

God did not create death,
  and he is sad whenever a living creature dies.
God made everything,
  and there is a reason for every living creature.
No deadly poison is in them,
  and the kingdom of death doesn't rule the earth.
Goodness will never die.

God created us to live forever,
  just as he does.
But the Devil was jealous and brought death into the world.

The word of the Lord.

RESPONSORIAL PSALM 30:4 and 5def, 10-11ab and 12bcd

℟. (2a) I will praise you, Lord, for you have rescued me.

Your faithful people, LORD,
will praise you with songs
and honor your holy name.
At night we may cry,
but when morning comes
we will celebrate.

℟. I will praise you, Lord, for you have rescued me.

Have pity, LORD! Help!
You have turned my sorrow
into joyful dancing.
I will never stop
singing your praises,
my LORD and my God.

℟. I will praise you, Lord, for you have rescued me.

THIRTEENTH SUNDAY IN ORDINARY TIME — B

SECOND READING

Your abundance should supply their want.

A reading from the second letter of Paul to the Corinthians 8:7, 9, 13-14

Brothers and sisters:
You do everything better than anyone else.
You have stronger faith.

You speak better and know more.
You are eager to give,
    and you love us better.
Now you must give more generously than anyone else.

You know that our Lord Jesus Christ
    was kind enough to give up all his riches and become poor,
    so that you could become rich.

I am not trying to make life easier for others
    by making life harder for you.
But it is only fair for you to share with them
    when you have so much,
    and they have so little.
Later, when they have more than enough, and you are in need,
    they can share with you.
Then everyone will have a fair share.

The word of the Lord.

ALLELUIA
See 2 Timothy 1:10

℟. Alleluia, alleluia.

**Our Savior Jesus Christ has done away with death
and brought us life through the gospel.**

℟. Alleluia, alleluia.

GOSPEL

Little girl, I say to you, arise.

✠ **A reading from the holy gospel according to Mark** 5:21-24, 35-43

Jesus got into the boat and crossed Lake Galilee.
   Then as he stood on the shore,
   a large crowd gathered around him.

The person in charge of the Jewish meeting place was also there.
His name was Jairus,
    and when he saw Jesus, he went over to him.
He kneeled at Jesus' feet and started begging him for help.
He said, "My daughter is about to die!
Please come and touch her,
    so she will get well and live."

Jesus went with Jairus.
Many people followed along and kept crowding around.

A little while later, some men came from Jairus' home and said,
"Your daughter has died!
Why bother the teacher anymore?"

Jesus heard what they said,
    and he said to Jairus,
"Don't worry. Just have faith!"

Jesus did not let anyone go with him
    except Peter and the two brothers, James and John.
They went home with Jairus and saw the people
    crying and making a lot of noise.

Then Jesus went inside and said to them,
"Why are you crying and carrying on like this?
The child is not dead.
She is just asleep."
But the people laughed at him.

After Jesus had sent them all out of the house,
    he took the girl's father and mother and his three disciples
        and went to where she was.
He took the twelve-year-old girl by the hand and said,

    "Talitha, koum!"
    which means, "Little girl, get up!"

The girl got right up and started walking around.

Everyone was greatly surprised.
But Jesus ordered them not to tell anyone what had happened.
Then he said, "Give her something to eat."

                              The gospel of the Lord.

[94] **THIRTEENTH SUNDAY IN ORDINARY TIME** C

FIRST READING

Elisha rose and followed Elijah.

A reading from the first book of Kings   19:16b, 19-21

God told Elijah the prophet:
"Choose Elisha, the son of Shaphat from Abel Meholah,
    to take your place as a prophet."
Elijah left and found Elisha plowing in a field with a pair of oxen.
There were eleven other men in front of him in the field,
    and each of them was also plowing with a pair of oxen.
Elijah went over to Elisha and put his robe on him.
Elisha left his oxen and ran after Elijah.
Then he said,
"Let me go and tell my father and mother good-by,
    and I will go with you."
Elijah answered, "Go back!
Did I tell you to do this?"

Elisha left him and went back.
He killed his two oxen and boiled them
    by making a fire with the wood from the plow and the yoke.
He gave the meat to the people,
    and they ate it.
Then he left with Elijah and became his servant.

The word of the Lord.

RESPONSORIAL PSALM   16:1-2ab and 5, 7-8, 11

℟. (see 5a) You are my inheritance, O Lord.

Protect me, LORD God!
I run to you for safety,
and I have said,
"Only you are my Lord!"
You, LORD, are all I want!
You are my choice,
and you keep me safe.

℟. You are my inheritance, O Lord.

I praise you, LORD,
for being my guide.
Even in the darkest night,
your teachings fill my mind.
I will always look to you,
as you stand beside me
and protect me from fear.

℟. You are my inheritance, O Lord.

You have shown me
the path to life,
and you make me glad
by being near to me.
Sitting at your right side,
I will always be joyful.

℟. You are my inheritance, O Lord.

SECOND READING

My brothers and sisters, you were called to freedom.

A reading from the letter of Paul to the Galatians   5:1, 13-15

Brothers and sisters:
Christ has set us free!
This means we are really free.
Now hold on to your freedom
and don't ever become slaves of the Law again.

My friends, you were chosen to be free.
So don't use your freedom as an excuse to do anything you want.
Use it as an opportunity to serve each other with love.
All that the Law says
     can be summed up in the command
        to love others as much as you love yourself.
But if you keep attacking each other like wild animals,
    you had better watch out or you will destroy yourselves.

                                            The word of the Lord.

ALLELUIA
1 Samuel 3:9; John 6:68c

℟. Alleluia, alleluia.

**Speak, O Lord, your servant is listening;
you have the words of everlasting life.**

℟. Alleluia, alleluia.

GOSPEL

I will follow you wherever you will go.

✜ **A reading from the holy gospel according to Luke**   9:57-62

Along the way to Jerusalem someone said to Jesus,
"I'll go anywhere with you!"

Jesus said, "Foxes have dens, and birds have nests,
 but the Son of Man doesn't have a place to call his own."

Jesus told someone else to come with him.
But the man said,
"Lord, let me wait until I bury my father."

Jesus answered, "Let the dead take care of the dead,
 while you go and tell about God's kingdom."

Then someone said to Jesus,
"I want to go with you, Lord,
 but first let me go back and take care of things at home."

Jesus answered,
"Anyone who starts plowing and keeps looking back
 isn't worth a thing in God's kingdom!"

The gospel of the Lord.

[95] FOURTEENTH SUNDAY IN ORDINARY TIME **A**

FIRST READING

See how humbly your king comes to you!

A reading from the book of the prophet Zechariah 9:9-10

The Lord says this:
Everyone in Jerusalem, celebrate and rejoice.
Your king has won the victory,
   and he is coming to you.
He is humble and rides on a donkey.
He comes on the colt of a donkey.

I, the Lord, will take away all war chariots and horses
   from Israel and Jerusalem.
Bows that were made for battle will be destroyed.

I will bring peace to nations,
   and your king will rule from sea to sea.
His kingdom will reach from the Euphrates River
   across all the earth.

                              The word of the Lord.

RESPONSORIAL PSALM 145:1-2, 8-9, 13cd-14

℟. (see 1) I will praise your name for ever, my king and my God.
or:
℟. Alleluia.

I will praise you,
my God and King,
and always honor your name.
I will praise you each day
and always honor your name.

℟. I will praise your name for ever, my king and my God.
or:
℟. Alleluia.

You are merciful, LORD!
You are kind and patient
and always loving.
You are good to everyone,
and you take care
of all your creation.

> ℟. I will praise your name for ever, my king and my God.
> or:
> ℟. Alleluia.

Our LORD, you keep your word
and do everything you say.
When someone stumbles or falls,
you give a helping hand.

> ℟. I will praise your name for ever, my king and my God.
> or:
> ℟. Alleluia.

SECOND READING

God's Spirit now lives in you.

A reading from the letter of Paul to the Romans 8:9, 11

Brothers and sisters:
You are no longer ruled by your desires,
   but by God's Spirit, who lives in you.
People who don't have the Spirit of Christ in them
      don't belong to him.

God raised Jesus to life!
God's Spirit now lives in you,
   and he will raise you to life by his Spirit.

The word of the Lord.

ALLELUIA

See Matthew 11:25

> ℟. Alleluia, alleluia.
>
> **Blessed are you, Father, Lord of heaven and earth;
> you have revealed to little ones the mysteries of the kingdom.**
>
> ℟. Alleluia, alleluia.

GOSPEL

I am gentle and humble of heart.

✣ A reading from the holy gospel according to Matthew   11:25-30

On one occasion Jesus said:
"My Father, Lord of heaven and earth,
 I am glad that you hid all this from wise and educated people
  and showed it to ordinary people.
Yes, Father, that is what pleased you.

"My Father has given me everything,
 and he is the only one who knows the Son.
The only one who truly knows the Father is the Son.
But the Son wants to tell others about the Father,
 so that they can know him too.

"If you are tired from carrying heavy burdens,
 come to me and I will give you rest.
Take the yoke I give you.
Put it on your shoulders and learn from me.
I am gentle and humble,
 and you will find rest.
This yoke is easy to bear,
 and this burden is light."

The gospel of the Lord.

[96] FOURTEENTH SUNDAY IN ORDINARY TIME   B

FIRST READING

The people are rebellious;
they shall know there will be a prophet in their midst.

A reading from the book of the prophet Ezekiel 2:2-5

As the Lord spoke,
his Spirit gave me the power to stand,
and I heard him say:

"You are a mere human,
   but I am sending you to the people of Israel.
All of them have rebelled against me,
   and they are still rebelling,
   just as their ancestors did.
They are stubborn and hardheaded.

"But I am the Lord God,
   and I am sending you to speak to them in my name.
They are stubborn.
So maybe they will listen
   and maybe they won't.
But at least they will know that a prophet has come to them."

The word of the Lord.

RESPONSORIAL PSALM   86:5-6, 15 and 16de

℟. (5a) Lord, you are good and forgiving.

You willingly forgive,
and your love is always there
for those who pray to you.
Please listen, Lord!
Answer my prayer for help.

℟. Lord, you are good and forgiving.

You, the Lord God,
are kind and merciful.

You don't easily get angry,
and your love
can always be trusted.
Look on me with kindness.
Make me strong and save me.

℟. Lord, you are good and forgiving.

SECOND READING

*I will boast in my weaknesses,
so that the power of Christ may dwell in me.*

A reading from the second letter of Paul to the Corinthians   12:7-10

Brothers and sisters:
I am now referring to the wonderful things I saw.

One of Satan's angels was sent to make me suffer terribly,
   so that I would not feel too proud.
Three times I begged the Lord to make this suffering go away.
But he replied, "My kindness is all you need.
My power is strongest when you are weak."

So if Christ keeps giving me his power,
   I will gladly brag about how weak I am.
Yes, I am glad to be weak or insulted or mistreated
       or to have troubles and sufferings,
   if it is for Christ.
Because when I am weak, I am strong.

The word of the Lord.

ALLELUIA   See Luke 4:18

℟. Alleluia, alleluia.

**The Spirit of the Lord now upon me
has sent me to bring good news to the poor.**

℟. Alleluia, alleluia.

GOSPEL

A prophet is without honor in his own country.

✚ A reading from the holy gospel according to Mark 6:1-6

Jesus left and returned to his hometown with his disciples. The next Sabbath he taught in the Jewish meeting place.

Many of the people who heard him were amazed and asked, "How can he do all this?
Where did he get such wisdom and the power to work these miracles?
Isn't he the carpenter, the son of Mary?
Aren't James, Joseph, Judas, and Simon his brothers?
Don't his sisters still live here in our town?"

The people were very unhappy because of what he was doing.
But Jesus said, "Prophets are honored by everyone,
> except the people of their hometown
> and their relatives and their own family."

Jesus could not work any miracles there,
> except to heal a few sick people by placing his hands on them.
He was surprised that the people did not have any faith.

The gospel of the Lord.

[97] **FOURTEENTH SUNDAY IN ORDINARY TIME** C

FIRST READING

I will send toward Jerusalem peace like a river.

A reading from the book of the prophet Isaiah 66:10-14c

If you love Jerusalem,
 be glad and celebrate.
If you were in sorrow because of the city,
 you can now rejoice.
She will nurse and comfort you, just like your own mother,
 until you are satisfied.
And you will fully enjoy her wonderful glory.

The Lord has promised,
"I will flood Jerusalem with the wealth of nations
 and make the city prosper.
Jerusalem will nurse you at her breast,
 carry you in her arms,
 and hold you in her lap.
I will comfort you there
 like a mother comforting her child.

"When you see this happen,
 you will celebrate.
And your strength will return faster than grass can sprout.
Then everyone will know the Lord is with you."

                              The word of the Lord.

RESPONSORIAL PSALM 66:1-3ab, 6-7a, 16 and 20

℟. (1) Let all the earth cry out to God with joy.

**Tell everyone on this earth
to shout praises to God!
Sing about his glorious name.
Honor him with praises.
Say to God, "Everything you do
is fearsome!"**

℟. Let all the earth cry out to God with joy.

**When God made the sea dry up,
our people walked across,
and because of him,
we celebrated there.
His mighty power rules forever.**

℟. Let all the earth cry out to God with joy.

**All who worship God,
come here and listen;
I will tell you everything
God has done for me.
Let's praise God!
He listened when I prayed,
and he is always kind.**

℟. Let all the earth cry out to God with joy.

ALLELUIA Colossians 3:15a, 16a

℟. Alleluia, alleluia.

**May the peace of Christ rule in your hearts,
and the fullness of his message live within you.**

℟. Alleluia, alleluia.

GOSPEL

Your peace will rest upon that person.

✢ A reading from the holy gospel according to Luke 10:1-9

The Lord chose seventy-two other followers
    and sent them out two by two to every town and village
    where he was about to go.

He said to them:
"A large crop is in the fields,
    but there are only a few workers.
Ask the Lord in charge of the harvest
    to send out workers to bring it in.
Now go,
    but remember, I am sending you like lambs into a pack of wolves.
Don't take along a moneybag or a traveling bag or sandals.
And don't waste time greeting people on the road.

"As soon as you enter a home, say,
'God bless this home with peace.'
If the people living there are peace-loving,
    your prayer for peace will bless them.
But if they are not peace-loving,
    your prayer will return to you.

"Stay with the same family,
    eating and drinking whatever they give you,
    because workers are worth what they earn.
Don't move around from house to house.

"If the people of a town welcome you,
    eat whatever they offer you.
Heal their sick and say,
'God's kingdom will soon be here!' "

                                  The gospel of the Lord.

[98] FIFTEENTH SUNDAY IN ORDINARY TIME **A**

FIRST READING

The rain makes the earth fruitful.

A reading from the book of the prophet Isaiah 55:10-11

The rain and the snow fall from the sky.
But they don't return without watering the earth
   that produces seeds to plant and grain to eat.
And that's how it is with my words.
They don't return to me without doing everything I sent them to do.

The word of the Lord.

RESPONSORIAL PSALM 65:9, 11-12, 13

℟. (Luke 8:8) The seed that falls on good ground
   will yield a fruitful harvest.

**Our God, you take care of the earth
and send rain to help the soil
grow all kinds of crops.
Your rivers never run dry,
and you prepare the earth
to produce much grain.**

℟. The seed that falls on good ground
   will yield a fruitful harvest.

**Wherever your footsteps
touch the earth,
a rich harvest is gathered.
Desert pastures blossom,
and mountains celebrate.**

℟. The seed that falls on good ground
   will yield a fruitful harvest.

Meadows are filled
with sheep and goats;
valleys overflow with grain
and echo with joyful songs.

> ℟. The seed that falls on good ground
> will yield a fruitful harvest.

SECOND READING

God's Spirit leads us to share in the glory of Christ.

A reading from the letter of Paul to the Romans   8:14-18

Brothers and sisters:
Only those people who are led by God's Spirit are his children.
God's Spirit doesn't make us slaves who are afraid of him.
Instead, we become his children and call him our Father.
God's Spirit makes us sure that we are his children.

His Spirit lets us know that together with Christ
> we will be given what God has promised.
We will also share in the glory of Christ,
> because we have suffered with him.

I am sure that what we are suffering now
> cannot compare with the glory that will be shown to us.

The word of the Lord.

ALLELUIA

> ℟. Alleluia, alleluia.

**The seed is the word of God, Christ is the sower;
all who come to him will live for ever.**

> ℟. Alleluia, alleluia.

GOSPEL

A sower went out to sow.

✣ A reading from the holy gospel according to Matthew   13:1-9

Jesus went out beside Lake Galilee,
  where he sat down to teach.
Such large crowds gathered around him that he had to sit in a boat,
  while the people stood on the shore.
Then he taught them many things by using stories.

He said: "A farmer went out to scatter seed in a field.
While the farmer was scattering the seed,
  some of it fell along the road and was eaten by birds.
Other seeds fell on thin, rocky ground and quickly started growing
  because the soil was not very deep.
But when the sun came up,
    the plants were scorched and dried up,
    because they did not have enough roots.

"Some other seeds fell where thorn bushes grew up and choked the plants.
But a few seeds did fall on good ground
  where the plants produced a hundred or sixty
    or thirty times as much as was scattered.

"If you have ears, pay attention!"

The gospel of the Lord.

[99] **FIFTEENTH SUNDAY IN ORDINARY TIME** B

FIRST READING
Go, prophesy to my people.

A reading from the book of the prophet Amos   7:10-15

Amaziah the priest of Bethel sent this message
    to Jeroboam the king of Israel:
"Amos is plotting against you in the very heart of Israel.
Our nation cannot put up with his message for very long.
Here is what he is saying,
'Jeroboam will be put to death,
    and the people will be taken to a foreign country.' "

Amaziah then told Amos,
"Take your visions and leave!
Go back to Judah and earn your living there as a prophet.
Don't do any more preaching at Bethel.
The king worships here,
    and this is our national temple."

Amos answered, "I'm not a prophet!
And I wasn't trained to be a prophet.
I raise livestock and take care of fig trees.
But the LORD told me to leave my herds
    and preach to the people of Israel."

The word of the Lord.

RESPONSORIAL PSALM   85:8abc and 9, 10-11, 12-13

    ℟. (8) Lord, show us your mercy and love, and grant us your salvation.

I will listen to you, LORD God,
because you promise peace
to those who are faithful.
You are ready to rescue
everyone who worships you,
so that you will live with us
in all of your glory.

    ℟. Lord, show us your mercy and love, and grant us your salvation.

Love and loyalty
will come together;
goodness and peace will unite.
Loyalty will sprout
from the ground;
justice will look down
from the sky above.

> ℟. Lord, show us your mercy and love, and grant us your salvation.

Our LORD, you will bless us;
our land will produce wonderful crops.
Justice will march in front,
make a path for you to follow.

> ℟. Lord, show us your mercy and love, and grant us your salvation.

SECOND READING

Before the world was made, God chose us in Christ.

A reading from the letter of Paul to the Ephesians   1:3-10

Brothers and sisters:
Praise the God and Father of our Lord Jesus Christ
   for the spiritual blessings that Christ has brought us
   from heaven!
Before the world was created,
   God had Christ choose us to live with him
      and to be his holy and innocent and loving people.
God was kind
   and decided that Christ would choose us
   to be God's own adopted children.
God was very kind to us because of the Son he dearly loves,
   and so we should praise God.

Christ sacrificed his life's blood to set us free,
   which means that our sins are forgiven.
Christ did this because God was so kind to us.

God has great wisdom and understanding,
> and by what Christ has done,
God has shown us his own mysterious ways.
Then when the time is right,
> God will do all that he has planned,
> and Christ will bring together everything in heaven and on earth.

The word of the Lord.

ALLELUIA See Ephesians 1:17-18

℟. Alleluia, alleluia.

May the Father of our Lord Jesus Christ
enlighten the eyes of our heart,
that we might see how great is the hope
to which we are called.

℟. Alleluia, alleluia.

GOSPEL

Jesus summoned the twelve and sent them out.

✠ A reading from the holy gospel according to Mark 6:7-13

Jesus called together his twelve apostles
> and sent them out two by two with power over evil spirits.
He told them, "You may take along a walking stick.
But don't carry food or a traveling bag or any money.
It's all right to wear sandals,
> but don't take along a change of clothes.

"When you are welcomed into a home,
> stay there until you leave that town.
If any place won't welcome you or listen to your message,
> leave and shake the dust from your feet as a warning to them."

The apostles left and started telling everyone to turn to God.
They forced out many demons and healed a lot of sick people
> by putting olive oil on them.

The gospel of the Lord.

[100] FIFTEENTH SUNDAY IN ORDINARY TIME   C

FIRST READING

The word is very near to you for your observance.

A reading from the book of Deuteronomy   30:10-14

Moses said to the people:
"You must obey the Lord your God
and follow all the laws and commands
   that are in the book of the Law.
You must trust him with all your heart and soul.

"What I am commanding you today is not too hard.
It isn't out of your reach somewhere up in the sky.
You don't have to ask yourselves,
'Who will go up to the sky and get it for us?
Who will bring it down and tell us what we must do?'

"What I am commanding you is not on the other side of the sea.
You don't have to ask yourselves,
'Who will cross the sea and get it for us?
Who will bring it here and tell us what to do?'
No! What I am commanding is as near as your mouth or your heart.
All you have to do is obey."

                                          The word of the Lord.

RESPONSORIAL PSALM   69:13, 29-30

℟. (see 33) Turn to the Lord in your need, and you will live.

I pray to you, Lord.
So when the time is right,
answer me and help me
with your wonderful love.

℟. Turn to the Lord in your need, and you will live.

I am mistreated and in pain.
Protect me, God,
and keep me safe!
I will praise the LORD God
with a song
and a thankful heart.

℟. Turn to the Lord in your need, and you will live.

SECOND READING

Christ is the head of his body, the Church.

A reading from the letter of Paul to the Colossians 1:18-20

Brothers and sisters:
Christ is the head of his body, which is the church.
He is the very beginning,
   the first to be raised from death,
   so that he would be above all others.

God himself was pleased to live fully in his Son.
And God was pleased for him to make peace
   by sacrificing his blood on the cross,
so that all beings in heaven and on earth
   would be brought back to God.

The word of the Lord.

ALLELUIA

See John 6:63, 68c

℟. Alleluia, alleluia.

Your words, Lord, are spirit and life;
you have the words of everlasting life.

℟. Alleluia, alleluia.

GOSPEL

Who is my neighbor?

✠ A reading from the holy gospel according to Luke   10:25-37

An expert in the Law of Moses stood up and asked Jesus a question to see what he would say.
"Teacher," he asked,
   "What must I do to have eternal life?"

Jesus answered, "What is written in the Scriptures?
How do you understand them?"

The man replied, "The Scriptures say,
'Love the Lord your God with all your heart, soul, strength, and mind.'
They also say, 'Love your neighbors as much as you love yourself.' "

Jesus said, "You have given the right answer.
If you do this, you will have eternal life."

But the man wanted to show that he knew what he was talking about.
So he asked Jesus, "Who are my neighbors?"

Jesus replied:
"As a man was going down from Jerusalem to Jericho,
   robbers attacked him and grabbed everything he had.
They beat him up and ran off, leaving him half dead.

"A priest happened to be going down the same road.
But when he saw the man,
   he walked by on the other side.
Later a temple helper came to the same place.
But when he saw the man who had been beaten up,
   he also went by on the other side.

"A man from Samaria then came traveling along that road.
When he saw the man,
   he felt sorry for him and went over to him.
He treated his wounds with olive oil and wine and bandaged them.
Then he put him on his own donkey and took him to an inn,
   where he took care of him.

"The next morning he gave the innkeeper two silver coins and said,
'Please take care of the man.
If you spend more than this on him,
    I will pay you when I return.' "

Then Jesus asked,
"Which of these three people was a real neighbor
    to the man who was beaten up by robbers?"

The teacher answered, "The one who showed pity."
Jesus said, "Go and do the same!"

                                          The gospel of the Lord.

[101] SIXTEENTH SUNDAY IN ORDINARY TIME **A**

FIRST READING

In place of sin you give repentance.

A reading from the book of Wisdom   12:13, 16-19

There is no God but you,
   and you care for all of us.
You don't have to prove that you judge fairly.

Your strength gives you the power to do right,
   and because you rule over all,
   you have pity on everyone.

When someone doubts how strong you are,
   you show your strength.
And you correct everyone who is too proud.

You are a powerful Master.
But you judge us with kindness and rule with great mercy,
   because you have the power to do whatever you want.

By doing such things,
   you have taught your people
   that those who do right must also care about others.
And you have given your children a wonderful hope
     by helping them turn from sin.

The word of the Lord.

RESPONSORIAL PSALM   86:5-6, 15-16de

℟. (5a) Lord, you are good and forgiving.

You willingly forgive,
and your love is always there
for those who pray to you.
Please listen, LORD!
Answer my prayer for help.

℟. Lord, you are good and forgiving.

You, the Lord God,
are kind and merciful.
You don't easily get angry,
and your love
can always be trusted.
Look on me with kindness.
Make me strong and save me.

℟. Lord, you are good and forgiving.

SECOND READING

*That very Spirit intercedes for us
with longings too deep for words.*

A reading from the letter of Paul to the Romans   8:26-27

Brothers and sisters:
In certain ways we are weak,
   but the Spirit is here to help us.
For example, when we don't know what to pray for,
   the Spirit prays for us in ways that cannot be put into words.
All of our thoughts are known to God.
He can understand what is in the mind of the Spirit,
   as the Spirit prays for God's people.

The word of the Lord.

ALLELUIA   See Matthew 11:25

℟. Alleluia, alleluia.

**Blessed are you, Father, Lord of heaven and earth;
you have revealed to little ones the mysteries of the kingdom.**

℟. Alleluia, alleluia.

GOSPEL

Let them grow together until the harvest.

✠ A reading from the holy gospel according to Matthew 13:24-30

Jesus told his disciples this story:
"The kingdom of heaven is like what happened
    when a farmer scattered good seed in a field.
But while everyone was sleeping,
    an enemy came and scattered weed seeds in the field and then left.
When the plants came up and began to ripen,
    the farmer's servants could see the weeds.

"The servants came and asked,
'Sir, didn't you scatter good seed in your field?
Where did these weeds come from?'
'An enemy did this,' he replied.

"His servants then asked,
'Do you want us to go out and pull up the weeds?'
'No!' he answered.
'You might also pull up the wheat.
Leave the weeds alone until harvest time.
Then I'll tell my workers to gather the weeds
    and tie them up and burn them.
But I'll have them store the wheat in my barn.' "

The gospel of the Lord.

[102] SIXTEENTH SUNDAY IN ORDINARY TIME B

FIRST READING

*The remnant of the flock I will gather to me,
to bring them back to their pastures.*

A reading from the book of the prophet Jeremiah   23:3-6

"I, the Lord, will bring the rest of my people back
from the lands where I have scattered them.
I will bring them home,
 and they will grow into a mighty nation.
I will choose leaders who will take care of them.
Every one of my people will be there,
 and they will never again be frightened or terrified.
I, the Lord, have spoken!

"I promise that the time will come
  when I will choose a king from the family of David.
He will be wise and will rule the land with justice and fairness.
As long as he is king, Judah will be safe,
 and Israel will live in peace.
The name of this king will be, 'The Lord is our Protector!' "

The word of the Lord.

RESPONSORIAL PSALM   23:1-3a, 3b-4, 6

℟. (1) The Lord is my shepherd; there is nothing I shall want.

You, Lord, are my shepherd.
I will never be in need.
You let me rest in fields
of green grass.
You lead me to streams
of peaceful water,
and you refresh my life.

℟. The Lord is my shepherd; there is nothing I shall want.

You are true to your name,
and you lead me
along the right paths.

I may walk through valleys
as dark as death,
but I won't be afraid.
You are with me,
and your shepherd's rod
makes me feel safe.

℟. The Lord is my shepherd; there is nothing I shall want.

Your kindness and love
will always be with me
every day of my life,
and I will live forever
in your house, LORD.

℟. The Lord is my shepherd; there is nothing I shall want.

ALLELUIA

John 10:27

℟. Alleluia, alleluia.

My sheep listen to my voice, says the Lord;
I know them, and they follow me.

℟. Alleluia, alleluia.

GOSPEL

They were like sheep without a shepherd.

✠ A reading from the holy gospel according to Mark 6:30-34

After the apostles returned to Jesus,
they told him everything they had done and taught.
But so many people were coming and going
   that Jesus and the apostles did not even have a chance to eat.
Then Jesus said, "Let's go to a place
   where we can be alone and get some rest."
They left in a boat for a place where they could be alone.
But many people saw them leave and figured out where they were going.
So people from every town ran on ahead and got there first.
When Jesus got out of the boat,
   he saw the large crowd that was like sheep without a shepherd.
He felt sorry for the people and started teaching them many things.

The gospel of the Lord.

[103] **SIXTEENTH SUNDAY IN ORDINARY TIME** C

FIRST READING

Lord, do not bypass your servant.

A reading from the book of Genesis 18:1-10a

One hot summer afternoon
> Abraham was sitting by the entrance to his tent
> near the sacred trees of Mamre,
>> when the Lord appeared to him.

Abraham looked up and saw three men standing nearby.
He quickly ran to meet them and bowed with his face to the ground.

He said, "Please come to my home where I can serve you.
I will have some water brought, so you can wash your feet,
> and then you can rest under the tree.
Let me get you some food to give you strength before you leave.
I would be honored to serve you."

They answered, "Thank you very much. We accept your offer."

Abraham hurried to his tent and said to Sarah,
"Hurry! Get a large sack of fine flour.
Then mix it and make some bread."

After saying this, he hurried off to his herd of cattle
>> and picked out one of the best calves,
> which his servant quickly prepared.
He served his guests some yogurt and milk,
> together with the meat.

While they were eating,
> he stood near them under the trees.
They asked him, "Where is your wife Sarah?"

He answered, "She is right there in the tent."

One of the guests was the Lord, and he said,
"I will come back next spring,
> and when I do, Sarah will already have a son."

The word of the Lord.

RESPONSORIAL PSALM
15:1-3a, 3bc and 5ef

℟. (1a) The just will live in the presence of the Lord.

**Who may stay in God's temple
or live on the holy mountain
of the LORD?
Only those who obey God
and do as they should.
They speak the truth
and don't spread gossip.**

℟. The just will live in the presence of the Lord.

**They treat others fairly
and don't say cruel things.
Those who do these things
will always stand firm.**

℟. The just will live in the presence of the Lord.

SECOND READING

God's mystery has been revealed to you.

A reading from the letter of Paul to the Colossians 1:27-28

Brothers and sisters:
   God did this because he wanted you Gentiles
      to understand his wonderful and glorious mystery.
And the mystery is that Christ lives in you,
   and he is your hope of sharing in God's glory.

**We announce the message about Christ,
   and we use all our wisdom to warn and teach everyone,
   so that all Christ's followers will grow and become mature.**

The word of the Lord.

ALLELUIA
See Luke 8:15

℟. Alleluia, alleluia.

**Blessed are they who have kept the word with a generous heart
and yield a harvest through perseverance.**

℟. Alleluia, alleluia.

GOSPEL

Martha took up the duties in the house.
Mary chose the better part.

✣ **A reading from the holy gospel according to Luke**　　10:38-42

The Lord and his disciples were traveling along
　　and came to a village.
When they got there,
　　a woman named Martha welcomed him into her home.
She had a sister named Mary,
　　who sat down in front of the Lord
　　　　and was listening to what he said.

Martha was worried about all that had to be done.
Finally, she went to Jesus and said,
"Lord, doesn't it bother you
　　that my sister has left me to do all the work by myself?
Tell her to come and help me!"

The Lord answered, "Martha, Martha!
You are worried and upset about so many things,
　　but only one thing is necessary.
Mary has chosen what is best,
　　and it will not be taken away from her."

　　　　　　　　　　　　　　　　The gospel of the Lord.

[104] SEVENTEENTH SUNDAY IN ORDINARY TIME — A

FIRST READING

You have asked for wisdom.

A reading from the first book of Kings 3:5, 7-12

One night at Gibeon, God appeared to Solomon in a dream and said, "Ask me for anything you want."

Solomon answered,
"My Lord and God, I am your servant.
You have made me king in place of my father David.
But I don't know any more about being king than a child would know.
And I must serve your chosen people,
> even though they are a great nation
>> with more people than can be counted.
Please make me wise enough to rule them well
> and know the difference between right and wrong.
No one is really able to rule this great nation of yours."

The Lord was pleased that Solomon had asked this, and he said:
"I will answer your prayer.
You will be wise and know more than anyone who has ever lived
> or ever will live.
You didn't ask to live a long time or to be rich,
> and you didn't ask for your enemies to be destroyed.
All you wanted was to be honest and fair."

The word of the Lord.

RESPONSORIAL PSALM 119:57 and 72, 127-128

℟. (97a) Lord, I love your commands.

You, Lord, are my choice,
and I will obey you.
I would rather obey you
than to have a thousand pieces of silver and gold.

℟. Lord, I love your commands.

Your laws mean more to me
than the finest gold.
I follow all of your commands,
but I hate anyone
who leads me astray.

℟. Lord, I love your commands.

SECOND READING

God predestined us to become true images of his Son.

A reading from the letter of Paul to the Romans 8:28-30

Brothers and sisters:
We know that God is always at work
  for the good of everyone who loves him.
They are the ones God has chosen for his purpose,
  and he has always known who his chosen ones would be.
He had decided to let them become like his own Son,
  so that his Son would be the first of many children.
God then accepted the people he had already decided to choose,
  and he has shared his glory with them.

The word of the Lord.

ALLELUIA

See Matthew 11:25

℟. Alleluia, alleluia.

**Blessed are you, Father, Lord of heaven and earth;
you have revealed to little ones the mysteries of the kingdom.**

℟. Alleluia, alleluia.

GOSPEL

He sold all that he had and bought the field.

✢ **A reading from the holy gospel according to Matthew** 13:44-46

Jesus said to his disciples:
"The kingdom of heaven is like what happens
   when someone finds treasure hidden in a field
   and buries it again.
A person like that is happy and goes and sells everything
   in order to buy that field.

"The kingdom of heaven is like what happens
   when a shop owner is looking for fine pearls.
After finding a very valuable one,
   the owner goes and sells everything
      in order to buy that pearl."

The gospel of the Lord.

[105] SEVENTEENTH SUNDAY IN ORDINARY TIME B

FIRST READING

They will eat and have some left over.

A reading from the second book of Kings 4:42-44

One day a man from the town of Baal Shalishah
 came with some food for Elisha.
The man brought him twenty loaves of barley bread
 that had been made from the first crop of grain.
He also brought some fresh heads of grain.

Elisha told his servant, "Let the people have it to eat."
His servant replied, "This isn't enough to feed a hundred people."
But Elisha told him, "Give the food to the people!
The Lord has said that when they are through eating,
 there will be some left over."

The servant gave them the food.
And when they had finished eating,
 there was some left over,
 just as the Lord had promised.

The word of the Lord.

RESPONSORIAL PSALM 145:10-11, 15-16

℟. (see 16) You open your hand to feed us, Lord;
 you answer all our needs.

**All creation will thank you,
and your loyal people
will praise you.
They will tell about
your marvelous kingdom
and your power.**

℟. You open your hand to feed us, Lord;
 you answer all our needs.

Everyone depends on you,
and when the time is right,
you provide them with food.
By your own hand you satisfy
the desires of all who live.

> ℟. You open your hand to feed us, Lord;
> you answer all our needs.

SECOND READING

There is one body, one Lord, one faith, one baptism.

A reading from the letter of Paul to the Ephesians 4:1-6

Brothers and sisters:
As a prisoner of the Lord,
> I beg you to live in a way that is worthy of the people
> > God has chosen to be his own.

Always be humble and gentle.
Patiently put up with each other and love each other.
Try your best to let God's Spirit keep your hearts united.
Do this by living at peace.

All of you are part of the same body.
There is only one Spirit of God,
> just as you were given one hope
> when you were chosen to be God's people.

We have only one Lord, one faith, and one baptism.
There is one God who is the Father of all people.
Not only is God above all others,
> but he works by using all of us,
> and he lives in all of us.

The word of the Lord.

ALLELUIA Luke 7:16

> ℟. Alleluia, alleluia.

A great prophet has appeared among us;
God has visited his people.

> ℟. Alleluia, alleluia.

GOSPEL

Jesus gave the people all the food they wanted.

✞ A reading from the holy gospel according to John 6:1-15

Jesus crossed Lake Galilee, which was also known as Lake Tiberias.
A large crowd had seen him work miracles to heal the sick,
 and those people went with him.
It was almost time for the Jewish festival of Passover,
 and Jesus went up on a mountain with his disciples and sat down.

When Jesus saw the large crowd coming toward him, he asked Philip,
"Where will we get enough food to feed all these people?"
He said this to test Philip,
 since he already knew what he was going to do.

Philip answered,
"Don't you know that it would take almost a year's wages
 just to buy only a little bread for each of these people?"
Andrew, the brother of Simon Peter, was one of the disciples.
He spoke up and said,
"There is a boy here who has five small loaves of barley bread
 and two fish.
But what good is that with all these people?"

The ground was covered with grass,
 and Jesus told his disciples to have everyone sit down.
About five thousand men were in the crowd.

Jesus took the bread in his hands and gave thanks to God.
Then he passed the bread to the people,
 and he did the same with the fish,
 until everyone had plenty to eat.
The people ate all they wanted,
 and Jesus told his disciples to gather up the leftovers,
 so that nothing would be wasted.
The disciples gathered them up and filled twelve large baskets
 with what was left over from the five barley loaves.

After the people had seen Jesus work this miracle,
 they began saying,
"This must be the Prophet who is to come into the world!"

Jesus realized that they would try to force him to be their king.
So he went up on a mountain, where he could be alone.

                                    The gospel of the Lord.

[106] SEVENTEENTH SUNDAY IN ORDINARY TIME C

FIRST READING

Lord, do not be angry if I speak.

A reading from the book of Genesis 18:20-32

The Lord said to Abraham,
  "I have heard that the people of Sodom and Gomorrah
    are doing all kinds of evil things.
Now I am going down to see if those people are really that bad.
If they aren't, I want to know about it."

The men turned and started toward Sodom.
But the Lord stayed with Abraham, who asked,
"Lord, when you destroy the wicked people,
    are you also going to destroy the good ones?
Would you spare the city if there are fifty good people in it?
Surely, you wouldn't let the good ones be killed
    when you destroy the bad ones.
You are the judge of the earth,
    and you do what is right."

The Lord replied, "If I find fifty good people in Sodom,
    I will save the city to keep them from being killed."

Abraham answered,
"Lord, I am nothing more than the dust of the earth.
Please forgive me for daring to speak to you like this.
But suppose there are only forty-five good people in Sodom.
Would you still wipe out the whole city?"

The Lord replied,
"If I find forty-five good people,
    I won't destroy the city."

Abraham asked the Lord,
"Suppose there are just forty good people?"
The Lord replied, "Just for them, I won't destroy the city."

Abraham said, "Lord, please don't be angry,
    if I ask you what you would do
        if there are only thirty good people in the city."
The Lord replied, "If I find thirty, I still won't destroy it."

Then Abraham said, "LORD, I don't have any right to ask.
But what would you do if you find only twenty?"
The LORD replied, "Because of them, I won't destroy the city."

Finally, Abraham said, "LORD, please don't become angry,
 if I speak just once more.
Suppose you find only ten good people there."

The LORD then replied,
"For the sake of ten good people,
 I still won't destroy the city."

The word of the Lord.

RESPONSORIAL PSALM   138:1-2a, 2bcdef-3, 7abde-8abc

℟. (3a) Lord, on the day I called for help, you answered me.

With all my heart
I praise you, LORD.
In the presence of angels
I sing your praises.
I worship at your holy temple.

℟. Lord, on the day I called for help, you answered me.

I praise you for your love
and your faithfulness.
You were true to your word
and made yourself more famous
than ever before.
When I asked for your help,
you answered my prayer
and gave me courage.

℟. Lord, on the day I called for help, you answered me.

I am surrounded by trouble,
but you protect me.
With your own powerful arm
you keep me safe.
You, LORD, will always
treat me with kindness.
Your love never fails.

℟. Lord, on the day I called for help, you answered me.

ALLELUIA Romans 8:15bc

℟. Alleluia, alleluia.

You have received the Spirit which makes us God's children, and in that Spirit we call God our Father.

℟. Alleluia, alleluia.

GOSPEL

Ask and you shall receive.

✣ A reading from the holy gospel according to Luke 11:1-10

When Jesus had finished praying,
one of his disciples said to him,
"Lord, teach us to pray,
just as John taught his followers to pray."

So Jesus told them, "Pray in this way:
'Father, help us to honor your name.
Come and set up your kingdom.
Give us each day the food we need.
Forgive our sins,
as we forgive everyone who has done wrong to us.
And keep us from being tempted.' "

Then Jesus went on to say:
"Suppose one of you goes to a friend in the middle
of the night and says,
'Let me borrow three loaves of bread.
A friend of mine has dropped in,
and I don't have a thing for him to eat.'
And suppose your friend answers, 'Don't bother me!
The door is bolted, and my children and I are in bed.
I cannot get up to give you something.'

"He may not get up and give you the bread,
just because you are his friend.
But he will get up and give you as much as you need,
simply because you are not ashamed to keep on asking.

"So I tell you to ask and you will receive,
   search and you will find,
   knock and the door will be opened for you.
Everyone who asks will receive,
   everyone who searches will find,
   and the door will be opened for everyone who knocks."

The gospel of the Lord.

[107] **EIGHTEENTH SUNDAY IN ORDINARY TIME**   **A**

FIRST READING

Hasten and eat.

A reading from the book of the prophet Isaiah   55:1-3

The Lord says this:
If you are thirsty,
   come and drink water!
If you don't have any money,
   buy food and eat it.
Come and buy wine and milk
   without paying a cent.
Why waste your money
   on something less than food?
Why work hard for something
   that doesn't satisfy?
Listen carefully to me,
   and you will enjoy
   the very best foods.
Listen carefully! Come to me,
   and you will live.
I will promise you
   the eternal love and loyalty
   that I promised David.

The word of the Lord.

RESPONSORIAL PSALM   145:8-9, 15-16

℟. (see 16) You open your hand to feed us, Lord; you answer all our needs.

You are merciful, Lord!
You are kind and patient
and always loving.
You are good to everyone,
and you take care
of all your creation.

℟. You open your hand to feed us, Lord; you answer all our needs.

Everyone depends on you,
and when the time is right,
you provide them with food.
By your own hand you satisfy
the desires of all who live.

℟. You open your hand to feed us, Lord; you answer all our needs.

SECOND READING

Nothing can come between us and the love of God made visible in Christ Jesus our Lord.

A reading from the letter of Paul to the Romans   8:35, 37-39

Brothers and sisters:
Can anything separate us from the love of Christ?
Can trouble, suffering, and hard times,
    or hunger and nakedness, or danger and death?

In everything we have won more than a victory
    because of Christ who loves us.

I am sure that nothing can separate us from God's love —
    not life or death, not angels or spirits,
    not the present or the future,
    and not powers above or powers below.
Nothing in all creation can separate us from God's love for us
    in Christ Jesus our Lord!

The word of the Lord.

ALLELUIA   Matthew 4:4b

℟. Alleluia, alleluia.

No one lives on bread alone,
but on every word that comes from the mouth of God.

℟. Alleluia, alleluia.

GOSPEL

They all ate and were satisfied.

✣ A reading from the holy gospel according to Matthew   14:13-21

After Jesus heard about John,
   he crossed Lake Galilee to go to some place
      where he could be alone.
But the crowds found out and followed him on foot from the towns.
When Jesus got out of the boat, he saw the large crowd.
He felt sorry for them and healed everyone who was sick.

That evening the disciples came to Jesus and said,
"This place is like a desert, and it is already late.
Let the crowds leave,
   so they can go to the villages and buy some food."

Jesus replied, "They don't have to leave.
Why don't you give them something to eat?"
But they said, "We have only five small loaves of bread
      and two fish."

Jesus asked his disciples to bring the food to him,
   and he told the crowd to sit down on the grass.
Jesus took the five loaves and the two fish.
He looked up toward heaven and blessed the food.
Then he broke the bread and handed it to his disciples,
   and they gave it to the people.

After everyone had eaten all they wanted,
   Jesus' disciples picked up twelve large baskets of leftovers.
There were about five thousand men who ate,
      not counting the women and children.

                              The gospel of the Lord.

[108] EIGHTEENTH SUNDAY IN ORDINARY TIME B

FIRST READING

I will rain bread from heaven upon you.

A reading from the book of Exodus 16:2-4, 12-15

After the people of Israel had escaped from Egypt
    and were in the desert,
  they all started complaining to Moses and Aaron.
They said, "We wish the Lord had killed us in Egypt.
When we lived there, we could at least sit down
    and eat all the bread and meat we wanted.
But you have brought us out here in the desert,
  where we are going to starve to death."

The Lord said to Moses:
"I will send bread down from heaven like rain for all of you.
Each day the people can go out and gather up
    only enough for that day.
By doing this, I'll find out if they will obey me.
I have heard my people complain.
Now tell them that each evening they will have meat,
  and each morning they will have more than enough bread.
The people will know that I am the Lord their God."

That evening birds came and landed everywhere in the camp.
The next morning dew covered the ground.
After the dew had gone, there were thin flakes
    that looked like frost all over the ground.
The people had never seen anything like this,
  and they started asking each other, "What is it?"
Moses told them,
"This is the food that the Lord has given you."

                                                       The word of the Lord.

RESPONSORIAL PSALM   78:3 and 4cdef, 23-24, 25 and 54ab

℟. (24b) The Lord gave them bread from heaven.

**These are things we learned
from our ancestors,
and we won't keep secret
the glorious deeds
and the mighty miracles
of the L**ORD**.**

℟. The Lord gave them bread from heaven.

**God gave a command
to the clouds,
and he opened the doors
in the skies.
From heaven he sent grain
that they called manna.**

℟. The Lord gave them bread from heaven.

**He gave them more than enough,
and each one of them ate
this special food.
God brought his people
to the sacred mountain.**

℟. The Lord gave them bread from heaven.

ALLELUIA   Matthew 4:4b

℟. Alleluia, alleluia.

**No one lives on bread alone,
but on every word that comes from the mouth of God.**

℟. Alleluia, alleluia.

GOSPEL

Work for food that gives eternal life.

✢ A reading from the holy gospel according to John   6:24-29

The people saw that Jesus and his disciples had left.
Then they got into the boats
   and went to Capernaum to look for Jesus.

They found him on the west side of the lake and asked,
"Rabbi, when did you get here?"

Jesus answered, "I tell you for certain
   that you are not looking for me because you saw the miracles,
   but because you ate all the food you wanted.
Don't work for food that spoils.
Work for food that gives eternal life.
The Son of Man will give you this food,
  because God the Father has given him the right to do so."

"What exactly does God want us to do?" the people asked.
Jesus answered, "God wants you to have faith in the one he sent."

                                                 The gospel of the Lord.

[109] EIGHTEENTH SUNDAY IN ORDINARY TIME   C

FIRST READING

    Seek the things that are above where Christ is.

A reading from the letter of Paul to the Colossians   3:1-4

Brothers and sisters:
   You have been raised to life with Christ.
Now set your heart on what is in heaven,
   where Christ rules at God's right side.
Think about what is up there,
   not about what is here on earth.

You died, which means that your life is hidden with Christ,
   who sits beside God.
Christ gives meaning to your life,
   and when he appears,
   you will also appear with him in glory.

                                       The word of the Lord.

RESPONSORIAL PSALM   147:1, 3-4, 5 and 7

℟. (Is. 30:18) Happy are all who long for the coming of the Lord.

**Shout praises to the Lord!
Our God is kind,
and it is right and good
to sing praises to him.**

℟. Happy are all who long for the coming of the Lord.

**He renews our hopes
and heals our bodies.
He decided how many stars
there would be in the sky
and gave each one a name.**

℟. Happy are all who long for the coming of the Lord.

**Our Lord is great and powerful!
He understands everything.
Celebrate and sing!**

Play your harps
for the L
ord our God.

℟. Happy are all who long for the coming of the Lord.

ALLELUIA Matthew 5:3

℟. Alleluia, alleluia.

**Blessed are the poor in spirit;
the kingdom of heaven is theirs!**

℟. Alleluia, alleluia.

GOSPEL

To whom will all this wealth of yours go?

✛ **A reading from the holy gospel according to Luke** 12:16-21

Jesus told the crowd this story:
"A rich man's farm produced a big crop,
  and he said to himself, 'What can I do?
I don't have a place large enough to store everything.'

"Later, he said, 'Now I know what I'll do.
I'll tear down my barns and build bigger ones,
  where I can store all my grain and other goods.
Then I'll say to myself,
"You have stored up enough good things to last for years to come.
Live it up! Eat, drink, and enjoy yourself." '

"But God said to him, 'You fool!
Tonight you will die.
Then who will get what you have stored up?'

"This is what happens to people who store up everything for themselves,
  but are poor in the sight of God."

The gospel of the Lord.

[110] NINETEENTH SUNDAY IN ORDINARY TIME **A**

FIRST READING

Go out and stand on the mountain before the Lord God.

A reading from the first book of Kings   19:9a, 11-13a

Elijah went into a cave and spent the night.
The L<small>ORD</small> said, "Elijah, go out and stand on the mountain.
I am going to pass that way."

At once a strong and mighty wind shook the mountain
    and shattered the rocks.
But the L<small>ORD</small> was not in the wind.

An earthquake shook the ground,
    but the L<small>ORD</small> was not in the earthquake.
After the earthquake there was a fire,
    but the L<small>ORD</small> was not in the fire.

After the fire,
    hardly a sound was heard.
Elijah covered his face with his robe
      and went out and stood at the entrance to the cave.

                              The word of the Lord.

RESPONSORIAL PSALM   85:8abc and 9, 10-11, 12-13

℟. (8) **Lord, show us your mercy and love, and grant us your salvation.**

I will listen to you, L<small>ORD</small> God,
because you promise peace
to those who are faithful.

You are ready to rescue
everyone who worships you,
so that you will live with us
in all of your glory.

℟. Lord, show us your mercy and love, and grant us your salvation.

**Love and loyalty
will come together;
goodness and peace will unite.
Loyalty will sprout
from the ground;
justice will look down
from the sky above.**

℟. Lord, show us your mercy and love, and grant us your salvation.

**Our Lord, you will bless us;
our land will produce
wonderful crops.
Justice will march in front,
making a path
for you to follow.**

℟. Lord, show us your mercy and love, and grant us your salvation.

ALLELUIA See Psalm 130:5

℟. Alleluia, alleluia.

**I hope in the Lord,
I trust in his word.**

℟. Alleluia, alleluia.

GOSPEL

Command me to come to you over the water.

✢ A reading from the holy gospel according to Matthew 14:22-33

Jesus made his disciples get into a boat and start back across the lake.
But he stayed until he had sent the crowds away.
Then he went up on a mountain where he could be alone and pray.
Later that evening, he was still there.

By this time the boat was a long way from the shore.
It was going against the wind and was being tossed around by the waves.
A little while before morning,
    Jesus came walking on the water toward his disciples.
When they saw him, they thought he was a ghost.
They were terrified and started screaming.

At once Jesus said to them, "Don't worry!
I am Jesus. Don't be afraid."

Peter replied, "Lord, if it is really you,
    tell me to come to you on the water."

"Come on!" Jesus said.
Peter then got out of the boat
    and started walking on the water toward him.

But when Peter saw how strong the wind was,
    he was afraid and started sinking.

"Lord, save me!" he shouted.

Right away Jesus reached out his hand.
He helped Peter up and said,
"You surely don't have much faith.
Why do you doubt?"

When Jesus and Peter got into the boat, the wind died down.
The men in the boat worshiped Jesus and said,
"You really are the Son of God!"

                                            The gospel of the Lord.

[111] NINETEENTH SUNDAY IN ORDINARY TIME B

FIRST READING

Strengthened by the food, Elijah walked to the mountain of the Lord.

A reading from the first book of Kings 19:4-8

Elijah walked through the desert for a whole day.
Finally, he came to a large bush and sat in its shade.
Then he prayed to die.
"Lord," he said, "I have had all I can take.
Let me die! I'm no better than my ancestors."
After saying this,
he lay in the shade of the bush and fell asleep.

Suddenly an angel touched Elijah and said, "Get up and eat!"
Elijah looked around,
and by his head was a jar of water
and some bread that had been baked over coals.
After eating and drinking, he lay back down.

Soon the Lord's angel came back and touched Elijah again.
This time the angel said, "Get up and eat,
or else the trip will be too hard for you."

The food gave Elijah strength,
and he traveled for forty more days
until he reached Mount Sinai, the mountain of God.

The word of the Lord.

RESPONSORIAL PSALM 34:1-2, 3-4, 7-8

℟. (9a) Taste and see the goodness of the Lord.

I will always praise the Lord.
With all my heart,
I will praise the Lord.
Let all who are helpless
listen and be glad.

℟. Taste and see the goodness of the Lord.

Honor the LORD with me!
Celebrate his great name.
I asked the LORD for help,
and he saved me
from all my fears.

℟. Taste and see the goodness of the Lord.

If you honor the LORD,
his angel will protect you.
Discover for yourself
that the LORD is kind.
Come to him for protection,
and you will be glad.

℟. Taste and see the goodness of the Lord.

SECOND READING

Walk in love, just as Christ.

A reading from the letter of Paul to the Ephesians   4:31—5:2

Brothers and sisters:
Stop being bitter and angry and mad at others.
Don't yell at one another or curse each other or ever be rude.
Instead, be kind and merciful,
    and forgive others, just as God forgave you because of Christ.

Do as God does.
After all, you are his dear children.
Let love be your guide.
Christ loved us and offered his life for us
    as a sacrifice that pleases God.

The word of the Lord.

ALLELUIA John 6:51

℟. Alleluia, alleluia.

**I am the living bread from heaven, says the Lord;
whoever eats this bread will live for ever.**

℟. Alleluia, alleluia.

GOSPEL

I am the living bread come down from heaven.

✢ **A reading from the holy gospel according to John** 6:48-51

Jesus said to the crowd:
"I am the bread that gives life!
Your ancestors ate manna in the desert,
    and later they died.
But the bread from heaven has come down,
    so that no one who eats it will ever die.

"I am that bread from heaven!
Everyone who eats it will live forever.
My flesh is the life-giving bread
    that I give to the people of this world."

The gospel of the Lord.

[112] NINETEENTH SUNDAY IN ORDINARY TIME C

FIRST READING

Abraham looked forward to the city designed and built by God.

A reading from the letter to the Hebrews 11:1-2, 8-12

Brothers and sisters:
Faith makes us sure of what we hope for
   and gives us proof of what we cannot see.
It was their faith that made our ancestors pleasing to God.

Abraham had faith and obeyed God.
He was told to go to the land that God had said would be his,
   and he left for a country he had never seen.

Because Abraham had faith,
   he lived as a stranger in the promised land.
He lived there in a tent,
   and so did Isaac and Jacob,
   who were later given the same promise.

Abraham did this,
   because he was waiting for the eternal city
      that God had planned and built.

Even when Sarah was too old to have children,
   she had faith that God would do what he had promised,
   and she had a son.
Her husband Abraham was almost dead,
   but he became the ancestor of many people.
In fact, there are as many of them as there are stars in the sky
   or grains of sand along the beach.

                                        The word of the Lord.

RESPONSORIAL PSALM
143:1, 8, 10

℟. (1a) O Lord, hear my prayer.

Listen, Lord, as I pray!
You are faithful and honest,
and will answer my prayer.

℟. O Lord, hear my prayer.

Each morning let me learn
more about your love
because I trust you.
I come to you in prayer,
asking for your guidance.

℟. O Lord, hear my prayer.

You are my God. Show me
what you want me to do,
and let your gentle Spirit
lead me in the right path.

℟. O Lord, hear my prayer.

ALLELUIA
Matthew 24:42a, 44

℟. Alleluia, alleluia.

Be watchful and ready:
you know not when the Son of Man is coming.

℟. Alleluia, alleluia.

GOSPEL

Be prepared.

✢ A reading from the holy gospel according to Luke   12:35-40

Jesus said to his disciples:
"Be ready and keep your lamps burning
    just like those servants who wait up
        for their master to return from a wedding feast.
As soon as he comes and knocks,
    they open the door for him.

"Servants are fortunate
    if their master finds them awake and ready when he comes!
I promise you that he will get ready
    and have his servants sit down so he can serve them.
Those servants are really fortunate if their master finds them ready,
    even though he comes late at night or early in the morning.

"You would surely not let a thief break into your home,
    if you knew when the thief was coming.
So always be ready!
You don't know when the Son of Man will come."

                                      The gospel of the Lord.

[113] TWENTIETH SUNDAY IN ORDINARY TIME   **A**

FIRST READING

I will lead the foreigners to my holy mountain.

A reading from the book of the prophet Isaiah   56:1, 6-7

The LORD said,
"Be honest and fair!

"Soon I will come to save you,
    and my saving power will be seen.
Foreigners will follow me.
They will love me and worship in my name.
They will respect the Sabbath and keep our agreement.

"Then I will bring them to my holy mountain
    and let them celebrate in my house of worship.
Their sacrifices and offerings will all be welcome on my altar.
And my house will be known as a house of worship for all nations."

The word of the Lord.

RESPONSORIAL PSALM   67:1-2, 4, 5 and 7

℟. (4) O God, let all the nations praise you!

**Our God, be kind and bless us!
Be pleased and smile.
Then everyone on earth
will learn to follow you,
and all nations will see
your power to save us.**

℟. O God, let all the nations praise you!

**Let the nations celebrate
with joyful songs,
because you judge fairly
and guide all nations.**

℟. O God, let all the nations praise you!

Make everyone praise you
and shout your praises.
Pray for his blessings to continue
and for everyone on earth
to worship our God.

℟. O God, let all the nations praise you!

ALLELUIA
See Matthew 4:23

℟. Alleluia, alleluia.

Jesus preached the good news of the kingdom
and healed all who were sick.

℟. Alleluia, alleluia.

GOSPEL

Woman, your faith is great.

✠ A reading from the holy gospel according to Matthew   15:21-28

Jesus went to the territory near the cities of Tyre and Sidon.
Suddenly a Canaanite woman from there came out shouting,
"Lord and Son of David, have pity on me!
My daughter is full of demons."

Jesus did not say a word.
But the woman kept following along and shouting,
    so his disciples came up and asked him to send her away.

Jesus said, "I was sent only to the people of Israel!
They are like a flock of lost sheep."

The woman came closer.
Then she kneeled down and begged,
"Lord, please help me!"

Jesus replied,
"It isn't right to take food away from children and feed it to dogs."

"Lord, that's true," the woman said,
    "but even dogs get the crumbs that fall from their owner's table."

Jesus answered, "Dear woman, you really do have a lot of faith,
    and you will be given what you want."

At that moment her daughter was healed.

The gospel of the Lord.

[114] TWENTIETH SUNDAY IN ORDINARY TIME B

FIRST READING

Come and eat my bread, drink the wine I have prepared.

A reading from the book of Proverbs 9:1-6

Wisdom has built her house with its seven columns.
She has prepared the meat and set out the wine.
Her feast is ready.

She has sent her servant women
 to announce her invitation from the highest hills.

"Everyone who is ignorant or foolish is invited!
All of you are welcome to my meat and wine.
If you want to live, give up your foolishness
and let understanding guide your steps."

The word of the Lord.

RESPONSORIAL PSALM 34:1-2, 9-10

℟. (9a) Taste and see the goodness of the Lord.

I will always praise the Lord.
With all my heart,
I will praise the Lord.
Let all who are helpless
listen and be glad.

℟. Taste and see the goodness of the Lord.

Honor the Lord!
You are his special people.
No one who honors the Lord
will ever be in need.
Young lions may go hungry
or even starve,
but if you trust the Lord,
you will never miss out
on anything good.

℟. Taste and see the goodness of the Lord.

SECOND READING

Be watchful that you may know the will of God.

A reading from the letter of Paul to the Ephesians 5:15-20

Brothers and sisters:
Act like people with good sense and not like fools.
These are evil times,
  so make every minute count.

Don't be stupid.
Instead, find out what the Lord wants you to do.
Don't destroy yourself by getting drunk,
  but let the Spirit fill your life.

When you meet together,
  sing psalms, hymns, and spiritual songs,
  as you praise the Lord with all your heart.
Always use the name of the Lord Jesus Christ
  to thank God the Father for everything.

The word of the Lord.

ALLELUIA John 6:56

℟. Alleluia, alleluia.
All who eat my flesh and drink my blood
live in me, and I in them, says the Lord.
℟. Alleluia, alleluia.

GOSPEL

My flesh is real food and my blood is real drink.

✛ A reading from the holy gospel according to John 6:51-58

Jesus said to the crowd:
"I am the bread from heaven!
Everyone who eats it will live forever.
My flesh is the life-giving bread
  that I give to the people of this world."

They started arguing with each other and asked,
"How can he give us his flesh to eat?"

Jesus answered:
"I tell you for certain that you won't live
    unless you eat the flesh and drink the blood of the Son of Man.
But if you do eat my flesh and drink my blood,
    you will have eternal life,
    and I will raise you to life on the last day.

"My flesh is the true food,
    and my blood is the true drink.
If you eat my flesh and drink my blood,
    you are one with me, and I am one with you.

"The living Father sent me,
    and I have life because of him.
Now everyone who eats my flesh will live because of me.

"The bread that comes down from heaven
      is not like what your ancestors ate.
They died,
    but whoever eats this bread will live forever."

The gospel of the Lord.

[115] TWENTIETH SUNDAY IN ORDINARY TIME C

FIRST READING

*You bore me to be a man of strife
for the whole world (Jeremiah 15:10).*

A reading from the book of the prophet Jeremiah   38:4-6, 8-10

The nation's leaders said to King Zedekiah,
"Jeremiah should be put to death!
He's saying things that are upsetting every soldier left in the city
    and everyone else as well.
He isn't trying to help anyone.
He just wants to cause trouble."

"Do what you want with him!" Zedekiah replied.
"I can't stop you."

So they took Jeremiah to the open courtyard where prisoners were kept.
Then they let him down with ropes
    into the cistern that belonged to Malchiah, the king's son.
There was no water in the cistern,
    and Jeremiah sank down in the mud.

Jeremiah's friend Ebedmelech went out of the palace
    and reported to the king,
"Your Majesty, those men were wrong
    to put Jeremiah the prophet down in a cistern.
There's no more food in the city,
    and he will starve to death."

The king then told Ebedmelech the Ethiopian,
"Take thirty men and pull Jeremiah out before he dies."

                                  The word of the Lord.

RESPONSORIAL PSALM   40:1, 2, 17

℟. (14b) Lord, come to my aid!

I patiently waited, LORD,
for you to hear my prayer.

    ℟. Lord, come to my aid!

You listened and pulled me
from a lonely pit
full of mud and mire.
You let me stand on a rock
with my feet firm.

> ℟. Lord, come to my aid!

I am poor and needy,
but, LORD God,
you care about me,
and you come to my rescue.
Please hurry and help.

> ℟. Lord, come to my aid!

SECOND READING

Let us persevere in running the race that lies ahead.

A reading from the letter to the Hebrews 12:1-4

Brothers and sisters:
Such a large crowd of witnesses is all around us!
So we must get rid of everything that slows us down,
> especially the sin that just won't let go.
And we must be determined to run the race that is ahead of us.

We must keep our eyes on Jesus,
> who leads us and makes our faith complete.
He endured the shame of being nailed to a cross,
> because he knew that later on he would be glad he did.
Now he is seated at the right side of God's throne!

So keep your mind on Jesus,
> who put up with many insults from sinners.
Then you won't get discouraged and give up.

None of you have yet been hurt in your battle against sin.

The word of the Lord.

ALLELUIA
John 10:27

℟. Alleluia, alleluia.

**My sheep listen to my voice, says the Lord;
I know them, and they follow me.**

℟. Alleluia, alleluia.

GOSPEL

I have come not to give peace, but discord.

✢ **A reading from the holy gospel according to Luke**   12:49-53

Jesus said to his disciples:
"I came to set fire to the earth,
   and I surely wish it were already on fire!

"I am going to be put to a hard test.
And I will have to suffer a lot of pain until it is over.

"Do you think that I came to bring peace to earth?
No indeed!
I came to make people choose sides.
A family of five will be divided,
      with two of them against the other three.
Fathers and sons will turn against one another,
      and mothers and daughters will do the same.
Mothers-in-law and daughters-in-law
      will also turn against each other."

The gospel of the Lord.

[116] TWENTY-FIRST SUNDAY IN ORDINARY TIME **A**

FIRST READING

From Christ, through him, and in him are all things.

A reading from the letter of Paul to the Romans 11:33-36

Brothers and sisters:
Who can measure the wealth and wisdom and knowledge of God?
Who can understand his decisions or explain what he does?

> "Has anyone ever known the thoughts of the Lord
> or given him advice?
> Has anyone loaned something to the Lord
> that must be repaid?"

Everything comes from the Lord.
All things were made because of him and will return to him.
Praise the Lord forever! Amen.

The word of the Lord.

RESPONSORIAL PSALM 138:1-2a, 2bc and 3, 6 and 8cde

℟. (8b) Lord, your love is eternal.

With all my heart
I praise you, LORD.
In the presence of angels
I sing your praises.
I worship at your holy temple.

℟. Lord, your love is eternal.

I praise you for your love
and your faithfulness.
When I asked for your help,
you answered my prayer
and gave me courage.

℟. Lord, your love is eternal.

Though you are above us all,
you care for humble people,
and you keep a close watch
on everyone who is proud.

Your love never fails.
You have made us what we are.
Don't give up on us now!

℟. Lord, your love is eternal.

ALLELUIA

Matthew 16:18

℟. Alleluia, alleluia.

You are Peter, the rock on which I will build my Church;
the gates of hell will not prevail against it.

℟. Alleluia, alleluia.

GOSPEL

You are Peter; to you I will give the keys of the kingdom of heaven.

✠ A reading from the holy gospel according to Matthew   16:13-20

When Jesus and his disciples were near the town of Caesarea Philippi, he asked them, "What do people say about the Son of Man?"

The disciples answered, "Some people say you are John the Baptist
 or maybe Elijah or Jeremiah or some other prophet."

Then Jesus asked them, "But who do you say I am?"

Simon Peter spoke up,
"You are the Messiah, the Son of the living God."

Jesus told him:
"Simon, son of Jonah, you are blessed!
You didn't discover this on your own.
It was shown to you by my Father in heaven.
So I will call you Peter, which means 'a rock.'
On this rock I will build my Church,
 and death itself will not have any power over it.
I will give you the keys to the kingdom of heaven,
 and God in heaven will allow whatever you allow on earth.
But he will not allow anything that you don't allow."

Jesus told his disciples not to tell anyone that he was the Messiah.

The gospel of the Lord.

[117] TWENTY-FIRST SUNDAY IN ORDINARY TIME B

FIRST READING

We will serve the Lord God, because he is our God.

A reading from the book of Joshua
24:1-2a, 15-17, 18b

Joshua brought together all the tribes of Israel at Shechem.
Then he told their leaders, judges, and officials
>   to come into the presence of God.

Joshua told all of them what the LORD, the God of Israel, had said.
He also told them, "If you don't want to serve the LORD,
>   then today you must choose the god you will serve.

You may choose the gods your ancestors worshiped
>   on the other side of the river.

Or you may even choose one of the gods of the Amorites,
>   since you are living in their land.

But as for me and everyone in my family,
>   we will serve the LORD!"

The people answered,
"We will never turn away from the LORD to serve other gods!
It was the LORD who brought us and our ancestors out of Egypt.
And with our own eyes we saw the powerful miracles he performed
>   to protect us during all the time
>   that we traveled through the nations.

The LORD is our God, and we will serve him too!"

The word of the Lord.

RESPONSORIAL PSALM
34:1-2, 17-18, 19-20

℟. (9a) Taste and see the goodness of the Lord.

I will always praise the LORD.
With all my heart,
I will praise the LORD.
Let all who are helpless
listen and be glad.

℟. Taste and see the goodness of the Lord.

When his people pray for help,
he listens and he rescues them
from their troubles.
The LORD is there to rescue
all who are discouraged
and have given up hope.

℟. Taste and see the goodness of the Lord.

The LORD's people
may suffer a lot,
but he will always
bring them safely through.
Not one of their bones
will ever be broken.

℟. Taste and see the goodness of the Lord.

SECOND READING

Honor your father and your mother.

A reading from the letter of Paul to the Ephesians   6:1-4

Children, you belong to the Lord,
and you do the right thing when you obey your parents.
The first commandment with a promise says,

"Obey your father and your mother,
and you will have a long and happy life."

Parents, don't be hard on your children.
Raise them properly.
Teach them and instruct them about the Lord.

The word of the Lord.

ALLELUIA

See John 6:63, 68c

℟. Alleluia, alleluia.

**Your words, Lord, are spirit and life;
you have the words of everlasting life.**

℟. Alleluia, alleluia.

GOSPEL

To whom shall we go?
You have the words of everlasting life.

✚ A reading from the holy gospel according to John   6:60-69

Many of Jesus' disciples heard him speak
        about the bread of life and said,
"This is too hard for anyone to understand."

Jesus knew that many of his disciples were grumbling.
So he asked, "Does this bother you?
What if you should see the Son of Man
        go up to heaven where he came from?

"The Spirit is the one who gives life!
Human strength can do nothing.
The words that I have spoken to you are from that life-giving Spirit.
But some of you refuse to have faith in me."

Jesus said this,
      because from the beginning he knew who would have faith in him.
He also knew which one would betray him.

Then Jesus said, "You cannot come to me,
      unless the Father makes you want to come.
That is why I have told these things to all of you."

Because of what Jesus said,
      many of his disciples turned their backs on him
            and stopped following him.

Jesus then asked his twelve disciples if they were going to leave him.
Simon Peter answered,
"Lord, there is no one else that we can go to!
Your words give eternal life.
We have faith in you,
      and we are sure that you are God's Holy One."

                              The gospel of the Lord.

[118] TWENTY-FIRST SUNDAY IN ORDINARY TIME   C

FIRST READING

The Lord disciplines those he loves.

A reading from the letter to the Hebrews   12:5a, 6-7, 11

Brothers and sisters:
You have forgotten that the Scriptures say to God's children,

> "When the Lord punishes you, don't make light of it.
> The Lord corrects the people he loves
> and disciplines those he calls his own."

Be patient when you are being corrected!
This is how the Lord treats his children.
Don't all parents correct their children?

It is never fun to be corrected.
In fact, at the time it is always painful.
But if we learn to obey by being corrected,
> we will do right and live at peace.

The word of the Lord.

RESPONSORIAL PSALM   119:165, 168, 171

℟. (165a) O Lord, great peace have they who love your law.

LORD, you give peace of mind
to all who love your Law.
Nothing can make them fall.

℟. O Lord, great peace have they who love your law.

You know everything I do.
You know I respect every law
you have given.

℟. O Lord, great peace have they who love your law.

If you will teach me your laws,
I will praise you.

℟. O Lord, great peace have they who love your law.

ALLELUIA
John 14:6

℟. Alleluia, alleluia.

I am the way, the truth, and the life, says the Lord;
no one comes to the Father, except through me.

℟. Alleluia, alleluia.

GOSPEL

*They will come from east and west to take their places
at the feast in the kingdom of God.*

✢ A reading from the holy gospel according to Luke
13:22-30

As Jesus was on his way to Jerusalem,
he taught the people in the towns and villages.
Someone asked him, "Lord, are only a few people going to be saved?"
Jesus answered:
"Do all you can to go in by the narrow door!
A lot of people will try to get in,
    but will not be able to.
Once the owner of the house gets up and locks the door,
    you will be left standing outside.
You will knock on the door and say,
'Sir, open the door for us!'

"But the owner will answer,
'I don't know a thing about you!'

"Then you will start saying,
'We dined with you, and you taught in our streets.'

"But he will say,
'I really don't know who you are!
Get away from me, all you evil people!'

"Then when you have been thrown outside,
    you will weep and grit your teeth
    because you will see Abraham and Isaac
        and all the prophets in God's kingdom.
People will come from all directions
    and sit down to feast in God's kingdom.
There the ones who are now least important will be the most important,
    and those who are now most important will be least important."

The gospel of the Lord.

[119] TWENTY-SECOND SUNDAY IN ORDINARY TIME **A**

FIRST READING

The word of the Lord God has meant derision for me.

A reading from the book of the prophet Jeremiah   20:7-9

Jeremiah spoke to the Lord and said:
"You tricked me, Lord, and I was really fooled.
With your mighty power you defeated me.

"No one ever stops sneering or telling jokes about me.
All I can say to anyone is, 'Death and destruction!'

"Your message has brought me insults and abuse.
Sometimes I say to myself,
   'I won't think about you or mention your name.'
But your message is like a fire burning inside me,
   and I can't keep quiet."

The word of the Lord.

RESPONSORIAL PSALM   63:1abc, 2-3, 4-5

℟. (2b) My soul is thirsting for you, O Lord my God.

You are my God. I worship you.
In my heart, I long for you,
as I would long for a stream.

℟. My soul is thirsting for you, O Lord my God.

I have seen your power
and your glory
in the place of worship.
Your love means more
than life to me,
and I praise you.

℟. My soul is thirsting for you, O Lord my God.

As long as I live,
I will pray to you.
I will sing joyful praises
and be filled with excitement
like a guest at a banquet.

℟. My soul is thirsting for you, O Lord my God.

SECOND READING

Offer your bodies as a living, holy sacrifice.

A reading from the letter of Paul to the Romans　　　　　12:1-2

Dear friends, God is good.
So I beg you to offer your bodies to him
　　as a living sacrifice, pure and pleasing.
That's the most sensible way to serve God.

Don't be like the people of this world,
　　but let God change the way you think.
Then you will know
　　　how to do everything that is good and pleasing to him.

The word of the Lord.

ALLELUIA　　　　　　　　　　　　　　　　　　See Ephesians 1:17-18

℟. Alleluia, alleluia.

May the Father of our Lord Jesus Christ
enlighten the eyes of our heart,
that we might see how great is the hope
to which we are called.

℟. Alleluia, alleluia.

GOSPEL

All who wish to follow me must deny themselves.

✢ A reading from the holy gospel according to Matthew   16:21-25

Jesus began telling his disciples what would happen to him.
He said, "I must go to Jerusalem.
There the nation's leaders, the chief priests,
    and the teachers of the Law of Moses will make me suffer terribly.
I will be killed,
    but three days later I will rise to life."

Peter took Jesus aside and told him to stop talking like that.
He said, "Lord, surely God won't let this happen to you!"

Jesus turned to Peter and said, "Satan, get away from me!
You're in my way because you think like everyone else
    and not like God."

Then Jesus said to his disciples:
"If any of you want to be my followers,
    you must forget about yourself.
You must take up your cross and follow me.
If you want to save your life,
    you will destroy it.

"But if you give up your life for me,
    you will find it."

                                      The gospel of the Lord.

[120] TWENTY-SECOND SUNDAY IN ORDINARY TIME B

FIRST READING

You may add nothing to the word which I speak to you; keep the commands of the Lord.

A reading from the book of Deuteronomy   4:1-2, 6-8

Moses said:
"People of Israel,
   listen carefully to the laws and commands that I am teaching you.
If you obey them, you will live,
   and you will take the land
     that the Lord God of your ancestors is giving you.
I am telling you what the Lord your God has commanded.
Don't add anything or take anything away.

"By faithfully obeying these commands,
   you will show other nations how wise and understanding you are.
They will learn about these laws and say,
   'This great nation is very wise and understanding.'

"No other great nation has a god who is close enough
     to answer their prayers,
   as the Lord God does for us.
And no other great nation has laws
   that are as fair as the ones I am giving you today."

The word of the Lord.

RESPONSORIAL PSALM   15:2-3a, 3bc and 5ef

℟. (1a) The just will live in the presence of the Lord.

**Only those who obey God
and do as they should
speak the truth
and don't spread gossip.**

℟. The just will live in the presence of the Lord.

They treat others fairly
and don't say cruel things.
Those who do these things
will always stand firm.

℟. The just will live in the presence of the Lord.

SECOND READING

Be doers of the word.

A reading from the letter of James 1:17-18, 21b-22

Brothers and sisters:
Every good and perfect gift comes down from the Father
who created all the lights in the heavens.
He is always the same and never makes dark shadows by changing.
He wanted us to be his own special people,
and so he sent the true message to give us new birth.

Be humble and accept the message that is planted in you to save you.

Obey God's message!
Don't fool yourselves by just listening to it.

The word of the Lord.

ALLELUIA James 1:18

℟. Alleluia, alleluia.

**The Father gave us birth by his message of truth,
that we might be as the first fruits of his creation.**

℟. Alleluia, alleluia.

GOSPEL

You forget the commandments of God and hold on to human tradition.

✚ **A reading from the holy gospel according to Mark** 7:1-5, 14-16, 21-23

Some Pharisees and several teachers of the Law of Moses from Jerusalem
  came and gathered around Jesus.
They noticed that some of his disciples
  ate without first washing their hands.

The Pharisees and all other Jewish people
  obey the teachings of their ancestors.
They always wash their hands in the proper way before eating.
None of them will eat anything they buy in the market
  until it is washed.
They also follow a lot of other teachings,
  such as washing cups, pitchers, and bowls.

The Pharisees and teachers asked Jesus,
"Why don't your disciples obey what our ancestors taught us to do?
Why do they eat without washing their hands?"

Jesus called the crowd together again and said,
"Pay attention and try to understand what I mean.
The food that you put into your mouth
  does not make you unclean and unfit to worship God.
The bad words that come out of your mouth are what make you unclean.

"Out of your heart come evil thoughts, vulgar deeds,
  stealing, murder, unfaithfulness in marriage,
  greed, meanness, deceit,
  indecency, envy, insults, pride, and foolishness.
All of these come from your heart,
  and they are what make you unfit to worship God."

            The gospel of the Lord.

[121] TWENTY-SECOND SUNDAY IN ORDINARY TIME C

FIRST READING

Humble yourself and you will find favor with the Lord.

A reading from the book of Sirach　　　　　　　　　　3:17-18, 20

My child, always be humble,
　and all of God's people will love you.
The more important you are,
　the more humble you should be.
This will please the Lord.
The Lord has great power,
　and it is praised by those who are humble.

The word of the Lord.

RESPONSORIAL PSALM　　　　　　　　　68:3-4acdef, 5-6abcd, 9-10

℟. (see 11b) God, in your goodness, you have made a home for the poor.

Our God, let your people be happy
and celebrate because of you.
Our God, you are the one
and we praise you.
Your name is the Lord,
and we celebrate
as we worship you.

℟. God, in your goodness, you have made a home for the poor.

Our God, from your sacred home
you take care of orphans
and protect widows.
You find families
for those who are lonely.
You set prisoners free
and let them prosper.

℟. God, in your goodness, you have made a home for the poor.

When your land was thirsty,
you sent showers
to refresh it.
Your people settled there,
and you were generous
to everyone in need.

℟. God, in your goodness, you have made a home for the poor.

ALLELUIA
Matthew 11:29ab

℟. Alleluia, alleluia.

Take my yoke upon you;
learn from me, for I am gentle and humble of heart.

℟. Alleluia, alleluia.

GOSPEL

*All who exalt themselves shall be humbled,
and all who humble themselves shall be exalted.*

✝ **A reading from the holy gospel according to Luke** 14:1, 7-14

One Sabbath Jesus was having dinner
 in the home of an important Pharisee,
and everyone was carefully watching Jesus.

Jesus saw how the guests had tried to take the best seats.
So he told them:
"When you are invited to a wedding feast,
 don't sit in the best place.
Someone more important may have been invited.
Then the one who invited you will come and say,
'Give your place to this other guest!'
You will be embarrassed and will have to sit in the worst place.

"When you are invited to be a guest,
 go and sit in the worst place.
Then the one who invited you may come and say,
'My friend, take a better seat!'
You will then be honored in front of all the other guests.
If you put yourself above others,
 you will be put down.
But if you humble yourself,
 you will be honored."

Then Jesus said to the man who had invited him:
"When you give a dinner or a banquet,
 don't invite your friends and family
  and relatives and rich neighbors.
If you do, they will invite you in return,
 and you will be paid back.
When you give a feast,
 invite the poor, the crippled, the lame, and the blind.
They cannot pay you back.
But God will bless you and reward you
 when his people rise from death."

The gospel of the Lord.

[122] TWENTY-THIRD SUNDAY IN ORDINARY TIME **A**

FIRST READING

*If you have not warned the wicked,
then I will hold you responsible for their death.*

A reading from the book of the prophet Ezekiel   33:7-9

The Lord said:
"Ezekiel, you are a mere human,
   but I have chosen you to be a watchman for the people of Israel.
So listen to what I say
   and then warn them for me.

"When I tell evil people that they will die because of their sins,
   you must try to make them turn from their evil ways.
If you don't warn them,
   you are responsible for what happens to them.
If you do warn them to turn from their evil ways, and they don't,
   then they will die.
But you won't be responsible."

The word of the Lord.

RESPONSORIAL PSALM   95:1-2, 6-7abcd, 7e-9

℟. (8) If today you hear God's voice, harden not your hearts.

Sing joyful songs to the LORD!
Praise the mighty rock
where we are safe.
Come to worship him
with thankful hearts
and songs of praise.

℟. If today you hear God's voice, harden not your hearts.

Bow down and worship
the LORD our Creator!
The LORD is our God,
and we are his people,
the sheep he takes care of
in his own pasture.

℟. If today you hear God's voice, harden not your hearts.

**Listen to God's voice today!
Don't be stubborn and rebel
as your ancestors did
at Meribah and at Massah
out in the desert.
For forty years
they tested God and saw
the things he did.**

℟. If today you hear God's voice, harden not your hearts.

SECOND READING

Love is the fulfillment of the law.

A reading from the letter of Paul to the Romans   13:8-10

Brothers and sisters:
Let love be your only debt!
**If you love others,
you have done all that the Law demands.**

In the Law there are many commands, such as,

"**Be faithful in marriage.
Do not murder. Do not steal.
Do not want what belongs to others.**"

But all of these are summed up in the command that says,
"**Love others as much as you love yourself.**"
No one who loves others will harm them.

So love is all that the Law demands.

The word of the Lord.

ALLELUIA   2 Corinthians 5:19

℟. Alleluia, alleluia.

**God was in Christ, to reconcile the world to himself;
and the good news of reconciliation he has entrusted to us.**

℟. Alleluia, alleluia.

GOSPEL

*If your brother or sister listens to you,
you will have won that person back.*

✞ **A reading from the holy gospel according to Matthew** 18:15-17

Jesus said to his disciples:
"If one of my followers sins against you,
  go and point out what was wrong.
But do it in private,
  just between the two of you.
If that person listens,
  you have won back a follower.
But if that one refuses to listen,
  take along one or two others.

"The Scriptures teach that every complaint must be proven true
    by two or more witnesses.
If the follower refuses to listen to them,
  report the matter to the church.

"Anyone who refuses to listen to the church
    must be treated like an unbeliever or a tax collector."

The gospel of the Lord.

[123] TWENTY-THIRD SUNDAY IN ORDINARY TIME B

FIRST READING

> Then the ears of those who are deaf shall be opened
> and the tongues of those who are mute shout for joy.

A reading from the book of the prophet Isaiah   35:4-7a

**The people were worried.
So the LORD told Isaiah to say to them:
Cheer up! Don't be afraid.
Your God is coming to punish your enemies.
God will take revenge on them and rescue you.**

**The blind will see,
   and the deaf will hear.
The disabled will leap about like deer,
   and tongues once silent will shout.
Water will rush through the desert.
Scorching sands will turn into lakes,
   and thirsty ground will become fountains.**

The word of the Lord.

RESPONSORIAL PSALM   146:6d-7, 7c-9a, 9bcd-10

℟. (1b) Praise the Lord, my soul!
or:
℟. Alleluia.

**God always keeps his word.
He gives justice to the poor
and food to the hungry.**

℟. Praise the Lord, my soul!
or:
℟. Alleluia.

**The LORD sets prisoners free
and heals blind eyes.
He gives a helping hand
to everyone who falls.
The LORD loves good people
and looks after strangers.**

℟. Praise the Lord, my soul!
or:
℟. Alleluia.

**He defends the rights
of orphans and widows,
but destroys the wicked.
The Lord God of Zion
will rule forever!
Shout praises to the Lord!**

℟. Praise the Lord, my soul!
or:
℟. Alleluia.

SECOND READING

Has not God chosen the poor of the world to inherit the kingdom?

A reading from the letter of James   2:1-5

**My friends,
if you have faith in our glorious Lord Jesus Christ,
   you won't treat some people better than others.**

**Suppose a rich person wearing fancy clothes and a gold ring
      comes to one of your meetings.
And suppose a poor person dressed in worn-out clothes also comes.**

**You must not give the best seat to the one in fancy clothes
         and tell the one who is poor
         to stand at the side or sit on the floor.
That is the same as saying that some people are better than others,
      and you would be acting like a crooked judge.**

**My dear friends, pay attention.
God has given a lot of faith to the poor people in this world.
He has also promised them a share in his kingdom
      that he will give to everyone who loves him.**

The word of the Lord.

TWENTY-THIRD SUNDAY IN ORDINARY TIME — B

ALLELUIA   See Matthew 4:23

℟. Alleluia, alleluia.

**Jesus preached the good news of the kingdom
and healed all who were sick.**

℟. Alleluia, alleluia.

GOSPEL

Jesus has made those who are deaf hear and those who are mute speak.

✠ A reading from the holy gospel according to Mark   7:31-37

Jesus left the region around Tyre
      and went by way of Sidon toward Lake Galilee.
He went through the land near the ten cities known as Decapolis.

Some people brought to him
      a man who was deaf and could hardly talk.
They begged Jesus just to touch him.

After Jesus had taken him aside from the crowd,
    he stuck his fingers in the man's ears.
Then he spit and put it on the man's tongue.
Jesus looked up toward heaven,
    and with a groan he said,
"Effatha!" which means "Open up!"
At once the man could hear,
    and he had no more trouble talking clearly.

Jesus told the people not to say anything about what he had done.
But the more he told them,
    the more they talked about it.
They were completely amazed and said,
"Everything he does is good!
He even heals people who cannot hear or talk."

                                                                     The gospel of the Lord.

[124] TWENTY-THIRD SUNDAY IN ORDINARY TIME C

FIRST READING

Who can comprehend the will of God?

A reading from the book of Wisdom 9:16c-18

No one really knows what is in the heavens.
And, Lord, we cannot know what you have planned,
unless you send down Wisdom and your Holy Spirit.

**Wisdom makes straight paths for those who live on earth.
She teaches us what pleases you,
and by Wisdom we are saved.**

The word of the Lord.

RESPONSORIAL PSALM 90:12-13, 14abc and 17

℟. (1) In every age, O Lord, you have been our refuge.

**Our Lord, teach us to use wisely
all the time we have.
Help us, Lord! Don't wait!
Pity your servants.**

℟. In every age, O Lord, you have been our refuge.

**When morning comes,
let your love satisfy
all our needs.
Our Lord and our God,
treat us with kindness
and let all go well for us.
Please let all go well!**

℟. In every age, O Lord, you have been our refuge.

ALLELUIA
Psalm 119:135

℟. Alleluia, alleluia.

**Let your face shine on your servant,
and teach me your laws.**

℟. Alleluia, alleluia.

GOSPEL

*Unless you are ready to give up all that you possess,
you cannot be my disciple.*

✠ **A reading from the holy gospel according to Luke** 14:25-27

Large crowds were walking along with Jesus,
when he turned and said:

"You cannot be my disciple
    unless you love me more than you love your father and mother,
    your wife and children, and your brothers and sisters.
You cannot come with me
    unless you love me more than you love your own life.

"You cannot be my disciple
    unless you carry your own cross and come with me."

The gospel of the Lord.

[125] TWENTY-FOURTH SUNDAY IN ORDINARY TIME **A**

FIRST READING

> Forgive your neighbor's faults, and when you pray,
> your sins will be forgiven.

A reading from the book of Sirach 28:2-5, 6b-7

If you forgive your friends when they mistreat you,
    your prayers will be answered and your sins forgiven.
If you stay angry with someone,
    don't expect the Lord to heal you.
Don't ask God to forgive you,
    if you don't have pity on others.
God won't forgive you,
    if you stay angry at someone.

So stop holding grudges and start obeying God.
Think about the commands and the promise of God Most High.
Then forget about the sins and the ignorance of others.

The word of the Lord.

RESPONSORIAL PSALM 103:1-2, 3-4, 11-12

℟. (8a) The Lord is kind and merciful.

With all my heart
I praise the LORD**,**
and with all that I am
I praise his holy name!
With all my heart
I praise the LORD**!**
I will never forget
how kind he has been.

℟. The Lord is kind and merciful.

The LORD forgives our sins,
heals us when we are sick,
and protects us from death.
His kindness and love
are a crown on our heads.

℟. The Lord is kind and merciful.

How great is God's love for all
who worship him?
Greater than the distance
between heaven and earth!
How far has the LORD taken
our sins from us?
Farther than the distance
from east to west!

℟. The Lord is kind and merciful.

SECOND READING

Whether alive or dead, we belong to the Lord.

A reading from the letter of Paul to the Romans 14:7-9

Brothers and sisters:
 Whether we live or die,
  it must be for God, rather than for ourselves.
Whether we live or die,
  it must be for the Lord.
Alive or dead,
  we still belong to the Lord.
This is because Christ died and rose to life,
  so that he would be the Lord of the dead and of the living.

The word of the Lord.

ALLELUIA

John 13:34

℟. Alleluia, alleluia.

I give you a new commandment:
love one another as I have loved you.

℟. Alleluia, alleluia.

GOSPEL

*I did not say to you to forgive seven times,
but seventy-seven times.*

✣ **A reading from the holy gospel according to Matthew**   18:21-35

Peter came up to the Lord and asked,
"How many times should I forgive
      someone who does something wrong to me?
Is seven times enough?"

Jesus answered:
"Not just seven times, but seventy-seven times!
This story will show you what the kingdom of heaven is like:

"One day a king decided to call in his officials
      and ask them to give an account of what they owed him.
As he was doing this,
   one official was brought in
      who owed him fifty million silver coins.
But he didn't have any money to pay what he owed.
The king ordered him to be sold,
      along with his wife and children and all he owned,
      in order to pay the debt.

"The official got down on his knees and began begging,
'Have pity on me, and I will pay you every cent I owe!'
The king felt sorry for him and let him go free.
He even told the official that he did not have to pay back the money.

"As the official was leaving,
   he happened to meet another official,
      who owed him a hundred silver coins.
So he grabbed the man by the throat.
He started choking him and said, 'Pay me what you owe!'

"The man got down on his knees and began begging,
'Have pity on me, and I will pay you back.'
But the first official refused to have pity.
Instead, he went and had the other official put in jail
   until he could pay what he owed.

"When some other officials found out what had happened,
    they felt sorry for the man who had been put in jail.

"Then they told the king what had happened.
The king called the first official back in and said,
'You're an evil man!
When you begged for mercy,
    I said you did not have to pay back a cent.
Don't you think you should show pity to someone else,
    as I did to you?'

"The king was so angry that he ordered the official to be tortured
    until he could pay back everything he owed.
That is how my Father in heaven will treat you,
    if you don't forgive each of my followers
        with all your heart."

The gospel of the Lord.

[126] TWENTY-FOURTH SUNDAY IN ORDINARY TIME B

FIRST READING

I gave my body to those who struck me.

A reading from the book of the prophet Isaiah   50:4-8a

The LORD All-Powerful gives me just the right words
>   to comfort the weary.
Each morning he makes me eager to learn his teaching.

The LORD All-Powerful made me willing to listen
>   and not rebel or run away.
And so, I let them beat my back and pull out my beard.
I didn't turn aside when they made fun of me
>   and spit in my face.

But the LORD God keeps me from being embarrassed.
And I refuse to give up,
>   because I know I will never be ashamed.
My Protector is nearby.
No one can stand here and accuse me of any wrong.

> The word of the Lord.

RESPONSORIAL PSALM   116:1-2, 5-6, 8-9

℟. (9a) I will walk in the presence of the Lord.

I love you, LORD!
You answered my prayers.
You paid attention to me,
and so I will pray to you
as long as I live.

℟. I will walk in the presence of the Lord.

You are kind, LORD,
and good and merciful.
You protect ordinary people,
and when I was helpless,
you saved me.

℟. I will walk in the presence of the Lord.

You, LORD, have saved
my life from death,
my eyes from tears,
my feet from stumbling.
Now I will walk at your side
in this land of the living.

℟. I will walk in the presence of the Lord.

SECOND READING

Faith without good works is dead.

A reading from the letter of James   2:14-18

My friends,
what good is it to say you have faith,
  when you don't do anything
    to show that you really do have faith?
Can that kind of faith save you?

If you know someone who doesn't have any clothes or food,
  you shouldn't just say, "I hope all goes well for you.
I hope you will be warm and have plenty to eat."

What good is it to say this,
  unless you do something to help?
Faith that doesn't lead us to do good deeds is all alone and dead!

Suppose someone disagrees and says,
"It is possible to have faith without doing kind deeds."

I would answer, "Prove that you have faith without doing kind deeds,
  and I will prove that I have faith by doing them."

The word of the Lord.

ALLELUIA   Galatians 6:14

℟. Alleluia, alleluia.

My only glory is the cross of our Lord Jesus Christ,
which crucifies the world to me and me to the world.

℟. Alleluia, alleluia.

GOSPEL

You must take up your cross and follow me.

✤ A reading from the holy gospel according to Mark   8:31-35

Jesus began telling his disciples what would happen to him.
He said, "The nation's leaders, the chief priests,
    and the teachers of the Law of Moses
    will make the Son of Man suffer terribly.
He will be rejected and killed,
    but three days later he will rise to life."

Then Jesus explained clearly what he meant.

Peter took Jesus aside and told him to stop talking like that.
But when Jesus turned and saw the disciples,
    he corrected Peter.
He said to him, "Satan, get away from me!
You are thinking like everyone else and not like God."

Jesus then told the crowd and the disciples to come closer,
    and he said:

"If any of you want to be my followers,
    you must forget about yourself.
You must take up your cross and follow me.
If you want to save your life,
    you will destroy it.
But if you give up your life for me and for the good news,
    you will save it."

The gospel of the Lord.

[127] TWENTY-FOURTH SUNDAY IN ORDINARY TIME C

FIRST READING

Christ came to save sinners.

A reading from the first letter of Paul to Timothy   1:12-15b

I thank Christ Jesus our Lord.
He has given me the strength for my work
    because he knew that he could trust me.

I used to say terrible and insulting things about him,
    and I was cruel.
But he had mercy on me
    because I didn't know what I was doing,
    and I had not yet put my faith in him.
Christ Jesus our Lord was very kind to me.
He has greatly blessed my life
    with faith and love just like his own.

Christ Jesus came into the world to save sinners,
    and I was the worst sinner of all!

                                          The word of the Lord.

RESPONSORIAL PSALM   111:1-2, 3-4, 7-8

℟. (7a) Your works, O Lord, are justice and truth.
or:
℟. Alleluia.

Shout praises to the Lord!
With all my heart
I will thank the Lord
when his people meet.
The Lord has done
many wonderful things!

Everyone who is pleased
with God's marvelous deeds
will keep them in mind.

> ℟. Your works, O Lord, are justice and truth.
> or:
> ℟. Alleluia.

Everything the Lord does
is glorious and majestic,
and his power to bring justice
will never end.
The Lord God is famous
for his wonderful deeds,
and he is kind and merciful.

> ℟. Your works, O Lord, are justice and truth.
> or:
> ℟. Alleluia.

God is always honest and fair,
and his laws can be trusted.
They are true and right
and will stand forever.

> ℟. Your works, O Lord, are justice and truth.
> or:
> ℟. Alleluia.

ALLELUIA   2 Corinthians 5:19

> ℟. Alleluia, alleluia.

**God was in Christ, to reconcile the world to himself;
and the good news of reconciliation he has entrusted to us.**

> ℟. Alleluia, alleluia.

GOSPEL

> There will be great rejoicing in heaven
> over one repentant sinner.

✢ A reading from the holy gospel according to Luke   15:11-32

Jesus told the people this story:
"Once a man had two sons.
The younger son said to his father,
'Give me my share of the property.'
So the father divided his property between his two sons.

"Not long after that,
    the younger son packed up everything he owned
        and left for a foreign country,
    where he wasted all his money in wild living.
He had spent everything,
    when a bad famine spread through that whole land.
Soon he had nothing to eat.

"He went to work for a man in that country,
    and the man sent him out to take care of his pigs.
He would have been glad to eat what the pigs were eating,
    but no one gave him a thing.

"Finally, he came to his senses and said,
'My father's workers have plenty to eat,
    and here I am, starving to death!
I will leave and go to my father and say to him,
"Father, I have sinned against God in heaven and against you.
I am no longer good enough to be called your son.
Treat me like one of your workers." '

"The younger son got up and started back to his father.
But when he was still a long way off,
    his father saw him and felt sorry for him.
He ran to his son and hugged and kissed him.

"The son said,
'Father, I have sinned against God in heaven and against you.
I am no longer good enough to be called your son.'

"But his father said to the servants,
'Hurry and bring the best clothes and put them on him.
Give him a ring for his finger and sandals for his feet.
Get the best calf and prepare it,
    so we can eat and celebrate.
This son of mine was dead,
    but has now come back to life.
He was lost and has now been found.'
And they began to celebrate.

"The older son had been out in the field.
But when he came near the house,
    he heard the music and dancing.
So he called one of the servants over and asked,
'What's going on here?'

"The servant answered,
'Your brother has come home safe and sound,
    and your father ordered us to kill the best calf.'
The older brother got so mad
    that he would not even go into the house.

"His father came out and begged him to go in.
But he said to his father,
'For years I have worked for you like a slave
    and have always obeyed you.
But you have never even given me a little goat,
    so that I could give a dinner for my friends.
This other son of yours wasted your money on bad women.
And now that he has come home,
    you ordered the best calf to be killed for a feast.'

"His father replied,
'My son, you are always with me,
    and everything I have is yours.
But we should be glad and celebrate!
Your brother was dead,
    but he is now alive.
He was lost and has now been found.' "

The gospel of the Lord.

[128] TWENTY-FIFTH SUNDAY IN ORDINARY TIME A

FIRST READING

My thoughts are not your thoughts.

A reading from the book of the prophet Isaiah   55:6-9

Turn to the Lord!
He can still be found.
Call out to him.
He is near.
Give up your wicked ways and your evil thoughts.
Return to the Lord our God.
He will be merciful and forgive all your sins.

The Lord says: "My thoughts and my ways are not like yours.
Just as the heavens are higher than the earth,
 my thoughts and my ways are higher than yours."

The word of the Lord.

RESPONSORIAL PSALM   145:2-3, 8-9, 17-18

℟. (18a) The Lord is near to all who call on him.

Lord, I will praise you each day
and always honor your name.
You are wonderful, Lord,
and you deserve all praise,
because you are much greater
than anyone can understand.

℟. The Lord is near to all who call on him.

You are merciful, Lord!
You are kind and patient
and always loving.
You are good to everyone,
and you take care
of all your creation.

℟. The Lord is near to all who call on him.

Our LORD, everything you do
is kind and thoughtful,
and you are near to everyone
whose prayers are sincere.

℟. The Lord is near to all who call on him.

ALLELUIA
See Acts 16:14b

℟. Alleluia, alleluia.

**Open our hearts, O Lord,
to listen to the words of your Son.**

℟. Alleluia, alleluia.

GOSPEL

Are you jealous because I am generous?

✣ A reading from the holy gospel according to Matthew   20:1-16a

As Jesus was telling what the kingdom of heaven would be like, he said:
"Early one morning a man went out to hire some workers for his vineyard.
After he had agreed to pay them the usual amount for a day's work,
   he sent them off to his vineyard.

"About nine that morning,
   the man saw some other people
      standing in the market with nothing to do.
He said he would pay them what was fair,
   if they would work in his vineyard.
So they went.

"At noon and again about three in the afternoon
   he returned to the market.
And each time he made the same agreement
   with others who were loafing around with nothing to do.

"Finally, about five in the afternoon
   the man went back and found some others standing there.
He asked them,
'Why have you been standing here all day long doing nothing?'

" 'Because no one has hired us,' they answered.
Then he told them to go work in his vineyard.

"That evening the owner of the vineyard
    told the man in charge of the workers
        to call them in and give them their money.
He also told the man to begin with the ones who were hired last.
When the workers arrived,
    the ones who had been hired at five in the afternoon
        were given a full day's pay.

"The workers who had been hired first
    thought they would be given more than the others.
But when they were given the same,
    they began complaining to the owner of the vineyard.
They said, 'The ones who were hired last worked for only one hour.
But you paid them the same that you did us.
And we worked in the hot sun all day long!'

"The owner answered one of them,
'Friend, I didn't cheat you.
I paid you exactly what we agreed on.
Take your money now and go!
What business is it of yours if I want to pay them
    the same that I paid you?
Don't I have the right to do what I want with my own money?

Why should you be jealous, if I want to be generous?' "

Jesus then said, "So it is!
Everyone who is now first will be last."

                                      The gospel of the Lord.

[129] TWENTY-FIFTH SUNDAY IN ORDINARY TIME B

FIRST READING

The harvest of justice is sown in peace by those who make peace.

A reading from the letter of James 3:17-18

Brothers and sisters:
The wisdom that comes from above
   leads us to be pure, friendly, gentle,
      sensible, kind, helpful, genuine, and sincere.
When peacemakers plant seeds of peace,
   they will harvest justice.

The word of the Lord.

RESPONSORIAL PSALM 122:1-2, 8-9

℟. (Sirach 36:18) Give peace, O Lord, to those who wait for you.

**It made me glad
to hear them say,
"Let's go to the house
of the L**ORD**!"
Jerusalem, we are standing
inside your gates.**

℟. Give peace, O Lord, to those who wait for you.

**Because of my friends
and my relatives,
I will pray for peace.
And because of the house
of the L**ORD **our God,
I will work for your good.**

℟. Give peace, O Lord, to those who wait for you.

ALLELUIA
See 2 Thessalonians 2:14

℟. Alleluia, alleluia.

God has called us with the gospel,
to share in the glory of our Lord Jesus Christ.

℟. Alleluia, alleluia.

GOSPEL

All who wish to be first must make themselves the servants of all.

✠ A reading from the holy gospel according to Mark   9:33-37

Jesus and his disciples went to his home in Capernaum.
After they were inside the house, Jesus asked them,
"What were you arguing about along the way?"
They had been arguing about which one of them was the greatest,
    and so they did not answer.

After Jesus sat down and told the twelve disciples
    to gather around him,
    he said, "If you want the place of honor,
    you must become a slave and serve others!"

Then Jesus had a child stand near him.
He put his arm around the child and said,
"When you welcome even a child because of me, you welcome me.
And when you welcome me,
    you welcome the one who sent me."

The gospel of the Lord.

[130] TWENTY-FIFTH SUNDAY IN ORDINARY TIME   C

FIRST READING

Love one another and serve the Lord.

A reading from the letter of Paul to the Romans 12:9-12

Brothers and sisters:
  Be sincere in your love for others.
Hate everything that is evil
  and hold tight to everything that is good.
Love each other as brothers and sisters
  and honor others more than you do yourself.

Never give up.
Eagerly follow the Holy Spirit and serve the Lord.
Let your hope make you glad.
Be patient in time of trouble and never stop praying.

The word of the Lord.

RESPONSORIAL PSALM 25:4-5ab, 5cd-6

℟. (4a) Teach me your ways, O Lord.

Show me your paths
and teach me to follow;
guide me by your truth
and instruct me.

℟. Teach me your ways, O Lord.

You keep me safe,
and I always trust you.
Please, LORD, remember,
you have always
been patient and kind.

℟. Teach me your ways, O Lord.

ALLELUIA
2 Corinthians 8:9

℟. Alleluia, alleluia.

**Jesus Christ was rich but he became poor,
to make you rich out of his poverty.**

℟. Alleluia, alleluia.

GOSPEL

You cannot be slaves both of God and of money.

✢ **A reading from the holy gospel according to Luke** 16:10-13

**Jesus said to his disciples:
"Anyone who can be trusted in little matters
   can also be trusted in important matters.
But anyone who is dishonest in little matters
   will be dishonest in important matters.
If you cannot be trusted with this wicked wealth,
   who will trust you with true wealth?
And if you cannot be trusted with what belongs to someone else,
   who will give you something that will be your own?**

**"You cannot be the slave of two masters.
You will like one more than the other
   or be more loyal to one than to the other.
You cannot serve God and money."**

The gospel of the Lord.

[131] TWENTY-SIXTH SUNDAY IN ORDINARY TIME **A**

FIRST READING

The sinner who decides to turn against sinfulness deserves to live.

A reading from the book of the prophet Ezekiel 18:25-28

The Lord says this:
People of Israel, you say,
"The Lord isn't fair!"
But you are the ones who are wrong.

I am fair,
    and if any of you stop doing right and start sinning,
        you will die because of your sins.
But if any of you turn from your sins and start doing right,
    you will be safe.
You won't die because of your sins,
    if you really think about the things you have done wrong
        and turn from them.

Do this, and you will go on living.

The word of the Lord.

RESPONSORIAL PSALM 25:4-5, 6-7, 8-9

℟. (6a) Remember your mercies, O Lord.

**Show me your paths
and teach me to follow;
guide me by your truth
and instruct me.
You keep me safe,
and I always trust you.**

℟. Remember your mercies, O Lord.

Please, Lord, remember,
you have always
been patient and kind.
Forget each wrong I did
when I was young.
Show how truly kind you are
and remember me.

℟. Remember your mercies, O Lord.

You are honest and merciful,
and you teach sinners
how to follow your path.
You lead humble people
to do what is right
and to stay on your path.

℟. Remember your mercies, O Lord.

SECOND READING

In your minds be as Christ Jesus.

A reading from the letter of Paul to the Philippians 2:1-5

Brothers and sisters:
Christ encourages you,
 and his love comforts you.
God's Spirit unites you,
 and you are concerned for others.
Now make me completely happy!
Live in harmony by showing love for each other.
Be united in what you think,
 as if you were only one person.

Don't be jealous or proud,
 but be humble and consider others more important than yourselves.
Care about them as much as you care about yourselves
 and think the same way that Christ Jesus did.

The word of the Lord.

ALLELUIA
John 10:27

℟. Alleluia, alleluia.

**My sheep listen to my voice, says the Lord;
I know them, and they follow me.**

℟. Alleluia, alleluia.

GOSPEL

The son went out moved by regret.

✤ A reading from the holy gospel according to Matthew   21:28-32

**Jesus said:
"I will tell you a story about a man who had two sons.
Then you can tell me what you think.**

"The father went to the older son and said,
'Go work in the vineyard today!'
His son told him that he would not do it,
   but later he changed his mind and went.
The man then told his younger son to go work in the vineyard.
The boy said he would, but he didn't go.
Which one of the sons obeyed his father?"

"The older one," the chief priests and leaders answered.

Then Jesus told them:
"You can be sure that tax collectors and bad women
   will get into the kingdom of God before you ever will!
When John the Baptist showed you how to do right,
   you would not believe him.
But these evil people did believe.
And even when you saw what they did,
   you still would not change your minds and believe."

The gospel of the Lord.

[132] TWENTY-SIXTH SUNDAY IN ORDINARY TIME B

FIRST READING

Are you jealous on my account?
Who decrees that all people may prophesy?

A reading from the book of Numbers 11:25-29

The LORD came down in a cloud and spoke with Moses.
   Then he took some of the Spirit's power that he had given to Moses,
   and he gave it to the seventy leaders.
The men prophesied,
   but they did it only this one time.

Two of the leaders had stayed in camp
   and had not gone out to the sacred tent.
They were Eldad and Medad.
But the Spirit also took control of them,
   and they prophesied.
A young man went and told Moses,
"Eldad and Medad are prophesying in camp."

Joshua son of Nun was still a boy when he first started helping Moses.
Joshua was there at the time and said to him,
"Master, make those men stop!"

Moses replied, "Are you saying this for my good?
I wish the LORD would give his Spirit to all his people
   and let them become his prophets!"

                               The word of the Lord.

RESPONSORIAL PSALM 66:1-3ab, 4-5, 16 and 20

℟. (1) Let all the earth cry out to God with joy.

Tell everyone on this earth
to shout praises to God!
Sing about his glorious name.
Honor him with praises.
Say to God, "Everything you do is fearsome!"

℟. Let all the earth cry out to God with joy.

"You are worshiped by everyone!
We all sing praises to you."

Come and see the fearsome things
our God has done!

> ℟. Let all the earth cry out to God with joy.

All who worship God,
come here and listen;
I will tell you everything
God has done for me.
Let's praise God!
He listened when I prayed,
and he was always kind.

> ℟. Let all the earth cry out to God with joy.

SECOND READING

> Your wealth is rotting.

A reading from the letter of James   5:1-6

Brothers and sisters:
You rich people should cry and weep!
Terrible things are going to happen to you.
Your treasures have already rotted,
> and moths have eaten your clothes.
Your money has rusted,
> and the rust will be evidence against you,
> as it burns your body like fire.

Yet you keep on storing up wealth in these last days.
You refused to pay the people who worked in your fields,
> and now their unpaid wages are shouting out against you.
The Lord All-Powerful has surely heard
> the cries of the workers who harvested your crops.

While here on earth,
> you have thought only of filling your own stomachs
> > and having a good time.
But now you are like fat cattle on their way to be butchered.
You have condemned and murdered innocent people,
> who couldn't even fight back.

The word of the Lord.

ALLELUIA

See John 17:17b, 17a

℟. Alleluia, alleluia.

**Your word, O Lord, is truth;
make us holy in the truth.**

℟. Alleluia, alleluia.

GOSPEL

Anyone who is not against us is for us.

✞ **A reading from the holy gospel according to Mark** 9:38-41

**The disciple John said to Jesus,
"Teacher, we saw a man using your name
to force demons out of people.
But he was not one of us,
and we told him to stop."**

**Jesus said to his disciples: "Don't stop him!
No one who works miracles in my name
will soon turn and say something bad about me.
Anyone who is not against us is for us.
And anyone who gives you a cup of water in my name,
just because you belong to me,
will surely be rewarded."**

The gospel of the Lord.

[133] TWENTY-SIXTH SUNDAY IN ORDINARY TIME   C

FIRST READING

Try to please God and be like him.

A reading from the first letter of Paul to Timothy 6:11b-12a

Try your best to please God and to be like him. Be faithful, loving, dependable, and gentle. Fight a good fight for the faith.

The word of the Lord.

RESPONSORIAL PSALM 25:4-5abc, 6 and 7cd

℟. (4a) Teach me your ways, O Lord.

**Show me your paths
and teach me to follow;
guide me by your truth
and instruct me.
You keep me safe.**

℟. Teach me your ways, O Lord.

**Please, Lord, remember,
you have always
been patient and kind.
Show how truly kind you are
and remember me.**

℟. Teach me your ways, O Lord.

ALLELUIA 2 Corinthians 8:9

℟. Alleluia, alleluia.

**Jesus Christ was rich but he became poor,
to make you rich out of his poverty.**

℟. Alleluia, alleluia.

GOSPEL

> Good things came to you and bad things to Lazarus;
> now he is comforted while you are in agony.

✚ A reading from the holy gospel according to Luke   16:19-31

Jesus told his disciples this story:
"There was once a rich man who wore expensive clothes
        and every day ate the best food.
But a poor beggar named Lazarus
        was brought to the gate of the rich man's house.
He was happy
        just to eat the scraps that fell from the rich man's table.

"His body was covered with sores,
    and dogs kept coming up to lick them.
The poor man died,
    and angels took him to the place of honor next to Abraham.

"The rich man also died and was buried.
He went to hell and was suffering terribly.
When he looked up and saw Abraham far off and Lazarus at his side,
    he said to Abraham, 'Have pity on me!
Send Lazarus to dip his finger in water and touch my tongue.
I'm suffering terribly in this fire.'

"Abraham answered,
'My friend, remember that while you lived,
    you had everything good,
    and Lazarus had everything bad.
Now he is happy, and you are in pain.
And besides, there is a deep ditch between us,
    and no one from either side can cross over.'

"But the rich man said,
'Abraham, then please send Lazarus to my father's home.
Let him warn my five brothers,
    so they won't come to this horrible place.'

"Abraham answered,
'Your brothers can read what Moses and the prophets wrote.
They should pay attention to that.'

"Then the rich man said, 'No, that's not enough!
If only someone from the dead would go to them,
    they would listen and turn to God.'

"So Abraham said,
'If they won't pay attention to Moses and the prophets,
    they won't listen even to someone who comes back from the dead.'"

The gospel of the Lord.

[134] TWENTY-SEVENTH SUNDAY IN ORDINARY TIME A

FIRST READING

The vineyard of the Lord God of hosts is the house of Israel.

A reading from the book of the prophet Isaiah 5:1-7

I will sing a song about the vineyard of my dear friend.
It was on the side of a fertile hill.
My friend dug the ground, removed the stones,
    and planted the best vines.
He built a watchtower and dug a place to press the grapes.
He hoped they would be good,
    but bitter grapes were all that grew.

Now listen, people of Jerusalem and of Judah!
You be the judge of me and my vineyard.
What more could I have done for my vineyard?
I hoped for good grapes,
    but bitter grapes were all that grew.

Now I will tell you what I am going to do.
I will cut down the hedge and tear down the wall.
My vineyard will be trampled and left in ruins.
It will turn into a desert, neither tended nor hoed,
    and it will be covered with thorns and briars.
I will command the clouds not to send it rain.

Israel is the vineyard of the LORD All-Powerful.
Judah is the garden that makes him rejoice.
He had hoped for honesty and for justice,
    but dishonesty and crying were all he found.

The word of the Lord.

RESPONSORIAL PSALM 80:8 and 11, 14de-15ab and 19

℟. (Isaiah 5:7a) The vineyard of the Lord is the house of Israel.

We were like a grapevine
you brought out of Egypt.
You chased other nations away
and planted us here.

Its branches stretched to the sea;
its new growth reached
to the river.

℟. The vineyard of the Lord is the house of Israel.

See what's happening
to this vine.
With your own hands
you planted its roots.
LORD God All-Powerful,
make us strong again!
Smile on us and save us.

℟. The vineyard of the Lord is the house of Israel.

SECOND READING

Do these things, and the God of peace will be with you.

A reading from the letter of Paul to the Philippians 4:6-9

Brothers and sisters:
Don't worry about anything,
but pray about everything.

With thankful hearts offer up your prayers and requests to God.
Then, because you belong to Christ Jesus,
God will bless you with peace
that no one can completely understand.
And this peace will control the way you think and feel.

Finally, my friends,
keep your minds on whatever is true, pure, right,
holy, friendly, and proper.
Don't ever stop thinking about what is truly worthwhile
and worthy of praise.
You know the teachings I gave you,
and you know what you heard me say and saw me do.

So follow my example.
And God, who gives peace, will be with you.

The word of the Lord.

ALLELUIA

See John 15:16

℟. Alleluia, alleluia.

I have chosen you from the world, says the Lord,
to go and bear fruit that will last.

℟. Alleluia, alleluia.

GOSPEL

A landowner leased his vineyard to other farmers.

✚ A reading from the holy gospel according to Matthew   21:33-43

Jesus told the chief priests and leaders to listen to this story:
"A land owner once planted a vineyard.
He built a wall around it and dug a pit to crush the grapes in.
He also built a lookout tower.

"Then he rented out his vineyard and left the country.

"When it was harvest time,
   the owner sent some servants to get his share of the grapes.
But the renters grabbed those servants.
They beat up one, killed one,
   and stoned one of them to death.
He then sent more servants than he did the first time.
But the renters treated them in the same way.

"Finally, the owner sent his own son to the renters,
   because he thought they would respect him.
But when they saw the man's son, they said,
'Someday he will own the vineyard.
Let's kill him!
Then we can have it all for ourselves.'
So they grabbed him, threw him out of the vineyard, and killed him."

Jesus asked, "When the owner of that vineyard comes,
   what do you suppose he will do to those renters?"

The chief priests and leaders answered,
"He will kill them in some horrible way.
Then he will rent out his vineyard to people
   who will give him his share of grapes at harvest time."

Jesus replied, "Surely you know that the Scriptures say,

> 'The stone that the builders tossed aside
> is now the most important stone of all.
> This is something the Lord has done,
> and it is amazing to us.'

"I tell you that God's kingdom will be taken from you
and given to people who will do what he demands."

The gospel of the Lord.

[135] **TWENTY-SEVENTH SUNDAY IN ORDINARY TIME** B

FIRST READING
        And they became two in one flesh.

   A reading from the book of Genesis   2:18-24

The LORD God said, "It isn't good for Adam to be alone!
I need to make the right kind of partner for him."

The LORD then took some earth and made all the animals and birds.
He brought them to Adam to see what names he would give to each of them.
Adam named all of the tame animals and all of the birds
    and the wild animals.
That's how they got their names.

Not one of the animals was the right kind of partner for Adam.
So the LORD God made him fall into a deep sleep,
    and he took out one of Adam's ribs.
Then after closing Adam's side,
    the LORD made a woman out of the rib.

The LORD God brought her to Adam,
    and Adam shouted, "Now here is someone like me!
She is part of my body, my own flesh and bones!
She came from me, a man.
So I will name her Woman!"

That's why a man will leave his own father and mother.
He marries a woman,
    and the two of them become like one person.

                                  The word of the Lord.

RESPONSORIAL PSALM   128:1-2, 3, 4-5

   ℟. (see 5) May the Lord bless us all the days of our lives.

The LORD will bless you
if you respect him
and obey his laws.
Your fields will produce,
and you will be happy
and all will go well.

   ℟. May the Lord bless us all the days of our lives.

Your wife will be as fruitful
as a grapevine,
and just as an olive tree
is rich with olives,
your home will be rich
with healthy children.

℟. May the Lord bless us all the days of our lives.

That is how the LORD will bless
everyone who respects him.
I pray that the LORD
will bless you from Zion
and let Jerusalem prosper
as long as you live.

℟. May the Lord bless us all the days of our lives.

ALLELUIA

1 John 4:12

℟. Alleluia, alleluia.

**If we love one another,
God will live in us in perfect love.**

℟. Alleluia, alleluia.

GOSPEL

The kingdom of God belongs to children like these.

✠ A reading from the holy gospel according to Mark   10:13-16

Some people brought their children to Jesus
so that he could bless them by placing his hands on them.
But his disciples told the people to stop bothering him.

When Jesus saw this, he became angry and said,
"Let the children come to me!
Don't try to stop them.
People who are like these little children belong to the kingdom of God.
I promise you that you cannot get into God's kingdom,
    unless you accept it the way a child does."

Then Jesus took the children in his arms
    and blessed them by placing his hands on them.

The gospel of the Lord.

[136] TWENTY-SEVENTH SUNDAY IN ORDINARY TIME   C

FIRST READING

The just will live by faithfulness.

A reading from the book of the prophet Habakkuk   1:2-3; 2:2-4

This was my prayer to God:
"Our LORD, how long must I beg for your help
   before you listen?
You won't help when I tell you about all of the violence.
Why do you make me watch such terrible injustice?
Violence and destruction, crime and cruelty are spreading everywhere."

Then the LORD told me,
"I will give you my message in the form of a vision.
Write it on a big clay tablet
   and make it easy to read.
At the time I have chosen,
   these things will happen.
You can trust what I say about the future.
It may take a long time,
   but keep on waiting,
   because it will happen.
I don't like proud people,
   but everyone who is faithful will please me and live."

The word of the Lord.

RESPONSORIAL PSALM   95:1-2, 6-7abcd, 7e-9

℟. (8) If today you hear God's voice, harden not your hearts.

Sing joyful songs to the LORD!
Praise the mighty rock
where we are safe.
Come to worship him
with thankful hearts
and songs of praise.

℟. If today you hear God's voice, harden not your hearts.

Bow down and worship
the LORD our Creator!
The LORD is our God,
and we are his people,
the sheep he takes care of
in his own pasture.

℟. If today you hear God's voice, harden not your hearts.

Listen to God's voice today!
Don't be stubborn and rebel
as your ancestors did
at Meribah and at Massah
out in the desert.
For forty years
they tested God and saw
the things he did.

℟. If today you hear God's voice, harden not your hearts.

SECOND READING

Never be ashamed of witnessing to the Lord.

A reading from the second letter of Paul to Timothy 1:6-8

I ask you to make full use of the gift that God gave you
when I placed my hands on you.
Use it well.
God's Spirit does not make cowards out of us.
The Spirit gives us power, love, and self-control.

Don't be ashamed to speak for our Lord.
And don't be ashamed of me,
    just because I am in jail for serving him.
Use the power that comes from God
    and join with me in suffering for telling the good news.

The word of the Lord.

ALLELUIA
1 Peter 1:25

℟. Alleluia, alleluia.

**The word of the Lord stands for ever;
it is the word given to you, the good news.**

℟. Alleluia, alleluia.

GOSPEL

If you had faith!

✢ A reading from the holy gospel according to Luke   17:5-10

The apostles said to the Lord,
"Make our faith stronger!"

Jesus replied:
"If you had faith no bigger than a tiny mustard seed,
    you could tell this mulberry tree to pull itself up, roots and all,
    and to plant itself in the ocean.
And it would!

"If your servant comes in from plowing or from taking care of the sheep,
    would you say, 'Welcome!
Come on in and have something to eat'?
No, you wouldn't say that.
You would say, 'Fix me something to eat.
Get ready to serve me, so I can have my meal.
Then later on you can eat and drink.'

"Servants don't deserve special thanks
    for doing what they are supposed to do.
And that's how it should be with you.
When you've done all you should,
    then say, 'We are merely servants,
    and we have simply done our duty.' "

                      The gospel of the Lord.

[137] TWENTY-EIGHTH SUNDAY IN ORDINARY TIME A

FIRST READING

*The Lord will prepare a feast
and will wipe away the tears from every cheek.*

A reading from the book of the prophet Isaiah   25:6-10a

On this mountain the LORD All-Powerful
 will prepare for all nations a feast of the finest foods.
Choice wines and the best meat will be served.
Here the LORD will strip away
 the funeral clothes that cover the nations.
The LORD All-Powerful will destroy the power of death
 and wipe away each tear.
No longer will his people be embarrassed everywhere.
The LORD has spoken!
On that day, people will say,
"The LORD God has saved us!
Let's celebrate.
We waited and waited, and now he is here."

The powerful arm of the LORD will protect this mountain.

The word of the Lord.

RESPONSORIAL PSALM   23:1-3a, 4abcd and 5ac, 6

℟. (6cd) I shall live in the house of the Lord all the days of my life.

You, LORD, are my shepherd.
I will never be in need.
You let me rest in fields
of green grass.
You lead me to streams
of peaceful water,
and you refresh my life.

℟. I shall live in the house of the Lord all the days of my life.

I may walk through valleys
as dark as death,
but I won't be afraid.

You are with me.
You treat me to a feast,
and you honor me as your guest.

℟. I shall live in the house of the Lord all the days of my life.

Your kindness and love
will always be with me
each day of my life,
and I will live forever
in your house, LORD.

℟. I shall live in the house of the Lord all the days of my life.

SECOND READING

I am able to do all things in Christ who strengthens me.

A reading from the letter of Paul to the Philippians 4:12-14, 19-20

Brothers and sisters:
I know what it is to be poor or to have plenty,
and I have lived under all kinds of conditions.
I know what it means to be full or to be hungry,
to have too much or too little.
Christ gives me the strength to face anything.

It was good of you to help me when I was having such a hard time.

I pray that God will take care of all your needs
with the wonderful blessings that come from Christ Jesus!
May God our Father be praised forever and ever. Amen.

The word of the Lord.

ALLELUIA

See Ephesians 1:17-18

℟. Alleluia, alleluia.

May the Father of our Lord Jesus Christ
enlighten the eyes of our heart,
that we might see how great is the hope
to which we are called.

℟. Alleluia, alleluia.

GOSPEL

Whomsoever you find invite to the wedding.

✢ A reading from the holy gospel according to Matthew 22:1-10

Jesus used this story to teach the people:
"The kingdom of heaven is like what happened
    when a king gave a wedding banquet for his son.
The king sent some servants to tell the invited guests
       to come to the banquet,
    but the guests refused.
He sent other servants to say to the guests,
'The banquet is ready!
My cattle and prize calves have all been prepared.
Everything is ready.
Come to the banquet!'

"But the guests did not pay any attention.
Some of them left for their farms,
    and some went to their places of business.
Others grabbed the servants, beat them up, and killed them.

"This made the king so furious that he sent an army to kill
       those murderers and burn down their city.
Then he said to the servants,
'It is time for the wedding banquet,
    and the invited guests don't deserve to come.
Go out to the street corners and tell everyone you meet
       to come to the banquet.'
They went out on the streets and brought in everyone they could find,
       good and bad alike.
And the banquet room was filled with guests."

                                              The gospel of the Lord.

[138] TWENTY-EIGHTH SUNDAY IN ORDINARY TIME B

FIRST READING

In comparison to wisdom, I held riches as nothing.

A reading from the book of Wisdom 7:7-11

I prayed for understanding,
  and it was given to me.
I asked God for Wisdom,
  and it came to me.

I valued Wisdom more than power and kingdoms.
Riches were nothing compared with Wisdom.
I considered her more valuable than priceless jewels.
Gold was nothing but sand,
  and silver was merely mud,
  when compared with Wisdom.

I loved her more than good health and beauty.
I preferred Wisdom to light,
  because she is much brighter.
Wisdom has countless treasures,
  and everything good is mine because of her.

The word of the Lord.

RESPONSORIAL PSALM 90:12 and 14, 16-17abc

℟. (14) Fill us with your love, O Lord, and we will sing for joy!

**Teach us to use wisely
all the time we have.
When morning comes,
let your love satisfy
all our needs.
Then we can celebrate
and be glad for what time
we have left.**

℟. Fill us with your love, O Lord, and we will sing for joy!

Do wonderful things for us,
your servants,
and show your mighty power
to our children.
Our Lord and our God,
treat us with kindness
and let all go well for us.

℟. Fill us with your love, O Lord, and we will sing for joy!

SECOND READING

The word of God discerns the thoughts and intentions of the heart.

A reading from the letter to the Hebrews 4:12-13

Brothers and sisters:
What God has said is not only alive and active!
It is sharper than any double-edged sword.
His word can cut through our spirits and souls
and through our joints and marrow,
until it discovers the desires and thoughts of our hearts.

Nothing is hidden from God!
He sees through everything,
and we will have to tell him the truth.

The word of the Lord.

ALLELUIA

Matthew 5:3

℟. Alleluia, alleluia.

**Blessed are the poor in spirit;
the kingdom of heaven is theirs!**

℟. Alleluia, alleluia.

GOSPEL

Go, sell everything you have and come follow me.

✠ A reading from the holy gospel according to Mark   10:17-27

As Jesus was walking down a road,
a man ran up to him.
He kneeled down, and asked,
"Good teacher, what can I do to have eternal life?"

Jesus replied, "Why do you call me good?
Only God is good.
You know the commandments.
'Do not murder.
Be faithful in marriage.
Do not steal.
Do not tell lies about others.
Do not cheat.
Respect your father and mother.' "

The man answered,
"Teacher, I have obeyed all these commandments
    since I was a young man."

Jesus looked closely at the man.
He liked him and said,
"There's one thing you still need to do.
Go sell everything you own.
Give the money to the poor,
    and you will have riches in heaven.
Then come with me."

When the man heard Jesus say this,
    he went away gloomy and sad because he was very rich.

Jesus looked around and said to his disciples,
"It's hard for rich people to get into God's kingdom!"
The disciples were shocked to hear this.
So Jesus told them again,
"It's terribly hard to get into God's kingdom!
In fact, it's easier for a camel to go through the eye of a needle
    than for a rich person to get into God's kingdom."

Jesus' disciples were even more amazed.
They asked each other,
"How can anyone ever be saved?"

Jesus looked at them and said,
"There are some things that people cannot do,
    but God can do anything."

The gospel of the Lord.

[139] TWENTY-EIGHTH SUNDAY IN ORDINARY TIME C

FIRST READING

Naaman returned to Elisha, the prophet, and acknowledged the Lord.

A reading from the second book of Kings 5:14-17

Naaman, the Syrian, did what God's prophet Elisha had told him to do.
He went down to the Jordan River
    and dipped in the water seven times.
Then he was well,
    and his skin looked as healthy as that of a young child.

Naaman and everyone with him went back to the prophet Elisha.
Naaman said, "Elisha, now I know
    that the only God in all the world is in Israel.
Please, sir, let me give you a gift."

Elisha replied, "I serve the living God,
    and I swear by him that I will not take a thing from you!"
Naaman kept begging him to accept something,
    but Elisha refused.

Naaman said, "Sir, if you won't accept a gift,
    then let me take back as much of Israel's soil
        as two mules can carry.
From now on I will give sacrifices and offerings only to the Lord."

The word of the Lord.

RESPONSORIAL PSALM 98:1, 2-3ab, 3cd-4

℟. (see 2b) The Lord has revealed to the nations his saving power.

Sing a new song to the Lord!
He has worked miracles,
and with his own powerful arm,
he has won the victory.

℟. The Lord has revealed to the nations his saving power.

The Lord has shown the nations
that he has the power to save
and to bring justice.
God has been faithful
in his love for Israel.

℟. The Lord has revealed to the nations his saving power.

His saving power is seen
everywhere on earth.
Tell everyone on this earth
to sing happy songs
in praise of the Lord.

℟. The Lord has revealed to the nations his saving power.

SECOND READING

If we hold firm, we shall reign with Christ.

A reading from the second letter of Paul to Timothy 2:11-13

Here is a true message:
"If we died with Christ,
  we will live with him.
If we don't give up,
  we will rule with him.
If we deny that we know him,
  he will deny that he knows us.
If we are not faithful,
  he will still be faithful.
Christ cannot deny who he is."

The word of the Lord.

ALLELUIA 1 Thessalonians 5:18

℟. Alleluia, alleluia.

**For all things give thanks to God,
because this is what he expects of you in Christ Jesus.**

℟. Alleluia, alleluia.

GOSPEL

It seems that no one has returned to give thanks to God except this foreigner.

✢ A reading from the holy gospel according to Luke   17:11-19

On his way to Jerusalem,
Jesus went along the border between Samaria and Galilee.
As he was going into a village,
  ten men with leprosy came toward him.
They stood at a distance and shouted,
"Jesus, Master, have pity on us!"

Jesus looked at them and said,
"Go show yourselves to the priests."

On their way they were healed.
When one of them discovered that he was healed,
  he came back, shouting praises to God.
He bowed down at the feet of Jesus and thanked him.
The man was from the country of Samaria.

Jesus asked, "Weren't ten men healed?
Where are the other nine?
Why was this foreigner the only one who came back to thank God?"

Then Jesus told the man, "You may get up and go.
Your faith has made you well."

                                    The gospel of the Lord.

[140] TWENTY-NINTH SUNDAY IN ORDINARY TIME **A**

FIRST READING

I have taken the hand of Cyrus to subdue nations before his countenance.

A reading from the book of the prophet Isaiah 45:1, 4-6

The Lord said to Cyrus, his chosen one,
"I have taken hold of your right hand
 to help you conquer nations and remove kings from power.
City gates will open for you.
Not one will stay closed.

"Cyrus, you don't even know me!
But I have called you by name and highly honored you,
 because of Jacob, my servant,
 and Israel, my chosen one.
Only I am the Lord!

"There is no other God.
I have made you strong,
 though you don't know me.
Now everyone from east to west will know that I am the Lord.
No other gods are real."

The word of the Lord.

RESPONSORIAL PSALM 96:1 and 3, 4-5, 9-10abef

℟. (7b) Give the Lord glory and honor.

Sing a new song to the Lord!
Everyone on this earth,
sing praises to the Lord.
Tell every nation on earth,
"The Lord is wonderful
and does marvelous things!"

℟. Give the Lord glory and honor.

"The LORD is great and deserves
our greatest praise!
He is the only God
worthy of our worship.
Other nations worship idols,
but the LORD created the heavens."

℟. Give the Lord glory and honor.

"Everyone on earth, now tremble
and worship the LORD,
majestic and holy."
Announce to the nations,
"The LORD is King!
God will judge the people
with fairness."

℟. Give the Lord glory and honor.

SECOND READING

We are mindful of your faith, hope, and love.

A reading from the first letter of Paul to the Thessalonians 1:1-5b

From Paul, Silas, and Timothy.
To the church in Thessalonica,
    the people of God the Father and of the Lord Jesus Christ.

I pray that God will be kind to you and will bless you with peace!

We thank God for you and always mention you in our prayers.
Each time we pray,
    we tell God our Father about your faith and loving work
        and about your firm hope in our Lord Jesus Christ.

My dear friends, God loves you,
    and we know he has chosen you to be his people.
When we told you the good news,
    it was with the power and assurance
        that come from the Holy Spirit,
        and not simply with words.

                                      The word of the Lord.

ALLELUIA
Philippians 2:15d,16a

℟. Alleluia, alleluia.

**Shine on the world like bright stars;
you are offering it the word of life.**

℟. Alleluia, alleluia.

GOSPEL

*Give to Caesar the things that belong to Caesar
and to God the things that are God's.*

✠ **A reading from the holy gospel according to Matthew**   22:15-21

The Pharisees got together and planned how they could trick Jesus
    into saying something wrong.
They sent some of their followers
    and some of Herod's followers to say to him,
"Teacher, we know that you are honest.
You teach the truth about what God wants people to do.
And you treat everyone with the same respect,
    no matter who they are.
Tell us what you think!
Should we pay taxes to the Emperor or not?"

Jesus knew their evil thoughts and said,
"Why are you trying to test me? You showoffs!
Let me see one of the coins used for paying taxes."

They brought him a silver coin, and he asked,
"Whose picture and name are on it?"

"The Emperor's," they answered.

Then Jesus told them,
"Give the Emperor what belongs to him
    and give God what belongs to God."

The gospel of the Lord.

[141] TWENTY-NINTH SUNDAY IN ORDINARY TIME — B

FIRST READING

Let us approach the throne of grace with confidence.

A reading from the letter to the Hebrews 4:14-16

Brothers and sisters:
We have a great high priest,
who has gone into heaven,
and he is Jesus the Son of God.
That is why we must hold on to what we have said about him.

Jesus understands every weakness of ours,
because he was tempted in every way that we are.
But he did not sin!

So whenever we are in need,
we should come bravely before the throne of our merciful God.
There we will be treated with undeserved kindness,
and we will find help.

The word of the Lord.

RESPONSORIAL PSALM 33:4-5, 20 and 22

℟. (22) Lord, let your mercy be on us, as we place our trust in you.

The LORD is truthful;
he can be trusted.
He loves justice and fairness,
and he is kind to everyone
everywhere on earth.

℟. Lord, let your mercy be on us, as we place our trust in you.

We depend on you, LORD,
to help and protect us.
Be kind and bless us!
We depend on you.

℟. Lord, let your mercy be on us, as we place our trust in you.

ALLELUIA Mark 10:45

℟. Alleluia, alleluia.
The Son of Man came to serve
and to give his life as a ransom for all.
℟. Alleluia, alleluia.

GOSPEL

The Son of Man came to give his life as a ransom for all.

✛ A reading from the holy gospel according to Mark   10:35-45

James and John, the sons of Zebedee,
    came up to Jesus and asked,
"Teacher, will you do us a favor?"

Jesus asked them what they wanted, and they answered,
"When you come into your glory,
    please let one of us sit at your right side
        and the other at your left."

Jesus told them, "You don't really know what you're asking!
Are you able to drink from the cup that I must soon drink from
    or be baptized as I must be baptized?"

"Yes, we are!" James and John answered.

Then Jesus replied,
"You certainly will drink from the cup from which I must drink.
And you will be baptized just as I must!
But it is not for me to say
    who will sit at my right side and at my left.
That is for God to decide."

When the ten other disciples heard this,
    they were angry with James and John.
But Jesus called the disciples together and said:

"You know that those foreigners who call themselves kings
    like to order their people around.
And their great leaders have full power over the people they rule.
But don't act like them.
If you want to be great,
    you must be the servant of all the others.
And if you want to be first,
    you must be everyone's slave.
The Son of Man did not come to be a slave master,
    but a slave who will give his life to rescue many people."

                                            The gospel of the Lord.

[142] TWENTY-NINTH SUNDAY IN ORDINARY TIME — C

FIRST READING

Proclaim the message and insist on it.

A reading from the second letter of Paul to Timothy   4:1-2

When Christ Jesus comes as king,
   he will be the judge of everyone,
whether they are living or dead.

So with God and Christ as witnesses,
   I command you to preach God's message.
Do it willingly,
   even if it is not the popular thing to do.

You must correct people and point out their sins.
But also cheer them up,
   and when you instruct them, always be patient.

The word of the Lord.

RESPONSORIAL PSALM   96:1-2a, 2b-3, 4-5

℟. (3) Proclaim God's marvelous deeds to all the nations.

Sing a new song to the Lord!
Everyone on this earth,
sing praises to the Lord,
sing and praise his name.

℟. Proclaim God's marvelous deeds to all the nations.

Day after day announce,
"The Lord has saved us!"
Tell every nation on earth,
"The Lord is wonderful
and does marvelous things!"

℟. Proclaim God's marvelous deeds to all the nations.

The Lord is great and deserves
our greatest praise!
He is the only God
worthy of our worship.

Other nations worship idols,
but the Lord created the heavens.

℟. Proclaim God's marvelous deeds to all the nations.

ALLELUIA Hebrews 4:12

℟. Alleluia, alleluia.

The word of God is living and active;
it probes the thoughts and motives of our heart.

℟. Alleluia, alleluia.

GOSPEL

God will see justice done to his chosen who cry to him.

✛ A reading from the holy gospel according to Luke   18:1-8

Jesus told his disciples a story
about how they should keep on praying and never give up:

"In a town there was once a judge who didn't fear God
or care about people.
In that same town there was a widow who kept going to the judge
and saying,
'Make sure that I get fair treatment in court.'

"For a while the judge refused to do anything.
Finally, he said to himself,
'Even though I don't fear God or care about people,
I will help this widow
because she keeps on bothering me.
If I don't help her,
she will wear me out.'"

The Lord said:
"Think about what that crooked judge said.
Won't God protect his chosen ones who pray to him day and night?
Won't he be concerned for them?
He will surely hurry and help them.
But when the Son of Man comes,
will he find on this earth anyone with faith?"

The gospel of the Lord.

[143] **THIRTIETH SUNDAY IN ORDINARY TIME** **A**

FIRST READING

> You turned away from idols to serve God and await his Son.

A reading from the first letter of Paul to the Thessalonians 1:5-8a

Brothers and sisters:
 When we told you the good news,
 it was with the power and assurance
  that come from the Holy Spirit,
  and not simply with words.

You knew what kind of people we were and how we helped you.
So, when you accepted the message,
 you followed our example and the example of the Lord.
You suffered, but the Holy Spirit made you glad.

You became an example for all the Lord's followers
  in Macedonia and Achaia.
And because of you,
 the Lord's message has spread everywhere in those regions.

The word of the Lord.

RESPONSORIAL PSALM 18:1-2, 46 and 50ce

℟. (2) I love you, Lord, my strength.

I love you, LORD God,
and you make me strong.
You are my mighty rock,
my fortress, my protector,
the rock where I am safe,
my shield, my powerful weapon,
and my place of shelter.

℟. I love you, Lord, my strength.

You are the living LORD!
I will praise you.
You are a mighty rock.
I will honor you
for keeping me safe.

Your faithful love for David
will never end.

℟. I love you, Lord, my strength.

ALLELUIA
John 14:23

℟. Alleluia, alleluia.

All who love me will keep my words,
and my Father will love them,
and we will come to them.

℟. Alleluia, alleluia.

GOSPEL

Love the Lord your God, and your neighbor as yourself.

✠ A reading from the holy gospel according to Matthew   22:34-40

After Jesus had made the Sadducees look foolish,
the Pharisees heard about it and got together.
One of them was an expert in the Jewish Law.
So he tried to test Jesus by asking,
"Teacher, what is the most important commandment in the Law?"

Jesus answered:
" 'Love the Lord your God with all your heart, soul, and mind.'
This is the first and most important commandment.
The second most important commandment is like this one.
And it is, 'Love others as much as you love yourself.'
All the Law of Moses and the Books of the Prophets
    are based on these two commandments."

The gospel of the Lord.

[144] THIRTIETH SUNDAY IN ORDINARY TIME B

FIRST READING

*I shall lead them back in mercy —
both those who are blind and those who are lame.*

A reading from the book of the prophet Jeremiah 31:7-9

The LORD says,
"Celebrate and rejoice for Israel, the greatest nation of all."
Offer praises and shout,
"Rescue your people, LORD!
Save what's left of Israel."

I will bring my people back from that country in the north
　　　and from everywhere else.
The blind and the lame will be there.
Expectant mothers and women who are about to give birth
　　　will return and be part of that great crowd.

They will cry and pray as I bring them home.
They won't stumble as I will lead them along a level road
　　　to streams of water.

I am a father to Israel,
　　　and they are my favorite children.

　　　　　　　　　　　　　　　The word of the Lord.

RESPONSORIAL PSALM 126:1-2ab, 4-5, 6

℟. (3) The Lord has done great things for us; we are filled with joy.

It seemed like a dream
when the LORD brought us back
to the city of Zion.
We celebrated with laughter
and joyful songs.

℟. The Lord has done great things for us; we are filled with joy.

Our LORD, we ask you to bless
our people again,
and let us be like streams
in the southern desert.

We cried as we went out
to plant our seeds.
Now let us celebrate
as we bring in the crops.

    ℟. The Lord has done great things for us; we are filled with joy.

We cried on the way
to plant our seeds,
but we will celebrate and shout
as we bring in the crops.

    ℟. The Lord has done great things for us; we are filled with joy.

SECOND READING

    You are a priest for ever, in the line of Melchizedek.

A reading from the letter to the Hebrews   5:1-6

Brothers and sisters:
Every high priest is appointed to help others
    by offering gifts and sacrifices to God because of their sins.
A high priest has weaknesses of his own,
    and he feels sorry for foolish and sinful people.
That is why he must offer sacrifices for his own sins
    and for the sins of others.

But no one can have the honor of being a high priest
    simply by wanting to be one.
Only God can choose a priest,
    and God is the one who chose Aaron.

That is how it was with Christ.
He became a high priest,
    but not just because he wanted the honor of being one.
It was God who told him,
"You are my Son, because today I have become your Father!"
In another place, God says,
"You are a priest forever just like Melchizedek."

                                    The word of the Lord.

THIRTIETH SUNDAY IN ORDINARY TIME — B

ALLELUIA See 2 Timothy 1:10

℟. Alleluia, alleluia.

Our Savior Jesus Christ has done away with death and brought us life through the gospel.

℟. Alleluia, alleluia.

GOSPEL

Master, grant that I may see.

✠ A reading from the holy gospel according to Mark   10:46-52

Jesus and his disciples went to Jericho.
And as they were leaving,
   they were followed by a large crowd.

A blind beggar by the name of Bartimaeus son of Timaeus
      was sitting beside the road.
When he heard that it was Jesus from Nazareth,
   he shouted, "Jesus, Son of David, have pity on me!"

Many people told the man to stop,
   but he shouted even louder,
"Son of David, have pity on me!"

Jesus stopped and said, "Call him over!"

They called out to the blind man and said,
"Don't be afraid! Come on!
He is calling for you."

The man threw off his coat as he jumped up and ran to Jesus.
Jesus asked, "What do you want me to do for you?"

The blind man answered, "Master, I want to see!"

Jesus told him, "You may go.
Your eyes are healed because of your faith."

Right away the man could see,
   and he went down the road with Jesus.

The gospel of the Lord.

[145] **THIRTIETH SUNDAY IN ORDINARY TIME**   C

FIRST READING

The prayer of the humble will penetrate the heavens.

A reading from the book of Sirach   35:12b-14, 16-17

The Lord doesn't have favorites,
   and you can't bribe him to cheat the poor.
But he hears the prayers of all who have been mistreated.
The Lord listens carefully to the prayers of orphans
   and the concerns of widows.

If you gladly obey God,
   your prayers will reach beyond the clouds.
The prayers of the humble go right through the clouds,
   and they are never satisfied
     till their prayers reach God.

The word of the Lord.

RESPONSORIAL PSALM   34:1-2, 17-18

℟. (7a) The Lord hears the cry of the poor.

I will always praise the LORD.
With all my heart,
I will praise the LORD.
Let all who are helpless
listen and be glad.

℟. The Lord hears the cry of the poor.

When his people pray for help,
he listens and he rescues them
from their troubles.
The LORD is there to rescue
all who are discouraged
and have given up hope.

℟. The Lord hears the cry of the poor.

SECOND READING

All that remains is the crown of righteousness reserved for me.

A reading from the second letter of Paul to Timothy   4:6-8

Now the time has come for me to die.
My life is like a drink offering being poured out on the altar.
I have fought well.
I finished the race,
   and I have been faithful.

So a crown will be given to me for pleasing the Lord.
He judges fairly,
   and on the day of judgment
   he will give a crown to me
      and to everyone else who wants him to appear with power.

The word of the Lord.

ALLELUIA   2 Corinthians 5:19

℟. Alleluia, alleluia.

God was in Christ, to reconcile the world to himself;
and the good news of reconciliation he has entrusted to us.

℟. Alleluia, alleluia.

GOSPEL

The tax collector went home justified, not the Pharisee.

✜ **A reading from the holy gospel according to Luke**   18:9-14

Jesus told a story to some people
   who thought they were better than others
   and who looked down on everyone else:

"Two men went into the temple to pray.
One was a Pharisee and the other a tax collector.

"The Pharisee stood over by himself and prayed,
'God, I thank you that I am not greedy, dishonest,
      and unfaithful in marriage like other people.
And I am really glad that I am not like that tax collector over there.
I go without eating for two days a week,
      and I give you one tenth of all I earn.'

"The tax collector stood off at a distance
      and did not think he was good enough
          even to look up toward heaven.
He was so sorry for what he had done
      that he pounded his chest and prayed,
'God, have pity on me!
I am such a sinner.'"

Then Jesus said, "When the two men went home,
      it was the tax collector and not the Pharisee
          who was pleasing to God.
If you put yourself above others,
      you will be put down.
But if you humble yourself,
      you will be honored."

                              The gospel of the Lord.

[146] THIRTY-FIRST SUNDAY IN ORDINARY TIME **A**

FIRST READING

You have strayed from the way,
you have caused many to stumble by your teaching.

A reading from the book of the prophet Malachi 2:8-10

The LORD says this:
Although I am the LORD All-Powerful,
  you priests have turned from following me.
Your teachings have led many people to do sinful things,
  and you have broken the promise that Levi made to me.

So I made everyone hate and despise you
  because you disobeyed me and did not treat all people alike.

Don't you know that we all have the same father?
Didn't the one God create us all?
So why do you cheat each other
    by breaking the promise that your ancestors made?

The word of the Lord.

RESPONSORIAL PSALM 25:4-5abc, 6 and 7cd, 8-9

℟. (4a) Teach me your ways, O Lord.

Show me your paths
and teach me to follow;
guide me by your truth
and instruct me.
You keep me safe.

℟. Teach me your ways, O Lord.

Please, LORD, remember,
you have always
been patient and kind.
Show how truly kind you are
and remember me.

℟. Teach me your ways, O Lord.

You are honest and merciful,
and you teach sinners
how to follow your path.
You lead humble people
to do what is right
and to stay on your path.

℟. Teach me your ways, O Lord.

SECOND READING

*We were eager to hand over to you not only the good news
but our lives as well.*

A reading from the first letter of Paul to the Thessalonians   2:7-9, 13

Brothers and sisters:
  We could have demanded help from you.
After all, Christ is the one who sent us.
We chose to be like children or like a mother nursing her baby.
We cared so much for you,
    and you became so dear to us,
      that we were willing to give our lives for you
        when we gave you God's message.

My dear friends,
    you surely haven't forgotten our hard work and hardships.
You remember how night and day we struggled to make a living,
    so that we could tell you God's message
      without being a burden to anyone.

We always thank God that you believed the message we preached.
It came from him,
    and it is not something made up by humans.
You accepted it as God's message,
    and now he is working in you.

The word of the Lord.

ALLELUIA   Matthew 23:9b,10b

℟. Alleluia, alleluia.
**You have one Father, your Father in heaven;
you have one teacher, the Lord Jesus Christ!**
℟. Alleluia, alleluia.

GOSPEL

The scribes and the Pharisees do not practice what they preach.

✣ **A reading from the holy gospel according to Matthew** 23:1-12

Jesus said to the crowds and to his disciples:
"The Pharisees and the teachers of the Law
>   are experts in the Law of Moses.
So obey everything they teach you,
>   but don't do as they do.
After all, they say one thing and do something else.

"They pile heavy burdens on people's shoulders
>   and won't lift a finger to help them.
Everything they do is just to show off in front of others.
They even make a big show
>   of wearing Scripture verses on their foreheads and arms,
>   and they wear big tassels for everyone to see.
They love the best seats at banquets
>   and the front seats in the meeting places.
And when they are in the market,
>   they like to have people greet them as their teachers.

"But none of you should be called a teacher.
You have only one teacher,
>   and all of you are like brothers and sisters.
Don't call anyone on earth your father.
All of you have the same Father in heaven.
None of you should be called the leader.
The Messiah is your only leader.

"Whoever is the greatest should be the servant of the others.
If you put yourself above others,
>   you will be put down.
But if you humble yourself,
>   you will be honored."

> The gospel of the Lord.

[147] THIRTY-FIRST SUNDAY IN ORDINARY TIME B

FIRST READING

Listen, Israel: You shall love the Lord with all your heart.

A reading from the book of Deuteronomy 6:2-6

Moses said to the people:
"You, your children,
 and all your descendants must respect the LORD.
And as long as you live,
 you must obey all of his laws and commands that I am teaching you.
If you do this,
 you will live a long time.

"People of Israel,
 listen carefully and obey all these laws.
Your nation will grow strong,
 and you will prosper in this land that is rich in milk
  and honey.
This is what the LORD God of your ancestors has promised you.

"Listen, people of Israel!
Only the LORD is our God.
You must love the LORD with all your heart, soul, and strength.
Don't forget anything that I am telling you today."

The word of the Lord.

RESPONSORIAL PSALM 18:1-2ab, 46

℟. (2) I love you, Lord, my strength.

I love you, LORD God,
and you make me strong.
You are my mighty rock,
my fortress, my protector.

℟. I love you, Lord, my strength.

You are the living LORD!
I will praise you.
You are a mighty rock.
I will honor you
for keeping me safe.

℟. I love you, Lord, my strength.

SECOND READING

Jesus is our high priest in heaven.

A reading from the letter to the Hebrews   7:26

Brothers and sisters:
   Jesus is the high priest we need.
He is holy and innocent and faultless,
   and not at all like us sinners.
Jesus is honored above all beings in heaven.

The word of the Lord.

ALLELUIA   John 14:23

℟. Alleluia, alleluia.

All who love me will keep my words,
and my Father will love them,
and we will come to them.

℟. Alleluia, alleluia.

GOSPEL

Love the Lord your God. Love your neighbor.

✠ A reading from the holy gospel according to Mark   12:28-31

One of the teachers of the Law of Moses came up
   while Jesus and the Sadducees were arguing.
When he heard Jesus give a good answer, he asked him,
"What is the most important commandment?"

Jesus answered, "The most important one says:
'People of Israel, you have only one Lord and God.
You must love him with all your heart, soul, mind, and strength.'
The second most important commandment says:
'Love others as much as you love yourself.'
No other commandment is more important than these."

The gospel of the Lord.

[148] THIRTY-FIRST SUNDAY IN ORDINARY TIME C

FIRST READING

You have mercy on all things because you love everything that exists.

A reading from the book of Wisdom   11:22—12:1

Our Lord, compared with you,
the world is a speck of dust too light for the scales.
And it quickly disappears like drops of morning dew.

You show mercy to everyone,
    and your power is absolute.
You overlook our sins,
    so that we will turn to you.

You created everything,
    and you love it all.
You would never make anything that you did not like.

Nothing would have lasted,
    unless you had wanted it to.
Only what you commanded to last could have endured.

Master, you love all who live,
    and you have pity on all of us,
    because everything is yours.
Your eternal Spirit is in everything.

                                The word of the Lord.

RESPONSORIAL PSALM   145:1-2, 8-9, 13cd-14

℟. (see 1) I will praise your name for ever, my king and my God.

I will praise you,
my God and King,
and always honor your name.
I will praise you each day
and always honor your name.

    ℟. I will praise your name for ever, my king and my God.

You are merciful, LORD!
You are kind and patient
and always loving.
You are good to everyone,
and you take care
of all your creation.

℟. I will praise your name for ever, my king and my God.

Our LORD, you keep your word
and do everything you say.
When someone stumbles or falls,
you give a helping hand.

℟. I will praise your name for ever, my king and my God.

SECOND READING

*May the name of our Lord Jesus Christ be glorified in you
and you in him.*

A reading from the second letter of Paul to the Thessalonians   1:11-12

Brothers and sisters:
 God chose you,
 and we keep praying that God will make you
  worthy of being his people.
We pray for God's power to help you do
 all the good things that you hope to do
 and that your faith makes you want to do.
Then, because God and our Lord Jesus Christ are so kind,
 you will bring honor to the name of our Lord Jesus,
 and he will bring honor to you.

The word of the Lord.

ALLELUIA   John 3:16

℟. Alleluia, alleluia.

**God loved the world so much, he gave us his only Son,
that all who believe in him might have eternal life.**

℟. Alleluia, alleluia.

GOSPEL

The Son of Man came to seek out and save what was lost.

✣ A reading from the holy gospel according to Luke   19:1-10

Jesus was going through Jericho,
  where a man named Zacchaeus lived.
He was in charge of collecting taxes and was very rich.

Jesus was heading his way,
  and Zacchaeus wanted to see what he was like.
But Zacchaeus was a short man and could not see over the crowd.
So he ran ahead and climbed up into a sycamore tree.

When Jesus got there, he looked up and said,
"Zacchaeus, hurry down!
I want to stay with you today."

Zacchaeus hurried down and gladly welcomed Jesus.

Everyone who saw this started grumbling,
"This man Zacchaeus is a sinner!
And Jesus is going home to eat with him."

Later that day Zacchaeus stood up and said to the Lord,
"I will give half of my property to the poor.
And I will now pay back four times as much
  to everyone I have ever cheated."

Jesus said to Zacchaeus,
"Today you and your family have been saved,
  because you are a true son of Abraham.
The Son of Man came to look for and to save
  people who are lost."

                                The gospel of the Lord.

[149] THIRTY-SECOND SUNDAY IN ORDINARY TIME A

FIRST READING

Wisdom is found by those who look for it.

A reading from the book of Wisdom 6:12-16

Wisdom shines brightly,
   and she is easily seen by all who love her
     and search for her.

Wisdom hurries to meet everyone who wants to be wise.
If you get up early and search,
   you will easily find her at your front door.

Keep your mind on Wisdom,
   and you will be very wise.
Keep thinking about her,
   and all of your worries will soon disappear.

Wisdom goes around searching for those who deserve her.
She meets them along the road and stays in their thoughts.

The word of the Lord.

RESPONSORIAL PSALM 63:1, 2-3, 6-7

℟. (2b) My soul is thirsting for you, O Lord my God.

You are my God. I worship you.
In my heart, I long for you,
as I would long for a stream
in a scorching desert.

℟. My soul is thirsting for you, O Lord my God.

I have seen your power
and your glory
in the place of worship.
Your love means more
than life to me,
and so I praise you.

℟. My soul is thirsting for you, O Lord my God.

I think about you
before I go to sleep,
and my thoughts turn to you
during the night.
You have helped me,
and I sing happy songs
in the shadow of your wings.

℟. My soul is thirsting for you, O Lord my God.

SECOND READING

Those who died, God will bring to life with Jesus.

A reading from the first letter of Paul to the Thessalonians   4:13-18

My friends, we want you to understand how it will be
    for those followers who have already died.
Then you won't grieve over them
    and be like people who don't have any hope.

We believe that Jesus died and was raised to life.
We also believe that when God brings Jesus back again,
    he will bring with him all who had faith in Jesus before they died.
Our Lord Jesus told us that when he comes,
    we won't go up to meet him
    ahead of his followers who have already died.

With a loud command and with the shout of the chief angel
    and a blast of God's trumpet,
    the Lord will return from heaven.
Then those who had faith in Christ before they died
    will be raised to life.
Next, all of us who are still alive
    will be taken up into the clouds together with them
    to meet the Lord in the sky.
From that time on we will all be with the Lord forever.

Encourage each other with these words.

                                                        The word of the Lord.

ALLELUIA

Matthew 24:42a, 44

℟. Alleluia, alleluia.

**Be watchful and ready:
you know not when the Son of Man is coming.**

℟. Alleluia, alleluia.

GOSPEL

Look, the bridegroom comes. Go out to meet him.

✛ A reading from the holy gospel according to Matthew   25:1-13

Jesus told his disciples this story about the kingdom of heaven:
"The kingdom of heaven is like what happened one night
    when ten girls took their oil lamps
      and went to a wedding to meet the groom.
Five of the girls were foolish and five were wise.
The foolish ones took their lamps, but no extra oil.
The ones who were wise took along extra oil for their lamps.

"The groom was late arriving,
    and the girls became drowsy and fell asleep.
Then in the middle of the night someone shouted,
'Here's the groom! Come to meet him!'

"When the girls got up and started getting their lamps ready,
    the foolish ones said to the others,
'Let us have some of your oil!
Our lamps are going out.'

"The girls who were wise answered,
'There's not enough oil for all of us!
Go and buy some for yourselves.'

"While the foolish girls were on their way to get some oil,
    the groom arrived.
The girls who were ready went into the wedding,
    and the doors were closed.
Later the other girls returned and shouted,
'Sir, sir! Open the door for us!'

"But the groom replied, 'I don't even know you!'

"So, my disciples, always be ready!
You don't know the day or the time
    when all this will happen."

                              The gospel of the Lord.

[150] THIRTY-SECOND SUNDAY IN ORDINARY TIME B

FIRST READING

*The widow made a little scone from her flour meal
and brought it to Elijah.*

A reading from the first book of Kings   17:10-16

Elijah went to Zarephath,
and near the city gate he saw a widow gathering sticks for a fire.
He asked her to bring him a cup of water.
When she started off to get the water, he asked,
"Would you also please bring me a piece of bread?"

The widow answered, "In the name of the living LORD your God,
I swear that I don't have any bread!
All I have is a handful of flour and a little olive oil.
I'm on my way home now with these few sticks
      to cook what I have for my son and me.
After that, we'll starve to death."

Elijah told the woman, "Don't worry!
Do as you have said
    and fix something for yourself and your son.
But first, make me a small piece of bread.
The LORD God of Israel has promised
      that your jar of flour won't become empty,
      and your jar of oil won't dry up
      before he sends rain for the crops."

The widow left and did exactly what Elijah had told her.
So every day Elijah and the widow and her family had food to eat.
There was always flour and oil,
    just as the LORD had promised and Elijah had said.

The word of the Lord.

RESPONSORIAL PSALM

146:6d-7b, 7c-8abc, 8d-9abc

℟. (1b) Praise the Lord, my soul!
or:
℟. Alleluia.

**God always keeps his word.
He gives justice to the poor
and food to the hungry.**

℟. Praise the Lord, my soul!
or:
℟. Alleluia.

**The LORD sets prisoners free
and heals blind eyes.
He gives a helping hand
to everyone who falls.**

℟. Praise the Lord, my soul!
or:
℟. Alleluia.

**The LORD loves good people
and looks after strangers.
He defends the rights
of orphans and widows.**

℟. Praise the Lord, my soul!
or:
℟. Alleluia.

ALLELUIA

Matthew 5:3

℟. Alleluia, alleluia.

**Blessed are the poor in spirit;
the kingdom of heaven is theirs!**

℟. Alleluia, alleluia.

GOSPEL

This poor widow has given more than all others.

✚ **A reading from the holy gospel according to Mark**   12:41-44

Jesus was sitting in the temple near the offering box
    and watching people put in their gifts.
He noticed that many rich people were giving a lot of money.

Finally, a poor widow came up
    and put in two coins that were worth only a few pennies.

Jesus told his disciples to gather around him.
Then he said:
"I tell you that this poor widow has put in more than all the others.
Everyone else gave what they didn't need.
But she is very poor and gave everything she had.
Now she doesn't have a cent to live on."

The gospel of the Lord.

[151] THIRTY-SECOND SUNDAY IN ORDINARY TIME C

FIRST READING

*The king of the world will receive us into life eternal
at the resurrection.*

A reading from the second book of Maccabees 7:1-2, 9-14

King Antiochus arrested seven Jewish brothers and their mother.
He had them beaten with heavy whips
   and tried to make them eat the meat of pigs,
 which was against their religion.
But one of them spoke up and said,
"Why are you torturing us like this?
We will die before we disobey the laws of our ancestors!"

When the second brother was almost dead,
   he said to the king,
"You're cruel!
You can kill us,
   but the King of this world will raise us back to life.
And then we will live forever,
   because we died, rather than disobey his laws."

When he died, they started torturing the third brother.
They told him, "Stick out your tongue!"

Right away he stuck out his tongue
   and bravely stretched out his arms as well.
He had a lot of courage and said,
"God in heaven gave these to me.
But I will give them up to obey his laws.
I know that he will give them back."

The king and all his troops were amazed at the young man's courage.
Here was someone willing to suffer.

After he was dead,
> the king's troops beat and tortured
>> the fourth brother in the same way.

But just before he died, he said,
"We are willing for you to kill us,
> because God has promised to raise us to life.

But you have no hope of being raised to life."

The word of the Lord.

RESPONSORIAL PSALM   17:1, 5-6, 8 and 15

    ℟. (15b) Lord, when your glory appears, my joy will be full.

I am innocent, LORD**!
Won't you listen as I pray
and beg for help?
I am honest!
Please hear my prayer.**

    ℟. Lord, when your glory appears, my joy will be full.

**I have followed you
without ever stumbling.
I pray to you, God,
because you will help me.
Listen and answer my prayer!**

    ℟. Lord, when your glory appears, my joy will be full.

**Protect me as you would
your very own eyes;
hide me in the shadow
of your wings.
I am innocent, L**ORD**,
and I will see your face!
When I awake, all I want
is to see you as you are.**

    ℟. Lord, when your glory appears, my joy will be full.

SECOND READING

May the Lord strengthen you in everything good that you do or say.

A reading from the second letter of Paul to the Thessalonians

2:16—3:5

Brothers and sisters:
God our Father loves us.
He is kind and has given us eternal comfort and a wonderful hope.
We pray that our Lord Jesus Christ and God our Father
    will encourage you and will help you
    always to do and say the right thing.

Finally, our friends, please pray for us.
This will help the message about the Lord to spread quickly,
    and others will respect it, just as you do.
Pray that we may be kept safe from worthless and evil people.
After all, not everyone has faith.

But the Lord can be trusted to make you strong
    and to protect you from harm.
He has made us sure that you are obeying what we taught you
    and that you will keep on obeying.
I pray that the Lord will guide you to be as loving as God
    and as patient as Christ.

                              The word of the Lord.

ALLELUIA

Revelation 1:5a, 6b

℟. Alleluia, alleluia.

**Jesus Christ is the firstborn from the dead;
glory and kingship be his for ever and ever.**

℟. Alleluia, alleluia.

GOSPEL

He is not a God of the dead but of the living.

✢ A reading from the holy gospel according to Luke   20:27-38

The Sadducees did not believe
> that people would rise to life after death.

So some of them came to Jesus and said:

"Teacher, Moses wrote
> that if a married man dies and has no children,
> his brother should marry the widow.

Their first son would then be thought of as the son of the dead brother.

"There were once seven brothers.
The first one married,
> but died without having any children.

The second one married his brother's widow,
> and he also died without having any children.

The same thing happened to the third one.

"Finally, all seven brothers married that woman
> and died without having any children.

At last the woman died.

"When God raises people from death,
> whose wife will this woman be?

All seven brothers had married her."

Jesus answered:
"The people in this world get married.
But in the future world no one who is worthy to rise from death
> will either marry or die.

They will be like the angels and will be God's children,
> because they have been raised to life.

"In the story about the burning bush,
> Moses clearly shows that people will live again.

He said, 'The Lord is the God worshiped by Abraham, Isaac, and Jacob.'
So the Lord is not the God of the dead,
> but of the living.

This means that anyone is alive as far as God is concerned."

> The gospel of the Lord.

[152] THIRTY-THIRD SUNDAY IN ORDINARY TIME **A**

FIRST READING

The day of the Lord is going to come like a thief in the night.

A reading from the first letter of Paul to the Thessalonians 5:1-6

Brothers and sisters:
  I don't need to write you
    about the time or date when all this will happen.
You surely know that the Lord's return
    will be as a thief coming at night.
People will think they are safe and secure.
But destruction will suddenly strike them
    like the pains of a woman about to give birth.
And they won't escape.

My dear friends, you don't live in darkness,
    and so that day won't surprise you like a thief.
All of you belong to the light and live in the day.
We don't live in the night or belong to the dark.
Others may sleep,
    but we should stay awake and be alert.

The word of the Lord.

RESPONSORIAL PSALM 27:1, 13-14

℟. (1a) The Lord is my light and my salvation.

You, LORD, are the light
that keeps me safe.
I am not afraid of anyone.
You protect me,
and I have no fears.

℟. The Lord is my light and my salvation.

LORD, I know I will live
to see how kind you are.
Trust the LORD!
Be brave and strong
and trust the LORD.

℟. The Lord is my light and my salvation.

THIRTY-THIRD SUNDAY IN ORDINARY TIME — A

ALLELUIA   John 15:4a, 5b

℟. Alleluia, alleluia.

**Live in me and let me live in you, says the Lord;
my branches bear much fruit.**

℟. Alleluia, alleluia.

GOSPEL

Because you have been faithful in small matters,
come into the joy of your master.

✠ A reading from the holy gospel according to Matthew   25:14-15, 19-21

Jesus told his disciples this story about the kingdom of God:
"The kingdom is like what happened when a man went away
      and put his three servants in charge of all he owned.
The man knew what each servant could do.
So he handed five thousand coins to the first servant,
    two thousand to the second,
    and one thousand to the third.
Then he left the country.

"Some time later the master of those servants returned.
He called them in and asked what they had done with his money.
The servant who had been given five thousand coins
      brought them in with the five thousand that he had earned.
He said, 'Sir, you gave me five thousand coins,
    and I have earned five thousand more.'

" 'Wonderful!' his master replied,
'You are a good and faithful servant.
I left you in charge of only a little,
    but now I will put you in charge of much more.
Come and share in my happiness!' "

                                                                The gospel of the Lord.

[153] THIRTY-THIRD SUNDAY IN ORDINARY TIME — B

FIRST READING

When that time comes your own people will be spared.

A reading from the book of the prophet Daniel 12:1-3

Prince Michael is the protector of your people,
   and he will appear when a time of terrible trouble comes.
That will be the worst time in all history.
Nothing like it has ever happened before.

But your people who have their names written in the book
   will be protected.
Many of those who lie dead in the ground will rise from death.
Some of them will be given eternal life,
   but others will receive nothing but eternal shame and disgrace.

Everyone who has been wise will shine as bright as the sky above,
   and everyone who has led others to please God
      will shine like the stars.

The word of the Lord.

RESPONSORIAL PSALM   16:5 and 8, 9-10, 11

℟. (1) Keep me safe, O God; you are my hope.

You, Lord, are all I want!
You are my choice,
and you keep me safe.
I will always look to you,
as you stand beside me
and protect me from fear.

℟. Keep me safe, O God; you are my hope.

With all my heart,
I will celebrate,
and I can safely rest.
I am your chosen one.
You won't leave me in the grave
or let my body decay.

℟. Keep me safe, O God; you are my hope.

You have shown me
the path to life,
and you make me glad
by being near to me.
Sitting at your right side,
I will always be joyful.

℟. Keep me safe, O God; you are my hope.

ALLELUIA
Luke 21:36

℟. Alleluia, alleluia.

Be watchful, pray constantly,
that you may be worthy to stand before the Son of Man.

℟. Alleluia, alleluia.

GOSPEL

The Son of Man shall gather his elect from the four winds.

✢ A reading from the holy gospel according to Mark 13:24-32

Jesus said to his disciples:
"In those days, right after that time of suffering,

'The sun will become dark,
and the moon will no longer shine.
The stars will fall,
and the powers in the sky will be shaken.'

"Then the Son of Man will be seen coming in the clouds
        with great power and glory.
He will send his angels to gather his chosen ones
        from all over the earth.

"Learn a lesson from a fig tree.
When its branches sprout and start putting out leaves,
        you know summer is near.
So when you see all these things happening,
        you will know that the time has almost come.
You can be sure that some of the people living today
        will still be alive when all this happens.

**The sky and the earth will not last forever,
    but my words will.**

**"No one knows the day or the time.
The angels in heaven don't know,
    and the Son himself doesn't know.
Only the Father knows."**

The gospel of the Lord.

[154] THIRTY-THIRD SUNDAY IN ORDINARY TIME — C

FIRST READING

The sun of righteousness will shine on you.

A reading from the book of the prophet Malachi   3:19-20

The Lord says this:
"That day will surely come!
It will be like a red-hot furnace,
 and its flames will burn up proud and evil people,
 as though they were straw.
The Lord All-Powerful has promised
  that not a branch or a root will be left.

"But if you honor my name,
 justice will shine like the sun,
 and its rays will bring healing."

The word of the Lord.

RESPONSORIAL PSALM   98:5-6, 7-8, 9

℟. (see 9) The Lord comes to rule the earth with justice.

Make music for him on harps.
Play beautiful melodies!
Sound the trumpets and horns
and celebrate with joyful songs
for our Lord and King!

℟. The Lord comes to rule the earth with justice.

Command the ocean to roar
with all of its creatures,
and the earth to shout
with all of its people.
Order the rivers
to clap their hands,
and all of the hills
to sing together.

℟. The Lord comes to rule the earth with justice.

Let them worship the LORD!
He is coming to judge
everyone on the earth,
and he will be honest and fair.

℟. The Lord comes to rule the earth with justice.

SECOND READING

Do not give anyone food who refuses to work.

A reading from the second letter of Paul to the Thessalonians 3:7-12

Brothers and sisters:
You surely know that you should follow our example.
We didn't waste our time loafing,
 and we didn't accept food from anyone without paying for it.
We didn't want to be a burden to any of you,
 so night and day we worked as hard as we could.

We had the right not to work,
 but we wanted to set an example for you.
We also gave you the rule that if you don't work,
 you don't eat.

Now we learn that some of you just loaf around and won't do any work,
 except the work of a busybody.
So, for the sake of our Lord Jesus Christ,
 we ask and beg these people to settle down
  and start working for a living.

The word of the Lord.

ALLELUIA

Luke 21:38

℟. Alleluia, alleluia.

**Lift up your heads and see;
your redemption is near at hand.**

℟. Alleluia, alleluia.

THIRTY-THIRD SUNDAY IN ORDINARY TIME — C

GOSPEL

Your endurance will win you your life.

✤ A reading from the holy gospel according to Luke   21:5-19

Some people were talking about the beautiful stones
    used to build the temple
    and about the gifts that had been placed in it.

Jesus said, "Do you see these stones?
The time is coming when not one of them will be left in place.
They will all be knocked down."

Some people asked, "Teacher, when will all this happen?
How can we know when these things are about to take place?"

Jesus replied:
"Don't be fooled by all those men
    who will come and claim to be me.
They will say, 'I am Christ!'
    and 'Now is the time!'
But don't follow them.
When you hear about wars and riots, don't be afraid.
These things will have to happen first,
    but that is not the end.

"Nations will go to war against one another,
    and kingdoms will attack each other.
There will be great earthquakes,
    and in many places people will starve to death
        and suffer terrible diseases.
All sorts of frightening things will be seen in the sky.

"Before all this happens,
    you will be arrested and punished.
You will be tried in the Jewish meeting places and put in jail.
Because of me
    you will be placed on trial before kings and governors.
But this will be your chance to tell about your faith.

"Don't worry about what you will say to defend yourselves.
I will give you the wisdom to know what to say.
None of your enemies will be able to oppose you
    or to say that you are wrong.

"You will be betrayed by your own parents,
    brothers, family, and friends.
Some of you will even be killed.
Because of me you will be hated by everyone.
But don't worry!
You will be saved by being faithful to me."

The gospel of the Lord.

[155] **Thirty-Fourth or Last Sunday in Ordinary Time** **A**
CHRIST THE KING

FIRST READING

The Lord will shepherd his flock.

A reading from the book of the prophet Ezekiel 34:11-12, 14-16abce

The LORD says this:
"I, the LORD God, will look for my people
 and take care of them myself.
As a shepherd looks for sheep that have wandered away,
 I will search for my scattered people.
I will rescue them from all the places where they went
 on that dark and gloomy day.

"My people will be like sheep grazing and resting
 in good pastures and on Israel's mountains.
I, the LORD All-Powerful, will lead them there and watch over them.

"I will look for the lost sheep
 and bring back the ones that have wandered off.
If any are hurt,
 I will bandage their wounds.
If any are weak,
 I will help them.
I will take good care of my people!"

The word of the Lord.

RESPONSORIAL PSALM 23:1-2ab, 2c-3, 5-6

℟. (1) The Lord is my shepherd; there is nothing I shall want.

You, LORD, are my shepherd.
I will never be in need.
You let me rest in fields
of green grass.

℟. The Lord is my shepherd; there is nothing I shall want.

You lead me to streams
of peaceful water,
and you refresh my life.
You are true to your name,
and you lead me
along the right paths.

℟. The Lord is my shepherd; there is nothing I shall want.

You treat me to a feast,
while my enemies watch.
You honor me as your guest,
and you fill my cup
until it overflows.
Your kindness and love
will always be with me
each day of my life,
and I will live forever
in your house, LORD.

℟. The Lord is my shepherd; there is nothing I shall want.

SECOND READING

Christ will hand over the kingdom to God the Father.

A reading from the first letter of Paul to the Corinthians   15:20-24a

Brothers and sisters:
Christ has been raised to life!
And he makes us certain
    that others will also be raised to life.

Just as we will die because of Adam,
    we will be raised to life because of Christ.
Adam brought death to all of us,
    and Christ will bring life to all of us.

But we must each wait our turn.
Christ was the first to be raised to life,
    and his people will be raised to life when he returns.
Then after Christ has destroyed all powers and forces,
    the end will come.

The word of the Lord.

ALLELUIA

Mark 11:9, 10

℟. Alleluia, alleluia.

Blessed is the one who inherits the kingdom of David our father; blessed is the one who comes in the name of the Lord.

℟. Alleluia, alleluia.

GOSPEL

The Son of Man will sit upon his seat of glory and he will separate all into two groups.

✠ A reading from the holy gospel according to Matthew   25:31-46

Jesus said to his disciples:
"When the Son of Man comes in his glory with all of his angels,
he will sit on his royal throne.

"The people of all nations will be brought before him,
    and he will separate them,
    as shepherds separate their sheep from their goats.

"He will place the sheep on his right and the goats on his left.
Then the king will say to those on his right,
'My father has blessed you!
Come and receive the kingdom that was prepared for you
        before the world was created.
When I was hungry, you gave me something to eat,
    and when I was thirsty, you gave me something to drink.
When I was a stranger, you welcomed me,
    and when I was naked, you gave me clothes to wear.
When I was sick, you took care of me,
    and when I was in jail, you visited me.'

"Then the ones who pleased the Lord will ask,
'When did we give you something to eat or drink?
When did we welcome you as a stranger or give you clothes to wear
        or visit you while you were sick or in jail?'

"The king will answer,
'Whenever you did it for any of my people,
        no matter how unimportant they seemed,
    you did it for me.'

"Then the king will say to those on his left,
'Get away from me!
You are under God's curse.
Go into the everlasting fire prepared for the devil and his angels!
I was hungry, but you did not give me anything to eat,
    and I was thirsty, but you did not give me anything to drink.
I was a stranger, but you did not welcome me,
    and I was naked, but you did not give me any clothes to wear.
I was sick and in jail, but you did not take care of me.'

"Then the people will ask,
'Lord, when did we fail to help you when you were hungry or thirsty
    or a stranger or naked or sick or in jail?'

"The king will say to them,
'Whenever you failed to help any of my people,
    no matter how unimportant they seemed,
    you failed to do it for me.'"

Then Jesus said, "Those people will be punished forever.
But the ones who pleased God will have eternal life."

                                              The gospel of the Lord.

[156] Thirty-Fourth or Last Sunday in Ordinary Time B

CHRIST THE KING

FIRST READING

His sovereignty is eternal.

A reading from the book of the prophet Daniel 7:13-14

During the night I had a vision,
and I saw what looked like the Son of Man,
coming with the clouds of heaven.

He came toward the Eternal God and was led into his presence,
where he was honored and given the power to rule as king.
People of every nation and language worshiped him.

He will rule forever,
and his kingdom will never be destroyed.

The word of the Lord.

RESPONSORIAL PSALM 93:1, 2 and 5

℟. (1a) The Lord is king; he is robed in majesty.

Our LORD, you are King!
Majesty and power
are your royal robes.
You put the world in place,
and it will never be moved.

℟. The Lord is king; he is robed in majesty.

You have always ruled,
and you are eternal.
Your decisions are firm,
and your temple will always
be beautiful and holy.

℟. The Lord is king; he is robed in majesty.

SECOND READING

*The ruler of the kings of the earth ...
made us a line of kings, priests to serve his God.*

A reading from the book of Revelation   1:5-8

May kindness and peace be yours from Jesus Christ,
     the faithful witness.

Jesus was the first to conquer death,
     and he is the ruler of all earthly kings.
Christ loves us,
     and by his blood he set us free from our sins.
He lets us rule as kings and serve God his Father as priests.
To him be glory and power forever and ever! Amen.

Look! He is coming with the clouds.
Everyone will see him,
     even the ones who stuck a sword through him.
All people on earth will weep because of him.
Yes, it will happen! Amen.

The Lord God says, "I am Alpha and Omega,
     the one who is and was and is coming.
I am God All-Powerful!"

                                        The word of the Lord.

ALLELUIA   Mark 11:9,10

℟. Alleluia, alleluia.

**Blessed is the one who inherits the kingdom of David our father;
blessed is the one who comes in the name of the Lord.**

℟. Alleluia, alleluia.

GOSPEL

You say that I am a king.

✠ A reading from the holy gospel according to John   18:33b-37

Pilate called Jesus over and asked,
"Are you the king of the Jews?"

Jesus answered,
"Are you asking this on your own
    or did someone tell you about me?"

"You know I'm not a Jew!" Pilate said.
"Your own people and the chief priests brought you to me.
What have you done?"

Jesus answered, "My kingdom does not belong to this world.
If it did,
    my followers would have fought
        to keep the Jewish leaders from handing me over to you.
No, my kingdom does not belong to this world."

"So you are a king," Pilate replied.

"You are saying that I am a king," Jesus told him.
"I was born into this world to tell about the truth.
And everyone who belongs to the truth knows my voice."

The gospel of the Lord.

[157] **Thirty-Fourth or Last Sunday in Ordinary Time** **C**
CHRIST THE KING

FIRST READING

They anointed David king of Israel.

A reading from the second book of Samuel 5:1-3

Israel's leaders met with David at Hebron and said,
"We are your close relatives.
Even when Saul was king,
  you led our nation in battle.
And the LORD promised that someday you would rule Israel
  and take care of us like a shepherd."

During the meeting,
  David made an agreement with the leaders,
  and asked the LORD to be their witness.
Then the leaders poured olive oil on David's head
  to show that he was now the king of Israel.

The word of the Lord.

RESPONSORIAL PSALM 47:1-2, 7-8

℟. (8a) God is king of all the earth.

All of you nations,
clap your hands and shout
joyful praises to God.
The LORD Most High is fearsome,
the ruler of all the earth.

℟. God is king of all the earth.

God is ruler of all the earth!
Praise God with songs.
God rules the nations
from his sacred throne.

℟. God is king of all the earth.

SECOND READING

The Father has taken us into the kingdom of his beloved Son.

A reading from the letter of Paul to the Colossians 1:15-18

Brothers and sisters:
Christ is exactly like God, who cannot be seen.
He is the first-born Son, superior to all creation.
Everything was created by him,
>everything in heaven and on earth,
>everything seen and unseen,
>including all forces and powers,
>and all rulers and authorities.

All things were created by God's Son,
>and everything was made for him.

God's Son was before all else,
>and by him everything is held together.

He is the head of his body, which is the church.
He is the very beginning,
>the first to be raised from death,
>so that he would be above all others.

The word of the Lord.

ALLELUIA Mark 11:9,10

℟. Alleluia, alleluia.

Blessed is the one who inherits the kingdom of David our father; blessed is the one who comes in the name of the Lord.

℟. Alleluia, alleluia.

GOSPEL

Lord, remember me when you come into your kingdom.

✠ A reading from the holy gospel according to Luke   23:35-43

While the crowd stood there watching Jesus,
the leaders insulted him by saying,
"He saved others.
Now he should save himself,
if he really is God's chosen Messiah!"

The soldiers made fun of Jesus and brought him some wine.
They said, "If you are the king of the Jews, save yourself!"
Above him was a sign that said,
"This is the King of the Jews."

One of the criminals hanging there also insulted Jesus by saying,
"Aren't you the Messiah?
Save yourself and save us!"

But the other criminal told the first one off,
"Don't you fear God?
Aren't you getting the same punishment as this man?
We got what was coming to us,
but he didn't do anything wrong."
Then he said to Jesus,
"Remember me when you come into power!"

Jesus replied,
"I promise that today you will be with me in paradise."

The gospel of the Lord.

SOLEMNITIES OF THE LORD DURING ORDINARY TIME

[158]   **Sunday after Pentecost**   **A**

HOLY TRINITY

FIRST READING

The Lord God, ruler of all, merciful and loving.

A reading from the book of Exodus   34:4b-6, 8-9

Moses did exactly what the LORD had told him.
   He got up early and carried the two stone tablets
      up the side of Mount Sinai.

The LORD came down in a cloud and stood beside Moses.
Then he said, "I am the LORD."
He also walked up and down in front of Moses and said,
"I am the LORD God,
      and I am kind and merciful.
I don't easily lose my temper,
      and my love can be trusted."

Moses quickly bowed low.
He worshiped and said,
"LORD, if you are pleased with me,
      then don't leave your people.
We are stubborn.
But I beg you to forgive our terrible sins
      and let us be your very own people."

                                     The word of the Lord.

RESPONSORIAL PSALM   Daniel 3:52, 53 and 56

    ℟. (52b) Glory and praise for ever!

**Lord God of our ancestors,
you are worthy of praise, the highest praise forever.
Your glorious and holy name
is also worthy of praise, the highest praise forever.**

    ℟. Glory and praise for ever!

**You are glorious and holy,
worthy of praise in your temple, the highest praise forever.**

You are worthy of praise
in the heavens, honored with hymns forever.

℟. Glory and praise for ever!

SECOND READING

<blockquote>The grace of our Lord Jesus Christ and the love of God
and the fellowship of the Holy Spirit be with you all.</blockquote>

A reading from the second letter of Paul to the Corinthians   13:11-13

Good-bye, my friends.
Do better and pay attention to what I have said.
Try to get along and live peacefully with each other.

Now I pray that God,
>who gives love and peace,
>will be with you.

Give each other a warm greeting.
All of God's people send their greetings.

I pray that the Lord Jesus Christ
>will bless you and be kind to you!

May God bless you with his love,
>and may the Holy Spirit join all your hearts together.

The word of the Lord.

ALLELUIA   See Revelation 1:8

℟. Alleluia, alleluia.

**Glory to the Father, the Son, and the Holy Spirit:
to God who is, who was, and who is to come.**

℟. Alleluia, alleluia.

GOSPEL

God sent his Son to save the world through him.

✣ A reading from the holy gospel according to John 3:16-17

Jesus told Nicodemus:
"God loved the people of this world so much
   that he gave his only Son,
so that everyone who has faith in him
   will have eternal life and never die.
God did not send his Son into the world to condemn its people.
He sent him to save them!"

The gospel of the Lord.

[159] **Sunday after Pentecost**
HOLY TRINITY
B

FIRST READING

*The Lord is God in heaven above and on earth below:
there is no other.*

A reading from the book of Deuteronomy   4:39-40

Moses said to the people:
"Today there is something you must learn and never forget.
The Lord God rules in heaven above and on earth below.
There is no other god.
Obey his laws and commands that I am teaching you today.
Then all will go well for you and your descendants.
You will always live in the land
    that the Lord your God is giving you forever."

The word of the Lord.

RESPONSORIAL PSALM   33:4-5, 6 and 9, 20 and 22

℟. (12b) Happy the people the Lord has chosen to be his own.

The Lord is truthful;
he can be trusted.
He loves justice and fairness,
and he is kind to everyone
everywhere on earth.

℟. Happy the people the Lord has chosen to be his own.

The Lord made the heavens
and everything in them
by his word.
As soon as he spoke
the world was created;
at his command,
the earth was formed.

℟. Happy the people the Lord has chosen to be his own.

We depend on you, LORD**,
to help and protect us.
Be kind and bless us!
We depend on you.**

℟. Happy the people the Lord has chosen to be his own.

SECOND READING

*You have received the Spirit that makes you God's children
and in that Spirit we call God: Abba, Father!*

A reading from the letter of Paul to the Romans　　　　　8:14-17

Brothers and sisters:
　**Only those people who are led by God's Spirit are his children.
God's Spirit doesn't make us slaves who are afraid of him.
Instead, we become his children and call him our Father.
God's Spirit makes us sure that we are his children.**

**His Spirit lets us know that together with Christ
　　we will be given what God has promised.
We will also share in the glory of Christ,
　　because we have suffered with him.**

　　　　　　　　　　　　　　　　　　　　The word of the Lord.

ALLELUIA　　　　　　　　　　　　　　　　　　　　See Revelation 1:8

℟. Alleluia, alleluia.

**Glory to the Father, the Son, and the Holy Spirit:
to God who is, who was, and who is to come.**

℟. Alleluia, alleluia.

GOSPEL

*Baptize them in the name of the Father,
and of the Son, and of the Holy Spirit.*

✚ **A reading from the holy gospel according to Matthew** 28:16-20

Jesus' eleven disciples went to a mountain in Galilee,
    where Jesus had told them to meet him.
They saw him and worshiped him,
    but some of them doubted.

Jesus came to them and said:
"I have been given all authority in heaven and on earth!
Go to the people of all nations and make them my disciples.
Baptize them in the name of the Father,
    the Son, and the Holy Spirit,
    and teach them to do everything I have told you.

"I will be with you always,
    even until the end of the world."

                              The gospel of the Lord.

Sunday after Pentecost
HOLY TRINITY

FIRST READING

Wisdom was born before the earth was made.

A reading from the book of Proverbs 8:22-31

From the very beginning, I was with the LORD.
I was there before he began to create the earth.
At the very first, the LORD gave life to me.
When I was born,
> there were no oceans or springs of water.
My birth was before mountains were formed or hills were put in place.
It happened long before God had made the earth
> or any of its fields or even the dust.

I was there when the LORD put the heavens in place
> and stretched the sky over the surface of the sea.
I was with him when he placed the clouds in the sky
> and created the springs that fill the ocean.
I was there when he set boundaries for the sea
> to make it obey him,
> and when he laid foundations to support the earth.

I was right beside the LORD, helping him plan and build.
I made him happy each day,
> and I was happy at his side.
I was pleased with his world and pleased with its people.

The word of the Lord.

RESPONSORIAL PSALM 8:3-4, 5-6, 7-8

℟. (2a) O Lord, our God, how wonderful your name in all the earth!

**I often think of the heavens
your hands have made,
and of the moon and stars
you put in place.
Then I ask, "Why do you care
about us humans?
Why are you concerned
for us weaklings?"**

℟. O Lord, our God, how wonderful your name in all the earth!

**You made us a little lower
than you yourself,
and you have crowned us
with glory and honor.
You let us rule everything
your hands have made.
And you put all of it
under our power —**

℟. O Lord, our God, how wonderful your name in all the earth!

**The sheep and the cattle,
and every wild animal,
the birds in the sky,
the fish in the sea,
and all ocean creatures.**

℟. O Lord, our God, how wonderful your name in all the earth!

ALLELUIA See Revelation 1:8

℟. Alleluia, alleluia.

**Glory to the Father, the Son, and the Holy Spirit:
to God who is, who was, and who is to come.**

℟. Alleluia, alleluia.

GOSPEL

Whatever the Father has is mine.
The Spirit will receive what I give and tell you about it.

✟ A reading from the holy gospel according to John 16:12-15

Jesus said to his disciples:
"I have much more to say to you,
   but right now it would be more than you could understand.
The Spirit shows what is true
      and will come and guide you into the full truth.

"The Spirit does not speak on his own.
He will tell you only what he has heard from me,
   and he will let you know what is going to happen.

"The Spirit will bring glory to me
      by taking my message and telling it to you.
Everything that the Father has is mine.
That is why I have said
      that the Spirit takes my message and tells it to you."

                              The gospel of the Lord.

[161] **Sunday after Trinity Sunday** **A**

THE BODY AND BLOOD OF CHRIST

FIRST READING

The Lord gave you food that you and your ancestors did not know.

A reading from the book of Deuteronomy   8:2-3, 14b-16a

Moses told the people:
"Don't forget how the LORD your God
   led you in the desert for forty years.
The LORD did this
   so that you would learn to depend on him.
And he wanted to know
   if you were truly willing to obey him.

"The LORD made you go hungry.
Then he gave you manna,
   a kind of food that you and your ancestors had never heard about.
He did this to teach you that people need more than food to live.
They need every word that the LORD has spoken.

"The LORD your God brought you out of Egypt,
   where you were slaves.
He led you safely through a big and terrible desert
      that was full of poisonous snakes and scorpions.

"The LORD gave you water from solid rock.
And in the desert he gave you manna,
   a kind of food your ancestors had never heard about.
He tested you like this to teach you to depend on him,
   so that all would go well for you."

                                        The word of the Lord.

RESPONSORIAL PSALM   147:12 and 14, 19-20

    ℟. (12) Praise the Lord, Jerusalem.
    or:
    ℟. Alleluia.

Everyone in Jerusalem,
come and praise
the LORD your God!

God lets you live in peace,
and he gives you
the very best wheat.

> ℟. Praise the Lord, Jerusalem.
> **or:**
> ℟. Alleluia.

God gave his laws and teachings
to the descendants of Jacob,
the nation of Israel.
But he has not given his laws
to any other nation.
Shout praises to the Lord!

> ℟. Praise the Lord, Jerusalem.
> **or:**
> ℟. Alleluia.

SECOND READING

Though we are many, we are one bread.

A reading from the first letter of Paul to the Corinthians   10:16-17

Brothers and sisters:
  When we drink from the cup that we ask God to bless,
    isn't that sharing in the blood of Christ?
When we eat the bread that we break,
    isn't that sharing in the body of Christ?
By sharing in the same loaf of bread,
    we become one body,
    even though there are many of us.

The word of the Lord.

ALLELUIA

John 6:51

> ℟. Alleluia, alleluia.
>
> **I am the living bread from heaven, says the Lord;
> whoever eats this bread will live for ever.**
>
> ℟. Alleluia, alleluia.

GOSPEL

My flesh is real food and my blood is real drink.

✣ A reading from the holy gospel according to John   6:51-58

Jesus said to the crowd:
"I am the bread from heaven!
Everyone who eats it will live forever.
My flesh is the life-giving bread
    that I give to the people of this world."

They started arguing with each other and asked,
"How can he give us his flesh to eat?"

Jesus answered:
"I tell you for certain that you won't live
    unless you eat the flesh and drink the blood of the Son of Man.
But if you do eat my flesh and drink my blood,
    you will have eternal life,
    and I will raise you to life on the last day.

"My flesh is the true food,
    and my blood is the true drink.
If you eat my flesh and drink my blood,
    you are one with me, and I am one with you.

"The living Father sent me,
    and I have life because of him.
Now everyone who eats my flesh will live because of me.

"The bread that comes down from heaven
    is not like what your ancestors ate.
They died,
    but whoever eats this bread will live forever."

                                            The gospel of the Lord.

[162] **Sunday after Trinity Sunday** **B**
THE BODY AND BLOOD OF CHRIST

FIRST READING

    This is the blood of the covenant that the Lord has made with you.

A reading from the book of Exodus   24:3-8

M oses told the people all of the Lord's commands and laws.
The people answered,
    "We will do everything the Lord has commanded!"
Then Moses wrote down all that the Lord had said.

The next morning Moses got up early
    and built an altar at the foot of the mountain.
He took a large stone for each of the twelve tribes of Israel
    and placed the stones there.
Then he sent some young men to burn offerings and sacrifice bulls
    as special offerings to the Lord.
Moses put half of the blood from the animals into some bowls
    and sprinkled the other half on the altar.

Moses read aloud from the book of the Lord's promises,
    and the people shouted,
"We will obey the Lord!
We will do everything he has commanded."

Then Moses took the blood that was in the bowls.
He sprinkled it on the people and told them,
"This blood shows that the Lord will keep all of his promises to you."

                                                      The word of the Lord.

THE BODY AND BLOOD OF CHRIST — B

RESPONSORIAL PSALM 116:12-13, 17-19ab

℟. (13) I will take the cup of salvation, and call on the name of the Lord.
or:
℟. Alleluia.

**What must I give you, LORD,
for being so good to me?
I will pour out an offering
of wine to you,
and I will pray in your name
because you have saved me.**

℟. I will take the cup of salvation, and call on the name of the Lord.
or:
℟. Alleluia.

**I will offer you a sacrifice
to show how grateful I am,
and I will pray.
I will keep my promise to you
when your people
gather at your temple in Jerusalem.**

℟. I will take the cup of salvation, and call on the name of the Lord.
or:
℟. Alleluia.

ALLELUIA John 6:51

℟. Alleluia, alleluia.

**I am the living bread from heaven, says the Lord;
whoever eats this bread will live for ever.**

℟. Alleluia, alleluia.

GOSPEL

This is my body. This is my blood.

✤ A reading from the holy gospel according to Mark   14:12-16, 22-26

It was the first day of the Feast of Thin Bread,
   and the Passover lambs were being killed.
Jesus' disciples asked him,
"Where do you want us to prepare the Passover meal?"

Jesus said to two of the disciples,
"Go into the city,
   where you will meet a man carrying a jar of water.
Follow him, and when he goes into a house,
   say to the owner,
'Our teacher wants to know if you have a room
     where he can eat the Passover meal with his disciples.'
The owner will take you upstairs and show you a large room
   furnished and ready for you to use.
Prepare the meal there."

The two disciples went into the city
   and found everything just as Jesus had told them.
So they prepared the Passover meal.

During the meal Jesus took some bread in his hands.
He blessed the bread and broke it.
Then he gave it to his disciples and said,
"Take this. It is my body."

Jesus picked up a cup of wine and gave thanks to God.
He then gave it to his disciples and said,
"Drink it!"
So they all drank some.

Then he said,
"This is my blood,
   which is poured out for many people,
   and with it God makes his agreement.
From now on I will not drink any wine,
   until I drink new wine in God's kingdom."

Then they sang a hymn and went out to the Mount of Olives.

                                       The gospel of the Lord.

[163]   Sunday after Trinity Sunday   **C**

THE BODY AND BLOOD OF CHRIST

FIRST READING

Melchizedek offered bread and wine.

A reading from the book of Genesis   14:18-20

King Melchizedek of Salem brought out some bread and wine. He was a priest of God Most High, and he said to Abraham,

> "I give you the blessing of God Most High,
> Creator of heaven and of the earth.
> All praise belongs to God Most High,
> who let you defeat your enemies."

Then Abraham gave him a tenth of everything.

The word of the Lord.

RESPONSORIAL PSALM   110:1, 3, 4

℟. (4b) You are a priest for ever, in the line of Melchizedek.

The LORD said to my Lord,
"Sit at my right side,
until I make your enemies
into a footstool for you."

℟. You are a priest for ever, in the line of Melchizedek.

Your glorious power
will be seen on the day
you begin to rule.
You will wear the sacred robes
and shine like the morning sun
in all of your strength.

℟. You are a priest for ever, in the line of Melchizedek.

The LORD has made a promise
that will never be broken:

"You will be a priest forever,
just like Melchizedek."

℟. You are a priest for ever, in the line of Melchizedek.

SECOND READING

Until the Lord comes, every time you eat this bread
and drink this cup, you proclaim his death.

A reading from the first letter of Paul to the Corinthians 11:23-26

Brothers and sisters:
I have already told you what the Lord Jesus did
> on the night he was betrayed.
And it came from the Lord himself.

He took some bread in his hands.
Then after he had given thanks,
> he broke it and said,
"This is my body, which is given for you.
Eat this and remember me."

After the meal,
> Jesus took a cup of wine in his hands and said,
"This is my blood,
> and with it God makes his new agreement with you.
Drink this and remember me."

The Lord meant that when you eat this bread and drink from this cup,
> you tell about his death until he comes.

The word of the Lord.

ALLELUIA John 6:51

℟. Alleluia, alleluia.

**I am the living bread from heaven, says the Lord;
whoever eats this bread will live for ever.**

℟. Alleluia, alleluia.

GOSPEL

They all ate and were filled.

✢ A reading from the holy gospel according to Luke 9:11b-17

Jesus welcomed the people.
He spoke to them about God's kingdom
    and healed everyone who was sick.

Late in the afternoon the twelve apostles came to Jesus and said,
"Send the crowd to the villages and farms around here.
They need to find a place to stay and something to eat.
There is nothing in this place.
It is like a desert!"

Jesus answered, "You give them something to eat."

But they replied,
"We have only five small loaves of bread and two fish.
If we are going to feed all these people,
    we will have to go and buy food."
There were about five thousand men in the crowd.

Jesus said to his disciples,
"Have the people sit in groups of fifty."

They did this,
    and all the people sat down.
Jesus took the five loaves and the two fish.
He looked up toward heaven and blessed the food.
Then he broke the bread and fish
    and handed them to his disciples to give to the people.

Everyone ate all they wanted.
What was left over filled twelve baskets.

                                        The gospel of the Lord.

[164] Friday after the Second Sunday after Pentecost **A**

THE SACRED HEART OF JESUS

FIRST READING

The Lord loves you and has chosen you.

A reading from the book of Deuteronomy   7:6-11

Moses told the people:
"You are the special people of the LORD your God.
The LORD has chosen you from all the people on earth
    to be his very own.
He wanted you and chose you,
    even though you are not a powerful nation.
In fact, you are weaker than any other nation.

"But the LORD had made a promise to your ancestors,
    and he kept it by caring for you.
With his own mighty arm
    he rescued you from the power of the king of Egypt,
    who had made you his slaves.

"Don't forget that the LORD your God is the only God.
He can be trusted to keep his merciful promise for thousands of years
    to everyone who loves and obeys him.
But he quickly and completely destroys anyone who hates him.
So be sure to obey the laws, commands, and rules
    that I am teaching you today."

The word of the Lord.

RESPONSORIAL PSALM   103:1-2, 3 and 5

℟. (see 17) The Lord's kindness is everlasting to those who fear him.

With all my heart
I praise the LORD,
and with all that I am
I praise his holy name!
With all my heart
I praise the LORD!

I will never forget
how kind he has been.

> ℟. The Lord's kindness is everlasting to those who fear him.

The LORD forgives our sins
and heals us when we are sick.
Each day that we live,
he provides for our needs
and gives us the strength
of a young eagle.

> ℟. The Lord's kindness is everlasting to those who fear him.

SECOND READING

God loved us first.

A reading from the first letter of John 4:7-11, 16b

My dear friends, we must love each other.
Love comes from God,
and when we love each other,
it shows that we have been given new life.

We are now God's children, and we know him.

God is love,
and anyone who doesn't love others has never known him.

God showed his love for us
when he sent his only Son into the world to give us life.

Real love is not our love for God, but his love for us.
God sent his Son to be the sacrifice by which our sins are forgiven.

Dear friends,
since God loved us this much,
we must love each other.

God is love.
If we keep on loving others,
we will stay one in our hearts with God,
and he will stay one with us.

The word of the Lord.

ALLELUIA

Matthew 11:29ab

℟. Alleluia, alleluia.

**Take my yoke upon you;
learn from me, for I am gentle and humble of heart.**

℟. Alleluia, alleluia.

GOSPEL

I am gentle and humble of heart.

✠ A reading from the holy gospel according to Matthew   11:25-30

On one occasion Jesus said:
"My Father, Lord of heaven and earth,
I am grateful that you hid all this
    from wise and educated people
    and showed it to ordinary people.
Yes, Father, that is what pleased you.

"My Father has given me everything,
    and he is the only one who knows the Son.
The only one who truly knows the Father is the Son.
But the Son wants to tell others about the Father,
    so that they can know him too.

"If you are tired from carrying heavy burdens,
    come to me and I will give you rest.
Take the yoke I give you.
Put it on your shoulders and learn from me.
I am gentle and humble,
    and you will find rest.
This yoke is easy to bear,
    and this burden is light."

The gospel of the Lord.

[165]   **Friday after the Second Sunday after Pentecost**   **B**

THE SACRED HEART OF JESUS

FIRST READING

My heart is saddened at the thought of parting.

A reading from the book of the prophet Hosea   11:1, 3-4, 8c-9

The Lord says this:
 When Israel was young,
  I loved him,
  and I rescued my son from Egypt.
I took my people by the hand and taught them to walk.

I was the one who healed them,
 but they did not know it.
I was loving and kind,
 and I made them want to come to me.
I freed them from slavery and tenderly fed them.

I have now changed my mind,
 and I feel sorry for you.
I am terribly angry,
 but I won't destroy Israel.
I am the holy God here with you!
I am not a mere human,
 and I won't show my anger.

                                                          The word of the Lord.

RESPONSORIAL PSALM   Isaiah 12:2-3, 4bcd, 5-6

℟. (3) You will draw water joyfully from the springs of salvation.

I trust the Lord to save me, and I won't be afraid.
My power and my strength come from the Lord God,
 and he has saved me.
When the Lord saves you,
 you will rejoice as you drink from refreshing streams.

℟. You will draw water joyfully from the springs of salvation.

On that day you will say,
"Our LORD, we are thankful, and we worship only you.
We will tell the nations how glorious you are
and what you have done."

℟. You will draw water joyfully from the springs of salvation.

"We will sing your praises everywhere
because of your wonderful deeds."
People of Jerusalem, celebrate and sing.
The famous LORD God of Israel is here with you.

℟. You will draw water joyfully from the springs of salvation.

SECOND READING

To know the love of Christ which is beyond all knowledge.

A reading from the letter of Paul to the Ephesians   3:14-19

Brothers and sisters:
I kneel in prayer to the Father.
All things in heaven and on earth receive their life from him.

God is wonderful and glorious.
I pray that his Spirit will make you become strong followers
    and that Christ will live in your hearts because of your faith.
Stand firm and be deeply rooted in his love.

I pray that you and all of God's people will understand
    what is called wide or long or high or deep.
I want you to know all about Christ's love,
    although it is too wonderful to be measured.
Then your lives will be filled with all that God is.

The word of the Lord.

ALLELUIA   Matthew 11:29ab

℟. Alleluia, alleluia.

Take my yoke upon you;
learn from me, for I am gentle and humble of heart.

℟. Alleluia, alleluia.

THE SACRED HEART OF JESUS — B

GOSPEL

> One of the soldiers pierced Jesus' side with a lance,
> and immediately there came out blood and water.

✣ A reading from the holy gospel according to John   19:31-37

The day after Jesus' death would be both a Sabbath and the Passover.
It was a special day for the Jewish people,
   and they did not want Jesus' body to stay on the cross
      during that day.
So they asked Pilate to break his legs and take his body down.

The soldiers first broke
   the legs of the other two men who were nailed there.
But when they came to Jesus,
   they saw that he was already dead,
   and they did not break his legs.

One of the soldiers stuck his spear into Jesus' side,
   and blood and water came out.

We know this is true,
   because it was told by someone who saw it happen.
Now you can have faith too.
All this happened so that the Scriptures would come true, which say,

      "No bone of his body will be broken"
            and,
   "They will see the one in whose side they stuck a spear."

The gospel of the Lord.

Friday after the Second Sunday after Pentecost
THE SACRED HEART OF JESUS

FIRST READING

I will watch over my sheep and tend them.

A reading from the book of the prophet Ezekiel   34:11-16abce

The Lord says this:
"I, the Lord God, will look for my people
    and take care of them myself.
As a shepherd looks for sheep that have wandered away,
    I will search for my scattered people.
I will rescue them from all the places where they went
    on that dark and gloomy day.
I will bring them back from the foreign countries
    and protect them on the mountains,
    in the valleys, and wherever they settle.

"My people will be like sheep grazing and resting
    in good pastures and on Israel's mountains.
I, the Lord All-Powerful, will lead them there and watch over them.

"I will look for the lost sheep
    and bring back the ones that have wandered off.
If any are hurt,
    I will bandage their wounds.
If any are weak,
    I will help them.
I will take good care of my people!"

                                           The word of the Lord.

RESPONSIVE PSALM 23:1-3a, 3b-4, 6

℟. (1) The Lord is my shepherd; there is nothing I shall want.

**You, Lord, are my shepherd.
I will never be in need.
You let me rest in fields
of green grass.
You lead me to streams
of peaceful water,
and you refresh my life.**

℟. The Lord is my shepherd; there is nothing I shall want.

**You are true to your name,
and you lead me
along the right paths.
I may walk through valleys
as dark as death,
but I won't be afraid.
You are with me,
and your shepherd's rod
makes me feel safe.**

℟. The Lord is my shepherd; there is nothing I shall want.

**Your kindness and love
will always be with me
each day of my life,
and I will live forever
in your house, Lord.**

℟. The Lord is my shepherd; there is nothing I shall want.

SECOND READING

God has entrusted his love to us.

A reading from the letter of Paul to the Romans   5:5-11

Brothers and sisters:
    Hope will never disappoint us.
All of this happens
    because God has given us the Holy Spirit,
    who fills our hearts with his love.

Christ died for us at a time when we were helpless and sinful.
No one is really willing to die for an honest person,
    though someone might be willing to die for a truly good person.
But God showed how much he loved us
    by having Christ die for us,
    even though we were sinful.

But there is more!
Now that God has accepted us because Christ sacrificed his life's blood,
    we will also be kept safe from God's anger.
Even when we were still God's enemies,
    he made peace with us,
    because his Son died for us.
Yet something even greater than friendship is ours.
Now that we are at peace with God,
    we will be saved by his Son's life.

And in addition to everything else,
    we are happy because God sent our Lord Jesus Christ
        to make peace with us.

The word of the Lord.

ALLELUIA   Matthew 11:29ab

℟. Alleluia, alleluia.

**Take my yoke upon you;
learn from me, for I am gentle and humble of heart.**

℟. Alleluia, alleluia.

GOSPEL

Share my joy: I have found my lost sheep!

✣ A reading from the holy gospel according to Luke   15:3-7

Jesus told the people this story:
"If any of you has a hundred sheep,
    and one of them gets lost,
    what will you do?
Won't you leave the ninety-nine in the field
      and go look for the lost sheep until you find it?
And when you find it,
    you will be so glad
      that you will put it on your shoulder and carry it home.
Then you will call in your friends and neighbors and say,
'Let's celebrate! I've found my lost sheep.' "

Jesus said,
"In the same way there is more happiness in heaven
      because of one sinner who turns to God
      than over ninety-nine good people who don't need to."

The gospel of the Lord.

COMMON TEXTS FOR SUNG RESPONSORIAL PSALMS

The psalm, as a rule, is drawn from the Lectionary because the individual psalm texts are directly connected with the individual readings: the choice of psalm depends therefore on the readings.

Nevertheless, in order that the children may be able to join in the responsorial psalm more readily, some texts of responses and psalms have been chosen, according to the different seasons of the year, for optional use, whenever the psalm is sung, in place of the text corresponding to the reading (see General Instruction of the Roman Missal, no. 36).

[167]

SEASON OF ADVENT

1

Psalm 25:4-5abc, 8-9, 10 and 14

℟. (1) To you, O Lord, I lift my soul.
or:
℟. Come, O Lord, and set us free.

**Show me your paths
and teach me to follow;
guide me by your truth
and instruct me.
You keep me safe.**

℟. To you, O Lord, I lift my soul.
or:
℟. Come, O Lord, and set us free.

**You are honest and merciful,
and you teach sinners
how to follow your path.
You lead humble people
to do what is right
and to stay on your path.**

℟. To you, O Lord, I lift my soul.
or:
℟. Come, O Lord, and set us free.

**In everything you do,
you are kind and faithful
to everyone who keeps
our agreement with you.
Our LORD, you are the friend
of your worshipers,**

**and you make an agreement
with all of us.**

> ℟. To you, O Lord, I lift my soul.
> or:
> ℟. Come, O Lord, and set us free.

2̄ Psalm 85:8-9, 10-11, 12-13

> ℟. (8a) Lord, show us your mercy and love.
> or:
> ℟. Come, O Lord, and set us free.

**I will listen to you, LORD God,
because you promise peace
to those who are faithful
and no longer foolish.
You are ready to rescue
everyone who worships you,
so that you will live with us
in all of your glory.**

> ℟. Lord, show us your mercy and love.
> or:
> ℟. Come, O Lord, and set us free.

**Love and loyalty
will come together,
and goodness and peace will unite.
Loyalty will sprout
from the ground;
justice will look down
from the sky above.**

> ℟. Lord, show us your mercy and love.
> or:
> ℟. Come, O Lord, and set us free.

**Our Lord, you will bless us;
our land will produce
wonderful crops.
Justice will march in front,
making a path
for you to follow.**

℟. Lord, show us your mercy and love.
or:
℟. Come, O Lord, and set us free.

SEASON OF CHRISTMAS

1

Psalm 98:1, 2-3ab, 3cd-4, 5-6

℟. (3cd) All the ends of the earth have seen the saving power of God.
or:
℟. Lord, today we have seen your glory.

Sing a new song to the LORD!
He has worked miracles,
and with his own powerful arm,
he has won the victory.

℟. All the ends of the earth have seen the saving power of God.
or:
℟. Lord, today we have seen your glory.

The LORD has shown the nations
that he has the power to save
and to bring justice.
God has been faithful
in his love for Israel.

℟. All the ends of the earth have seen the saving power of God.
or:
℟. Lord, today we have seen your glory.

His saving power is seen
everywhere on earth.
Tell everyone on this earth
to sing happy songs
in praise of the LORD.

℟. All the ends of the earth have seen the saving power of God.
or:
℟. Lord, today we have seen your glory.

Make music for him on harps.
Play beautiful melodies!

Sound the trumpets and horns
and celebrate with joyful songs
for our LORD and King!

> ℟. All the ends of the earth have seen the saving power of God.
> or:
> ℟. Lord, today we have seen your glory.

SEASON OF LENT

1

Psalm 51:1-2, 10-11, 12 and 15

> ℟. (see 3a) Be merciful, O Lord, for we have sinned.
> or:
> ℟. Remember, O Lord, your faithfulness and love.

You are kind, God!
Please have pity on me.
You are always merciful!
Please wipe away my sins.
Wash me clean from all
of my sin and guilt.

> ℟. Be merciful, O Lord, for we have sinned.
> or:
> ℟. Remember, O Lord, your faithfulness and love.

Create pure thoughts in me
and make me faithful again.
Don't chase me away from you
or take your Holy Spirit
away from me.

> ℟. Be merciful, O Lord, for we have sinned.
> or:
> ℟. Remember, O Lord, your faithfulness and love.

Make me as happy as you did
when you saved me;
make me want to obey!
Help me to speak,
and I will praise you, Lord.

℟. Be merciful, O Lord, for we have sinned.
or:
℟. Remember, O Lord, your faithfulness and love.

2   Psalm 91:1-2, 10-11, 14-15

℟. (see 15b) Be with me, Lord, when I am in trouble.
or:
℟. Remember, O Lord, your faithfulness and love.

**Live under the protection
of God Most High
and stay in the shadow
of God All-Powerful.
Then you will say to the LORD,
"You are my fortress,
my place of safety;
you are my God,
and I trust you."**

℟. Be with me, Lord, when I am in trouble.
or:
℟. Remember, O Lord, your faithfulness and love.

**No terrible disasters
will strike you or your home.
God will command his angels
to protect you
wherever you go.**

℟. Be with me, Lord, when I am in trouble.
or:
℟. Remember, O Lord, your faithfulness and love.

**The Lord says, "If you love me
and truly know who I am,
I will rescue you
and keep you safe.
When you are in trouble,
call out to me.
I will answer and be there
to protect and honor you."**

℟. Be with me, Lord, when I am in trouble.
or:
℟. Remember, O Lord, your faithfulness and love.

[3]   Psalm 130:1-2, 5-6ab, 6def, 7

℟. (7bc) With the Lord there is mercy, and fullness of redemption.
or:
℟. Remember, O Lord, your faithfulness and love.

From a sea of troubles
I call out to you, Lord.
Won't you please listen
as I beg for mercy?

℟. With the Lord there is mercy, and fullness of redemption.
or:
℟. Remember, O Lord, your faithfulness and love.

With all my heart,
I am waiting, Lord, for you!
I trust your promises.
I wait for you more eagerly
than a soldier on guard duty.

℟. With the Lord there is mercy, and fullness of redemption.
or:
℟. Remember, O Lord, your faithfulness and love.

Yes, I wait more eagerly
than a soldier on guard duty
waits for the dawn.

℟. With the Lord there is mercy, and fullness of redemption.
or:
℟. Remember, O Lord, your faithfulness and love.

Israel, trust the Lord!
He is always merciful,
and he has the power
to save you.

℟. With the Lord there is mercy, and fullness of redemption.
or:
℟. Remember, O Lord, your faithfulness and love.

SEASON OF EASTER

1

Psalm 118:1-2, 15c-16ab, 17, 22-23

℟. (24) This is the day the Lord has made; let us rejoice and be glad.
or:
℟. Alleluia.

Tell the LORD
how thankful you are,
because he is kind
and always merciful.
Let Israel shout,
"God is always merciful!"

℟. This is the day the Lord has made; let us rejoice and be glad.
or:
℟. Alleluia.

The LORD **is powerful!**
With his mighty arm
the LORD **wins victories!**

℟. This is the day the Lord has made; let us rejoice and be glad.
or:
℟. Alleluia.

And so my life is safe,
and I will live to tell
what the LORD **has done.**

℟. This is the day the Lord has made; let us rejoice and be glad.
or:
℟. Alleluia.

The stone that the builders
tossed aside
has now become
the most important stone.
The LORD **has done this,**
and it is amazing to us.

℟. This is the day the Lord has made; let us rejoice and be glad.
or:
℟. Alleluia.

2

Psalm 66:1-3a, 4-5, 6-7a

℟. (1) Let all the earth cry out to God with joy, alleluia.
or:
℟. Alleluia.

Tell everyone on this earth to shout praises to God!
Sing about his glorious name.
Honor him with praises.
Say to God, "Everything you do is fearsome!"

℟. Let all the earth cry out to God with joy, alleluia.
or:
℟. Alleluia.

"You are worshiped by everyone!
We all sing praises to you."
Come and see the fearsome things
our God has done!

℟. Let all the earth cry out to God with joy, alleluia.
or:
℟. Alleluia.

When God made the sea dry up,
our people walked across,
and because of him,
we celebrated there.
His mighty power rules forever.

℟. Let all the earth cry out to God with joy, alleluia.
or:
℟. Alleluia.

ORDINARY TIME

1

Psalm 19:7, 8

℟. (John 6:68c) Lord, you have the words of everlasting life.

The Law of the Lord is perfect;
it gives us new life.
His teachings last forever,
and they give wisdom to ordinary people.

℟. Lord, you have the words of everlasting life.

The Lord's instruction is right;
it makes our hearts glad.
His commands shine brightly,
and they give us light.

℟. Lord, you have the words of everlasting life.

2

Psalm 27:1, 4, 13-14

℟. (1a) The Lord is my light and my salvation.

You, Lord, are the light
that keeps me safe.
I am not afraid of anyone.
You protect me,
and I have no fears.

℟. The Lord is my light and my salvation.

I ask only one thing, Lord:
Let me live in your house
every day of my life
to see how wonderful you are
and to pray in your temple.

℟. The Lord is my light and my salvation.

I know that I will live
to see how kind you are.
Trust the Lord!
Be brave and strong
and trust the Lord.

℟. The Lord is my light and my salvation.

3

Psalm 34:1-2, 3 and 5, 7-8

℟. (2) I will bless the Lord at all times.

I will always praise the Lord.
With all my heart,
I will praise the Lord.
Let all who are helpless
listen and be glad.

℟. I will bless the Lord at all times.

Honor the LORD with me!
Celebrate his great name.
Keep your eyes on the LORD!
You will shine like the sun
and never blush with shame.

℟. I will bless the Lord at all times.

If you honor the LORD,
his angel will protect you.
Discover for yourself
that the LORD is kind.
Come to him for protection,
and you will be glad.

℟. I will bless the Lord at all times.

4

Psalm 63:1, 2-3, 4-5, 7-8

℟. (2b) My soul is thirsting for you, O Lord my God.

You are my God. I worship you.
In my heart, I long for you,
as I would long for a stream
in a scorching desert.

℟. My soul is thirsting for you, O Lord my God.

I have seen your power
and your glory
in the place of worship.
Your love means more
than life to me,
and I praise you.

℟. My soul is thirsting for you, O Lord my God.

As long as I live,
I will pray to you.
I will sing joyful praises
and be filled with excitement
like a guest at a banquet.

℟. My soul is thirsting for you, O Lord my God.

You have helped me,
and I sing happy songs

in the shadow of your wings.
I stay close to you,
and your powerful arm
supports me.

℟. My soul is thirsting for you, O Lord my God.

5

Psalm 95:1-2, 3-5, 6-7

℟. (8) If today you hear God's voice, harden not your hearts.

Sing joyful songs to the LORD!
Praise the mighty rock
where we are safe.
Come to worship him
with thankful hearts
and songs of praise.

℟. If today you hear God's voice, harden not your hearts.

The LORD is the greatest God,
king over all other gods.
He holds the deepest part
of the earth in his hands,
and the mountain peaks
belong to him.
The ocean is the Lord's
because he made it,
and with his own hands
he formed the dry land.

℟. If today you hear God's voice, harden not your hearts.

Bow down and worship
the LORD our Creator!
The LORD is our God,
and we are his people,
the sheep he takes care of
in his own pasture.
Listen to God's voice today!

℟. If today you hear God's voice, harden not your hearts.

6 Psalm 100:1-2, 3, 5

℟. (3c) We are God's people: the sheep of his flock.

**Shout praises to the Lord,
everyone on this earth.
Be joyful and sing
as you come in
to worship the Lord!**

℟. We are God's people: the sheep of his flock.

**You know the Lord is God!
He created us,
and we belong to him;
we are his people,
the sheep in his pasture.**

℟. We are God's people: the sheep of his flock.

**The Lord is good!
His love and faithfulness
will last forever.**

℟. We are God's people: the sheep of his flock.

7 Psalm 103:1-2, 8 and 10, 12-13

℟. (8a) The Lord is kind and merciful.

**With all my heart
I praise the Lord,
and with all that I am
I praise his holy name!
With all my heart
I praise the Lord!
I will never forget
how kind he has been.**

℟. The Lord is kind and merciful.

**The Lord is merciful!
He is kind and patient,
and his love never fails.
He doesn't punish us
as our sins deserve.**

℟. The Lord is kind and merciful.

How far has the LORD taken
our sins from us?
Farther than the distance
from east to west!
Just as parents are kind
to their children,
the LORD is kind
to all who worship him.

℟. The Lord is kind and merciful.

8   Psalm 145:1-2, 8-9, 10-11, 13cd-14

℟. (see 1) I will praise your name for ever, my king and my God.

I will praise you,
my God and King,
and always honor your name.
I will praise you each day
and always honor your name.

℟. I will praise your name for ever, my king and my God.

You are merciful, LORD!
You are kind and patient
and always loving.
You are good to everyone,
and you take care
of all your creation.

℟. I will praise your name for ever, my king and my God.

All creation will thank you,
and your loyal people
will praise you.
They will tell about
your marvelous kingdom
and your power.

℟. I will praise your name for ever, my king and my God.

Our LORD, you keep your word
and do everything you say.
When someone stumbles or falls,
you give a helping hand.

℟. I will praise your name for ever, my king and my God.

Last Weeks in Ordinary Time

☐9 Psalm 122:1-2, 6-7, 8-9

℟. (see 1) Let us go rejoicing to the house of the Lord.

**It made me glad
to hear them say,
"Let's go to the house
of the Lord!"
Jerusalem, we are standing
inside your gates.**

℟. Let us go rejoicing to the house of the Lord.

**Jerusalem, we pray
that you will have peace,
and that all will go well
for those who love you.
May there be peace
inside your city walls
and in your palaces.**

℟. Let us go rejoicing to the house of the Lord.

**Because of my friends
and my relatives,
I will pray for peace.
And because of the house
of the Lord our God,
I will work for your good.**

℟. Let us go rejoicing to the house of the Lord.

WEEKDAY READINGS

SEASON OF ADVENT

[172] **"Prepare for the Coming of the Lord"**

FIRST READING

The Lord God will be gracious to you when he hears your cry.

A reading from the book of the prophet Isaiah 30:19b-21

The LORD is kind,
    and as soon as he hears you crying,
    he will come to help you.

The LORD has caused you trouble and sorrow
    by not giving you enough bread and water.
But now you will see the LORD.
He is your guide,
    and he will no longer be hidden from you.

Whether you turn to the right or to the left,
    you will hear a voice saying,
"This is the road! Now follow it."

                                        The word of the Lord.

RESPONSORIAL PSALM   25:4-5abc, 8-9, 10 and 14

℟. (1) To you, O Lord, I lift my soul.

Show me your paths
and teach me to follow;
guide me by your truth
and instruct me.
You keep me safe.

℟. To you, O Lord, I lift my soul.

You are honest and merciful,
and you teach sinners
how to follow your path.
You lead humble people
to do what is right
and to stay on your path.

℟. To you, O Lord, I lift my soul.

In everything you do,
you are kind and faithful
to everyone who keeps
our agreement with you.
Our LORD, you are the friend
of your worshipers,
and you make an agreement
with all of us.

℟. To you, O Lord, I lift my soul.

ALLELUIA   Psalm 85:8

℟. Alleluia, alleluia.

**Lord, show us your mercy and love,
and grant us your salvation.**

℟. Alleluia, alleluia.

GOSPEL

See that you are prepared.

✢ A reading from the holy gospel according to Luke   12:35-38

Jesus said to his disciples:
"Be ready and keep your lamps burning
> just like those servants who wait up
> > for their master to return from a wedding feast.
As soon as he comes and knocks,
> they open the door for him.

"Servants are fortunate
> if their master finds them awake and ready when he comes!
I promise you that he will get ready
> and have his servants sit down so he can serve them.
Those servants are really fortunate if their master finds them ready,
> even though he comes late at night or early in the morning."

The gospel of the Lord.

[173] # "The Kingdom of Heaven Is Near"

FIRST READING

The Lord God will be gracious to you when he hears your cry.

A reading from the book of the prophet Isaiah 30:19, 23-24, 26

People of Jerusalem,
  you don't need to cry anymore.
The LORD is kind,
  and as soon as he hears you crying,
  he will come to help you.

He will send rain to water the seeds you have planted,
  and your fields will produce more crops than you need.
When that time comes,
  your cattle will graze in open pastures.

Even the oxen and donkeys that plow your fields
    will be fed grain that has been prepared in a special way.
And it will be placed there for them with shovels and pitchforks.

On the day the LORD binds up his people's injuries
    and heals the wounds he has caused,
  the moon will be bright as the sun.
The light of the sun will be seven times brighter than usual,
  and it will be like the light of seven days all at once.

The word of the Lord.

RESPONSORIAL PSALM 147:1, 3-4, 5 and 7

℟. (Isaiah 30:18) Happy are all who long for the coming of the Lord.

Shout praises to the LORD!
Our God is kind,
and it is right and good
to sing praises to him.

℟. Happy are all who long for the coming of the Lord.

He renews our hopes
and heals our bodies.
He decided how many stars
there would be in the sky
and gave each one a name.

℟. Happy are all who long for the coming of the Lord.

Our Lord is great and powerful!
He understands everything.
Celebrate and sing!
Play your harps
for the Lord our God.

℟. Happy are all who long for the coming of the Lord.

ALLELUIA Psalm 85:8

℟. Alleluia, alleluia.

Lord, show us your mercy and love,
and grant us your salvation.

℟. Alleluia, alleluia.

GOSPEL

When Jesus saw the crowds, he felt sorry for them.

✠ A reading from the holy gospel according to Matthew 9:35—10:1, 5a, 6-7

Jesus went to every town and village.
He taught in their meeting places
    and preached the good news about God's kingdom.
Jesus also healed every kind of disease and sickness.

When he saw the crowds,
    he felt sorry for them.
They were confused and helpless,
    like sheep without a shepherd.

He said to his disciples,
"A large crop is in the fields,
> but there are only a few workers.
Ask the Lord in charge of the harvest
> to send out workers to bring it in."

Jesus called together his twelve disciples.
He gave them the power to force out evil spirits
> and to heal every kind of disease and sickness.

Jesus sent out the twelve apostles with these instructions:
"Go only to the people of Israel,
> because they are like a flock of lost sheep.

"As you go,
> announce that the kingdom of heaven will soon be here."

The gospel of the Lord.

[174] "The Kingdom of God Is Within You"

FIRST READING

The Lord God is almighty and gives strength to the weary.

A reading from the book of the prophet Isaiah   40:25-26, 29-31

The Holy God asks,
"Who can compare with me?
Is anyone my equal?"

Look at the stars in the sky.
Who created all of these?
Who leads them like an army and gives them each a name?
The LORD is so strong and mighty that none of the stars are missing.

The LORD gives strength to all who are weary.
Even young people tire out, then stumble and fall.
But all who trust the LORD will find new strength.
They will be strong like eagles that soar about on wings.
They will walk and run and not feel weary or tired.

The word of the Lord.

RESPONSORIAL PSALM   33:4-5, 20 and 22

℟. (22) Lord, let your mercy be on us, as we place our trust in you.

The LORD is truthful;
he can be trusted.
He loves justice and fairness,
and he is kind to everyone
everywhere on earth.

℟. Lord, let your mercy be on us, as we place our trust in you.

We depend on you, LORD,
to help and protect us.
Be kind and bless us!
We depend on you.

℟. Lord, let your mercy be on us, as we place our trust in you.

ALLELUIA

Psalm 85:8

℟. Alleluia, alleluia.

Lord, show us your mercy and love,
and grant us your salvation.

℟. Alleluia, alleluia.

GOSPEL

Go back and tell John what you have seen and heard.

✜ A reading from the holy gospel according to Luke

7:17-26

News about Jesus spread all over Judea
and everywhere else in that part of the country.

John's followers told John
everything that was being said about Jesus.
So he sent two of them to ask the Lord,
"Are you the one we should be looking for?
Or must we wait for someone else?"

When these messengers came to Jesus, they said,
"John the Baptist sent us to ask,
'Are you the one we should be looking for?
Or are we supposed to wait for someone else?'"

At that time Jesus was healing many people who were sick
or in pain or were troubled by evil spirits,
and he was giving sight to a lot of blind people.

Jesus said to the messengers sent by John,
"Go and tell John what you have seen and heard.
Blind people are now able to see,
and those who are lame can walk.
People who have leprosy are being healed,
and those who are deaf can now hear.
The dead are raised to life,
and the poor are hearing the good news.
God will bless everyone who does not reject me because of what I do."

After John's messengers had gone,
>   Jesus began speaking to the crowds about John:

"What kind of person did you go out to the desert to see?
Was he like tall grass blown about by the wind?
What kind of man did you really go out to see?
Was he someone dressed in fine clothes?
People who wear expensive clothes and live in luxury
>   are in the king's palace.

"What then did you go out to see?
Was he a prophet?
He certainly was!
I tell you that he was more than a prophet."

>   The gospel of the Lord.

[175]   **"My Heart Praises the Lord"**

FIRST READING

Our merciful God always comforts us.

A reading from the second letter of Paul to the Corinthians   1:3-4

Brothers and sisters:
Praise God, the Father of our Lord Jesus Christ!

The Father is a merciful God,
    who always gives us comfort.
He comforts us when we are in trouble,
    so that we can share that same comfort with others in trouble.

The word of the Lord.

RESPONSORIAL PSALM   34:1-2, 3-4

℟. (9a) Taste and see the goodness of the Lord.

I will always praise the Lord.
With all my heart,
I will praise the Lord.
Let all who are helpless
listen and be glad.

℟. Taste and see the goodness of the Lord.

Honor the Lord with me!
Celebrate his great name.
I asked the Lord for help,
and he saved me
from all my fears.

℟. Taste and see the goodness of the Lord.

ALLELUIA   Psalm 85:8

℟. Alleluia, alleluia.

Lord, show us your mercy and love,
and grant us your salvation.

℟. Alleluia, alleluia.

GOSPEL

The Almighty has done great things for me.

✣ A reading from the holy gospel according to Luke 1:46-56

Mary said:
"With all my heart I praise the Lord,
 and I am glad because of God my Savior.
He cares for me, his humble servant.
From now on, all people will say God has blessed me.
God All-Powerful has done great things for me,
 and his name is holy.

"He always shows mercy to everyone who worships him.
The Lord has used his powerful arm to scatter those who are proud.
He drags strong rulers from their thrones
 and puts humble people in places of power.
He gives the hungry good things to eat,
 and he sends the rich away with nothing in their hands.
He helps his servant Israel and is always merciful to his people.
He made this promise to our ancestors,
 to Abraham and his family forever!"

Mary stayed with Elizabeth about three months.
Then she went back home.

The gospel of the Lord.

SEASON OF LENT

[176] **"Pray, Fast, and Share"**

FIRST READING
Is this not the sort of fast that pleases me?

A reading from the book of the prophet Isaiah   58:6-9

The Lord says this:
I'll tell you what it really means
   to worship the Lord.
Remove the chains of prisoners who are chained unjustly.
Free those who are abused!

Share your food with everyone who is hungry;
   share your home with the poor and homeless.
Give clothes to those in need;
   don't turn away your relatives.

Then your light will shine like the dawning sun,
   and you will quickly be healed.
Your honesty will protect you as you advance,
   and the glory of the Lord will defend you from behind.
Then you will call for help,
   and the Lord will answer, "Here I am!"

Don't oppress others or falsely accuse them or say cruel things.

                                The word of the Lord.

RESPONSORIAL PSALM   27:1, 11ab and 13

   ℟. (1a) The Lord is my light and my salvation.

You, Lord, are the light
that keeps me safe.
I am not afraid of anyone.
You protect me,
and I have no fears.

   ℟. The Lord is my light and my salvation.

Teach me to follow, Lord,
and lead me on the right path.
I know I will live
to see how kind you are.

   ℟. The Lord is my light and my salvation.

VERSE BEFORE THE GOSPEL   Matthew 4:17

℟. Glory and praise to you, Lord Jesus Christ.

Repent, says the Lord;
the kingdom of heaven is at hand.

℟. Glory and praise to you, Lord Jesus Christ.

GOSPEL

A

        Your Father, who sees all that is done in secret,
                will reward you.

✞ A reading from the holy gospel according to Matthew   6:1-6, 16-18

Jesus said to his disciples:
"When you do good deeds,
    don't try to show off.
If you do, you won't get a reward from your Father in heaven.

"When you give to the poor,
    don't blow a loud horn.
That's what showoffs do in the meeting places and on the street corners,
    because they are always looking for praise.
I promise you that they already have their reward.

"When you give to the poor,
    don't let anyone know about it.
Then your gift will be given in secret.
Your Father knows what is done in secret,
    and he will reward you.

"When you pray,
    don't be like those showoffs who love to stand up and pray
        in the meeting places and on the street corners.
They do this just to look good.
I promise you that they already have their reward.

"When you pray,
    go into a room alone and close the door.
Pray to your Father in private.
He knows what is done in private,
    and he will reward you.

"When you go without eating,
>	don't try to look gloomy as those showoffs do
>		when they go without eating.
I promise you that they already have their reward.

"Instead, comb your hair and wash your face.
Then others won't know that you are going without eating.
But your Father sees what is done in private,
>	and he will reward you."

The gospel of the Lord.

OR

B

Your Father, who sees all that is done in secret,
will reward you.

✛ A reading from the holy gospel according to Matthew   6:1-4

Jesus said to his disciples:
"When you do good deeds,
>	don't try to show off.
If you do, you won't get a reward from your Father in heaven.

"When you give to the poor,
>	don't blow a loud horn.
That's what showoffs do in the meeting places and on the street corners,
>	because they are always looking for praise.
I promise you that they already have their reward.

"When you give to the poor,
>	don't let anyone know about it.
Then your gift will be given in secret.
Your Father knows what is done in secret,
>	and he will reward you."

The gospel of the Lord.

OR

C
    Your Father, who sees all that is done in secret,
    will reward you.

✛ **A reading from the holy gospel according to Matthew**   6:1, 5-6

Jesus said to his disciples:
"When you do good deeds,
   don't try to show off.
If you do, you won't get a reward from your Father in heaven.

"When you pray,
   don't be like those showoffs who love to stand up and pray
     in the meeting places and on the street corners.
They do this just to look good.
I promise you that they already have their reward.

"When you pray,
   go into a room alone and close the door.
Pray to your Father in private.
He knows what is done in private,
   and he will reward you."

The gospel of the Lord.

OR

D
    Your Father, who sees all that is done in secret,
    will reward you.

✛ **A reading from the holy gospel according to Matthew**   6:1, 16-18

Jesus said to his disciples:
"When you do good deeds,
   don't try to show off.
If you do, you won't get a reward from your Father in heaven.

"When you go without eating,
   don't try to look gloomy as those showoffs do
     when they go without eating.
I promise you that they already have their reward.

"Instead, comb your hair and wash your face.
Then others won't know that you are going without eating.
But your Father sees what is done in private,
    and he will reward you."

                                The gospel of the Lord.

[177] "What We Do for Others We Do for Jesus"

FIRST READING

The disciples decided to send relief during the famine,
each to contribute what they could afford,
to the brothers and sisters living in Judea.

A reading from the Acts of the Apostles 11:27-30

Some prophets from Jerusalem came to Antioch.
One of them was Agabus.
With the help of the Spirit,
   he told that there would be a terrible famine
      everywhere in the world.
And it happened when Claudius was Emperor.
The followers in Antioch decided to send whatever help they could
      to the followers in Judea.
So they had Barnabas and Saul take their gifts
      to the church leaders in Jerusalem.

The word of the Lord.

RESPONSORIAL PSALM 25:4-5ab, 5cd-6

℟. (4a) Teach me your ways, O Lord.

Show me your paths
and teach me to follow;
guide me by your truth
and instruct me.

℟. Teach me your ways, O Lord.

You keep me safe,
and I always trust you.
Please, LORD, remember,
you have always been patient and kind.

℟. Teach me your ways, O Lord.

VERSE BEFORE THE GOSPEL Matthew 4:17

℟. Glory and praise to you, Lord Jesus Christ.

Repent, says the Lord;
the kingdom of heaven is at hand.

℟. Glory and praise to you, Lord Jesus Christ.

GOSPEL

Whatever you have done to the very least of my brothers and sisters, you have done to me.

✚ A reading from the holy gospel according to Matthew 25:31-40

Jesus said to his disciples:
"When the Son of Man comes in his glory with all of his angels,
he will sit on his royal throne.

"The people of all nations will be brought before him,
and he will separate them,
as shepherds separate their sheep from their goats.

"He will place the sheep on his right and the goats on his left.
Then the king will say to those on his right,
'My father has blessed you!
Come and receive the kingdom that was prepared for you
before the world was created.
When I was hungry, you gave me something to eat,
and when I was thirsty, you gave me something to drink.
When I was a stranger, you welcomed me,
and when I was naked, you gave me clothes to wear.
When I was sick, you took care of me,
and when I was in jail, you visited me.'

"Then the ones who pleased the Lord will ask,
'When did we give you something to eat or drink?
When did we welcome you as a stranger or give you clothes to wear
or visit you while you were sick or in jail?'

"The king will answer,
'Whenever you did it for any of my people,
no matter how unimportant they seemed,
you did it for me.'"

The gospel of the Lord.

[178]   **"Forgive One Another"**

FIRST READING

Have charity, which is the bond of perfection.

A reading from the letter of Paul to the Colossians   3:12-14

Brothers and sisters:
God loves you and has chosen you as his own special people.
So be gentle, kind, humble, meek, and patient.
Put up with each other,
    and forgive anyone who does you wrong,
    just as Christ has forgiven you.
Love is more important than anything else.
It is what ties everything completely together.

                                           The word of the Lord.

RESPONSORIAL PSALM   51:1 and 10, 12 and 15

℟. (see 3a) Be merciful, O Lord, for we have sinned.

You are kind, God!
Please have pity on me.
You are always merciful!
Please wipe away my sins.
Create pure thoughts in me
and make me faithful again.

℟. Be merciful, O Lord, for we have sinned.

Make me as happy as you did
when you saved me;
make me want to obey!
Help me to speak,
and I will praise you, Lord.

℟. Be merciful, O Lord, for we have sinned.

VERSE BEFORE THE GOSPEL

Matthew 4:17

℟. Glory and praise to you, Lord Jesus Christ.

**Repent, says the Lord;
the kingdom of heaven is at hand.**

℟. Glory and praise to you, Lord Jesus Christ.

GOSPEL

This is how you should pray.

✠ **A reading from the holy gospel according to Matthew** 6:7-15

Jesus said to his disciples:
  "When you pray,
    don't talk on and on as people do who don't know God.
They think God likes to hear long prayers.
Don't be like them.
Your Father knows what you need before you ask.

"You should pray like this:

>   Our Father in heaven,
>   help us to honor your name.
>   Come and set up your kingdom,
>   so that everyone on earth will obey you,
>   as you are obeyed in heaven.
>   Give us our food for today.
>   Forgive our sins,
>   as we forgive others.
>   Keep us from being tempted and protect us from evil.

"If you forgive others for the wrongs they do to you,
  your Father in heaven will forgive you.
But if you don't forgive others,
  your Father will not forgive your sins."

The gospel of the Lord.

[179] **"Ask and You Will Receive"**

FIRST READING

We will thank you because of your wonderful deeds.

A reading from the book of the prophet Isaiah 12:4b-5

When the Lord comes you will say,
"Our Lord, we are thankful,
and we worship only you.
We will tell the nations how glorious you are and what you have done.
We will sing your praises everywhere because of your wonderful deeds."

The word of the Lord.

RESPONSORIAL PSALM 126:1-2ab, 2cde-3

℟. (3) The Lord has done great things for us; we are filled with joy.

**It seemed like a dream
when the Lord brought us back
to the city of Zion.
We celebrated with laughter
and joyful songs.**

℟. The Lord has done great things for us; we are filled with joy.

**In foreign nations it was said,
"The Lord has worked miracles
for his people."
And so we celebrated
because the Lord had indeed
worked miracles for us.**

℟. The Lord has done great things for us; we are filled with joy.

VERSE BEFORE THE GOSPEL Matthew 4:17

℟. Glory and praise to you, Lord Jesus Christ.

**Repent, says the Lord;
the kingdom of heaven is at hand.**

℟. Glory and praise to you, Lord Jesus Christ.

GOSPEL

Ask and you will receive.

✣ A reading from the holy gospel according to Matthew   7:7-11

Jesus said to his disciples:
"Ask, and you will receive.
Search, and you will find.
Knock, and the door will be opened for you.

"Everyone who asks will receive.
Everyone who searches will find.
And the door will be opened for everyone who knocks.

"Would any of you give your hungry child a stone,
    if the child asked for some bread?
Would you give your child a snake if the child asked for a fish?
As bad as you are,
    you still know how to give good gifts to your children.
But your heavenly Father is even more ready to give good things
    to people who ask."

The gospel of the Lord.

[180] **"Be at Peace with Everyone"**

FIRST READING

Please forgive all the wrong we have done.

A reading from the book of Genesis 50:15-21

After Jacob died,
Joseph's brothers said to each other,
"What if Joseph still hates us and wants to get even with us
  for all the cruel things we did to him?"

So they sent a message to Joseph.
It said: "Before our father Jacob died, he told us,
'You did some cruel and terrible things to Joseph!
But you must ask him to forgive you.'"

"Now we ask you to please forgive all the terrible things we did.
After all, we serve the same God that your father worshiped."

When Joseph heard this, he started crying.

Right then Joseph's brothers came and bowed down to the ground
  in front of him.
They said, "We are your slaves."

But Joseph told them, "Don't be afraid!
I have no right to change what God has decided.
You tried to harm me,
  but God made it turn out for the best,
  so that he could save all these people, as he is now doing.
So then, don't be afraid.
I will take care of you and your children."

When Joseph said this, his brothers felt better.

The word of the Lord.

RESPONSIAL PSALM   122:1-2, 6-7, 8-9

℟. (Sirach 36:18) Give peace, O Lord, to those who wait for you.

It made me glad
to hear them say,
"Let's go to the house
of the Lord!"
Jerusalem, we are standing
inside your gates.

℟. Give peace, O Lord, to those who wait for you.

Jerusalem, we pray
that you will have peace,
and that all will go well
for those who love you.
May there be peace
inside your city walls
and in your palaces.

℟. Give peace, O Lord, to those who wait for you.

Because of my friends
and my relatives,
I will pray for peace.
And because of the house
of the Lord our God,
I will work for your good.

℟. Give peace, O Lord, to those who wait for you.

VERSE BEFORE THE GOSPEL   Matthew 4:17

℟. Glory and praise to you, Lord Jesus Christ.

Repent, says the Lord;
the kingdom of heaven is at hand.

℟. Glory and praise to you, Lord Jesus Christ.

GOSPEL

*Those who are angry with their brother or sister
will answer for it before the law.*

✣ A reading from the holy gospel according to Matthew   5:20-24

Jesus said to his disciples:
"You must obey God's commands better than the Pharisees
   and the teachers of the Law obey them.
If you don't,
   I promise you that you will never get into the kingdom
     of heaven.

"You know that our ancestors were told,
'Do not murder' and 'A murderer must be brought to trial.'
But I promise you that if you are angry with someone,
   you will have to stand trial.
If you call someone a fool,
   you will be taken to court.
And if you say that someone is worthless,
   you will be in danger of the fires of hell.

"So if you are about to place your gift on the altar
   and remember that someone is angry with you,
   leave your gift there in front of the altar.
Make peace with that person,
   then come back and offer your gift to God."

The gospel of the Lord.

[181] "Love Everyone"

FIRST READING

Do your best to live at peace with everyone.

A reading from the letter of Paul to the Romans 12:17-18, 21

Brothers and sisters:
   Don't mistreat someone who has mistreated you.
But try to earn the respect of others,
   and do your best to live at peace with everyone.

**Don't let evil defeat you,
   but defeat evil with good.**

The word of the Lord.

RESPONSORIAL PSALM 85:8abc and 9, 10-11, 12-13

℟. (8) Lord, show us your mercy and love, and grant us your salvation.

I will listen to you, LORD **God,
because you promise peace
to those who are faithful.
You are ready to rescue
everyone who worships you,
so that you will live with us
in all of your glory.**

℟. Lord, show us your mercy and love, and grant us your salvation.

**Love and loyalty
will come together;
goodness and peace will unite.
Loyalty will sprout
from the ground;
justice will look down
from the sky above.**

℟. Lord, show us your mercy and love, and grant us your salvation.

Our L ORD, you will bless us;
our land will produce
wonderful crops.
Justice will march in front,
making a path
for you to follow.

> ℟. Lord, show us your mercy and love, and grant us your salvation.

VERSE BEFORE THE GOSPEL
Matthew 4:17

> ℟. Glory and praise to you, Lord Jesus Christ.

**Repent, says the Lord;
the kingdom of heaven is at hand.**

> ℟. Glory and praise to you, Lord Jesus Christ.

GOSPEL

Be perfect as your heavenly Father is perfect.

✜ A reading from the holy gospel according to Matthew   5:43-48

Jesus said to his disciples:
"You have heard people say,
'Love your neighbors and hate your enemies.'
But I tell you to love your enemies
   and pray for anyone who mistreats you.
Then you will be acting like your Father in heaven.

"He makes the sun rise on both good and bad people.
And he sends rain for the ones who do right
   and for the ones who do wrong.

"If you love only those people who love you,
   will God reward you for that?
Even tax collectors love their friends.
If you greet only your friends,
   what's so great about that?
Don't even unbelievers do that?
But you must always act like your Father in heaven."

The gospel of the Lord.

[182]   **"Love of God and Love of Neighbor"**

FIRST READING

> The Lord wants you to serve him with all your heart and soul.

A reading from the book of Deuteronomy   10:12-14

Moses told the people:
"People of Israel,
  what does the LORD your God want from you?
The LORD wants you to worship and obey him
    and to love and serve him with all your heart and soul.
For your own good you must obey his laws and commands
  that I am teaching you today.

"Everything belongs to the LORD your God.
The highest heavens are his,
  and so are the earth and everything on it."

The word of the Lord.

RESPONSORIAL PSALM   19:7, 8ab and 9cd, 10

℟. (9a) The precepts of the Lord give joy to the heart.

The Law of the LORD is perfect;
it gives us new life.
His teachings last forever,
and they give wisdom
to ordinary people.

℟. The precepts of the Lord give joy to the heart.

The LORD's instruction is right;
it makes our hearts glad.
All of his decisions
are correct and fair.

℟. The precepts of the Lord give joy to the heart.

They are worth more
than the finest gold
and are sweeter than honey
from a honeycomb.

℟. The precepts of the Lord give joy to the heart.

VERSE BEFORE THE GOSPEL   Matthew 4:17

℟. Glory and praise to you, Lord Jesus Christ.

**Repent, says the Lord;
the kingdom of heaven is at hand.**

℟. Glory and praise to you, Lord Jesus Christ.

GOSPEL

The Lord our God is one Lord and you shall love the Lord your God.

✢ **A reading from the holy gospel according to Mark**   12:28b-31

When one of the teachers of the Law of Moses
heard Jesus give a good answer, he asked him,
"What is the most important commandment?"

**Jesus answered, "The most important one says:
'People of Israel, you have only one Lord and God.
You must love him with all your heart, soul, mind, and strength.'
The second most important commandment says:
'Love others as much as you love yourself.'
No other commandment is more important than these."**

                                                                     The gospel of the Lord.

[183]   **"Trust in the Lord"**

FIRST READING
         It is good to wait in silence for the Lord God to save.

     A reading from the book of Lamentations   3:22-25

We would have been destroyed,
    if the Lord had not been kind.
But his mercy never fails.
The Lord can always be trusted to show mercy each morning.

Deep in my heart I say,
"The Lord is all I need.
I can depend on him!"

The Lord is good to everyone who trusts and worships him.

                                            The word of the Lord.

RESPONSORIAL PSALM   33:1-2, 4-5, 21-22

     ℟. (22) Lord, let your mercy be on us, as we place our trust in you.

You are the Lord's people.
Obey him and celebrate!
He deserves your praise.
Praise the Lord with harps!
Use harps with ten strings
to make music for him.

     ℟. Lord, let your mercy be on us, as we place our trust in you.

The Lord is truthful;
he can be trusted.
He loves justice and fairness,
and he is kind to everyone
everywhere on earth.

     ℟. Lord, let your mercy be on us, as we place our trust in you.

You make our hearts glad
because we trust you,
the only God.

Be kind and bless us!
We depend on you.

℟. Lord, let your mercy be on us, as we place our trust in you.

VERSE BEFORE THE GOSPEL
Matthew 4:17

℟. Glory and praise to you, Lord Jesus Christ.

**Repent, says the Lord;
the kingdom of heaven is at hand.**

℟. Glory and praise to you, Lord Jesus Christ.

GOSPEL

Go, your son will live.

✟ A reading from the holy gospel according to John 4:46-53

While Jesus was in Galilee,
he returned to the village of Cana,
where he had turned the water into wine.

There was an official in Capernaum whose son was sick.
And when the man heard that Jesus had come from Judea,
he went and begged him to keep his son from dying.

Jesus told the official,
"You won't have faith
unless you see miracles and wonders!"

The man replied, "Lord, please come before my son dies!"

Jesus then said, "Your son will live.
Go on home to him."

The man believed Jesus and started back home.

Some of the official's servants met him along the road and told him,
"Your son is better!"

He asked them when the boy got better, and they answered,
"The fever left him yesterday at one o'clock."

The boy's father realized that at one o'clock the day before
Jesus had told him,
"Your son will live!"

So the man and everyone in his family put their faith in Jesus.

The gospel of the Lord.

[184]   **"Jesus Brings Together All People"**

FIRST READING
I will make them into one nation.

A reading from the book of the prophet Ezekiel   37:21-22, 24

I, the Lord God, will gather the people of Israel
    and bring them back home
from the nations where they have gone.
I will make them into one nation on the hills of Israel.

Only one king will rule over them,
    and they will never again be divided into two nations.
My servant David will be their king and only ruler,
    and they will eagerly obey my laws and commands.

The word of the Lord.

RESPONSORIAL PSALM   33:4-5, 12-13 and 14b, 20 and 22

℟. (12b) Happy the people the Lord has chosen to be his own.

The Lord is truthful;
he can be trusted.
He loves justice and fairness,
and he is kind to everyone
everywhere on earth.

℟. Happy the people the Lord has chosen to be his own.

The Lord blesses each nation
that worships only him.
He blesses his chosen ones.
The Lord looks at the world,
and he watches us all.

℟. Happy the people the Lord has chosen to be his own.

We depend on you, Lord,
to help and protect us.
Be kind and bless us!
We depend on you.

℟. Happy the people the Lord has chosen to be his own.

VERSE BEFORE THE GOSPEL
Matthew 4:17

℟. Glory and praise to you, Lord Jesus Christ.

**Repent, says the Lord;
the kingdom of heaven is at hand.**

℟. Glory and praise to you, Lord Jesus Christ.

GOSPEL

*Jesus was going to die to gather together in unity
the scattered children of God.*

✢ **A reading from the holy gospel according to John** 11:47-52

The chief priests and the Pharisees
  called the council together and said,
"What should we do?
This man is working a lot of miracles.
If we don't stop him now,
  everyone will put their faith in him.
Then the Romans will come and destroy our temple and our nation."

One of the council members was Caiaphas,
  who was also high priest that year.

He spoke up and said, "You people don't have any sense at all!
Don't you know it is better for one person to die for the people
  than for our whole nation to be destroyed?"

Caiaphas did not say this on his own.
As high priest that year,
  he was prophesying that Jesus would die for the nation.

Yet Jesus would not die just for the Jewish nation.
He would die to bring together all of God's scattered people.

The gospel of the Lord.

SEASON OF EASTER

[185] # "Witnesses of the Resurrection"

FIRST READING

God raised this man Jesus to life, and all of us are witnesses to it.

A reading from the Acts of the Apostles   2:32-33

On the day of Pentecost Peter told the people:
"All of us can tell you that God has raised Jesus to life!

"Jesus was taken up to sit at the right side of God,
    and he was given the Holy Spirit,
    just as the Father had promised.

"Jesus is also the one who has given the Spirit to us,
    and that is what you are now seeing and hearing."

The word of the Lord.

RESPONSORIAL PSALM   96:1-2a, 2b-3, 11-12ab

℟. (3) Proclaim God's marvelous deeds to all the nations.

**Sing a new song to the Lord!
Everyone on this earth,
sing praises to the Lord,
sing and praise his name.**

℟. Proclaim God's marvelous deeds to all the nations.

**Day after day announce,
"The Lord has saved us!"
Tell every nation on earth,
"The Lord is wonderful
and does marvelous things!"**

℟. Proclaim God's marvelous deeds to all the nations.

**Tell the heavens and the earth
to be glad and celebrate!
Command the ocean to roar
with all of its creatures
and the fields to rejoice
with all of their crops.**

℟. Proclaim God's marvelous deeds to all the nations.

ALLELUIA

See John 6:63c, 68c

℟. Alleluia, alleluia.

Your words, Lord, are spirit and life:
you have the words of everlasting life.

℟. Alleluia, alleluia.

GOSPEL

I have seen the Lord and he said these things to me.

✠ A reading from the holy gospel according to John   20:11-18

Mary Magdalene stood crying outside the tomb.
She was still weeping,
　　when she stooped down and saw two angels inside.
They were dressed in white and were sitting where Jesus' body had been.
One was at the head and the other was at the foot.

The angels asked Mary, "Why are you crying?"

She answered, "They have taken away my Lord's body!
I don't know where they have put him."

As soon as Mary said this,
　　she turned around and saw Jesus standing there.
But she did not know who he was.
Jesus asked her, "Why are you crying?
Who are you looking for?"

She thought he was the gardener and said,
"Sir, if you have taken his body away,
　　please tell me, so I can go and get him."

Then Jesus said to her, "Mary!"

She turned and said to him, "Rabboni."
The Aramaic word "Rabboni" means "Teacher."

Jesus told her, "Don't hold on to me!
I have not yet gone to the Father.
But tell my disciples that I am going to the one
　　　who is my Father and my God,
　　　as well as your Father and your God."
Mary Magdalene then went and told the disciples
　　　that she had seen the Lord.
She also told them what he had said to her.

　　　　　　　　　　　　　　The gospel of the Lord.

[186] # "The Power of Jesus' Name"

FIRST READING

What I have, I give you:
in the name of Jesus stand up and walk.

A reading from the Acts of the Apostles 3:1-10

At the time of prayer,
 which was about three o'clock in the afternoon,
  Peter and John were going into the temple.
A man who had been born lame was being carried to the temple door.
Each day he was placed beside this door,
  known as the Beautiful Gate.
He sat there and begged from the people who were going in.

The man saw Peter and John entering the temple,
  and he asked them for money.
But they looked straight at him and said,
"Look up at us!"

The man stared at them and thought he was going to get something.
But Peter said, "I don't have any silver or gold!
But I will give you what I do have.
In the name of Jesus Christ from Nazareth,
  get up and start walking."
Peter then took him by the right hand and helped him up.

At once the man's feet and ankles became strong,
  and he jumped up and started walking.
He went with Peter and John into the temple,
  walking and jumping and praising God.

Everyone saw him walking around and praising God.
They knew that he was the beggar
    who had been lying beside the Beautiful Gate,
  and they were completely surprised.
They could not imagine what had happened to the man.

                                    The word of the Lord.

RESPONSORIAL PSALM 98:1, 2, 5-6

℟. (3cd) All the ends of the earth have seen the saving power of God.

Sing a new song to the Lord!
He has worked miracles,
and with his own powerful arm,
he has won the victory.

℟. All the ends of the earth have seen the saving power of God.

The Lord has shown the nations
that he has the power to save
and to bring justice.

℟. All the ends of the earth have seen the saving power of God.

Make music for him on harps.
Play beautiful melodies!
Sound the trumpets and horns
and celebrate with joyful songs
for our Lord and King!

℟. All the ends of the earth have seen the saving power of God.

ALLELUIA See John 6:63c, 68c

℟. Alleluia, alleluia.

Your words, Lord, are spirit and life:
you have the words of everlasting life.

℟. Alleluia, alleluia.

GOSPEL

If you have faith in me, you will do even greater things.

✢ A reading from the holy gospel according to John   14:12-14

Jesus said to his disciples:
"I tell you for certain that if you have faith in me,
you will do the same things that I am doing.

"You will do even greater things,
now that I am going back to the Father.

"Ask me, and I will do whatever you ask.
This way the Son will bring honor to the Father.
I will do whatever you ask me to do."

The gospel of the Lord.

[187]   **"One in Christ Jesus"**

FIRST READING

        The whole group of believers was united, heart and soul.

A reading from the Acts of the Apostles   4:32-35

**The followers of Jesus all felt the same way about everything.
None of them claimed that their belongings were their own,
    and they shared everything they had with each other.**

**In a powerful way the apostles told everyone
    that the Lord Jesus was now alive.**

**God greatly blessed his followers,
    and no one went in need of anything.
Everyone who owned land or houses would sell them
    and bring the money to the apostles.
Then they would give the money to anyone who needed it.**

                                       The word of the Lord.

RESPONSORIAL PSALM   145:10-11, 15-16, 17-18

    ℟. (18a) The Lord is near to all who call on him.

**All creation will thank you,
and your loyal people
will praise you.
They will tell about
your marvelous kingdom
and your power.**

    ℟. The Lord is near to all who call on him.

**Everyone depends on you,
and when the time is right,
you provide them with food.
By your own hand you satisfy
the desires of all who live.**

    ℟. The Lord is near to all who call on him.

Our LORD, everything you do
is kind and thoughtful,
and you are near to everyone
whose prayers are sincere.

℟. The Lord is near to all who call on him.

ALLELUIA

See John 6:63c, 68c

℟. Alleluia, alleluia.

Your words, Lord, are spirit and life:
you have the words of everlasting life.

℟. Alleluia, alleluia.

GOSPEL

May they be completely one.

✜ A reading from the holy gospel according to John   17:21-23

Jesus prayed to God:
"I want all of my followers to be one with each other,
just as I am one with you and you are one with me.
I also want them to be one with us.
Then the people of this world will believe that you sent me.

"I have honored my followers in the same way that you honored me,
in order that they may be one with each other,
just as we are one.

"I am one with them,
and you are one with me,
so that they may become completely one.
Then this world's people will know that you sent me.
They will know that you love my followers as much as you love me."

The gospel of the Lord.

[188]

"Followers of Jesus"

FIRST READING

Go and tell the people everything about this new life.

A reading from the Acts of the Apostles 5:17-21

The high priest and all the other Sadducees who were with him became jealous.
They arrested the apostles and put them in the city jail.

But that night an angel from the Lord opened the doors of the jail
    and led the apostles out.
The angel said, "Go to the temple and tell the people everything
    about this new life."
So they went into the temple before sunrise and started teaching.

The word of the Lord.

RESPONSORIAL PSALM 34:1-2, 3-4, 7-8

℟. (7a) The Lord hears the cry of the poor.

I will always praise the LORD.
With all my heart,
I will praise the LORD.
Let all who are helpless
listen and be glad.

℟. The Lord hears the cry of the poor.

Honor the LORD with me!
Celebrate his great name.
I asked the LORD for help,
and he saved me
from all my fears.

℟. The Lord hears the cry of the poor.

If you honor the LORD,
his angel will protect you.
Discover for yourself
that the LORD is kind.

Come to him for protection,
and you will be glad.

℟. The Lord hears the cry of the poor.

ALLELUIA See John 6:63c, 68c

℟. Alleluia, alleluia.

**Your words, Lord, are spirit and life:
you have the words of everlasting life.**

℟. Alleluia, alleluia.

GOSPEL

You do not belong to the world because I have chosen you out of it.

✢ A reading from the holy gospel according to John 15:18-21

Jesus said to his disciples:
"If the people of this world hate you,
   just remember that they hated me first.
If you belonged to the world,
   its people would love you.
But you don't belong to the world.

"I have chosen you to leave the world behind,
   and that is why its people hate you.

"Remember how I told you
   that servants are not greater than their master.
So if people mistreat me, they will mistreat you.
If they do what I say, they will do what you say.

"People will do to you exactly what they did to me.
They will do it because you belong to me,
   and they don't know the one who sent me."

The gospel of the Lord.

[189]   **"Obedience to God"**

FIRST READING

We do not obey people. We obey God.

A reading from the Acts of the Apostles   5:27-32

When the apostles were brought before the Jewish council,
the high priest said to them,
"We told you plainly not to teach in the name of Jesus.
But look what you have done!
You have been teaching all over Jerusalem,
    and you are trying to blame us for his death."

Peter and the apostles replied:

"We don't obey people. We obey God.
You killed Jesus by nailing him to a cross.
But the God our ancestors worshiped raised him to life
    and made him our Leader and Savior.
Then God gave him a place at his right side,
    so that the people of Israel would turn back to him
        and be forgiven.
We are here to tell you about all this,
    and so is the Holy Spirit,
    who is God's gift to everyone who obeys God."

                                            The word of the Lord.

RESPONSORIAL PSALM   119:1-2, 7 and 24

    ℟. (1b) Happy are they who follow the law of the Lord!

Our Lord, you bless everyone
who lives right
and obeys your Law.
You bless all of those
who follow your commands
from deep in their hearts.

    ℟. Happy are they who follow the law of the Lord!

I will do right and praise you
by learning to respect
your perfect laws.

Your laws are my greatest joy!
I follow their advice.

℟. Happy are they who follow the law of the Lord!

ALLELUIA See John 6:63c, 68c

℟. Alleluia, alleluia.

**Your words, Lord, are spirit and life:
you have the words of everlasting life.**

℟. Alleluia, alleluia.

GOSPEL

If you love me you will obey me.

✠ A reading from the holy gospel according to John   14:21-26

Jesus said to his disciples:
"If you love me, you will do what I have said,
   and my Father will love you.
I will also love you and show you what I am like."

The other Judas, not Judas Iscariot, then spoke up and asked,
"Lord, what do you mean by saying
      that you will show us what you are like,
      but you will not show the people of this world?"

Jesus replied:
"If anyone loves me, they will obey me.
Then my Father will love them,
   and we will come to them and live in them.
But anyone who doesn't love me,
   won't obey me.
What they have heard me say doesn't really come from me,
   but from the Father who sent me.

"I have told you these things while I am still with you.
But the Holy Spirit will come and help you,
   because the Father will send the Spirit to take my place.
The Spirit will teach you everything
   and will remind you of what I said while I was with you."

                                        The gospel of the Lord.

[190] "There Are Other Sheep Who Belong to Me"

FIRST READING

This man is my chosen instrument to bring my name before the Gentiles.

A reading from the Acts of the Apostles 9:1-20

Saul kept on threatening to kill the Lord's followers.
He even went to the high priest
    and asked for letters to the Jewish leaders in Damascus.
He did this because he wanted to arrest and take to Jerusalem
    any man or woman who had accepted the Lord's Way.

When Saul had almost reached Damascus,
    a bright light from heaven suddenly flashed around him.
He fell to the ground and heard a voice that said,
"Saul! Saul! Why are you so cruel to me?"

"Who are you?" Saul asked.

"I am Jesus," the Lord answered.
"I am the one you are so cruel to.
Now get up and go into the city,
    where you will be told what to do."

The men with Saul stood there speechless.
They had heard the voice,
    but they had not seen anyone.
Saul got up from the ground,
    and when he opened his eyes,
    he could not see a thing.
Someone then led him by the hand to Damascus,
    and for three days he was blind and did not eat or drink.

A follower named Ananias lived in Damascus,
    and the Lord spoke to him in a vision.
Ananias answered, "Lord, here I am."

The Lord said to him,
"Get up and go to the house of Judas on Straight Street.
When you get there,
    you will find a man named Saul from the city of Tarsus.
Saul is praying,
    and he has seen a vision.

He saw a man named Ananias coming to him and putting his hands on him,
so that he could see again."

Ananias replied, "Lord, a lot of people have told me
    about the terrible things this man has done
    to your followers in Jerusalem.
Now the chief priests have given him the power to come here
    and arrest anyone who worships in your name."

The Lord said to Ananias, "Go!
I have chosen him to tell foreigners, kings,
    and the people of Israel about me.
I will show him how much he must suffer for worshiping in my name."

Ananias left and went into the house where Saul was staying.
Ananias placed his hands on him and said,
"Saul, the Lord Jesus has sent me.
He is the same one who appeared to you along the road.
He wants you to be able to see and to be filled with the Holy Spirit."

Suddenly something like fish scales fell from Saul's eyes,
    and he could see.
He got up and was baptized.
Then he ate and felt much better.

For several days Saul stayed with the Lord's followers in Damascus.
Soon he went to the Jewish meeting places
    and started telling people that Jesus is the Son of God.

                                          The word of the Lord.

RESPONSORIAL PSALM   117:1, 2

℟. (Mark 16:15) Go out to all the world and tell the good news.

All of you nations,
come praise the LORD**!**
Let everyone praise him.

℟. Go out to all the world and tell the good news.

His love for us is wonderful,
his faithfulness never ends.
Shout praises to the LORD!

℟. Go out to all the world and tell the good news.

ALLELUIA
See John 6:63c, 68c

℟. Alleluia, alleluia.

Your words, Lord, are spirit and life:
you have the words of everlasting life.

℟. Alleluia, alleluia.

GOSPEL

The good shepherd lays down his life for his sheep.

✢ A reading from the holy gospel according to John 10:14-16

Jesus said:
"I am the good shepherd.
I know my sheep, and they know me.
Just as the Father knows me,
  I know the Father,
  and I give up my life for my sheep.

"I have other sheep that are not in this sheep pen.
I must bring them together too,
  when they hear my voice.
Then there will be one flock of sheep and one shepherd."

The gospel of the Lord.

[191]   **"Believe in Jesus"**

FIRST READING

*The disciples preached to the Greeks,
proclaiming the good news of the Lord Jesus.*

A reading from the Acts of the Apostles   11:19-22, 26c

Some of the Lord's followers had been scattered
    because of the terrible trouble that started
    when Stephen was killed.
They went as far as Phoenicia, Cyprus, and Antioch,
    but they told the message only to the Jews.
Some of the followers from Cyprus and Cyrene went to Antioch
    and started telling Gentiles the good news
    about the Lord Jesus.
The Lord's power was with them,
    and many people turned to the Lord and put their faith in him.

News of what was happening reached the church in Jerusalem.
Then they sent Barnabas to Antioch.

There in Antioch the Lord's followers were first called Christians.

                                       The word of the Lord.

RESPONSORIAL PSALM   37:3-4, 5-6

    ℟. (39a) The salvation of the just comes from the Lord.

Trust the LORD and live right!
The land will be yours,
and you will be safe.
Do what the LORD wants,
and he will give you
your heart's desire.

    ℟. The salvation of the just comes from the Lord.

Let the LORD lead you
and trust him to help.
Then it will be as clear
as the noonday sun
that you were right.

℟. The salvation of the just comes from the Lord.

ALLELUIA

See John 6:63c, 68c

℟. Alleluia, alleluia.

**Your words, Lord, are spirit and life:
you have the words of everlasting life.**

℟. Alleluia, alleluia.

GOSPEL

The Spirit of truth will be my witness.

✠ **A reading from the holy gospel according to John** 15:26—16:1

**Jesus said to his disciples:
"I will send you the Spirit
who comes from the Father and shows what is true.
The Spirit will help you and will tell you about me.
Then you will also tell others about me,
because you have been with me from the beginning.**

"I am telling you this to keep you from being afraid."

The gospel of the Lord.

[192]   **"Preaching About Jesus"**

FIRST READING

> Believe in the Lord Jesus, and you will be saved,
> and your household too.

A reading from the Acts of the Apostles   16:22-34

The crowd joined in the attack on Paul and Silas.
Then the officials tore the clothes off the two men
    and ordered them to be beaten with a whip.

After they had been badly beaten,
    they were put in jail,
    and the jailer was told to guard them carefully.
The jailer did as he was told.
He put them deep inside the jail
    and chained their feet to heavy blocks of wood.

About midnight Paul and Silas were praying and singing praises to God,
    while the other prisoners listened.
Suddenly a strong earthquake shook the jail to its foundations.
The doors opened,
    and the chains fell from all the prisoners.

When the jailer woke up and saw that the doors were open,
    he thought that the prisoners had escaped.
He pulled out his sword and was about to kill himself.
But Paul shouted, "Don't harm yourself!
No one has escaped."

The jailer asked for a torch and went into the jail.

He was shaking all over as he kneeled down in front of Paul and Silas.
After he had led them out of the jail, he asked,
"What must I do to be saved?"

They replied, "Have faith in the Lord Jesus and you will be saved!
This is also true for everyone who lives in your home."
Then Paul and Silas told him and everyone else in his house
    about the Lord.

While it was still night,
    the jailer took them to a place
    where he could wash their cuts and bruises.

Then he and everyone in his home were baptized.
They were very glad that they had put their faith in God.

After this, the jailer took Paul and Silas to his home
and gave them something to eat.

The word of the Lord.

RESPONSORIAL PSALM 96:1-2, 3 and 10

℟. (Mark 16:15) Go out to all the world and tell the good news.

Sing a new song to the Lord!
Everyone on this earth,
sing praises to the Lord,
sing and praise his name.
Day after day announce,
"The Lord has saved us!"

℟. Go out to all the world and tell the good news.

Tell every nation on earth,
"The Lord is wonderful
and does marvelous things!"
Announce to the nations,
"The Lord is King!
The world stands firm,
never to be shaken,
and he will judge its people
with fairness."

℟. Go out to all the world and tell the good news.

ALLELUIA See John 6:63c, 68c

℟. Alleluia, alleluia.

Your words, Lord, are spirit and life:
you have the words of everlasting life.

℟. Alleluia, alleluia.

GOSPEL

Jesus sent them to proclaim the kingdom of God and to heal the sick.

✣ **A reading from the holy gospel according to Luke** 9:1-6

Jesus called together his twelve apostles
    and gave them complete power over all demons and diseases.
Then he sent them to tell about God's kingdom and to heal the sick.

He told them, "Don't take anything with you!
Don't take a walking stick or a traveling bag or food or money
    or even a change of clothes.
When you are welcomed into a home,
    stay there until you leave that town.
If people won't welcome you,
    leave the town and shake the dust from your feet
        as a warning to them."

The apostles left and went from village to village,
    telling the good news and healing people everywhere.

The gospel of the Lord.

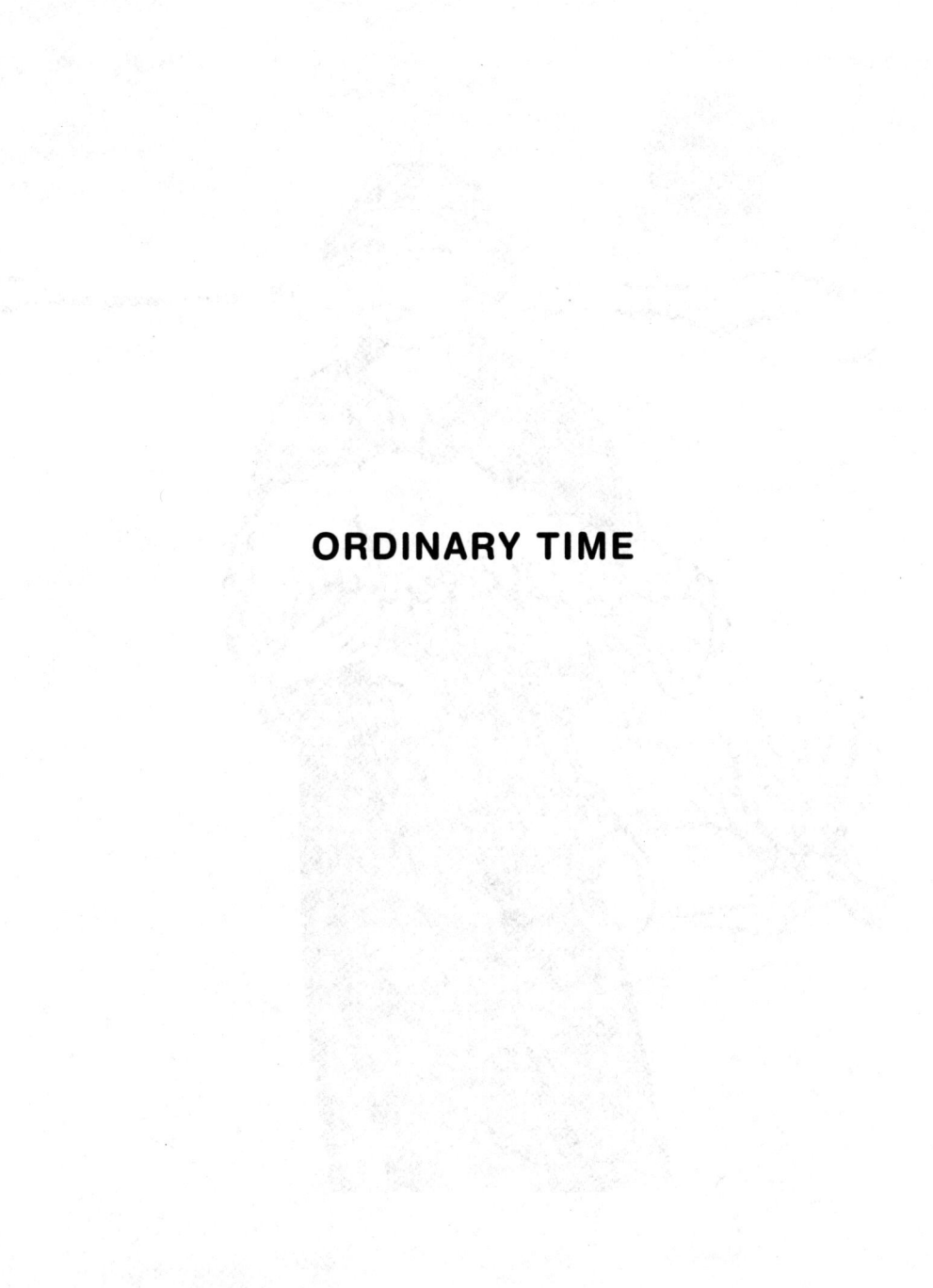

ORDINARY TIME

In Ordinary Time the gospel acclamation is chosen from the texts given at no. 232 on page 697.

[193] ## "Light for the World"

FIRST READING

Act like people of the light and make your light shine.

A reading from the letter of Paul to the Ephesians   5:8-10

Brothers and sisters:
> You used to be like people living in the dark,
but now you are people of the light
> because you belong to the Lord.
So act like people of the light
> and make your light shine.
Be good and honest and truthful,
> as you try to please the Lord.

The word of the Lord.

RESPONSORIAL PSALM   27:1, 13-14

℟. (1a) The Lord is my light and my salvation.

**You, LORD, are the light
that keeps me safe.
I am not afraid of anyone.
You protect me,
and I have no fears.**

℟. The Lord is my light and my salvation.

**I know I will live
to see how kind you are.
Trust the LORD!
Be brave and strong
and trust the LORD!**

℟. The Lord is my light and my salvation.

GOSPEL

You are the light of the world.

✙ **A reading from the holy gospel according to Matthew** 5:14-16

Jesus said to his disciples:
"You are like light for the whole world.
A city built on top of a hill cannot be hidden,
    and no one would light a lamp and put it under a clay pot.
A lamp is placed on a lamp stand,
    where it can give light to everyone in the house.
Make your light shine,
    so that others will see the good that you do
        and will praise your Father in heaven."

The gospel of the Lord.

"Love Everyone"

FIRST READING

Love is the greatest gift.

A reading from the first letter of Paul to the Corinthians   13:4-7

Brothers and sisters:
Love is kind and patient,
never jealous, boastful, proud, or rude.
Love isn't selfish or quick tempered.
It doesn't keep a record of wrongs that others do.
Love rejoices in the truth, but not in evil.
Love is always supportive, loyal, hopeful, and trusting.
Love never fails!

The word of the Lord.

RESPONSORIAL PSALM   116:5 and 7, 9 and 12

℟. (9a) Now I will walk at your side.

You are kind, Lord,
so good and merciful.
You have treated me so kindly
that I don't need
to worry anymore.

℟. Now I will walk at your side.

Now I will walk at your side
in this land of the living.
What must I give you, Lord,
for being so good to me?

℟. Now I will walk at your side.

GOSPEL

Be perfect as your heavenly Father is perfect.

✣ **A reading from the holy gospel according to Matthew**   5:43-48

Jesus said to his disciples:
"You have heard people say,
'Love your neighbors and hate your enemies.'
But I tell you to love your enemies
     and pray for anyone who mistreats you.
Then you will be acting like your Father in heaven.

"He makes the sun rise on both good and bad people.
And he sends rain for the ones who do right
     and for the ones who do wrong.

"If you love only those people who love you,
    will God reward you for that?
Even tax collectors love their friends.
If you greet only your friends,
    what's so great about that?
Don't even unbelievers do that?
But you must always act like your Father in heaven."

                                      The gospel of the Lord.

[195] **"This Is How You Should Pray"**

FIRST READING

Let prayers be offered for everyone to God.

A reading from the first letter of Paul to Timothy   2:1-4

First of all,
  I ask you to pray for everyone.
Ask God to help and bless them all,
  and tell God how thankful you are for each of them.

Pray for kings and others in power,
  so that we may live quiet and peaceful lives
    as we worship and honor God.
This kind of prayer is good,
  and it pleases God our Savior.

God wants everyone to be saved and to know the whole truth.

The word of the Lord.

RESPONSORIAL PSALM   25:1-2ab and 4, 5-6

℟. (1) To you, O Lord, I lift my soul.

I offer you my heart, Lord God,
and I trust you.
Don't make me ashamed.
Show me your paths
and teach me to follow.

℟. To you, O Lord, I lift my soul.

Guide me by your truth
and instruct me.
You keep me safe,
and I always trust you.
Please, Lord, remember,
you have always been patient and kind.

℟. To you, O Lord, I lift my soul.

GOSPEL

This is how you should pray.

✣ A reading from the holy gospel according to Matthew   6:7-13

Jesus said to his disciples:
"When you pray,
  don't talk on and on as people do who don't know God.
They think God likes to hear long prayers.
Don't be like them.
Your Father knows what you need before you ask.

"You should pray like this:

>Our Father in heaven,
>help us to honor your name.
>Come and set up your kingdom,
>so that everyone on earth will obey you,
>as you are obeyed in heaven.
>Give us our food for today.
>Forgive our sins,
>as we forgive others.
>Keep us from being tempted and protect us from evil."

The gospel of the Lord.

"Store Up Riches in Heaven"

FIRST READING

Look for the things that are in heaven, where Christ is.

A reading from the letter of Paul to the Colossians   3:1-2

Brothers and sisters:
   You have been raised to life with Christ.
Now set your heart on what is in heaven,
   where Christ rules at God's right side.
Think about what is up there,
   not about what is here on earth.

The word of the Lord.

RESPONSORIAL PSALM   119:1-2, 14-15

℟. (1b) Happy are they who follow the law of the Lord!

Our Lord, you bless everyone
who lives right
and obeys your Law.
You bless all of those
who follow your commands
from deep in their hearts.

℟. Happy are they who follow the law of the Lord!

Obeying your instructions
brings as much happiness
as being rich.
I will study your teachings
and follow your footsteps.

℟. Happy are they who follow the law of the Lord!

GOSPEL

Where your treasure is, there will your heart be also.

✢ **A reading from the holy gospel according to Matthew**   6:19-21

Jesus said to his disciples:
   "Don't store up treasures on earth!
Moths and rust can destroy them,
   and thieves can break in and steal them.

"Instead, store up your treasures in heaven,
   where moths and rust cannot destroy them,
   and thieves cannot break in and steal them.

"Your heart will always be where your treasure is."

                                    The gospel of the Lord.

[197]   **"I Will Take Care of You"**

FIRST READING

I will take care of you.

A reading from the book of the prophet Isaiah   46:4

Even when you are old and gray,
   I will still be the same,
   and I will take care of you.

I created you,
   and I will carry you and always keep you safe.

                                     The word of the Lord.

RESPONSORIAL PSALM   23:1-3a, 3b-4, 6

℟. (1) The Lord is my shepherd; there is nothing I shall want.

You, LORD, are my shepherd.
I will never be in need.
You let me rest in fields
of green grass.
You lead me to streams
of peaceful water,
and you refresh my life.

℟. The Lord is my shepherd; there is nothing I shall want.

You are true to your name,
and you lead me
along the right paths.
I may walk through valleys
as dark as death,
but I won't be afraid.
You are with me,
and your shepherd's rod
makes me feel safe.

℟. The Lord is my shepherd; there is nothing I shall want.

Your kindness and love
will always be with me
each day of my life,

and I will live forever
in your house, LORD.

℟. The Lord is my shepherd; there is nothing I shall want.

GOSPEL

Do not worry about tomorrow.

✛ A reading from the holy gospel according to Matthew 6:25b-33

Jesus said to his disciples:
"Don't worry about having something to eat, drink, or wear.
Isn't life more than food or clothing?
Look at the birds in the sky!
They don't plant or harvest.
They don't even store grain in barns.
Yet your Father in heaven takes care of them.
Aren't you worth more than birds?

"Can worry make you live longer?
Why worry about clothes?
Look how the wild flowers grow.
They don't work hard to make their clothes.
But I tell you that Solomon with all his wealth
    was not as well clothed as one of them.
God gives such beauty to everything that grows in the fields,
    even though it is here today and thrown into a fire tomorrow.
He will surely do even more for you!
Why do you have such little faith?

"Don't worry and ask yourselves,
'Will we have anything to eat?
Will we have anything to drink?
Will we have clothes to wear?'
Only people who don't know God are always worrying about such things.
Your Father in heaven knows that you need all of these.
But more than anything else,
    put God's work first and do what he wants.
Then all the other things will be yours as well."

The gospel of the Lord.

[198] "Forgive as the Lord Has Forgiven You"

FIRST READING

Forgive anyone who does you wrong, just as Christ has forgiven you.

A reading from the letter of Paul to the Colossians 3:12-13

Brothers and sisters:
God loves you and has chosen you as his own special people.
So be gentle, kind, humble, meek, and patient.
Put up with each other,
> and forgive anyone who does you wrong,
> just as Christ has forgiven you.

The word of the Lord.

RESPONSORIAL PSALM 103:1-2, 3 and 8, 11-12

℟. (8a) The Lord is kind and merciful.

With all my heart
I praise the LORD,
and with all that I am
I praise his holy name!
With all my heart
I praise the LORD!
I will never forget
how kind he has been.

℟. The Lord is kind and merciful.

The LORD forgives our sins,
heals us when we are sick.
The LORD is merciful!
He is kind and patient,
and his love never fails.

℟. The Lord is kind and merciful.

How great is God's love for all
who worship him?
Greater than the distance
between heaven and earth!

How far has the LORD taken
our sins from us?
Farther than the distance
from east to west!

℟. The Lord is kind and merciful.

GOSPEL

Take the beam out of your own eye first.

✠ A reading from the holy gospel according to Matthew   7:1-5

Jesus said to his disciples:
 "Don't condemn others,
  and God will not condemn you.
God will be as hard on you as you are on others!
He will treat you exactly as you treat them.

"You can see the speck in your friend's eye,
  but you don't notice the log in your own eye.
How can you say,
'My friend, let me take the speck out of your eye,'
  when you don't see the log in your own eye?
You're nothing but showoffs!
First, take the log out of your own eye.
Then you can see how to take the speck out of your friend's eye."

The gospel of the Lord.

[199]   # "My Burden Is Light"

FIRST READING

    Fill your minds with everything that is holy.

A reading from the letter of Paul to the Philippians   4:8-9

My friends,
   keep your minds on whatever is true, pure, right,
      holy, friendly, and proper.
Don't ever stop thinking about what is truly worthwhile
      and worthy of praise.
You know the teachings I gave you,
   and you know what you heard me say and saw me do.

So follow my example.
And God, who gives peace, will be with you.

                                               The word of the Lord.

RESPONSORIAL PSALM   19:7, 8

   ℟. (9a) The precepts of the Lord give joy to the heart.

The Law of the Lord is perfect;
it gives us new life.
His teachings last forever,
and they give wisdom
to ordinary people.

   ℟. The precepts of the Lord give joy to the heart.

The Lord's instruction is right;
it makes our hearts glad.
His commands shine brightly,
and they give us light.

   ℟. The precepts of the Lord give joy to the heart.

GOSPEL

I am gentle and humble of heart.

✚ **A reading from the holy gospel according to Matthew** 11:29-30

Jesus said to his disciples:
   "Take the yoke I give you.
Put it on your shoulders and learn from me.
I am gentle and humble,
   and you will find rest.
This yoke is easy to bear,
   and this burden is light."

The gospel of the Lord.

[200]   **"Treasures of Heaven"**

FIRST READING

God has something stored up for you in heaven.

A reading from the first letter of Peter   1:3-4

Brothers and sisters:
Praise God, the Father of our Lord Jesus Christ.
God is so good,
> **and by raising Jesus from death,**
>> **he has given us new life and a hope that lives on.**

God has something stored up for you in heaven,
> **where it will never decay or be ruined or disappear.**

The word of the Lord.

RESPONSORIAL PSALM   112:1, 3, 4

℟. (1a) Happy are those who fear the Lord.

Shout praises to the Lord!
The Lord blesses everyone
who worships him and gladly
obeys his teachings.

℟. Happy are those who fear the Lord.

They will get rich and prosper
and will always be remembered
for their fairness.

℟. Happy are those who fear the Lord.

They will be so kind
and merciful and good,
that they will be like a light
in the dark for others
who do the right thing.

℟. Happy are those who fear the Lord.

GOSPEL

He sold all that he had and bought the field.

✤ **A reading from the holy gospel according to Matthew**   13:44-46

Jesus said to his disciples:
"The kingdom of heaven is like what happens
   when someone finds treasure hidden in a field
   and buries it again.
A person like that is happy and goes and sells everything
   in order to buy that field.

"The kingdom of heaven is like what happens
   when a shop owner is looking for fine pearls.
After finding a very valuable one,
  the owner goes and sells everything
   in order to buy that pearl."

                                    The gospel of the Lord.

[201]   **"Trust in the Lord"**

FIRST READING

We waited and waited and now the Lord is here.

A reading from the book of the prophet Isaiah   25:6-7, 9

On this mountain the L<small>ORD</small> All-Powerful
     will prepare for all nations a feast of the finest foods.
Choice wines and the best meat will be served.
Here the L<small>ORD</small> will strip away
     the funeral clothes that cover the nations.

On that day, people will say,
"The L<small>ORD</small> God has saved us!
Let's celebrate.
We waited and waited, and now he is here."

                                             The word of the Lord.

RESPONSORIAL PSALM   91:1-2, 9 and 11

℞. (see 2b) In you, my God, I place my trust.

Live under the protection
of God Most High
and stay in the shadow
of God All-Powerful.
Then you will say to the L<small>**ORD**</small>**,**
"You are my fortress,
my place of safety;
you are my God,
and I trust you."

    ℞. In you, my God, I place my trust.

The L<small>**ORD**</small> **Most High**
is your fortress.
Run to him for safety.
God will command his angels
to protect you
wherever you go.

    ℞. In you, my God, I place my trust.

GOSPEL

Order me to come to you across the water.

✣ **A reading from the holy gospel according to Matthew** 14:22-33

Jesus made his disciples get into a boat and start back across the lake.
But he stayed until he had sent the crowds away.
Then he went up on a mountain where he could be alone and pray.
Later that evening, he was still there.

By this time the boat was a long way from the shore.
It was going against the wind and was being tossed around by the waves.
A little while before morning,
 Jesus came walking on the water toward his disciples.
When they saw him, they thought he was a ghost.
They were terrified and started screaming.

At once Jesus said to them, "Don't worry!
I am Jesus. Don't be afraid."

Peter replied, "Lord, if it is really you,
 tell me to come to you on the water."

"Come on!" Jesus said.
Peter then got out of the boat
 and started walking on the water toward him.

But when Peter saw how strong the wind was,
 he was afraid and started sinking.

"Lord, save me!" he shouted.

Right away Jesus reached out his hand.
He helped Peter up and said,
"You surely don't have much faith.
Why do you doubt?"

When Jesus and Peter got into the boat, the wind died down.
The men in the boat worshiped Jesus and said,
"You really are the Son of God!"

The gospel of the Lord.

[202] # "Gifts Received from God"

FIRST READING

*Each one of you has received a special gift;
put yourselves at the service of others.*

A reading from the first letter of Peter 4:10-11

Brothers and sisters:
Each of you has been blessed with one of God's many wonderful gifts
   to be used in the service of others.
So use your gift well.

If you have the gift of speaking,
   preach God's message.
If you have the gift of helping others,
   do it with the strength that God supplies.

Everything should be done in a way that will bring honor to God
      because of Jesus Christ,
   who is glorious and powerful forever. Amen.

The word of the Lord.

RESPONSORIAL PSALM 37:3 and 4, 5 and 26

℟. (39a) The salvation of the just comes from the Lord.

Trust the L<small>ORD</small> and live right!
The land will be yours,
and you will be safe.
Do what the L<small>ORD</small> wants,
and he will give you
your heart's desire.

℟. The salvation of the just comes from the Lord.

Let the L<small>ORD</small> lead you
and trust him to help.
Good people gladly give and lend,
and their children
turn out good.

℟. The salvation of the just comes from the Lord.

GOSPEL

Because you have been faithful in small matters,
come into the joy of your master.

✢ A reading from the holy gospel according to Matthew 25:14-29

Jesus told his disciples this story about the kingdom of God:
"The kingdom is like what happened when a man went away
    and put his three servants in charge of all he owned.
The man knew what each servant could do.
So he handed five thousand coins to the first servant,
    two thousand to the second,
    and one thousand to the third.
Then he left the country.

"As soon as the man had gone,
    the servant with the five thousand coins
        used them to earn five thousand more.
The servant who had two thousand coins did the same with his money
    and earned two thousand more.
But the servant with one thousand coins dug a hole
    and hid his master's money in the ground.

"Some time later the master of those servants returned.
He called them in and asked what they had done with his money.
The servant who had been given five thousand coins
    brought them in with the five thousand that he had earned.
He said, 'Sir, you gave me five thousand coins,
    and I have earned five thousand more.'

" 'Wonderful!' his master replied.
'You are a good and faithful servant.
I left you in charge of only a little,
    but now I will put you in charge of much more.
Come and share in my happiness!'

"Next, the servant who had been given two thousand coins
    came in and said,
'Sir, you gave me two thousand coins,
    and I have earned two thousand more.'

" 'Wonderful!' his master replied.
'You are a good and faithful servant.
I left you in charge of only a little,
> but now I will put you in charge of much more.
Come and share in my happiness!'

"The servant who had been given one thousand coins
> then came in and said,
'Sir, I know that you are hard to get along with.
You harvest what you don't plant
> and gather crops where you have not scattered seed.
I was frightened and went out and hid your money in the ground.
Here is every single coin!'

"The master of the servant told him,
'You are lazy and good-for-nothing!
You know that I harvest what I don't plant
> and gather crops where I have not scattered seed.
You could have at least put my money in the bank,
> so that I could have earned interest on it.'

"Then the master said,
'Now your money will be taken away
> and given to the servant with ten thousand coins!
Everyone who has something will be given more,
> and they will have more than enough.
But everything will be taken from those who don't have anything.' "

The gospel of the Lord.

[203] # "The Word That I Speak"

FIRST READING

My word carries out my will.

A reading from the book of the prophet Isaiah   55:10-11

The rain and the snow fall from the sky.
But they don't return without watering the earth
    that produces seeds to plant and grain to eat.
And that's how it is with my words.
They don't return to me without doing everything I sent them to do.

The word of the Lord.

RESPONSORIAL PSALM   65:9, 11-12, 13

℟. (Luke 8:8) The seed that falls on good ground will yield a fruitful harvest.

Our God, you take care of the earth
and send rain to help the soil
grow all kinds of crops.
Your rivers never run dry,
and you prepare the earth
to produce much grain.

℟. The seed that falls on good ground will yield a fruitful harvest.

Wherever your footsteps
touch the earth,
a rich harvest is gathered.
Desert pastures blossom,
and mountains celebrate.

℟. The seed that falls on good ground will yield a fruitful harvest.

Meadows are filled
with sheep and goats;
valleys overflow with grain
and echo with joyful songs.

℟. The seed that falls on good ground will yield a fruitful harvest.

GOSPEL

The sower went out to sow seed.

✣ A reading from the holy gospel according to Mark   4:1-9

The next time Jesus taught beside Lake Galilee,
   a big crowd gathered.
It was so large that he had to sit in a boat out on the lake,
   while the people stood on the shore.
He used stories to teach them many things,
   and this is part of what he taught:

"Now listen!
A farmer went out to scatter seed in a field.
While the farmer was scattering the seed,
   some of it fell along the road and was eaten by birds.

"Other seeds fell on thin, rocky ground and quickly started growing
   because the soil was not very deep.
But when the sun came up,
   the plants were scorched and dried up,
   because they did not have enough roots.

"Some other seeds fell where thorn bushes grew up
      and choked out the plants.
So they did not produce any grain.

"But a few seeds did fall on good ground
      where the plants grew and produced thirty or sixty
      or even a hundred times as much as was scattered."

Then Jesus said, "If you have ears, pay attention."

                              The gospel of the Lord.

[204]   **"I Will Help You"**

FIRST READING

The God of Israel saves and protects you.

A reading from the book of the prophet Isaiah   41:14

The LORD says this:
"People of Israel, don't worry,
though others may say,
'Israel is only a worm!'
I am the holy God of Israel,
who saves and protects you."

The word of the Lord.

RESPONSORIAL PSALM   90:1-2, 14 and 16

℟. (1) In every age, O Lord, you have been our refuge.

Our LORD, in all generations
you have been our home.
You have always been God—
long before the birth
of the mountains,
even before you created
the earth and the world.

℟. In every age, O Lord, you have been our refuge.

When morning comes,
let your love satisfy
all our needs.
Then we can celebrate
and be glad for what time
we have left.
Do wonderful things for us,
your servants,
and show your mighty power
to our children.

℟. In every age, O Lord, you have been our refuge.

GOSPEL

*Who can this be?
Even the wind and the sea obey him.*

✣ **A reading from the holy gospel according to Mark**   4:35-41

Jesus said to his disciples, "Let's cross to the east side."
So they left the crowd,
   and his disciples started across the lake with him in the boat.

Some other boats followed along.
Suddenly a windstorm struck the lake.
Waves started splashing into the boat,
   and it was about to sink.

Jesus was in the back of the boat with his head on a pillow,
   and he was asleep.
His disciples woke him and said,
"Teacher, don't you care that we're about to drown?"

Jesus got up and ordered the wind and the waves to be quiet.
The wind stopped,
   and everything was calm.

Jesus asked his disciples, "Why were you afraid?
Don't you have any faith?"

Now they were more afraid than ever and said to each other,
"Who is this?
Even the wind and the waves obey him!"

The gospel of the Lord.

[205] **"The Lord Will Help You"**

FIRST READING

A The Lord God will be gracious to you when he hears your cry.

A reading from the book of the prophet Isaiah 30:19-20, 23-24, 26

People of Jerusalem,
   you don't need to cry anymore.
The Lord is kind,
   and as soon as he hears your cries for help,
   he will come.

The Lord has brought trouble and sorrow
   by not giving you enough bread and water.
But now you will again see the Lord, your teacher,
   and he will guide you.

The Lord will send rain to water the seeds you have planted—
   your fields will produce more crops than you need,
   and your cattle will graze in open pastures.

Even the oxen and donkeys that plow your fields
   will be fed the finest grain.

Then the Lord will bind up his people's injuries
   and heal the wounds he has caused.
The moon will shine as bright as the sun,
   and the sun will shine seven times brighter than usual.
It will be like the light of seven days all at once.

The word of the Lord.

OR

B

My prayer is that you know about God's great power for us.

A reading from the letter of Paul to the Ephesians 1:15-16a, 18-19a

Brothers and sisters:
 I have heard about your faith in the Lord Jesus
     and your love for all of God's people.
So I never stop being grateful for you.

My prayer is that light will flood your hearts
     and that you will understand the hope that was given to you
         when God chose you.
Then you will discover the glorious blessings that will be yours
     together with all of God's people.

I want you to know about the great and mighty power
     that God has for us followers.

The word of the Lord.

RESPONSORIAL PSALM   121:1-2, 5-6, 7-8

℟. (see 2) Our help is from the Lord, who made heaven and earth.

I look to the hills!
Where will I find help?
It will come from the LORD,
who created the heavens
and the earth.

℟. Our help is from the Lord, who made heaven and earth.

The LORD is your protector,
there at your right side
to shade you from the sun.
You won't be harmed
by the sun during the day
or by the moon at night.

℟. Our help is from the Lord, who made heaven and earth.

The LORD will protect you
and keep you safe
from all dangers.
The LORD will protect you
now and always
wherever you are.

℟. Our help is from the Lord, who made heaven and earth.

GOSPEL

Little girl, I say to you, arise.

✠ **A reading from the holy gospel according to Mark** 5:21-24, 35b-36, 38-42

Jesus got into the boat and crossed Lake Galilee.
Then as he stood on the shore,
    a large crowd gathered around him.

The person in charge of the Jewish meeting place was also there.
His name was Jairus,
    and when he saw Jesus, he went over to him.
He kneeled at Jesus' feet and started begging him for help.
He said, "My daughter is about to die!
Please come and touch her,
    so she will get well and live."

Jesus went with Jairus.
Many people followed along and kept crowding around.

Some men came from Jairus' home and said,
"Your daughter has died!
Why bother the teacher anymore?"

Jesus heard what they said,
    and he said to Jairus,
"Don't worry. Just have faith!"

They went home with Jairus and saw the people
    crying and making a lot of noise.

Then Jesus went inside and said to them,
"Why are you crying and carrying on like this?
The child is not dead.
She is just asleep."
But the people laughed at him.

After Jesus had sent them all out of the house,
    he took the girl's father and mother and his three disciples
        and went to where she was.
He took the twelve-year-old girl by the hand and said,

    "Talitha, koum!"
    which means, "Little girl, get up!"

The girl got right up and started walking around.

The gospel of the Lord.

[206] **"We Are Called God's Children"**

FIRST READING

Whoever lives in God is a child of God.

A reading from the first letter of John   2:29b—3:1a

Beloved:
You know that everyone who does right is a child of God.

Think how much the Father loves us.
He loves us so much that he lets us be called his children,
    as we truly are.

The word of the Lord.

RESPONSORIAL PSALM   119:129-130, 133 and 135

℟. (135a) Lord, let your face shine on me.

**Your teachings are wonderful,
and I respect them all.
Understanding your word
brings light to the minds
of ordinary people.**

℟. Lord, let your face shine on me.

**Keep your promise
and don't let me stumble
or let sin control my life.
Smile on me, your servant,
and teach me your laws.**

℟. Lord, let your face shine on me.

GOSPEL

*Whenever you have accepted graciously a small child,
you have accepted me.*

✣ **A reading from the holy gospel according to Mark** 9:33-37

Jesus and his disciples went to his home in Capernaum.
After they were inside the house, Jesus asked them,
"What were you arguing about along the way?"
They had been arguing about which one of them was the greatest,
and so they did not answer.

After Jesus sat down and told the twelve disciples
    to gather around him,
he said, "If you want the place of honor,
you must become a slave and serve others!"

Then Jesus had a child stand near him.
He put his arm around the child and said,
"When you welcome even a child because of me, you welcome me.
And when you welcome me,
    you welcome the one who sent me."

The gospel of the Lord.

[207]   **"Jesus Blessed the Children"**

FIRST READING

I am your God; I will protect you.

A reading from the book of the prophet Isaiah   41:10

The Lord says this:
Don't be afraid!
I am with you.
Don't tremble with fear.
I am your God.
I will help you to be strong,
    as I protect you with my arm and give you victories.

The word of the Lord.

RESPONSORIAL PSALM   17:1abc and 5, 6 and 8

    ℟. (6b) Lord, bend your ear and hear my prayer.

I am innocent, LORD!
Won't you listen as I pray
and beg for help?
I have followed you,
without ever stumbling.

    ℟. Lord, bend your ear and hear my prayer.

I pray to you, God,
because you will help me.
Listen and answer my prayer!
Protect me as you would
your very own eyes;
hide me in the shadow
of your wings.

    ℟. Lord, bend your ear and hear my prayer.

GOSPEL

Jesus blessed the children.

✢ A reading from the holy gospel according to Mark 10:13-16

Some people brought their children to Jesus
so that he could bless them by placing his hands on them.
But his disciples told the people to stop bothering him.

When Jesus saw this, he became angry and said,
"Let the children come to me!
Don't try to stop them.
People who are like these little children belong to the kingdom of God.
I promise you that you cannot get into God's kingdom,
unless you accept it the way a child does."

Then Jesus took the children in his arms
and blessed them by placing his hands on them.

The gospel of the Lord.

[208] **"I Want to See Again"**

FIRST READING

I will lead and guide those who are blind.

A reading from the book of the prophet Isaiah   42:16

The LORD says this:
I will lead the blind on roads they have never seen,
   and I will guide them on paths they have never traveled.
Their road is dark and rough,
   but I will give light and make the road smooth.
This is a promise I will never break.

The word of the Lord.

RESPONSORIAL PSALM   27:1, 8 and 11ab

℟. (1) The Lord is my light and my salvation.

You, LORD, are the light
that keeps me safe.
I am not afraid of anyone.
You protect me,
and I have no fears.

℟. The Lord is my light and my salvation.

My heart tells me to pray.
I am eager to see your face.
Teach me to follow, LORD,
and lead me on the right path.

℟. The Lord is my light and my salvation.

GOSPEL

> Master, let me see again.

✝ A reading from the holy gospel according to Mark   10:46-52

Jesus and his disciples went to Jericho.
And as they were leaving,
> they were followed by a large crowd.

A blind beggar by the name of Bartimaeus son of Timaeus
> was sitting beside the road.
When he heard that it was Jesus from Nazareth,
> he shouted, "Jesus, Son of David, have pity on me!"

Many people told the man to stop,
> but he shouted even louder,
"Son of David, have pity on me!"

Jesus stopped and said, "Call him over!"

They called out to the blind man and said,
"Don't be afraid! Come on!
He is calling for you."

The man threw off his coat as he jumped up and ran to Jesus.
Jesus asked, "What do you want me to do for you?"

The blind man answered, "Master, I want to see!"

Jesus told him, "You may go.
Your eyes are healed because of your faith."

Right away the man could see,
> and he went down the road with Jesus.

The gospel of the Lord.

[209] **"They Were Extremely Generous"**

FIRST READING

They were glad to give generously.

A reading from the second letter of Paul to the Corinthians 8:1-3a, 12

My friends, we want you to know that the churches in Macedonia have shown others how kind God is.
Although they were going through hard times and were very poor,
   they were glad to give generously.
They gave as much as they could afford and even more.

It doesn't matter how much you have.
What matters is how much you are willing to give from what you have.

The word of the Lord.

RESPONSORIAL PSALM 103:1-2, 5 and 11

℟. (8a) The Lord is kind and merciful.

With all my heart
I praise the LORD,
and with all that I am
I praise his holy name!
With all my heart
I praise the LORD!
I will never forget
how kind he has been.

℟. The Lord is kind and merciful.

Each day that we live,
he provides for our needs
and gives us the strength
of a young eagle.
How great is God's love for all
who worship him?
Greater than the distance
between heaven and earth!

℟. The Lord is kind and merciful.

GOSPEL

This poor widow has given more than all others.

✣ A reading from the holy gospel according to Mark   12:41-44

Jesus was sitting in the temple near the offering box
   and watching people put in their gifts.
He noticed that many rich people were giving a lot of money.

Finally, a poor widow came up
   and put in two coins that were worth only a few pennies.

Jesus told his disciples to gather around him.
Then he said:
"I tell you that this poor widow has put in more than all the others.
Everyone else gave what they didn't need.
But she is very poor and gave everything she had.
Now she doesn't have a cent to live on."

                              The gospel of the Lord.

[210]   **"Kind Is the Lord"**

FIRST READING

The Lord is waiting to show you how kind he is.

A reading from the book of the prophet Isaiah   30:18

The LORD God is waiting to show you how kind he is
     and to have pity on you.
The LORD always does right,
     and he blesses everyone who trusts him.

                                                     The word of the Lord.

RESPONSORIAL PSALM   33:1-2, 4-5, 21-22

℟. (22) Lord, let your mercy be on us, as we place our trust in you.

**You are the LORD's people.
Obey him and celebrate!
He deserves your praise.
Praise the LORD with harps!
Use harps with ten strings
to make music for him.**

℟. Lord, let your mercy be on us, as we place our trust in you.

**The LORD is truthful;
he can be trusted.
He loves justice and fairness,
and he is kind to everyone
everywhere on earth.**

℟. Lord, let your mercy be on us, as we place our trust in you.

**You make our hearts glad
because we trust you,
the only God.
Be kind and bless us!
We depend on you.**

℟. Lord, let your mercy be on us, as we place our trust in you.

GOSPEL

This man deserves your help.

✠ A reading from the holy gospel according to Luke   7:1-10

After Jesus had finished teaching the people,
   he went to Capernaum.
In that town an army officer's servant was sick and about to die.
The officer liked this servant very much.
And when he heard about Jesus,
   he sent some Jewish leaders
      to ask him to come and heal the servant.

The leaders went to Jesus and begged him to do something.
They said, "This man deserves your help!
He loves our nation and even built us a meeting place."
So Jesus went with them.

When Jesus was not far from the house,
   the officer sent some friends to tell him,
"Lord, don't go to any trouble for me!
I am not good enough for you to come into my house.
And I am certainly not worthy to come to you.
Just say the word, and my servant will get well.
I have officers who give orders to me,
   and I have soldiers who take orders from me.
I can say to one of them, 'Go!' and he goes.
I can say to another, 'Come!' and he comes.
I can say to my servant, 'Do this!'
   and he will do it."

When Jesus heard this,
   he was so surprised
      that he turned and said to the crowd following him,
"In all of Israel I've never found anyone with this much faith!"

The officer's friends returned and found the servant well.

The gospel of the Lord.

[211] **"I Will Save You"**

FIRST READING
                        I will save you.

A reading from the book of the prophet Isaiah   43:1-3a, 5

The Lord says this:
Descendants of Jacob,
   I, the Lord, created you and formed your nation.

Israel, don't be afraid.
I will rescue you.
I have called you by name,
   and you belong to me.

When you cross deep rivers,
   I will be with you,
   and you won't drown.
When you walk through fire,
   you won't be burned or scorched by the flames.

I am the Lord, your God,
   the Holy One of Israel,
   the God who saves you.
Don't be afraid!
I am with you.

From the east and the west I will bring you together.

                                            The word of the Lord.

RESPONSORIAL PSALM   116:1-2, 5 and 12

    ℟. (9a) Now I will walk at your side.

I love you, Lord!
You answered my prayers.
You paid attention to me,
and so I will pray to you
as long as I live.

    ℟. Now I will walk at your side.

You are kind, LORD,
so good and merciful.
What must I give you, LORD,
for being so good to me?

℟. Now I will walk at your side.

GOSPEL

God has come to his people.

✣ A reading from the holy gospel according to Luke 7:11-17

Jesus and his disciples were on their way to the town of Nain,
and a big crowd was going along with them.
As they came near the gate of the town,
they saw people carrying out the body of a widow's only son.
Many people from the town were walking along with her.

When the Lord saw the woman,
he felt sorry for her and said, "Don't cry!"

Jesus went over and touched the stretcher
on which the people were carrying the dead boy.
They stopped, and Jesus said,
"Young man, get up!"
The boy sat up and began to speak.
Jesus then gave him back to his mother.

Everyone was frightened and praised God.
They said, "A great prophet is here with us!
God has come to his people."

News about Jesus spread all over Judea
and everywhere else in that part of the country.

The gospel of the Lord.

[212]   **"God Is Love"**

FIRST READING

God is love.

A reading from the first letter of John   4:7-10

My dear friends, we must love each other.
  Love comes from God,
    and when we love each other,
    it shows that we have been given new life.

We are now God's children, and we know him.

God is love,
    and anyone who doesn't love others has never known him.

God showed his love for us
    when he sent his only Son into the world to give us life.

Real love is not our love for God, but his love for us.
God sent his Son to be the sacrifice by which our sins are forgiven.

The word of the Lord.

RESPONSORIAL PSALM   90:12 and 14, 16-17abc

℟. (14) Fill us with your love, O Lord, and we will sing for joy!

Teach us to use wisely
all the time we have.
When morning comes,
let your love satisfy
all our needs.
Then we can celebrate
and be glad for what time
we have left.

℟. Fill us with your love, O Lord, and we will sing for joy!

Do wonderful things for us,
your servants,
and show your mighty power
to our children.

Our Lord and our God,
treat us with kindness
and let all go well for us.

℟. Fill us with your love, O Lord, and we will sing for joy!

GOSPEL

*Her many sins were forgiven her,
because she has shown great love.*

✢ A reading from the holy gospel according to Luke   7:36-50

A Pharisee invited Jesus to have dinner with him.
So Jesus went to the Pharisee's home and got ready to eat.

When a sinful woman in that town found out that Jesus was there,
    she bought an expensive bottle of perfume.
Then she came and stood behind Jesus.
She cried and started washing his feet with her tears
    and drying them with her hair.
The woman kissed his feet and poured the perfume on them.

The Pharisee who had invited Jesus saw this and said to himself,
"If this man really were a prophet,
    he would know what kind of woman is touching him!
He would know that she is a sinner."

Jesus said to the Pharisee,
"Simon, I have something to say to you."

"Teacher, what is it?" Simon replied.

Jesus told him, "Two people were in debt to a moneylender.
One of them owed him five hundred silver coins,
    and the other owed him fifty.
Since neither of them could pay him back,
    the moneylender said that they didn't have to pay him anything.
Which one of them will like him more?"

Simon answered,
"I suppose it would be the one who had owed more
    and didn't have to pay it back."

"You are right," Jesus said.

He turned toward the woman and said to Simon,
"Have you noticed this woman?
When I came into your home,
    you didn't give me any water so I could wash my feet.
But she has washed my feet with her tears
    and dried them with her hair.

"You didn't greet me with a kiss,
    but from the time I came in,
    she has not stopped kissing my feet.

"You didn't even pour olive oil on my head,
    but she has poured expensive perfume on my feet.

"So I tell you that all her sins are forgiven,
    and that is why she has shown great love.
But anyone who has been forgiven only a little
      will show only a little love."

Then Jesus said to the woman,
"Your sins are forgiven."

Some other guests started saying to one another,
"Who is this who dares to forgive sins?"

But Jesus told the woman,
"Because of your faith, you are now saved.
May God give you peace!"

                                      The gospel of the Lord.

[213] **"Sent to Preach the Kingdom of God"**

FIRST READING

Go now to those to whom I send you.

A reading from the book of the prophet Jeremiah 1:4-8

The Lord said to Jeremiah,
"Before I gave you life,
   and before you were born,
   I chose you to be a prophet to the nations."

Jeremiah replied,
"Lord God, how can I speak for you? I'm too young."

The Lord answered, "Don't say you're too young.
Go to everyone I send you to
   and tell them everything I command you.
Don't be afraid of them!
I, the Lord, will be with you to keep you safe."

The word of the Lord.

RESPONSORIAL PSALM 96:1-2a, 2b-3, 7-8a

℟. (3) Proclaim God's marvelous deeds to all the nations.

Sing a new song to the Lord!
Everyone on this earth,
sing praises to the Lord,
sing and praise his name.

℟. Proclaim God's marvelous deeds to all the nations.

Day after day announce,
"The Lord has saved us!"
Tell every nation on earth,
"The Lord is wonderful
and does marvelous things!"

℟. Proclaim God's marvelous deeds to all the nations.

Tell everyone of every nation,
"Praise the glorious power
of the Lord.
He is wonderful! Praise him!"

℟. Proclaim God's marvelous deeds to all the nations.

GOSPEL

Jesus sent them to proclaim the kingdom of God and to heal the sick.

✜ A reading from the holy gospel according to Luke 9:1-6

Jesus called together his twelve apostles
    and gave them complete power over all demons and diseases.
Then he sent them to tell about God's kingdom and to heal the sick.

He told them, "Don't take anything with you!
Don't take a walking stick or a traveling bag or food or money
    or even a change of clothes.
When you are welcomed into a home,
    stay there until you leave that town.
If people won't welcome you,
    leave the town and shake the dust from your feet
        as a warning to them."

The apostles left and went from village to village,
    telling the good news and healing people everywhere.

The gospel of the Lord.

"Who Is My Neighbor?"

FIRST READING

We must love one another.

A reading from the first letter of John   3:11, 18

Beloved:
From the beginning you were told
that we must love each other.

Children, you show love for others by truly helping them,
and not merely by talking about it.

The word of the Lord.

RESPONSORIAL PSALM   37:3 and 4, 5 and 26

℟. (39a) The salvation of the just comes from the Lord.

Trust the Lord and live right!
The land will be yours,
and you will be safe.
Do what the Lord wants,
and he will give you
your heart's desire.

℟. The salvation of the just comes from the Lord.

Let the Lord lead you
and trust him to help.
Good people gladly give and lend,
and their children
turn out good.

℟. The salvation of the just comes from the Lord.

GOSPEL

Who is my neighbor?

✢ A reading from the holy gospel according to Luke   10:25-37

An expert in the Law of Moses stood up and asked Jesus a question to see what he would say.

"Teacher," he asked,
   "What must I do to have eternal life?"

Jesus answered, "What is written in the Scriptures?
How do you understand them?"

The man replied, "The Scriptures say,
'Love the Lord your God with all your heart, soul, strength, and mind.'
They also say, 'Love your neighbors as much as you love yourself.'"

Jesus said, "You have given the right answer.
If you do this, you will have eternal life."

But the man wanted to show that he knew what he was talking about.
So he asked Jesus, "Who are my neighbors?"

Jesus replied:
"As a man was going down from Jerusalem to Jericho,
   robbers attacked him and grabbed everything he had.
They beat him up and ran off, leaving him half dead.

"A priest happened to be going down the same road.
But when he saw the man,
   he walked by on the other side.
Later a temple helper came to the same place.
But when he saw the man who had been beaten up,
   he also went by on the other side.

"A man from Samaria then came traveling along that road.
When he saw the man,
   he felt sorry for him and went over to him.
He treated his wounds with olive oil and wine and bandaged them.
Then he put him on his own donkey and took him to an inn,
   where he took care of him.

"The next morning he gave the innkeeper two silver coins and said,
'Please take care of the man.
If you spend more than this on him,
    I will pay you when I return.' "

Then Jesus asked,
"Which of these three people was a real neighbor
    to the man who was beaten up by robbers?"

The teacher answered, "The one who showed pity."
Jesus said, "Go and do the same!"

The gospel of the Lord.

[215] **"Ask and You Will Receive"**

FIRST READING

The prayer of the just has great power.

A reading from the letter of James   5:16c-18

Brothers and sisters:
The prayer of an innocent person is powerful,
and it can help a lot.

Elijah was just as human as we are,
    and for three and a half years
        his prayers kept the rain from falling.
But when he did pray for rain,
    it fell from the skies and made the crops grow.

The word of the Lord.

RESPONSORIAL PSALM   145:10-11, 15-16

℟. (16) You open your hand to feed us, Lord; you answer all our needs.

All creation will thank you,
and your loyal people
will praise you.
They will tell about
your marvelous kingdom
and your power.

℟. You open your hand to feed us, Lord; you answer all our needs.

Everyone depends on you,
and when the time is right,
you provide them with food.
By your own hand you satisfy
the desires of all who live.

℟. You open your hand to feed us, Lord; you answer all our needs.

GOSPEL

Ask and you shall receive.

✠ A reading from the holy gospel according to Luke   11:5-10

Jesus said to his disciples:
"Suppose one of you goes to a friend in the middle
   of the night and says,
'Let me borrow three loaves of bread.
A friend of mine has dropped in,
   and I don't have a thing for him to eat.'
And suppose your friend answers, 'Don't bother me!
The door is bolted, and my children and I are in bed.
I cannot get up to give you something.'

"He may not get up and give you the bread,
   just because you are his friend.
But he will get up and give you as much as you need,
   simply because you are not ashamed to keep on asking.

"So I tell you to ask and you will receive,
   search and you will find,
   knock and the door will be opened for you.
Everyone who asks will receive,
   everyone who searches will find,
   and the door will be opened for everyone who knocks."

The gospel of the Lord.

[216] **"Become Stronger in Your Faith"**

FIRST READING
>Be strong in your faith.

A reading from the letter of Paul to the Colossians   2:6-7

Brothers and sisters:
You have accepted Christ Jesus as your Lord.
Now keep on following him.
Plant your roots in Christ and let him be the foundation for your life.

Be strong in your faith,
    just as you were taught.
And be grateful.

                                            The word of the Lord.

RESPONSORIAL PSALM   46:1-2, 7-8

℟. (see 1) God is our help in times of trouble.

God is our mighty fortress,
always ready to help
in times of trouble.
And so, we won't be afraid!
Let the earth tremble
and the mountains tumble
into the deepest sea.

℟. God is our help in times of trouble.

The LORD All-Powerful
is with us.
The God of Jacob
is our fortress.
Come! See the fearsome things
the LORD has done on earth.

℟. God is our help in times of trouble.

GOSPEL

I will fertilize it to make it grow.

✠ A reading from the holy gospel according to Luke 13:6-9

Jesus told the people this story:
"A man had a fig tree growing in his vineyard.
One day he went out to pick some figs,
    but he didn't find any.
So he said to the gardener,
'For three years I have come looking for figs on this tree,
    and I haven't found any yet.
Chop it down!
Why should it take up space?'

"The gardener answered,
'Master, leave it for another year.
I'll dig around it and put some manure on it to make it grow.
Maybe it will have figs on it next year.
If it doesn't, you can have it cut down.'"

The gospel of the Lord.

[217]   **"Show Faith by Actions"**

FIRST READING

Faith without good works is dead.

A reading from the letter of James   2:14-18

My friends,
what good is it to say you have faith,
  when you don't do anything
    to show that you really do have faith?
Can that kind of faith save you?

If you know someone who doesn't have any clothes or food,
  you shouldn't just say, "I hope all goes well for you.
I hope you will be warm and have plenty to eat."

What good is it to say this,
  unless you do something to help?
Faith that doesn't lead us to do good deeds is all alone and dead!

Suppose someone disagrees and says,
"It is possible to have faith without doing kind deeds."

I would answer, "Prove that you have faith without doing kind deeds,
  and I will prove that I have faith by doing them."

The word of the Lord.

RESPONSORIAL PSALM   146:6d-7ab, 7c-9a

℟. (1b) Praise the Lord, my soul!

God always keeps his word.
He gives justice to the poor
and food to the hungry.

℟. Praise the Lord, my soul!

The LORD sets prisoners free
and heals blind eyes.
He gives a helping hand
to everyone who falls.
The LORD loves good people
and looks after strangers.

℟. Praise the Lord, my soul!

GOSPEL

*Do not invite just your friends,
but the poor and those who are crippled.*

✢ A reading from the holy gospel according to Luke   14:12-14

Jesus said to the man who had invited him to dinner:
"When you give a dinner or a banquet,
  don't invite your friends and family
    and relatives and rich neighbors.
If you do, they will invite you in return,
  and you will be paid back.
When you give a feast,
  invite the poor, the crippled, the lame, and the blind.
They cannot pay you back.
But God will bless you and reward you
  when his people rise from death."

The gospel of the Lord.

[218] # "The Good Shepherd"

FIRST READING

A   *The Lord cares for his nation as a shepherd cares for sheep.*

A reading from the book of the prophet Isaiah　　　　40:10-11

Look!
The powerful Lord God is coming to rule with his mighty arm.
He will reward some people and punish others.

The Lord cares for his nation,
　　as shepherds care for sheep.
He carries the lambs close to his chest,
　　while gently leading the mother sheep.

　　　　　　　　　　　　　　　　The word of the Lord.

OR

B   *I will watch over my sheep and tend them.*

A reading from the book of the prophet Ezekiel　　　　34:11-15

The Lord says this:
"I, the Lord God, will look for my people
　　and take care of them myself.
As a shepherd looks for sheep that have wandered away,
　　I will search for my scattered people.
I will rescue them from all the places where they went
　　on that dark and gloomy day.

> I will bring them back from the foreign countries
> > and protect them on the mountains,
> > in the valleys, and wherever they settle.
>
> "My people will be like sheep grazing and resting
> > in good pastures and on Israel's mountains.
> I, the Lord All-Powerful, will lead them there and watch over them."

The word of the Lord.

RESPONSORIAL PSALM   100:1-2, 3, 5

℟. (3) **We are God's people: the sheep of his flock.**

**Shout praises to the Lord,
everyone on this earth.
Be joyful and sing
as you come in
to worship the Lord!**

℟. We are God's people: the sheep of his flock.

**You know the Lord is God!
He created us,
and we belong to him;
we are his people,
the sheep in his pasture.**

℟. We are God's people: the sheep of his flock.

**The Lord is good!
His love and faithfulness
will last forever.**

℟. We are God's people: the sheep of his flock.

GOSPEL

Share my joy: I have found my lost sheep!

✢ A reading from the holy gospel according to Luke   15:1-7

Tax collectors and sinners were all crowding around to listen to Jesus. So the Pharisees and the teachers of the Law of Moses started grumbling, "This man is friendly with sinners.
He even eats with them."

Then Jesus told them this story:

"If any of you has a hundred sheep,
    and one of them gets lost,
    what will you do?
Won't you leave the ninety-nine in the field
       and go look for the lost sheep until you find it?
And when you find it,
    you will be so glad
       that you will put it on your shoulder and carry it home.
Then you will call in your friends and neighbors and say,
'Let's celebrate! I've found my lost sheep.' "

Jesus said,
"In the same way there is more happiness in heaven
       because of one sinner who turns to God
       than over ninety-nine good people who don't need to."

                                        The gospel of the Lord.

[219]   **"Give Thanks to God"**

FIRST READING

Keep thanking God because of Jesus Christ.

A reading from the first letter of Paul to the Thessalonians   5:16-18

Brothers and sisters:
Always be joyful and never stop praying.
Whatever happens, keep thanking God because of Jesus Christ.
This is what God wants you to do.

The word of the Lord.

RESPONSORIAL PSALM   138:1-2a, 2bcdef

℟. (2bc) Lord, I thank you for your faithfulness and love.

**With all my heart
I praise you, Lord.
In the presence of angels
I sing your praises.
I worship at your holy temple.**

℟. Lord, I thank you for your faithfulness and love.

**I praise you for your love
and your faithfulness.
You were true to your word
and made yourself more famous
than ever before.**

℟. Lord, I thank you for your faithfulness and love.

GOSPEL

It seems that no one has returned to give thanks to God.

✣ **A reading from the holy gospel according to Luke**   17:11-19

On his way to Jerusalem,
Jesus went along the border between Samaria and Galilee.
As he was going into a village,
   ten men with leprosy came toward him.
They stood at a distance and shouted,
"Jesus, Master, have pity on us!"

Jesus looked at them and said,
"Go show yourselves to the priests."

On their way they were healed.
When one of them discovered that he was healed,
   he came back, shouting praises to God.
He bowed down at the feet of Jesus and thanked him.
The man was from the country of Samaria.

Jesus asked, "Weren't ten men healed?
Where are the other nine?
Why was this foreigner the only one who came back to thank God?"

Then Jesus told the man, "You may get up and go.
Your faith has made you well."

The gospel of the Lord.

"Pray Always"

FIRST READING

Pray always by the power of the Spirit.

A reading from the letter of Paul to the Ephesians 6:18b-19a, 20b

Brothers and sisters:
Always pray by the power of the Spirit.
Stay alert and keep praying for God's people.

**Pray that I will be given the message to speak.
And pray that I will be brave and will speak as I should.**

The word of the Lord.

RESPONSORIAL PSALM 25:1-2ab and 4, 5-6

℟. (1) To you, O Lord, I lift my soul.

**I offer you my heart, Lord God,
and I trust you.
Don't make me ashamed.
Show me your paths
and teach me to follow.**

℟. To you, O Lord, I lift my soul.

**Guide me by your truth
and instruct me.
You keep me safe,
and I always trust you.
Please, Lord, remember,
you have always
been patient and kind.**

℟. To you, O Lord, I lift my soul.

GOSPEL

God will see justice done to his chosen who cry to him.

✠ A reading from the holy gospel according to Luke　　18:1-8a

Jesus told his disciples a story
   about how they should keep on praying and never give up:

"In a town there was once a judge who didn't fear God
   or care about people.
In that same town there was a widow who kept going to the judge
   and saying,
'Make sure that I get fair treatment in court.'

"For a while the judge refused to do anything.
Finally, he said to himself,
'Even though I don't fear God or care about people,
   I will help this widow
      because she keeps on bothering me.
If I don't help her,
   she will wear me out.' "

The Lord said:
"Think about what that crooked judge said.
Won't God protect his chosen ones who pray to him day and night?
Won't he be concerned for them?
He will surely hurry and help them."

　　　　　　　　　　　　　　　　　　　The gospel of the Lord.

[221]   **"God Loves Us"**

FIRST READING

The Lord was loving and kind to his people.

A reading from the book of the prophet Hosea   11:3-4

The Lord says this:
I took my people by the hand and taught them to walk.

I was the one who healed them,
>but they did not know it.

I was loving and kind,
>and I made them want to come to me.

I freed them from slavery and tenderly fed them.

>>>>>> **The word of the Lord.**

RESPONSORIAL PSALM   116:5 and 7, 9 and 12

℟. (9a) Now I will walk at your side.

You are kind, LORD,
so good and merciful.
You have treated me so kindly
that I don't need
to worry anymore.

℟. Now I will walk at your side.

Now I will walk at your side
in this land of the living.
What must I give you, LORD,
for being so good to me?

℟. Now I will walk at your side.

GOSPEL

God so loved the world that he gave his only Son.

✠ A reading from the holy gospel according to John   3:16-17

Jesus told Nicodemus:
"God loved the people of this world so much
>that he gave his only Son,
so that everyone who has faith in him
>will have eternal life and never die.

God did not send his Son into the world to condemn its people.
He sent him to save them!"

>>>>>> **The gospel of the Lord.**

[222] **"We Are the People of God"**

FIRST READING

A   They will be my people, says the Lord.

A reading from the book of the prophet Jeremiah   31:33

The L<small>ORD</small> says this:
"This is the agreement that I, the L<small>ORD</small>,
   will make with the people of Israel:
I will write my laws on their hearts and minds.
I will be their God, and they will be my people."

                                                    The word of the Lord.

                                                 OR

B   You are God's chosen people.

A reading from the first letter of Peter   2:9-10

Brothers and sisters:
   You are God's chosen and special people.
You are a group of royal priests and a holy nation.
God has brought you out of darkness into his marvelous light.
Now you must tell all the wonderful things that he has done.

The Scriptures say, "Once you were nobody.
Now you are God's people.
At one time no one had pity on you.
Now God has treated you with kindness."

                                                    The word of the Lord.

RESPONSORIAL PSALM   100:1-2, 3, 5

   ℟. (3) We are God's people: the sheep of his flock.

**Shout praises to the L<small>ORD</small>,
everyone on this earth.
Be joyful and sing
as you come in
to worship the L<small>ORD</small>!**

   ℟. We are God's people: the sheep of his flock.

You know the LORD is God!
He created us,
and we belong to him;
we are his people,
the sheep in his pasture.

℟. We are God's people: the sheep of his flock.

The LORD is good!
His love and faithfulness
will last forever.

℟. We are God's people: the sheep of his flock.

GOSPEL

I give you a new commandment: love one another.

✠ A reading from the holy gospel according to John　　13:34-35

Jesus said to his disciples:
"I am giving you a new command.
You must love each other,
    just as I have loved you.
If you love each other,
    everyone will know that you are my disciples."

The gospel of the Lord.

[223]   ## "The Spirit Has Given Us Life"

FIRST READING

The Spirit has given us life.

A reading from the letter of Paul to the Galatians   5:22-23, 25-26

Brothers and sisters:
God's Spirit makes us loving, happy, peaceful,
   patient, kind, good, faithful,
   gentle, and self-controlled.
There is no law against behaving in any of these ways.

God's Spirit has given us life,
   and so we should follow the Spirit.
But don't be conceited or make others jealous
   by claiming to be better than they are.

The word of the Lord.

RESPONSORIAL PSALM   16:1-2ab and 5, 7-8, 11

℟. (11a) Lord, you will show us the path of life.

Protect me, Lord God!
I run to you for safety,
and I have said,
"Only you are my Lord!"
You, Lord, are all I want!
You are my choice,
and you keep me safe.

℟. Lord, you will show us the path of life.

I praise you, Lord,
for being my guide.
Even in the darkest night,
your teachings fill my mind.
I will always look to you,
as you stand beside me
and protect me from fear.

℟. Lord, you will show us the path of life.

You have shown me
the path to life,
and you make me glad
by being near to me.
Sitting at your right side,
I will always be joyful.

℟. Lord, you will show us the path of life.

GOSPEL

The Holy Spirit will teach you all things.

✢ **A reading from the holy gospel according to John** 14:15-17

Jesus said to his disciples:
"If you love me, you will do as I command.
Then I will ask the Father to send you the Holy Spirit
    who will help you and always be with you.
The Spirit will show you what is true.

"The people of this world cannot accept the Spirit,
    because they don't see or know him.
But you know the Spirit, who is with you
    and will keep on living in you."

The gospel of the Lord.

[224] **"Peace I Leave with You"**

FIRST READING

A
All creation will be at peace.

A reading from the book of the prophet Isaiah   11:1b, 5-9

The LORD says this:
Someone from David's family will someday be king.
Honesty and fairness will be his royal robes.

Leopards and young goats, and wolves and lambs
    will lie down and rest in the same field.
Calves and lions will eat together and be cared for by a child.
Cows and bears will share the same pasture,
    and their young will rest side by side.
Lions will eat straw just like oxen.

Young children will play near snake holes.
They will stick their hands into dens of poisonous snakes
    without being harmed.
No one will be hurt or killed on the LORD's holy mountain.

Just as water fills the sea,
    the land will be filled with people who know and honor the LORD.

The word of the Lord.

OR

B
Live in peace together,
the peace that comes from Christ.

A reading from the letter of Paul to the Colossians   3:15-16

Brothers and sisters:
Each one of you is part of the body of Christ,
    and you were chosen to live together in peace.
So let the peace that comes from Christ control your thoughts.
And be grateful.

Let the message about Christ completely fill your lives,
    while you use all your wisdom to teach and instruct each other.
With thankful hearts,
    sing psalms, hymns, and spiritual songs to God.

The word of the Lord.

RESPONSORIAL PSALM 122:1-2, 8-9

℟. (Sirach 36:18) Give peace, O Lord, to those who wait for you.

**It made me glad
to hear them say,
"Let's go to the house
of the Lord!"
Jerusalem, we are standing
inside your gates.**

℟. Give peace, O Lord, to those who wait for you.

**Because of my friends
and my relatives,
I will pray for peace.
And because of the house
of the Lord our God,
I will work for your good.**

℟. Give peace, O Lord, to those who wait for you.

GOSPEL

My peace I give to you.

✤ A reading from the holy gospel according to John 14:27

Jesus said to his disciples:
  "I give you peace,
    the kind of peace that only I can give.
It is not like the peace that this world can give.
So don't be worried or afraid."

The gospel of the Lord.

[225] **"One with Jesus"**

FIRST READING

Together you are Christ's body.

A reading from the first letter of Paul to the Corinthians   12:12-13

Brothers and sisters:
The body of Christ has many different parts,
    just as any other body does.
Some of us are Jews,
    and others are Gentiles.
Some of us are slaves,
    and others are free.
But God's Spirit baptized each of us
    and made us part of the body of Christ.
Now we each drink from that same Spirit.

The word of the Lord.

RESPONSORIAL PSALM   80:8ab and 9-10ab, 14d-15ab and 19

℟. (Isaiah 5:7a) The vineyard of the Lord is the house of Israel.

**We were like a grapevine
you brought out of Egypt.
You cleared the ground,
and we put our roots deep,
spreading over the land.
Shade from this vine
covered the mountains.**

℟. The vineyard of the Lord is the house of Israel.

**See what's happening
to this vine.
With your own hands
you planted its roots.
L**ORD** God All-Powerful,
make us strong again!
Smile on us and save us.**

℟. The vineyard of the Lord is the house of Israel.

GOSPEL

>Those who live in me, and I in them, will bear much fruit.

✢ A reading from the holy gospel according to John   15:1-5

Jesus said to his disciples:
"I am the true vine,
   and my Father is the gardener.
He cuts away every branch of mine that does not produce fruit.
But he trims clean every branch that does produce fruit,
   so that it will produce even more fruit.

"You are already clean because of what I have said to you.

"Stay joined to me,
   and I will stay joined to you.
Just as a branch cannot produce fruit
     unless it stays joined to the vine,
   you cannot produce fruit unless you stay joined to me.

"I am the vine, and you are the branches.
If you stay joined to me, and I stay joined to you,
   then you will produce lots of fruit.
But you cannot do anything without me."

The gospel of the Lord.

[226] "May Your Joy Be Complete"

FIRST READING

We are happy because God sent Jesus Christ to make peace with us.

A reading from the letter of Paul to the Romans 5:10b-11

Brothers and sisters:
 Now that we are at peace with God,
 we will be saved by his Son's life.

And in addition to everything else,
 we are happy because God sent our Lord Jesus Christ
  to make peace with us.

The word of the Lord.

RESPONSORIAL PSALM 89:1-2, 15-16

℟. (2a) For ever I will sing the goodness of the Lord.

Our Lord, I will sing
of your love forever.
Everyone yet to be born
will hear me praise
your faithfulness.
I will tell them, "God's love
can always be trusted,
and his faithfulness lasts
as long as the heavens."

℟. For ever I will sing the goodness of the Lord.

Our Lord, you bless those
who join in the festival
and walk in the brightness
of your presence.
We are happy all day
because of you,
and your saving power
brings honor to us.

℟. For ever I will sing the goodness of the Lord.

GOSPEL

I have told you this to make you as happy as I am.

✢ A reading from the holy gospel according to John 15:9-11

Jesus said to his disciples:
"I have loved you,
   just as my Father has loved me.
So make sure that I keep on loving you.
If you obey me,
I will keep loving you,
   just as my Father keeps loving me,
   because I have obeyed him.

"I have told you this to make you as completely happy as I am."

The gospel of the Lord.

[227] **"You Are My Friends"**

FIRST READING

We are called children of God, and that is what we are.

A reading from the first letter of John 3:1, 23

Beloved:
Think how much the Father loves us.
He loves us so much that he lets us be called his children,
  as we truly are.
But since the people of this world did not know who Christ is,
  they don't know who we are.

God wants us to have faith in his Son Jesus Christ
    and to love each other.
This is also what Jesus taught us to do.

The word of the Lord.

RESPONSORIAL PSALM 85:8, 9-10

℟. (9b) The Lord speaks of peace to his people.

**I will listen to you, Lord God,
because you promise peace
to those who are faithful
and no longer foolish.**

℟. The Lord speaks of peace to his people.

**You are ready to rescue
everyone who worships you,
so that you will live with us
in all of your glory.
Love and loyalty
will come together;
goodness and peace will unite.**

℟. The Lord speaks of peace to his people.

GOSPEL

You are my friends.

✠ A reading from the holy gospel according to John   15:12-15

Jesus said to his disciples:
"Now I tell you to love each other,
   as I have loved you.
The greatest way to show love for friends is to die for them.
And you are my friends, if you obey me.

"Servants don't know what their master is doing,
   and so I don't speak to you as my servants.
I speak to you as my friends,
   and I have told you everything that my Father has told me."

The gospel of the Lord.

Last Weeks in Ordinary Time

[228] **"Entering the Kingdom of Heaven"**

FIRST READING

Faith without good works is dead.

A reading from the letter of James 2:14-17

My friends,
what good is it to say you have faith,
when you don't do anything
to show that you really do have faith?
Can that kind of faith save you?

If you know someone who doesn't have any clothes or food,
you shouldn't just say, "I hope all goes well for you.
I hope you will be warm and have plenty to eat."

What good is it to say this,
unless you do something to help?
Faith that doesn't lead us to do good deeds is all alone and dead!

The word of the Lord.

RESPONSORIAL PSALM 40:1 and 3ab, 8 and 11

℟. (8a and 9a) Here am I, Lord; I come to do your will.

I patiently waited, LORD,
for you to hear my prayer.
You listened and you gave me a new song,
a song of praise to you.

℟. Here am I, Lord; I come to do your will.

I enjoy pleasing you.
Your Law is in my heart.
You, LORD, never fail
to have pity on me;
your love and faithfulness
always keep me secure.

℟. Here am I, Lord; I come to do your will.

GOSPEL

Whoever does the will of the Father will enter the kingdom of heaven.

✚ A reading from the holy gospel according to Matthew   7:21, 24-27

Jesus said to his disciples:
"Not everyone who calls me their Lord
    will get into the kingdom of heaven.
Only the ones who obey my Father in heaven will get in.

"Anyone who hears and obeys these teachings of mine
    is like a wise person who built a house on solid rock.
Rain poured down, rivers flooded,
    and winds beat against that house.
But it did not fall,
    because it was built on solid rock.

"Anyone who hears my teachings and does not obey them
    is like a foolish person who built a house on sand.
The rain poured down, the rivers flooded,
    and the winds blew and beat against that house.
Finally, it fell with a crash."

                                                      The gospel of the Lord.

[229] "The Banquet of the Kingdom"

FIRST READING

The Lord will prepare a banquet for all nations.

A reading from the book of the prophet Isaiah 25:6, 9

On this mountain the Lord All-Powerful will prepare for all nations a feast of the finest foods. Choice wines and the best meat will be served.

On that day, people will say, "The Lord God has saved us! Let's celebrate. We waited and waited, and now he is here."

The word of the Lord.

RESPONSORIAL PSALM 34:1-2, 3-4

℟. (9a) Taste and see the goodness of the Lord.

I will always praise the Lord. With all my heart, I will praise the Lord. Let all who are helpless listen and be glad.

℟. Taste and see the goodness of the Lord.

Honor the Lord with me! Celebrate his great name. I asked the Lord for help, and he saved me from all my fears.

℟. Taste and see the goodness of the Lord.

GOSPEL

*Many will come from the east and west
and take their place in the kingdom of heaven.*

✢ A reading from the holy gospel according to Matthew   8:5-11

When Jesus was going into the town of Capernaum,
an army officer came up to him and said,
"Lord, my servant is at home in such terrible pain
that he can't even move."

"I will go and heal him," Jesus replied.

But the officer said,
"Lord, I'm not good enough for you to come into my house.
Just give the order,
and my servant will get well.

"I have officers who give orders to me,
and I have soldiers who take orders from me.
I can say to one of them, 'Go!' and he goes.
I can say to another, 'Come!' and he comes.
I can say to my servant, 'Do this!' and he will do it."

When Jesus heard this,
he was so surprised that he turned and said to the crowd
following him,
"I tell you that in all of Israel
I've never found anyone with this much faith!
Many people will come from everywhere
to enjoy the feast in the kingdom of heaven
with Abraham, Isaac, and Jacob."

The gospel of the Lord.

[230]   **"The Lord Is Coming Soon"**

FIRST READING
The Lord is near.

A reading from the letter of Paul to the Philippians   4:4-7

Brothers and sisters:
Always be glad because of the Lord!
I will say it again: Be glad.

Always be gentle with others.
The Lord will soon be here.
Don't worry about anything,
    but pray about everything.

With thankful hearts offer up your prayers and requests to God.
Then, because you belong to Christ Jesus,
    God will bless you with peace
        that no one can completely understand.
And this peace will control the way you think and feel.

The word of the Lord.

RESPONSORIAL PSALM   85:8abc and 9, 10-11

    ℟. (8) Lord, show us your mercy and love, and grant us your salvation.

I will listen to you, LORD God,
because you promise peace
to those who are faithful.
You are ready to rescue
everyone who worships you,
so that you will live with us
in all of your glory.

    ℟. Lord, show us your mercy and love, and grant us your salvation.

Love and loyalty
will come together;
goodness and peace will unite.

Loyalty will sprout
from the ground;
justice will look down
from the sky above.

℟. Lord, show us your mercy and love, and grant us your salvation.

GOSPEL

Be prepared.

✠ A reading from the holy gospel according to Luke   12:35-40

Jesus said to his disciples:
"Be ready and keep your lamps burning
    just like those servants who wait up
    for their master to return from a wedding feast.
As soon as he comes and knocks,
    they open the door for him.

"Servants are fortunate
    if their master finds them awake and ready when he comes!
I promise you that he will get ready
    and have his servants sit down so he can serve them.
Those servants are really fortunate if their master finds them ready,
    even though he comes late at night or early in the morning.

"You would surely not let a thief break into your home,
    if you knew when the thief was coming.
So always be ready!
You don't know when the Son of Man will come."

                                        The gospel of the Lord.

[231] "The Kingdom of God Is Among You"

FIRST READING

Christ's power is at work in our hearts.

A reading from the letter of Paul to the Ephesians   3:16b-17, 20-21

Brothers and sisters:
  I pray that God's Spirit will make you become strong followers
  and that Christ will live in your hearts because of your faith.
Stand firm and be deeply rooted in his love.

I pray that Christ Jesus and the church
    will forever bring praise to God.
His power at work in us
    can do far more than we dare ask or imagine. Amen.

The word of the Lord.

RESPONSORIAL PSALM   126:1-2ab, 2cde-3

℟. (3) The Lord has done great things for us.

It seemed like a dream
when the L<small>ORD</small> brought us back
to the city of Zion.
We celebrated with laughter
and joyful songs.

℟. The Lord has done great things for us.

In foreign nations it was said,
"The L<small>ORD</small> has worked miracles
for his people."
And so we celebrated
because the L<small>ORD</small> had indeed
worked miracles for us.

℟. The Lord has done great things for us.

GOSPEL

The kingdom of God is among you.

✢ A reading from the holy gospel according to Luke   17:20-21

Some Pharisees asked Jesus when God's kingdom would come.
Jesus answered, "God's kingdom is not something you can see.
There is no use saying, 'Look! Here it is'
    or 'Look! There it is.'
God's kingdom is here with you."

The gospel of the Lord.

GOSPEL ACCLAMATIONS FOR WEEKDAYS IN ORDINARY TIME

[232] Any of the following gospel acclamations may be chosen for use at weekday Masses during Ordinary Time.

1
1 Samuel 3:9; John 6:68c

℟. Alleluia, alleluia.

**Speak, O Lord, your servant is listening;
you have the words of everlasting life.**

℟. Alleluia, alleluia.

2
Psalm 25:4b, 5a

℟. Alleluia, alleluia.

**Teach me your paths, my God,
and lead me in your truth.**

℟. Alleluia, alleluia.

3
Matthew 4:4b

℟. Alleluia, alleluia.

**No one lives on bread alone,
but on every word that comes from the mouth of God.**

℟. Alleluia, alleluia.

4
See Matthew 11:25

℟. Alleluia, alleluia.

**Blessed are you, Father, Lord of heaven and earth;
you have revealed to little ones the mysteries of the kingdom.**

℟. Alleluia, alleluia.

5
See John 6:63c, 68c

℟. Alleluia, alleluia.

**Your words, Lord, are spirit and life:
you have the words of everlasting life.**

℟. Alleluia, alleluia.

6 John 8:12

℟. Alleluia, alleluia.

**I am the light of the world, says the Lord;
whoever follows me will have the light of life.**

℟. Alleluia, alleluia.

7 John 14:6

℟. Alleluia, alleluia.

**I am the way, the truth, and the life, says the Lord;
no one comes to the Father, except through me.**

℟. Alleluia, alleluia.

8 See Acts 16:14b

℟. Alleluia, alleluia.

**Open our hearts, O Lord,
to listen to the words of your Son.**

℟. Alleluia, alleluia.

9 1 John 2:5

℟. Alleluia, alleluia.

**Whoever keeps the word of Christ
grows perfect in the love of God.**

℟. Alleluia, alleluia.

Last Weeks in Ordinary Time

10 Matthew 24:42a, 44

℟. Alleluia, alleluia.

**Be watchful and ready:
you know not when the Son of Man is coming.**

℟. Alleluia, alleluia.

PROPER OF SAINTS

[233] For celebrations in honor of the saints, in addition to the texts referred to in individual cases, the readings given in the common of the saints may always be selected.

JANUARY

January 1
[234] **Octave of Christmas**
MARY, MOTHER OF GOD

Solemnity

See the Proper of Seasons, no. 15, p. 73.

January 2
[235] **Basil the Great and Gregory Nazianzen,**
bishops, doctors of the Church

Memorial

From the Common of Pastors or the Common of Doctors of the Church, p. 808 or 812.

January 4
[236] **Elizabeth Ann Seton,**
married woman, religious founder

Memorial

From the Common of Saints [For Religious], p. 815.

January 5
[237] **John Neumann,**
bishop, religious, missionary

Memorial

From the Common of Pastors, p. 808.

January 6
[238] **Blessed André Bessette,**
religious

From the Common of Saints [For Religious], p. 815.

701

702 PROPER OF SAINTS

January 7
[239] **Raymond of Penyafort,**
presbyter, religious

From the Common of Pastors, p. 808.

January 13
[240] **Hilary,**
bishop, doctor of the Church

From the Common of Pastors or the Common of Doctors of the Church, p. 808 or 812.

January 17
[241] **Anthony,**
abbot

Memorial

From the Common of Saints [For Religious], p. 815.

January 20
[242] **Fabian,**
pope, martyr

From the Common of Martyrs or the Common of Pastors [For a Pope], p. 804 or 808.

[243] **Sebastian,**
martyr

From the Common of Martyrs, p. 804.

January 21
[244] **Agnes,**
virgin, martyr

Memorial

From the Common of Martyrs or the Common of Saints, p. 804 or 815.

January 22
[245] **Vincent,**
deacon, martyr

From the Common of Martyrs, p. 804.

January 24
Francis de Sales,
bishop, religious founder, doctor of the Church

Memorial

From the Common of Pastors or the Common of Doctors of the Church, p. 808 or 812.

January 25
The Conversion of Paul,
apostle

Feast

FIRST READING

*Rise and be baptized and wash away your sins,
calling on the name of Jesus.*

A reading from the Acts of the Apostles   22:3-16

Paul told the people:
"I am a Jew, born and raised in the city of Tarsus in Cilicia.
I was a student of Gamaliel and was taught
    to follow every single law of our ancestors.
In fact, I was just as eager to obey God as any of you are today.

"I made trouble for everyone who followed the Lord's Way,
    and I even had some of them killed.
I had others arrested and put in jail.
I didn't care if they were men or women.
The high priest and all the council members
    can tell you that this is true.
They even gave me letters to the Jewish leaders in Damascus,
    so that I could arrest people there
        and bring them to Jerusalem to be punished.

"One day about noon I was getting close to Damascus,
    when a bright light from heaven suddenly flashed around.
I fell to the ground and heard a voice asking me,
'Saul, Saul, why are you so cruel to me?'

" 'Who are you?' I answered.

"The Lord replied, 'I am Jesus from Nazareth!
I am the one you are so cruel to.'

The men who were traveling with me saw the light,
> but did not hear the voice.

"I asked, 'Lord, what do you want me to do?'

"Then he told me, 'Get up and go to Damascus.
When you get there, you will be told what to do.'

"The light had been so bright that I couldn't see.
And the other men had to lead me by the hand to Damascus.

"In that city there was a man named Ananias,
> who faithfully obeyed the Law of Moses
>> and was well liked by all the Jewish people living there.

He came to me and said,
'Saul, my friend, you can now see again!'
At once I could see.

"Then Ananias told me,
'The God that our ancestors worshiped
> has chosen you to know what he wants done.

He has chosen you to see the One Who Obeys God
> and to hear his voice.

You must tell everyone what you have seen and heard.
What are you waiting for?
Get up! Be baptized,
> and wash away your sins by praying to the Lord.' "

The word of the Lord.

RESPONSORIAL PSALM 117:1, 2

℟. (Mark 16:15) Go out to all the world and tell the good news.

**All of you nations,
come praise the L**ORD**!
Let everyone praise him.**

℟. Go out to all the world and tell the good news.

**His love for us is wonderful,
his faithfulness never ends.
Shout praises to the L**ORD**!**

℟. Go out to all the world and tell the good news.

ALLELUIA   See John 15:16

℟. Alleluia, alleluia.

**I have chosen you from the world, says the Lord,
to go and bear fruit that will last.**

℟. Alleluia, alleluia.

GOSPEL

Go out to all the world and tell the good news.

✟ A reading from the holy gospel according to Mark   16:15-18

Jesus told his disciples:
  **"Go and preach the good news to everyone in the world.
Anyone who believes and is baptized will be saved.
But anyone who refuses to believe me will be condemned.**

**"Everyone who believes me will be able to do wonderful things.
By using my name they will force out demons,**
    **and they will speak new languages.
They will handle snakes and will drink poison and not be hurt.
They will also heal sick people by placing their hands on them."**

                                                      The gospel of the Lord.

January 26

Timothy and Titus,
bishops

                                                                                                     Memorial

The first reading for this memorial is proper.

From the Common of Pastors, p. 808, except:

FIRST READING

A   I have in mind your faith, which is openly sincere.

A reading from the second letter of Paul to Timothy   1:1-8

**From Paul, an apostle of Christ Jesus.
God himself chose me to be an apostle,**
    and he gave me the promised life that Jesus Christ makes possible.

Timothy, you are like a dear child to me.
I pray that God our Father and our Lord Christ Jesus
>> will be kind and merciful to you
>> and will bless you with peace.

Night and day I mention you in my prayers.
I am always grateful for you,
> as I pray to the God
>> my ancestors and I have served with a clear conscience.

I remember how you cried, and I want to see you,
> because that will make me truly happy.
I also remember the genuine faith of your mother Eunice.
Your grandmother Lois had the same sort of faith,
> and I am sure that you have it as well.

So I ask you to make full use of the gift that God gave you
> when I placed my hands on you.
Use it well.
God's Spirit does not make cowards out of us.
The Spirit gives us power, love, and self-control.

Don't be ashamed to speak for our Lord.
And don't be ashamed of me,
> just because I am in jail for serving him.
Use the power that comes from God
> and join with me in suffering for telling the good news.

> > > > > > > > > The word of the Lord.

OR

B

To Titus, my beloved son in a common faith.

A reading from the letter of Paul to Titus 1:1-5

From Paul, a servant of God and an apostle of Jesus Christ.
I encourage God's own people to have more faith
> and to understand the truth about religion.
Then they will have the hope of eternal life that God promised long ago.
And God never tells a lie!

> So, at the proper time,
> > God our Savior gave this message
> > > and told me to announce what he had said.
>
> Titus, because of our faith,
> > you are like a son to me.
> I pray that God our Father and Christ Jesus our Savior
> > will be kind to you and will bless you with peace!
>
> I left you in Crete to do what had been left undone
> > and to appoint leaders for the churches in each town.

The word of the Lord.

January 27
Angela Merici,
virgin, religious founder

From the Common of Saints [For Educators], p. 815.

January 28
Thomas Aquinas,
presbyter, religious, doctor of the Church

Memorial

From the Common of Doctors of the Church or the Common of Pastors, p. 812 or 808.

January 31
John Bosco,
presbyter, religious founder

Memorial

From the Common of Pastors or the Common of Saints [For Educators], p. 808 or 815.

FEBRUARY

February 2
The Presentation of the Lord

[252]

Feast

FIRST READING

The Lord whom you seek will come to his temple.

A reading from the book of the prophet Malachi   3:1-2b

The LORD All-Powerful says,
"I will send my messenger to prepare the way for me.
Then suddenly the LORD you are longing for will come to his temple.
The messenger you are eagerly looking for
   will come and announce my promise to you.
Who can face him on that day?
Who will be able to stand?"

The word of the Lord.

RESPONSORIAL PSALM   24:7, 10

℟. (10b) The Lord of hosts: he is king of glory!

Open the ancient gates,
so that the glorious king
may come in.

℟. The Lord of hosts: he is king of glory!

Who is this glorious king?
He is our LORD,
the All-Powerful!

℟. The Lord of hosts: he is king of glory!

ALLELUIA   Luke 2:32

℟. Alleluia, alleluia.

This is the light of revelation to the nations
and the glory of your people Israel.

℟. Alleluia, alleluia.

GOSPEL

My eyes have seen your saving power.

✣ A reading from the holy gospel according to Luke   2:22-32

The time came for Mary and Joseph to do what the Law of Moses says
    a mother is supposed to do after her baby is born.

They took Jesus to the temple in Jerusalem
    and presented him to the Lord,
  just as the Law of the Lord says,
"Each first-born baby boy belongs to the Lord."
The Law of the Lord also says that parents have to offer a sacrifice,
    giving at least a pair of doves or two young pigeons.
So that is what Mary and Joseph did.

At this time a man named Simeon was living in Jerusalem.
Simeon was a good man.
He loved God and was waiting for God to save the people of Israel.
God's Spirit came to him and told him that he would not die
    until he had seen Christ the Lord.

When Mary and Joseph brought Jesus to the temple
    to do what the Law of Moses says should be done for a new baby,
    the Spirit told Simeon to go into the temple.
Simeon took the baby Jesus in his arms and praised God, saying,

    "Lord, I am your servant,
    and now I can die in peace,
    because you have kept your promise to me.

    "With my own eyes I have seen
    what you have done to save your people,
    and foreign nations will also see this.

    "Your mighty power is a light for all nations,
    and it will bring honor to your people Israel."

                             The gospel of the Lord.

February 3
[253] **Blase,**
bishop, martyr

From the Common of Martyrs or the Common of Pastors, p. 804 or 808.

[254] **Ansgar,**
bishop, missionary

From the Common of Pastors [For Missionaries], p. 808.

February 5
[255] **Agatha,**
virgin, martyr

Memorial

From the Common of Martyrs or the Common of Saints, p. 804 or 815.

February 6
[256] **Paul Miki,** religious, missionary, martyr, **and his companions,** martyrs

Memorial

From the Common of Martyrs, p. 804.

February 8
[257] **Jerome Emiliani,**
presbyter, religious founder

From the Common of Saints [For Educators], p. 815.

February 10
[258] **Scholastica,**
virgin, religious

Memorial

From the Common of Saints [For Religious], p. 815.

February 11
[259] **Our Lady of Lourdes**

From the Common of the Blessed Virgin Mary, p. 795.

February 14
[260] **Cyril,** religious, missionary,
and Methodius, bishop, missionary

Memorial

From the Common of Pastors [For Missionaries] or the Common of Saints, p. 808 or 815.

February 17
[261] **Seven Founders of the Order of Servites,**
religious

From the Common of Saints [For Religious], p. 815.

February 21
[262] **Peter Damian,**
bishop, religious, doctor of the Church

From the Common of Doctors of the Church or the Common of Pastors or the Common of Saints [For Religious], p. 812, or 808, or 815.

February 22
[263] **The Chair of the Apostle Peter**

Feast

FIRST READING

*I myself am one of your leaders
and a witness to the sufferings of Christ.*

A reading from the first letter of Peter 5:1-4

Church leaders, I am writing to encourage you.
  I too am a leader, as well as a witness of Christ's suffering,
  and I will share in his glory when it is shown to us.

Just as shepherds watch over their sheep,
  you must watch over everyone God has placed in your care.

Do it willingly in order to please God,
  and not simply because you think you must.
Let it be something you want to do,
  instead of something you do merely to make money.

> Don't be bossy to those people who are in your care,
>> but set an example for them.
> Then when Christ the Chief Shepherd returns,
>> you will be given a crown that will never lose its glory.

The word of the Lord.

RESPONSORIAL PSALM   23:1-3a, 3b-4, 6

℟. (1) The Lord is my shepherd; there is nothing I shall want.

**You, Lord, are my shepherd.
I will never be in need.
You let me rest in fields
of green grass.
You lead me to streams
of peaceful water,
and you refresh my life.**

℟. The Lord is my shepherd; there is nothing I shall want.

**You are true to your name,
and you lead me
along the right paths.
I may walk through valleys
as dark as death,
but I won't be afraid.
You are with me,
and your shepherd's rod
makes me feel safe.**

℟. The Lord is my shepherd; there is nothing I shall want.

**Your kindness and love
will always be with me
each day of my life,
and I will live forever
in your house, Lord.**

℟. The Lord is my shepherd; there is nothing I shall want.

ALLELUIA Matthew 16:18

℟. Alleluia, alleluia.

**You are Peter, the rock on which I will build my Church;
the gates of hell will not prevail against it.**

℟. Alleluia, alleluia.

GOSPEL

You are Peter; and to you I will give
the keys of the kingdom of heaven.

✢ A reading from the holy gospel according to Matthew   16:13-19a

When Jesus and his disciples were near the town of Caesarea Philippi, he asked them, "What do people say about the Son of Man?"

The disciples answered, "Some people say you are John the Baptist or maybe Elijah or Jeremiah or some other prophet."

Then Jesus asked them, "But who do you say I am?"

Simon Peter spoke up,
"You are the Messiah, the Son of the living God."

Jesus told him:
"Simon, son of Jonah, you are blessed!
You didn't discover this on your own.
It was shown to you by my Father in heaven.
So I will call you Peter, which means 'a rock.'
On this rock I will build my Church,
   and death itself will not have any power over it.
I will give you the keys to the kingdom of heaven,
   and God in heaven will allow whatever you allow on earth."

The gospel of the Lord.

February 23

Polycarp,
bishop, martyr

Memorial

From the Common of Martyrs or the Common of Pastors, p. 804 or 808.

MARCH

March 3
[265] **Blessed Katharine Drexel,**
virgin, religious founder

From the Common of Saints [For Religious; For Those Who Work for the Underprivileged], p. 815.

March 4
[266] **Casimir**

From the Common of Saints, p. 815.

March 7
[267] **Perpetua and Felicity,**
martyrs

Memorial

From the Common of Martyrs, p. 804.

March 8
[268] **John of God,**
religious founder

From the Common of Saints [For Religious; For Those Who Work for the Underprivileged], p. 815.

March 9
[269] **Frances of Rome,**
married woman, religious founder

From the Common of Saints [For Religious], p. 815.

March 17
[270] **Patrick,**
bishop, missionary

From the Common of Pastors [For Missionaries], p. 808.

March 18
[271] **Cyril of Jerusalem,**
bishop, doctor of the Church

From the Common of Pastors or the Common of Doctors of the Church, p. 808 or 812.

March 19
JOSEPH, HUSBAND OF THE VIRGIN MARY
Solemnity

FIRST READING

The Lord God will give to him the throne
of his father, David (Luke 1:32).

A reading from the second book of Samuel   7:4-5a, 12-14a, 16

One night, the LORD told Nathan to go to David
and give him this message:

"I'll choose one of your sons to be king
when you reach the end of your life
and are buried near your ancestors.

"I'll make him a strong ruler,
and no one will be able to take his kingdom away from him.

"He will be the one to build a temple for me.
I will be his father,
and he will be my son.

"When he does wrong,
I'll see that he is corrected.
I will make sure that one of your descendants will always be king."

The word of the Lord.

RESPONSORIAL PSALM   89:1-2, 3-4

℟. (37) The son of David will live for ever.

Our LORD, I will sing
of your love forever.
Everyone yet to be born
will hear me praise
your faithfulness.
I will tell them, "God's love
can always be trusted,
and his faithfulness lasts
as long as the heavens."

℟. The son of David will live for ever.

You said, "David, my servant,
is my chosen one,
and this is the agreement
I made with him:
David, one of your descendants
will always be king."

℟. The son of David will live for ever.

VERSE BEFORE THE GOSPEL   Psalm 84:5

℟. Glory and praise to you, Lord Jesus Christ.

**Blessed are they who dwell in your house, O Lord;
they sing your praise without end!**

℟. Glory and praise to you, Lord Jesus Christ.

GOSPEL
A   Joseph did as the angel of the Lord commanded him.

✢ A reading from the holy gospel according to Matthew   1:16, 18-21, 24a

Jacob was the father of Joseph who was the husband of Mary.
   She was the mother of Jesus, who is called the Messiah.
This is how Jesus Christ was born.
A young woman named Mary was engaged to Joseph from King
       David's family.
But before they were married,
   she learned that she was going to have a baby by God's Holy Spirit.
Joseph was a good man and did not want to embarrass Mary
       in front of everyone.
So he decided to quietly call off the wedding.
While Joseph was thinking about this,
   an angel from the Lord came to him in a dream.
The angel said, "Joseph, the baby that Mary will have
       is from the Holy Spirit.
Go ahead and marry her.
Then after her baby is born, name him Jesus,
   because he will save his people from their sins."
After Joseph woke up, he and Mary were soon married.

                                    The gospel of the Lord.

OR

B   See how your father and I have been in sorrow seeking you.

✤ **A reading from the holy gospel according to Luke** 2:41-51

Every year Jesus' parents went to Jerusalem for Passover.
And when Jesus was twelve years old,
   they all went there as usual for the celebration.

After Passover his parents left,
   but they did not know that Jesus had stayed on in the city.
They thought he was traveling with some other people,
   and they went a whole day before they started looking for him.

When they could not find him with their relatives and friends,
   they went back to Jerusalem and started looking for him there.

Three days later they found Jesus sitting in the temple,
   listening to the teachers and asking them questions.
Everyone who heard him was surprised at how much he knew
   and at the answers he gave.

When his parents found him, they were amazed.
His mother said, "Son, why have you done this to us?
Your father and I have been very worried,
   and we have been searching for you!"

Jesus answered, "Why did you have to look for me?
Didn't you know that I would be in my Father's house?"
But they did not understand what he meant.

Jesus went back to Nazareth with his parents and obeyed them.

                                                         The gospel of the Lord.

March 23

[273]   **Toribio de Mogrovejo,**
                        bishop

From the Common of Pastors, p. 808.

March 25

THE ANNUNCIATION OF THE LORD

Solemnity

FIRST READING

God appointed me to preach the good news about his Son, our Lord Jesus Christ.

A reading from the letter of Paul to the Romans   1:1c-4

Brothers and sisters:
God appointed me to preach the good news
that he promised long ago
by what his prophets said in the holy Scriptures.
This good news is about his Son, our Lord Jesus Christ!
As a human, he was from the family of David.
But the Holy Spirit proved that Jesus is the powerful Son of God,
because he was raised from death.

The word of the Lord.

RESPONSORIAL PSALM   40:7-8, 9

℟. (8a and 9a) Here am I, Lord; I come to do your will.

I said, "I am here
to do what is written
about me in the book,
where it says,
'I enjoy pleasing you.
Your Law is in my heart.' "

℟. Here am I, Lord; I come to do your will.

When your people worshiped,
you know I told them,
"Our LORD always helps!"

℟. Here am I, Lord; I come to do your will.

VERSE BEFORE THE GOSPEL   John 1:14ab

℟. Glory and praise to you, Lord Jesus Christ.

The Word of God became flesh and dwelt among us;

and we saw his glory.

℟. Glory and praise to you, Lord Jesus Christ.

GOSPEL

You will conceive and bear a son.

✢ A reading from the holy gospel according to Luke　　1:26-38

God sent the angel Gabriel to the town of Nazareth in Galilee
with a message for a virgin named Mary.
She was engaged to Joseph from the family of King David.
The angel greeted Mary and said,
"You are truly blessed! The Lord is with you."

Mary was confused by the angel's words and wondered what they meant.
Then the angel told Mary, "Don't be afraid!
God is pleased with you, and you will have a son.
His name will be Jesus.
He will be great and will be called the Son of God Most High.
The Lord God will make him king,
　　as his ancestor David was.
He will rule the people of Israel forever,
　　and his kingdom will never end."

Mary asked the angel, "How can this happen?
I am not married!"

The angel answered, "The Holy Spirit will come down to you,
　　and God's power will come over you.
So your child will be called the holy Son of God.

"Your relative Elizabeth is also going to have a son,
　　even though she is old.
No one thought she could ever have a baby,
　　but in three months she will have a son.
Nothing is impossible for God!"

Mary said, "I am the Lord's servant!
Let it happen as you have said."

And the angel left her.

　　　　　　　　　　　　　　　　　　　　The gospel of the Lord.

APRIL

April 2
[275] **Francis of Paola,**
hermit, religious founder

From the Common of Saints [For Religious], p. 815.

April 4
[276] **Isidore of Seville,**
bishop, doctor of the Church

From the Common of Pastors or the Common of Doctors of the Church, p. 808 or 812.

April 5
[277] **Vincent Ferrer,**
presbyter, religious, missionary

From the Common of Pastors [For Missionaries], p. 808.

April 7
[278] **John Baptist de la Salle,**
presbyter, religious founder

Memorial

From the Common of Pastors or the Common of Saints [For Educators], p. 808 or 815.

April 11
[279] **Stanislaus,**
bishop, martyr

Memorial

From the Common of Martyrs or the Common of Pastors, p. 804 or 808.

April 13
[280] **Martin I,**
pope, martyr

From the Common of Martyrs or the Common of Pastors [For a Pope], p. 804 or 808.

April 21
[281] **Anselm,**
bishop, religious, doctor of the Church

From the Common of Pastors or the Common of Doctors of the Church, p. 808 or 812.

April 23
[282] **George,**
martyr

From the Common of Martyrs, p. 804.

April 24
[283] **Fidelis of Sigmaringen,**
presbyter, religious, martyr

From the Common of Martyrs or the Common of Pastors, p. 804 or 808.

April 25
[284] **Mark,**
evangelist

Feast

FIRST READING

My son, Mark, sends you greetings.

A reading from the first letter of Peter   5:12-14

Brothers and sisters:
   Silvanus helped me write this short letter,
   and I consider him a faithful follower of the Lord.
I wanted to encourage you and tell you how kind God really is,
   so that you will keep on having faith in him.

Greetings from the Lord's followers in Babylon.
They are God's chosen ones.

Mark, who is like a son to me, sends his greetings too.

Give each other a warm greeting.
I pray that God will give peace to everyone who belongs to Christ.

                                      The word of the Lord.

RESPONSORIAL PSALM
89:1 and 5, 15-16

℟. (2a) For ever I will sing the goodness of the Lord.

**Our LORD, I will sing
of your love forever.
Everyone yet to be born
will hear me praise
your faithfulness.
Our LORD, let the heavens
now praise your miracles,
and let all of your angels
praise your faithfulness.**

℟. For ever I will sing the goodness of the Lord.

**Our LORD, you bless those
who join in the festival
and walk in the brightness
of your presence.
We are happy all day
because of you,
and your saving power
brings honor to us.**

℟. For ever I will sing the goodness of the Lord.

ALLELUIA
1 Corinthians 1:23a,24b

℟. Alleluia, alleluia.

**We preach a Christ who was crucified;
he is the power and wisdom of God.**

℟. Alleluia, alleluia.

GOSPEL

Tell the good news to all the world.

✠ A reading from the holy gospel according to Mark
16:15-20

Jesus told his disciples:
**"Go and preach the good news to everyone in the world.
Anyone who believes me and is baptized will be saved.
But anyone who refuses to believe me will be condemned.**

"Everyone who believes me will be able to do wonderful things.
By using my name they will force out demons,
   and they will speak new languages.
They will handle snakes and will drink poison and not be hurt.
They will also heal sick people by placing their hands on them."

After the Lord Jesus had said these things to the disciples,
   he was taken back up to heaven
   where he sat down at the right side of God.
Then the disciples left and preached everywhere.
The Lord was with them,
   and the miracles they worked proved that their message was true.

The gospel of the Lord.

April 28
Peter Chanel,
presbyter, religious, missionary, martyr

From the Common of Martyrs or the Common of Pastors [For Missionaries], p. 804 or 808.

April 29
Catherine of Siena,
virgin, doctor of the Church

Memorial

From the Common of Saints or the Common of Doctors of the Church, p. 815 or 812.

April 30
Pius V,
pope, religious

From the Common of Pastors [For a Pope], p. 808.

MAY

May 1
[288]   **Joseph the Worker**

The gospel for this optional memorial is proper.

FIRST READING

A   Fill the earth and subdue it.

A reading from the book of Genesis   1:26—2:3

God said, "Now we will make humans.
We will use ourselves as a pattern,
   and they will be like us.
We will let them rule over fish, birds, animals,
      and everything that crawls on the earth."

So God used himself as a pattern and made men and women.
He gave them his blessing and said, "Have a lot of children!
Fill the earth with people and bring it under your control.
Rule over the fish in the sea, the birds in the sky,
      and all the living things that crawl on the earth."

God told the men and women,
"I have provided all kinds of grain and fruit for you to eat.
And I have given the green plants
      as food for everything else that breathes.
These plants will be food for the wild animals, for the birds,
      and for everything that crawls on the earth."

God looked at what he had done.
All of it was very good!

Evening and morning came, and that was the end of the sixth day.

So heaven and earth and everything else was created.

On the seventh day God stopped working and rested.
God blessed the seventh day and made it special,
      because on that day he had rested from all his work.

The word of the Lord.

OR

B

*Whatever the task, do it with all your heart,
as serving the Lord and not any human master.*

A reading from the letter of Paul to the Colossians   3:17, 23-24

Brothers and sisters:
Whatever you say or do should be done in the name of the Lord Jesus,
as you give thanks to God the Father because of him.
Do your work willingly,
as though you were serving the Lord himself,
and not just your earthly master.
In fact, the Lord Christ is the one you are really serving,
and you know that he will reward you.

The word of the Lord.

RESPONSORIAL PSALM   90:2, 14 and 16

℟. (17c) Lord, give success to the work of our hands.

Our Lord, you have always been God—
long before the birth
of the mountains,
even before you created
the earth and the world.

℟. Lord, give success to the work of our hands.

When morning comes,
let your love satisfy
all our needs.
Then we can celebrate
and be glad for what time
we have left.
Do wonderful things for us,
your servants,
and show your mighty power
to our children.

℟. Lord, give success to the work of our hands.

ALLELUIA   Psalm 68:20

℟. Alleluia, alleluia.

Blessed be the Lord day after day,
the God who saves us and bears our burdens.

℟. Alleluia, alleluia.

GOSPEL

Is this not the son of the carpenter?

✠ **A reading from the holy gospel according to Matthew** 13:54-58

Jesus went to his hometown.
 He taught in their meeting place,
  and the people were so amazed that they asked,
"Where does he get all this wisdom and the power to work these miracles?
Isn't he the son of the carpenter?
Isn't Mary his mother,
  and aren't James, Joseph, Simon, and Judas his brothers?
Don't his sisters still live here in our town?
How can he do all this?"

So the people were very unhappy because of what he was doing.

But Jesus said, "Prophets are honored by everyone,
  except the people of their hometown and their own family."
And because the people did not have any faith,
  Jesus did not work many miracles there.

The gospel of the Lord.

May 2

[289]   **Athanasius,**
bishop, doctor of the Church

Memorial

From the Common of Pastors or the Common of Doctors of the Church, p. 808 or 812.

May 3

[290]   **Philip and James,**
apostles

Feast

From the Common of Apostles, p. 801.

May 12

[291]   **Nereus and Achilleus,**
martyrs

From the Common of Martyrs, p. 804.

[292]   **Pancras,**
martyr

From the Common of Martyrs, p. 804.

May 14

[293] **Matthias,**
apostle

Feast

From the Common of Apostles, p. 801, except:

FIRST READING

The lot fell to Matthias,
and he was numbered with the eleven apostles.

A reading from the Acts of the Apostles   1:15-17, 20a, 20c-26

One day there were about a hundred and twenty of the Lord's followers
   meeting together,
and Peter stood up to speak to them.

He said:
"My friends, long ago by the power of the Holy Spirit,
   David said something about Judas,
   and what he said has now happened.
Judas was one of us and had worked with us,
   but he brought the mob to arrest Jesus.
In the book of Psalms David said,
'Leave his house empty.'

"It also says, 'Let someone else have his job.'

"So we need someone else to help us tell others
   that Jesus has been raised from death.
He must also be one of the men who was with us from the very beginning.
He must have been with us
   from the time the Lord Jesus was baptized by John
   until the day he was taken to heaven."

Two men were suggested:
One of them was Joseph Barsabbas, known as Justus,
   and the other was Matthias.
Then they all prayed,
"Lord, you know what everyone is like!
Show us the one you have chosen to be an apostle
   and to serve in place of Judas,
   who got what he deserved."

They drew names,
and Matthias was chosen to join the group of the eleven apostles.

The word of the Lord.

May 15

[294] **Isidore the Farmer,**
married man

From the Common of Saints, p. 815.

May 18

[295] **John I,**
pope, martyr

From the Common of Martyrs or the Common of Pastors [For a Pope], p. 804 or 808.

May 20

[296] **Bernardine of Siena,**
presbyter, religious, missionary

From the Common of Pastors [For Missionaries], p. 808.

May 25

[297] **Bede the Venerable,**
presbyter, religious, doctor of the Church

From the Common of Pastors or the Common of Doctors of the Church, p. 808 or 812.

[298] **Gregory VII,**
pope, religious

From the Common of Pastors [For a Pope], p. 808.

[299] **Mary Magdalene de' Pazzi,**
virgin, religious

From the Common of Saints [For Religious], p. 815.

May 26

[300] **Philip Neri,**
presbyter

Memorial

From the Common of Pastors or the Common of Saints [For Religious], p. 808 or 815.

May 27
[301] **Augustine of Canterbury,**
bishop, religious, missionary

From the Common of Pastors [For Missionaries], p. 808.

May 31
[302] **The Visit of the Virgin Mary to Elizabeth**

Feast

FIRST READING

A The Lord, the King of Israel, is among you.

A reading from the book of the prophet Zephaniah 3:17-18a

The LORD your God wins victory after victory,
  and he is with you.
He celebrates and rejoices because of you,
  and he will silently show you his love.

The LORD has promised,
"Your festivals will no longer be a time of sorrow."

The word of the Lord.

OR

B Contribute to the needs of God's people,
and practice hospitality.

A reading from the letter of Paul to the Romans 12:9-16b

Brothers and sisters:
  Be sincere in your love for others.
Hate everything that is evil
  and hold tight to everything that is good.
Love each other as brothers and sisters
  and honor others more than you do yourself.

Never give up.
Eagerly follow the Holy Spirit and serve the Lord.
Let your hope make you glad.
Be patient in time of trouble and never stop praying.

> Take care of God's needy people
>> and welcome strangers into your home.
>
> Ask God to bless everyone who mistreats you.
> Ask him to bless them and not to curse them.
> When others are happy, be happy with them,
>> and when they are sad, be sad.
> Be friendly with everyone.
> Don't be proud and feel that you are smarter than others.

The word of the Lord.

RESPONSORIAL PSALM — Isaiah 12:2, 4, 5-6

℟. (6b) Among you is the great and Holy One of Israel.

I trust the LORD **to save me,
and I won't be afraid.
My power and my strength come from the L**ORD **God,
and he has saved me.**

℟. Among you is the great and Holy One of Israel.

On that day you will say, "Our LORD**, we are thankful,
and we worship only you.
We will tell the nations how glorious you are
and what you have done."**

℟. Among you is the great and Holy One of Israel.

**"We will sing your praises everywhere
because of your wonderful deeds."
People of Jerusalem, celebrate and sing.
The famous L**ORD **God of Israel is here with you.**

℟. Among you is the great and Holy One of Israel.

ALLELUIA — See Luke 1:45

℟. Alleluia, alleluia.

**Blessed are you, O Virgin Mary, for your firm believing
that the promises of the Lord would be fulfilled.**

℟. Alleluia, alleluia.

GOSPEL

Why should I be honored with a visit from the mother of my Lord?

✣ A reading from the holy gospel according to Luke   1:39-56

Mary hurried to a town in the hill country of Judea.
She went to Zechariah's home,
>where she greeted Elizabeth.

When Elizabeth heard Mary's greeting,
>her baby moved within her.

The Holy Spirit came upon Elizabeth.
Then in a loud voice she said to Mary:
"God has blessed you more than any other woman!
He has also blessed the child you will have.
Why should the mother of my Lord come to me?
As soon as I heard your greeting,
>my baby became happy and moved within me.

The Lord has blessed you
>because you believed that he will keep his promise."

Mary said:
"With all my heart I praise the Lord,
>and I am glad because of God my Savior.

He cares for me, his humble servant.
From now on, all people will say God has blessed me.
God All-Powerful has done great things for me,
>and his name is holy.

"He always shows mercy to everyone who worships him.
The Lord has used his powerful arm to scatter those who are proud.
He drags strong rulers from their thrones
>and puts humble people in places of power.

He gives the hungry good things to eat,
>and he sends the rich away with nothing in their hands.

He helps his servant Israel and is always merciful to his people.
He made this promise to our ancestors,
>to Abraham and his family forever!"

Mary stayed with Elizabeth about three months.
Then she went back home.

>>>The gospel of the Lord.

[303] The Immaculate Heart of Mary
(Saturday following the Second Sunday after Pentecost)

The gospel for this optional memorial is proper.

From the Common of the Blessed Virgin Mary, p. 795, except:

GOSPEL

Mary treasured all these things in her heart.

✛ A reading from the holy gospel according to Luke   2:41-51

Every year Jesus' parents went to Jerusalem for Passover. And when Jesus was twelve years old,
> they all went there as usual for the celebration.

After Passover his parents left,
> but they did not know that Jesus had stayed on in the city.

They thought he was traveling with some other people,
> and they went a whole day before they started looking for him.

When they could not find him with their relatives and friends,
> they went back to Jerusalem and started looking for him there.

Three days later they found Jesus sitting in the temple,
> listening to the teachers and asking them questions.

Everyone who heard him was surprised at how much he knew
> and at the answers he gave.

When his parents found him, they were amazed.
His mother said, "Son, why have you done this to us?
Your father and I have been very worried,
> and we have been searching for you!"

Jesus answered, "Why did you have to look for me?
Didn't you know that I would be in my Father's house?"
But they did not understand what he meant.

Jesus went back to Nazareth with his parents and obeyed them.

The gospel of the Lord.

JUNE

June 1
[304] **Justin,**
martyr

Memorial

From the Common of Martyrs, p. 804.

June 2
[305] **Marcellinus and Peter,**
martyrs

From the Common of Martyrs, p. 804.

June 3
[306] **Charles Lwanga,** catechist, martyr, **and his companions,** martyrs

Memorial

From the Common of Martyrs, p. 804.

June 5
[307] **Boniface,**
bishop, religious, missionary, martyr

Memorial

From the Common of Martyrs or the Common of Pastors [For Missionaries], p. 804 or 808.

June 6
[308] **Norbert,**
bishop, religious founder

From the Common of Pastors or the Common of Saints [For Religious], p. 808 or 815.

June 9
[309] **Ephrem of Syria,**
deacon, doctor of the Church

From the Common of Doctors of the Church, p. 812.

June 11
Barnabas,
apostle

Memorial

The first reading for this memorial is proper.
From the Common of Apostles, p. 801, except:

FIRST READING

Barnabas was a good man, filled with the Holy Spirit and with faith.

A reading from the Acts of the Apostles   11:21-26; 13:1-3

The Lord's power was with the followers of Jesus,
   and many people turned to the Lord and put their faith in him.

News of what was happening reached the church in Jerusalem.
Then they sent Barnabas to Antioch.

When Barnabas got there
   and saw what God had been kind enough to do for them,
he was very glad.
So he begged them to remain faithful to the Lord with all their hearts.

Barnabas was a good man of great faith,
   and he was filled with the Holy Spirit.
Many more people turned to the Lord.

Barnabas went to Tarsus to look for Saul.
He found Saul and brought him to Antioch,
   where they met with the church for a whole year
   and taught many of its people.
There in Antioch the Lord's followers were first called Christians.

The church at Antioch had several prophets and teachers.
They were Barnabas, Simeon, also called Niger,
   Lucius from Cyrene,
   Manaen, who was Herod's close friend, and Saul.

While they were worshiping the Lord and going without eating,
   the Holy Spirit told them,
"Appoint Barnabas and Saul to do the work
   for which I have chosen them."

Everyone prayed and went without eating for a while longer.
Next, they placed their hands on Barnabas and Saul
   to show that they had been appointed to this work.
Then everyone sent them on their way.

The word of the Lord.

June 13

Anthony of Padua,

presbyter, religious, doctor of the Church

[311]

Memorial

From the Common of Pastors or the Common of Doctors of the Church or the Common of Saints [For Religious], p. 808, or 812, or 815.

June 19

Romuald,

abbot, religious founder

[312]

From the Common of Saints [For Religious], p. 815.

June 21

Aloysius Gonzaga,

religious

[313]

Memorial

From the Common of Saints [For Religious], p. 815.

June 22

Paulinus of Nola,

bishop

[314]

From the Common of Pastors, p. 808.

---

[315] **John Fisher,** bishop, martyr,
and Thomas More, married man, martyr

From the Common of Martyrs, p. 804.

June 24
THE BIRTH OF JOHN THE BAPTIST
Solemnity

FIRST READING

Before I formed you in the womb, I knew you.

A reading from the book of the prophet Jeremiah 1:4-8

The Lord said to Jeremiah,
"Before I gave you life,
 and before you were born,
  I chose you to be a prophet to the nations."

Jeremiah replied,
"Lord God, how can I speak for you? I'm too young."

The Lord answered, "Don't say you're too young.
Go to everyone I send you to
 and tell them everything I command you.
Don't be afraid of them!
I, the Lord, will be with you to keep you safe."

The word of the Lord.

RESPONSORIAL PSALM 139:1-3, 13-14abc, 14de-15

℟. (14a) I praise you for I am wonderfully made.

**You have looked deep
into my heart, Lord,
and you know all about me.
You know when I am resting or when I am working,
and from heaven
you discover my thoughts.
You notice everything I do
and everywhere I go.**

℟. I praise you for I am wonderfully made.

**You are the one
who put me together
inside my mother's body,
and I praise you
because of the wonderful way
you created me.**

℟. I praise you for I am wonderfully made.

Everything you do is marvelous!
Of this I have no doubt.
Nothing about me
is hidden from you!
I was secretly woven together
deep in the earth below.

℟. I praise you for I am wonderfully made.

ALLELUIA See Luke 1:76

℟. Alleluia, alleluia.

You, child, shall be called the prophet of the Most High,
for you will go before the Lord to prepare his way.

℟. Alleluia, alleluia.

GOSPEL

A son is born to you and you will name him John.

✣ A reading from the holy gospel according to Luke 1:5-17

When Herod was king of Judea,
there was a priest by the name of Zechariah
    from the priestly group of Abijah.
His wife Elizabeth was from the family of Aaron.
Both of them were good people and pleased the Lord God
    by obeying all that he had commanded.
But they did not have children.
Elizabeth could not have any,
    and both Zechariah and Elizabeth were already old.

One day Zechariah's group of priests were on duty,
    and he was serving God as a priest.
According to the custom of the priests,
    he had been chosen to go into the Lord's temple that day
        and to burn incense,
    while the people stood outside praying.

All at once an angel from the Lord came and appeared to Zechariah
    at the right side of the altar.
Zechariah was confused and afraid when he saw the angel.

But the angel told him: "Don't be afraid, Zechariah!
God has heard your prayers.
Your wife Elizabeth will have a son,
> and you must name him John.
His birth will make you very happy,
> and many people will be glad.
Your son will be a great servant of the Lord.
He must never drink wine or beer,
> and the power of the Holy Spirit will be with him
> > from the time he is born.

"John will lead many people in Israel
> to turn back to the Lord their God.
He will go ahead of the Lord
> with the same power and spirit that Elijah had.
And because of John,
> parents will be more thoughtful of their children.
And people who now disobey God will begin to think as they ought to.
That is how John will get people ready for the Lord."

The gospel of the Lord.

June 27

[317] **Cyril of Alexandria,**
bishop, doctor of the Church

From the Common of Pastors or the Common of Doctors of the Church, p. 808 or 812.

June 28

[318] **Irenaeus,**
bishop, martyr

Memorial

From the Common of Martyrs or the Common of Doctors of the Church, p. 804 or 812.

June 29
PETER AND PAUL,
apostles

Solemnity

FIRST READING

Now I know it is indeed true:
the Lord has saved me from the power of Herod.

A reading from the Acts of the Apostles　　　　12:1-11

King Herod caused terrible suffering for some members of the church.
He ordered soldiers to cut off the head of James, the brother of John.
When Herod saw that this pleased the Jewish people,
   he had Peter arrested during the Feast of Thin Bread.
He put Peter in jail and ordered four squads of soldiers to guard him.
Herod planned to put him on trial in public after the feast.

While Peter was being kept in jail,
   the church never stopped praying to God for him.

The night before Peter was to be put on trial,
   he was asleep and bound by two chains.
A soldier was guarding him on each side,
   and two other soldiers were guarding the entrance to the jail.
Suddenly an angel from the Lord appeared,
   and light flashed around in the cell.
The angel poked Peter in the side and woke him up.
Then he said, "Quick! Get up!"

The chains fell off his hands, and the angel said,
"Get dressed and put on your sandals."
Peter did what he was told.
Then the angel said, "Now put on your coat and follow me."
Peter left with the angel,
   but he thought everything was only a dream.
They went past the two groups of soldiers,
   and when they came to the iron gate to the city,
   it opened by itself.
They went out and were going along the street,
   when all at once the angel disappeared.

Peter now realized what had happened, and he said,
"I am certain that the Lord sent his angel to rescue me from Herod
   and from everything the Jewish leaders planned to do to me."

                                       The word of the Lord.

RESPONSIAL PSALM 34:3-4, 5-6, 7-8

℟. (5b) The Lord set me free from all my fears.

Honor the LORD **with me!
Celebrate his great name.
I asked the L**ORD **for help,
and he saved me
from all my fears.**

℟. The Lord set me free from all my fears.

Keep your eyes on the LORD**!
You will shine like the sun
and never blush with shame.
I was a nobody, but I prayed,
and the L**ORD **saved me
from all my troubles.**

℟. The Lord set me free from all my fears.

If you honor the LORD**,
his angel will protect you.
Discover for yourself
that the L**ORD **is kind.
Come to him for protection,
and you will be glad.**

℟. The Lord set me free from all my fears.

SECOND READING

The Lord will bring me safely into his heavenly kingdom.

A reading from the second letter of Paul to Timothy 4:17-18

**The Lord stood beside me.
He gave me the strength to tell his full message,
   so that all Gentiles would hear it.
And I was kept safe from hungry lions.**

**The Lord will always keep me from being harmed by evil,
   and he will bring me safely into his heavenly kingdom.
Praise him forever and ever! Amen.**

The word of the Lord.

ALLELUIA Matthew 16:18

℟. Alleluia, alleluia.

You are Peter, the rock on which I will build my Church;
the gates of hell will not prevail against it.

℟. Alleluia, alleluia.

GOSPEL

You are Peter; to you I will give the keys of the kingdom of heaven.

✛ A reading from the holy gospel according to Matthew   16:13-19

When Jesus and his disciples were near the town of Caesarea Philippi, he asked them, "What do people say about the Son of Man?"

The disciples answered, "Some people say you are John the Baptist
 or maybe Elijah or Jeremiah or some other prophet."

Then Jesus asked them, "But who do you say I am?"

Simon Peter spoke up,
"You are the Messiah, the Son of the living God."

Jesus told him:
"Simon, son of Jonah, you are blessed!
You didn't discover this on your own.
It was shown to you by my Father in heaven.
So I will call you Peter, which means 'a rock.'
On this rock I will build my Church,
 and death itself will not have any power over it.
I will give you the keys to the kingdom of heaven,
 and God in heaven will allow whatever you allow on earth.
But he will not allow anything that you don't allow."

The gospel of the Lord.

June 30
First Martyrs of Rome

From the Common of Martyrs, p. 804.

JULY

July 1
[321] **Blessed Junípero Serra,**
presbyter, religious, missionary

From the Common of Pastors [For Missionaries] or the Common of Saints [For Religious], p. 808 or 815.

July 3
[322] **Thomas,**
apostle

Feast

From the Common of Apostles, p. 801, except:

GOSPEL

My Lord and my God.

✠ A reading from the holy gospel according to John   20:24-29

Although Thomas the Twin was one of the twelve disciples,
he was not with the others when Jesus appeared to them.
So they told him, "We have seen the Lord!"

But Thomas said, "First, I must see the nail scars in his hands
      and touch them with my finger.
I must put my hand where the spear went into his side.
I won't believe unless I do this!"

A week later the disciples were together again.
This time Thomas was with them.
Jesus came in while the doors were still locked
      and stood in the middle of the group.
He greeted his disciples and said to Thomas,
"Put your finger here and look at my hands!
Put your hand into my side.
Stop doubting and have faith!"

Thomas replied, "You are my Lord and my God!"

Jesus said, "Thomas, do you have faith because you have seen me?
The people who have faith in me without seeing me
      are the ones who are really blessed!"

                                      The gospel of the Lord.

[323]

July 4
Elizabeth of Portugal,
married woman

From the Common of Saints [For Those Who Work for the Underprivileged], p. 815.

[324]

Independence Day

Mass For Peace and Justice, p. 869.

---

[325]

July 5
Anthony Mary Zaccaria,
presbyter, religious founder

From the Common of Pastors or the Common of Saints [For Educators or For Religious], p. 808 or 815.

---

[326]

July 6
Maria Goretti,
virgin, martyr

From the Common of Martyrs or the Common of Saints, p. 804 or 815.

---

[327]

July 11
Benedict,
abbot, religious founder

Memorial

From the Common of Saints [For Religious], p. 815.

---

[328]

July 13
Henry,
married man

From the Common of Saints, p. 815.

---

[329]

July 14
Blessed Kateri Tekakwitha,
virgin

Memorial

From the Common of Saints, p. 815.

July 15
[330] **Bonaventure,**
bishop, religious, doctor of the Church

Memorial

From the Common of Pastors or the Common of Doctors of the Church, p. 808 or 812.

July 16
[331] **Our Lady of Mount Carmel**

From the Common of the Blessed Virgin Mary, p. 795.

July 21
[332] **Lawrence of Brindisi,**
presbyter, religious, doctor of the Church

From the Common of Pastors or the Common of Doctors of the Church, p. 808 or 812.

July 22
[333] **Mary Magdalene,**
disciple of the Lord

Memorial

The gospel for this memorial is proper.

From the Common of Saints, p. 815, except:

GOSPEL

Woman, why are you weeping? Whom are you seeking?

✤ **A reading from the holy gospel according to John** 20:1-2, 11-18

On Sunday morning while it was still dark,
Mary Magdalene went to the tomb
and saw that the stone had been rolled away from the entrance.
She ran to Simon Peter and to Jesus' favorite disciple and said,
"They have taken the Lord from the tomb!
We don't know where they have put him."

Mary Magdalene stood crying outside the tomb.
She was still weeping, when she stooped down and saw two angels inside.
They were dressed in white and were sitting where Jesus' body had been.
One was at the head and the other was at the foot.

The angels asked Mary, "Why are you crying?"

She answered, "They have taken away my Lord's body!
I don't know where they have put him."

As soon as Mary said this,
    she turned around and saw Jesus standing there.
But she did not know who he was.
Jesus asked her, "Why are you crying?
Who are you looking for?"

She thought he was the gardener and said,
"Sir, if you have taken his body away,
    please tell me, so I can go and get him."

Then Jesus said to her, "Mary!"

She turned and said to him, "Rabboni."
The Aramaic word "Rabboni" means "Teacher."

Jesus told her, "Don't hold on to me!
I have not yet gone to the Father.
But tell my disciples that I am going to the one
    who is my Father and my God,
    as well as your Father and your God."
Mary Magdalene then went and told the disciples
    that she had seen the Lord.
She also told them what he had said to her.

The gospel of the Lord.

July 23
Bridget of Sweden,
married woman, religious founder

From the Common of Saints [For Religious], p. 815.

July 25
James,
apostle

From the Common of Apostles, p. 801.

July 26
Joachim and Ann,
parents of the Virgin Mary

Memorial

From the Common of Saints, p. 815.

July 29
Martha,
disciple of the Lord

Memorial

The gospel for this memorial is proper.

From the Common of Saints, p. 815, except:

GOSPEL

I believe that you are the Christ, the Son of the living God.

✣ A reading from the holy gospel according to John   11:17-27

When Jesus got to Bethany,
he found that Lazarus had already been in the tomb four days.
Bethany was only about two miles from Jerusalem,
    and many people had come from the city to comfort Martha and Mary
      because their brother had died.

When Martha had heard that Jesus had arrived,
    she went out to meet him,
    but Mary stayed in the house.
Martha said to Jesus, "Lord, if you had been here,
    my brother would not have died.
Yet even now I know that God will do anything you ask."

Jesus told her, "Your brother will live again!"

Martha answered,
"I know that he will be raised to life on the last day,
    when all the dead are raised."

Jesus then said,
"I am the one who raises the dead to life!
Everyone who has faith in me will live,
    even if they die.
And everyone who lives because of faith in me will never die.
Do you believe this?"

"Yes, Lord!" she replied.
"I believe that you are Christ, the Son of God.
You are the one we hoped would come into the world."

The gospel of the Lord.

July 30
Peter Chrysologus,
bishop, doctor of the Church

From the Common of Pastors or the Common of Doctors of the Church, p. 808 or 812.

July 31
Ignatius of Loyola,
presbyter, religious founder

Memorial

From the Common of Pastors or the Common of Saints [For Religious], p. 808 or 815.

AUGUST

August 1
[340] **Alphonsus Ligouri,**
bishop, religious founder, doctor of the Church

Memorial

From the Common of Pastors or the Common of Doctors of the Church, p. 808 or 812.

August 2
[341] **Eusebius of Vercelli,**
bishop

From the Common of Pastors, p. 808.

August 4
[342] **John Mary Vianney,**
presbyter

Memorial

From the Common of Pastors, p. 808.

August 5
[343] **The Dedication of the Basilica of Saint Mary in Rome**

From the Common of the Blessed Virgin Mary, p. 795.

August 6
[344] **The Transfiguration of the Lord**

Feast

FIRST READING

We heard this voice from out of heaven.

A reading from the second letter of Peter   1:16-19

Brothers and sisters:
When we told you about the power
    and the return of our Lord Jesus Christ,
we were not telling clever stories that someone had made up.
But with our own eyes we saw his true greatness.

God, our great and wonderful Father, truly honored him by saying,
"This is my own dear Son, and I am pleased with him."

We were there with Jesus on the holy mountain
    and heard this voice speak from heaven.

All of this makes us even more certain
    that what the prophets said is true.
So you should pay close attention to their message,
   as you would to a lamp shining in some dark place.
You must keep on paying attention until daylight comes
    and the morning star rises in your hearts.

The word of the Lord.

RESPONSORIAL PSALM   97:1-2, 5-6, 9

℟. (1a and 9a) **The Lord is king, the most high over all the earth.**

**The Lord is King!
Tell the earth to celebrate
and all islands to shout.
Dark clouds surround him,
and his throne is supported
by justice and fairness.**

℟. The Lord is king, the most high over all the earth.

**Mountains melt away like wax
in the presence of the Lord
of all the earth.
The heavens announce,
"The Lord brings justice!"
Everyone sees God's glory.**

℟. The Lord is king, the most high over all the earth.

**The Lord rules the whole earth,
and he is more glorious
than all the false gods.**

℟. The Lord is king, the most high over all the earth.

ALLELUIA   Matthew 17:5c

℟. Alleluia, alleluia.

**This is my beloved Son, in whom is all my delight;
hear him.**

℟. Alleluia, alleluia.

GOSPEL

A

Jesus' face shone like the sun.

✢ A reading from the holy gospel according to Matthew 17:1-9

Jesus took Peter and the brothers James and John with him.
   They went up on a very high mountain where they could be alone.
There in front of the disciples Jesus was completely changed.
His face was shining like the sun,
   and his clothes became white as light.

All at once Moses and Elijah were there talking with Jesus.
So Peter said to him, "Lord, it is good for us to be here!
Let us make three shelters,
   one for you, one for Moses, and one for Elijah."

While Peter was still speaking,
   the shadow of a bright cloud passed over them.
From the cloud a voice said,
"This is my own dear Son, and I am pleased with him.
Listen to what he says!"

When the disciples heard the voice,
   they were so afraid that they fell flat on the ground.
But Jesus came over and touched them.
He said, "Get up and don't be afraid!"
When they opened their eyes, they saw only Jesus.

On their way down from the mountain,
   Jesus warned his disciples not to tell anyone what they had seen
   until after the Son of Man had been raised from death.

The gospel of the Lord.

B

This is my beloved Son.

✢ A reading from the holy gospel according to Mark 9:2-10

Jesus took Peter, James, and John with him.
   They went up on a high mountain,
      where they could be alone.
There in front of the disciples,
   Jesus was completely changed.

And his clothes became much whiter
> than any bleach on earth could make them.

Then Moses and Elijah were there talking with Jesus.

Peter said to Jesus, "Teacher, it is good for us to be here!
Let us make three shelters,
> one for you, one for Moses, and one for Elijah."

But Peter and the others were terribly frightened,
> and he did not know what he was talking about.

The shadow of a cloud passed over and covered them.
From the cloud a voice said, "This is my Son, and I love him.
Listen to what he says!"
At once the disciples looked around,
> but they saw only Jesus.

As Jesus and his disciples were coming down the mountain,
> he told them not to say a word about what they had seen,
> until the Son of Man had been raised from death.

So they kept it to themselves.
But they wondered what he meant by the words "raised from death."

> The gospel of the Lord.

C

As he prayed the appearance of his face was changed.

✢ A reading from the holy gospel according to Luke   9:28-36

Jesus took Peter, John, and James with him
> and went up on a mountain to pray.

While he was praying,
> his face changed, and his clothes became shining white.

Suddenly Moses and Elijah were there speaking with him.
They appeared in heavenly glory
> and talked about all that Jesus' death
> in Jerusalem would mean.

Peter and the other two disciples had been sound asleep.
All at once they woke up and saw how glorious Jesus was.
They also saw the two men who were with him.

Moses and Elijah were about to leave, when Peter said to Jesus,
"Master, it is good for us to be here!

Let us make three shelters,
>one for you, one for Moses, and one for Elijah."
But Peter did not know what he was talking about.

While Peter was still speaking,
>a shadow from a cloud passed over them,
>and they were frightened as the cloud covered them.
From the cloud a voice spoke, "This is my chosen Son.
Listen to what he says!"

After the voice had spoken,
>Peter, John, and James saw only Jesus.
For some time they kept quiet
>and did not say anything about what they had seen.

>>>The gospel of the Lord.

August 7
Sixtus II, pope, martyr, and his companions, martyrs

[345]

From the Common of Martyrs, p. 804.

[346]
Cajetan,
presbyter, religious founder

From the Common of Pastors or the Common of Saints [For Religious], p. 808 or 815.

August 8
Dominic,
presbyter, religious founder

[347]

Memorial

From the Common of Pastors [For Missionaries] or the Common of Saints [For Religious], p. 808 or 815.

August 10
Lawrence,
deacon, martyr

[348]

Feast

From the Common of Martyrs, p. 804.

August 11
[349] Clare,
virgin, religious founder

Memorial

From the Common of Saints [For Religious], p. 815.

August 13
[350] Pontian, pope, martyr,
and Hippolytus, presbyter, martyr

From the Common of Martyrs or the Common of Pastors, p. 804 or 808.

August 14
[351] Maximilian Mary Kolbe,
presbyter, religious, martyr

Memorial

From the Common of Martyrs or the Common of Pastors, p. 804 or 808.

August 15
[352] THE ASSUMPTION OF THE VIRGIN MARY INTO HEAVEN

Solemnity

From the Common of the Blessed Virgin Mary, p. 795, except:

GOSPEL

> The Almighty has done great things for me;
> the Lord has lifted up the lowly.

✢ A reading from the holy gospel according to Luke   1:39-56

Mary hurried to a town in the hill country of Judea.
　She went into Zechariah's home,
　　where she greeted Elizabeth.
When Elizabeth heard Mary's greeting,
　her baby moved within her.

The Holy Spirit came upon Elizabeth.
Then in a loud voice she said to Mary:
"God has blessed you more than any other woman!
He has also blessed the child you will have.
Why should the mother of my Lord come to me?

As soon as I heard your greeting,
> my baby became happy and moved within me.

The Lord has blessed you
> because you believed that he will keep his promise."

Mary said:
"With all my heart I praise the Lord,
> and I am glad because of God my Savior.

He cares for me, his humble servant.
From now on, all people will say God has blessed me.
God All-Powerful has done great things for me,
> and his name is holy.

"He always shows mercy to everyone who worships him.
The Lord has used his powerful arm to scatter those who are proud.
He drags strong rulers from their thrones
> and puts humble people in places of power.

He gives the hungry good things to eat,
> and he sends the rich away with nothing in their hands.

He helps his servant Israel and is always merciful to his people.
He made this promise to our ancestors,
> to Abraham and his family forever!"

Mary stayed with Elizabeth about three months.
Then she went back home.

> The gospel of the Lord.

August 16

[353] **Stephen of Hungary,**
married man

From the Common of Saints, p. 815.

August 18

[354] **Jane Frances de Chantal,**
married woman, religious founder

From the Common of Saints [For Religious], p. 815.

August 19
[355] **John Eudes,**
presbyter, religious founder

From the Common of Pastors or the Common of Saints, p. 808 or 815.

August 20
[356] **Bernard,**
abbot, doctor of the Church

Memorial

From the Common of Doctors of the Church or the Common of Saints [For Religious], p. 812 or 815.

August 21
[357] **Pius X,**
pope

Memorial

From the Common of Pastors [For a Pope], p. 808.

August 22
[358] **The Queenship of the Virgin Mary**

Memorial

From the Common of the Blessed Virgin Mary, p. 795.

August 23
[359] **Rose of Lima,**
virgin

From the Common of Saints [For Religious], p. 815.

August 24
[360] **Bartholomew,**
apostle

Feast

From the Common of Apostles, p. 801.

August 25
[361] **Louis of France,**
married man

From the Common of Saints, p. 815.

[August 25]
Joseph Calasanz,
presbyter, religious founder

From the Common of Pastors or the Common of Saints [For Religious], p. 808 or 815.

August 27
Monica,
married woman

Memorial

From the Common of Saints, p. 815.

August 28
Augustine,
bishop, doctor of the Church

Memorial

From the Common of Pastors or the Common of Doctors of the Church, p. 808 or 812.

August 29
The Martyrdom of John the Baptist

Memorial

The gospel for this memorial is proper.

From the Common of Martyrs, p. 804, except:

GOSPEL

I want you to give me the head of John the Baptist on a dish.

✠ **A reading from the holy gospel according to Mark**   6:17-29

Herod had earlier married Herodias,
the wife of his brother Philip.
But John had told him,
"It isn't right for you to take your brother's wife!"
So, in order to please Herodias,
   Herod arrested John and put him in prison.

Herodias had a grudge against John and wanted to kill him.
But she could not do it
   because Herod was afraid of John and protected him.

He knew that John was a good and holy man.
Even though Herod was confused by what John said,
    he was glad to listen to him.
And he often did.

Finally, Herodias got her chance
    when Herod gave a great birthday celebration for himself
        and invited his officials, his army officers,
            and the leaders of Galilee.

The daughter of Herodias came in and danced for Herod and his guests.
She pleased them so much that Herod said,
"Ask for anything, and it's yours!
I swear that I will give you as much as half of my kingdom,
    if you want it."

The girl left and asked her mother,
"What do you think I should ask for?"

Her mother answered, "The head of John the Baptist!"

The girl hurried back and told Herod,
"Right now on a platter I want the head of John the Baptist!"

The king was very sorry for what he had said.
But he did not want to break the promise he had made
        in front of his guests.
At once he ordered a guard to cut off John's head there in prison.
The guard put the head on a platter and took it to the girl.
Then she gave it to her mother.

When John's followers learned that he had been killed,
    they took his body and put it in a tomb.

                                The gospel of the Lord.

SEPTEMBER

September 3
[366] **Gregory the Great,**
pope, religious, doctor of the Church

Memorial

From the Common of Pastors [For a Pope] or the Common of Doctors of the Church, p. 808 or 812.

September 8
[367] **The Birth of the Virgin Mary**

Feast

From the Common of the Blessed Virgin Mary, p. 795.

September 9
[368] **Peter Claver,**
presbyter, religious, missionary

Memorial

From the Common of Pastors or the Common of Saints [For Those Who Work for the Underprivileged], p. 808 or 815.

September 13
[369] **John Chrysostom,**
bishop, doctor of the Church

Memorial

From the Common of Pastors or the Common of Doctors of the Church, p. 808 or 812.

September 14
[370] **The Holy Cross**

Feast

FIRST READING

When those that were afflicted looked upon the serpent, they were healed.

A reading from the book of Numbers 21:4b-9

One day the people of Israel got angry
 and started insulting Moses and God.
They said, "Did you bring us out of Egypt
 just to let us die in the desert?
There's no bread or water in this place.
We are sick of this awful food!"

So the Lord sent poisonous snakes to attack the people,
> and many of them were bitten and died.

The others came to Moses and said,
"We were wrong to insult you and the Lord.
Please pray for the Lord to take these snakes away."

Moses prayed for the people.
Then the Lord said,
"Make a snake out of bronze and put it on a pole.
The people who are bitten can look at the snake,
> and they won't die."
So Moses made a bronze snake and put it on a pole.
Everyone who looked at the snake lived,
> even after being bitten by a poisonous snake.

The word of the Lord.

RESPONSORIAL PSALM 88:4-5, 14-15abc

℟. (7a) Our Lord and God, you keep me safe.

Lord God, I am as good as dead
and completely helpless.
I am no better off
than those in the grave,
those you have forgotten
and no longer help.

℟. Our Lord and God, you keep me safe.

Why do you reject me?
Why do you turn from me?
Ever since I was a child,
I have been sick
and close to death.

℟. Our Lord and God, you keep me safe.

ALLELUIA

℟. Alleluia, alleluia.

We adore you, O Christ, and we praise you,
> because by your cross you have redeemed the world.

℟. Alleluia, alleluia.

GOSPEL

The Son of Man must be lifted up.

✢ A reading from the holy gospel according to John 3:13-17

Jesus told Nicodemus:
"No one has gone up to heaven except the Son of Man,
   who came down from there.
And the Son of Man must be lifted up,
   just as that metal snake was lifted up by Moses in the desert.
Then everyone who has faith in the Son of Man will have eternal life.

"God loved the people of this world so much
      that he gave his only Son,
   so that everyone who has faith in him
      will have eternal life and never die.
God did not send his Son into the world to condemn its people.
He sent him to save them!"

The gospel of the Lord.

September 15
Our Lady of Sorrows

Memorial

The gospel for this memorial is proper.

From the Common of the Blessed Virgin Mary, p. 795, except:

GOSPEL

*How that loving mother was pierced with grief and anguish
when she saw the sufferings of her son (Stabat Mater).*

✢ A reading from the holy gospel according to John 19:25-27

Jesus' mother stood beside his cross
   with her sister and Mary the wife of Clopas.
Mary Magdalene was standing there too.

When Jesus saw his mother and his favorite disciple with her,
    he said to his mother,
"This man is now your son."
Then he said to the disciple,
"She is now your mother."

From then on, that disciple took her into his own home.

The gospel of the Lord.

September 16
Cornelius, pope, martyr,
and Cyprian, bishop, martyr

Memorial

From the Common of Martyrs or the Common of Pastors, p. 804 or 808.

September 17
Robert Bellarmine,
bishop, religious, doctor of the Church

From the Common of Pastors or the Common of Doctors of the Church, p. 808 or 812.

September 19
Januarius,
bishop, martyr

From the Common of Martyrs or the Common of Pastors, p. 804 or 808.

September 20
Andrew Kim Taegon, presbyter, martyr,
Paul Chong Hasang, catechist, martyr,
and their companions, martyrs

Memorial

From the Common of Martyrs, p. 804.

September 21
Matthew,
apostle, evangelist

Feast

From the Common of Apostles, p. 801, except:

GOSPEL

Follow me. And standing up, Matthew followed Jesus.

✤ A reading from the holy gospel according to Matthew   9:9-13

As Jesus was leaving Capernaum,
he saw a tax collector named Matthew
   sitting at the place for paying taxes.
Jesus said to him, "Come with me."
Matthew got up and went with him.

Later, Jesus and his disciples were having dinner at Matthew's house.
Many tax collectors and other sinners were also there.
Some Pharisees asked Jesus' disciples,
"Why does your teacher eat with tax collectors and other sinners?"

Jesus heard them and answered,
"Healthy people don't need a doctor,
   but sick people do.
Go and learn what the Scriptures mean when they say,
'Instead of offering sacrifices to me,
I want you to be merciful to others.'
I didn't come to invite good people to be my followers.
I came to invite sinners."

The gospel of the Lord.

September 26
Cosmas and Damian,
martyrs

From the Common of Martyrs, p. 804.

September 27
Vincent de Paul,
presbyter, religious founder

Memorial

From the Common of Pastors [For Missionaries] or the Common of Saints [For Those Who Work for the Underprivileged], p. 808 or 815.

September 28
Wenceslaus,
martyr

From the Common of Martyrs, p. 804.

Lawrence Ruiz, married man, martyr, and his companions, martyrs

From the Common of Martyrs, p. 804.

September 29
Michael, Gabriel, and Raphael,
archangels

Feast

FIRST READING

Michael and his angels battled with the dragon.

A reading from the book of Revelation 12:7-12a

A war broke out in heaven.
Michael and his angels
 were fighting against the dragon and its angels.

But the dragon lost the battle.
It and its angels were forced out of their places in heaven
 and were thrown down to the earth.
Yes, that old snake and his angels were thrown out of heaven!

That snake, who fools everyone on earth,
 is known as the devil and Satan.

Then I, John, heard a voice from heaven shout,
"Our God has shown his saving power,
 and his kingdom has come!
God's own Chosen One has shown his authority.

Satan accused our people in the presence of God day and night.
Now he has been thrown out!

"Our people defeated Satan because of the blood of the Lamb
    and the message of God.
They were willing to give up their lives.

"The heavens should rejoice,
    together with everyone who lives there.
But pity the earth and the sea,
    because the devil was thrown down to the earth."

                              The word of the Lord.

RESPONSORIAL PSALM   138:1-2ab, 2c-3, 4-5

℟. (1c) In the sight of the angels I will sing your praises, Lord.

With all my heart
I praise you, LORD.
In the presence of angels
I sing your praises.
I worship at your holy temple
and praise you for your love.

℟. In the sight of the angels I will sing your praises, Lord.

I praise you for your faithfulness.
You were true to your word
and made yourself more famous
than ever before.
When I asked for your help,
you answered my prayer
and gave me courage.

℟. In the sight of the angels I will sing your praises, Lord.

All kings on earth
have heard your promises, LORD,
and they will praise you.
You are so famous
that they will sing about
the things you have done.

℟. In the sight of the angels I will sing your praises, Lord.

ALLELUIA
Psalm 103:21

℟. Alleluia, alleluia.

**Bless the Lord, all you angels,
you ministers who do God's will.**

℟. Alleluia, alleluia.

GOSPEL

*Above the Son of Man you will see the angels of God
ascending and descending.*

✠ A reading from the holy gospel according to John   1:47-51

**When Jesus saw Nathanael coming toward him, he said,
"Here is a true descendant of our ancestor Israel.
And he is not deceitful."**

"How do you know me?" Nathanael asked.

**Jesus answered, "Before Philip called you,
    I saw you under the fig tree."**

Nathanael said, "Rabbi, you are the Son of God and the King of Israel!"

**Jesus answered, "Did you believe me
        just because I said that I saw you under the fig tree?
You will see something even greater.
I tell you for certain that you will see heaven open
        and God's angels going up and coming down on the Son of Man."**

The gospel of the Lord.

September 30
Jerome,
presbyter, doctor of the Church

Memorial

From the Common of Pastors or the Common of Doctors of the Church, p. 808 or 812.

OCTOBER

October 1

[383] **Thérèse of the Child Jesus,**
virgin, religious

Memorial

From the Common of Saints [For Religious], p. 815.

October 2

[384] **The Guardian Angels**

Memorial

The gospel for this memorial is proper.

FIRST READING

My angel will go before you.

A reading from the book of Exodus 23:20-21a

The Lord told Moses:
"I am sending an angel ahead of you.
The angel will protect you as you travel
    and will bring you to the place I have made ready.
But you must obey him and do what he says."

The word of the Lord.

RESPONSORIAL PSALM 91:1-2, 3-4, 5-6, 10-11

℟. (11) The Lord has put angels in charge of you, to guard you in all your ways.

Live under the protection
of God Most High
and stay in the shadow
of God All-Powerful.
Then you will say to the LORD,
"You are my fortress,
my place of safety;
you are my God,
and I trust you."

℟. The Lord has put angels in charge of you, to guard you in all your ways.

The Lord will keep you safe
from secret traps
and deadly diseases.
He will spread his wings over you
and keep you secure.
His faithfulness is like
a shield or a city wall.

> ℟. The Lord has put angels in charge of you, to guard you in all your ways.

You won't need to worry
about dangers at night
or arrows during the day.
And you won't fear diseases
that strike in the dark
or sudden disaster at noon.

> ℟. The Lord has put angels in charge of you, to guard you in all your ways.

No terrible disasters
will strike you
or your home.
God will command his angels
to protect you
wherever you go.

> ℟. The Lord has put angels in charge of you, to guard you in all your ways.

ALLELUIA   Psalm 103:21

> ℟. Alleluia, alleluia.

Bless the Lord, all you angels,
you ministers who do God's will.

> ℟. Alleluia, alleluia.

768 PROPER OF SAINTS

GOSPEL

Their angels in heaven are always in the presence of my Father, who is in heaven.

✠ A reading from the holy gospel according to Matthew   18:1-5, 10

The disciples came to Jesus and asked him
    who would be the greatest in the kingdom of heaven.
Jesus called a child over and had the child stand near him.

Then he said: "I promise you this.
If you don't change and become like this child,
    you will never get into the kingdom of heaven.
But if you are as humble as this child,
    you are the greatest in the kingdom of heaven.
And when you welcome one of these children because of me,
    you welcome me.

"Don't be cruel to any of these little ones!
I promise you that their angels are always with my Father in heaven."

The gospel of the Lord.

October 4

[385] **Francis of Assisi,**
religious founder

Memorial

From the Common of Saints [For Religious], p. 815.

October 6

[386] **Bruno,**
presbyter, hermit, religious founder

From the Common of Pastors or the Common of Saints [For Religious], p. 808 or 815.

[387] **Blessed Marie-Rose Durocher,**
virgin, religious founder

From the Common of Saints [For Religious], p. 815.

October 7

[388] **Our Lady of the Rosary**

Memorial

From the Common of the Blessed Virgin Mary, p. 795.

October 9

[389] **Denis,** bishop, martyr, **and his companions,** martyrs

From the Common of Martyrs, p. 804.

[390] **John Leonardi,**
presbyter, religious founder

From the Common of Pastors or the Common of Saints [For Those Who Work for the Underprivileged], p. 808 or 815.

October 14

[391] **Callistus I,**
pope, martyr

From the Common of Martyrs or the Common of Pastors [For a Pope], p. 804 or 808.

October 15

[392] **Teresa of Jesus,**
virgin, religious, doctor of the Church

Memorial

From the Common of Saints [For Religious] or the Common of Doctors of the Church, p. 815 or 812.

October 16

[393] **Hedwig,**
married woman, religious

From the Common of Saints [For Religious], p. 815.

[394] **Margaret Mary Alacoque,**
virgin, religious

From the Common of Saints [For Religious], p. 815.

October 17

[395] **Ignatius of Antioch,**
bishop, martyr

Memorial

From the Common of Martyrs or the Common of Pastors, p. 804 or 808.

October 18
Luke,
evangelist

Feast

From the Common of Apostles, p. 801, except:

GOSPEL

The harvest is rich, but the laborers are few.

✣ A reading from the holy gospel according to Luke   10:1-9

The Lord chose seventy-two other followers
    and sent them out two by two to every town and village
    where he was about to go.

He said to them:
"A large crop is in the fields,
    but there are only a few workers.
Ask the Lord in charge of the harvest
    to send out workers to bring it in.
Now go,
    but remember, I am sending you like lambs into a pack of wolves.
Don't take along a moneybag or a traveling bag or sandals.
And don't waste time greeting people on the road.

"As soon as you enter a home, say,
'God bless this home with peace.'
If the people living there are peace-loving,
    your prayer for peace will bless them.
But if they are not peace-loving,
    your prayer will return to you.

"Stay with the same family,
      eating and drinking whatever they give you,
    because workers are worth what they earn.
Don't move around from house to house.

"If the people of a town welcome you,
    eat whatever they offer you.
Heal their sick and say,
'God's kingdom will soon be here!' "

                                        The gospel of the Lord.

October 19
[397] **Isaac Jogues and John de Brébeuf,**
presbyters, religious, missionaries, martyrs,
and their companions, martyrs

Memorial

From the Common of Martyrs or the Common of Pastors [For Missionaries], p. 804 or 808.

October 20
[398] **Paul of the Cross,**
presbyter, religious founder

From the Common of Pastors or the Common of Saints [For Religious], p. 808 or 815.

October 23
[399] **John of Capistrano,**
presbyter, religious founder

From the Common of Pastors [For Missionaries], p. 808.

October 24
[400] **Anthony Mary Claret,**
bishop, religious founder

From the Common of Pastors [For Missionaries], p. 808.

October 28
[401] **Simon and Jude,**
apostles

Feast

From the Common of Apostles, p. 801.

NOVEMBER

November 1

[402] **ALL SAINTS**

Solemnity

FIRST READING

*I saw an immense crowd, beyond hope of counting,
of people from every nation, race, tribe, and language.*

A reading from the book of Revelation   7:9-10

I, John, saw a large crowd with more people than could be counted. They were from every race, tribe, nation, and language,
and they stood before the throne and before the Lamb.
They wore white robes and held palm branches in their hands,
  as they shouted,

> "Our God, who sits upon the throne,
> has the power to save his people,
> and so does the Lamb."

The word of the Lord.

RESPONSORIAL PSALM   24:1-2, 3-4, 5-6

℟. (see 6) Lord, this is the people that longs to see your face.

The earth and everything on it
belong to the LORD.
The world and its people
belong to him.
The LORD placed it all
on the oceans and rivers.

℟. Lord, this is the people that longs to see your face.

Who may climb the LORD's hill
or stand in his holy temple?
Only those who do right
for the right reasons,
and don't worship idols
or tell lies under oath.

℟. Lord, this is the people that longs to see your face.

The LORD God, who saves them,
will bless and reward them,
because they worship and serve
the God of Jacob.

℟. Lord, this is the people that longs to see your face.

ALLELUIA   Matthew 11:28

℟. Alleluia, alleluia.

**Come to me, all you that labor and are burdened,
and I will give you rest, says the Lord.**

℟. Alleluia, alleluia.

GOSPEL

Rejoice and be glad, for your reward will be great in heaven.

✙ A reading from the holy gospel according to Matthew   5:1-12ab

When Jesus saw the crowds,
he went up on the side of a mountain and sat down.

Jesus' disciples gathered around him, and he taught them:

"God blesses those people who depend only on him.
They belong to the kingdom of heaven!

"God blesses those people who grieve.
They will find comfort!

"God blesses those people who are humble.
The earth will belong to them!

"God blesses those people who want to obey him
     more than to eat or drink.
They will be given what they want!

"God blesses those people who are merciful.
They will be treated with mercy!

"God blesses those people whose hearts are pure.
They will see him!

"God blesses those people who make peace.
They will be called his children!

"God blesses those people who are treated badly for doing right.
They belong to the kingdom of heaven.

"God will bless you when people insult you, mistreat you,
    and tell all kinds of evil lies about you because of me.
Be happy and excited!
You will have a great reward in heaven."

The gospel of the Lord.

November 2
[403] **The Commemoration of All the Faithful Departed**
(All Souls)

From the Masses for the Dead, p. 882.

November 3
[404] **Martin de Porres,**
religious

From the Common of Saints [For Religious], p. 815.

November 4
[405] **Charles Borromeo,**
bishop

Memorial

From the Common of Pastors, p. 808.

November 9
[406] **The Dedication of the Lateran Basilica in Rome**

Feast

From the Common of the Dedication of a Church, p. 791.

November 10
[407] **Leo the Great,**
pope, doctor of the Church

Memorial

From the Common of Pastors [For a Pope] or the Common of Doctors of the Church, p. 808 or 812.

[408]

November 11

Martin of Tours,
bishop

Memorial

From the Common of Pastors or the Common of Saints [For Religious], p. 808 or 815.

---

[409]

November 12

Josaphat,
bishop, religious, martyr

Memorial

From the Common of Martyrs or the Common of Pastors, p. 804 or 808.

---

[410]

November 13

Frances Xavier Cabrini,
virgin, religious, missionary

Memorial

From the Common of Saints [For Religious], p. 815.

---

[411]

November 15

Albert the Great,
bishop, religious, doctor of the Church

From the Common of Pastors or the Common of Doctors of the Church, p. 808 or 812.

---

[412]

November 16

Margaret of Scotland,
married woman

From the Common of Saints [For Those Who Work for the Underprivileged], p. 815.

[413]

Gertrude the Great,
virgin, religious

From the Common of Saints [For Religious], p. 815.

---

[414]

November 17

Elizabeth of Hungary,
married woman, religious

Memorial

From the Common of Saints [For Those Who Work for the Underprivileged], p. 815.

November 18
The Dedication of the Basilicas of the Apostles Peter and Paul in Rome

The readings for this optional memorial are proper.

FIRST READING

So we came to Rome.

A reading from the Acts of the Apostles 28:11-16

Three months after reaching Malta
    we sailed in a ship that had been docked there for the winter.
The ship was from Alexandria in Egypt
    and was known as "The Twin Gods."
We arrived in Syracuse and stayed for three days.
From there we sailed to Rhegium.

The next day a south wind began to blow,
    and two days later we arrived in Puteoli.
There we found some of the Lord's followers,
    who begged us to stay with them.
A week later we left for the city of Rome.

Some of the followers in Rome heard about us and came to meet us
    at the Market of Appius and at the Three Inns.
When Paul saw them,
    he thanked God and was encouraged.

We arrived in Rome,
    and Paul was allowed to live in a house by himself
        with a soldier to guard him.

The word of the Lord.

RESPONSORIAL PSALM 98:1, 2-3, 4-6

℟. (see 2b) The Lord has revealed to the nations his saving power.

Sing a new song to the LORD!
He has worked miracles,
and with his own powerful arm,
he has won the victory.

℟. The Lord has revealed to the nations his saving power.

**The LORD has shown the nations
that he has the power to save
and to bring justice.
God has been faithful
in his love for Israel,
and his saving power is seen
everywhere on earth.**

℟. The Lord has revealed to the nations his saving power.

**Tell everyone on this earth
to sing happy songs
in praise of the LORD.
Make music for him on harps.
Play beautiful melodies!
Sound the trumpets and horns
and celebrate with joyful songs
for our LORD and King!**

℟. The Lord has revealed to the nations his saving power.

ALLELUIA

℟. Alleluia, alleluia.

**We praise you, O God; we acclaim you as Lord;
the glorious company of apostles praise you.**

℟. Alleluia, alleluia.

GOSPEL

Order me to come to you across the water.

✢ A reading from the holy gospel according to Matthew   14:22-33

**Jesus made his disciples get into a boat and start back across the lake. But he stayed until he had sent the crowds away.
Then he went up on a mountain where he could be alone and pray. Later that evening, he was still there.**

By this time the boat was a long way from the shore.
It was going against the wind and was being tossed around by the waves.
A little while before morning,
>Jesus came walking on the water toward his disciples.
When they saw him, they thought he was a ghost.
They were terrified and started screaming.

At once Jesus said to them, "Don't worry!
I am Jesus. Don't be afraid."

Peter replied, "Lord, if it is really you,
>tell me to come to you on the water."

"Come on!" Jesus said.
Peter then got out of the boat
>and started walking on the water toward him.

But when Peter saw how strong the wind was,
>he was afraid and started sinking.

"Lord, save me!" he shouted.
Right away Jesus reached out his hand.
He helped Peter up and said,
"You surely don't have much faith.
Why do you doubt?"

When Jesus and Peter got into the boat, the wind died down.
The men in the boat worshiped Jesus and said,
"You really are the Son of God!"

>>The gospel of the Lord.

[November 18]

[416]   **Rose Philippine Duchesne,**
>virgin, religious, missionary

From the Common of Saints [For Religious], p. 815.

November 21
[417] **The Presentation of the Virgin Mary**

Memorial

From the Common of the Blessed Virgin Mary, p. 795.

November 22
[418] **Cecilia,**
virgin, martyr

Memorial

From the Common of Martyrs or the Common of Saints, p. 804 or 815.

November 23
[419] **Clement I,**
pope, martyr

From the Common of Martyrs or the Common of Pastors [For a Pope], p. 804 or 808.

[420] **Columban,**
abbot, missionary

From the Common of Pastors [For Missionaries] or the Common of Saints [For Religious], p. 808 or 815.

[421] **Blessed Miguel Agustín Pro,**
presbyter, religious, martyr

From the Common of Martyrs or the Common of Pastors, p. 804 or 808.

November 24
[422] **Andrew Dung-Lac,** presbyter, martyr,
and his companions, martyrs

Memorial

From the Common of Martyrs, p. 804.

November 30
[423] **Andrew,**
apostle

Feast

From the Common of Apostles, p. 801, except:

GOSPEL

Immediately they left their nets and followed Jesus.

✠ A reading from the holy gospel according to Matthew   4:18-22

While Jesus was walking along the shore of Lake Galilee,
  he saw two brothers.
One was Simon, also known as Peter,
  and the other was Andrew.
They were fishermen, and they were casting their net into the lake.

Jesus said to them, "Come with me!
I will teach you how to bring in people instead of fish."
Right then the two brothers dropped their nets and went with him.

Jesus walked on until he saw James and John, the sons of Zebedee.
They were in a boat with their father, mending their nets.
Jesus asked them to come with him too.
Right away they left the boat and their father and went with Jesus.

Jesus went all over Galilee,
  teaching in the Jewish meeting places
  and preaching the good news about God's kingdom.

The gospel of the Lord.

Fourth Thursday in November
[424] **Thanksgiving Day**

Mass in Thanksgiving, p. 857.

DECEMBER

December 3
[425] **Francis Xavier,**
presbyter, religious, missionary

Memorial

From the Common of Pastors [For Missionaries], p. 808.

December 4
[426] **John of Damascus,**
presbyter, doctor of the Church

From the Common of Pastors or the Common of Doctors of the Church, p. 808 or 812.

December 6
[427] **Nicholas,**
bishop

From the Common of Pastors, p. 808.

December 7
[428] **Ambrose,**
bishop, doctor of the Church

Memorial

From the Common of Pastors or the Common of Doctors of the Church, p. 808 or 812.

December 8
[429] **THE IMMACULATE CONCEPTION OF THE VIRGIN MARY**

Solemnity

FIRST READING

I will put enmity between your offspring and her offspring.

A reading from the book of Genesis   3:9-15, 20

The Lord called out to Adam and asked, "Where are you?"

Adam answered, "I was naked,
 and when I heard you walking through the garden,
 I was afraid and hid!"

"How did you know you were naked?" God asked.
"Did you eat from the tree I told you not to?"

Adam said, "It was that woman you put here with me!
She gave me some of the fruit, and I ate it."

The LORD God then asked her, "What have you done?"

The woman answered,
"The snake tricked me into eating some of that fruit."

The LORD God said to the snake:
"Because of what you have done,
> you will suffer a greater curse than the cattle
>> and the wild animals.
For as long as you live,
> you will crawl on your stomach and eat dirt from the ground.
You and this woman will hate each other.
Your descendants and hers will always be enemies.
One of them will crush your head,
> and you will bite him on the heel."

Adam named his wife Eve,
> because she would become the mother of all people.

The word of the Lord.

RESPONSORIAL PSALM   98:1, 2-3ab, 3cd-4

℟. (1a) Sing to the Lord a new song, for he has done marvelous deeds.

**Sing a new song to the LORD!
He has worked miracles,
and with his own powerful arm,
he has won the victory.**

℟. Sing to the Lord a new song, for he has done marvelous deeds.

**The LORD has shown the nations
that he has the power to save
and to bring justice.
God has been faithful
in his love for Israel.**

℟. Sing to the Lord a new song, for he has done marvelous deeds.

**His saving power is seen
everywhere on earth.**

Tell everyone on this earth
to sing happy songs
in praise of the Lord.

℟. Sing to the Lord a new song, for he has done marvelous deeds.

ALLELUIA See Luke 1:28

℟. Alleluia, alleluia.

Hail, Mary, full of grace, the Lord is with you;
blessed are you among women.

℟. Alleluia, alleluia.

GOSPEL

Rejoice, favored one, the Lord is with you.

✠ A reading from the holy gospel according to Luke 1:26-38

God sent the angel Gabriel to the town of Nazareth in Galilee
with a message for a virgin named Mary.
She was engaged to Joseph from the family of King David.
The angel greeted Mary and said,
"You are truly blessed! The Lord is with you."

Mary was confused by the angel's words
and wondered what they meant.
Then the angel told Mary, "Don't be afraid!
God is pleased with you, and you will have a son.
His name will be Jesus.
He will be great and will be called the Son of God Most High.
The Lord God will make him king,
as his ancestor David was.
He will rule the people of Israel forever,
and his kingdom will never end."

Mary asked the angel, "How can this happen?
I am not married!"

The angel answered, "The Holy Spirit will come down to you,
and God's power will come over you.
So your child will be called the holy Son of God.

"Your relative Elizabeth is also going to have a son,
even though she is old.

No one thought she could ever have a baby,
>   but in three months she will have a son.
Nothing is impossible for God!"

Mary said, "I am the Lord's servant!
Let it happen as you have said."

And the angel left her.

> The gospel of the Lord.

December 9
[430] **Blessed Juan Diego (Cuatitlatoatzin),**
hermit

From the Common of Saints, p. 815.

December 11
[431] **Damasus I,**
pope

From the Common of Pastors [For a Pope], p. 808.

December 12
[432] **Our Lady of Guadalupe**

Feast

From the Common of the Blessed Virgin Mary, p. 795.

December 13
[433] **Lucy,**
virgin, martyr

Memorial

From the Common of Martyrs or the Common of Saints, p. 804 or 815.

December 14
[434] **John of the Cross,**
presbyter, doctor of the Church

Memorial

From the Common of Pastors or the Common of Doctors of the Church, p. 808 or 812.

December 21
Peter Canisius,
presbyter, religious, doctor of the Church

From the Common of Pastors or the Common of Doctors of the Church, p. 808 or 812.

December 23
John of Kanty,
presbyter

From the Common of Pastors, p. 808.

December 26
Stephen,
first martyr

Feast

From the Common of Martyrs, p. 804, except:

FIRST READING

I can see heaven thrown open.

A reading from the Acts of the Apostles 6:8-10; 7:54-60

God gave Stephen
  the power to work great miracles and wonders among the people.
But some Jews from Cyrene and Alexandria
  were members of a group who called themselves "Free Men."
They started arguing with Stephen.
Some others from Cilicia and Asia also argued with him.
But they were no match for Stephen,
  who spoke with the great wisdom that the Spirit gave him.

Those who heard Stephen's speech were angry and furious.
But Stephen was filled with the Holy Spirit.
He looked toward heaven,
  where he saw our glorious God and Jesus standing at his right side.
Then Stephen said, "I see heaven open
  and the Son of Man standing at the right side of God!"

The council members shouted and covered their ears.
At once they all attacked Stephen and dragged him out of the city.
Then they started throwing stones at him.

The men who had brought charges against him
> put their coats at the feet of a young man named Saul.

As Stephen was being stoned to death, he called out,
"Lord Jesus, please welcome me!"
He kneeled down and shouted,
"Lord, don't blame them for what they have done."
Then he died.

> The word of the Lord.

December 27

[438]

John,

apostle, evangelist

Feast

From the Common of Apostles, p. 801, except:

GOSPEL

The other disciple outran Peter and came first to the tomb.

✜ A reading from the holy gospel according to John   20:2-8

On Sunday morning Mary Magdalene ran to Simon Peter
> and to Jesus' favorite disciple and said,
"They have taken the Lord from the tomb!
We don't know where they have put him."

Peter and the other disciple started for the tomb.
They ran side by side,
> until the other disciple ran faster than Peter and got there first.
He bent over and saw the strips of linen cloth lying inside the tomb,
> but he did not go in.

When Simon Peter got there,
> he went into the tomb and saw the strips of cloth.
He also saw the piece of cloth that had been used to cover Jesus' face.
It was rolled up and in a place by itself.
The disciple who got there first then went into the tomb,
> and when he saw it, he believed.

> The gospel of the Lord.

December 28

The Holy Innocents,
martyrs

Feast

From the Common of Martyrs, p. 804, except:

GOSPEL

Herod killed all the male children who were in Bethlehem.

✤ A reading from the holy gospel according to Matthew   2:13-18

After the wise men had gone,
an angel from the Lord appeared to Joseph in a dream.
The angel said, "Get up!
Hurry and take the child and his mother to Egypt!
Stay there until I tell you to return,
    because Herod is looking for the child and wants to kill him."

That night Joseph got up and took his wife and the child to Egypt,
    where they stayed until Herod died.
So the Lord's promise came true, just as the prophet had said,
"I called my son out of Egypt."

When Herod found out that the wise men from the east had tricked him,
    he was very angry.
He gave orders for his men to kill
    all the boys who lived in or near Bethlehem
    and were two years old and younger.

So the Lord's promise came true,
    just as the prophet Jeremiah had said,
"In Ramah a voice was heard crying and weeping loudly.
Rachel was mourning for her children,
    and she refused to be comforted,
    because they were dead."

                                                  The gospel of the Lord.

December 29
Thomas Becket,
bishop, martyr

From the Common of Martyrs or the Common of Pastors, p. 804 or 808.

December 31
Sylvester I,
pope

From the Common of Pastors [For a Pope], p. 808.

COMMONS

COMMON OF THE DEDICATION OF A CHURCH

[442] **OLD TESTAMENT READING**

My house will be called a house of prayer for all the peoples.

A reading from the book of the prophet Isaiah   56:1, 6-7

The LORD said,
"Be honest and fair!

"Soon I will come to save you,
    and my saving power will be seen.
Foreigners will follow me.
They will love me and worship in my name.
They will respect the Sabbath and keep our agreement.

"Then I will bring them to my holy mountain
    and let them celebrate in my house of worship.
Their sacrifices and offerings will all be welcome on my altar.
And my house will be known as a house of worship for all nations."

The word of the Lord.

[443] **NEW TESTAMENT READING**

1

*Through the Lord, the whole building is bound together
as one holy temple.*

A reading from the letter of Paul to the Ephesians   2:20-22

Brothers and sisters:
You are like a building with the apostles and prophets as the foundation
    and with Christ as the most important stone.
Christ is the one who holds the building together
    and makes it grow into a holy temple for the Lord.
And you are part of that building Christ has built
    as a place for God's own Spirit to live.

The word of the Lord.

2. Behold, the home of God is among his people.

A reading from the book of Revelation 21:1-4

I, John, saw a new heaven and a new earth.
The first heaven and the first earth had disappeared,
  and so had the sea.
Then I saw New Jerusalem, that holy city,
  coming down from God in heaven.
It was like a bride dressed in her wedding gown
  and ready to meet her husband.

I heard a loud voice shout from the throne:
"God's home is now with his people.
He will live with them,
  and they will be his own.
Yes, God will make his home among his people.
He will wipe all tears from their eyes,
  and there will be no more death, suffering, crying, or pain.
These things of the past are gone forever."

The word of the Lord.

[444] **RESPONSORIAL PSALM**

Psalm 84:2, 3, 4-5, 10

℟. (2) How lovely is your dwelling place, Lord, mighty God!
or:
℟. (Revelation 21:3b) Here God lives among his people.

Deep in my heart I long
for your temple,
and with all that I am
I sing joyful songs to you.

℟. How lovely is your dwelling place, Lord, mighty God!
or:
℟. Here God lives among his people.

Lord God All-Powerful,
my King and my God,
sparrows find a home
near your altars;
swallows build nests there
to raise their young.

> ℟. How lovely is your dwelling place, Lord, mighty God!
> or:
> ℟. Here God lives among his people.

You bless everyone
who lives in your house,
and they sing your praises.
You bless all who depend
on you for their strength
and all who deeply desire
to visit your temple.

> ℟. How lovely is your dwelling place, Lord, mighty God!
> or:
> ℟. Here God lives among his people.

One day in your temple
is better than a thousand
anywhere else.
I would rather serve
in your house,
than live in the homes
of the wicked.

> ℟. How lovely is your dwelling place, Lord, mighty God!
> or:
> ℟. Here God lives among his people.

[445] ALLELUIA VERSE AND VERSE BEFORE THE GOSPEL

See Matthew 7:8

In my house, says the Lord, everyone who asks will receive;
whoever seeks shall find;
and to those who knock it shall be opened.

GOSPEL

Today salvation has come to this house.

✠ A reading from the holy gospel according to Luke   19:1-10

Jesus was going through Jericho,
   where a man named Zacchaeus lived.
He was in charge of collecting taxes and was very rich.

Jesus was heading his way,
   and Zacchaeus wanted to see what he was like.
But Zacchaeus was a short man and could not see over the crowd.
So he ran ahead and climbed up into a sycamore tree.

When Jesus got there, he looked up and said,
"Zacchaeus, hurry down!
I want to stay with you today."

Zacchaeus hurried down and gladly welcomed Jesus.

Everyone who saw this started grumbling,
"This man Zacchaeus is a sinner!
And Jesus is going home to eat with him."

Later that day Zacchaeus stood up and said to the Lord,
"I will give half of my property to the poor.
And I will now pay back four times as much
   to everyone I have ever cheated."

Jesus said to Zacchaeus,
"Today you and your family have been saved,
   because you are a true son of Abraham.
The Son of Man came to look for and to save
   people who are lost."

                                    The gospel of the Lord.

COMMON OF THE BLESSED VIRGIN MARY

[447] **OLD TESTAMENT READING**

\[1\]
A son is given to us.

A reading from the book of the prophet Isaiah   9:2-3a, 6-7a

Those who walked in the dark have seen a bright light.
And it shines upon everyone who lives in the land of darkest shadows.

Our LORD, you have made your nation stronger.
Because of you, its people are glad and celebrate.

For us a child has been born.
A son has been given to us,
    and he will be our ruler.
His names will be:
    Wonderful Adviser and Mighty God,
    Eternal Father and Prince of Peace.

His power will never end,
    and peace will last forever.

The word of the Lord.

\[2\]
Rejoice, daughter of Zion, for I am coming.

A reading from the book of the prophet Zechariah   2:14-15

The LORD said, "Everyone in Jerusalem, celebrate and shout!
    I am coming to live with you."

Many nations will turn to the LORD and become his people,
    and he will live with all of you.
Then you will know that the LORD All-Powerful has sent me.

The word of the Lord.

[448] **NEW TESTAMENT READING**

\[1\]
*They all joined in continuous prayer
together with Mary, the mother of Jesus.*

A reading from the Acts of the Apostles   1:12-13a, 14

The apostles returned to Jerusalem from the Mount of Olives,
    which was about a half mile from Jerusalem.
Then they went upstairs to the room where they had been staying.

The apostles often met together
and prayed with a single purpose in mind.
The women and Mary the mother of Jesus would meet with them,
and so would his brothers.

The word of the Lord.

2

Before the world was made, God chose us in Christ.

A reading from the letter of Paul to the Ephesians   1:3-6

Brothers and sisters:
Praise the God and Father of our Lord Jesus Christ
for the spiritual blessings that Christ has brought us
from heaven!
Before the world was created,
God let Christ choose us to live with him
and to be his holy and innocent and loving people.
God was kind
and decided that Christ would choose us
to be God's own adopted children.
God was very kind to us because of the Son he dearly loves,
and so we should praise God.

The word of the Lord.

[449]

RESPONSORIAL PSALM

1

Psalm 113:1-2, 3-4, 5-6, 7-8

℟. (see 2) Blessed be the name of the Lord for ever.
or:
℟. Alleluia.

Shout praises to the LORD!
Everyone who serves him,
come and praise his name.
Let the name of the LORD
be praised now and forever.

℟. Blessed be the name of the Lord for ever.
or:
℟. Alleluia.

From dawn until sunset
the name of the LORD

deserves to be praised.
The Lord is far above
all of the nations;
he is more glorious
than the heavens.

> ℟. Blessed be the name of the Lord for ever.
> or:
> ℟. Alleluia.

No one can compare
with the Lord our God.
His throne is high above,
and he looks down to see
the heavens and the earth.

> ℟. Blessed be the name of the Lord for ever.
> or:
> ℟. Alleluia.

God lifts the poor and needy
from dust and ashes,
and he lets them take part
in ruling his people.

> ℟. Blessed be the name of the Lord for ever.
> or:
> ℟. Alleluia.

2

Luke 1:47-48b, 48c-49, 50-51, 52-53, 54-55

> ℟. (49) The Almighty has done great things for me,
>   and holy is his name.

With all my heart I praise the Lord,
and I am glad because of God my Savior.
He cares for me, his humble servant.

> ℟. The Almighty has done great things for me,
>   and holy is his name.

From now on,
all people will say God has blessed me.
God All-Powerful has done great things for me,
and his name is holy.

℟. The Almighty has done great things for me,
　　and holy is his name.

**He always shows mercy
to everyone who worships him.
The Lord has used his powerful arm
to scatter those who are proud.**

℟. The Almighty has done great things for me,
　　and holy is his name.

**He drags strong rulers from their thrones
and puts humble people in places of power.
He gives the hungry good things to eat,
and he sends the rich away with nothing in their hands.**

℟. The Almighty has done great things for me,
　　and holy is his name.

**He helps his servant Israel
and is always merciful to his people.
He made this promise to our ancestors,
to Abraham and his family forever!**

℟. The Almighty has done great things for me,
　　and holy is his name.

[450] ALLELUIA VERSE AND VERSE BEFORE THE GOSPEL

See Luke 1:28

**Hail, Mary, full of grace, the Lord is with you;
blessed are you among women.**

[451] GOSPEL

[1]　　　　　　You will conceive and bear a son.

✠ A reading from the holy gospel according to Luke　　　1:26-38

God sent the angel Gabriel to the town of Nazareth in Galilee
　　with a message for a virgin named Mary.
**She was engaged to Joseph from the family of King David.
The angel greeted Mary and said,
"You are truly blessed! The Lord is with you."**

Mary was confused by the angel's words
   and wondered what they meant.
Then the angel told Mary, "Don't be afraid!
God is pleased with you, and you will have a son.
His name will be Jesus.
He will be great and will be called the Son of God Most High.
The Lord God will make him king,
   as his ancestor David was.
He will rule the people of Israel forever,
   and his kingdom will never end."

Mary asked the angel, "How can this happen?
I am not married!"

The angel answered, "The Holy Spirit will come down to you,
   and God's power will come over you.
So your child will be called the holy Son of God.

"Your relative Elizabeth is also going to have a son,
   even though she is old.
No one thought she could ever have a baby,
   but in three months she will have a son.
Nothing is impossible for God!"

Mary said, "I am the Lord's servant!
Let it happen as you have said."

And the angel left her.

The gospel of the Lord.

2

Your father and I have been looking for you.

✚ A reading from the holy gospel according to Luke   2:41-51

Every year Jesus' parents went to Jerusalem for Passover.
   And when Jesus was twelve years old,
   they all went there as usual for the celebration.

After Passover his parents left,
   but they did not know that Jesus had stayed on in the city.
They thought he was traveling with some other people,
   and they went a whole day before they started looking for him.

When they could not find him with their relatives and friends,
   they went back to Jerusalem and started looking for him there.

Three days later they found Jesus sitting in the temple,
> listening to the teachers and asking them questions.
Everyone who heard him was surprised at how much he knew
> and at the answers he gave.

When his parents found him, they were amazed.
His mother said, "Son, why have you done this to us?
Your father and I have been very worried,
> and we have been searching for you!"

Jesus answered, "Why did you have to look for me?
Didn't you know that I would be in my Father's house?"
But they did not understand what he meant.

Jesus went back to Nazareth with his parents and obeyed them.

> **The gospel of the Lord.**

---

3 Woman, this is your son. This is your mother.

✠ **A reading from the holy gospel according to John** 19:25-27

Jesus' mother stood beside his cross
> with her sister and Mary the wife of Clopas.
Mary Magdalene was standing there too.

When Jesus saw his mother and his favorite disciple with her,
> he said to his mother,
"This man is now your son."
Then he said to the disciple,
"She is now your mother."

From then on, that disciple took her into his own home.

> **The gospel of the Lord.**

COMMON OF APOSTLES

[452]

NEW TESTAMENT READING

1

What I have, I give you; in the name of Jesus stand up and walk.

A reading from the Acts of the Apostles 3:1-10

At the time of prayer,
which was about three o'clock in the afternoon,
    Peter and John were going into the temple.
A man who had been born lame was being carried to the temple door.
Each day he was placed beside this door,
    known as the Beautiful Gate.
He sat there and begged from the people who were going in.

The man saw Peter and John entering the temple,
    and he asked them for money.
But they looked straight at him and said,
"Look up at us!"

The man stared at them and thought he was going to get something.
But Peter said, "I don't have any silver or gold!
But I will give you what I do have.
In the name of Jesus Christ from Nazareth,
    get up and start walking."
Peter then took him by the right hand and helped him up.

At once the man's feet and ankles became strong,
    and he jumped up and started walking.
He went with Peter and John into the temple,
    walking and jumping and praising God.

Everyone saw him walking around and praising God.
They knew that he was the beggar
      who had been lying beside the Beautiful Gate,
    and they were completely surprised.
They could not imagine what had happened to the man.

                                          The word of the Lord.

☐2   You are like a building
        with the apostles and prophets as the foundation.

A reading from the letter of Paul to the Ephesians 2:20-22

Brothers and sisters:
 You are like a building
    with the apostles and prophets as the foundation
    and with Christ as the most important stone.
Christ is the one who holds the building together
    and makes it grow into a holy temple for the Lord.
And you are part of that building Christ has built
    as a place for God's own Spirit to live.

                                    The word of the Lord.

[453]   **RESPONSORIAL PSALM**

                                    Psalm 19:1-2, 3-4abcd

℟. (5a) Their message goes through all the earth.

**The heavens keep telling
the wonders of God,
and the skies declare
what he has done.
Each day informs
the following day;
each night announces
to the next.**

℟. Their message goes through all the earth.

**They don't speak a word,
and there is never
the sound of a voice.
Yet their message reaches
all the earth,
and it travels
around the world.**

℟. Their message goes through all the earth.

[455]

[454] ALLELUIA VERSE AND VERSE BEFORE THE GOSPEL

See Luke 11:28

> Blessed are they who hear the word of God
> and keep it.

[455]
GOSPEL

1

Anyone among you who wishes to be first must be your servant.

✢ A reading from the holy gospel according to Matthew   20:26b-28

Jesus said to his disciples:
"If you want to be great,
    you must be the servant of all the others.
And if you want to be first,
    you must be the slave of the rest.

"The Son of Man did not come to be a slave master,
    but a slave who will give his life to rescue many people."

                                                      The gospel of the Lord.

2

Jesus spent the night in prayer.
He chose twelve from them whom he named apostles.

✢ A reading from the holy gospel according to Luke   6:12-16

Jesus went off to a mountain to pray,
    and he spent the whole night there.

The next morning he called his disciples together
    and chose twelve of them to be his apostles.

One was Simon, and Jesus named him Peter.
Another was Andrew, Peter's brother.
There were also James, John, Philip, Bartholomew,
    Matthew, Thomas, and James the son of Alphaeus.

The rest of the apostles were Simon, known as the Eager One,
    Jude, who was the son of James,
    and Judas Iscariot, who later betrayed Jesus.

                                                      The gospel of the Lord.

COMMON OF MARTYRS

[456] ## OLD TESTAMENT READING

*Because of her hope in the Lord,
this admirable mother bore their deaths with honor.*

A reading from the second book of Maccabees   7:1, 20-23

King Antiochus arrested seven Jewish brothers and their mother.
He had them beaten with heavy whips
    and tried to make them eat the meat of pigs,
  which was against their religion.

The mother of these young men was a wonderful woman,
  and she deserves to be remembered with praise.
She saw all seven of her sons die on the same day,
  but she was brave and never gave up her hope in the LORD.
She cheered each of her sons
    by speaking to them in their native language.

This mother was very special.
With the feelings of a woman and with the courage of a man,
  she told her sons:
"I don't understand how you grew inside me.
I didn't give you life and breath or give shape to your bodies.
The Creator of the world made all people and started everything.
Now you are giving up your lives,
  so that you can obey his laws.
But he will be merciful and give life and breath back to you."

                                              The word of the Lord.

[457] ## NEW TESTAMENT READING

1

Lord Jesus, receive my spirit.

A reading from the Acts of the Apostles   7:55-60

Stephen was filled with the Holy Spirit.
He looked toward heaven,
  where he saw our glorious God and Jesus standing at his right side.
Then Stephen said, "I see heaven open
  and the Son of Man standing at the right side of God!"

The council members shouted and covered their ears.
At once they all attacked Stephen and dragged him out of the city.
Then they started throwing stones at him.
The men who had brought charges against him
>> put their coats at the feet of a young man named Saul.

As Stephen was being stoned to death, he called out,
"Lord Jesus, please welcome me!"
He kneeled down and shouted,
"Lord, don't blame them for what they have done."
Then he died.

>> The word of the Lord.

2

We are said to be dying and yet here we are alive.

A reading from the second letter of Paul to the Corinthians 6:4-10

Brothers and sisters:
In everything and in every way
>> we show that we truly are God's servants.

We have always been patient,
>> though we have had a lot of trouble, suffering, and hard times.
We have been beaten, put in jail, and hurt in riots.
We have worked hard and have gone without sleep or food.
But we have kept ourselves pure
>> and have been understanding, patient, and kind.

The Holy Spirit has been with us,
>> and our love has been real.
We have spoken the truth,
>> and God's power has worked in us.
In all our struggles we have said and done only what is right.

Whether we were honored or dishonored or praised or cursed,
>> we always told the truth about ourselves.
But some people said we did not.

We were unknown to others, but well known to you.
We seem to be dying,
>> and yet we are still alive.
We have been punished, but never killed,
>> and we are always happy, even in times of suffering.

Although we are poor,
>> we have made many people rich.

And though we own nothing,
    everything is ours.

The word of the Lord.

[458]   **RESPONSORIAL PSALM**

☐1   Psalm 31:1-2a, 2bcde-3, 19

℟. (6a) Into your hands, O Lord, I entrust my spirit.

**I come to you, Lord,
for protection.
Don't let me be ashamed.
Do as you have promised
and rescue me.
Listen to my prayer.**

℟. Into your hands, O Lord, I entrust my spirit.

**Hurry to save me.
Be my mighty rock
and the fortress
where I am safe.
You, Lord God,
are my mighty rock
and my fortress.
Lead me and guide me,
so that your name
will be honored.**

℟. Into your hands, O Lord, I entrust my spirit.

**You are wonderful,
and while everyone watches,
you store up blessings for all
who honor and trust you.**

℟. Into your hands, O Lord, I entrust my spirit.

☐2   Psalm 34:1-2, 3-4, 7-8

℟. (5b) The Lord set me free from all my fears.

**I will always praise the Lord.
With all my heart,
I will praise the Lord.**

Let all who are helpless
listen and be glad.

> ℟. The Lord set me free from all my fears.

Honor the Lord with me!
Celebrate his great name.
I asked the Lord for help,
and he saved me
from all my fears.

> ℟. The Lord set me free from all my fears.

If you honor the Lord,
his angel will protect you.
Discover for yourself
that the Lord is kind.
Come to him for protection,
and you will be glad.

> ℟. The Lord set me free from all my fears.

[459] ALLELUIA VERSE AND VERSE BEFORE THE GOSPEL

2 Corinthians 1:3b-4a

Blessed be the Father of mercies and the God of all comfort,
who consoles us in all our afflictions.

[460] GOSPEL

If a grain of wheat falls on the ground and dies,
it yields a rich harvest.

✢ A reading from the holy gospel according to John   12:24-26

Jesus said to his disciples:
   "I tell you for certain that a grain of wheat that falls on the ground
      will never be more than one grain unless it dies.
But if it dies, it will produce lots of wheat.

"If you love your life, you will lose it.
If you give it up in this world,
   you will be given eternal life.

"If you serve me, you must go with me.
My servants will be with me wherever I am.
If you serve me, my Father will honor you."

The gospel of the Lord.

COMMON OF PASTORS

[461]
OLD TESTAMENT READING

*As a shepherd keeps all his flock in view,
so shall I keep my sheep in view.*

A reading from the book of the prophet Ezekiel 34:11-16abce

The Lord says this:
"I, the Lord God, will look for my people
    and take care of them myself.
As a shepherd looks for sheep that have wandered away,
    I will search for my scattered people.
I will rescue them from all the places where they went
    on that dark and gloomy day.
I will bring them back from the foreign countries
    and protect them on the mountains,
    in the valleys, and wherever they settle.

"My people will be like sheep grazing and resting
    in good pastures and on Israel's mountains.
I, the Lord All-Powerful, will lead them there and watch over them.

"I will look for the lost sheep
    and bring back the ones that have wandered off.
If any are hurt,
    I will bandage their wounds.
If any are weak,
    I will help them.
I will take good care of my people!"

                                                    The word of the Lord.

[462]
RESPONSORIAL PSALM

[1]   Psalm 23:1-3a, 3b-4, 6

℟. (1) The Lord is my shepherd; there is nothing I shall want.

You, Lord, are my shepherd.
I will never be in need.
You let me rest in fields
of green grass.
You lead me to streams
of peaceful water,
and you refresh my life.

℟. The Lord is my shepherd; there is nothing I shall want.

**You are true to your name,
and you lead me
along the right paths.
I may walk through valleys
as dark as death,
but I won't be afraid.
You are with me,
and your shepherd's rod
makes me feel safe.**

℟. The Lord is my shepherd; there is nothing I shall want.

**Your kindness and love
will always be with me
each day of my life,
and I will live forever
in your house, Lord.**

℟. The Lord is my shepherd; there is nothing I shall want.

2

Psalm 96:1-2a, 2b-3, 7-8a, 10

℟. (3) Proclaim God's marvelous deeds to all the nations.

**Sing a new song to the Lord!
Everyone on this earth,
sing praises to the Lord,
sing and praise his name.**

℟. Proclaim God's marvelous deeds to all the nations.

**Day after day announce,
"The Lord has saved us!"
Tell every nation on earth,
"The Lord is wonderful
and does marvelous things!"**

℟. Proclaim God's marvelous deeds to all the nations.

**Tell everyone of every nation,
"Praise the glorious power
of the Lord.
He is wonderful! Praise him!"**

℟. Proclaim God's marvelous deeds to all the nations.

Announce to the nations,
"The Lord is King!
The world stands firm,
never to be shaken,
and he will judge its people
with fairness."

℟. Proclaim God's marvelous deeds to all the nations.

[463] ALLELUIA VERSE AND VERSE BEFORE THE GOSPEL

Matthew 28:19a, 20b

Go and teach all people my gospel;
I am with you always, until the end of the world.

[464]   GOSPEL
[For Missionaries]

☐ 1

Go and teach all people my gospel.

✠ A reading from the holy gospel according to Matthew   28:16-20

Jesus' eleven disciples went to a mountain in Galilee,
   where Jesus had told them to meet him.
They saw him and worshiped him,
   but some of them doubted.

Jesus came to them and said:
"I have been given all authority in heaven and on earth!
Go to the people of all nations and make them my disciples.
Baptize them in the name of the Father,
   the Son, and the Holy Spirit,
   and teach them to do everything I have told you.

"I will be with you always,
   even until the end of the world."

The gospel of the Lord.

☐ 2

I will make you fishers of people.

✠ A reading from the holy gospel according to Mark   1:14-20

After John was arrested,
   Jesus went to Galilee and told the good news that comes from God.
He said, "The time has come!

God's kingdom will soon be here.
Turn back to God and believe the good news!"

As Jesus was walking along the shore of Lake Galilee,
    he saw Simon and his brother Andrew.
They were fishermen and were casting their nets into the lake.
Jesus said to them, "Come with me!
I will teach you how to bring in people instead of fish."
Right then the two brothers dropped their nets and went with him.

Jesus walked on and soon saw James and John, the sons of Zebedee.
They were in a boat, mending their nets.
At once Jesus asked them to come with him.
They left their father in the boat with the hired workers
    and went with him.

The gospel of the Lord.

[For a Pope]

3
           Feed my lambs, feed my sheep.

✣ **A reading from the holy gospel according to John**   21:15-17

When Jesus and his disciples had finished eating, he asked,
    "Simon son of John, do you love me more than the others do?"

Simon Peter answered, "Yes, Lord, you know I do!"
"Then feed my lambs," Jesus said.

Jesus asked a second time, "Simon son of John, do you love me?"
Peter answered, "Yes, Lord, you know I love you!"
"Then take care of my sheep," Jesus told him.

Jesus asked a third time, "Simon son of John, do you love me?"

Peter was hurt because Jesus had asked him three times if he loved him.
So he told Jesus, "Lord, you know everything.
You know I love you."

Jesus replied, "Feed my sheep."

The gospel of the Lord.

COMMON OF DOCTORS OF THE CHURCH

[465] ## OLD TESTAMENT READING

I give you a heart wise and shrewd.

A reading from the first book of Kings   3:11-14

The Lord said to Solomon:
"I will answer your prayer.
You will be wise and know more than anyone who has ever lived
    or ever will live.
You didn't ask to live a long time or to be rich,
    and you didn't ask for your enemies to be destroyed.
All you wanted was to be honest and fair.

"But I will give you more than you have asked for.
I will make you rich and respected.
You will be the most famous king of your time.
And if you obey me and keep all my laws and commands,
    as your father David did,
    I will give you a long life."

                                      The word of the Lord.

[466] ## NEW TESTAMENT READING

[1]

Unity in the work of service, building up the body of Christ.

A reading from the letter of Paul to the Ephesians   4:1-7

Brothers and sisters:
As a prisoner of the Lord,
    I beg you to live in a way that is worthy of the people
        God has chosen to be his own.
Always be humble and gentle.
Patiently put up with each other and love each other.
Try your best to let God's Spirit keep your hearts united.
Do this by living at peace.

All of you are part of the same body.
There is only one Spirit of God,
    just as you were given one hope
        when you were chosen to be God's people.

We have only one Lord, one faith, and one baptism.
There is one God who is the Father of all people.
Not only is God above all others,
> but he works by using all of us,
> and he lives in all of us.

Christ has generously divided out his gifts to us.

The word of the Lord.

☐2

God chose some of us so that his people would learn to serve
and his body grow strong.

A reading from the letter of Paul to the Ephesians   4:11-13

Brothers and sisters:
  Christ chose some of us to be apostles, prophets,
> missionaries, pastors, and teachers,
so that his people would learn to serve
> and his body would grow strong.

This will continue until we are united by our faith
> and by our understanding of the Son of God.
Then we will be mature, just as Christ is,
> and we will be completely like him.

The word of the Lord.

RESPONSORIAL PSALM

Psalm 19:7, 8

℟. (John 6:63c) Your words, Lord, are spirit and life.

The Law of the LORD is perfect;
it gives us new life.
His teachings last forever,
and they give wisdom
to ordinary people.

  ℟. Your words, Lord, are spirit and life.

The LORD's instruction is right;
it makes our hearts glad.
His commands shine brightly,
and they give us light.

  ℟. Your words, Lord, are spirit and life.

[468] **ALLELUIA VERSE AND VERSE BEFORE THE GOSPEL**

> The seed is the word of God, Christ is the sower;
> all who come to him will live for ever.

[469] **GOSPEL**

The sower went out to sow seed.

✢ A reading from the holy gospel according to Mark   4:1-9

The next time Jesus taught beside Lake Galilee,
   a big crowd gathered.
It was so large that he had to sit in a boat out on the lake,
   while the people stood on the shore.
He used stories to teach them many things,
   and this is part of what he taught:

"Now listen!
A farmer went out to scatter seed in a field.
While the farmer was scattering the seed,
   some of it fell along the road and was eaten by birds.

"Other seeds fell on thin, rocky ground and quickly started growing
   because the soil was not very deep.
But when the sun came up,
   the plants were scorched and dried up,
   because they did not have enough roots.

"Some other seeds fell where thorn bushes grew up
      and choked out the plants.
So they did not produce any grain.

"But a few seeds did fall on good ground
      where the plants grew and produced thirty or sixty
      or even a hundred times as much as was scattered."

Then Jesus said, "If you have ears, pay attention."

The gospel of the Lord.

COMMON OF SAINTS

[470] **NEW TESTAMENT READING**

[For Religious]

☐1 The whole group of believers was united, heart and soul.

A reading from the Acts of the Apostles 4:32-35

The followers of Jesus all felt the same way about everything.
None of them claimed that their belongings were their own,
 and they shared everything they had with each other.

In a powerful way the apostles told everyone
 that the Lord Jesus was now alive.

God greatly blessed his followers,
 and no one went in need of anything.
Everyone who owned land or houses would sell them
 and bring the money to the apostles.
Then they would give the money to anyone who needed it.

The word of the Lord.

☐2 God has chosen what is weak by human reckoning.

A reading from the first letter of Paul to the Corinthians 1:26-31

My dear friends,
 remember what you were when God chose you.
The people of this world didn't think that many of you were wise.
Only a few of you were in places of power,
 and not many of you came from important families.

But God chose the foolish things of this world to put the wise to shame.
He chose the weak things of this world to put the powerful to shame.

What the world thinks is worthless, useless, and nothing at all
  is what God has used
   to destroy what the world considers important.
God did all this to keep anyone from bragging to him.
You are God's children.
He sent Christ Jesus to save us
 and to make us wise, acceptable, and holy.

So if you want to brag,
> do what the Scriptures say and brag about the Lord.

The word of the Lord.

3 — Love never ends.

A reading from the first letter of Paul to the Corinthians 13:4-13

Brothers and sisters:
> Love is kind and patient,
> > never jealous, boastful, proud, or rude.
>
> Love isn't selfish or quick tempered.
> It doesn't keep a record of wrongs that others do.
> Love rejoices in the truth, but not in evil.
> Love is always supportive, loyal, hopeful, and trusting.
> Love never fails!
>
> Everyone who prophesies will stop,
> > and unknown languages will no longer be spoken.
>
> All that we know will be forgotten.
> We don't know everything,
> > and our prophecies are not complete.
>
> But what is perfect will someday appear,
> > and what is not perfect will then disappear.
>
> When we were children,
> > we thought and reasoned as children do.
>
> But when we grew up,
> > we quit our childish ways.
>
> Now all we can see of God is like a cloudy picture in a mirror.
> Later we will see him face to face.
> We don't know everything,
> > but then we will,
> > > just as God completely understands us.
>
> For now there are faith, hope, and love.
> But of these three, the greatest is love.

The word of the Lord.

4

Fill your minds with everything that is holy.

A reading from the letter of Paul to the Philippians   4:4-9

Brothers and sisters:
Always be glad because of the Lord!
I will say it again: Be glad.

Always be gentle with others.
The Lord will soon be here.
Don't worry about anything,
    but pray about everything.

With thankful hearts offer up your prayers and requests to God.
Then, because you belong to Christ Jesus,
    God will bless you with peace
        that no one can completely understand.
And this peace will control the way you think and feel.

Finally, my friends,
    keep your minds on whatever is true, pure, right,
        holy, friendly, and proper.
Don't ever stop thinking about what is truly worthwhile
    and worthy of praise.
You know the teachings I gave you,
    and you know what you heard me say and saw me do.

So follow my example.
And God, who gives peace, will be with you.

The word of the Lord.

5

*Each one of you has received a special gift;
put yourselves at the service of others.*

A reading from the first letter of Peter   4:7b-11

Brothers and sisters:
Be serious and be sensible enough to pray.

Most important of all, you must sincerely love each other,
    because love wipes away many sins.

Welcome people into your home and don't grumble about it.

Each of you has been blessed with one of God's many wonderful gifts
> to be used in the service of others.
So use your gift well.

If you have the gift of speaking,
> preach God's message.
If you have the gift of helping others,
> do it with the strength that God supplies.

Everything should be done in a way that will bring honor to God
> because of Jesus Christ,
> > who is glorious and powerful forever. Amen.

The word of the Lord.

6

We should lay down our lives for our brothers and sisters.

A reading from the first letter of John   3:16-18

Beloved:
> We know what love is because Jesus gave his life for us.
That's why we must give our lives for each other.

If we have all we need and see one of our own people in need,
> we must have pity on that person,
> or else we cannot say we love God.

Children, you show love for others by truly helping them,
> and not merely by talking about it.

The word of the Lord.

7

This is the victory over the world—our faith.

A reading from the first letter of John   5:2-5

Beloved:
> If we love and obey God,
> we know that we will love his children.
We show our love for God by obeying his commandments,
> and they are not hard to follow.

Every child of God can defeat the world,
> **and our faith is what gives us this victory.**
No one can defeat the world
> **without having faith in Jesus as the Son of God.**

> The word of the Lord.

RESPONSORIAL PSALM

1

Psalm 34:1-2, 3-4, 8-9

℟. (2a) I will bless the Lord at all times.
or:
℟. (9a) Taste and see the goodness of the Lord.

I will always praise the LORD.
With all my heart,
I will praise the LORD.
Let all who are helpless
listen and be glad.

℟. I will bless the Lord at all times.
or:
℟. Taste and see the goodness of the Lord.

Honor the LORD with me!
Celebrate his great name.
I asked the LORD for help,
and he saved me
from all my fears.

℟. I will bless the Lord at all times.
or:
℟. Taste and see the goodness of the Lord.

Discover for yourself
that the LORD is kind.
Come to him for protection,
and you will be glad.
Honor the LORD!
You are his special people.
No one who honors the LORD
will ever be in need.

℟. I will bless the Lord at all times.
or:
℟. Taste and see the goodness of the Lord.

[2] Psalm 103:1-2, 3-4, 17-18a

℟. (1a) O bless the Lord, my soul!

With all my heart
I praise the LORD,
and with all that I am
I praise his holy name!
With all my heart
I praise the LORD!
I will never forget
how kind he has been.

℟. O bless the Lord, my soul!

The LORD forgives our sins,
heals us when we are sick,
and protects us from death.
His kindness and love
are a crown on our heads.

℟. O bless the Lord, my soul!

The LORD is always kind
to those who worship him,
and he keeps his promises
to their descendants
who faithfully obey him.

℟. O bless the Lord, my soul!

[472] ALLELUIA VERSE AND VERSE BEFORE THE GOSPEL

Matthew 23:11, 12

**Whoever is greatest among you will serve the rest.
All who humble themselves shall be exalted.**

[473] GOSPEL

[1]

Unless you become like children,
you will not enter the kingdom of heaven.

✢ A reading from the holy gospel according to Matthew   18:1-4

The disciples came to Jesus and asked him
    who would be the greatest in the kingdom of heaven.
Jesus called a child over and had the child stand near him.

Then he said: "I promise you this.
If you don't change and become like this child,
    you will never get into the kingdom of heaven.
But if you are as humble as this child,
    you are the greatest in the kingdom of heaven."

The gospel of the Lord.

[For Those Who Work for the Underprivileged]

2

Whatever you have done to the very least
of my brothers and sisters, you have done to me.

✣ A reading from the holy gospel according to Matthew   25:31-40

Jesus said to his disciples:
"When the Son of Man comes in his glory with all of his angels,
    he will sit on his royal throne.

"The people of all nations will be brought before him,
    and he will separate them,
    as shepherds separate their sheep from their goats.

"He will place the sheep on his right and the goats on his left.
Then the king will say to those on his right,
'My father has blessed you!
Come and receive the kingdom that was prepared for you
    before the world was created.
When I was hungry, you gave me something to eat,
    and when I was thirsty, you gave me something to drink.
When I was a stranger, you welcomed me,
    and when I was naked, you gave me clothes to wear.
When I was sick, you took care of me,
    and when I was in jail, you visited me.'

"Then the ones who pleased the Lord will ask,
'When did we give you something to eat or drink?
When did we welcome you as a stranger or give you clothes to wear
    or visit you while you were sick or in jail?'

"The king will answer,
'Whenever you did it for any of my people,
    no matter how unimportant they seemed,
    you did it for me.' "

The gospel of the Lord.

[For Educators]

3 Whenever you have accepted graciously a small child,
you have accepted me.

✢ A reading from the holy gospel according to Mark   9:33-37

Jesus and his disciples went to his home in Capernaum.
After they were inside the house, Jesus asked them,
"What were you arguing about along the way?"
They had been arguing about which one of them was the greatest,
and so they did not answer.

After Jesus sat down and told the twelve disciples
to gather around him,
he said, "If you want the place of honor,
you must become a slave and serve others!"

Then Jesus had a child stand near him.
He put his arm around the child and said,
"When you welcome even a child because of me, you welcome me.
And when you welcome me,
you welcome the one who sent me."

The gospel of the Lord.

[For Religious]

4 It has pleased the Father to give you the kingdom.

✢ A reading from the holy gospel according to Luke   12:32-34

Jesus said to his disciples:
"My little group of disciples, don't be afraid!
Your Father wants to give you the kingdom.

"Sell what you have and give the money to the poor.
Make yourselves moneybags that never wear out.
Make your treasure safe in heaven,
where thieves cannot steal it and moths cannot destroy it.
Your heart will always be where your treasure is."

The gospel of the Lord.

SACRAMENTS

BAPTISM

[474]   **OLD TESTAMENT READING**

> I shall pour clean water over you
> and you will be cleansed from all your sins.

A reading from the book of the prophet Ezekiel   36:24-28

The Lord says this:
"I will bring all of you back home
    from those foreign nations and countries.
I will sprinkle you with clean water,
    and you will be clean.
I will wash away everything that makes you unclean,
    and I will remove your idols.

"I will give you a new heart and a new mind.
In place of your stone heart,
    I will give you a heart with feeling.
I will put my Spirit in you
    and make you eager to obey my teachings and laws.
You will live in the land that I gave your ancestors.
You will be my people, and I will be your God."

                                          The word of the Lord.

[475]   **NEW TESTAMENT READING**

[1]
> In the one Spirit we were all baptized into one body.

A reading from the first letter of Paul to the Corinthians   12:12-13

Brothers and sisters:
   The body of Christ has many different parts,
    just as any other body does.
Some of us are Jews, and others are Gentiles.
Some of us are slaves, and others are free.
But God's Spirit baptized each of us
    and made us part of the body of Christ.
Now we each drink from that same Spirit.

                                          The word of the Lord.

2

All baptized in Christ have put on Christ.

A reading from the letter of Paul to the Galatians 3:26-28

Brothers and sisters:
All of you are God's children because of your faith in Christ Jesus.
And when you were baptized,
    it was as though you had put on Christ
        in the same way you put on new clothes.
Faith in Christ Jesus is what makes each of you equal with each other,
    whether you are a Jew or a Greek,
    a slave or a free person,
    a man or a woman.

                                  The word of the Lord.

[476]

1

RESPONSORIAL PSALM

                                          Psalm 23:1-3a, 3b-4, 5-6

℟. (1) The Lord is my shepherd; there is nothing I shall want.

**You, Lord, are my shepherd.
I will never be in need.
You let me rest in fields
of green grass.
You lead me to streams
of peaceful water,
and you refresh my life.**

℟. The Lord is my shepherd; there is nothing I shall want.

**You are true to your name,
and you lead me
along the right paths.
I may walk through valleys
as dark as death,
but I won't be afraid.
You are with me,
and your shepherd's rod
makes me feel safe.**

℟. The Lord is my shepherd; there is nothing I shall want.

**You treat me to a feast,
while my enemies watch.**

You honor me as your guest,
and you fill my cup
until it overflows.
Your kindness and love
will always be with me
each day of my life,
and I will live forever
in your house, Lord.

℟. The Lord is my shepherd; there is nothing I shall want.

2⃞ Psalm 27:1, 4, 13-14

℟. (1a) The Lord is my light and my salvation.

You, Lord, are the light
that keeps me safe.
I am not afraid of anyone.
You protect me,
and I have no fears.

℟. The Lord is my light and my salvation.

I ask only one thing, Lord:
Let me live in your house
every day of my life
to see how wonderful you are
and to pray in your temple.

℟. The Lord is my light and my salvation.

I know that I will live
to see how kind you are.
Trust the Lord!
Be brave and strong
and trust the Lord!

℟. The Lord is my light and my salvation.

[477] ALLELUIA VERSE AND VERSE BEFORE THE GOSPEL

John 14:6

I am the way, the truth, and the life, says the Lord;
no one comes to the Father, except through me.

GOSPEL

1

This is the greatest and the first commandment.

✠ A reading from the holy gospel according to Matthew   22:35-40

One of the Pharisees was an expert in the Jewish Law.
He tried to test Jesus by asking,
"Teacher, what is the most important commandment in the Law?"

Jesus answered:
" 'Love the Lord your God with all your heart, soul, and mind.'
This is the first and most important commandment.
The second most important commandment is like this one.
And it is, 'Love others as much as you love yourself.'
All the Law of Moses and the Books of the Prophets
    are based on these two commandments."

The gospel of the Lord.

2

Do not keep the children from me.

✠ A reading from the holy gospel according to Mark   10:13-16

Some people brought their children to Jesus
so that he could bless them by placing his hands on them.
But his disciples told the people to stop bothering him.
When Jesus saw this, he became angry and said,
"Let the children come to me!
Don't try to stop them.
People who are like these little children belong to the kingdom of God.
I promise you that you cannot get into God's kingdom,
    unless you accept it the way a child does."
Then Jesus took the children in his arms
    and blessed them by placing his hands on them.

The gospel of the Lord.

3

Those who live in me, and I in them, will bear much fruit.

✠ A reading from the holy gospel according to John   15:1-4

Jesus said to his disciples:
"I am the true vine,
    and my Father is the gardener.
He cuts away every branch of mine that does not produce fruit.
But he trims clean every branch that does produce fruit,
    so that it will produce even more fruit.

"You are already clean because of what I have said to you.

"Stay joined to me,
    and I will stay joined to you.
Just as a branch cannot produce fruit
        unless it stays joined to the vine,
    you cannot produce fruit unless you stay joined to me."

The gospel of the Lord.

4

Those who live in me, and I in them, will bear much fruit.

✢ **A reading from the holy gospel according to John**   15:5-8

Jesus said to his disciples:
  "I am the vine, and you are the branches.
If you stay joined to me, and I stay joined to you,
    then you will produce lots of fruit.
But you cannot do anything without me.

"If you don't stay joined to me,
    you will be thrown away.
You will be like dry branches
        that are gathered up and burned in a fire.

"Stay joined to me and let my teachings become part of you.
Then you can pray for whatever you want,
    and your prayer will be answered.

"When you become fruitful disciples of mine,
    my Father will be honored."

The gospel of the Lord.

5

I have loved you as my Father has loved me.

✢ **A reading from the holy gospel according to John**   15:9-11

Jesus said to his disciples:
  "I have loved you,
    just as my Father has loved me.
So make sure that I keep on loving you.
If you obey me,
    I will keep loving you,
    just as my Father keeps loving me,
    because I have obeyed him.

"I have told you this to make you as completely happy as I am."

The gospel of the Lord.

CONFIRMATION

(Holy Spirit)

[479]

OLD TESTAMENT READING

1

I will place a new Spirit in your midst.

A reading from the book of the prophet Ezekiel 36:24-28

The Lord says this:
"I will bring all of you back home
    from those foreign nations and countries.
I will sprinkle you with clean water,
    and you will be clean.
I will wash away everything that makes you unclean,
    and I will remove your idols.

"I will give you a new heart and a new mind.
In place of your stone heart,
    I will give you a heart with feeling.
I will put my Spirit in you
    and make you eager to obey my teachings and laws.
You will live in the land that I gave your ancestors.
You will be my people, and I will be your God."

The word of the Lord.

2

I will pour out my Spirit on all people.

A reading from the book of the prophet Joel 3:1-3a

The LORD said:
"When that time comes,
    I will give my Spirit to everyone.
Your sons and daughters will prophesy.

"Your young men will see visions,
    and your old men will have dreams.
In those days I will give my Spirit to my servants, both men and women.
I will work miracles in the sky above and wonders on the earth below."

The word of the Lord.

NEW TESTAMENT READING

1

*They were all filled with the Holy Spirit,
and began to speak different languages.*

A reading from the Acts of the Apostles   2:1-6, 14, 22b-23, 32-33

On the day of Pentecost
   all the Lord's followers were together in one place.
Suddenly there was a noise from heaven like the sound of a mighty wind!
It filled the house where they were meeting.
Then they saw what looked like fiery tongues moving in all directions,
   and a tongue came and settled on each person there.
The Holy Spirit took control of everyone,
   and they began speaking
      whatever languages the Spirit let them speak.

Many religious Jews from every country in the world
   were living in Jerusalem.
And when they heard this noise, a crowd gathered.
But they were surprised,
   because they were hearing everything in their own languages.

Peter stood with the eleven apostles
   and spoke in a loud and clear voice to the crowd:
"Friends and everyone else living in Jerusalem,
   listen carefully to what I have to say!

"God proved that he sent Jesus to you
   by having him work miracles, wonders, and signs.
All of you know this.

"God had already planned and decided
   that Jesus would be handed over to you.
So you took him and had evil men put him to death on a cross.

"All of us can tell you that God has raised Jesus to life!

"Jesus was taken up to sit at the right side of God,
   and he was given the Holy Spirit,
   just as the Father had promised.
Jesus is also the one who has given the Spirit to us,
   and that is what you are now seeing and hearing."

                                      The word of the Lord.

2

The Spirit and our spirit bear united witness that we are children of God.

A reading from the letter of Paul to the Romans 8:14-17

Brothers and sisters:
Only those people who are led by God's Spirit are his children.
God's Spirit doesn't make us slaves who are afraid of him.
Instead, we become his children and call him our Father.
God's Spirit makes us sure that we are his children.

His Spirit lets us know that together with Christ
> we will be given what God has promised.
We will also share in the glory of Christ,
> because we have suffered with him.

The word of the Lord.

3

There is one and the same Spirit giving to each as the Spirit wills.

A reading from the first letter of Paul to the Corinthians 12:4-13

Brothers and sisters:
There are different kinds of spiritual gifts,
> but they all come from the same Spirit.
There are different ways to serve the same Lord,
> and we can each do different things.
Yet the same God works in all of us and helps us in everything we do.

The Spirit has given each of us a special way of serving others.
Some of us can speak with wisdom,
> while others can speak with knowledge,
> but these gifts come from the same Spirit.

To others the Spirit has given great faith
> or the power to heal the sick
> or the power to work mighty miracles.

Some of us are prophets,
> and some of us recognize when God's Spirit is present.
Others can speak different kinds of languages,
> and still others can tell what these languages mean.

But it is the Spirit who does all this
> and decides which gifts to give to each of us.

The body of Christ has many different parts,
> just as any other body does.
Some of us are Jews,
> and others are Gentiles.
Some of us are slaves,
> and others are free.
But God's Spirit baptized each of us
> and made us part of the body of Christ.
Now we each drink from that same Spirit.

> The word of the Lord.

RESPONSORIAL PSALM

1

Psalm 104:1abc and 24bcd, 30-31

℟. (30) Lord, send out your Spirit, and renew the face of the earth.

I praise you, LORD God,
with all my heart.
You are glorious and majestic.
Our LORD, you made so many things;
the whole earth is covered
with your living creatures.

℟. Lord, send out your Spirit, and renew the face of the earth.

You created all of them
by your Spirit,
and you give new life
to the earth.
Our LORD, we pray
that your glory
will last forever
and that you will be pleased
with what you have done.

℟. Lord, send out your Spirit, and renew the face of the earth.

2

Psalm 23:1-3a, 3b-4, 5, 6

℟. (1) The Lord is my shepherd; there is nothing I shall want.

You, LORD, are my shepherd.
I will never be in need.

You let me rest in fields
of green grass.
You lead me to streams
of peaceful water,
and you refresh my life.

℟. The Lord is my shepherd; there is nothing I shall want.

You are true to your name,
and you lead me
along the right paths.
I may walk through valleys
as dark as death,
but I won't be afraid.
You are with me,
and your shepherd's rod
makes me feel safe.

℟. The Lord is my shepherd; there is nothing I shall want.

You treat me to a feast,
while my enemies watch.
You honor me as your guest,
and you fill my cup
until it overflows.

℟. The Lord is my shepherd; there is nothing I shall want.

Your kindness and love
will always be with me
each day of my life,
and I will live forever
in your house, LORD.

℟. The Lord is my shepherd; there is nothing I shall want.

[482] ALLELUIA VERSE AND VERSE BEFORE THE GOSPEL

John 14:16

I will ask the Father
and he will send you the Holy Spirit,
to be with you for ever.

GOSPEL

1

The Spirit of truth will be with you for ever.

✢ A reading from the holy gospel according to John   14:15-17

Jesus said to his disciples:
"If you love me, you will do as I command.
Then I will ask the Father to send you the Holy Spirit
    who will help you and always be with you.
The Spirit will show you what is true.

"The people of this world cannot accept the Spirit,
    because they don't see or know him.
But you know the Spirit, who is with you
    and will keep on living in you."

The gospel of the Lord.

2

The Holy Spirit will teach you everything.

✢ A reading from the holy gospel according to John   14:23-26

Jesus said:
"If anyone loves me, they will obey me.
Then my Father will love them,
    and we will come to them and live in them.
But anyone who doesn't love me,
    won't obey me.
What they have heard me say doesn't really come from me,
    but from the Father who sent me.

"I have told you these things while I am still with you.
But the Holy Spirit will come and help you,
    because the Father will send the Spirit to take my place.
The Spirit will teach you everything
    and will remind you of what I said while I was with you."

The gospel of the Lord.

HOLY EUCHARIST

[484] ## NEW TESTAMENT READING

*They continued in fellowship with the apostles
and in the breaking of bread.*

A reading from the Acts of the Apostles   2:42-47

The followers of Jesus spent their time learning from the apostles,
   and they were like family to each other.
They also broke bread and prayed together.

Everyone was amazed at the many miracles and wonders
   that the apostles worked.

All the Lord's followers often met together,
   and they shared everything they had.
They would sell their property and possessions
   and give the money to whoever needed it.
Day after day they met together in the temple.
They broke bread together in different homes
   and shared their food happily and freely,
   while praising God.
Everyone liked them,
   and each day the Lord added to their group
   others who were being saved.

                                                 The word of the Lord.

[485] ## RESPONSORIAL PSALM

[1]   Psalm 23:1-3a, 3b-4, 5, 6

℟. (1) The Lord is my shepherd; there is nothing I shall want.

**You, Lord, are my shepherd.
I will never be in need.
You let me rest in fields
of green grass.
You lead me to streams
of peaceful water,
and you refresh my life.**

   ℟. The Lord is my shepherd; there is nothing I shall want.

You are true to your name,
and you lead me
along the right paths.
I may walk through valleys
as dark as death,
but I won't be afraid.
You are with me,
and your shepherd's rod
makes me feel safe.

℟. The Lord is my shepherd; there is nothing I shall want.

You treat me to a feast,
while my enemies watch.
You honor me as your guest,
and you fill my cup
until it overflows.

℟. The Lord is my shepherd; there is nothing I shall want.

Your kindness and love
will always be with me
each day of my life,
and I will live forever
in your house, LORD.

℟. The Lord is my shepherd; there is nothing I shall want.

2 Psalm 34:1-2, 3-4, 5-6, 9-10

℟. (9a) Taste and see the goodness of the Lord.

I will always praise the LORD.
With all my heart,
I will praise the LORD.
Let all who are helpless
listen and be glad.

℟. Taste and see the goodness of the Lord.

Honor the LORD with me!
Celebrate his great name.
I asked the LORD for help,
and he saved me
from all my fears.

℟. Taste and see the goodness of the Lord.

Keep your eyes on the L<small>ORD</small>!
You will shine like the sun
and never blush with shame.
I was a nobody, but I prayed,
and the L<small>ORD</small> saved me
from all my troubles.

℟. Taste and see the goodness of the Lord.

Honor the L<small>ORD</small>!
You are his special people.
No one who honors the L<small>ORD</small>
will ever be in need.
Young lions may go hungry
or even starve,
but if you trust the L<small>ORD</small>,
you will never miss out
on anything good.

℟. Taste and see the goodness of the Lord.

3

Psalm 145:10-11, 15-16, 17-18

℟. (16) You open your hand to feed us, Lord; you answer all our needs.

All creation will thank you,
and your loyal people
will praise you.
They will tell about
your marvelous kingdom
and your power.

℟. You open your hand to feed us, Lord; you answer all our needs.

Everyone depends on you,
and when the time is right,
you provide them with food.
By your own hand you satisfy
the desires of all who live.

℟. You open your hand to feed us, Lord; you answer all our needs.

Our L<small>ORD</small>, everything you do
is kind and thoughtful,

and you are near to everyone
whose prayers are sincere.

℟. You open your hand to feed us, Lord; you answer all our needs.

[486] ALLELUIA VERSE AND VERSE BEFORE THE GOSPEL

John 6:51

I am the living bread from heaven, says the Lord;
whoever eats this bread will live for ever.

[487] GOSPEL

1

This is my body. This is my blood.

✛ A reading from the holy gospel according to Mark   14:12-16, 22-26

It was the first day of the Feast of Thin Bread,
   and the Passover lambs were being killed.
Jesus' disciples asked him,
"Where do you want us to prepare the Passover meal?"

Jesus said to two of the disciples,
"Go into the city,
   where you will meet a man carrying a jar of water.
Follow him, and when he goes into a house,
   say to the owner,
'Our teacher wants to know if you have a room
   where he can eat the Passover meal with his disciples.'
The owner will take you upstairs and show you a large room
   furnished and ready for you to use.
Prepare the meal there."

The two disciples went into the city
   and found everything just as Jesus had told them.
So they prepared the Passover meal.

During the meal Jesus took some bread in his hands.
He blessed the bread and broke it.
Then he gave it to his disciples and said,
"Take this. It is my body."

Jesus picked up a cup of wine and gave thanks to God.
He then gave it to his disciples and said,
"Drink it!"
So they all drank some.

Then he said,
"This is my blood,
> which is poured out for many people,
> and with it God makes his agreement.
From now on I will not drink any wine,
> until I drink new wine in God's kingdom."

Then they sang a hymn and went out to the Mount of Olives.

The gospel of the Lord.

|2|

My flesh is real food and my blood is real drink.

✠ A reading from the holy gospel according to John   6:51-58

Jesus said to the crowd:
> "I am the bread from heaven!
Everyone who eats it will live forever.
My flesh is the life-giving bread
> that I give to the people of this world."

They started arguing with each other and asked,
"How can he give us his flesh to eat?"

Jesus answered:
"I tell you for certain that you won't live
> unless you eat the flesh and drink the blood of the Son of Man.
But if you do eat my flesh and drink my blood,
> you will have eternal life,
> and I will raise you to life on the last day.

"My flesh is the true food,
> and my blood is the true drink.
If you eat my flesh and drink my blood,
> you are one with me, and I am one with you.

"The living Father sent me,
> and I have life because of him.
Now everyone who eats my flesh will live because of me.

"The bread that comes down from heaven
> is not like what your ancestors ate.
They died,
> but whoever eats this bread will live forever."

The gospel of the Lord.

RECONCILIATION

[488]

NEW TESTAMENT READING

1

You were once in darkness;
now you are light in the Lord;
so walk as children of the light.

A reading from the letter of Paul to the Ephesians   5:1-2, 8-10

Brothers and sisters:
  Do as God does.
After all, you are his dear children.
Let love be your guide.
Christ loved us and offered his life for us
      as a sacrifice that pleases God.

You used to be like people living in the dark,
    but now you are people of the light
    because you belong to the Lord.
So act like people of the light
    and make your light shine.
Be good and honest and truthful,
    as you try to please the Lord.

The word of the Lord.

2

What use is it if someone says that he or she believes
and does not manifest it in works?

A reading from the letter of James   2:14-17

My friends,
  what good is it to say you have faith,
    when you don't do anything
      to show that you really do have faith?
Can that kind of faith save you?

If you know someone who doesn't have any clothes or food,
    you shouldn't just say, "I hope all goes well for you.
I hope you will be warm and have plenty to eat."

What good is it to say this,
    unless you do something to help?
Faith that doesn't lead us to do good deeds is all alone and dead!

The word of the Lord.

3

> Those who conquer will inherit all this,
> and I will be their God, and they will be my children.

A reading from the book of Revelation 21:1-8

I, John, saw a new heaven and a new earth.
The first heaven and the first earth had disappeared,
and so had the sea.
Then I saw New Jerusalem, that holy city,
    coming down from God in heaven.
It was like a bride dressed in her wedding gown
    and ready to meet her husband.

I heard a loud voice shout from the throne:
"God's home is now with his people.
He will live with them,
    and they will be his own.
Yes, God will make his home among his people.
He will wipe all tears from their eyes,
    and there will be no more death, suffering, crying, or pain.
These things of the past are gone forever."

Then the one sitting on the throne said:
"I am making everything new.
Write down what I have said.
My words are true and can be trusted.
Everything is finished!

"I am Alpha and Omega,
    the beginning and the end.
I will freely give water from the life-giving fountain
    to everyone who is thirsty.
All who win the victory will be given these blessings.
I will be their God, and they will be my people.

"But I will tell you what will happen to cowards
    and to everyone who is unfaithful or dirty-minded
    or who murders or is sexually immoral
    or uses witchcraft or worships idols or tells lies.
They will be thrown into that lake of fire and burning sulphur.
This is the second death."

The word of the Lord.

RESPONSORIAL PSALM

Psalm 25:4-5abc, 8-9, 10 and 14

1

℟. (1) To you, O Lord, I lift my soul.

**Show me your paths
and teach me to follow;
guide me by your truth
and instruct me.
You keep me safe.**

℟. To you, O Lord, I lift my soul.

**You are honest and merciful,
and you teach sinners
how to follow your path.
You lead humble people
to do what is right
and to stay on your path.**

℟. To you, O Lord, I lift my soul.

**In everything you do,
you are kind and faithful
to everyone who keeps
our agreement with you.
Our Lord, you are the friend
of your worshipers,
and you make an agreement
with all of us.**

℟. To you, O Lord, I lift my soul.

2

Psalm 119:1-2, 4-5, 17-18, 33-34

℟. (1) Happy are they who follow the law of the Lord!

**Our Lord, you bless everyone
who lives right
and obeys your Law.
You bless all of those
who follow your commands
from deep in their hearts.**

℟. Happy are they who follow the law of the Lord!

**You have ordered us always
to obey your teachings;**

I don't ever want to stray
from your laws.

℟. Happy are they who follow the law of the Lord!

Treat me with kindness, Lord,
so that I may live
and do what you say.
Open my mind
and let me discover
the wonders of your Law.

℟. Happy are they who follow the law of the Lord!

Point out your rules to me,
and I won't disobey
even one of them.
Help me to understand your Law;
I promise to obey it
with all my heart.

℟. Happy are they who follow the law of the Lord!

ALLELUIA VERSE AND VERSE BEFORE THE GOSPEL

Psalm 33:22

Lord, let your mercy be on us,
as we place our trust in you.

GOSPEL

1

Let your light shine before all.

✠ A reading from the holy gospel according to Matthew   5:13-16

Jesus said to his disciples:
"You are like salt for everyone on earth.
But if salt no longer tastes like salt,
   how can it make food salty?
All it is good for is to be thrown out and walked on.

"You are like light for the whole world.
A city built on top of a hill cannot be hidden,
   and no one would light a lamp and put it under a clay pot.
A lamp is placed on a lamp stand,
   where it can give light to everyone in the house.

Make your light shine,
> so that others will see the good that you do
> and will praise your Father in heaven."

The gospel of the Lord.

2

Father, I have sinned.

✣ A reading from the holy gospel according to Luke   15:1-3, 11b-32

Tax collectors and sinners were all crowding around to listen to Jesus.
So the Pharisees and the teachers of the Law of Moses
> started grumbling,
"This man is friendly with sinners.
He even eats with them."

Then Jesus told them this story:

"Once a man had two sons.
The younger son said to his father,
'Give me my share of the property.'
So the father divided his property between his two sons.

"Not long after that,
> the younger son packed up everything he owned
>> and left for a foreign country,
>
> where he wasted all his money in wild living.

He had spent everything,
> when a bad famine spread through that whole land.

Soon he had nothing to eat.

"He went to work for a man in that country,
> and the man sent him out to take care of his pigs.

He would have been glad to eat what the pigs were eating,
> but no one gave him a thing.

"Finally, he came to his senses and said,
'My father's workers have plenty to eat,
> and here I am, starving to death!

I will leave and go to my father and say to him,
"Father, I have sinned against God in heaven and against you.
I am no longer good enough to be called your son.
Treat me like one of your workers." '

"The younger son got up and started back to his father.
But when he was still a long way off,
> his father saw him and felt sorry for him.

He ran to his son and hugged and kissed him.

"The son said,
'Father, I have sinned against God in heaven and against you.
I am no longer good enough to be called your son.'

"But his father said to the servants,
'Hurry and bring the best clothes and put them on him.
Give him a ring for his finger and sandals for his feet.
Get the best calf and prepare it,
    so we can eat and celebrate.
This son of mine was dead,
    but has now come back to life.
He was lost and has now been found.'
And they began to celebrate.

"The older son had been out in the field.
But when he came near the house,
    he heard the music and dancing.
So he called one of the servants over and asked,
'What's going on here?'

"The servant answered,
'Your brother has come home safe and sound,
    and your father ordered us to kill the best calf.'
The older brother got so mad
    that he would not even go into the house.

"His father came out and begged him to go in.
But he said to his father,
'For years I have worked for you like a slave
    and have always obeyed you.
But you have never even given me a little goat,
    so that I could give a dinner for my friends.
This other son of yours wasted your money on bad women.
And now that he has come home,
    you ordered the best calf to be killed for a feast.'

"His father replied,
'My son, you are always with me,
    and everything I have is yours.
But we should be glad and celebrate!
Your brother was dead,
    but he is now alive.
He was lost and has now been found.' "

The gospel of the Lord.

MASSES FOR VARIOUS NEEDS AND OCCASIONS

BEGINNING OF THE SCHOOL YEAR

[492]   **NEW TESTAMENT READING**

Do not give any food to those who refuse to work.

A reading from the second letter of Paul to the Thessalonians 3:6-12, 16

My dear friends,
in the name of the Lord Jesus,
   I beg you not to have anything to do
      with any of your people who loaf around
      and refuse to obey the instructions we gave you.

You surely know that you should follow our example.
We didn't waste our time loafing,
   and we didn't accept food from anyone without paying for it.
We didn't want to be a burden to any of you,
   so night and day we worked as hard as we could.

We had the right not to work,
   but we wanted to set an example for you.
We also gave you the rule that if you don't work,
   you don't eat.

Now we learn that some of you just loaf around and won't do any work,
   except the work of a busybody.
So, for the sake of our Lord Jesus Christ,
   we ask and beg these people to settle down
      and start working for a living.

I pray that the Lord, who gives peace,
   will keep blessing you with peace no matter where you are.
May the Lord be with all of you.

The word of the Lord.

[493]   **RESPONSORIAL PSALM**

Psalm 95:1-2, 3-5, 6-7abcd

℟. (see 2) Let us come before the Lord and praise him.

Sing joyful songs to the LORD!
Praise the mighty rock
where we are safe.

Come to worship him
with thankful hearts
and songs of praise.

℟. Let us come before the Lord and praise him.

The LORD is the greatest God,
king over all other gods.
He holds the deepest part
of the earth in his hands,
and the mountain peaks
belong to him.
The ocean is the Lord's
because he made it,
and with his own hands
he formed the dry land.

℟. Let us come before the Lord and praise him.

Bow down and worship
the LORD our Creator!
The LORD is our God,
and we are his people,
the sheep he takes care of
in his own pasture.

℟. Let us come before the Lord and praise him.

[494] **ALLELUIA VERSE AND VERSE BEFORE THE GOSPEL**

Philippians 3:8-9

I count all things worthless but this:
to gain Jesus Christ and to be found in him.

[495] **GOSPEL**

1

He sold all that he had and bought the field.

✠ A reading from the holy gospel according to Matthew   13:44-46

Jesus said to his disciples:
"The kingdom of heaven is like what happens
when someone finds treasure hidden in a field
and buries it again.
A person like that is happy and goes and sells everything
in order to buy that field.

"The kingdom of heaven is like what happens
>when a shop owner is looking for fine pearls.
After finding a very valuable one,
>the owner goes and sells everything
>>in order to buy that pearl."

The gospel of the Lord.

2

>Because you have been faithful in small matters,
>come into the joy of your master.

☩ A reading from the holy gospel according to Matthew 25:14-30

Jesus told his disciples this story about the kingdom of God:
"The kingdom is also like what happened when a man went away
>and put his three servants in charge of all he owned.
The man knew what each servant could do.
So he handed five thousand coins to the first servant,
>two thousand to the second,
>and one thousand to the third.
Then he left the country.

"As soon as the man had gone,
>the servant with the five thousand coins
>>used them to earn five thousand more.
The servant who had two thousand coins did the same with his money
>and earned two thousand more.
But the servant with one thousand coins dug a hole
>and hid his master's money in the ground.

"Some time later the master of those servants returned.
He called them in and asked what they had done with his money.
The servant who had been given five thousand coins
>brought them in with the five thousand that he had earned.
He said, 'Sir, you gave me five thousand coins,
>and I have earned five thousand more.'

" 'Wonderful!' his master replied.
'You are a good and faithful servant.
I left you in charge of only a little,
>but now I will put you in charge of much more.
Come and share in my happiness!'

"Next, the servant who had been given two thousand coins
>   came in and said,
'Sir, you gave me two thousand coins,
>   and I have earned two thousand more.'

" 'Wonderful!' his master replied.
'You are a good and faithful servant.
I left you in charge of only a little,
>   but now I will put you in charge of much more.
Come and share in my happiness!'

"The servant who had been given one thousand coins
>   then came in and said,
'Sir, I know that you are hard to get along with.
You harvest what you don't plant
>   and gather crops where you have not scattered seed.
I was frightened and went out and hid your money in the ground.
Here is every single coin!'

"The master of the servant told him,
'You are lazy and good-for-nothing!
You know that I harvest what I don't plant
>   and gather crops where I have not scattered seed.
You could have at least put my money in the bank,
>   so that I could have earned interest on it.'

"Then the master said,
'Now your money will be taken away
>   and given to the servant with ten thousand coins!
Everyone who has something will be given more,
>   and they will have more than enough.
But everything will be taken from those who don't have anything.
You are a worthless servant,
>   and you will be thrown out into the dark
>   where people will cry and grit their teeth in pain.' "

The gospel of the Lord.

3

The Holy Spirit will teach you everything.

✣ **A reading from the holy gospel according to John** 14:23-26

Jesus said:
"**If anyone loves me, they will obey me.**
Then my Father will love them,
    and we will come to them and live in them.
But anyone who doesn't love me,
    won't obey me.
What they have heard me say doesn't really come from me,
    but from the Father who sent me.

"**I have told you these things while I am still with you.**
But the Holy Spirit will come and help you,
    because the Father will send the Spirit to take my place.
The Spirit will teach you everything
        and will remind you of what I said while I was with you."

The gospel of the Lord.

END OF THE SCHOOL YEAR

[496] ## OLD TESTAMENT READING

Let me sing the praises of the Lord's goodness.

A reading from the book of the prophet Isaiah 63:7

I will tell all the kind deeds that the Lord has done,
because they deserve praise.
The Lord has shown mercy to the people of Israel.
He has been loving and kind.

The word of the Lord.

[497] ## NEW TESTAMENT READING

Above all have love, which is the bond of perfection.

A reading from the letter of Paul to the Colossians 3:12, 15b-17

Brothers and sisters:
God loves you and has chosen you as his own special people.
So be gentle, kind, humble, meek, and patient.

Let the peace that comes from Christ control your thoughts.
And be grateful.

Let the message about Christ completely fill your lives,
while you use all your wisdom to teach and instruct each other.
With thankful hearts,
sing psalms, hymns, and spiritual songs to God.
Whatever you say or do should be done in the name of the Lord Jesus,
as you give thanks to God the Father because of him.

The word of the Lord.

[498] ## RESPONSORIAL PSALM

[1] Psalm 113:1-2, 3-4, 5-6

℟. (see 2) Blessed be the name of the Lord for ever.

Shout praises to the Lord!
Everyone who serves him,
come and praise his name.
Let the name of the Lord
be praised now and forever.

℟. Blessed be the name of the Lord for ever.

**From dawn until sunset
the name of the L**ORD
**deserves to be praised.
The L**ORD **is far above
all of the nations;
he is more glorious
than the heavens.**

℟. Blessed be the name of the Lord for ever.

**No one can compare
with the L**ORD **our God.
His throne is high above,
and he looks down to see
the heavens and the earth.**

℟. Blessed be the name of the Lord for ever.

2   Psalm 150:1-2, 3-4, 5-6

℟. (6) Let everything that breathes praise the Lord!
or:
℟. Alleluia.

Shout praises to the LORD**!
Praise God in his temple.
Praise him in heaven,
his mighty fortress.
Praise our God!
His deeds are wonderful,
too marvelous to describe.**

℟. Let everything that breathes praise the Lord!
or:
℟. Alleluia.

**Praise God with trumpets
and all kinds of harps.
Praise him with tambourines and dancing,
with stringed instruments and woodwinds.**

℟. Let everything that breathes praise the Lord!
or:
℟. Alleluia.

Praise God with cymbals,
with clashing cymbals.
Let every living creature
praise the LORD.
Shout praises to the LORD!

   ℟. Let everything that breathes praise the Lord!
   or:
   ℟. Alleluia.

[499] ALLELUIA VERSE AND VERSE BEFORE THE GOSPEL

Psalm 66:16

Come and listen,
and I will tell what great things God has done for me.

[500] GOSPEL

1

When the mustard seed grows it is the biggest shrub of all
and the birds of the air come and nest in its branches.

✠ A reading from the holy gospel according to Matthew   13:31-32

Jesus told the people this story:
   "The kingdom of heaven is like what happens
     when a farmer plants a mustard seed in a field.
Although it is the smallest of all seeds,
   it grows larger than any garden plant and becomes a tree.
Birds even come and nest on its branches."

The gospel of the Lord.

2

Tell what the Lord has done for you.

✠ A reading from the holy gospel according to Mark   5:18-20

When Jesus was getting into the boat,
   the man who had been healed of the evil spirit
     begged to go with him.
But Jesus would not let him.

Instead, he said, "Go home to your family
   and tell them how much the Lord has done for you
   and how good he has been to you."

The man went away into the region near the ten cities known as Decapolis
   and began telling everyone how much Jesus had done for him.
Everyone who heard what happened was amazed.

The gospel of the Lord.

IN THANKSGIVING

[501] ## OLD TESTAMENT READING

God does great deeds everywhere.

A reading from the book of Sirach 50:22-24

Now let's praise the God of all
who always does such wonderful things
    and treats us with mercy from the day of our birth.
Pray for God to make us happy
    and let Israel live in peace from this day onward.
Ask God to show mercy and save our nation now.

                                         The word of the Lord.

[502] ## RESPONSORIAL PSALM

1
                                                 Psalm 67:1-2, 4

℟. (4a) O God, let all the nations praise you!

**Our God, be kind and bless us!
Be pleased and smile.
Then everyone on earth
will learn to follow you,
and all nations will see
your power to save us.**

℟. O God, let all the nations praise you!

**Let the nations celebrate
with joyful songs,
because you judge fairly
and guide all nations.**

℟. O God, let all the nations praise you!

2
                                        Psalm 113:1-2, 3-4, 5-6

℟. (see 2) Blessed be the name of the Lord for ever.
or:
℟. Alleluia.

**Shout praises to the LORD!
Everyone who serves him,**

come and praise his name.
Let the name of the LORD
be praised now and forever.

> ℟. Blessed be the name of the Lord for ever.
> or:
> ℟. Alleluia.

From dawn until sunset
the name of the LORD
deserves to be praised.
The LORD is far above
all of the nations;
he is more glorious
than the heavens.

> ℟. Blessed be the name of the Lord for ever.
> or:
> ℟. Alleluia.

No one can compare
with the LORD our God.
His throne is high above,
and he looks down to see
the heavens and the earth.

> ℟. Blessed be the name of the Lord for ever.
> or:
> ℟. Alleluia.

[503] ALLELUIA VERSE AND VERSE BEFORE THE GOSPEL

Psalm 138:1bc

> I will give thanks to you with all my heart, O Lord,
> for you have answered me.

[504]

GOSPEL

The man with leprosy threw himself at the feet of Jesus and thanked him.

✝ A reading from the holy gospel according to Luke   17:11-19

On his way to Jerusalem,
Jesus went along the border between Samaria and Galilee.
As he was going into a village,
    ten men with leprosy came toward him.
They stood at a distance and shouted,
"Jesus, Master, have pity on us!"

Jesus looked at them and said,
"Go show yourselves to the priests."

On their way they were healed.
When one of them discovered that he was healed,
    he came back, shouting praises to God.
He bowed down at the feet of Jesus and thanked him.
The man was from the country of Samaria.

Jesus asked, "Weren't ten men healed?
Where are the other nine?
Why was this foreigner the only one who came back to thank God?"

Then Jesus told the man, "You may get up and go.
Your faith has made you well."

The gospel of the Lord.

FOR VOCATIONS

[505]

OLD TESTAMENT READING

1

I shall be with you.

A reading from the book of Exodus 3:1-6, 9-12

One day Moses was taking care of the sheep of Jethro his father-in-law,
who was the priest of Midian.
Moses led the sheep along the edge of the desert to Sinai,
    the mountain of God.
Suddenly the Lord's angel appeared to him from a burning bush.
Moses saw that the bush was on fire,
    but it was not burning up.
He said to himself, "This is strange!
I'll go over and see why the bush is not burning up."

When the Lord saw Moses coming near the bush,
    he called out to him.

Moses answered, "Lord, here I am."

God replied, "Don't come any closer.
Take off your sandals,
    because the ground where you are standing is holy.
I am the God who was worshiped by your ancestors,
    Abraham, Isaac, and Jacob."

Moses was too afraid to look at God, and he hid his face.

The Lord said, "My people have cried out to me,
    and I have seen how cruelly the Egyptians treat them.
Now go to the king.
I am sending you to bring my people out of his country."

But Moses said to God,
"Who am I to go to the king and bring your people out of Egypt?"

God replied,
"I will be with you,
    and you will lead my people out of Egypt.
Then you will know that I am the one who sent you,
    and you will worship me on this mountain."

                                  The word of the Lord.

2⃣ Speak, O Lord, your servant is listening.

A reading from the first book of Samuel 3:1-10

Samuel served the Lord by helping Eli the priest.
But in those days the Lord did not often speak to people
    or appear to them in dreams.

One night Eli, who was almost blind, was in bed as usual.
Samuel was sleeping on a mat
    in the place of worship near the sacred chest.
The lamp was still burning when the Lord called out to Samuel.

"Here I am," Samuel answered.
He ran to Eli and said,
"Here I am, sir. What can I do for you?"

Eli replied, "I didn't call you. Go back to bed."
So Samuel went back.

Once more the Lord called Samuel's name.
Samuel got up.
He went to Eli and said,
"Here I am. What can I do for you?"

But Eli told him, "Son, I didn't call you.
Now go back to sleep."

Samuel did not realize that the Lord was speaking,
    because this was the first time the Lord had spoken to him.
When the Lord spoke a third time that night,
    Samuel again went to Eli and said,
"Here I am. What can I do for you?"

Eli now knew that it was the Lord who was speaking to Samuel.
So Eli told him, "Go back to bed.
If someone speaks to you again,
    answer, 'Lord, I am your servant.
Speak, and I will listen.' "
Once again Samuel went back and lay down.

The Lord came and stood beside Samuel.
Then he called out as he had done before, "Samuel! Samuel!"

The boy replied, "Lord, I am your servant.
Speak, and I will listen."

                                         The word of the Lord.

3   Go to those to whom I send you.

A reading from the book of the prophet Jeremiah   1:4-9

The Lord said to Jeremiah,
"Before I gave you life,
and before you were born,
I chose you to be a prophet to the nations."

I replied, "Lord God, how can I speak for you? I'm too young."

The Lord answered, "Don't say you're too young.
Go to everyone I send you to
   and tell them everything I command you.
Don't be afraid of them!
I, the Lord, will be with you to keep you safe."

Then the Lord reached out his hand.
He touched my lips and said,
"I have now given you the words to say."

                                   The word of the Lord.

[506]   **RESPONSORIAL PSALM**

                                                Psalm 27:1, 4

℟. (8b) I long to see your face, O Lord.

You, Lord, are the light
that keeps me safe.
I am not afraid of anyone.
You protect me,
and I have no fears.

℟. I long to see your face, O Lord.

I ask only one thing, Lord:
Let me live in your house
every day of my life
to see how wonderful you are
and to pray in your temple.

℟. I long to see your face, O Lord.

[507] **ALLELUIA VERSE AND VERSE BEFORE THE GOSPEL**

                                                See John 15:16

I have chosen you from the world, says the Lord,
   to go and bear fruit that will last.

GOSPEL

[508]

① The harvest is rich, but the laborers are few.

✣ A reading from the holy gospel according to Matthew 9:35-38

Jesus went to every town and village.
He taught in their meeting places
    and preached the good news about God's kingdom.
Jesus also healed every kind of disease and sickness.

When he saw the crowds,
    he felt sorry for them.
They were confused and helpless,
    like sheep without a shepherd.

He said to his disciples,
"A large crop is in the fields,
    but there are only a few workers.
Ask the Lord in charge of the harvest
    to send out workers to bring it in."

The gospel of the Lord.

② You will not be without persecutions
but you will be repaid a hundred times over in this life
and in the world to come, you will have eternal life.

✣ A reading from the holy gospel according to Mark 10:28-30

Peter said to Jesus,
    "Remember, we left everything to be your followers!"
Jesus told him:
"You can be sure that anyone who gives up home or brothers or sisters
    or mother or father or children or land
    for me and for the good news will be rewarded.
In this world they will be given a hundred times as many houses
    and brothers and sisters
    and mothers and children
    and pieces of land,
    though they will also be mistreated.

"And in the world to come,
    they will have eternal life."

The gospel of the Lord.

[For Vocations to Holy Orders]

3   From this moment on, you will be fishers of people.

✢ A reading from the holy gospel according to Luke   5:1-11

Jesus was standing on the shore of Lake Gennesaret,
    teaching the people as they crowded around him
    to hear God's message.
Near the shore he saw two boats
    left there by some fishermen who had gone to wash their nets.
Jesus got into the boat that belonged to Simon
    and asked him to row it out a little way from the shore.
Then Jesus sat down in the boat to teach the crowd.

When Jesus had finished speaking, he told Simon,
"Row the boat out into the deep water
    and let your nets down to catch some fish."

"Master," Simon answered,
    "we have worked hard all night long and have not caught a thing.
But if you tell me to, I will let the nets down."

They did it and caught so many fish that their nets began ripping apart.
Then they signaled for their partners in the other boat
    to come and help them.
The men came,
    and together they filled the two boats so full
    that they both began to sink.

When Simon Peter saw this happen,
    he kneeled down in front of Jesus and said,
"Lord, don't come near me!
I am a sinner."

Peter and everyone with him
    were completely surprised at all the fish they had caught.
His partners James and John, the sons of Zebedee, were surprised too.

Jesus told Simon, "Don't be afraid!
From now on you will bring in people instead of fish."
The men pulled their boats up on the shore.
Then they left everything and went with Jesus.

                    The gospel of the Lord.

FOR UNITY OF CHRISTIANS

[509]
OLD TESTAMENT READING

*I shall take you from among the nations,
and I shall give you a new heart.*

A reading from the book of the prophet Ezekiel   36:24-28

The Lord says this:
"I will bring all of you back home
    from those foreign nations and countries.
I will sprinkle you with clean water,
    and you will be clean.
I will wash away everything that makes you unclean,
    and I will remove your idols.

"I will give you a new heart and a new mind.
In place of your stone heart,
    I will give you a heart with feeling.
I will put my Spirit in you
    and make you eager to obey my teachings and laws.
You will live in the land that I gave your ancestors.
You will be my people, and I will be your God."

                                          The word of the Lord.

[510]
RESPONSORIAL PSALM

[1]

                                                   Psalm 23:1-3a, 3b-4, 5, 6

℟. (1) The Lord is my shepherd; there is nothing I shall want.

**You, LORD, are my shepherd.
I will never be in need.
You let me rest in fields
of green grass.
You lead me to streams
of peaceful water,
and you refresh my life.**

℟. The Lord is my shepherd; there is nothing I shall want.

**You are true to your name,
and you lead me
along the right paths.**

I may walk through valleys
as dark as death,
but I won't be afraid.
You are with me,
and your shepherd's rod
makes me feel safe.

℟. The Lord is my shepherd; there is nothing I shall want.

You treat me to a feast,
while my enemies watch.
You honor me as your guest,
and you fill my cup
until it overflows.

℟. The Lord is my shepherd; there is nothing I shall want.

Your kindness and love
will always be with me
each day of my life,
and I will live forever
in your house, Lord.

℟. The Lord is my shepherd; there is nothing I shall want.

2

Psalm 100:1-2, 3, 4, 5

℟. (3c) We are God's people: the sheep of his flock.
or:
℟. (2c) Come with joy into the presence of the Lord.

Shout praises to the Lord,
everyone on this earth.
Be joyful and sing
as you come in
to worship the Lord!

℟. We are God's people: the sheep of his flock.
or:
℟. Come with joy into the presence of the Lord.

You know the Lord is God!
He created us,
and we belong to him;
we are his people,
the sheep in his pasture.

℟. We are God's people: the sheep of his flock.
or:
℟. Come with joy into the presence of the Lord.

Be thankful and praise the Lord
as you enter his temple.

℟. We are God's people: the sheep of his flock.
or:
℟. Come with joy into the presence of the Lord.

The Lord is good!
His love and faithfulness
will last forever.

℟. We are God's people: the sheep of his flock.
or:
℟. Come with joy into the presence of the Lord.

[511] ALLELUIA VERSE AND VERSE BEFORE THE GOSPEL

Colossians 3:15

May the peace of Christ rule in your hearts,
that peace to which all of you are called as one body.

[512] GOSPEL

1

Theirs is the kingdom of heaven.

✢ **A reading from the holy gospel according to Matthew**   5:1-12ab

When Jesus saw the crowds,
he went up on the side of a mountain and sat down.

Jesus' disciples gathered around him, and he taught them:

"God blesses those people who depend only on him.
They belong to the kingdom of heaven!

"God blesses those people who grieve.
They will find comfort!

"God blesses those people who are humble.
The earth will belong to them!

"God blesses those people who want to obey him
> more than to eat or drink.
They will be given what they want!

"God blesses those people who are merciful.
They will be treated with mercy!

"God blesses those people whose hearts are pure.
They will see him!

"God blesses those people who make peace.
They will be called his children!

"God blesses those people who are treated badly for doing right.
They belong to the kingdom of heaven.

"God will bless you when people insult you, mistreat you,
> and tell all kinds of evil lies about you because of me.
Be happy and excited!
You will have a great reward in heaven."

> The gospel of the Lord.

2

> Where two or three meet in my name,
> I shall be there with them.

✠ A reading from the holy gospel according to Matthew 18:19-22

Jesus said to his disciples:
"I promise that when any two of you on earth
> agree about something you are praying for,
my Father in heaven will do it for you.
Whenever two or three of you come together in my name,
> I am there with you."

Peter came up to the Lord and asked,
"How many times should I forgive someone
> who does something wrong to me?
Is seven times enough?"

Jesus answered:
"Not just seven times, but seventy-seven times!"

> The gospel of the Lord.

FOR PEACE AND JUSTICE

[513] ## OLD TESTAMENT READING

The effect of justice will be peace.

A reading from the book of the prophet Isaiah 32:15-20

When the Spirit is given to us from heaven,
 deserts will become orchards,
 and orchards will turn into fertile forests.
Honesty and justice will prosper in the deserts and orchards.

Then justice will produce unending peace and quiet.
My people will live in peace, secure and undisturbed,
 even if hailstones flatten forests and cities.
They will have my blessing,
 as they plant their crops beside streams
 and let their donkeys roam freely about.

The word of the Lord.

[514] ## NEW TESTAMENT READING

1

May the peace of God guard your hearts and your thoughts.

A reading from the letter of Paul to the Philippians 4:6-9

Brothers and sisters:
 Don't worry about anything,
 but pray about everything.

With thankful hearts offer up your prayers and requests to God.
Then, because you belong to Christ Jesus,
 God will bless you with peace
 that no one can completely understand.
And this peace will control the way you think and feel.

Finally, my friends,
 keep your minds on whatever is true, pure, right,
 holy, friendly, and proper.
Don't ever stop thinking about what is truly worthwhile
 and worthy of praise.
You know the teachings I gave you,
 and you know what you heard me say and saw me do.

So follow my example.
And God, who gives peace, will be with you!

                                                         The word of the Lord.

2

                May the peace of Christ rule in your hearts.

A reading from the letter of Paul to the Colossians   3:12-15

Brothers and sisters:
  God loves you and has chosen you as his own special people.
So be gentle, kind, humble, meek, and patient.
Put up with each other,
     and forgive anyone who does you wrong,
     just as Christ has forgiven you.
Love is more important than anything else.
It is what ties everything completely together.

Each one of you is part of the body of Christ,
     and you were chosen to live together in peace.
So let the peace that comes from Christ control your thoughts.
And be grateful.

                                                          The word of the Lord.

RESPONSORIAL PSALM

1

                                                         Psalm 72:1-2, 7-8, 12-13

    ℟. (see 7) Justice shall flourish in his time,
           and fullness of peace for ever.

Please help the king
to be honest and fair
just like you, our God.
Let him be honest and fair
with all your people,
especially the poor.

    ℟. Justice shall flourish in his time,
       and fullness of peace for ever.

Let the king be fair
with everyone,
and let there be peace
until the moon
falls from the sky.

Let his kingdom reach
from sea to sea,
from the Euphrates River
across all the earth.

℟. Justice shall flourish in his time,
and fullness of peace for ever.

Do this because the king
rescues the homeless
when they cry out,
and he helps everyone
who is poor and in need.
The king has pity
on the weak and helpless
and protects those in need.

℟. Justice shall flourish in his time,
and fullness of peace for ever.

2 Psalm 122:1-2, 8-9

℟. (see Sirach 36:18) Give peace, O Lord, to those who wait for you.

It made me glad to hear them say,
"Let's go to the house
of the LORD!"
Jerusalem, we are standing
inside your gates.

℟. Give peace, O Lord, to those who wait for you.

Because of my friends
and my relatives,
I will pray for peace.
And because of the house
of the LORD our God,
I will work for your good.

℟. Give peace, O Lord, to those who wait for you.

[516] ALLELUIA VERSE AND VERSE BEFORE THE GOSPEL

Matthew 5:9

Blessed are the peacemakers;
they shall be called children of God.

GOSPEL

Blessed are the peacemakers: they shall be called children of God.

✟ **A reading from the holy gospel according to Matthew**   5:1-12ab

When Jesus saw the crowds,
he went up on the side of a mountain and sat down.

Jesus' disciples gathered around him, and he taught them:

"God blesses those people who depend only on him.
They belong to the kingdom of heaven!

"God blesses those people who grieve.
They will find comfort!

"God blesses those people who are humble.
The earth will belong to them!

"God blesses those people who want to obey him
      more than to eat or drink.
They will be given what they want!

"God blesses those people who are merciful.
They will be treated with mercy!

"God blesses those people whose hearts are pure.
They will see him!

"God blesses those people who make peace.
They will be called his children!

"God blesses those people who are treated badly for doing right.
They belong to the kingdom of heaven.

"God will bless you when people insult you, mistreat you,
      and tell all kinds of evil lies about you because of me.
Be happy and excited!
You will have a great reward in heaven."

                                                The gospel of the Lord.

FOR PRODUCTIVE LAND AND AFTER THE HARVEST

[518] **OLD TESTAMENT READING**

1

Let the earth produce vegetation and seed-bearing plants.

A reading from the book of Genesis 1:11-12

God said to the earth,
"Make all kinds of green things grow!
Produce grain and fruit trees."

So the earth made all kinds of green things grow.
It produced grain and fruit trees.

The word of the Lord.

2

You will have all you want to eat.

A reading from the book of Deuteronomy 8:7-10

Moses told the people:
"The Lord your God is bringing you into a good land.
It has a lot of streams and springs
    that flow from underground rivers in the valleys and hills.
Wheat and barley grow there,
    and you will also find grapes, figs,
        pomegranates, olives, and honey.

"You will have all you want to eat,
    and you will never run out of food.
You can make iron from the stones in that land,
    and from its hills you can dig copper.

"You will have all you want to eat,
    and you will praise the Lord your God
        for giving you this good land."

The word of the Lord.

[519] **NEW TESTAMENT READING**

God will provide bread for people to eat.

A reading from the second letter of Paul to the Corinthians 9:8-11

Brothers and sisters:
God can bless you with everything you need,
and you will always have more than enough
to do all kinds of good things for others.

The Scriptures say,

"God freely gives his gifts to the poor,
and always does right."

God gives seed to farmers and provides everyone with food.
He will increase what you have,
so that you can give even more to those in need.

You will be blessed in every way,
and you will be able to keep on being generous.
Then many people will thank God when we deliver your gift.

The word of the Lord.

[520] **RESPONSORIAL PSALM**

Psalm 147:5 and 7, 8

℟. (1) Shout praises to the Lord! Our God is kind.

Our Lord is great and powerful!
He understands everything.
Celebrate and sing!
Play your harps
for the Lord our God.

℟. Shout praises to the Lord! Our God is kind.

He fills the sky with clouds
and sends rain to the earth,
so that the hills
will be green with grass.

℟. Shout praises to the Lord! Our God is kind.

[521] **ALLELUIA VERSE AND VERSE BEFORE THE GOSPEL**

Psalm 126:5

Those who sow in tears
shall reap with shouts of joy.

[522]   **GOSPEL**

*Life is not made secure by worldly possessions
even when a person owns them in abundance.*

✢ A reading from the holy gospel according to Luke   12:15-21

Jesus said to the crowd, "Don't be greedy!
Owning a lot of things won't make your life safe."

So Jesus told them this story:

"A rich man's farm produced a big crop,
    and he said to himself, 'What can I do?
I don't have a place large enough to store everything.'

"Later, he said, 'Now I know what I'll do.
I'll tear down my barns and build bigger ones,
    where I can store all my grain and other goods.
Then I'll say to myself,
"You have stored up enough good things to last for years to come.
Live it up! Eat, drink, and enjoy yourself." '

"But God said to him, 'You fool!
Tonight you will die.
Then who will get what you have stored up?'

"This is what happens to people who store up everything for themselves,
    but are poor in the sight of God."

The gospel of the Lord.

FOR REFUGEES AND EXILES

[523] ## OLD TESTAMENT READING

Be sure to welcome strangers into your home.

A reading from the letter to the Hebrews   13:1-3, 14-16

Brothers and sisters:
   Keep being concerned about each other
     as the Lord's followers should.

Be sure to welcome strangers into your home.
By doing this, some people have welcomed angels as guests,
    without even knowing it.

Remember the Lord's people who are in jail and be concerned for them.
Don't forget those who are suffering,
    but imagine that you are there with them.

On this earth we don't have a city that lasts forever,
    but we are waiting for such a city.

Our sacrifice is to keep offering praise to God in the name of Jesus.
But don't forget to help others and to share your possessions with them.
This too is like offering a sacrifice that pleases God.

                       The word of the Lord.

[524] ## RESPONSORIAL PSALM

Psalm 121:1-2, 5-6, 7-8

℟. (2) Our help is from the Lord, who made heaven and earth.

**I look to the hills!
Where will I find help?
It will come from the Lord,
who created the heavens
and the earth.**

℟. Our help is from the Lord, who made heaven and earth.

**The Lord is your protector,
there at your right side
to shade you from the sun.
You won't be harmed**

by the sun during the day
or by the moon at night.

℟. Our help is from the Lord, who made heaven and earth.

The LORD will protect you
and keep you safe
from all dangers.
The LORD will protect you
now and always
wherever you are.

℟. Our help is from the Lord, who made heaven and earth.

[525] ALLELUIA VERSE AND VERSE BEFORE THE GOSPEL

2 Corinthians 1:3b-4a

Blessed be the Father of mercies and the God of all comfort,
who consoles us in all our afflictions.

[526] GOSPEL

Who is my neighbor?

✠ A reading from the holy gospel according to Luke   10:25-37

An expert in the Law of Moses stood up and asked Jesus a question to see what he would say.
"Teacher," he asked,
"What must I do to have eternal life?"

Jesus answered, "What is written in the Scriptures?
How do you understand them?"

The man replied, "The Scriptures say,
'Love the Lord your God with all your heart, soul, strength, and mind.'
They also say, 'Love your neighbors as much as you love yourself.'"

Jesus said, "You have given the right answer.
If you do this, you will have eternal life."

But the man wanted to show that he knew what he was talking about.
So he asked Jesus, "Who are my neighbors?"

Jesus replied:
"As a man was going down from Jerusalem to Jericho,
    robbers attacked him and grabbed everything he had.
They beat him up and ran off, leaving him half dead.

"A priest happened to be going down the same road.
But when he saw the man,
    he walked by on the other side.
Later a temple helper came to the same place.
But when he saw the man who had been beaten up,
    he also went by on the other side.

"A man from Samaria then came traveling along that road.
When he saw the man,
    he felt sorry for him and went over to him.
He treated his wounds with olive oil and wine and bandaged them.
Then he put him on his own donkey and took him to an inn,
    where he took care of him.

"The next morning he gave the innkeeper two silver coins and said,
'Please take care of the man.
If you spend more than this on him,
    I will pay you when I return.' "

Then Jesus asked,
"Which of these three people was a real neighbor
    to the man who was beaten up by robbers?"

The teacher answered, "The one who showed pity."
Jesus said, "Go and do the same!"

                                    The gospel of the Lord.

FOR THE SICK

[527]
NEW TESTAMENT READING

The prayer of faith will save the one who is ill.

A reading from the letter of James   5:13-16

Brothers and sisters:
If you are having trouble, you should pray.
And if you are feeling good, you should sing praises.

If you are sick, ask the church leaders to come and pray for you.
Ask them to pour olive oil on you in the name of the Lord.
If you have faith when you pray for sick people,
    they will get well.
The Lord will heal them,
    and if they have sinned, he will forgive them.

If you have sinned,
    you should tell each other what you have done.
Then you can pray for one another and be healed.

The prayer of an innocent person is powerful,
    and it can help a lot.

                              The word of the Lord.

[528]
RESPONSORIAL PSALM

1
                            Psalm 25:4-5abc, 8-9, 10 and 14, 15-16

    ℟. (1) To you, O Lord, I lift my soul.

**Show me your paths
and teach me to follow;
guide me by your truth
and instruct me.
You keep me safe.**

    ℟. To you, O Lord, I lift my soul.

**You are honest and merciful,
and you teach sinners
how to follow your path.
You lead humble people
to do what is right
and to stay on your path.**

℟. To you, O Lord, I lift my soul.

**In everything you do,
you are kind and faithful
to everyone who keeps
our agreement with you.
Our L**ORD**, you are the friend
of your worshipers,
and you make an agreement
with all of us.**

℟. To you, O Lord, I lift my soul.

**I always look to you,
because you rescue me
from every trap.
I am lonely and troubled.
Show that you care
and have pity on me.**

℟. To you, O Lord, I lift my soul.

2

Psalm 34:1-2, 3-4, 16 and 18

℟. (9a) Taste and see the goodness of the Lord.

I will always praise the LORD**.
With all my heart,
I will praise the L**ORD**.
Let all who are helpless
listen and be glad.**

℟. Taste and see the goodness of the Lord.

Honor the LORD **with me!
Celebrate his great name.
I asked the L**ORD **for help,
and he saved me
from all my fears.**

℟. Taste and see the goodness of the Lord.

**God despises evil people,
and he will wipe them all
from the earth,
till they are forgotten.**

The LORD is there to rescue
all who are discouraged
and have given up hope.

℟. Taste and see the goodness of the Lord.

[529] ALLELUIA VERSE AND VERSE BEFORE THE GOSPEL

Matthew 8:17

Christ bore our sickness,
and endured our suffering.

[530] GOSPEL

Christ bore our sickness.

✛ A reading from the holy gospel according to Matthew   8:14-17

Jesus went to the home of Peter,
  where he found that Peter's mother-in-law
    was sick in bed with fever.
He took her by the hand,
  and the fever left her.
Then she got up and served Jesus a meal.

That evening many people with demons in them were brought to Jesus.
And with only a word he forced out the evil spirits
  and healed everyone who was sick.

So God's promise came true,
  just as the prophet Isaiah had said,

    "He healed our diseases and made us well."

The gospel of the Lord.

FOR THE DEAD

[531] ## OLD TESTAMENT READING

The Lord God will destroy death for ever.

A reading from the book of the prophet Isaiah 25:6a, 7-9

On this mountain the LORD All-Powerful
> will prepare for all nations a feast of the finest foods.

Here the LORD will strip away
> the funeral clothes that cover the nations.

The LORD All-Powerful will destroy the power of death
> and wipe away each tear.

No longer will his people be embarrassed everywhere.
The LORD has spoken!

On that day, people will say,
"The LORD God has saved us!
Let's celebrate.
We waited and waited, and now he is here."

The word of the Lord.

[532] ## NEW TESTAMENT READING

1

*The Father chose us in Christ,
before the creation of the world, to be holy.*

A reading from the letter of Paul to the Ephesians 1:3-5

Brothers and sisters:
> Praise the God and Father of our Lord Jesus Christ
>> for the spiritual blessings that Christ has brought us
>> from heaven!

Before the world was created,
> God let Christ choose us to live with him
>> and to be his holy and innocent and loving people.

God was kind
> and decided that Christ would choose us
> to be God's own adopted children.

The word of the Lord.

2

We shall stay with the Lord for ever.

A reading from the first letter of Paul to the Thessalonians 4:13-14, 18

My friends, we want you to understand how it will be
for those followers who have already died.
Then you won't grieve over them
and be like people who don't have any hope.

We believe that Jesus died and was raised to life.
We also believe that when God brings Jesus back again,
he will bring with him all who had faith in Jesus before they died.

Encourage each other with these words.

The word of the Lord.

3

We shall see God as he really is.

A reading from the first letter of John 3:1-2

Beloved:
Think how much the Father loves us.
He loves us so much that he lets us be called his children,
as we truly are.
But since the people of this world did not know who Christ is,
they don't know who we are.

My dear friends, we are already God's children,
though what we will be has not yet been seen.
But we do know that when Christ returns,
we will be like him,
because we will see him as he truly is.

The word of the Lord.

4

Blessed are those who die in the Lord.

A reading from the book of Revelation 14:13

I, John, heard a voice from heaven say,
"Put this in writing.
From now on, the Lord will bless everyone who has faith in him
when they die."

The Spirit answered, "Yes, they will rest from their hard work,
and they will be rewarded for what they have done."

The word of the Lord.

RESPONSORIAL PSALM

[533]

1

Psalm 23:1-3a, 3b-4, 5, 6

℟. (1) The Lord is my shepherd; there is nothing I shall want.

You, LORD, are my shepherd.
I will never be in need.
You let me rest in fields
of green grass.
You lead me to streams
of peaceful water,
and you refresh my life.

℟. The Lord is my shepherd; there is nothing I shall want.

You are true to your name,
and you lead me
along the right paths.
I may walk through valleys
as dark as death,
but I won't be afraid.
You are with me,
and your shepherd's rod
makes me feel safe.

℟. The Lord is my shepherd; there is nothing I shall want.

You treat me to a feast,
while my enemies watch.
You honor me as your guest,
and you fill my cup
until it overflows.

℟. The Lord is my shepherd; there is nothing I shall want.

Your kindness and love
will always be with me
each day of my life,
and I will live forever
in your house, LORD.

℟. The Lord is my shepherd; there is nothing I shall want.

2

Psalm 27:1, 4, 13-14

℟. (1a) The Lord is my light and my salvation.

You, LORD, are the light that keeps me safe.
I am not afraid of anyone.
You protect me, and I have no fears.

℟. The Lord is my light and my salvation.

I ask only one thing, Lord:
Let me live in your house every day of my life
to see how wonderful you are
and to pray in your temple.

℟. The Lord is my light and my salvation.

I know that I will live to see how kind you are.
Trust the Lord!
Be brave and strong and trust the Lord!

℟. The Lord is my light and my salvation.

[534] ALLELUIA VERSE AND VERSE BEFORE THE GOSPEL

John 11:25a, 26

I am the resurrection and the life, says the Lord,
whoever believes in me will not die for ever.

[535] GOSPEL

1

You have hidden these things from the learned and the clever
and have revealed them to children.

✣ A reading from the holy gospel according to Matthew   11:25-26, 28-30

On one occasion Jesus said:
"My Father, Lord of heaven and earth,
I am grateful that you hid all this from wise and educated people
and showed it to ordinary people.
Yes, Father, that is what pleased you."

Then Jesus said:
"If you are tired from carrying heavy burdens,
come to me and I will give you rest.
Take the yoke I give you.
Put it on your shoulders and learn from me.
I am gentle and humble,
and you will find rest.
This yoke is easy to bear,
and this burden is light."

The gospel of the Lord.

2

Young man, I say to you, arise.

✣ A reading from the holy gospel according to Luke   7:11-17

Jesus and his disciples were on their way to the town of Nain,
and a big crowd was going along with them.

As they came near the gate of the town,
   they saw people carrying out the body of a widow's only son.
Many people from the town were walking along with her.

When the Lord saw the woman,
   he felt sorry for her and said, "Don't cry!"

Jesus went over and touched the stretcher
     on which the people were carrying the dead boy.
They stopped, and Jesus said,
"Young man, get up!"
The man sat up and began to speak.
Jesus then gave him back to his mother.

Everyone was frightened and praised God.
They said, "A great prophet is here with us!
God has come to his people."

News about Jesus spread all over Judea
     and everywhere else in that part of the country.

The gospel of the Lord.

3

I am the resurrection and the life.

✠ A reading from the holy gospel according to John   11:21-27

Martha said to Jesus,
   "Lord, if you had been here,
   my brother would not have died.
Yet even now I know that God will do anything you ask."

Jesus told her, "Your brother will live again!"

Martha answered,
"I know that he will be raised to life on the last day,
   when all the dead are raised."

Jesus then said,
"I am the one who raises the dead to life!
Everyone who has faith in me will live,
   even if they die.
And everyone who lives because of faith in me will never die.
Do you believe this?"

"Yes, Lord!" she replied.
"I believe that you are Christ, the Son of God.
You are the one we hoped would come into the world."

The gospel of the Lord.

INDEXES

INDEX OF READINGS

This Index lists all the readings together with the year, Lectionary number (where applicable), and page (in bold). The readings with no listing for the year are those for weekdays, saints, sacraments, and various needs and occasions.

Reading	Year	No.	Page
Genesis			
1:11-12		518	**873**
1:26—2:3		288	**724**
2:7-9; 3:1-7	A	18	**83**
2:18-24	B	135	**436**
3:9-15	B	84	**286**
3:9-15, 20		429	**781**
9:8-15	B	19	**86**
12:1-4a	A	21	**91**
14:18-20	C	163	**522**
18:1-10a	C	103	**343**
18:20-32	C	106	**352**
50:15-21		180	**578**
Exodus			
3:1-6, 9-12		505	**860**
3:1-8a, 13-15	C	26	**105**
16:2-4, 12-15	B	108	**359**
17:3-7	A	24	**98**
19:1-6a	A	86	**293**
20:1-3, 7-8, 12-17	B	25	**102**
23:20-21a		384	**766**
24:3-8	B	162	**519**
34:4b-6, 8-9	A	158	**507**
Leviticus			
19:1-2, 17-18	A	74	**260**
Numbers			
6:22-27	ABC	15	**73**
11:25-29	B	132	**426**
21:4b-9		370	**758**
Deuteronomy			
4:1-2, 6-8	B	120	**391**
4:39-40	B	159	**510**
5:12-15	B	81	**278**
6:2-6	B	147	**469**
7:6-11	A	164	**525**
8:2-3, 14b-16a	A	161	**516**
8:7-10		518	**873**
10:12-14		182	**583**
11:18, 26-28	A	80	**276**
18:18-19	B	66	**238**
26:4-10	C	20	**88**
30:10-14	C	100	**334**
Joshua			
24:1-2a, 15-17, 18b	B	117	**383**

Reading	Year	No.	Page
1 Samuel			
3:1-10		505	**861**
3:4-10, 19	B	60	**221**
16:1b, 6-7, 10-13a	A	27	**108**
26:2, 7-9, 12-13, 22-23	C	76	**266**
2 Samuel			
5:1-3	C	157	**501**
7:4-5a, 12-14a, 16	C	272	**715**
12:7-10, 13-14	C	88	**299**
1 Kings			
3:5, 7-12	A	104	**346**
3:11-14		465	**812**
8:41-43	C	82	**281**
17:10-16	B	150	**478**
17:17-24	C	85	**290**
19:4-8	B	111	**367**
19:9a, 11-13a	A	110	**364**
19:16b, 19-21	C	94	**316**
2 Kings			
4:8-11, 14-16a	A	92	**310**
4:42-44	B	105	**349**
5:14-17	C	139	**448**
Nehemiah			
8:1-4a, 5-6, 8-10	C	64	**232**
2 Maccabees			
7:1, 20-23		456	**804**
7:1-2, 9-14	C	151	**481**
Job			
7:1-4, 6-7	B	69	**246**
38:1, 8-11	B	90	**304**
Proverbs			
8:22-31	C	160	**513**
9:1-6	B	114	**375**
Wisdom			
1:13-15; 2:23-24a	B	93	**313**
6:12-16	A	149	**474**
7:7-11	B	138	**444**
9:16c-18	C	124	**403**
11:22—12:1	C	148	**471**
12:13, 16-19	A	101	**338**
Sirach			
3:2-6	ABC	14	**70**

Reading	Year	No.	Page
3:17-18, 20	C	121	**394**
15:15-20	A	71	**252**
27:6-7	C	79	**274**
28:2-5, 6b-7	A	125	**405**
35:12b-14, 16-17	C	145	**463**
50:22-24		501	**857**
Isaiah			
2:1-5	A	1	**35**
5:1-7	A	134	**432**
6:1-2a, 3-8	C	70	**249**
9:2-3a, 6-7a		447	**795**
9:2-4	A	62	**227**
9:2-4, 6-7	ABC	13	**67**
11:1b, 5-9		224	**680**
11:1-4a, 5-6, 9b	A	4	**42**
12:4b-5		179	**576**
25:6, 9		229	**690**
25:6-7, 9		201	**629**
25:6-10a	A	137	**441**
25:6a, 7-9		531	**882**
30:18		210	**650**
30:19, 23-24, 26		173	**557**
30:19-20, 23-24, 26		205	**638**
30:19b-21		172	**555**
32:15-20		513	**869**
35:1-2, 5-6ab, 10	A	7	**50**
35:4-7a	B	123	**400**
40:3-5	B	5	**45**
40:10-11		218	**668**
40:25-26, 29-31		174	**560**
41:10		207	**644**
41:14		204	**636**
42:1-2, 4, 6-7	ABC	17	**78**
42:16		208	**646**
43:1-3a, 5		211	**652**
43:18-21	C	32	**124**
43:22-25	B	75	**263**
45:1, 4-6	A	140	**451**
46:4		197	**621**
49:3, 5-6	A	59	**219**
49:14-15	A	77	**269**
50:4-8a	B	126	**409**
50:6-7	A	33	**128**
"	B	34	**134**
"	C	35	**139**
55:1-3	A	107	**356**
55:6-9	A	128	**416**

INDEX OF READINGS

Reading	Year	No.	Page
55:10-11	A	98	**328**
"		203	**634**
56:1, 6-7	A	113	**373**
"		442	**791**
58:6-9		176	**567**
58:7-10	A	68	**243**
60:1-6	ABC	16	**75**
61:1-2	B	8	**53**
62:1-3	C	61	**224**
63:7		496	**854**
66:10-14c	C	97	**325**

Jeremiah

Reading	Year	No.	Page
1:4-5, 17ab, 18-19	C	67	**240**
1:4-8		213	**657**
"		316	**736**
1:4-9		505	**862**
17:7-8	C	73	**257**
20:7-9	A	119	**388**
20:10-12a, 13	A	89	**302**
23:3-6	B	102	**341**
31:7-9	B	144	**460**
31:31-34	B	31	**122**
31:33		222	**676**
33:14-16	C	3	**40**
38:4-6, 8-10	C	115	**378**

Lamentations

Reading	Year	No.	Page
3:22-25		183	**585**

Baruch

Reading	Year	No.	Page
5:1-5, 7	C	6	**47**

Ezekiel

Reading	Year	No.	Page
2:2-5	B	96	**322**
17:22-24	B	87	**296**
18:25-28	A	131	**423**
33:7-9	A	122	**397**
34:11-12, 14-16abce	A	155	**494**
34:11-15		218	**668**
34:11-16abce	C	166	**531**
"		461	**808**
36:24-28		474	**825**
"		479	**830**
"		509	**865**
37:12-14	A	30	**118**
37:21-22, 24		184	**587**

Daniel

Reading	Year	No.	Page
7:13-14	B	156	**498**
12:1-3	B	153	**487**

Hosea

Reading	Year	No.	Page
2:16b, 17b, 21-22	B	78	**272**
6:3-6	A	83	**283**
11:1, 3-4, 8c-9	B	165	**528**
11:3-4		221	**675**

Joel

Reading	Year	No.	Page
3:1-3a		479	**830**

Amos

Reading	Year	No.	Page
7:10-15	B	99	**331**

Jonah

Reading	Year	No.	Page
3:1-5, 10	B	63	**230**

Micah

Reading	Year	No.	Page
5:1-3	C	12	**63**

Habakkuk

Reading	Year	No.	Page
1:2-3; 2:2-4	C	136	**438**

Zephaniah

Reading	Year	No.	Page
2:3; 3:12-13	A	65	**235**
3:14-15	C	9	**56**
3:17-18a		302	**729**

Zechariah

Reading	Year	No.	Page
2:14-15		447	**795**
9:9-10	A	95	**319**

Malachi

Reading	Year	No.	Page
2:8-10	A	146	**466**
3:1-2b		252	**708**
3:19-20	C	154	**490**

Matthew

Reading	Year	No.	Page
1:16, 18-21, 24a		272	**716**
1:18-24	A	10	**60**
2:1-12	ABC	16	**77**
2:13-15, 19-23	ABC	14	**72**
2:13-18		439	**787**
3:1-9, 11	A	4	**44**
4:1-11	A	18	**85**
4:17-23	A	62	**229**
4:18-22		423	**780**
5:1-12ab	A	65	**237**
"		402	**773**
"		512	**867**
"		517	**872**
5:13-16	A	68	**245**
"		491	**844**
5:14-16		193	**614**
5:20-24		180	**580**
5:23-24	A	71	**254**
5:38-48	A	74	**262**
5:43-48		181	**582**
"		194	**616**
6:1, 5-6		176	**570**
6:1, 16-18		176	**570**
6:1-4		176	**569**
6:1-6, 16-18		176	**568**
6:7-13		195	**618**
6:7-15		178	**575**
6:19-21		196	**620**
6:24-34	A	77	**270**
6:25b-33		197	**622**
7:1-5		198	**624**
7:7-11		179	**577**
7:21, 24-27		228	**689**
7:21-27	A	80	**277**
8:5-11		229	**691**
8:14-17		530	**881**
9:9-13	A	83	**285**
"		376	**762**
9:35-38		508	**863**
9:35—10:1, 5a, 6-7		173	**558**
9:36—10:8	A	86	**295**
10:26-31	A	89	**303**
10:40-42	A	92	**312**
11:2-11	A	7	**52**
11:25-26, 28-30		535	**885**
11:25-30	A	95	**321**
"	A	164	**527**
11:29-30		199	**626**
13:1-9	A	98	**330**
13:24-30	A	101	**340**
13:31-32		500	**856**
13:44-46	A	104	**348**
"		200	**628**
"		495	**850**
13:54-58		288	**726**
14:13-21	A	107	**358**
14:22-33	A	110	**366**
"		201	**630**
"		415	**777**
15:21-28	A	113	**374**
16:13-19		319	**741**
16:13-19a		263	**713**
16:13-20	A	116	**382**
16:21-25	A	119	**390**
17:1-9	A	21	**92**
"	A	344	**750**
18:1-4		473	**820**
18:1-5, 10		384	**768**
18:15-17	A	122	**399**
18:19-22		512	**868**
18:21-35	A	125	**407**
20:1-16a	A	128	**417**
20:26b-28		455	**803**
21:1-11	A	33	**127**
21:28-32	A	131	**425**
21:33-43	A	134	**434**
22:1-10	A	137	**443**
22:15-21	A	140	**453**
22:34-40	A	143	**459**
22:35-40		478	**828**

INDEX OF READINGS

Reading	Year	No.	Page
23:1-12	A	146	468
24:37-44	A	1	36
25:1-13	A	149	476
25:14-15, 19-21	A	152	486
25:14-29		202	632
25:14-30		495	851
25:31-40		177	573
"		473	821
25:31-46	A	155	496
27:11-54	A	33	129
28:16-20	A	52	199
"	B	159	512
"		464	810

Mark

Reading	Year	No.	Page
1:1-8	B	5	46
1:12-15	B	19	87
1:14-20	B	63	231
"		464	810
1:21-28	B	66	239
1:29-39	B	69	248
1:40-45	B	72	256
2:1-12	B	75	264
2:18-22	B	78	273
2:23-28	B	81	280
3:20-21, 31-35	B	84	289
3:20-26, 31-35	B	84	288
4:1-9		203	635
"		469	814
4:30-34	B	87	298
4:35-41	B	90	306
"		204	637
5:18-20		500	856
5:21-24, 35b-36, 38-42		205	640
5:21-24, 35-43	B	93	314
6:1-6	B	96	324
6:7-13	B	99	333
6:17-29		365	756
6:30-34	B	102	342
7:1-5, 14-16, 21-23	B	120	393
7:31-37	B	123	402
8:31-35	B	126	411
9:2-10	B	22	94
"	B	344	750
9:33-37	B	129	420
"		206	643
"		473	822
9:38-41	B	132	428
10:13-16	B	135	437
"		207	645
"		478	828
10:17-27	B	138	446
10:28-30		508	863
10:35-45	B	141	455
10:46-52	B	144	462
"		208	647
11:1-10	B	34	133
12:28-31	B	147	470
12:28b-31		182	584
12:41-44	B	150	480
"		209	649
13:24-32	B	153	488
13:33-37	B	2	39
14:12-16, 22-26	B	162	521
"		487	839
15:1-39	B	34	135
16:15-18		247	705
16:15-20	B	53	202
"		284	722

Luke

Reading	Year	No.	Page
1:5-17		316	737
1:26-38	B	11	62
"		274	719
"		429	783
"		451	798
1:39-45	C	12	64
1:39-56		302	731
"		352	753
1:46-56		175	564
2:1-14	ABC	13	69
2:16-21	ABC	15	74
2:22-32		252	709
2:41-51		272	717
"		303	732
"		451	799
3:1a, 2-6	C	6	49
3:10-16, 18	C	9	58
3:15-16, 21-22	ABC	17	80
4:1-13	C	20	90
4:14-21	C	64	234
4:20b-24, 28-30	C	67	242
5:1-11	C	70	251
"		508	864
6:12-16		455	803
6:17, 20-23	C	73	259
6:27-37	C	76	267
6:39-45	C	79	275
7:1-10	C	82	282
"		210	651
7:11-17	C	85	292
"		211	653
"		535	885
7:17-26		174	561
7:36-50	C	88	300
"		212	655
9:1-6		192	609
"		213	658
9:11b-17	C	163	524
9:18-24	C	91	308
9:28-36	C	23	96
"	C	344	751
9:57-62	C	94	318
10:1-9	C	97	327
"		396	770
10:25-37	C	100	336
"		214	660
"		526	877
10:38-42	C	103	345
11:1-10	C	106	354
11:5-10		215	663
12:15-21		522	875
12:16-21	C	109	363
12:32-34		473	822
12:35-38		172	556
12:35-40	C	112	372
"		230	693
12:49-53	C	115	380
13:6-9	C	26	107
"		216	665
13:22-30	C	118	387
14:1, 7-14	C	121	396
14:12-14		217	667
14:25-27	C	124	404
15:1-3, 11b-32	C	29	115
"		491	845
15:1-7		218	670
15:3-7	C	166	534
15:11-32	C	127	414
16:10-13	C	130	422
16:19-31	C	133	430
17:5-10	C	136	440
17:11-19	C	139	450
"		219	672
"		504	859
17:20-21		231	694
18:1-8	C	142	457
18:1-8a		220	674
18:9-14	C	145	464
19:1-10	C	148	473
"		446	794
19:28-40	C	35	138
20:27-38		151	484
21:5-19	C	154	492
21:25-28, 34-36	C	3	41
23:1-49	C	35	140
23:35-43	C	157	503
24:13-35	A	40	161
24:35-48	B	41	166
24:50-53	C	54	205

INDEX OF READINGS

Reading	Year	No.	Page
John			
1:19-28	B	8	55
1:29-34	A	59	220
1:35-42	B	60	223
1:47-51		381	765
2:1-12	C	61	226
2:13-22	B	25	104
3:13-17		370	760
3:16-17	B	28	113
"	A	158	509
"		221	675
4:5-15, 19b-26, 39a, 40-42	A	24	100
4:46-53		183	586
6:1-15	B	105	351
6:24-29	B	108	361
6:48-51	B	111	369
6:51-58	B	114	376
"	A	161	518
"		487	840
6:60-69	B	117	385
8:2-11	C	32	126
9:1, 6-12, 35-38	A	27	110
10:1-10	A	43	172
10:11-16	B	44	175
10:14-16		190	604
10:27-30	C	45	177
11:3-7, 17, 20-27, 31-45	A	30	119
11:17-27		337	746
11:21-27		535	886
11:47-52		184	588
12:24-26	B	31	123
"		460	807
13:31a, 33-35	C	48	187
13:34-35		222	677
14:1-12	A	46	180
14:12-14		186	595
14:15-17		223	679
"		483	835
14:15-21	A	49	190
14:21-26		189	601
14:23-26	C	51	196
"		483	835
"		495	853
14:27		224	681
15:1-4		478	828
15:1-5		225	683
15:1-5, 7-8	B	47	184
15:5-8		478	829
15:9-11		226	685
"		478	829
15:9-14	B	50	193
15:12-15		227	687
15:18-21		188	599
15:26—16:1		191	606
16:12-15	C	160	515
17:6-9	A	55	208
17:11	B	56	211
17:20-21	C	57	213
17:21-23		187	597
18:33b-37	B	156	500
19:25-27		371	760
"		451	800
19:31-37	B	165	530
20:1-2, 11-18		333	744
20:1-9	ABC	36	150
20:2-8		438	786
20:11-18		185	592
20:19-23	ABC	58	216
20:19-29	A	37	153
"	B	38	156
"	C	39	158
20:24-29		322	742
21:1-14	C	42	168
21:15-17		464	811
Acts			
1:8-11	A	52	197
"	B	53	200
"	C	54	203
1:12-13a, 14		448	795
1:12-14	A	55	206
1:15-17, 20a, 20c-26	B	56	209
"		293	727
2:1-6, 14, 22b-23, 32-33		480	831
2:1-11	ABC	58	214
2:14, 22-24	A	40	160
2:14a, 36-41	A	43	170
2:32-33		185	591
2:42-47	A	37	151
"		484	836
3:1-10		186	593
"		452	801
3:13-15, 17-19	B	41	164
4:8-12	B	44	173
4:32-35	B	38	154
"		187	596
"		470	815
5:12-16	C	39	157
5:17-21		188	598
5:27-32		189	600
5:27b-32, 40b-41	C	42	167
6:1-7a	A	46	178
6:8-10; 7:54-60		437	785
7:55-60	C	57	212
"		457	804
8:5-8, 14-17	A	49	188
9:1-20		190	602
9:26-28	B	47	182
10:25-26, 34-35, 44-48	B	50	191
10:34-38	ABC	17	79
10:34a, 37-43	ABC	36	147
11:19-22, 26c		191	605
11:21-26; 13:1-3		310	734
11:27-30		177	572
12:1-11		319	739
13:43-44, 47-48	C	45	176
14:21-27	C	48	185
16:22-34		192	607
22:3-16		247	703
28:11-16		415	776
Romans			
1:1c-4		274	718
1:2-4	A	10	59
4:18-21	A	83	284
5:5-11	C	166	533
5:6-11	A	86	294
5:10b-11		226	684
6:3-4, 8-9	A	92	311
8:9, 11	A	95	320
8:14-17	B	159	511
"		480	832
8:14-18	A	98	329
8:26-27	A	101	339
8:28-30	A	104	347
8:31, 38-39	B	22	93
8:35, 37-39	A	107	357
11:33-36	A	116	381
12:1-2	A	119	389
12:9-12	C	130	421
12:9-16b		302	729
12:17-18, 21		181	581
13:8-10	A	122	398
13:11-13a	A	1	36
14:7-9	A	125	406
15:4-6	A	4	43
16:25-27	B	11	61
1 Corinthians			
1:3-9	B	2	38
1:10-13, 17	A	62	228
1:26-31	A	65	236
"		470	815
2:1-5	A	68	244
2:6-10	A	71	253

892 INDEX OF READINGS

Reading	Year	No.	Page
3:18-20	A	74	261
5:6b-8	ABC	36	149
9:16-18	B	69	247
10:16-17	A	161	517
10:31—11:1	B	72	255
11:23-26	C	163	523
12:4-7, 12-13	ABC	58	215
12:4-11	C	61	225
12:4-13		480	832
12:12-13		225	682
"		475	825
12:12-14, 27	C	64	233
13:4-7		194	615
13:4-8a, 11-13	C	67	241
13:4-13		470	816
15:3-8, 11	C	70	250
15:12, 16-20	C	73	258
15:20-24a	A	155	495

2 Corinthians

Reading	Year	No.	Page
1:3-4		175	563
4:6-11	B	81	279
4:16—5:1	B	84	287
5:6-10	B	87	297
5:14-17	B	90	305
5:17-19	C	29	114
6:4-10		457	805
8:1-3a 12		209	648
8:7, 9, 13-14	B	93	314
9:8-11		519	874
12:7-10	B	96	323
13:11-13	A	158	508

Galatians

Reading	Year	No.	Page
1:11-12, 15-19	C	85	291
3:26-28		475	826
3:26-29	C	91	307
5:1, 13-15	C	94	317
5:22-23, 25-26		223	678

Ephesians

Reading	Year	No.	Page
1:3-5		532	882
1:3-6		448	796
1:3-10	B	99	332
1:15-16a, 18-19a		205	639
1:17-21	A	52	198
"	B	53	201
"	C	54	204
2:4-10	B	28	112
2:20-22		443	791
"		452	802
3:14-19	B	165	529
3:16b-17, 20-21		231	694

Reading	Year	No.	Page
4:1-6	B	105	350
4:1-7		466	812
4:11-13		466	813
4:31—5:2	B	111	368
5:1-2, 8-10	A	27	110
"		488	841
5:8-10		193	613
5:15-20	B	114	376
6:1-4	B	117	384
6:18b-19a, 20b		220	673

Philippians

Reading	Year	No.	Page
1:4-6	C	6	48
2:1-5	A	131	424
3:12-14	C	32	125
3:20—4:1	C	23	95
4:4-7	C	9	57
"		230	692
4:4-9		470	817
4:6-9	A	134	433
"		514	869
4:8-9		199	625
4:12-14, 19-20	A	137	442

Colossians

Reading	Year	No.	Page
1:15-18	C	157	502
1:18-20	C	100	335
1:27-28	C	103	344
2:6-7		216	664
3:1-4	ABC	36	149
"	C	109	362
3:12-13		198	623
3:12-14		178	574
3:12-15		514	870
3:12, 15b-17		497	854
3:12-17	ABC	14	71
3:15-16		224	680
3:17, 23-24		288	725

1 Thessalonians

Reading	Year	No.	Page
1:1-5b	A	140	452
1:5-8a	A	143	458
2:7-9, 13	A	146	467
4:13-14, 18		532	883
4:13-18	A	149	475
5:1-6	A	152	485
5:16-18		219	671
5:16-24	B	8	54

2 Thessalonians

Reading	Year	No.	Page
1:11-12	C	148	472
2:16—3:5	C	151	483
3:6-12, 16		492	849
3:7-12	C	154	491

1 Timothy

Reading	Year	No.	Page
1:12-15b	C	127	412
2:1-4		195	617
6:11b-12a	C	133	429

2 Timothy

Reading	Year	No.	Page
1:1-8		248	705
1:6-8	C	136	439
2:11-13	C	139	449
4:1-2	C	142	456
4:6-8	C	145	464
4:17-18		319	740

Titus

Reading	Year	No.	Page
1:1-5		248	706
3:4-6	ABC	13	68

Hebrews

Reading	Year	No.	Page
4:12-13	B	138	445
4:14-16	B	141	454
5:1-6	B	144	461
7:26	B	147	470
11:1-2, 8-12	C	112	370
12:1-4	C	115	379
12:5a, 6-7, 11	C	118	386
13:1-3, 14-16		523	876

James

Reading	Year	No.	Page
1:17-18, 21b-22	B	120	392
2:1-5	B	123	401
2:14-17		228	688
"		488	841
2:14-18	B	126	410
"		217	666
3:17-18	B	129	419
5:1-6	B	132	427
5:7-10	A	7	51
5:13-16		527	879
5:16c-18		215	662

1 Peter

Reading	Year	No.	Page
1:3-4	A	37	152
"		200	627
2:9-10		222	676
4:7b-11		470	817
4:10-11		202	631
4:13-16	A	55	207
5:1-4		263	711
5:12-14		284	721

2 Peter

Reading	Year	No.	Page
1:16-19		344	748

1 John

Reading	Year	No.	Page
2:29b—3:1a		206	642
3:1-2	B	44	174

INDEX OF RESPONSORIAL PSALMS 893

Reading	Year	No.	Page	Reading	Year	No.	Page	Reading	Year	No.	Page
3:1-2		532	883	4:7-11, 16b	A	164	526	12:7-12a		381	763
3:1, 23		227	686	4:11-13	B	56	210	14:13		532	883
3:11, 18		214	659	5:1-3	B	38	155	21:1-4	C	48	186
3:16-18		470	818	5:2-5		470	818	"		443	792
3:18	B	47	183	**Revelation**				21:1-8		488	842
4:7-10	B	50	192	1:5-8	B	156	499	21:10-14, 22-23	C	51	194
"		212	654	7:9-10		402	772				

INDEX OF RESPONSORIAL PSALMS

Psalm	Page
4: 1ab + 1ef, 3, 6cd-7a (R. 7b)	165
8:3-4, 5-6, 7-8 (R. 2a)	514
15:1-3a, 3bc + 5ef (R. 1a)	344
15:2-3a, 3bc + 5ef (R. 1a)	391
16:1-2ab + 5, 7-8, 11 (R. see 5a)	316
16:1-2ab + 5, 7-8, 11 (R. 11a)	678
16:5 + 8, 9-10, 11 (R. 1)	487
17:1abc + 5, 6 + 8 (R. 6b)	644
17:1, 5-6, 8 + 15 (R. 15b)	482
18:1-2ab, 46 (R. 2)	469
18:1-2, 46 + 50ab (R. 2)	160
18:1-2, 46 + 50ce (R. 2)	458
19:1-2, 3-4abce (R. 5a)	802
19:7, 8ab + 9cd, 10 (R. 9a)	583
19:7, 8 (R. 9a)	625
19:7, 8 (R. Jn 6:63c)	813
19:7, 8 (R. Jn 6:68c)	544
19:7, 8, 9cd-10ab (R. Jn 6:68c)	103
19:7, 8, 14 (R. see Jn 6:63c)	233
22:7-8, 16c-17a, 18, 19 + 22 (R. 2a)	128
	134, 139
22:27, 30-31 (R. 26a)	182
23:1-2ab, 2c-3, 5-6 (R. 1)	494
23:1-3a, 3b-4, 5, 6 (R. 1)	826, 833, 836, 884
23:1-3a, 3b-4, 5-6 (R. 1)	865
23:1-3a, 3b-4, 5b-6c (R. 1)	109
23:1-3a, 3b-4, 6 (R. 1)	170
	341, 532, 621, 712, 808
23:1-3a, 4abcd + 5ac, 6 (R. 6cd)	441
24:1-2, 3-4abc (R. 7c + 10b)	59
24:1-2, 3-4, 5-6 (R. see 6)	772
24:7, 10 (R. 10b)	708
25:1-2ab + 4, 5-6 (R. 1)	617, 673
25:4-5ab, 5cd-6 (R. 4a)	421, 572
25:4-5abc, 6 + 7cd (R. 4a)	429
25:4-5abc, 6 + 7cd (R. 6a)	112
25:4-5abc, 6 + 7cd (R. see 10)	86
25:4-5abc, 6 + 7cd, 8-9 (R. 4a)	230, 466
25:4-5abc, 8-9, 10 + 14 (R. 1)	555, 843
25:4-5abc, 8-9, 10 + 14 (R. 1 or R. Come, O Lord, and set us free.)	537
25:4-5abc, 8-9, 10 + 14, 15-16 (R. 1)	879
25:4-5, 6-7, 8-9 (R. 6a)	423
25:4-5, 8-9 (R. 1b)	40
27:1, 4abc (R. 1a)	227
27:1, 4abc, 7-8 (R. 13a)	206
27:1, 4 (R. 8b)	862
27:1, 4, 13-14 (R. 1a)	545, 827, 884
27:1, 8 + 11ab (R. 1)	646
27:1, 11ab + 13 (R. 1a)	567
27:1, 13-14 (R. 1a)	485, 613

Psalm	Page
29:3abde-4, 3cde + 9ef-10 (R. 11b)	78
30:1ab + 2 + 4, 10-11ab + 12bcd (R. 2a)	167
30:4 + 5def, 10-11 ab + 12 bcd (R. 2a)	290
	313
31:1-2a, 2bcde - 3, 19 (R. 6a)	806
31:1 + 2b, 3 + 16 (R. 3b)	276
32:1 + 5ab, 7 + 11 (R. see 5c)	299
32:1, 5ab, 11 (R. 7a)	255
33:1-2, 4-5, 21-22 (R. 22)	585, 650
33:4-5, 6 + 9, 20 + 22 (R. 12b)	510
33:4-5, 12-13 + 14b, 20 + 22 (R. 12b)	587
33:4-5, 20 + 22 (R. 22)	91, 454, 560
34:1-2, 3-4 (R. 9a)	563, 690
34:1-2, 3-4, 5-6, 9-10 (R. 9a)	837
34:1-2, 3-4, 7-8 (R. 5b)	806
34:1-2, 3-4, 7-8 (R. 7a)	598
34:1-2, 3-4, 7-8 (R. 9a)	367
34:1-2, 3-4, 8-9 (R. 2a or R. 9a)	819
34:1-2, 3-4, 16 + 18 (R. 9a)	880
34:1-2, 3 + 5, 7-8 (R. 2)	545
34:1-2, 9-10 (R. 9a)	375
34:1-2, 17-18 (R. 7a)	463
34:1-2, 17-18, 19-20 (R. 9a)	383
34:3-4, 5-6, 7-8 (R. 5b)	740
37:3-4, 5-6 (R. 39a)	605
37:3 + 4, 5 + 26 (R. 39a)	631, 659
40:1, 2, 17 (R. 14b)	378
40:1 + 2de, 3, 17 (R. 5a)	257
40:1 + 3ab, 8 + 11 (R. 8a + 9a)	219, 222, 688
40:7-8, 9 (R. 8a + 9a)	718
41:1-2abcd, 3 + 13 (R. 5)	263
46:1-2, 7-8 (R. see 1)	664
47:1-2, 5-6, 7-8 (R. 6a)	197, 200, 203
47:1-2, 7-8 (R. 8a)	501
47:1-2, 7-8 (R. 8)	61
50:8-9, 14-15 (R. 23b)	283
51:1 + 10, 12 + 15 (R. see 3a)	574
51:1, 10, 12 (R. 12a)	122
51:1, 10, 12, 15 (R. 3a)	84
51:1-2, 10-11, 12 + 15 (R. see 3a or R. Remember, O Lord, your faithfulness and love.)	540
62:1-2, 7-8abc (R. 6a)	269
63:1abc, 2-3, 4-5 (R. 2b)	388
63:1, 2-3, 4-5, 7-8 (R. 2b)	546
63:1, 2-3, 6-7 (R. 2b)	474
65:9, 11-12, 13 (R. Lk 8:8)	328, 634
66:1-3a, 4-5, 6-7a (R. 1)	544
66:1-3ab, 4-5, 16 + 20 (R. 1)	188, 426
66:1-3ab, 6-7a, 16 + 20 (R. 1)	326
67:1-2, 5 + 7 (R. 2a)	73

Psalm	Page
67:1-2, 4 (R. 4a)	857
67:1-2, 4, 5 + 7 (R. 4)	373
67:1-2, 4, 5 + 7 (R. 6a)	195
68:3-4acdef, 5-6abcd, 9-10 (R. see 11b)	394
69:13, 16, 29b-30a (R. 14c)	302
69:13, 29-30 (R. see 33)	334
71:1-2, 3abcd, 3ef + 5a (R. see 15ab)	240
72:1-2, 7-8, 12-13 (R. see 7)	870
72:1, 2, 10abc, 10de-11 (R. see 11)	76
72:1 + 8, 17 (R. 7)	42
78:3 + 4cdef, 23-24, 25 + 54ab (R. 24b)	360
80:1acdef + 2c, 14-15ab (R. 3)	63
80:8ab + 9-10ab, 14d-15ab + 19 (R. Is 5:7a)	682
80:8 + 11, 14de-15ab + 19 (R. Is 5:7a)	432
81:2-3, 4-5abcd (R. 2a)	278
84:2, 3, 4-5, 10 (R. 2 or R. Rv 21:3b)	792
85:8abc + 9, 10-11 (R. 8)	692
85:8abc + 9, 10-11, 12-13 (R. 8)	331
	364, 581
85:8, 9, 10 (R. 9b)	114
85:8, 9, 10 (R. Sir 36:16)	38
85:8, 9-10 (R. 9b)	686
85:8-9, 10-11 (R. 8)	45
85:8-9, 10-11, 12-13 (R. 8a or R. Come, O Lord, and set us free.)	538
86:5-6, 15 + 16de (R. 5a)	322
86:5-6, 15-16de (R. 5a)	338
88:4-5, 14-15abc (R. 7a)	759
89:1-2, 3-4 (R. 37)	715
89:1-2, 15-16 (R. 2a)	310, 684
89:1 + 5, 15-16 (R. 2a)	722
90:1-2, 14 + 16 (R. 1)	636
90:2, 14 + 16	725
90:12-13, 14abc + 17 (R. 1)	403
90:12 + 14, 16-17abc (R. 14)	444, 654
91:1-2, 3-4, 5-6, 10-11 (R. 11)	766
91:1-2, 9 + 11 (R. see 2b)	629
91:1-2, 10-11 (R. see 15b)	89
91:1-2, 10-11, 14-14 (R. see 15b or R. Remember, O Lord, your faithfulness and love.)	541
92:1-2, 12-13 (R. see 2a)	274, 296
93:1, 2 + 5 (R. 1a)	498
95:1-2, 3-5, 6-7abcd (R. see 2)	849
95:1-2, 3-5, 6-7 (R. 8)	547
95:1-2, 6-7abcd (R. 8)	238
95:1-2, 6-7abcd, 7e-9c (R. 8)	397, 438
95:1-2, 7e-9c (R. 8)	99
96:1-2a, 2b-3, 4-5 (R. 3)	456
96:1-2a, 2b-3, 7-8a (R. 3)	224, 657

INDEX OF ALLELUIA VERSES AND VERSES BEFORE THE GOSPEL

Psalm	Page
96:1-2a, 2b-3, 7-8a, 10 (R. 3)	809
96:1-2a, 2b-3, 11-12a (R. Lk 2:11)	67
96:1-2a, 2b-3, 11-12ab (R. 3)	591
96:1-2, 3 + 10 (R. Mk 16:15)	608
96:1 + 3, 4-5, 9-10abef (R. 7b)	451
97:1, 6, 9 (R. 1a + 9a)	212
97:1-2, 5-6, 9 (R. 1a + 9a)	749
98:1, 2-3ab (R. 1a)	782
98:1, 2-3ab, 3cd-4 (R. see 2b)	448
98:1, 2-3ab, 3cd-4, 5-6 (R. 3cd or R. Lord, today we have seen your glory.)	539
98:1-2, 3cd-4 (R. see 2b)	191
98:1, 2-3, 4-6 (R. see 2b)	776
98:1, 2, 5-6 (R. 3cd)	594
98:5-6, 7-8, 9 (R. see 9)	490
100:1-2, 3, 4, 5, (R. 3c or R. 2c)	866
100:1-2, 3, 5 (R. 3)	669, 676
100:1-2, 3, 5 (R. 3c)	176, 293, 307, 548
103:1-2, 3-4, 11-12 (R. 8a)	405
103:1-2, 3-4, 17-18a (R. 1a)	820
103:1-2, 3 + 5 (R. see 17)	525
103:1-2, 3 + 8, 11-12 (R. 8a)	623
103:1-2, 3 + 13 (R. 8a)	260, 267, 272
103:1-2, 5 + 11 (R. 8a)	648
103:1-2, 6-7, 8 + 11 (R. 8a)	106
103:1-2, 8 + 10, 12-13 (R. 8a)	548
103:1-2, 8 + 11 (R. 8a)	93
103:1-2, 19-20ac (R. 19a)	210
104:1abc + 24, 30-31 (R. see 30)	215
104:1abc + 24bcd, 30 (R. 30)	833
107:23-24, 25 + 28, 29-30 (R. 1b)	304
110:1, 3, 4 (R. 4b)	522
111:1-2, 3-4, 7-8 (R. 7a)	412
112:1, 3, 4 (R. 1a)	627

Psalm	Page
112:4-5, 8ab + 9 (R. 4a)	243
113:1-2, 3-4, 5-6 (R. see 2)	854, 857
113:1-2, 3-4, 5-6, 7-8 (R. see 2)	796
116:1-2, 5-6, 8-9 (R. 9a)	409
116:1-2, 5 + 12 (R. 9a)	652
116:5 + 7, 9 + 12 (R. 9a)	615, 675
116:12-13, 17-19ab (R. 13)	520
117:1, 2 (R. Mk 16:15)	281, 603, 704
118:1-2, 15c-16ab, 17, 22-23 (R. 24)	543
118:1-2, 15c-16ab + 17, 22-23 (R. 24)	148
118:1 + 21, 22-23 (R. 22)	173
118:2 + 4, 13-14 (R. 1)	157
118:2-4, 22-24 (R. 1)	151, 154
119:1-2, 4-5, 17-18, 33-34 (R. 1)	843
119:1-2, 4-5, 33-34 (R. 1b)	252
119:1-2, 7 + 24 (R. 1b)	600
119:57 + 72, 127-128 (R. 97a)	346
119:129-130, 133 + 135 (R. 135a)	642
119:165, 168, 171 (R. 165a)	386
121:1-2, 5-6, 7-8 (R. 2)	876
121:1-2, 5-6, 7-8 (R. see 2)	639
122:1-2, 6-7, 8-9 (R. see 1)	550
122:1-2, 6-7, 8-9 (R. Sir 36:18)	579
122:1-2, 8-9 (R. see 1)	35
122:1-2, 8-9 (R. Sir 36:18)	419, 681, 871
126:1-2ab, 2cd-3 (R. 3a or R. 3)	124
126:1-2ab, 2cde-3 (R. 3)	47, 576, 694
126:1-2ab, 4-5, 6 (R. 3)	460
128:1-2, 3, 4-5 (R. see 1)	70
128:1-2, 3, 4-5 (R. see 5)	436
130:1-2, 3-4, 5 + 6d-7a (R. 7b)	286
130:1-2, 5-6ab, 6def, 7 (R. 7bc or R. Remember, O Lord, your faithfulness and love.)	542
130:1-2, 5 + 7bcd (R. 7bc)	118

Psalm	Page
138:1acd-2a, 4-5 (R. 1c)	249
138:1-2a, 2bc + 3, 6 + 8cde (R. 8b)	381
138:1-2a, 2bcdef (R. 2bc)	671
138:1-2a, 2bcdef-3, 7abde-8abc (R. 3a)	353
138:1-2a, 2bcdef, 2c-3, 4-5 (R. 1c)	764
139:1-3, 13-14abc, 14de-15 (R. 14a)	736
143:1, 8, 10 (R. 1a)	371
145:1-2, 8-9, 10-11, 13cd-14 (R. see 1)	549
145:1-2, 8-9, 13cd-14 (R. see 1)	319, 471
145:2-3, 8-9, 17-18 (R. 18a)	416
145:8-9, 10 + 12 (R. see 1)	185
145:8-9, 15-16 (R. see 16)	356
145:10-11, 15-16 (R. see 16)	349, 662
145:10-11, 15-16, 17-18 (R. 16)	179, 838
145:10-11, 15-16, 17-18 (R. 18a)	596
146:6d-7ab, 7c-8abc, 10 (R. Is 35:4)	50
146:6d-7ab, 7c-9a (R. 1b)	666
146:6d-7ab, 7c-9a (R. Mt 5:3)	235
146:6d-7b, 7c-8abc, 8d-9abc (R. 1b)	479
146:6d-7, 7c-9a, 9bcd-10 (R. 1b)	400
147:1, 3-4, 5 + 7 (R. Is 30:18)	95
	362, 557
147:1, 4, 5 + 7 (R. see 3a)	246
147:5 + 7, 8 (R. 1)	874
147:12 + 14, 19-20 (R. 12)	516
150:1-2, 3-4, 5-6 (R. 6)	855

CANTICLES

	Page
Is 12:2, 4bcd, 6 (R. 6)	56
Is 12:2, 4, 5-6 (R. 6b)	730
Is 12:2-3, 4bcd, 5-6 (R. 3)	528
Dn 3:52, 53 + 56 (R. 52b)	507
Lk 1:47-48b, 48c-49, 50-51, 52-53, 54-55 (R. 49)	797
Lk 1:47 + 49, 53-54 (R. Is 61:10b)	53

INDEX OF ALLELUIA VERSES AND VERSES BEFORE THE GOSPEL

Reference	Page
1 Sm 3:9; Jn 6:63c	318
Ps 33:22	844
Ps 66:16	856
Ps 68:20	725
Ps 84:5	716
Ps 85:8	36, 39, 41, 556, 558, 561, 563
Ps 103:21	765, 767
Ps 119:135	404
Ps 126:5	875
Ps 130:5 (see)	365
Ps 138:1bc	858
Is 61:1	51, 54, 57
Ez 18:31	103
Jl 2:12-13	125
Mt 1:23	60
Mt 2:2	76
Mt 4:4b	84, 87, 89, 357, 360
Mt 4:16	239
Mt 4:17	107, 568, 572, 575, 576, 579, 582, 584, 586, 588
Mt 4:19	250
Mt 4:23 (see)	228, 374, 402

Reference	Page
Mt 5:3	363, 445, 479
Mt 5:9	871
Mt 5:12a	236
Mt 7:8 (see)	793
Mt 8:17	247, 881
Mt 11:25 (see)	254, 320, 339, 347
Mt 11:28	773
Mt 11:29ab	395, 527, 529, 533
Mt 16:18	382, 713, 741
Mt 17:5 (see)	92, 94, 96
Mt 17:5c	749
Mt 23:9b, 10b	467
Mt 23:11, 12	820
Mt 24:42a, 44	371, 476
Mt 28:19a, 20b	199, 202, 205, 810
Mk 1:15	231, 294
Mk 9:7 (see)	79
Mk 10:45	454
Mk 11:9, 10	496, 499, 502
Lk 1:28 (see)	783, 798
Lk 1:38	61, 64
Lk 1:45 (see)	730
Lk 1:76 (see)	737

Reference	Page
Lk 2:10-11	68
Lk 2:32	708
Lk 3:4, 6	43, 46, 48
Lk 4:18	234, 242, 264, 284
Lk 4:18 (see)	323
Lk 6:23ab	258
Lk 7:16	255, 292, 305, 350
Lk 8:15 (see)	344
Lk 11:28 (see)	803
Lk 15:18	115
Lk 21:36	488
Lk 21:38	491
Lk 24:32 (see)	161, 165, 168
Jn 1:14a, 12a	220
Jn 1:14ab	718
Jn 1:41, 17b	222
Jn 2:42, 15 (see)	99
Jn 3:16	113, 281, 472
Jn 6:51	369, 517, 520, 523, 839
Jn 6:56	376
Jn 6:63c, 68c(see)	592, 594, 597, 599, 601, 604, 606, 608
Jn 6:63, 68c	335, 384

Reference	Page
Jn 8:12	110, 244
Jn 10:14	171, 174, 177
Jn 10:27	308, 342, 380, 425
Jn 11:25a, 26	885
Jn 11:25, 26	119
Jn 12:26	123
Jn 12:31b-32	288
Jn 13:34	187, 267, 406
Jn 14:6	180, 387, 827
Jn 14:16	834
Jn 14:18 (see)	207, 211, 213
Jn 14:23	189, 193, 196, 459, 470
Jn 15:4a, 5b	183, 486
Jn 15:5	
Jn 15:16 (see)	434, 705, 862
Jn 15:26b, 27a	303
Jn 17:17b, 17a (see)	280, 428
Jn 20:29	152, 155, 158
Acts 16:14b (see)	417
Rom 8:15bc	354
1 Cor 1:23a, 24b	722
1 Cor 5:7b-8a	150
2 Cor 1:3b-4a	807, 877

ALPHABETICAL INDEX OF CELEBRATIONS

Reference	Page	Reference	Page	Reference	Page	Reference	Page
2 Cor 5:19	398, 413, 464	Col 3:15a, 16a	326	Heb 4:12	270, 457	Rv 1:5a, 6b	483
2 Cor 8:9	422, 429	Col 3:15a, 16	72	Jas 1:18	273, 392	Rv 1:8 (see)	508, 511, 514
Gal 6:14	410	Col 3:15	867	1 Pt 1:25	440	Come, Holy Spirit	216
Eph 1:17-18 (see)	333, 389, 442	1 Thes 5:18	449	1 Pt 2:9	312	Seed is the word of God, The	297
Phil 2:8-9	129, 135, 140	2 Thes 2:14 (see)	225, 420	1 Jn 2:5	261		329, 814
Phil 2:15d, 16a	274, 453	2 Tm 1:10 (see)	314, 462	1 Jn 4:10b	300	We adore you, O Christ	759
Phil 3:8-9	850	Heb 1:1-2	74	1 Jn 4:12	437	We praise you, O God	777

ALPHABETICAL INDEX OF CELEBRATIONS

Name	Page
Achilleus	726
Advent	33-64, 537-539, 555-564
Agatha	710
Agnes	702
Albert the Great	775
All Saints	772
All Souls	774
Aloysuis Gonzaga	735
Alphonsus Ligouri	748
Ambrose	781
André Bessette, Bl.	701
Andrew	780
Andrew Dung-Lac	779
Andrew Kim Taegon	761
Angela Merici	707
Ann	746
Annunciation of the Lord, The	718
Anselm	721
Ansgar	710
Anthony	702
Anthony Mary Claret	771
Anthony of Padua	735
Anthony Mary Zaccaria	743
Ascension, The	197, 200, 203
"Ask and You Will Receive"	576
"Ask and You Will Receive"	662
Assumption of the Virgin Mary into Heaven, The	753
Athanasius	726
Augustine	756
Augustine of Canterbury	729
"Banquet of the Kingdom, The"	690
Baptism	825
Baptism of the Lord, The	78
Barnabas	734
Bartholomew	755
Basil the Great	701
"Be at Peace with Everyone"	578
"Become Stronger in Your Faith"	664
Bede the Venerable	728
Beginning of the School Year	849
"Believe in Jesus"	605
Benedict	743
Bernard	755
Bernardine of Siena	728

Name	Page
Birth of John the Baptist, The	736
Birth of the Lord, The	67
Birth of the Virgin Mary, The	758
Blase	710
Body & Blood of Christ	516, 519, 522
Bonaventure	744
Boniface	733
Bridget of Sweden	745
Bruno	768
Cajetan	752
Callistus I	769
Casimir	714
Catherine of Siena	723
Cecilia	779
Chair of the Apostle Peter	711
Charles Borromeo	774
Charles Lwanga	733
Christ the King	494, 498, 501
Christmas, Season of	65-80, 539-540
Clare	753
Clement I	779
Columban	779
Commemoration of All the Faithful Departed, The	774
Common of Apostles	801
Common of the Blessed Virgin	795
Common of the Dedication of a Church	791
Common of Doctors of the Church	812
Common of Martyrs	804
Common of Pastors	808
Common of Saints	815
Commons	789-822
Confirmation	830
Conversion of Paul, The	703
Cornelius	761
Cosmas	762
Cross, The Holy	758
Cyprian	761
Cyril	711
Cyril of Alexandria	738
Cyril of Jerusalem	714
Damasus I	784
Damian	762

Name	Page
Dedication of the Basilica of Saint Mary in Rome, The	748
Dedication of the Basilicas of the Apostles Peter and Paul	776
Dedication of the Lateran Basilica in Rome, The	774
Denis	769
Dominic	752
Easter, Season of	145-216, 543-544, 589-609
Elizabeth of Hungary	775
Elizabeth of Portugal	743
Elizabeth Ann Seton	701
End of the School Year	854
"Entering Kingdom of Heaven"	688
Ephrem of Syria	733
Epiphany of the Lord, The	75
Eusebius of Vercelli	748
Fabian	702
Felicity	714
Fidelis of Sigmaringen	721
First Martyrs of Rome	741
"Followers of Jesus"	598
For the Dead	882
For Peace and Justice	869
For Productive Land and After the Harvest	873
For Refugees and Exiles	876
For the Sick	879
For Unity of Christians	865
For Vocations	860
"Forgive as the Lord Has Forgiven You"	623
"Forgive One Another"	574
Frances Xavier Cabrini	775
Frances of Rome	714
Francis of Assisi	768
Francis of Paola	720
Francis de Sales	703
Francis Xavier	781
Gabriel	763
George	721
Gertrude the Great	775
"Gifts Received from God"	631
"Give Thanks to God"	671

Name	Page
"God Is Love"	654
"God Loves Us"	675
"Good Shepherd, The"	668
Gregory VII	728
Gregory the Great	758
Gregory Nazianzen	701
Guardian Angels, The	766
Hedwig	769
Henry	743
Hilary	702
Hippolytus	753
Holy Eucharist	836
Holy Family, The	70
Holy Innocents, The	787
Holy Spirit Confirmation	830
Pentecost Sunday	214
"I Want to See Again"	646
"I Will Help You"	636
"I Will Save You"	652
"I Will Take Care of You"	621
Ignatius of Antioch	769
Ignatius of Loyola	747
Immaculate Conception	781
Immaculate Heart of Mary, The	732
In Thanksgiving	857
Independence Day	743
Irenaeus	738
Isaac Jogues	771
Isidore the Farmer	728
Isidore of Seville	720
James the Greater	745
James the Less	726
Jane Frances de Chantal	754
Januarius	761
Jerome	765
Jerome Emiliani	710
"Jesus Blessed the Children"	644
"Jesus Brings Together All People"	587
Jesus Christ the Lord Annunciation	718
Ascension	197, 200, 203
Baptism	78
Birth	67
Body and Blood	516, 519, 522

896 ALPHABETICAL INDEX OF CELEBRATIONS

Name	Page
Christ the King	494, 498, 501
Cross, the Holy	758
Dedication of Lateran Basilica	774
Epiphany	75
Holy Family	70
Presentation	708
Resurrection	147
Sacred Heart	525, 528, 531
Transfiguration	748
Joachim	746
John	786
John I	728
John the Baptist	
Birth	736
Martyrdom	756
John Baptist de la Salle	720
John Bosco	707
John de Brébeuf	771
John of Capistrano	771
John Chrysostom	758
John of the Cross	784
John of Damascus	781
John Eudes	755
John Fisher	735
John of God	714
John of Kanty	785
John Leonardi	769
John Neumann	701
John Mary Vianney	748
Josaphat	775
Joseph, Husband of the Virgin Mary	
Solemnity	715
Worker	724
Joseph Calasanz	756
Juan Diego (Cuatitlatoatzin), Bl.	784
Jude	771
Junipero Serra, Bl.	742
Justin	733
Kateri Tekakwitha, Bl.	743
Katharine Drexel, Bl.	714
"Kind Is the Lord"	650
"Kingdom of God Is Among You"	694
"Kingdom of God Is Within You"	560
"Kingdom of Heaven Is Near, The"	557
Lawrence	752
Lawrence of Brindisi	744
Lawrence Ruiz	763
Lent	81-143, 540-542, 565-588
Leo the Great	774
"Light for the World"	613
"Lord Is Coming Soon, The"	692
"Lord Will Help You, The"	638
Louis of France	755
"Love Everyone"	581
"Love Everyone"	615

Name	Page
"Love of God and ... of Neighbor"	583
Lucy	784
Luke	770
Marcellinus	733
Margaret Mary Alacoque	769
Margaret of Scotland	775
Maria Goretti	743
Marie-Rose Durocher, Bl.	768
Mark	721
Martha	746
Martin I	720
Martin de Porres	774
Martin of Tours	775
Martyrdom of John the Baptist, The	756
Mary, The Blessed Virgin	
Assumption	753
Birth	758
Common	795
Dedication of Saint Mary	748
Immaculate Conception	781
Immaculate Heart	732
Mother of God	701
Our Lady of Guadalupe	784
Our Lady of Lourdes	710
Our Lady of Mount Carmel	744
Our Lady of the Rosary	768
Our Lady of Sorrows	760
Presentation	779
Queenship	755
Visit to Elizabeth	729
Mary Magdalene	744
Mary Magdalene de' Pazzi	728
Matthew	762
Matthias	727
Maximilian Mary Kolbe	753
"May Your Joy Be Complete"	684
Methodius	711
Michael	763
Miguel Agustín Pro, Bl.	779
Monica	756
"My Burden Is Light"	625
"My Heart Praises the Lord"	563
Nereus	726
Nicholas	781
Norbert	733
"Obedience to God"	600
"One in Christ Jesus"	596
"One with Jesus"	682
Ordinary Time	217-503, 544-550, 611-698
Our Lady of Guadalupe	784
Our Lady of Lourdes	710
Our Lady of Mount Carmel	744
Our Lady of the Rosary	768
Our Lady of Sorrows	760

Name	Page
Pancras	726
Patrick	714
Paul	
Conversion	703
Dedication of the Basilica of Peter and Paul	776
Peter and Paul	739
Paul of the Cross	771
Paul Chong Hasang	761
Paul Miki	710
Paulinus of Nola	735
"Peace I Leave with You"	680
Perpetua	714
Peter, apostle	
Chair of Peter	711
Dedication of the Basilica of Peter and Paul	776
Peter and Paul	739
Peter, martyr	733
Peter Canisius	785
Peter Chanel	723
Peter Chrysologus	747
Peter Claver	758
Peter Damian	711
Philip	726
Philip Neri	728
Pius V	723
Pius X	755
Polycarp	713
Pontian	753
"Power of Jesus' Name, The"	593
"Pray Always"	673
"Pray, Fast, and Share"	567
"Preaching About Jesus"	607
"Prepare for Coming of Lord"	555
Presentation of the Lord, The	708
Presentation of the Virgin Mary, The	779
Proper of Saints	699-788
Proper of Seasons	31-504
Queenship of the Virgin Mary	755
Raphael	763
Raymond of Penyafort	702
Reconciliation	841
Resurrection of the Lord (Easter Sunday)	147
Robert Bellarmine	761
Romuald	735
Rose of Lima	755
Rose Philippine Duchesne	778
Sacraments	823-846
Sacred Heart of Jesus	525, 528, 531
Saints, Common of	789-822
Saints, Proper of	699-788
Scholastica	710
Sebastian	702

Name	Page
"Sent To Preach the Kingdom of God"	657
Seven Founders of the Order of Servites	711
"Show Faith by Actions"	666
Simon	771
Sixtus II	752
Solemnities of the Lord during Ordinary Time	505-534
Solemnity of Mary, Mother of God	701
"Spirit Has Given Us Life, The"	678
Stanislaus	720
Stephen	785
Stephen of Hungary	754
"Store Up Riches in Heaven"	619
Sundays	33-503
(See also Calendar	24-30)
Sylvester I	788
Teresa of Jesus	769
Thanksgiving Day	780
"There Are Other Sheep Who Belong to Me"	602
Thérèse of the Child Jesus	766
"They Were Extremely Generous"	648
"This Is How You Should Pray"	617
Thomas	742
Thomas Aquinas	707
Thomas Becket	788
Thomas More	735
Timothy	705
Titus	705
Toribio de Mogrovejo	717
Transfiguration of the Lord, The	748
"Treasures of Heaven"	627
Trinity, Holy	507, 510, 513
"Trust in the Lord"	585
"Trust in the Lord"	629
Various Needs and Occasions, Masses for	847-886
Vincent	702
Vincent Ferrer	720
Vincent de Paul	763
Visit of the Virgin Mary to Elizabeth, The	729
"We Are Called God's Children"	642
"We Are the People of God"	676
Weekdays	551-694
Wenceslaus	763
"What We Do for Others We Do for Jesus"	572
"Who Is My Neighbor?"	659
"Witnesses of the Resurrection"	591
"Word That I Speak, The"	634
"You Are My Friends"	686